The WESTERN HERITAGE

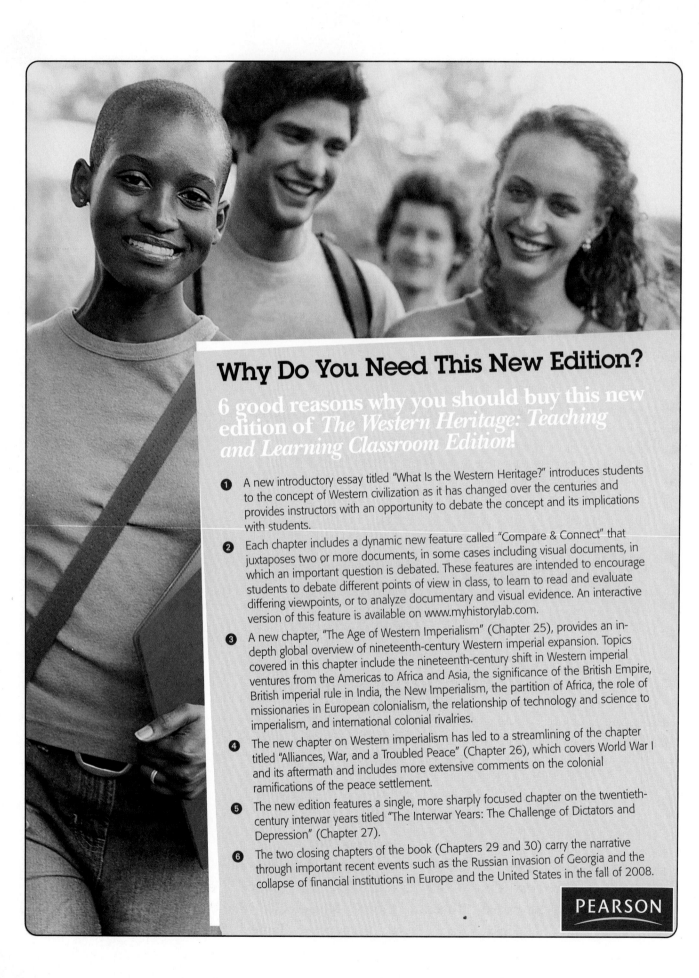

Why Do You Need This New Edition?

6 good reasons why you should buy this new edition of *The Western Heritage: Teaching and Learning Classroom Edition!*

1. A new introductory essay titled "What Is the Western Heritage?" introduces students to the concept of Western civilization as it has changed over the centuries and provides instructors with an opportunity to debate the concept and its implications with students.

2. Each chapter includes a dynamic new feature called "Compare & Connect" that juxtaposes two or more documents, in some cases including visual documents, in which an important question is debated. These features are intended to encourage students to debate different points of view in class, to learn to read and evaluate differing viewpoints, or to analyze documentary and visual evidence. An interactive version of this feature is available on www.myhistorylab.com.

3. A new chapter, "The Age of Western Imperialism" (Chapter 25), provides an in-depth global overview of nineteenth-century Western imperial expansion. Topics covered in this chapter include the nineteenth-century shift in Western imperial ventures from the Americas to Africa and Asia, the significance of the British Empire, British imperial rule in India, the New Imperialism, the partition of Africa, the role of missionaries in European colonialism, the relationship of technology and science to imperialism, and international colonial rivalries.

4. The new chapter on Western imperialism has led to a streamlining of the chapter titled "Alliances, War, and a Troubled Peace" (Chapter 26), which covers World War I and its aftermath and includes more extensive comments on the colonial ramifications of the peace settlement.

5. The new edition features a single, more sharply focused chapter on the twentieth-century interwar years titled "The Interwar Years: The Challenge of Dictators and Depression" (Chapter 27).

6. The two closing chapters of the book (Chapters 29 and 30) carry the narrative through important recent events such as the Russian invasion of Georgia and the collapse of financial institutions in Europe and the United States in the fall of 2008.

PEARSON

The WESTERN HERITAGE

TEACHING AND LEARNING CLASSROOM EDITION

BRIEF SIXTH EDITION

VOLUME 2: SINCE 1648

Donald Kagan
YALE UNIVERSITY

Steven Ozment
HARVARD UNIVERSITY

Frank M. Turner
YALE UNIVERSITY

Prentice Hall

Boston   Columbus   Indianapolis   New York   San Francisco   Upper Saddle River
Amsterdam   Cape Town   Dubai   London   Madrid   Milan   Munich
Paris   Montreal   Toronto   Delhi   Mexico City   Sao Paulo   Sydney
Hong Kong   Seoul   Singapore   Taipei   Tokyo

VP, Editorial Director: Leah Jewell
Executive Editor: Charles Cavaliere
Editorial Project Manager: Rob DeGeorge
Production Project Manager: Lynn Savino Wendel
Editorial Assistant: Lauren Aylward
Director of Marketing: Brandy Dawson
Senior Managing Editor: Ann Marie McCarthy
Copy Editor: Martha Williams
Proofreader: Donna Mulder
Senior Operations Supervisor: Mary Ann Gloriande
Senior Art Director: Maria Lange
Text Designer: Jill Little
Cover Designer: John Christiana/Corrin Skidds
AV Project Manager: Mirella Signoretto

Manager, Visual Research: Beth Brenzel
Manager, Rights and Permissions: Zina Arabia
Image Permission Coordinator: Michelina Viscusi
Manager, Cover Visual Research & Permissions: Karen Sanatar
Cover Art: Karl Marx/Bettmann/Corbis
Media Director: Brian Hyland
Lead Media Project Manager: Sarah Kinney
Supplements Editor: Emsal Hasan
Composition, Full-Service Project Management: Rebecca Dunn, Prepare, Inc.
Printer/Binder: Webcrafters Inc.
Cover Printer: Lehigh-Phoenix Color

This book was set in 10/13 Goudy Regular.

Credits and acknowledgments borrowed from other sources and reproduced, with permission, in this textbook appear on appropriate page within text.

Library of Congress Cataloging-in-Publication Data

Kagan, Donald.
  The Western heritage/Donald Kagan, Steven Ozment, Frank M. Turner. —Teaching and learning classroom edition, Brief 6th ed.
    p. cm.
  "Combined volume."
  Includes bibliographical references and index.
  ISBN 978-0-205-72891-6 (combined)—ISBN 978-0-205-73210-4 (exam)—ISBN 978-0-205-72892-3 (volume one)—
  ISBN 978-0-205-72893-0 (volume two)
  1. Civilization, Western—History—Textbooks. I. Ozment, Steven E. II. Turner, Frank M. (Frank Miller), 1944 III. Title.
CB245.K28 2010b
909'.09821–dc22   2009014281

10 9 8 7 6 5 4 3 2 1

Prentice Hall
is an imprint of

www.pearsonhighered.com

ISBN 10:0-205-72893-6
ISBN 13:978-0-205-72893-0

18 The French Revolution   440

19 The Age of Napoleon and the Triumph of Romanticism   466

PART 5 Toward the Modern World, 1850–1939

22 The Age of Nation-States 540

23 The Building of European Supremacy: Society and Politics to World War I 564

Students undertaking the study of the Western heritage on the threshold of the second decade of the twenty-first century do so at a remarkable historical moment. In 2008, the United States elected its first African American president, a Democrat backed by larger Democratic congressional majorities pledged to undertaking major new policy directions at home and abroad. Both the Western and non-Western worlds confront a changing global economy that gave birth to a financial crisis with the most serious implications for economic stability since the 1930s. The August 2008 invasion of Georgia by Russian Federation troops signaled the possibility of a move from a period of relative quietude to one of military resurgence that may bring into question numerous strategic military assumptions that prevailed for almost two decades after the collapse of the Soviet Union. The United States and Western Europe, after several years of controversial military engagement in Iraq and Afghanistan, continue efforts to reshape foreign policy with an emphasis on diplomacy instead of preemptive warfare. Christians in the Northern and Southern Hemispheres continue to be sharply divided as they debate the character of their faith and its relationship to other faiths and the social questions of the day. A growing consensus of opinion recognizes the dangers posed by environmental change.

The authors of this volume continue to believe that the heritage of Western civilization remains a major point of departure for understanding and defining the challenges of this no longer new century. The unprecedented globalization of daily life that is a hallmark of our era has occurred largely through the spread of Western influences. From the sixteenth century onward, the West has exerted vast influences throughout the globe for both good and ill, and today's global citizens continue to live in the wake of that impact. It is the goal of this book to introduce its readers to the Western heritage, so that they may be better informed and more culturally sensitive citizens of the increasingly troubled and challenging global age. The events of recent years and the hostility that has arisen in many parts of the world to the power and influence of the West require new efforts to understand how the West sees itself and how other parts of the world see the West.

Since *The Western Heritage* first appeared, we have sought to provide our readers with a work that does justice to the richness and variety of Western civilization and its many complexities. We hope that such an understanding of the West will foster lively debate about its character, values, institutions, and global influence. Indeed, we believe such a critical outlook on their own culture has characterized the peoples of the West since the dawn of history. Through such debates we define ourselves and the values of our culture. Consequently, we welcome the debate and hope that *The Western Heritage: Teaching and Learning Classroom Edition*, Brief Sixth Edition, can help foster an informed discussion through its history of the West's strengths and weaknesses, and the controversies surrounding Western history. To further that debate, we have included a new introductory essay entitled "What Is the Western Heritage?" to introduce students to the concept of the West and to allow instructors and students to have a point of departure for debating this concept in their course of study.

We also believe that any book addressing the experience of the West must also look beyond its historical European borders. Students reading this book come from a wide variety of cultures and experiences. They live in a world of highly interconnected economies and instant communication between cultures. In this emerging multicultural society it seems both appropriate and necessary to recognize how Western civilization has throughout its history interacted with other cultures, both influencing and being influenced by them. For this reason, we have introduced to this edition a new chapter on the nineteenth-century European age of imperialism. Further examples of Western interaction with other parts of the world, such as with Islam, appear throughout the text.

In this edition as in past editions, our goal has been to present Western civilization fairly, accurately, and in a way that does justice to this great, diverse legacy of human enterprise. History has many facets, no single one of which can alone account for the others. Any attempt to tell the story of the West from a single overarching perspective, no matter how timely, is bound to neglect or suppress some important parts of this story. Like all other authors of introductory texts, we have had to make choices, but we have attempted to provide the broadest possible introduction to Western civilization.

GOALS OF THE TEXT

Our primary goal has been to present a strong, clear, narrative account of the central developments in Western history. We have also sought to call attention to certain critical themes:

- The capacity of Western civilization, from the time of the Greeks to the present, to transform itself through self-criticism.

- The development in the West of political freedom, constitutional government, and concern for the rule of law and individual rights.

- The shifting relations among religion, society, and the state.

- The development of science and technology and their expanding impact on Western thought, social institutions, and everyday life.

- The major religious and intellectual currents that have shaped Western culture.

We believe that these themes have been fundamental in Western civilization, shaping the past and exerting a continuing influence on the present.

Flexible Presentation   *The Western Heritage: Teaching and Learning Classroom Edition*, Brief Sixth Edition, is designed to accommodate a variety of approaches to a course in Western civilization, allowing teachers to stress what is most important to them. Some teachers will ask students to read all the chapters. Others will select among them to reinforce assigned readings and lectures. We believe the "Compare & Connect" and "Encountering the Past" features may also be adopted selectively by instructors for purposes of classroom presentation and debate and as the basis for short written assignments.

Integrated Social, Cultural, and Political History
The Western Heritage provides one of the richest accounts of the social history of the West available today, with strong coverage of family life, the changing roles of women, and the place of the family in relation to broader economic, political, and social developments. This coverage reflects the explosive growth in social historical research in the past half-century, which has enriched virtually all areas of historical study.

We have also been told repeatedly by teachers that no matter what their own historical specialization, they believe that a political narrative gives students an effective tool to begin to understand the past. Consequently, we have sought to integrate such a strong political narrative with our treatment of the social, cultural, and intellectual factors in Western history.

We also believe that religious faith and religious institutions have been fundamental to the development of the West. No other survey text presents so full an account of the religious and intellectual development of the West. People may be political and social beings, but they are also reasoning and spiritual beings. What they think and believe are among the most important things we can know about them. Their ideas about God, society, law, gender, human nature, and the physical world have changed over the centuries and continue to change. We cannot fully grasp our own approach to the world without understanding the religious and intellectual currents of the past and how they influenced our thoughts and conceptual categories. We seek to recognize the impact of religion in the expansion of the West, including the settlement the Americas in the sixteenth century and the role of missionaries in nineteenth-century Western imperialism.

Clarity and Accessibility   Good narrative history requires clear, vigorous prose. As with earlier editions, we have paid careful attention to our writing, subjecting every paragraph to critical scrutiny. Our goal has been to make the history of the West accessible to students without compromising vocabulary or conceptual level. We hope this effort will benefit both teachers and students.

THE BRIEF SIXTH EDITION

NEW TO THIS EDITION

- We include a new introductory essay entitled "What Is the Western Heritage?" designed to introduce students to the concept of Western civilization as it has changed over the centuries and at the same to provide instructors the opportunity to debate this concept and its implications with their students.

- Each chapter includes a new feature entitled **"Compare & Connect"** that juxtaposes two or more documents in which an important question is debated or a comparison between a document and an illustration is presented. Each "Compare & Connect" feature contains three to five questions on each of the documents, one of which asks students to make connections between and among the viewpoints presented in the feature. These features are intended to encourage students to debate different points of view in class and to learn to read and evaluate differing viewpoints or to analyze documentary and visual evidence. An interactive version of this feature is available on www.myhistorylab.com.

- An entirely new chapter, "The Age of Western Imperialism" (Chapter 25), provides an in-depth global overview of nineteenth-century Western imperial expansion. Topics covered in this chapter include the nineteenth-century shift in Western imperial ventures from the Americas to Africa and Asia, the significance of the British Empire, British imperial rule in India, the New Imperialism, the partition of Africa, the role of missionaries in European colonialism, the relationship of technology and science to imperialism, and international colonial rivalries.

- The new chapter on imperialism has led to a streamlining of the chapter on World War I and its aftermath as well as more extensive comments on the colonial ramifications of the peace settlement (Chapter 26).

- A single, more sharply focused chapter on the twentieth-century interwar years (Chapter 27) has replaced two longer chapters on this period.

- The two closing chapters of the book (Chapters 29 and 30) carry the narrative through important recent events such as the Russian invasion of Georgia and the collapse of financial institutions in Europe and the United States in the fall of 2008.

ONGOING FEATURES THAT ENLIVEN STUDENT INTEREST AND UNDERSTANDING

"Encountering the Past"   Each chapter includes an essay on a significant issue of everyday life or popular culture. These essays explore a variety of subjects, including gladiatorial bouts and medieval games, smoking in early modern Europe, and the politics of rock music in the late twentieth century. These thirty essays, each of which includes an illustration and study questions, expand *The Western Heritage*'s rich coverage of social and cultural history.

Recent Scholarship   As in previous editions, changes in this edition reflect our determination to incorporate the most recent developments in historical scholarship and the concerns of professional historians.

Maps and Illustrations   To help students understand the relationship between geography and history, approximately half of the maps include relief features. One or two maps in each chapter feature interactive

exercises that can be found in MyHistoryLab. All maps have been carefully edited for accuracy. The text also contains close to 500 color and black and white illustrations, many of which are new to the Brief Sixth Edition.

Pedagogical Features   This edition retains the pedagogical features of previous editions, including glossary terms, chapter review questions, and questions accompanying all "Compare & Connect" and "Encountering the Past" features in the text. Each of these features is designed to make the text more accessible to students and to reinforce key concepts.

- **Summary** sections at the end of each chapter summarize the major themes of each chapter.

- **Chapter Review** questions help students focus on and interpret the broader themes of a chapter. These also can be used for class discussion and essay topics.

- **Chronologies** within each chapter help students organize a time sequence for key events.

- **Overview Tables** in each chapter summarize complex issues.

- **Quick Reviews,** found at key places in the margins of each chapter, encourage students to review important concepts.

- **Key Terms,** boldfaced in the text, are listed (with page reference) at the end of each chapter and defined in the book's glossary.

- **Suggested Readings** at the end of the book have been updated with new titles reflecting recent scholarship.

- **Map Explorations** and **Critical-Thinking Questions** prompt students to engage with maps, often in an interactive fashion. Each Map Exploration can be found at www.myhistorylab.com.

A Note on Dates and Transliterations   This edition of *The Western Heritage* continues the practice of using B.C.E. (before the common era) and C.E. (common era) instead of B.C. (before Christ) and A.D. (anno Domini, the year of the Lord) to designate dates. We also follow the most accurate currently accepted English transliterations of Arabic words. For example, today *Koran* has been replaced by the more accurate

Qur'an; similarly *Muhammad* is preferable to *Mohammed* and *Muslim* to *Moslem*.

ANCILLARY INSTRUCTIONAL MATERIALS

The ancillary instructional materials that accompany *The Western Heritage: Teaching and Learning Classroom Edition*, Brief Sixth Edition, are designed to reinforce and enliven the richness of the past and inspire students with the excitement of studying the history of Western civilization.

FOR INSTRUCTORS

Instructor's Manual   The *Instructor's Manual* contains chapter summaries, key points and vital concepts, and information on audiovisual resources that can be used in developing and preparing lecture presentations. (ISBN 0-205-73241-0)

Test Item File   The Test Item File includes over 1,500 multiple-choice, identification, map, and essay test questions. (ISBN 0-205-73240-2)

MyTest   MyTest is a browser-based test management program. The program allows instructors to select items from the Test Item File in order to create tests. It also allows for online testing. (ISBN 0-205-73298-4)

The Instructor's Resource Center (www.pearsonhighered.com)   Text-specific materials, such as the Instructor's Manual and the Test Item File, are available for downloading by adopters.

FOR INSTRUCTORS AND STUDENTS

myhistorylab MyHistoryLab (www.myhistorylab.com)   MyHistoryLab provides students with an online package complete with the electronic textbook and numerous study aids. With several hundred primary sources, many of which are assignable and link to a gradebook, pre- and post-tests that link to a gradebook and result in individualized study plans, videos and images, as well as map activities with gradable quizzes, the site offers students a unique, interactive experience that brings history to life. The comprehensive site also includes a History Bookshelf with fifty of the most commonly assigned books in history classes and a History Toolkit with tutorials and helpful links. Other features include gradable assignments and chapter review materials as well as a Test Item File.

FOR STUDENTS

 The Primary Source: Documents in Western Civilization **DVD**   This DVD-ROM offers a rich collection of textual and visual sources—many never before available to a wide audience—and serves as an indispensable tool for working with sources. Extensively developed with the guidance of historians and teachers, *Primary Source: Documents in Western Civilization* includes over 800 sources in Western civilization history—from cave art, to text documents, to satellite images of Earth from space. All sources are accompanied by headnotes and focus questions and are searchable by topic, region, or theme. In addition, a built-in tutorial guides students through the process of working with documents. The DVD can be bundled with *The Western Heritage: Teaching and Learning Classroom Edition*, Brief Sixth Edition, at no charge. Please contact your Pearson Arts and Sciences representative for ordering information. (ISBN 0-13-134407-2)

Two-volume print version of *Primary Source: Documents in Western Civilization* is also available:

Primary Sources in Western Civilization, Volume 1: *To 1700, Second Edition* (ISBN 0-13-175583-8)

Primary Sources in Western Civilization, Volume 2: *Since 1400, Second Edition* (ISBN 0-13-175584-6)

Please contact your Pearson Arts and Sciences representative for ordering information.

Lives and Legacies: Biographies in Western Civilization, **Second Edition**   Extensively revised, *Lives and Legacies* includes brief, focused biographies of sixty individuals whose lives provide insight into the key developments of Western civilization. Each biography includes an introduction, prereading questions, and suggestions for additional reading. Available in two volumes:

Lives and Legacies, Volume 1, Second Edition (ISBN 0-205-64915-7)

Lives and Legacies, Volume 2, Second Edition (ISBN 0-205-64914-9)

Western Civilization Study Site (www.ablongman.com/longmanwesterncivilization/)   This course-based, open-access online companion provides both students and professors with links for further research as well as test questions in multiple choice, true/false, and fill-in-the-blank formats.

Penguin Classics Selected titles from the renowned Penguin Classics series can be bundled with *The Western Heritage: Teaching and Learning Classroom Edition*, Brief Sixth Edition, for a nominal charge. Please contact your Pearson Arts and Sciences sales representative for details.

Longman Atlas of Western Civilization This 52-page atlas features carefully selected historical maps that provide comprehensive coverage for the major historical periods. Contact your Pearson Arts and Sciences representative for details. (ISBN 0-321-21626-1)

DK ***The Prentice Hall Atlas of Western Civilization*, Second Edition** Produced in collaboration with Dorling Kindersley, the leader in cartographic publishing, the updated second edition of *The Prentice Hall Atlas of Western Civilization* applies the most innovative cartographic techniques to present Western civilization in all of its complexity and diversity. Copies of the atlas can be bundled with *The Western Heritage: Teaching and Learning Classroom Edition*, Brief Sixth Edition, for a nominal charge. Contact your Pearson Arts and Sciences sales representative for details. (ISBN 0-13-604246-5)

 A Guide to Your History Course: What Every Student Needs to Know Written by Vincent A. Clark, this concise, spiral-bound guidebook orients students to the issues and problems they will face in the history classroom. Available at a discount when bundled with *The Western Heritage: Teaching and Learning Classroom Edition*, Brief Sixth Edition. (ISBN 0-13-185087-3)

***A Short Guide to Writing about History*, Seventh Edition** Written by Richard Marius, late of Harvard University, and Melvin E. Page, Eastern Tennessee State University, this engaging and practical text helps students get beyond merely compiling dates and facts. Covering both brief essays and the documented resource paper, the text explores the writing and researching processes, identifies different modes of historical writing, including argument, and concludes with guidelines for improving style. (ISBN 0-205-67370-8)

Interpretations of the Western World (www.pearsoncustom.com/custom-library/interpretations-of-the-western-world) The selections in this customizable database of secondary source readings are grouped together topically so instructors can assign readings that illustrate different points of view on a given historical debate.

ACKNOWLEDGMENTS

We are grateful to the scholars and teachers whose thoughtful and often detailed comments helped shape this revision:

Mark Baker, California State University, Bakersfield
Fred Baumgartner, Virginia Tech
Jane Bishop, The Citadel, The Military College of South Carolina
Eugene Boia, Cleveland State University
Kristen Burkholder, Oklahoma State University
Joseph Byrnes, Oklahoma State University
Anthony Cardoza, Loyola University, Chicago
Marcus Cox, The Citadel, The Military College of South Carolina
Delores Davison, Foothill College
Paul Deslandes, University of Vermont
Petra DeWitt, University of Missouri, Rolla
Richard Eller, Catawaba Valley Community College
Axel Fair-Schulz, State University of New York at Potsdam
Sean Field, University of Vermont
Shannon Fogg, Missouri S&T
Stephen Gibson, Ranken Technical College
Stephanie Hallock, Harford Community College
Michael Hickey, Bloomsburg University
Anthony Heideman, Range Community College
William Hudon, Bloomsburg University
Terry Jones, Oklahoma State University
Kevin Keating, Broward Community College
Michael Khodarkovsky, Loyola University, Chicago
Martha Kinney, Suffolk County Community College
Helena Krohn, Tidewater Community College
Eugene Larson, Los Angeles Pierce College
Karl Loewenstein, University of Wisconsin, Oshkosh
Arthur Lysiak, Bloomsburg University
William Martin, University of Utah
Lisa McClain, Boise State University
Daniel Miller, University of West Florida
Eva Mo, Meridian Junior College
Michelle Mouton, University of Wisconsin, Oshkosh
Tonia Sharlach Nash, Oklahoma State University
Charles Odahl, Boise State University
Mark Orsag, Doane College
Michael Pascale, SUNY at Suffolk, Farmingdale College
Neal Pease, University of Wisconsin, Milwaukee

Norman Raiford, Greenville Technical College

Pete Rottier, Cleveland State University

Thomas Rowland, University of Wisconsin at Oshkosh

Michael Rutz, University of Wisconsin, Oshkosh

Stephen Ruzicka, University of North Carolina at
    Greensboro

Mark Schumann, Eastern Michigan University

Patrick Speelman, The Citadel, The Military College of
    South Carolina

Frank W. Thackeray, Indiana University Southeast

Daniel Trifan, Missouri Western State University

Miriam Vivian, California State University, Bakersfield

Andrew Zimmerman, George Washington University

We would like to thank the dedicated people who helped produce this new edition. Our acquisitions editor, Charles Cavaliere; our development editor, Gerald Lombardi; our project manager, Rob DeGeorge; our production liaison, Lynn Savino Wendel; Maria Lange, who created the beautiful new design of this edition; Mary Ann Gloriande, our operations specialist; and Rebecca Dunn, production editor.

D.K.

S.O.

F.M.T.

Donald Kagan is Sterling Professor of History and Classics at Yale University, where he has taught since 1969. He received the A.B. degree in history from Brooklyn College, the M.A. in classics from Brown University, and the Ph.D. in history from Ohio State University. During 1958–1959 he studied at the American School of Classical Studies as a Fulbright Scholar. He has received three awards for undergraduate teaching at Cornell and Yale. He is the author of a history of Greek political thought, *The Great Dialogue* (1965); a four-volume history of the Peloponnesian war, *The Origins of the Peloponnesian War* (1969); *The Archidamian War* (1974); *The Peace of Nicias and the Sicilian Expedition* (1981); *The Fall of the Athenian Empire* (1987); a biography of Pericles, *Pericles of Athens and the Birth of Democracy* (1991); *On the Origins of War* (1995); and *The Peloponnesian War* (2003). He is coauthor, with Frederick W. Kagan, of *While America Sleeps* (2000). With Brian Tierney and L. Pearce Williams, he is the editor of *Great Issues in Western Civilization*, a collection of readings. He was awarded the National Humanities Medal for 2002 and was chosen by the National Endowment for the Humanities to deliver the Jefferson Lecture in 2004.

Steven Ozment is McLean Professor of Ancient and Modern History at Harvard University. He has taught Western Civilization at Yale, Stanford, and Harvard. He is the author of eleven books. *The Age of Reform, 1250–1550* (1980) won the Schaff Prize and was nominated for the 1981 National Book Award. Five of his books have been selections of the History Book Club: *Magdalena and Balthasar: An Intimate Portrait of Life in Sixteenth Century Europe* (1986); *Three Behaim Boys: Growing Up in Early Modern Germany* (1990); *Protestants: The Birth of a Revolution* (1992); *The Burgermeister's Daughter: Scandal in a Sixteenth Century German Town* (1996); and *Flesh and Spirit: Private Life in Early Modern Germany* (1999). His most recent publications are *Ancestors: The Loving Family of Old Europe* (2001); *A Mighty Fortress: A New History of the German People* (2004); and "Why We Study Western Civ," *The Public Interest 158* (2005).

Frank M. Turner is John Hay Whitney Professor of History at Yale University and Director of the Beinecke Rare Book and Manuscript Library at Yale University, where he served as University Provost from 1988 to 1992. He received his B.A. degree at the College of William and Mary and his Ph.D. from Yale. He has received the Yale College Award for Distinguished Undergraduate Teaching. He has directed a National Endowment for the Humanities Summer Institute. His scholarly research has received the support of fellowships from the National Endowment for the Humanities and the Guggenheim Foundation and the Woodrow Wilson Center. He is the author of *Between Science and Religion: The Reaction to Scientific Naturalism in Late Victorian England* (1974); *The Greek Heritage in Victorian Britain* (1981), which received the British Council Prize of the Conference on British Studies and the Yale Press Governors Award; *Contesting Cultural Authority: Essays in Victorian Intellectual Life* (1993); and *John Henry Newman: The Challenge to Evangelical Religion* (2002). He has also contributed numerous articles to journals and has served on the editorial advisory boards of *The Journal of Modern History, Isis*, and *Victorian Studies*. He edited *The Idea of a University* by John Henry Newman (1996); *Reflections on the Revolution in France* by Edmund Burke (2003); and *Apologia Pro Vita Sua* and *Six Sermons by John Henry Newman* (2008). Between 1996 and 2006, he served as a Trustee of Connecticut College and between 2004 and 2008 as a member of the Connecticut Humanities Council. In 2003, Professor Turner was appointed Director of the Beinecke Rare Book and Manuscript Library at Yale University.

WHAT IS THE WESTERN HERITAGE?

This book invites students and instructors to explore the Western Heritage. What is that heritage? The Western Heritage emerges from an evolved and evolving story of human actions and interactions, peaceful and violent, that arose in the eastern Mediterranean and then spread across the western Mediterranean into northern Europe and eventually to the American continents, and in their broadest impact, to the peoples of Africa and Asia as well.

The Western Heritage as a distinct portion of world history descends from the ancient Greeks. They saw their own political life based on open discussion of law and policy as different from that of Mesopotamia, Persia, and Egypt, where kings ruled without regard to public opinion. The Greeks invented the concept of citizenship, defining it as engagement in some form of self-government. Furthermore, through their literature and philosophy, the Greeks established the conviction, which became characteristic of the West, that reason can shape and analyze physical nature, politics, and morality.

The city of Rome, spreading its authority through military conquest across the Mediterranean world, embraced Greek literature and philosophy. Through their conquests and imposition of their law, the Romans created the Western world as a vast empire stretching from Egypt and Syria in the east to Britain in the west. Although the Roman Republic, governed by a Senate and popular political institutions, gave way after civil wars to the autocratic rule of the Roman Empire, the idea of a free republic of engaged citizens governed by public law and constitutional arrangements limiting political authority survived centuries of arbitrary rule by emperors. As in the rest of the world, the Greeks, the Romans, and virtually all other ancient peoples excluded women and slaves from political life and tolerated considerable social inequality.

In the early fourth century C.E., the Emperor Constantine reorganized the Roman Empire in two fundamental ways that reshaped the West. First, he moved the imperial capital from Rome to Constantinople (Istanbul), establishing separate emperors in the east and west. Thereafter, large portions of the western empire became subject to the rulers of Germanic tribes. In the confusion of these times, most of the texts embodying ancient philosophy, literature, and history became lost in the West, and for centuries Western Europeans were intellectually severed from that ancient heritage, which would later be recovered in a series of renaissances, or cultural rebirths, beginning in the eighth century.

Constantine's second fateful major reshaping of the West was his recognition of Christianity as the official religion of the empire. Christianity had grown out of the ancient monotheistic religion of the Hebrew people living in ancient Palestine. With the ministry of Jesus of Nazareth and the spread of his teachings by the Apostle Paul, Christianity had established itself as one of many religions in the empire. Because Christianity was monotheistic, Constantine's official embrace of it led to the eradication of pagan polytheism. Thereafter, the West became more or less coterminous with Latin Christianity, or that portion of the Christian Church acknowledging the Bishop of Rome as its head.

As the emperors' rule broke down, bishops became the effective political rulers in many parts of Western Europe. But the Christian Church in the West never governed without negotiation or conflict with secular rulers, and religious law never replaced secular law. Nor could secular rulers govern if they ignored the influence of the church. Hence, from the fourth century C.E. to the present day, rival claims to political and moral authority between ecclesiastical and political officials have characterized the West.

In the seventh century the Christian West faced a new challenge from the rise of Islam. This new monotheistic religion originating in the teachings of the prophet Muhammad arose on the Arabian Peninsula and spread through rapid conquests across North Africa and eventually into Spain, turning the Mediterranean into what one historian has termed "a Muslim lake." Between the eleventh and the thirteenth centuries, Christians attempted to reclaim the Holy Land from Muslim control in church-inspired military crusades that still resonate negatively in the Islamic world.

It was, however, in the Muslim world that most of the texts of ancient Greek and Latin learning survived and were studied, while intellectual life languished in the West. Commencing in the twelfth century, knowledge of those texts began to work its way back into Western Europe. By the fourteenth century European thinkers redefined themselves and their intellectual ambitions by recovering the literature and science

In his painting *The School of Athens*, the great Italian Renaissance painter Raphael portrayed the ancient Greek philosopher Plato and his student Aristotle engaged in debate. Plato, who points to the heavens, believed in a set of ideal truths that exists in its own realm distinct from the earth. Aristotle urged that all philosophy must be in touch with lived reality and confirms this position by pointing to the earth. Such debate has characterized the intellectual, political, and social experience of the West. Indeed, the very concept of "Western Civilization" has itself been subject to debate, criticism, and change over the centuries.

© Scala/Art Resource, NY

from the ancient world, reuniting Europe with its Graeco-Roman past.

From the twelfth through the eighteenth centuries, a new European political system slowly arose based on centralized monarchies characterized by large armies, navies, and bureaucracies loyal to the monarch and by the capacity to raise revenues. Whatever the personal ambitions of individual rulers, for the most part these monarchies recognized both the political role of local or national assemblies drawn from the propertied elites and the binding power of constitutional law on themselves. Also, in each of these monarchies, church officials and church law played important roles in public life. The monarchies, their military, and their expanding commercial economies became the basis for the extension of European and Western influence around the globe.

In the late fifteenth and early sixteenth centuries, two transforming events occurred. The first was the European discovery and conquest of the American continents, thus opening the Americas to Western institutions, religion, and economic exploitation. Over time the labor shortages of the Americas led to the forced migration of millions of Africans as slaves to the "New World." By the mid–seventeenth century, the West consequently embraced the entire transatlantic world and its multiracial societies.

Second, shortly after the American encounter, a religious schism erupted within Latin Christianity. Reformers rejecting both many medieval Christian doctrines as unbiblical and the primacy of the Pope in Rome established Protestant churches across much of northern Europe. As a consequence, for almost two centuries religious warfare between Protestants and Roman

Catholics overwhelmed the continent as monarchies chose to defend one side or the other. This religious turmoil meant that the Europeans who conquered and settled the Americas carried with them particularly energized religious convictions, with Roman Catholics dominating Latin America and English Protestants most of North America.

By the late eighteenth century, the idea of the West denoted a culture increasingly dominated by two new forces. First, science arising from a new understanding of nature achieved during the sixteenth and seventeenth centuries persuaded growing numbers of the educated elite that human beings can rationally master nature for ever-expanding productive purposes improving the health and well-being of humankind. From this era to the present, the West has been associated with advances in technology, medicine, and scientific research. Second, during the eighteenth century, a drive for economic improvement that vastly increased agricultural production and then industrial manufacturing transformed economic life, especially in Western Europe and later the United States. Both of these economic developments went hand in hand with urbanization and the movement of the industrial economy into cities where the new urban populations experienced major social dislocation.

During these decades certain Western European elites came to regard advances in agricultural and manufacturing economies that were based on science and tied to commercial expansion as "civilized" in contrast to cultures that lacked those characteristics. From these ideas emerged the concept of Western Civilization defined to suggest that peoples dwelling outside Europe or inside Europe east of the Elbe River were less than civilized. Whereas Europeans had once defined themselves against the rest of the world as free citizens and then later as Christians, they now defined themselves as "civilized." Europeans would carry this self-assured superiority into their nineteenth- and early-twentieth-century encounters with the peoples of Asia, Africa, and the Pacific.

During the last quarter of the eighteenth century, political revolution erupted across the transatlantic world. The British colonies of North America revolted. Then revolution occurred in France and spread across much of Europe. From 1791 through 1830, the Wars of Independence liberated Latin America from its European conquerors. These revolutions created bold new modes of political life, rooting the legitimacy of the state in some form of popular government and generally written constitutions. Thereafter, despite the presence of authoritarian governments on the European continent, the idea of the West, now including the new republics of the United States and Latin America, became associated with liberal democratic governments.

Furthermore, during the nineteenth century, most major European states came to identify themselves in terms of nationality—language, history, and ethnicity—rather than loyalty to a monarch. Nationalism eventually inflamed popular opinion and unloosed unprecedented political ambition by European governments.

These ambitions led to imperialism and the creation of new overseas European empires in the late nineteenth century. For the peoples living in European-administered Asian and African colonies, the idea and reality of the West embodied foreign domination and often disadvantageous involvement in a world economy. When in 1945 the close of World War II led to a sharp decline in European imperial authority, colonial peoples around the globe challenged that authority and gained independence. These former colonial peoples, however, often still suspected the West of seeking to control them. Hence, anticolonialism like colonialism before it redefined the West far from its borders.

Late-nineteenth-century nationalism and imperialism also unleashed with World War I in 1914 unprecedented military hostilities among European nations that spread around the globe, followed a quarter-century later by an even greater world war. As one result of World War I, revolution occurred in Russia with the establishment of the communist Soviet Union. During the interwar years a Fascist Party seized power in Italy and a Nazi Party took control of Germany. In response to these new authoritarian regimes, Western European powers and the United States identified themselves with liberal democratic constitutionalism, individual freedom, commercial capitalism, science and learning freely pursued, and religious liberty, all of which they defined as the Western Heritage. During the Cold War, conceived of as an East-West, democratic versus communist struggle that concluded with the collapse of the Soviet Union in 1991, the Western powers led by the United States continued to embrace those values in conscious opposition to the Soviet government, which since 1945 had also dominated much of Eastern Europe.

Since 1991, the West has again become redefined in the minds of many people as a world political and economic order dominated by the United States. Europe clearly remains the West, but political leadership has moved to North America. That American domination and recent American foreign policy have led throughout the West and elsewhere to much criticism of the United States.

Such self-criticism itself embodies one of the most important and persistent parts of the Western Heritage. From the Hebrew prophets and Socrates to the critics of European imperialism, American foreign policy, social inequality, and environmental devastation, voices in the West have again and again been raised to criticize often in the most strident manner the policies of Western governments and the thought, values, social conditions, and inequalities of Western societies.

Consequently, we study the Western Heritage not because the subject always or even primarily presents an admirable picture, but because the study of the Western Heritage like the study of all history calls us to an integrity of research, observation, and analysis that clarifies our minds and challenges our moral sensibilities. The challenge of history is the challenge of thinking, and it is to that challenge that his book invites its readers.

QUESTIONS

1. How have people in the West defined themselves in contrast with civilizations of the ancient East, and later in contrast with Islamic civilization, and still later in contrast with less economically developed regions of the world? Have people in the West historically viewed their own civilization to be superior to civilizations in other parts of the world? Why or why not?

2. How did the Emperor Constantine's adoption of Christianity as the official religion of the Roman Empire change the concept of the West? Is the presence of Christianity still a determining characteristic of the West?

3. How has the geographical location of what has been understood as the West changed over the centuries?

4. In the past two centuries Western nations established empires around the globe. How did these imperial ventures and the local resistance to them give rise to critical definitions of the West that contrasted with the definitions that had developed in Europe and the United States? How have those non-Western definitions of the West contributed to self-criticism within Western nations?

5. How useful is the concept of Western civilization in understanding today's global economy and global communications made possible by the Internet? Is the idea of Western civilization synonymous with the concept of modern civilization? Do you think the concept of the West will once again be redefined ten years from now?

To view a video of the authors discussing the Western heritage, go to www.myhistorylab.com

The WESTERN HERITAGE

European State Consolidation in the Seventeenth and Eighteenth Centuries

Peter the Great (r. 1682–1725), seeking to make Russia a military power, reorganized the country's political and economic structures. His reign saw Russia enter fully into European power politics.

The Apotheosis of Tsar Peter the Great 1672–1725 by unknown artist, 1710. Historical Museum, Moscow, Russia/E.T. Archive

How would you reconcile this image of Peter the Great with his reputation as a modernizer and reformer?

THE NETHERLANDS: GOLDEN AGE TO DECLINE *page 322*

WHAT WAS the Dutch Golden Age and what led to its decline?

TWO MODELS OF EUROPEAN POLITICAL DEVELOPMENT *page 323*

WHAT FACTORS led to the different political paths taken by England and France in the seventeenth century?

CONSTITUTIONAL CRISIS AND SETTLEMENT IN STUART ENGLAND *page 323*

HOW DID conflicts over taxation and religion lead to civil war in Stuart England?

RISE OF ABSOLUTE MONARCHY IN FRANCE: THE WORLD OF LOUIS XIV *page 328*

WHY WERE efforts to establish absolute monarchy successful in France but unsuccessful in England?

CENTRAL AND EASTERN EUROPE *page 335*

WHAT WERE the main characteristics that defined the Polish, Austrian, and Prussian states in the seventeenth and eighteenth centuries?

RUSSIA ENTERS THE EUROPEAN POLITICAL ARENA *page 338*

HOW DID Peter the Great transform Russia into a powerful, centralized nation?

THE OTTOMAN EMPIRE *page 341*

WHAT WAS the attitude of the Ottoman rulers toward religion in their empire and how was this reflected in their policies?

etween the early seventeenth and mid–twentieth centuries, no region so dominated other parts of the world politically, militarily, and economically as Europe. Such had not been the case before this period, nor would it be so after World War II. This era of European dominance coincided with a shift of power with Europe itself from the Mediterranean—in particular, Spain and Portugal—to the states of northern Europe.

By the mid–1700s, five states—Great Britain, France, Austria, Prussia, and Russia—organized themselves politically and came to dominate Europe, and later, large areas of the world through military might and economic strength. These states arose at the expense of Spain, Portugal, the United Provinces of the Netherlands, Poland, Sweden, the Ottoman Empire, and the Holy Roman Empire. ■

THE NETHERLANDS: GOLDEN AGE TO DECLINE

WHAT WAS the Dutch Golden Age and what led to its decline?

The seven provinces that became the United Provinces of the Netherlands emerged as a nation after revolting against Spain in 1572. During the seventeenth century, the Dutch engaged in a series of naval wars with England. Then, in 1672, the armies of Louis XIV invaded the Netherlands. Prince William III of Orange (1650–1702), the grandson of William the Silent (1533–1584) and the hereditary chief executive, or *stadtholder*, of Holland, the most important of the provinces, rallied the Dutch and eventually led the entire European coalition against France. As a part of that strategy, he answered the invitation of Protestant English aristocrats in 1688 to assume, along with his wife Mary, the English throne.

During both the seventeenth and eighteenth centuries, the political and economic life of the Netherlands differed from that of the rest of Europe. The other major nations pursued paths toward strong central government. By contrast, the Netherlands was formally a republic. Each of the provinces retained considerable authority. The Dutch deeply distrusted monarchy and the ambitions of the House of Orange. Nonetheless, when confronted with major military challenges, the Dutch would permit the House of Orange and, most notably, William III to assume dominant leadership. When William died in 1702 and the wars with France ended in 1714, the Dutch reverted to their republican structures.

Although the provinces making up the Netherlands were traditionally identified with the Protestant cause in Europe, toleration marked Dutch religious life. While governments in other European states attempted to impose a single religion on their people or tore themselves apart in religious conflict, in the Netherlands peoples of differing religious faiths lived together peacefully.

URBAN PROSPERITY

Beyond the climate of religious toleration, what most amazed seventeenth-century contemporaries about the Dutch Republic was its economic prosperity. Its remarkable economic achievement was built on the foundations of high urban consolidation, transformed agriculture, extensive trade and finance, and an overseas commercial empire.

In the Netherlands, more people lived in cities than in any other area of Europe. Key transformations in Dutch farming that served as the model for the rest of Europe made this urban transformation possible. During the seventeenth century, the Dutch drained and reclaimed land from the sea, which they used for highly profitable farming.

The technologically advanced fleet of the Dutch East India Company, shown here at anchor in Amsterdam, linked the Netherlands' economy with that of Southeast Asia.

Andries van Eertvelt (1590–1652), *The Return to Amsterdam of the Fleet of the Dutch East India Company in 1599*. Oil on copper. Johnny van Haeften Gallery, London, UK. The Bridgeman Art Library

What role did naval power play in producing the Golden Age of the Netherlands?

Dutch fishermen dominated the market for herring and supplied much of the continent's dried fish. The Dutch also supplied textiles to many parts of Europe. The overseas trades also supported a vast shipbuilding and ship supply industry. The most advanced financial system of the day supported all of this trade, commerce, and manufacturing.

The final foundation of Dutch prosperity was a seaborne empire. Dutch traders established a major presence in East Asia, particularly in spice-producing areas of Java, the Moluccas, and Sri Lanka. The vehicle for this penetration was the Dutch East Indies Company (chartered in 1602). The company eventually displaced Portuguese dominance in the spice trade of East Asia and for many years prevented English traders from establishing a major presence there.

ECONOMIC DECLINE

The decline in political influence of the United Provinces of the Netherlands occurred in the eighteenth century. After the death of William III of Britain in 1702, unified political leadership vanished. Naval supremacy slowly but steadily passed to the British. The fishing industry declined, and the Dutch lost their technological superiority in shipbuilding. Similar stagnation overtook the Dutch domestic industries.

What saved the United Provinces from becoming completely insignificant in European affairs was its continued financial dominance. Well past the middle of the eighteenth century, Dutch banks continued to finance European trade, and the Amsterdam stock exchange remained an important financial institution.

TWO MODELS OF EUROPEAN POLITICAL DEVELOPMENT

The United Netherlands, like Venice and the Swiss cantons, was a republic governed without a monarch. Elsewhere in Europe, monarchy of two fundamentally different patterns predominated in response to the military challenges of international conflict. The two models became known as *parliamentary monarchy* and *political absolutism*. England embodied the first, and France, the second. The political forces that led to the creation of these two models had arisen from military concerns. During the second half of the sixteenth century, changes in military organization, weapons, and tactics sharply increased the cost of warfare. Because their traditional sources of income could not finance these growing expenses, in addition to the other costs of government, monarchs sought new revenues. Only monarchies that succeeded in building a secure financial base that was not deeply dependent on the support of noble estates, diets, or assemblies achieved absolute rule. The French monarchy succeeded in this effort, whereas the English monarchy failed. That success and failure led to the two models of government—*absolutism* in France and *parliamentary monarchy* in England—that shaped subsequent political development in Europe.

CONSTITUTIONAL CRISIS AND SETTLEMENT IN STUART ENGLAND

JAMES I

In 1603 James VI, the son of Mary Stuart, Queen of Scots, who had been King of Scotland since 1567 succeeded without opposition or incident the childless Elizabeth I as James I of England. He also inherited a large royal debt and a fiercely divided church. A strong believer in the divine right of kings, he expected to rule with a minimum of consultation beyond his own royal court.

 WHAT FACTORS led to the different political paths taken by England and France in the seventeenth century?

political absolutism Government by a ruler with absolute authority.

parliamentary monarchy Rule by a monarch with some parliamentary guidance or input.

 HOW DID conflicts over taxation and religion lead to civil war in Stuart England?

Parliament met only when the monarch summoned it, which James hoped to do rarely. In place of parliamentarily approved revenues, James developed other sources of income, largely by levying new custom duties known as *impositions*. Members of Parliament regarded this as an affront to their authority over the royal purse, but they did not seek a serious confrontation. Rather, throughout James's reign they wrangled and negotiated.

The religious problem also festered under James. Since the days of Elizabeth, **Puritans** within the Church of England had sought to eliminate elaborate religious ceremonies and replace the hierarchical episcopal system of church governance under bishops appointed by the king with a more representative Presbyterian form like that of the Calvinist churches in Scotland and on the Continent. At the Hampton Court Conference of January 1604, James rebuffed the Puritans and firmly declared his intention to maintain and even enhance the Anglican episcopacy.

Religious dissenters began to leave England. In 1620, Puritan separatists founded Plymouth Colony on Cape Cod Bay in North America, preferring flight from England to Anglican conformity. Later in the 1620s, a larger, better financed group of Puritans left England to found the Massachusetts Bay Colony.

James's court became a center of scandal and corruption. He governed by favorites, of whom the most influential was the duke of Buckingham, whom rumor made the king's homosexual lover. Buckingham controlled royal patronage and openly sold peerages and titles to the highest bidders—a practice that angered the nobility because it cheapened their rank.

James's foreign policy roused further opposition and doubt about his Protestant loyalty. In 1604, he concluded a much needed peace with Spain, England's longtime adversary. The war had been ruinously expensive, but his subjects considered the peace a sign of pro-Catholic sentiment. James's unsuccessful attempt to relax penal laws against Catholics further increased suspicions, as did his wise hesitancy in 1618 to rush English troops to the aid of German Protestants at the outbreak of the Thirty Years' War. In 1624, shortly before James's death, England again went to war against Spain, largely in response to parliamentary pressures.

Puritans English Protestants who advocated the "further reformation" of the Anglican Church.

Overview   **Two Models of Government**

	FRANCE'S ABSOLUTISM	ENGLAND'S PARLIAMENTARY MONARCHY
RELIGIOUS FACTORS	Louis XIV, with the support of Catholics, crushed Protestantism for religious uniformity.	A strong Protestant religious movement known as Puritanism limited the monarchy.
INSTITUTIONAL DIFFERENCES	Opposition to the monarchy lacked a tradition of liberties, representation, or bargaining tools.	Parliament was to be consulted, and it appealed to concepts of liberty when conflicts arose.
ECONOMIC POLICIES	Louis XIV made French nobility dependent on his good will by supporting their status.	Political groups invoked traditional liberties to resist the monarchy's economic intrusions.
ROLE OF PERSONALITIES	Louis XIV had guidance from Cardinals Mazarin and Richelieu, training him to be hardworking.	The four Stuart monarchs, acting on whims, had trouble simply making people trust them.

ENCOUNTERING THE PAST

EARLY CONTROVERSY OVER TOBACCO AND SMOKING

King James defended sports from the Puritan charge that all amusements were sinful when enjoyed on the Sabbath, but the king did not favor all popular pleasures. He was ardently opposed to tobacco, one of the novelties that Europeans discovered in the Americas. Tobacco smoking excited opposition almost from the start. Spanish missionaries associated it with pagan religious practices. Sir Francis Bacon (1561–1626) noted it was addictive, and it was condemned by both Christian and Muslim clerics. None of this, however, impeded the spreading use of the pipe.

In 1604, James published a work that left smokers in no doubt as to his opinion of them and their practice. In *A Counterblast to Tobacco* he wrote, "Have you not reason then to be ashamed, and to forbear this filthy novelty . . . ? In your abuse thereof sinning against God, harming yourselves in person . . . [with a] custom loathsome to the eye, hateful to the nose, harmful to the brain, dangerous to the lungs, and the black stinking fume thereof, nearest resembling the horrible Stygian smoke of the pit that is bottomless." [*A Counterblast to Tobacco* (1604), reprinted by the Rodale Press, London, 1954, p. 36.] James tried to stem the use of tobacco by heavily taxing it. When this had the result of encouraging smugglers, James lowered the tax. That, however, produced a stream of revenue that became increasingly important to his government. In 1614, he made the importation of tobacco a royal monopoly, and by 1619, Virginia was shipping 40,000 pounds of tobacco to England annually. James's government, like modern ones, put itself in the odd position of depending on taxes imposed to stop the practice that produced those taxes.

Practically from the moment of its introduction into Europe tobacco smoking was controversial. Here a court jester is portrayed as exhaling rabbits from a pipe as three pipe-smoking gentlemen look on.

© Christel Gerstenberg/Corbis

What activities did early modern writers associate with tobacco smoking?

CHARLES I

Parliament had favored the war with Spain but would not adequately finance it because its members distrusted the monarchy. Unable to gain adequate funds from Parliament, Charles I (r. 1625–1649), like his father, resorted to extra-parliamentary measures. These included levying new tariffs and duties, attempting to collect discontinued taxes, and subjecting English property owners to a so-called forced loan (a tax theoretically to be repaid) and then imprisoning those who refused to pay.

When Parliament met in 1628, its members would grant new funds only if Charles recognized the Petition of Right. This document required that henceforth there should be no forced loans or taxation without the consent of Parliament, that no freeman should be imprisoned without due cause, and that troops should not be billeted in private homes. Charles agreed to the petition, but whether he would keep his word was doubtful. The next year after further disputes, Charles dissolved Parliament and did not recall it until 1640.

Years of Personal Rule Charles might have ruled indefinitely without Parliament had not his religious policies provoked war with Scotland. James I had allowed a wide variety of religious observances in England, Scotland, and Ireland; by contrast, Charles hoped to impose religious conformity at least within England and Scotland. In 1637, Charles and his

QUICK REVIEW

Charles I (r. 1625–1649)

- 1629: Charles dissolves Parliament in face of criticism of his policies

- Unable to wage foreign wars without funds granted by Parliament

- 1640: Efforts to enforce religious conformity within England and Scotland force Charles to reconvene Parliament

King CHARLES the FIRST in the HOUSE of COMMONS, demanding the FIVE impeached MEMBERS to be delivered up to his AUTHORITY.

One of the key moments in the conflict between Charles I and Parliament occurred in January 1642 when Charles personally arrived at the House of Commons intent on arresting five members who had been responsible for opposing him. They had already escaped. Thereafter Charles departed London to raise his army. The event was subsequently often portrayed in English art. The present illustration is from an eighteenth-century engraving.

The Granger Collection, New York

How did Charles I see the relationship between himself and Parliament?

Oliver Cromwell's New Model Army defeated the royalists in the English Civil War. After the execution of Charles I in 1649, Cromwell dominated the short-lived English republic, conquered Ireland and Scotland, and ruled as Lord Protector from 1653 until his death in 1658.

Dorling Kindersley Media Library

What kind of government did Cromwell think was best for England?

high-church Archbishop William Laud (1573–1645), against the opposition of both the English Puritans and the Presbyterian Scots, tried to impose on Scotland the English episcopal system and a prayer book almost identical to the Anglican Book of Common Prayer.

The Scots rebelled, and Charles, with insufficient resources for war, was forced in 1640 to call Parliament. It refused even to consider funds for war until the king agreed to redress a long list of political and religious grievances. The king, in response, immediately dissolved that Parliament—hence its name, the Short Parliament (April–May 1640). When the Scots defeated an English army at the Battle of Newburn in the summer of 1640, Charles reconvened Parliament—this time on its terms—for a long and fateful duration.

THE LONG PARLIAMENT AND CIVIL WAR

The landowners and the merchant classes represented in Parliament had long resented the king's financial measures and paternalistic rule. The Puritans in Parliament resented his religious policies and distrusted the influence of his Roman Catholic wife. What became known as the Long Parliament (1640–1660) thus acted with widespread support and general unanimity when it convened in November 1640.

Parliament abolished the courts that had enforced royal policy and prohibited the levying of new taxes without its consent. In addition, Parliament resolved that no more than three years should elapse between its meetings and that the king could not dissolve it without its own consent.

In January 1642, Charles invaded Parliament, intending to arrest certain of his opponents, but they escaped. The king then left London and began to raise an army. Shocked, a majority of the House of Commons passed the Militia Ordinance, which gave Parliament authority to raise an army of its own. The die was now cast. For the next four years (1642–1646), civil war engulfed England with the king's supporters known as Cavaliers and the parliamentary opposition as Roundheads.

OLIVER CROMWELL AND THE PURITAN REPUBLIC

Two factors led finally to Parliament's victory. The first was an alliance with Scotland in 1643 that committed Parliament to a Presbyterian system of church government. The second was the reorganization of the parliamentary army under Oliver Cromwell (1599–1658), a country squire of iron discipline and strong, independent religious sentiment.

Defeated militarily by June 1645, Charles for the next several years tried to take advantage of divisions within Parliament, but Cromwell and his army foiled him. Members who might have been sympathetic to the monarch were expelled from Parliament in December 1648. After a trial by a special court, Charles was executed on January 30, 1649, as a public criminal. Parliament then abolished the monarchy, the House of Lords, and the Anglican Church.

From 1649 to 1660, England became officially a Puritan republic, although Cromwell dominated it. When in 1653, the House of Commons wanted to disband his expensive army of 50,000 men, Cromwell instead disbanded Parliament. He ruled thereafter as Lord Protector.

Cromwell's military dictatorship, however, proved no more effective than Charles's rule and became just as harsh and hated. People deeply resented his Puritan prohibitions of drunkenness, theatergoing, and dancing. Political liberty vanished in the name of religious conformity. When Cromwell died in 1658, the English were ready by 1660 to restore both the Anglican Church and the monarchy.

CHARLES II AND THE RESTORATION OF THE MONARCHY

After negotiations with the army, Charles II (r. 1660–1685) returned to England amid great rejoicing. England returned to the status quo of 1642, with a hereditary monarch, a Parliament of Lords and Commons that met only when the king summoned it, and the Anglican Church, with its bishops and prayer book, supreme in religion.

The king, however, had secret Catholic sympathies and favored religious toleration. He wanted to allow loyal Catholics and Puritans to worship freely. Yet ultraroyalists in Parliament between 1661 and 1665, through a series of laws known as the Clarendon Code, excluded Roman Catholics, Presbyterians, and Independents from the official religious and political life of the nation.

In 1670 by the Treaty of Dover, England and France formally allied against the Dutch, their chief commercial competitor. In a secret portion of this treaty, Charles pledged to announce his conversion to Catholicism as soon as conditions in England permitted this to happen. In return for this announcement (which Charles never made), Louis XIV promised to pay Charles a substantial subsidy. In an attempt to unite the English people behind the war with Holland, and as a sign of good faith to Louis XIV, Charles issued a Declaration of Indulgence in 1672, suspending all laws against Roman Catholics and non-Anglican Protestants. Parliament refused to fund the war, however, until Charles rescinded the measure. After he did so, Parliament passed the Test Act requiring all civil and military officials of the crown to swear an oath against the doctrine of transubstantiation—which no loyal Roman Catholic could honestly do. Parliament had aimed the Test Act largely at the king's brother, James, duke of York, heir to the throne and a recent, devout convert to Catholicism.

In 1678, a notorious liar named Titus Oates swore before a magistrate that Charles's Catholic wife, through her physician, was plotting with Jesuits and Irishmen to kill the king so James could assume the throne. Parliament believed Oates. In the ensuing hysteria, known as the Popish Plot, several innocent people were tried and executed.

More suspicious than ever of Parliament, Charles II turned again to increased customs duties and the assistance of Louis XIV for extra income. By these means, he was able to rule from 1681 to 1685 without recalling Parliament.

THE "GLORIOUS REVOLUTION"

When James II (r. 1685–1688) became king, he immediately demanded the repeal of the Test Act. When Parliament balked, he dissolved it and proceeded to appoint Catholics to high positions in both his court and the army. In 1687, he issued another Declaration of Indulgence suspending all religious tests and permitting free worship. In June 1688, James imprisoned seven Anglican bishops who had refused to publicize his suspension of laws against the Catholics. Each of these actions represented a direct royal attack on the local authority of nobles, landowners, the church, and other corporate bodies whose members believed they possessed particular legal privileges.

The English had hoped that James would be succeeded by Mary (r. 1689–1694), his Protestant eldest daughter. She was the wife of William III of Orange, the leader of European opposition to Louis XIV. But on June 20, James II's Catholic second wife gave birth to a son. There was now a Catholic male heir to the throne. The Parliamentary opposition invited William to invade England to preserve its "traditional liberties," that is, the Anglican Church and parliamentary government.

William of Orange arrived with his army in November 1688 and was received with considerable popular support. James fled to France, and Parliament, in 1689, proclaimed William III and Mary II the new monarchs, thus completing the "**Glorious Revolution**." William and Mary, in turn, recognized a Bill of Rights that limited the powers of the monarchy and guaranteed the civil liberties of the English privileged classes. The Bill of Rights also prohibited Roman Catholics from occupying the English throne. The Toleration Act of 1689 permitted worship by all Protestants and outlawed only Roman Catholics and those who denied the Christian doctrine of the Trinity.

Glorious Revolution   Parliament's 1688 declaration of a vacant throne and proclamation that William and Mary were its heirs.

The parliamentary measure closing this century of strife was the Act of Settlement (1701), which provided for the English crown to go to the Protestant House of Hanover in Germany if Queen Anne (r. 1702–1714), the second daughter of James II and the heir to the childless William III, died without issue. Thus, at Anne's death in 1714, the Elector of Hanover became King George I of Great Britain (r. 1714–1727) since England and Scotland had been combined in an Act of Union in 1707.

THE AGE OF WALPOLE

George I almost immediately confronted a challenge to his title. James Edward Stuart (1688–1766), the Catholic son of James II, landed in Scotland in December 1715 but met defeat less than two months later.

Despite the victory over the Stuart pretender, the political situation after 1715 remained in flux until Sir Robert Walpole (1676–1745) took over the helm of government. Walpole maintained peace abroad and promoted the status quo at home. Britain's foreign trade spread from New England to India. Because the central government refrained from interfering with the local political influence of nobles and other landowners, they were willing to serve as local government administrators, judges, and military commanders, and to collect and pay the taxes to support a powerful military force, particularly a strong navy. As a result, Great Britain became not only a European power of the first order but eventually a world power as well.

The power of the British monarchs and their ministers had real limits. Parliament could not wholly ignore popular pressure. Newspapers and public debate flourished. Free speech could be exercised, as could freedom of association. There was no large standing army. There existed significant religious toleration. Walpole's enemies could and did openly oppose his policies, which would not have been possible on the Continent. Consequently, the English state combined considerable military power with both religious and political liberty. British political life became the model for all progressive Europeans who questioned the absolutist political developments of the Continent.

RISE OF ABSOLUTE MONARCHY IN FRANCE: THE WORLD OF LOUIS XIV

WHY WERE efforts to establish absolute monarchy successful in France but unsuccessful in England?

The French monarchy, which had faced numerous challenges from strong, well-armed nobles and discontented Protestants during the first half of the seventeenth century, only gradually achieved the firm authority for which it became renowned later in the century. The groundwork for Louis XIV's (r. 1643–1715) absolutism had been laid by two powerful chief ministers, Cardinal Richelieu (1585–1642) under Louis XIII (r. 1610–1643), and then by Cardinal Mazarin (1602–1661). Both Richelieu and Mazarin attempted to impose direct royal administration on France. The centralizing policies of Richelieu and then of Mazarin, however, finally provoked a series of widespread rebellions among French nobles between 1649 and 1652 known as the *Fronde* (after the slingshots used by street boys).

Though unsuccessful, these rebellions convinced Louis XIV and his advisors that heavy-handed policies could endanger the throne. Thereafter Louis would concentrate unprecedented authority in the monarchy, but he would be more subtle than his predecessors. His genius was to make the monarchy the most important and powerful political institution in France while also assuring the nobles and other wealthy groups of their social standing and influence on the local level.

Fronde Widespread rebellions in France between 1649 and 1652 (named after a slingshot used by street ruffians) aimed at reversing the drift toward absolute monarchy and preserving local autonomy.

YEARS OF PERSONAL RULE

On the death of Mazarin in 1661, Louis XIV assumed personal control of the government at the age of twenty-three. Louis devoted enormous personal energy to his political tasks. He ruled through councils that controlled foreign affairs, the army, domestic administration, and economic regulations. Each day he spent hours with the ministers of these councils, whom he chose from families long in royal service or from among people just beginning to rise in the social structure. Unlike the more ancient noble families, the latter had no real or potential power bases in the provinces and depended solely on the king for their standing in both government and society.

Louis made sure, however, that the nobility and other major social groups would benefit from the growth of his own authority. Although he controlled foreign affairs and limited the influence of noble institutions on the monarchy, he never tried to abolish those institutions or limit their local authority. The crown, for example, usually conferred informally with regional judicial bodies, called *parlements*, before making rulings that would affect them. Likewise, the crown would rarely enact economic regulations without consulting local opinion.

Gold Fleur-de-Lis with Gold Crown.

Neil Lukas © Dorling Kindersley, Courtesy of l'Etablissement Public du Musée et du Domaine National de Versailles

Why was it so important to Louis XIV to look like a king at all times?

VERSAILLES

Louis and his advisors became masters of propaganda and political image creation. Louis never missed an opportunity to impress the grandeur of his crown on the French people, but most especially on the French nobility. The central element of the image of the monarchy was the palace of Versailles, which, when completed, was the largest secular structure in Europe. More than any other monarch of the day, Louis XIV used the physical setting of his court to exert political control. Versailles was a temple to royalty, designed and decorated to proclaim the glory of the Sun King, as Louis was known. A spectacular estate with magnificent fountains and gardens, it housed thousands of the more important nobles, royal officials, and servants. Some nobles paid for their own residence at the palace, thus depleting their resources; others required royal patronage to remain in residence. In either case they became dependent on the monarch. Although it consumed over half Louis's annual revenues, Versailles paid significant political dividends.

Because Louis ruled personally, he was himself the chief source of favors and patronage in France. To emphasize his prominence, he organized life at court around every aspect of his own daily routine. Elaborate etiquette governed every detail of life at Versailles. Moments near the king were important to most court nobles because they were effectively excluded from the real business of government. The king's rising and dressing were times of rare intimacy, when nobles could whisper their special requests in his ear. Fortunate nobles held his night candle when he went to his bed.

Palace of Versailles, garden facade. The terrace later became part of the Hall of Mirrors.

Chateau de Versailles, France/The Bridgeman Art Library

What political motives were behind the transformation of Versailles into the seat of the French monarchy?

KING BY DIVINE RIGHT

An important source for Louis's concept of royal authority was his devout tutor, the political theorist Bishop Jacques-Bénigne Bossuet (1627–1704). Bossuet defended what he called the **"divine right of kings"** and cited examples of Old Testament rulers divinely appointed by and answerable only to God. Although kings might be duty bound to reflect God's will in their rule, yet as God's regents on earth they could not be bound to the dictates of mere nobles and parliaments. Such assumptions lay behind Louis XIV's alleged declaration: "*L'état, c'est moi*" ("I am the state"). (See "Compare & Connect: The Debate over the Origin and Character of Political Authority," pages 330–331.)

divine right of kings   The belief that God appoints kings and that kings are accountable only to God for how they use their power.

THE DEBATE OVER THE ORIGIN AND CHARACTER OF POLITICAL AUTHORITY

During the second half of the seventeenth century a profound dispute occurred among European political philosophers over the origin and character of political authority. Some political philosophers, here illustrated by the French bishop Jacques-Bénigne Bossuet, contended that monarchs governed absolutely by virtue of authority derived from God. Other philosophers, here illustrated by the English writer John Locke, contended that political authority originated in the consent of the governed and that such authority was inherently limited in its scope.

QUESTIONS

1. Why might Bossuet have wished to make such extravagant claims for absolute royal power? How might these claims be transferred to any form of government?

2. How does Bossuet's argument for absolute royal authority lead also to the need for a single uniform religion in France?

3. Why does Locke find an absolute monarch in conflict with his subjects and they with him?

4. How do Locke's views serve to provide a foundation for parliamentary government?

5. How might subjects governed according to Bossuet's and Locke's principles relate differently to their monarchs and to the officials of monarchs administering their local communities?

I. BISHOP BOSSUET DEFENDS THE DIVINE RIGHT OF KINGS

The revolutions of the seventeenth century caused many to fear anarchy far more than tyranny, among them the influential French bishop Jacques-Bénigne Bossuet (1627–1704), the leader of French Catholicism in the second half of the seventeenth century. Louis XIV made him court preacher and tutor to his son, for whom Bossuet wrote a celebrated universal history. In the following excerpt, Bossuet defends the divine right and absolute power of kings. He depicts kings as embracing in their person the whole body of the state and the will of the people they govern and, as such, as being immune from judgment by any mere mortal.

The royal power is absolute. . . . The prince need render account of his acts to no one. "I counsel thee to keep the king's commandment, and that in regard of the oath of God. Be not hasty to go out of his sight; stand not on an evil thing for he doeth whatsoever pleaseth him. Where the word of a king is, there is power; and who may say unto him, What doest thou? Whoso keepeth the commandment shall feel no evil thing" [Eccles. 8:2–5]. Without this absolute authority the king could neither do good nor repress evil. It is necessary that his power be such that no one can hope to escape him, and finally, the only protection of individuals against the public authority should be their innocence. This confirms the teaching of St. Paul: "Wilt thou then not be afraid of the power? Do that which is good" [Rom. 13:3].

God is infinite, God is all. The prince, as prince, is not regarded as a private person: he is a public personage, all the state is in him; the will of all the people is included in his. As all perfection and all strength are united in God, so all the power of individuals is united in the person of the prince. What grandeur that a single man should embody so much! . . .

Behold an immense people united in a single person; behold this holy power, paternal and absolute; behold the secret cause which governs the whole body of the state, contained in a single head: you see the image of God in the king, and you have the idea of royal majesty. God is holiness itself, goodness itself, and power itself. In these things lies the majesty of God. In the image of these things lies the majesty of the prince.

Source: From *Politics Drawn from the Very Words of Holy Scripture*, as quoted in James Harvey Robinson, ed., *Readings in European History*, vol. 2 (Boston: Athenaeum, 1906), pp. 275–276.

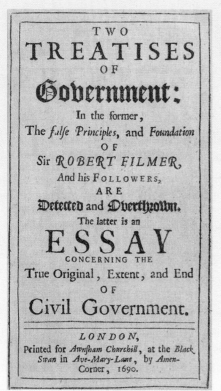

Title Page from *Two Treatises of Government* by John Locke, London, 1690.

Courtesy of the Library of Congress (Rosenwald Collection, Rare Book and Special Collections Division)

How did Locke challenge traditional notions of European monarchy?

II. JOHN LOCKE DENOUNCES THE IDEA OF ABSOLUTE MONARCHY

John Locke (1632–1704) was the most important English philosopher of the late seventeenth century. As will be seen in Chapter 14, he wrote on a wide variety of subjects including both political philosophy and religious toleration. In 1690 he published his second Treatise of Civil Government. In this work he defended limitations on government and rooted political authority in the consent of the governed. He drafted the treatise in the late 1670s in response to Tory assertions of absolute monarchy set forth by supporters of Charles II. The treatise was published in the wake of the Revolution of 1688 and was read at the time as a justification of that event. Locke's thought would almost a century later influence the American Declaration of Independence. In the passages below Locke explains that under absolute monarchy citizens must submit to an authority from which they can make no appeal. Consequently, there is a necessary conflict between citizens and the absolute monarchy. It was to escape such conflict and to secure property and liberty that human beings had left the state of nature to found civil society.

Man being born . . . with a title to perfect freedom, and an uncontrolled enjoyment of all the rights and privileges of the law of nature, equally with any other man, or number of men in the world, hath by nature a power, not only to preserve his property, that is, his life, liberty and estate, against the injuries and attempts of other men; but to judge of, and punish the breaches of that law in others, as he is persuaded the offence deserve . . . [T]here and there only is political society, where every one of the members hath quitted this natural power, resigned it up into the hands of the community in all cases that excludes him not from appealing for protection to the law established by it. And thus all private judgment of every particular member being excluded, the community comes to be umpire, by settled standing rules, indifferent, and the same to all parties; and by men having authority from the community, for the execution of those rules, decides all the differences that may happen between any members of that society concerning any matter of right . . .

Whenever therefore any number of men are so united into one society, as to quit every one his executive power of the law of nature, and to resign it to the public, there and there only is a political, or civil society. . . .

Hence it is evident, that absolute monarchy, which by some men is counted the only government in the world, is indeed inconsistent with civil society, and so can be no form of civil government at all; for the end of civil society, being to avoid, and remedy those inconveniencies of the state of nature, which necessarily follow from every man's being judge in his own case, by setting up a known authority, to which every one of that society may appeal upon any injury received, or controversy that may arise, and which every one of the society ought to obey; whereever any persons are, who have not such an authority to appeal to, for the decision of any difference between them, there those persons are still in the state of nature; and so is every absolute prince, in respect of those who are under his dominion.

For he being supposed to have all, both legislative and executive power in himself alone, there is no judge to be found, no appeal lies open to any one, who may fairly, and indifferently, and with authority decide, and from whose decision relief and redress may be expected of any injury or inconveniency, that may be suffered from the prince, or by his order: so that such a man, however intitled, czar, or grand seignior, or how you please, is as much in the state of nature, with all under his dominion, as he is with the rest of mankind: for where-ever any two men are, who have no standing rule, and common judge to appeal to on earth, for the determination of controversies of right betwixt them, there they are still in the state of nature, and under all the inconveniencies of it. . .

Source: John Locke, *Of Civil Government*, paragraphs 87, 89, 90, 91 in *Two Treatises of Government*, a new ed. (London: C. and J. Rivington et al., 1824), pp. 179–183.

Louis XIV of France came to symbolize absolute monarchy though such government was not as absolute as the term implied. This state portrait was intended to convey the grandeur of the king and of his authority. The portrait was brought into royal council meetings when the king himself was absent.

Hyacinthe Rigaud (1659–1743), *Portrait of Louis XIV.* Louvre, Paris, France. Dorling Kindersley Media Library/Max Alexander. © Dorling Kindersley, courtesy of l'Etablissement public du musée et du domaine national de Versailles

What does this portrait tell us about Louis XIV's ideas about kingship?

Given power from god,

Gallican Liberties   The French Roman Catholic Church's ecclesiastical independence of papal authority in Rome.

Jansenism   Appearing in the 1630s, it followed the teachings of St. Augustine, who stressed the role divine grace played in human salvation.

Despite these claims, Louis's rule did not exert the oppressive control over the daily lives of his subjects that police states would do in the nineteenth and twentieth centuries. His absolutism functioned primarily in the classic areas of European state action—the making of war and peace, the regulation of religion, and the oversight of economic activity.

LOUIS'S EARLY WARS

By the late 1660s, France was superior to any other European nation in population, administrative bureaucracy, army, and national unity. Because of the economic policies of Jean-Baptiste Colbert (1619–1683), his most brilliant minister, Louis could afford to raise and maintain a large and powerful army. Louis was particularly concerned to secure France's northern borders along the Spanish Netherlands, the Franche-Comté, Alsace, and Lorraine from which foreign armies had invaded France and could easily do so again. Louis was also determined to frustrate Habsburg ambitions that endangered France and, as part of that goal, sought to secure his southern borders toward Spain. Whether reacting to external events or pursuing his own ambitions, Louis's pursuit of French interests threatened and terrified neighboring states and led them to form coalitions against France.

The early wars of Louis XIV included conflicts with Spain and the United Netherlands. The first was the War of the Devolution in which Louis supported the alleged right of his first wife, Marie Thérèse, to inherit the Spanish Netherlands. In 1667, Louis's armies invaded Flanders and the Franche-Comté. He was repulsed by the Triple Alliance of England, Sweden, and the United Provinces. By the Treaty of Aix-la-Chapelle (1668), he gained control of certain towns bordering the Spanish Netherlands.

In 1670, with the secret Treaty of Dover, England and France became allies against the Dutch. Louis invaded the Netherlands again in 1672. The Prince of Orange, the future William III of England, forged an alliance with the Holy Roman Emperor, Spain, Lorraine, and Brandenburg against Louis, now regarded as a menace to the whole of Western Europe, Catholic and Protestant alike. The war ended inconclusively with the Peace of Nijmwegen, signed with different parties in successive years (1678, 1679). France gained more territory, including the Franche-Comté.

LOUIS'S REPRESSIVE RELIGIOUS POLICIES

Louis believed that political unity and stability required religious conformity. To that end he carried out repressive actions against both Roman Catholics and Protestants.

Suppression of the Jansenists   The French crown and the French Roman Catholic church had long jealously guarded their ecclesiastical independence or "**Gallican Liberties**" from papal authority in Rome. However, after the conversion to Roman Catholicism of Henry IV in 1593, the Jesuits, fiercely loyal to the authority of the pope, had monopolized the education of French upper-class men, and their devout students promoted the religious reforms and doctrines of the Council of Trent.

A Roman Catholic religious movement known as **Jansenism** arose in the 1630s in opposition to the theology and the political influence of the Jesuits. Jansenists adhered to the teachings of St. Augustine (354–430) that had also influenced many Protestant doctrines. Serious and uncompromising, they particularly opposed Jesuit teachings about free will. They believed with Augustine that original sin had so corrupted humankind that individuals could by their own effort do nothing good nor contribute anything to their own salvation.

On May 31, 1653, Pope Innocent X declared heretical five Jansenist theological propositions on grace and salvation. In 1660, Louis permitted the papal bull banning Jansenism to be enforced in France. Thereafter, Jansenists either retracted their views or went underground.

By persecuting the Jansenists, Louis XIV turned his back on the long tradition of protecting the Gallican Liberties of the French Church and fostered within the French Church a core of opposition to royal authority. This had long-term political significance. During the eighteenth century after the death of Louis XIV, the Parlement of Paris and other French judicial bodies would reassert their authority in opposition to the monarchy. These courts were sympathetic to the Jansenists because of their common resistance to royal authority. Jansenism, because of its austere morality, then also came to embody a set of religious and moral values that contrasted with what eighteenth-century public opinion saw as the corruption of the mid-eighteenth-century French royal court.

Revocation of the Edict of Nantes   After the Edict of Nantes in 1598, relations between the Catholic majority (nine-tenths of the French population) and the Protestant minority had remained hostile. After the Peace of Nijmwegen, Louis launched a methodical campaign against the Huguenots in an effort to unify France religiously. Louis hounded Huguenots out of public life, banning them from government office and excluding them from such professions as printing and medicine. He used financial incentives to encourage them to convert to Catholicism. In 1681, he bullied them by quartering troops in their towns. Finally, in October 1685, Louis revoked the Edict of Nantes, and extensive religious repression followed. Protestant churches and schools were closed, Protestant ministers exiled, nonconverting laity were condemned to be galley slaves, and Protestant children were baptized by Catholic priests.

The revocation was a major blunder. Henceforth, Protestants across Europe considered Louis a fanatic who must be resisted at all costs. More than a quarter million people, many of whom were highly skilled, left France. They formed new communities abroad and joined the resistance to Louis in England, Germany, Holland, and the New World. As a result of the revocation of the Edict of Nantes and the ongoing persecution of Jansenists, France became a symbol of religious repression in contrast to England's reputation for moderate, if not complete, religious toleration.

LOUIS'S LATER WARS

The League of Augsburg and the Nine Years' War   After the Treaty of Nijmwegen in 1678–1679, Louis maintained his army at full strength and restlessly probed beyond his borders. In 1681 his forces occupied the free city of Strasbourg on the Rhine River, prompting new defensive coalitions to form against him. One of these, the League of Augsburg, grew to include England, Spain, Sweden, the United Provinces, and the major German states. Between 1689 and 1697, the League and France battled each other in the Nine Years' War, while England and France struggled to control North America. The Peace of Ryswick, signed in September 1697, which ended the war, secured Holland's borders and thwarted Louis's expansion into Germany.

War of the Spanish Succession   On November 1, 1700, the last Habsburg king of Spain, Charles II (r. 1665–1700), died without direct heirs. He left his entire inheritance to Louis's grandson Philip of Anjou, who became Philip V of Spain (r. 1700–1746). Spain and the vast trade with its American empire appeared to have fallen to France. In September 1701, England, Holland, and the Holy Roman Empire formed the Grand Alliance to preserve the balance of power by once and for all securing Flanders as a neutral barrier between Holland and France and by gaining for the emperor, who was also a Habsburg, his fair share of the Spanish inheritance. Louis soon increased the political stakes by recognizing the Stuart claim to the English throne.

In 1701 the War of the Spanish Succession (1701–1714) began, and it soon enveloped Western Europe. John Churchill, the Duke of Marlborough (1650–1722) bested Louis's soldiers in every major engagement, although French arms triumphed in Spain. After 1709 the war became a bloody stalemate.

Portrait of Françoise d'Aubigne, Marquise de Maíntenon (1635–1719), Mistress and Second Wife of Louis XIV, by Pierre Mignard (1612–1695).

Portrait of Françoise d'Aubigne, Marquise de Maintenon (1635–1719), Mistress and Second Wife of Louis XIV, c. 1694. Oil on canvas, 128 ∞ 97 cm. Inv.: MV 3637. Chateaux de Versailles et de Trianon, Versailles. Bridgeman-Giraudon/Art Resource, NY

What role did elite women play in the court of Louis XIV?

MAP 13–1   **Europe in 1714**   The War of the Spanish Succession ended a year before the death of Louis XIV. The Bourbons had secured the Spanish throne, but Spain had forfeited its possessions in Flanders and Italy.

How did the territorial makeup of Europe change during the long reign of Louis XIV?

France finally made peace with England at Utrecht in July 1713, and with Holland and the emperor at Rastatt in March 1714. Philip V remained king of Spain, but England got Gibraltar and the island of Minorca, making it a Mediterranean power. (See Map 13–1.) Louis also recognized the right of the House of Hanover to the English throne.

FRANCE AFTER LOUIS XIV

Despite its military reverses in the War of the Spanish Succession, France remained a great power. It was less strong in 1715 than in 1680, but it still possessed the largest European population, an advanced, if troubled, economy, and the administrative structure bequeathed it by Louis XIV. Moreover, even if France and its resources had been drained by the last of Louis's wars, the other major states of Europe were similarly debilitated. Louis XIV was succeeded by his five-year-old great-grandson Louis XV (r. 1715–1774). The young boy's uncle, the duke of Orléans, became regent and remained so until his death in 1720. The regency, marked by financial and moral scandals, further undermined the faltering prestige of the monarchy.

John Law and the Mississippi Bubble   The duke of Orléans was a gambler, and for a time he turned over the financial management of the kingdom to John Law (1671–1729), a Scottish mathematician and fellow gambler. Law believed an increase in the paper-money supply would stimulate France's economic recovery. With the permission of the regent, he established a bank in Paris that issued paper money. Law then organized a monopoly, called the Mississippi Company, on trading privileges with the French colony of Louisiana in North America.

The Mississippi Company also took over the management of the French national debt. The company issued shares of its own stock in exchange for government bonds, which had fallen sharply in value. To redeem large quantities of bonds, Law encouraged speculation in the Mississippi Company stock. In 1719, the price of the stock rose handsomely. Smart investors, however, took their profits by selling their stock in exchange for paper money from Law's bank, which they then sought to exchange for gold. The bank, however, lacked enough gold to redeem all the paper money brought to it.

In February 1720, all gold payments were halted in France. Soon thereafter, Law himself fled the country. The Mississippi Bubble, as the affair was called, had burst. The fiasco brought disgrace on the government that had sponsored Law. The Mississippi Company was later reorganized and functioned profitably, but fear of paper money and speculation marked French economic life for decades.

Renewed Authority of the *Parlements*   The duke of Orléans made a second decision that also lessened the power of the monarchy. He attempted to draw the French nobility once again into the decision-making processes of the government. He set up a system of councils on which nobles were to serve along with bureaucrats. The experiment failed. Nonetheless, the chief feature of eighteenth-century French political life was the attempt of the nobility to use its authority to limit the power of the monarchy. The most effective instrument in this process was the ***parlements***, or courts dominated by the nobility.

Throughout the eighteenth century, *parlements* succeeded in identifying their authority and resistance to the monarchy with wider public opinion. This situation meant that until the revolution in 1789, the *parlements* became natural centers not only for aristocratic, but also for popular resistance to royal authority. In a vast transformation from the days of Louis XIV, the *parlements* rather than the monarchy would come to be seen as more nearly representing the nation.

By 1726, the general political direction of the nation had come under the authority of Cardinal Fleury (1653–1743). He worked to maintain the authority of the monarchy, including ongoing repression of the Jansenists, while continuing to preserve the local interests of the French nobility. Like Walpole in Britain, he pursued economic prosperity at home and peace abroad. Again like Walpole, after 1740, Fleury could not prevent France from entering a worldwide colonial conflict. (See Chapter 17.)

parlements   French political institutions with customary rights of consultation and deliberation.

CENTRAL AND EASTERN EUROPE

Central and eastern Europe were economically much less advanced than western Europe. Except for the Baltic ports, the economy was agrarian. There were fewer cities and many more large estates worked by serfs.

During the sixteenth and early seventeenth centuries, the political authorities in this region, which lay largely east of the Elbe River, were weak. During the last half of the seventeenth century, however, three strong dynasties, whose rulers aspired to the absolutism then being constructed in France, emerged in central and eastern Europe. They were Austria, Prussia, and Russia. By contrast, Poland during the eighteenth century became the single most conspicuous example in Europe of a land that failed to establish a viable centralized government.

WHAT WERE the main characteristics that defined the Polish, Austrian, and Prussian states in the seventeenth and eighteenth centuries?

POLAND: ABSENCE OF STRONG CENTRAL AUTHORITY

In no other part of Europe was the failure to maintain a competitive political position so complete as in Poland. The Polish monarchy was elective, but the deep distrust and divisions among the nobility usually prevented their electing a king from among

Sejm Central legislative body to which the Polish nobles belonged.

themselves. Most of the Polish monarchs were foreigners and the tools of foreign powers. The Polish nobles did have a central legislative body called the ***Sejm***, or diet. The diet, however, had a practice known as the *liberum veto*, whereby the staunch opposition of any single member, who might have been bribed by a foreign power, could require the body to disband. Such opposition, termed "exploding the diet," was most often the work of a group of dissatisfied nobles rather than of one person. Nonetheless, the requirement of unanimity was a major stumbling block to effective government. The price of this noble liberty would eventually be the disappearance of Poland from the map of Europe in the late eighteenth century.

THE HABSBURG EMPIRE AND THE PRAGMATIC SANCTION

The close of the Thirty Years' War marked a fundamental turning point in the history of the Austrian Habsburgs. Previously, in alliance with their Spanish cousins, they had hoped to bring all of Germany under their control and back to the Catholic fold. In this they had failed, and the decline of Spanish power meant that the Austrian Habsburgs were on their own. (See Map 13–2.)

After 1648, the Habsburg family retained a firm hold on the title of Holy Roman Emperor, but the power of the emperor depended less on the force of arms than on the cooperation he could elicit from the various political bodies in the empire. While establishing their new dominance among the German states, the Habsburgs also began to consolidate their power and influence within their hereditary possessions outside the Holy Roman Empire, which included the Crown of Saint Wenceslas, encompassing the kingdom of Bohemia (in the modern Czech Republic) and the duchies of Moravia and Silesia; and the Crown of Saint Stephen, which ruled Hungary, Croatia, and Transylvania.

In each of their many territories the Habsburgs ruled by virtue of a different title—king, archduke, duke—and they needed the cooperation of the local nobility, which was not always forthcoming. They repeatedly had to bargain with nobles in one part of Europe to maintain their position in another. Their domains were so geographically diverse and the people who lived in them of so many different languages and customs that almost no grounds existed on which to unify them politically.

MAP 13–2 The Austrian Habsburg Empire, 1521–1772 The empire had three main units—Austria, Bohemia, and Hungary. Expansion was mainly eastward: eastern Hungary from the Ottomans (seventeenth century) and Galicia from Poland (1772). Meantime, Silesia was lost after 1740, but the Habsburgs remained Holy Roman Emperors.

Why was expansion of the Austrian Habsburg Empire mostly eastward?

Despite these internal difficulties, Leopold I (r. 1658–1705) managed to resist the advances of the Ottoman Empire into central Europe, which included a siege of Vienna in 1683, and to thwart the aggression of Louis XIV. He achieved Ottoman recognition of his sovereignty over Hungary in 1699 and extended his territorial holdings over much of the Balkan peninsula and western Romania. These conquests allowed the Habsburgs to hope to develop Mediterranean trade through the port of Trieste on the northern coast of the Adriatic Sea and helped compensate for their loss of effective power over the Holy Roman Empire. Strength in the East gave them greater political leverage in Germany. Joseph I (r. 1705–1711) continued Leopold's policies.

When Charles VI (r. 1711–1740) succeeded Joseph, a new problem was added to the chronic one of territorial diversity. He had no male heir, and there was only the weakest of precedents for a female ruler of the Habsburg domains. Charles feared that on his death the Austrian Habsburg lands might fall prey to the surrounding powers, as had those of the Spanish Habsburgs in 1700. He was determined to prevent that disaster and to provide his domains with the semblance of legal unity. To those ends, he devoted most of his reign to seeking the approval of his family, the estates of his realms, and the major foreign powers for a document called the **Pragmatic Sanction**.

Pragmatic Sanction   Document recognizing Charles VI's daughter Maria Theresa as his heir.

This instrument provided the legal basis for a single line of inheritance within the Habsburg dynasty through Charles VI's daughter Maria Theresa (r. 1740–1780). When Charles VI died in October 1740, he believed that he had secured legal unity for the Habsburg Empire and a safe succession for his daughter. Despite the Pragmatic Sanction, however, his failure to provide his daughter with a strong army or a full treasury left her inheritance open to foreign aggression. In December 1740, Frederick II of Prussia invaded the Habsburg province of Silesia in eastern Germany. Maria Theresa had to fight for her inheritance.

PRUSSIA AND THE HOHENZOLLERNS

The rise of Prussia occurred within the German power vacuum created by the Peace of Westphalia. It is the story of the extraordinary Hohenzollern family, which had ruled Brandenburg since 1417. Through inheritance the family had acquired the duchy of Cleves, and the counties of Mark and Ravensburg in 1614, East Prussia in 1618, and Pomerania in 1648. Except for Pomerania, none of these lands shared a border with Brandenburg. Still, by the late seventeenth century, the geographically scattered Hohenzollern holdings represented a block of territory within the Holy Roman Empire, second in size only to that of the Habsburgs.

The person who began to forge these areas into a modern state was Frederick William (r. 1640–1688), who became known as the Great Elector. He established himself and his successors as the central uniting power by breaking the local noble estates, organizing a royal bureaucracy, and building a strong army.

Between 1655 and 1660, Sweden and Poland fought each other across the Great Elector's holdings in Pomerania and East Prussia. Frederick William had neither an adequate army nor the tax revenues to confront this threat. In 1655, the Brandenburg estates refused to grant him new taxes; however, he proceeded to collect them by military force. In 1659, a different grant of taxes, originally made in 1653, elapsed; Frederick William continued to collect them as well as those he had imposed by his own authority. He used the money to build an army, which allowed him to continue to enforce his will without the approval of the nobility. Similar coercion took place against the nobles in his other territories.

There was, however, a political and social trade-off between the Elector and his various nobles. In exchange for their obedience to the Hohenzollerns, the **Junkers**, or German noble landlords, received the right to demand obedience from their serfs. Frederick William also tended to choose as the local administrators of the tax structure

Junkers   (Prussian nobles) They were allowed to demand absolute obedience from the serfs on their estates in exchange for their support of the Hohenzollerns.

men who would normally have been members of the noble branch of the old parliament. As the years passed, Junkers increasingly dominated the army officer corps, and this situation became even more pronounced during the eighteenth century. All officials and army officers took an oath of loyalty directly to the Elector. The army and the Elector thus came to embody the otherwise absent unity of the state.

The achievement of a royal title was one of the few state-building accomplishments of the Elector's heir, Frederick I (r. 1688–1713). In the War of the Spanish Succession, he put his army at the disposal of the Habsburg Holy Roman Emperor Leopold I. In exchange, the emperor permitted Frederick to assume the title of "King in Prussia" in 1701.

His successor, Frederick William I (r. 1713–1740), was both the most eccentric monarch to rule the Hohenzollern domains and one of the most effective. He organized the bureaucracy along military lines. The Prussian military grew from about 39,000 in 1713 to over 80,000 in 1740, making it the third or fourth largest army in Europe. Separate laws applied to the army and to civilians. Laws, customs, and royal attention made the officer corps the highest social class of the state. Military service thus attracted the sons of Junkers. In this fashion the army, the Junker nobility, and the monarchy became forged into a single political entity.

Although Frederick William I built the best army in Europe, he avoided conflict. His army was a symbol of Prussian power and unity, not an instrument for foreign adventures or aggression. At his death in 1740, he passed to his son Frederick II, later known as Frederick the Great (r. 1740–1786), this superb military machine but not the wisdom to refrain from using it. Almost immediately on coming to the throne, Frederick II upset the Pragmatic Sanction and invaded Silesia. He thus crystallized the Austrian-Prussian rivalry for the control of Germany that would dominate central European affairs for over a century.

QUICK REVIEW
Frederick William's Army

- Grew from 39,000 in 1713 to over 80,000 in 1740
- Separate laws applied to the army and civilians
- The officer corps became the highest social class of the state

RUSSIA ENTERS THE EUROPEAN POLITICAL ARENA

HOW DID Peter the Great transform Russia into a powerful, centralized nation?

The emergence of Russia in the late seventeenth century as an active European power was a wholly new factor in European politics.

THE ROMANOV DYNASTY

The reign of Ivan IV (r. 1533–1584), later known as Ivan the Terrible, had commenced well but ended badly. About midway in his reign he underwent a personality change that led him to move from a program of sensible reform of law, government, and the army toward violent personal tyranny. A period known as the "Time of Troubles" followed upon his death. In 1613, hoping to end the uncertainty, an assembly of nobles elected as tsar a seventeen-year-old boy named Michael Romanov (r. 1613–1645). Thus began the dynasty that ruled Russia until 1917.

Michael Romanov and his two successors, Aleksei (r. 1654–1676) and Theodore II (r. 1676–1682), brought stability and modest bureaucratic centralization to Russia. The country remained, however, weak and impoverished. After years of turmoil, the *boyars*, the old nobility, still largely controlled the bureaucracy. Furthermore, the government and the tsars faced the danger of mutiny from the *streltsy*, or guards of the Moscow garrison.

PETER THE GREAT

In 1682, Peter (r. 1682–1725)—ten years old at the time—ascended the fragile Russian throne as co-ruler with his half brother. He and the sickly Ivan V had come to power on the shoulders of the *streltsy*, who expected to be rewarded for their support. Violence and bloodshed had surrounded the disputed succession. Matters became even more confused when the boys' sister, Sophia, was named regent. Peter's followers overthrew her in 1689. From that date onward, Peter ruled personally, although in theory he shared the crown until Ivan died in 1696. The dangers and turmoil of his youth convinced Peter of two things: First, the power of the tsar must be made secure from the jealousy of the *boyars* and the greed of the *streltsy*; second, Russian military power must be increased.

Northwestern Europe, particularly the military resources of the maritime powers, fascinated Peter I, who eventually became known as Peter the Great. In 1697, he made a famous visit in transparent disguise to western Europe. An imitator of the first order, Peter returned to Moscow determined to copy what he had seen abroad, for he knew warfare would be necessary to make Russia a great power. Yet he understood his goal would require him to confront the long-standing power and traditions of the Russian nobles.

Taming the *Streltsy* and *Boyars*   In 1698, while Peter was abroad, the *streltsy* had rebelled. On his return, Peter brutally suppressed the revolt. Approximately a thousand of the rebels were put to death, and their corpses remained on public display to discourage disloyalty. Peter then set about building a new military. He drafted an unprecedented 130,000 soldiers, and by the end of his reign he had a well-disciplined army of 300,000.

Peter also made a sustained attack on the *boyars* and their attachment to traditional Russian culture. After his European journey, he personally shaved the long beards of the court *boyars* and sheared off the customary long hand-covering sleeves of their shirts and coats, which had made them the butt of jokes among other European courts. Peter became highly skilled at balancing one group off against another while never completely excluding any as he set about to organize Russian government and military forces along the lines of the more powerful European states.

Developing a Navy   In the mid-1690s, Peter oversaw the construction of ships to protect his interests in the Black Sea against the Ottoman Empire. In 1695, he began a war with the Ottomans and captured Azov on the Black Sea in 1696. Part of the reason for Peter's trip to western Europe in 1697 was to learn how to build still better warships, this time for combat on the Baltic. The construction of a Baltic fleet was essential in Peter's struggles with Sweden that over the years accounted for many of his major steps toward westernizing his realm.

Russian Expansion in the Baltic: The Great Northern War   Following the end of the Thirty Years' War in 1648, Sweden had consolidated its control of the Baltic, thus preventing Russian possession of a port on that sea and permitting Polish and German access to the sea only on Swedish terms.

In 1697, Charles XII (r. 1697–1718) came to the Swedish throne. He was headstrong, to say the least, and perhaps insane. In 1700, Peter the Great began a drive to the west against Swedish territory to gain a foothold on the Baltic. The result was the Great Northern War (1700–1721). By 1709, Peter had decisively defeated the Swedes at the Battle of Poltava in Ukraine. Thereafter, the Swedes could maintain only a holding action against their enemies. When the Great Northern War came to a close in 1721, the Peace of Nystad confirmed the Russian conquest of Estonia, Livonia, and part of Finland. Henceforth, Russia possessed ice-free ports and a permanent influence on European affairs.

Founding St. Petersburg   At one point, the domestic and foreign policies of Peter the Great intersected. This was at the site on the Gulf of Finland where he founded his new capital city of St. Petersburg in 1703. There he built government structures and compelled the *boyars* to construct town houses. He thus imitated those European monarchs who had copied Louis XIV by constructing smaller versions of Versailles. The

Table of Ranks Issued by Peter the Great to draw nobles into state service, it made rank in the bureaucracy or military, not lineage, the determinant of an individual's social status.

founding of St. Petersburg went beyond establishing a central imperial court, however; it symbolized a new Western orientation of Russia and Peter's determination to hold his position on the Baltic coast.

The Case of Peter's Son Aleksei Peter's son Aleksei had been born to his first wife whom he had divorced in 1698. By 1716, Peter was becoming convinced that his opponents looked to Aleksei as a focus for their possible sedition while Russia remained at war with Sweden. There was some truth to these concerns because the next year Aleksei went to Vienna where he attempted to enter into a vague conspiracy with the Habsburg emperor Charles VI.

Peter, who was investigating official corruption, realized his son might become a rallying point for those he accused. Early in 1718, when Aleksei reappeared in St. Petersburg, the tsar began to look into his son's relationships with Charles VI. During this six-month investigation, Peter personally interrogated Aleksei, who was eventually condemned to death and died under mysterious circumstances on June 26, 1718.

Reforms of Peter the Great's Final Years The interrogations surrounding Aleksei had revealed greater degrees of court opposition than Peter had suspected. Recognizing he could not eliminate his opponents the way he had attacked the *streltsy* in 1698, Peter undertook radical administrative reforms designed to bring the nobility and the Russian Orthodox Church more closely under the authority of persons loyal to the tsar.

Administrative Colleges In December 1717, Peter reorganized his domestic administration to sustain his own personal authority and to fight rampant corruption. To achieve this goal, Peter looked to Swedish institutions called *colleges*—bureaus of several persons operating according to written instructions rather than departments headed by a single minister. He created eight of these colleges to oversee matters such as the collection of taxes, foreign relations, war, and economic affairs. Each college was to receive advice from a foreigner. Peter divided the members of these colleges between nobles and persons he was certain would be personally loyal to himself.

Table of Ranks Peter made another major administrative reform with important consequences when in 1722 he published a **Table of Ranks**, which was intended to draw the nobility into state service. That table equated a person's social position and privileges with his rank in the bureaucracy or the military, rather than with his lineage among the traditional landed nobility. Peter thus made the social standing of individual *boyars* a function of their willingness to serve the central state.

Achieving Secular Control of the Church Peter also moved to suppress the independence of the Russian Orthodox Church. In 1721, Peter simply abolished the position of *patriarch*, the bishop who had been head of the church. In its place he established a government department called the *Holy Synod*, which

EVENTS AND REIGNS

1533–1584	Ivan the Terrible
1584–1613	Time of Troubles
1613	Michael Romanov becomes tsar
1640–1688	Frederick William, the Great Elector
1643–1715	Louis XIV, the Sun King
1648	Independence of the Netherlands recognized
1682–1725	Peter the Great
1683	Turkish siege of Vienna
1688–1713	Frederick I of Prussia
1697	Peter the Great's European tour
1700–1721	The Great Northern War
1703	Saint Petersburg founded
1711–1740	The Great Northern War
1703	Saint Petersburg founded
1711–1740	Charles VI, the Pragmatic Sanction
1713	War of the Spanish Succession ends
1713–1740	Frederick William I of Prussia
1714	George I founds England's Hanoverian dynasty
1715	Louis XV becomes king of France
1720–1741	Robert Walpole dominates British politics
1726–1743	Cardinal Fleury
1727	George II
1740	Maria Theresa succeeds to the Habsburg throne
1740	Frederick II invades Silesia

consisted of several bishops headed by a layman, called the *procurator general*. This body would govern the church in accordance with the tsar's secular requirements.

For all the numerous decisive actions Peter had taken since 1718, he still had not settled on a successor. Consequently, when he died in 1725, there was no clear line of succession to the throne. For more than thirty years, soldiers and nobles again determined who ruled Russia. Peter had laid the foundations of a modern Russia, but not the foundations of a stable state.

Ottoman Empire The authority Instanbul's Ottoman Turkish sultan exercised over the Balkans, the Middle East, and North Africa from the end of the Middle Ages to World War I.

THE OTTOMAN EMPIRE

Governing a remarkably diverse collection of peoples that ranged from Baghdad eastward across the Arabian peninsula, Anatolia, the Balkan peninsula, and across North Africa from Egypt to Algiers, the **Ottoman Empire** was the largest and most stable political entity to arise in or near Europe following the collapse of the Roman Empire. (See Map 13–3.) It had achieved this power between the eleventh and early sixteenth centuries as Ottoman tribes migrated eastward from the steppes of Asia.

WHAT WAS the attitude of the Ottoman rulers toward religion in their empire and how was this reflected in their policies?

MAP 13–3 The Ottoman Empire in the Late Seventeenth Century By the 1680s, the Ottoman Empire had reached its maximum extent, but the Ottoman failure to capture Vienna in 1683 marked the beginning of a long and inexorable decline that ended with the empire's collapse after World War I.

From the late 1600s until 1918, which non-Turkish peoples would rise up against Turkish rule in the Ottoman Empire?

RELIGIOUS TOLERATION AND OTTOMAN GOVERNMENT

The Ottoman Empire was the dominant political power in the Muslim world after 1516, when it administered the holy cities of Mecca and Medina as well as Jerusalem, and arranged the safety of Muslim pilgrimages to Mecca. Yet its population was exceedingly diverse ethnically, linguistically, and religiously with significant numbers of Orthodox and Roman Catholic Christians and, after the late fifteenth century, thousands of Jews from Spain.

millets Communities of the officially recognized religions that governed portions of the Ottoman Empire.

The Ottomans extended far more religious toleration to their subjects than existed anywhere in Europe. The Ottoman sultans governed their empire through units, called **millets**, of officially recognized religious communities. Various laws and regulations applied to the persons who belonged to a particular millet rather than to a particular administrative territory. Non-Islamic persons in the empire, known as *dhimmis*, or followers of religions tolerated by law, could practice their religion and manage their internal community affairs through their own religious officials. They were, however, also second-class citizens generally unable to rise in the service of the empire, subject to certain restrictions, and required to pay special taxes. Nonetheless, they often attained economic success because they possessed the highest level of commercial skills in the empire. Because the Ottomans discouraged their various peoples from interacting with each other, the Islamic population rarely acquired these and other skills from their non-Islamic neighbors.

The Ottoman dynasty also kept itself separated from the most powerful families of the empire by recruiting military leaders and administrative officers from groups whom the sultans believed would be personally loyal to them. For example, through a practice known as the *devshirme*, the Ottomans, until the end of the seventeenth century, recruited their most elite troops from Christian communities usually in the Balkans. Christian boys so recruited were raised as Muslims and organized into elite military units, the most famous of which were infantry troops called *Janissaries*. It was thought these troops would be extremely loyal to the sultan and the state because they owed their life and status to the sultan. As a result of this policy, entry into the elite military organizations and advancement in the administrative structures of the empire remained generally closed to the native Islamic population and most especially to members of the most elite Islamic families. Thus, in contrast to Europe, few people from the socially leading families gained military, administrative, or political experience in the central institutions of the empire but remained primarily linked to local government in provincial cities.

The Role of the *Ulama*   Again in contrast to the long-standing tension between church and state in Europe, Islamic religious authorities played a significant and enduring role in the political, legal, and administrative life of the Ottoman Empire. Islamic scholars, or *Ulama*, dominated not only Ottoman religious institutions but also schools and courts of law. There essentially existed a trade-off between Ottoman political and religious authorities. The sultan and his administrative officials would consult these Islamic scholars for advice with regard to how their policies and the behavior of their subjects accorded with Islamic law and the Qur'an. In turn, the *Ulama* would support the Ottoman state while the latter deferred to their judgments. This situation would prove a key factor in the fate of the Ottoman Empire. From the late seventeenth century onward, the *Ulama* urged the sultans to conform to traditional life even as the empire confronted a rapidly changing and modernizing Europe. The Janissaries also resisted changes that might undermine their own privileged status.

QUICK REVIEW

The *Ulama*

- *Ulama:* Dominant group of Muslim scholars
- Sultan and his advisors consulted with *Ulama*
- *Ulama* advised against modernization and adoption of European ideas

THE END OF OTTOMAN EXPANSION

From the fifteenth century onward, the Ottoman Empire had tried to push further westward into Europe. The Ottomans made their deepest military invasion into Europe in 1683, when they unsuccessfully besieged Vienna. Although that defeat proved to be decisive, many observers at the time thought it the result only of an overreach of power by the Ottomans rather than as a symptom of a deeper decline, which was actually the case.

Gradually, from the seventeenth century onward, the authority of the grand vizier, the major political figure after the sultan, began to grow. This development meant that more and more authority lay with the administrative and military bureaucracy. Rivalries for power among army leaders and nobles, as well as their flagrant efforts to enrich themselves, weakened the effectiveness of the government. About the same time local elites in the various provincial cities of the empire began to assert their own influence.

External factors also accounted for both the blocking of Ottoman expansion in the late seventeenth century and then its slow decline thereafter. During the European Middle Ages, the Islamic world had far outdistanced Europe in learning, science, and military prowess. From the fifteenth century onward, however, Europeans had begun to make rapid advances in technology, wealth, and scientific knowledge. For example, they designed ships for the difficult waters of the Atlantic and thus eventually opened trade routes to the East around Africa and reached the Americas. As trade expanded, Europeans achieved new commercial skills, founded trading posts in South Asia, established the plantation economies and precious metal mines of the Americas, and became much wealthier. By the seventeenth century, Europeans, particularly the Dutch and Portuguese, imported directly from Asia or America commodities such as spices, sugar, and coffee that they had previously acquired through the Ottoman Empire. During the same decades, Europeans developed greater military and naval power and new weapons.

During the 1690s, the Ottomans unsuccessfully fought a league of European states including Austria, Venice, Malta, Poland, and Tuscany, joined by Russia, which, as we have already seen, was emerging as a new aggressive power to the north. In early 1699, the defeated Ottomans negotiated the Treaty of Carlowitz, which required them to surrender significant territory lying not at the edges, but at the heart of their empire in Europe, including most of Hungary, to the Habsburgs. This treaty meant not only the loss of territory, but also of the revenue the Ottomans had long drawn from those regions. From this time onward, Russia and the Ottomans would duel for control of regions around the Black Sea with Russia achieving ever greater success by the close of the eighteenth century.

Despite these defeats, the Ottomans remained deeply inward looking, continuing to regard themselves as superior to the once underdeveloped European West. The Ottoman leaders, isolated from both their own leading Muslim subjects and from Europe, failed to understand what was occurring far beyond their immediate borders, especially European advances in military technology. When during the eighteenth century the Ottoman Empire began to recognize the new situation, it tended to borrow European technology and import foreign advisers, thus failing to develop its own infrastructure. Moreover, the powerful influence of the *Ulama* worked against imitation of Christian Europe. This influence by Muslim religious teachers occurred just as governments, such as that of Peter the Great, and secular intellectuals across Europe, through the influence of the Enlightenment (see Chapter 17), were increasingly diminishing the influence of the Christian churches in political and economic affairs. Consequently, European intellectuals began to view the once feared Ottoman Empire as a declining power and Islam as a backward-looking religion.

Devshirme. An Ottoman portrayal of the *Devshirme.* This miniature painting from about 1558 depicts the recruiting of young Christian children for the Sultan's elite Janissary corps.

British Library, London, UK/Bridgeman Art Library

What was the relationship between the Ottoman government and its Christian subjects?

SUMMARY

WHAT WAS the Dutch Golden Age and what led to its decline?

The Netherlands: Golden Age to Decline By the mid–eighteenth century, Britain and France had emerged as the dominant powers in Western Europe and Spain had lost influence. The United Netherlands had enjoyed a Golden Age in the seventeenth century, and it was more urbanized than any other area of Europe. Dutch agriculture and financial systems were models for the rest of Europe, and the Dutch were the leading traders of Europe. After the death of William of Orange in 1702, the loose republican system that had given the Netherlands valuable flexibility turned into a handicap in the absence of leadership. *page 322*

WHAT FACTORS led to the different political paths taken by England and France in the seventeenth century?

Two Models of European Political Development In the seventeenth century, England and France developed two different forms of government that served as models for other European countries in the eighteenth century. In England, nobles and the wealthy were politically active and had a tradition of broad liberties, representation, and bargaining with the monarch through Parliament. The English nobility felt little admiration or affection for the Stuart monarchs. In France, members of the French nobility believed the strength of Louis XIV served their personal interests as well as those of the king. This led to the so-called absolutism of the French monarchy, which became the country's sole significant national institution. *page 323*

HOW DID conflicts over taxation and religion lead to civil war in Stuart England?

Constitutional Crisis and Settlement in Stuart England In the first half of the seventeenth century, many of the English suspected that their leaders were Catholic sympathizers. Oliver Cromwell led opposition in a civil war from 1642 to 1646, and then ruled until 1658. In 1660, the Stuart monarchy was restored under Charles II. His relationship with Parliament was testy. His brother and successor, the Catholic James II, was not as astute as Charles II. In 1688, members of Parliament invited William III of Orange to invade England and take the throne. After the success of the "Glorious Revolu-

tion," in 1689, William and Mary recognized a Bill of Rights, limiting the monarchy's powers, guaranteeing civil liberties to some, formalizing Parliament's role, and barring Catholics from the throne. The 1689 Toleration Act allowed Protestants freedom to worship but denied Catholics similar privileges. The monarchy in Great Britain passed to the house of Hanover, and George I sought support from the Whigs. Robert Walpole functioned as George's prime minister. Parliament checked royal influence and provided strong central political authority. Britain's economy was strong, and political life was remarkably free. *page 323*

WHY WERE efforts to establish absolute monarchy successful in France but unsuccessful in England?

Rise of Absolute Monarchy in France: The World of Louis XIV Louis XIV's monarchy gathered unprecedented power on the national level in the area of foreign and military affairs, domestic administration, and economic regulation. At the same time, Louis was careful to allow nobles to retain their local power and privileges. He ensured loyalty to the crown by employing nobles in his administration and crafted a political image as the "Sun King" based at Versailles. At this palace, Louis built a system of patronage that effectively excluded many nobles from government, even as it occupied them in ritual and ceremony all designed to promote Louis's personal rule and divine right monarchy. Louis's armies instilled fear in France's neighbors, prompting several alliances to be formed against France throughout his reign. He repressed the anti-Jesuit Jansenists and revoked the Edict of Nantes, which had ensured toleration of French Protestants. These policies reinforced Europe's image of Louis as a repressive fanatic and sowed the seeds of domestic opposition to the monarchy, not only among Jansenist sympathizers, but also in noble and judicial bodies. *page 328*

WHAT WERE the main characteristics that defined the Polish, Austrian, and Prussian states in the seventeenth and eighteenth centuries?

Central and Eastern Europe The economies and political structures of central and eastern Europe were weaker than those of the West. Late in the seventeenth century, Poland could not develop a strong central authority, while Austria, Prussia, and Russia emerged as political and military powers. The Habsburg Empire expanded so much that by the eighteenth and nineteenth centuries, Habsburg power and influence were based more on territories outside of Germany than within. Political unity was in short supply. The Hohenzollerns created a Prussian army that, according to an axiom, possessed the nation, rather than the other way around. *page 335*

HOW DID Peter the Great transform Russia into a powerful, centralized nation?

Russia Enters the European Political Arena In the seventeenth century, Russia became one of the nations of Europe, and the Romanov dynasty was founded. Russia's old nobility, the *boyars*, retained considerable authority until Peter (later Peter the Great) assumed personal rule in 1689. Peter was zealous in his efforts to westernize Russia, to curb the power of the *boyars* and Moscow garrison guards (the *streltsy*), and to increase the nation's military strength. He was remark-

ably successful in most of his efforts. His critical failure was that, when he died in 1725, he had not appointed a successor; for decades after his death, power reverted to nobles and soldiers. *page 338*

WHAT WAS the attitude of the Ottoman rulers toward religion in their empire and how was this reflected in their policies?

The Ottoman Empire The Ottoman Empire was diverse ethnically, linguistically, and religiously and offered more religious freedom than could be found anywhere in Europe. Social and political structures prevented leading families from interacting meaningfully with the ruling elite, which limited the infusion of new ideas and personalities into government. Military defeats in the late seventeenth century marked the beginning of the end for the Ottoman Empire. *page 341*

REVIEW QUESTIONS

1. Why did Britain and France remain leading powers while the United Netherlands declined? How did the structure of British government change under the political leadership of Walpole?

2. What similarities and differences do you see between the systems of government and religious policies in place in England and France at the end of the seventeenth century? What accounts for the path each nation took?

3. Why did the English king and Parliament come into conflict in the 1640s? What was the "Glorious Revolution"? How did England in 1700 differ from England in 1600?

4. How did Louis XIV consolidate his monarchy? How successful was his foreign policy? What were the domestic and international consequences of his religious policies?

5. How did Peter the Great's plan for building a greater Russia compare with the conduct of the Ottoman leaders who allowed their empire to decline?

6. How was the Hohenzollern family able to forge a conglomerate of diverse landholdings into the state of Prussia? How do the Hohenzollerns and the Habsburgs compare in the ways they dealt with the problems that confronted their domains?

7. What sorts of political and diplomatic problems did questions about successions to thrones create for various states between 1685 and 1740?

KEY TERMS

divine right of kings (p. 329)
Fronde (p. 328)
Gallican Liberties (p. 332)
Glorious Revolution (p. 327)
Jansenism (p. 332)
Junkers (p. 337)
millets (p. 342)
Ottoman Empire (p. 341)

parlements(p. 335)
parliamentary monarchy (p. 323)
political absolutism (p. 323)
Pragmatic Sanction (p. 337)
Puritans (p. 324)
Sejm (p. 336)
Table of Ranks (p. 340)

For additional learning resources related to this chapter, please go to **www.myhistorylab.com**

PEARSON
myhistorylab

14

New Directions in Thought and Culture in the Sixteenth and Seventeenth Centuries

The great Dutch artist Rembrandt van Rijn (1606–1669) recorded the contemporary life of the United Provinces of the Netherlands during its Golden Age. The new sciences including medicine made much progress in the Netherlands, which was a center for publishing and instrument making and known for its religious toleration. *The Anatomy Lesson of Dr. Tulp* (1632) presents the dissection of a cadaver of an executed criminal by the noted Dutch physician Dr. Nicolass Tulp who stands on the right surrounded by other members of the Amsterdam Guild of Surgeons. Such dissections were a controversial part of new emerging medical education with only one a year permitted in Amsterdam. The dramatic use of light and darkness is characteristic of the painting of the baroque style.

Rembrandt van Rijn (1606–1669). *The Anatomy Lesson of Dr. Tulp.* Mauritshuis, The Hague, The Netherlands. SCALA/Art Resource, NY

What does this painting tell us about the development of medical education in the seventeenth century?

uring the sixteenth and seventeenth centuries, science created a new view of the universe that challenged many previously held beliefs. Earth moved from the center of the universe and became only one of several planets orbiting a sun that was only one of countless stars. This new cosmology forced people to re-think humanity's place in the larger scheme of things. The new scientific ideas came into apparent conflict with traditional religion and raised doubts about the grounds for faith and morality. Europeans discovered the world was a much more complex place than their ancestors had imagined. The telescope opened the heavens to them while the microscope disclosed the existence of a realm of microorganisms. A spate of scientific discoveries added to the intellectual dislocation already created by the Reformation and contact with the New World. ■

THE SCIENTIFIC REVOLUTION

WHAT WAS the scientific revolution?

scientific revolution The emergence in the sixteenth century of rational and empirical methods of research that challenged traditional thought and promoted the rise of science and technology.

The process that established the new view of the universe is normally termed the *scientific revolution*. The revolution-in-science metaphor must be used carefully, however. Not everything associated with the "new" science was necessarily new. Sixteenth- and seventeenth-century natural philosophers were often reexamining and rethinking theories and data from the ancient world and the late Middle Ages. Moreover, the word *revolution* normally denotes rapid, collective political change involving many people. The scientific revolution was not rapid. It was a complex movement with many false starts and brilliant people suggesting wrong as well as useful ideas. Nor did it involve more than a few hundred people who labored in widely separated studies and crude laboratories located in Poland, Italy, Denmark, Bohemia, France, and Great Britain. Furthermore, the achievements of the new science were not simply the function of isolated brilliant scientific minds. The leading figures of the scientific revolution often drew on the aid of artisans and craftspeople to help them construct new instruments for experimentation and to carry out those experiments. Finally, because the practice of science involves social activity as well as knowledge, the revolution also saw the establishment of new social institutions to support the emerging scientific enterprise.

Natural knowledge was only in the process of becoming science as we know it today during the era of the scientific revolution. In fact the word *scientist*, which was only coined in the 1830s, did not yet exist in the seventeenth century, nor did anything resembling the modern scientific career. Individuals devoted to natural philosophy might work in universities or in the court of a prince or even in their own homes and workshops. Only in the second half of the seventeenth century did formal societies and academies devoted to the pursuit of natural philosophy come into existence.

Although new knowledge emerged in many areas during the sixteenth and seventeenth centuries, including medicine, chemistry, and natural history, the scientific achievements that most captured the learned imagination and persuaded people of the cultural power of natural knowledge were those that occurred in astronomy.

NICOLAUS COPERNICUS REJECTS AN EARTH-CENTERED UNIVERSE

Nicolaus Copernicus (1473–1543) was a Polish priest and an astronomer. In 1543, the year of his death, Copernicus published *On the Revolutions of the Heavenly Spheres*. What Copernicus's work did was to provide an intellectual springboard for a complete criticism of the then-dominant view of the position of Earth in the universe. He had undertaken this task to help the papacy reform the calendar, so that it could correctly calculate the date for Easter based on a more accurate understanding of astronomy.

The Ptolemaic System   In Copernicus's time, the standard explanation of the place of Earth in the heavens combined the mathematical astronomy of Ptolemy, contained in his work entitled the *Almagest* (150 C.E.), with the physical cosmology of Aristotle. Over the centuries, commentators on Ptolemy's work had developed several alternative **Ptolemaic systems**, on the basis of which they made mathematical calculations relating to astronomy. Most of these writers assumed Earth was the center of the universe, an outlook known as *geocentrism*. Drawing on Aristotle, these commentators assumed that above Earth lay a series of concentric spheres, one of which contained the moon, another the sun, and still others the planets and the stars. At the outer regions of these spheres lay the realm of God and the angels. Earth had to be the center because of its heaviness. The stars and the other heavenly bodies had to be enclosed in the spheres so they could move, since nothing could move unless something was actually moving it. The state of rest was presumed to be natural; motion required explanation.

The Ptolemaic model gave rise to many problems, which had long been recognized. For example, at certain times the planets appeared to be going backwards. Complex mathematical models were developed to account for this phenomenon. Other intellectual, but nonobservational, difficulties related to the immense speed at which the spheres had to move around Earth. To say the least, the Ptolemaic systems were cluttered. They were effective, however, as long as one assumed Aristotelian physics to be correct.

Copernicus's Universe   Copernicus's *On the Revolutions of the Heavenly Spheres* challenged the Ptolemaic picture in the most conservative manner possible. He adopted many elements of the Ptolemaic model but transferred them to a *heliocentric* (sun-centered) model, which assumed Earth moved about the sun in a circle. The repositioning of the Earth had not been Copernicus's goal. Rather, he appears to have set out to achieve new intelligibility and mathematical elegance in astronomy by rejecting Aristotle's cosmology and by removing the earth from the center of the universe. His system was no more accurate than the existing ones for predicting the location of the planets. He had used no new evidence. The major impact of his work was to provide another way of confronting some of the difficulties inherent in Ptolemaic astronomy. The Copernican system did not immediately replace the old astronomy, but it allowed other people who were also discontented with the Ptolemaic view to think in new directions. Indeed, for at least a century, only a minority of natural philosophers and astronomers embraced the Copernican system.

Scenographia: Systematis Copernicani Astrological Chart, ca. 1543.

British Library, London, UK/Bridgeman Art Library

What was the relationship between astronomy and astrology in the sixteenth century?

Ptolemaic system   Astronomical theory, named after Greek astronomer Ptolemy, that assumed Earth was the center point of a ball-shaped universe composed of concentric layers of rotating crystalline spheres to which the heavenly bodies were attached.

QUICK REVIEW

On the Revolutions of the Heavenly Spheres

- Copernicus's work meant as a revision of Ptolemy's model
- If Earth was assumed to rotate around the sun, the model would be vastly simplified
- Model slow to attract adherents

TYCHO BRAHE AND JOHANNES KEPLER MAKE NEW SCIENTIFIC OBSERVATIONS

The Danish astronomer Tycho Brahe (1546–1601) took the next major step toward the conception of a sun-centered system. He did not embrace Copernicus's view of the universe and actually spent most of his life advocating an Earth-centered system. Brahe's contribution was the construction of scientific instruments with which he made more extensive naked-eye observations of the planets than anyone else had ever done. His labors produced a vast body of astronomical data from which his successors could work.

When Brahe died, his assistant, Johannes Kepler (1571–1630), a German astronomer, took possession of these tables. Kepler was a convinced Copernican and a more consistently rigorous advocate of a heliocentric model than Copernicus himself had been. Like Copernicus, Kepler was deeply influenced by Renaissance Neoplatonism, which held the sun in special honor. In keeping with this outlook, Kepler was determined to find in Brahe's numbers mathematical harmonies that would support a sun-centered universe. Based on the mathematical relationships that emerged from his study of Brahe's observations, Kepler set forth the first astronomical model that actually portrayed motion—that is, the path of the planets—and those orbits were elliptical, not circular. Kepler published his findings in his 1609 book entitled *The New Astronomy*. He had used Copernicus's sun-centered universe and Brahe's empirical data to solve the problem of planetary motion.

Kepler had also defined a new problem. None of the available theories could explain why the planetary orbits were elliptical or, for that matter, why planetary motion was orbital at all rather than simply moving off along a tangent. That solution awaited the work of Sir Isaac Newton.

GALILEO GALILEI ARGUES FOR A UNIVERSE OF MATHEMATICAL LAWS

From Copernicus to Brahe to Kepler, there had been little new information about the heavens that might not have been known to Ptolemy. In 1609, however, the same year that Kepler published *The New Astronomy*, an Italian mathematician and natural philosopher named Galileo Galilei (1564–1642) first turned a telescope on the heavens. Using that recently invented Dutch instrument, he saw stars where none had been known to exist, mountains on the moon, spots moving across the sun, and moons orbiting Jupiter. The heavens were far more complex than anyone had suspected. In the *Starry Messenger* (1610) and *Letters on Sunspots* (1613), he used his considerable rhetorical skills to argue that his newly observed physical evidence, particularly the phases of Venus, required a Copernican interpretation of the heavens.

Galileo's career illustrates that the forging of the new science involved more than just presenting arguments and evidence. In 1610, he had left the University of Padua for Florence, where he became the philosopher and mathematician to the Grand Duke of Tuscany, who was a Medici. Galileo was now pursuing natural philosophy in a princely court and had become dependent on princely patronage. To win such support both for his continued work and for his theories, he named the moons of Jupiter after the Medicis. As a natural philosopher working with the new telescope, he had literally presented recently discovered heavenly bodies to his patron. By his political skills and his excellent prose, he had transformed himself into a high-profile advocate of Copernicanism. Galileo's problems with the Roman Catholic Church (see page 000) arose from both his ideas and his flair for self-advertisement.

Galileo not only popularized the Copernican system but also articulated the concept of a universe subject to mathematical laws. More than any other writer of the century, he argued that nature displayed mathematical regularity in its most minute details. For Galileo, the universe was rational; however, its rationality was not that of medieval scholastic logic, but of mathematics. Copernicus had thought that the heavens conformed to mathematical regularity; Galileo saw this regularity throughout physical nature.

A world of quantities was replacing one of qualities. The new natural philosophy portrayed nature as cold, rational, mathematical, and mechanistic. What was real and lasting was what was mathematically measurable. For many people, the power of the mathematical arguments that appeared irrefutable proved more persuasive than the new information from physical observation that produced so much controversy. Few intellectual shifts have wrought such momentous changes for Western civilization.

ISAAC NEWTON DISCOVERS THE LAWS OF GRAVITATION

The question that continued to perplex seventeenth-century scientists who accepted the theories of Copernicus, Kepler, and Galileo was how the planets and other heavenly bodies moved in an orderly fashion. It was this issue of planetary motion that the Englishman Isaac Newton (1642–1727) addressed and, in so doing, established a basis for physics that endured for more than two centuries.

In 1687, Newton published *The Mathematical Principles of Natural Philosophy*, better known by its Latin title of *Principia Mathematica*. Galileo's mathematical bias permeated Newton's thought, as did his view that inertia applied to bodies both at rest and in motion. Newton reasoned that the planets and all other physical objects in the universe moved through mutual attraction, or gravity. Every object in the universe affected every other object through gravity. The attraction of gravity explained why the planets moved in an orderly, rather than a chaotic, manner. Newton demonstrated this relationship mathematically; he made no attempt to explain the nature of gravity itself.

Newton was a mathematical genius, but he also upheld the importance of empirical data and observation. Like Francis Bacon, he believed in empiricism—that one must observe phenomena before attempting to explain them. The final test of any theory or hypothesis for him was whether it described what was actually observed. Newton was a great opponent of the rationalism of the French philosopher René Descartes (see page 000), which he believed included insufficient guards against error. Consequently, as Newton's own theory of universal gravitation became increasingly accepted, so, too, was Baconian empiricism.

Sir Isaac Newton's experiments dealing with light passing through a prism became a model for writers praising the experimental method.
CORBIS/Bettmann

In what sense was Newton's work the culmination of the scientific revolution?

PHILOSOPHY RESPONDS TO CHANGING SCIENCE

The revolution in scientific thought contributed directly to a major reexamination of Western philosophy. Several of the most important figures in the scientific revolution, such as Bacon and Descartes, were also philosophers discontented with the scholastic heritage. Newton's interests likewise extended to philosophy; he wrote broadly on many topics, including scientific method and theology.

WHAT IMPACT did the new science have on philosophy?

NATURE AS MECHANISM

If a single idea informed all of these philosophers, though in different ways, it was the idea of *mechanism*. The proponents of the new science sought to explain the world in terms of mechanical metaphors, or the language of machinery. Nature conceived as machinery removed much of the mystery of the world and the previous assumption of the presence of divine purpose in nature. The qualities that seemed to inhere in matter came to be understood as the result of mechanical arrangement. Some writers came to understand God as a kind of divine watchmaker or mechanic who had arranged the world as a machine that would thereafter function automatically. The drive to a mechanical understanding of

Published in 1620, *Novum Organum* ("new organ or instrument") by Francis Bacon is one of the most important works of the scientific revolution. In this and other works Bacon attacked the long-held belief that most truth had already been discovered. This allegorical image, from the frontispiece of *Novum Organum*, shows a ship striking out for unknown territories, seeking, as did Bacon, for a new understanding of the natural world. The ship is flanked by the mythical pillars of Hercules that stand at the point where the Mediterranean meets the Atlantic—the realm of the unknown and unexplored.

Courtesy of the Library of Congress

What sort of future did Bacon imagine for the human race?

empiricism   The use of experiment and observation derived from sensory evidence to construct scientific theory or philosophy of knowledge.

nature also meant that the language of science and of natural philosophy would become largely that of mathematics.

This new mode of thinking transformed physical nature from a realm in which Europeans looked for symbolic or sacramental meaning related to the divine into a realm where they looked for utility or usefulness. Natural knowledge became the path toward the physical improvement of human beings through their ability to command and manipulate the processes of nature. Many people associated with the new science also believed such knowledge would strengthen the power of their monarchs.

FRANCIS BACON: THE EMPIRICAL METHOD

Bacon (1561–1626) was an Englishman of almost universal accomplishment. He was a lawyer, a high royal official, and the author of histories, moral essays, and philosophical discourses. Traditionally, he has been regarded as the father of **empiricism** and of experimentation in science. Much of this reputation was actually unearned. Bacon was not a natural philosopher, except in the most amateur fashion. His real accomplishment was setting an intellectual tone and helping create a climate conducive to scientific work.

In books such as *The Advancement of Learning* (1605), the *Novum Organum* (1620), and *The New Atlantis* (1627), Bacon attacked the scholastic belief that most truth had already been discovered and only required explanation, as well as the scholastic reverence for authority in intellectual life. He urged contemporaries to strike out on their own in search of a new understanding of nature. Bacon was one of the first major European writers to champion innovation and change.

Bacon believed that human knowledge should produce useful results—deeds rather than words. In particular, knowledge of nature should be enlisted to improve the human condition. These goals required modifying or abandoning scholastic modes of learning and thinking. Scholastic philosophers could not escape from their syllogisms to examine the foundations of their thought and intellectual presuppositions. Bacon urged that philosophers and investigators of nature examine the evidence of their senses before constructing logical speculations. By directing natural philosophy toward an examination of empirical evidence, Bacon hoped it would achieve new knowledge and thus new capabilities for humankind.

Bacon boldly compared himself with Columbus, plotting a new route to intellectual discovery. The comparison is significant, because it displays the consciousness of a changing world that appears so often in writers of the late sixteenth and early seventeenth centuries. They were rejecting the past not from simple contempt or arrogance, but rather from a firm understanding that the world was much more complicated than their medieval forebearers had thought. Neither Europe nor European thought could remain self-contained. Like the new worlds on the globe, new worlds of the mind were also emerging.

Most of the people in Bacon's day, including the intellectuals influenced by humanism, thought that the best era of human history lay in antiquity. Bacon dissented vigorously from that view. He looked to a future of material improvement achieved through the empirical examination of nature. His own theory of induction from empirical evidence was unsystematic, but his insistence on appealing to experience influenced others whose methods were more productive. He and others of his outlook received almost daily support from the reports not only of European explorers, but also of ordinary seamen who now sailed all over the world and could describe wondrous cultures, as well as plants and animals, unknown to the European ancients.

Bacon believed that expanding natural knowledge had a practical purpose and its goal was human improvement. Some scientific investigation does have this character. Much pure research does not. Bacon, however, linked science and material progress in the public mind. This was a powerful idea that still influences Western civilization. It has made science and those who can appeal to the authority of science major forces for change and innovation. As a person actively associated with politics, Bacon also believed the pursuit of new knowledge would increase the power of governments and monarchies. Again, his thought in this area opened the way for the eventual strong links between governments and the scientific enterprise.

> **QUICK REVIEW**
> **The Empirical Method**
>
> * Francis Bacon believed Scholasticism did nothing more than arrange old ideas
> * Thinkers should reexamine the foundations of their thought
> * Reliance on empirical evidence would yield the best results

RENÉ DESCARTES: THE METHOD OF RATIONAL DEDUCTION

Descartes (1596–1650) was a gifted mathematician who invented analytic geometry. His most important contribution, however, was to develop a scientific method that relied more on deduction—reasoning from general principle to arrive at specific facts—than empirical observation and induction.

In 1637, he published his *Discourse on Method*, in which he rejected scholastic philosophy and education and advocated thought founded on a mathematical model. (See "Compare & Connect: Descartes and Swift Debate the Scientific Enterprise," pages 354–355.) In the *Discourse*, he began by saying he would doubt everything except those propositions about which he could have clear and distinct ideas. This approach rejected all forms of intellectual authority, except the conviction of his own reason. Descartes concluded that he could not doubt his own act of thinking and his own existence. From this base, he proceeded to deduce the existence of God. The presence of God was important to Descartes because God guaranteed the correctness of clear and distinct ideas. Since God was not a deceiver, the ideas of God-given reason could not be false.

On the basis of such an analysis, Descartes concluded that human reason could fully comprehend the world. He divided existing things into two basic categories: thinking things and things occupying space—mind and body, respectively. Thinking was the defining quality of the mind, and extension (the property by which things occupy space) was the defining quality of material bodies. Human reason could grasp and understand the world of extension, which became the realm of the natural philosopher. That world had no place for spirits, divinity, or anything nonmaterial.

Descartes's emphasis on deduction, rational speculation, and internal reflection by the mind, all of which he explored more fully in his *Meditations* of 1641, has influenced philosophers from his time to the present. His deductive methodology, however, eventually lost favor to scientific induction, whereby scientists draw generalizations derived from and test hypotheses against empirical observations.

Queen Christina of Sweden (r. 1632–1654), shown here with the French philosopher and scientist René Descartes, was one of many women from the elite classes interested in the new science. In 1649 she invited Descartes to live at her court in Stockholm, but he died a few months after moving to Sweden.

Pierre-Louis the Younger Dumesnil (1698–1781), *Christina of Sweden (1626–89) and Her Court: Detail of the Queen and René Descartes (1596–1650) at the Table*. Oil on canvas. Chateau de Versailles, France/Bridgeman Art Library

What role did monarchs like Christina play in promoting scientific research?

DESCARTES AND SWIFT DEBATE THE SCIENTIFIC ENTERPRISE

Throughout the seventeenth and eighteenth century, various writers asserted that the growth of natural knowledge held the promise of improving the human situation. Others, who did not dispute the truth or correctness of the new natural knowledge, nonetheless questioned whether it could actually improve the human situation. In these two documents the French philosopher René Descartes upholds the former position while many decades later the English satirist Jonathan Swift questions the usefulness of the new natural knowledge pursued by the Royal Society of London and by implication by other European scientific academies.

QUESTIONS

1. How does Descartes compare the usefulness of science with previous speculative philosophy?

2. What, if any, limits does he place on the extension of scientific knowledge?

3. Why might Swift have so emphasized what he saw as the impracticality of science?

4. How might Swift's presentation be seen as manifesting jealousy of a literary figure toward the growing influence of science?

5. How does Swift's passage serve as an effort to refute the promise of science championed by Bacon and Descartes?

An Illustration from *Discourse on Method*, by René Descartes (1637).

Courtesy of the Library of Congress

What place did mathematics have in Descartes's vision of the universe?

I. DESCARTES EXPLORES THE PROMISE OF EXPANDING NATURAL KNOWLEDGE

In 1637, Descartes published his Discourse on Method. *He wrote against what he believed to be the useless speculations of scholastic philosophy. He championed the careful investigation of physical nature on the grounds that it would expand the scope of human knowledge beyond anything previously achieved and, in doing so, make human beings the masters of nature. This passage contains much of the broad intellectual and cultural argument that led to the ever-growing influence and authority of science from the seventeenth century onward.*

My speculations were indeed truly pleasing to me; but I recognize that other men have theirs, which perhaps please them even more. As soon, however, as I had acquired some general notions regarding physics, and on beginning to make trial of them in various special difficulties had observed how far they can carry us and how much they differ from the principles hitherto employed, I believed that I could not keep them hidden without grievously sinning against the law which lays us under obligation to promote, as far as in us lies, the general good of all mankind. For they led me to see that it is possible to obtain knowledge highly useful in life, and that in place of the speculative philosophy taught in the Schools we can have a practical philosophy, by means of which, knowing the force and the actions of fire, water, air, and of the stars, of the heavens, and of all the bodies that surround us—knowing them as distinctly as we know the various crafts of the artisans—we may in the same fashion employ them in all the uses for which they are suited, thus rendering ourselves the masters and possessors of nature. This is to be desired, not only with a view to the invention of an infinity of arts by which we would be enabled to enjoy without heavy labor the fruits of the earth and all its conveniences, but above all for the preservation of health, which is, without doubt, of all blessings in this life, the first of all goods and the foundation on which the others rest. For the mind is so dependent on the temper and disposition of the bodily organisms that if any means can ever be found to render men wiser and more capable than they have hitherto been, I believe that it is in the science of medicine that the means must be sought. . . . With no wish to depreciate it, I am yet sure there is no one, even of those engaged in the profession, who does not admit that all we know is almost nothing in comparison with what remains to be discovered; and that we could be freed from innumerable maladies, both of body and of mind, and even perhaps from the infirmities of age, if we had sufficient knowledge of their causes and of the remedies provided by nature.

Source: From René Descartes, *Discourse on Method*, in *Descartes's Philosophical Writings*, ed. by Norman Kemp Smith (New York: The Modern Library, 1958), pp. 130–131. Reprinted by permission of Macmillan Press Ltd.

II. JONATHAN SWIFT SATIRIZES SCIENTIFIC SOCIETIES

Swift, the greatest author of English satire in the eighteenth century, was a deeply pessimistic person who thought much of the promise held forth for scientific enterprise would never be realized. In the third voyage of Gulliver's Travels, *published in 1726, Swift portrays Gulliver as visiting the land of Lagardo where he encounters a learned academy filled with scholars pursuing outlandish projects. Swift lists the efforts of a whole series of Projectors, each of which is more impractical than the next. This passage in which Swift pillories the various people who hoped to receive patronage for projects from persons associated with the Royal Society of London remains one of the most famous satires of science in the English language. That Swift wrote it is a testimony to the cultural authority that science had achieved by the early eighteenth century.*

Gulliver reports a conversation he encountered while visiting Lagardo:

"The Sum of his Discourse was to this Effect. That about Forty Years ago, certain Persons went up to *Laputa*, either upon Business or Diversion; and after five Months Continuance, came back with a very little Smattering in Mathematics, but full of Volatile Spirits acquired in that Airy Region. That these Persons upon their Return, began to dislike the Management of every Thing below; and fell into Schemes of putting all Arts, Sciences, Languages, and Mechanics upon a new Foot. To this End they procured a Royal Patent for erecting an Academy of *Projectors* in *Lagado*; And the Humour prevailed so strongly among the People, that there is not a Town of any Consequence in the Kingdom without such an Academy. In these Colleges, the Professors contrive new Rules and Methods of Agriculture and Building, and new Instruments and Tools for all Trades and Manufactures, whereby, as they undertake, one Man shall do the Work of Ten; a Palace may be built in a Week, of Materials so durable as to last for ever without repairing. All the Fruits of the Earth shall come to Maturity at whatever Season we think fit to chuse; and increase an Hundred Fold more than they do at present; with innumerable other happy Proposals. The only Inconvenience is, that none of these Projects are yet brought to Perfection; and in the mean time, the whole Country lies miserably waste, the Houses in Ruins, and the People without Food or Cloaths. By all which, instead of being discouraged they are Fifty Times more violently bent upon prosecuting their Schemes, driven equally on by Hope and Depair. . . ."

Gulliver then reports what he found occurring in the rooms of an academy in Lagardo:

"The first Man I saw . . . had been Eight Years upon a Project for extracting Sun-Beams out of Cucumbers, which were to be put into Vials hermetically sealed, and let out to warm the Air in raw inclement Summers. . . .

"I saw another at work to calcine ice into Gunpowder . . .

"There was another most ingenius Architect who had contrived a new Method for building Houses, by beginning at the Roof, and working downwards to the Foundation. . . .

In another Apartment I was highly pleased with a Projector, who had found a Device of plowing the Ground with Hogs, to save the Charges of Plows, Cattle, and Labour. The Method is this: In an Acre of Ground you bury at six Inches Distance, and eight deep, a quantity of Acorns, Dates, Chesnuts, and other Masts or Vegetables whereof these Animals are fondest; then you drive six Hundred or more of them into the Field, where in a few Days they will root up the whole Ground in search of their Food, and make it fit for sowing, at the same time manuring it with their Dung. It is true, upon Experiment they found the Charge and Trouble very great, and they had little or no Crop. However, it is not doubted that this Invention may be capable of great Improvement."

Source: Jonathan Swift, *Gulliver's Travels*, Part III, chaps. iv and v (New York: The Heritage Press, 1960), pp. 193–194, 197–199.

THOMAS HOBBES: APOLOGIST FOR ABSOLUTE GOVERNMENT

Nowhere did the impact of the methods of the new science so deeply affect political thought as in the thought of Thomas Hobbes (1588–1679), the most original political philosopher of the seventeenth century.

An urbane and much-traveled man, Hobbes enthusiastically supported the new scientific movement. During the 1630s, he visited Paris, where he came to know Descartes, and Italy, where he spent time with Galileo. He took special interest in the works of William Harvey (1578–1657), who was famous for his discovery of the circulation of blood through the body.

Hobbes had written works of political philosophy before the English Civil War, but the turmoil of that struggle led him in 1651 to publish his influential work *Leviathan*. His aim was to provide a rigorous philosophical justification for a strong central political authority. Hobbes portrayed human beings and society in a thoroughly materialistic and mechanical way. He traced all psychological processes to bare sensation and regarded all human motivations as egoistical, intended to increase pleasure and minimize pain.

According to Hobbes, human beings in their natural state are inclined to a "perpetual and restless desire" for power. Because all people want and, in their natural state, possess a natural right to everything, their equality breeds enmity, competition, diffidence, and perpetual quarreling—"a war of every man against every man." Hobbes, contrary to Aristotle and Christian thinkers like Thomas Aquinas (1225–1274), rejected the view that human beings are naturally sociable. Rather, they are self-centered creatures who lack a master. Thus, whereas earlier and later philosophers saw the original human state as a paradise from which humankind had fallen, Hobbes saw it as a state of natural, inevitable conflict in which neither safety, security, nor any final authority existed. Human beings in this state of nature were constantly haunted by fear of destruction and death.

Human beings escaped this terrible state of nature, according to Hobbes, only by entering into a particular kind of political contract according to which they agreed to live in a commonwealth tightly ruled by a recognized sovereign. This contract obliged every person, for the sake of peace and self-defense, to agree to set aside personal rights to all things and to be content with as much liberty against others as he or she would allow others against himself or herself.

Because, however, words and promises are insufficient to guarantee this agreement, the contract also established the coercive use of force by the sovereign to compel compliance. Believing the dangers of anarchy to be always greater than those of tyranny, Hobbes thought that rulers should be absolute and unlimited in their power, once established as authority. Hobbes's political philosophy has no room for protest in the name of individual conscience or for individual appeal to some other legitimate authority beyond the sovereign.

The specific structure of this absolute government was not of enormous concern to Hobbes. He believed absolute authority might be lodged in either a monarch or a legislative body, but once that person or body had been granted authority, there existed no argument for appeal. For all practical purposes, obedience to the Hobbesian sovereign was absolute.

Hobbes's argument for an absolute political authority that could assure order aroused sharp opposition. Monarchists objected to his willingness to assign sovereign authority to a legislature.

The Famous Title Page Illustration for Hobbes's *Leviathan*. The ruler is pictured as absolute lord of his lands, but note that the ruler incorporates the mass of individuals whose self-interests are best served by their willing consent to accept him and cooperate with him.

Courtesy of the Library of Congress

How did Hobbes see the relationship between a monarch and his or her subjects?

Republicans rejected his willingness to accept a monarchical authority. Many Christian writers, including those who supported the divine right of kings, furiously criticized his materialist arguments for an absolute political authority. Other Christian writers attacked his refusal to recognize the authority of either God or the church as standing beside or above his secular sovereign. The religious critique of Hobbes meant that his thought had little immediate practical impact, but his ideas influenced philosophical literature from the late seventeenth century onward.

JOHN LOCKE: DEFENDER OF MODERATE LIBERTY AND TOLERATION

Locke (1632–1704) proved to be the most influential philosophical and political thinker of the seventeenth century. Although he was less original than Hobbes, his political writings became a major source of criticism of absolutism and provided a foundation for later liberal political philosophy in both Europe and America. His philosophical works dealing with human knowledge became the most important work of psychology for the eighteenth century.

Locke wrote two treatises on government that were eventually published in 1690. In the first of these, he rejected arguments for absolute government that based political authority on the patriarchal model of fathers ruling over a family. After the publication of this treatise, no major political philosopher again appealed to the patriarchal model. In that regard, though not widely read today, Locke's *First Treatise of Government* proved enormously important by clearing the philosophical decks, so to speak, of a long-standing traditional argument that could not stand up to rigorous analysis.

In his *Second Treatise of Government*, Locke presented an extended argument for a government that must necessarily be both responsible for and responsive to the concerns of the governed. Locke portrayed the natural human state as one of perfect freedom and equality in which everyone enjoyed, in an unregulated fashion, the natural rights of life, liberty, and property. Locke, contrary to Hobbes, regarded human beings in their natural state as creatures of reason and basic goodwill rather than of uncontrolled passion and selfishness. For Locke, human beings possess a strong capacity for dwelling more or less peacefully in society before they enter a political contract. What they experience in the state of nature is not a state of war, but a condition of competition and modest conflict that requires a political authority to sort out problems rather than to impose sovereign authority. They enter into the contract to form political society to secure and preserve the rights, liberty, and property that they already possess prior to the existence of political authority. In this respect, government exists to protect the best achievements and liberty of the state of nature, not to overcome them. Thus, by its very foundation, Locke's government is one of limited authority.

The conflict that Hobbes believed characterized the state of nature emerged for Locke only when rulers failed to preserve people's natural freedom and attempted to enslave them by absolute rule. The relationship between rulers and the governed is that of trust, and if the rulers betray that trust, the governed have the right to replace them.

In his *Letter Concerning Toleration* (1689), Locke used the premises of the as yet unpublished *Second Treatise* to defend extensive religious toleration among Christians, which he saw as an answer to the destructive religious conflict of the past two centuries. To make his case for toleration, Locke claimed that each individual was required to work out his or her own religious salvation and these efforts might lead various people to join different religious groups. For its part, government existed by its very nature to preserve property, not to make religious decisions for its citizens. Consequently, Locke urged a wide degree of religious toleration among differing voluntary Christian groups. He did not, however, extend toleration to Roman Catholics, whom he believed to have given allegiance to a foreign prince (i.e., the pope), to non-Christians, or to atheists, whom he believed could not be trusted to keep their word. Despite these limitations, Locke's *Letter Concerning Toleration* established a powerful foundation for the future extension of toleration, religious liberty, and the separation of church and state.

Finally, just as Newton had set forth laws of astronomy and gravitation, Locke hoped to elucidate the basic structures of human thought. He did so in the most immediately influential of his books, his *Essay Concerning Human Understanding* (1690), which became the major work of European psychology during the eighteenth century. There, Locke portrayed a person's mind at birth as a blank tablet whose content would be determined by sense experience. It was a reformer's psychology, which contended that the human condition could be improved by changing the environment.

Locke's view of psychology rejected the Christian understanding of original sin, yet he believed his psychology had preserved religious knowledge. He thought such knowledge came through divine revelation in Scripture and also from the conclusions that human reason could draw from observing nature. He hoped this interpretation of religious knowledge would prevent human beings from falling into what he regarded as fanaticism arising from the claims of alleged private revelations and irrationality arising from superstition. For Locke, reason and revelation were compatible and together could sustain a moderate religious faith that would avoid religious conflict.

THE NEW INSTITUTIONS OF EXPANDING NATURAL KNOWLEDGE

WHAT WAS the social and political context for scientific inquiry in the seventeenth century?

One of the most fundamental features of the expansion of science was the emerging idea that *genuinely new knowledge* about nature and humankind could be discovered. The proponents of the new natural knowledge and the new philosophy sought to pursue what Bacon called the advancement of learning. New knowledge would be continuously created. This outlook required new institutions.

Colbert was Louis XIV's most influential minister. He sought to expand the economic life of France and to associate the monarchy with the emerging new science from which he hoped might flow new inventions and productive technology. Here he is portrayed presenting members of the French Academy of Science to the monarch on the founding of the French Academy.

Henri Testelin (1616–1695) (after Le Brun). Minister of Finance Colbert presenting the members of the Royal Academy of Science (founded in 1667) to Louis XIV. Study for a tapestry. Photo: Gerard Blot. Chateaux de Versailles et de Triaanon, Versailles, France. Reunion des Musées Nationaux/Art Resource, NY

What role did Colbert believe science could play in the development of the French economy?

The expansion of natural knowledge had powerful social implications. Both the new science and the philosophical outlook associated with it opposed Scholasticism and Aristotelianism. These were not simply disembodied philosophical outlooks, but ways of approaching the world of knowledge most scholars in the universities of the day still believed in.

Not surprisingly, the advanced thinkers of the seventeenth century often criticized the universities. Some of the criticism of universities was exaggerated. Medical faculties, on the whole, welcomed the advancement of learning in their fields of study. Most of the natural philosophers had themselves received their education at universities. Moreover, however slowly new ideas might penetrate universities, the expanding world of natural knowledge would be taught to future generations. With that diffusion of science into the universities came new supporters of scientific knowledge beyond the small group of natural philosophers themselves. Universities also provided much of the physical and financial support for teaching and investigating natural philosophy and employed many scientists, the most important of whom was Newton himself.

Yet because of the reluctance of universities to rapidly assimilate the new science, its pioneers quickly understood that they required a framework for cooperating and sharing information that went beyond existing intellectual institutions. Consequently, they and their supporters established what have been termed "institutions of sharing" that allowed information and ideas associated with the new science to be gathered, exchanged, and debated. The most famous of these institutions was the Royal Society of London, founded in 1660, whose members consciously saw themselves as following the path Bacon had laid out almost a half century earlier. In addition to these major institutions, the new science was discussed and experiments were carried out in many local societies and academies.

These societies met regularly to hear papers and observe experiments. These groups also published information relating to natural philosophy and often organized libraries for their members. Perhaps most important, they attempted to separate the discussion and exploration of natural philosophy from the religious and political conflicts of the day. They intended science to exemplify an arena for the polite exchange of ideas and for civil disagreement and debate.

The activities of the societies also constituted a kind of crossroads between their own members always drawn from the literate classes, and people outside the elite classes, whose skills and practical knowledge might be important for advancing the new science. The latter included craftspeople who could manufacture scientific instruments, sailors whose travels had taken them to foreign parts and who might report on the plants and animals they had seen there, and workers who had practical knowledge of problems in the countryside.

The work, publications, and interaction of the scientific societies with both the government and private business established a distinct role and presence for scientific knowledge in European social life. By 1700, that presence was relatively modest, but it would grow steadily during the coming decades. The groups associated with the new science saw themselves as championing modern practical achievements of applied knowledge and urging religious toleration, mutual forbearance, and political liberty. Such people would form the social base for the eighteenth-century movement known as the **Enlightenment**.

Enlightenment   The eighteenth-century movement led by the *philosophes* that held that change and reform were both desirable through the application of reason and science.

WOMEN IN THE WORLD OF THE SCIENTIFIC REVOLUTION

WHAT ROLE did women play in the scientific revolution?

The same factors that had long excluded women from participating in most intellectual life continued to exclude them from working in the emerging natural philosophy. Traditionally, the institutions of European intellectual life had all but excluded women. Women could and did exercise influence over princely courts where natural philosophers, such as Galileo, sought patronage, but they usually did not determine those patronage decisions or benefit from them. Queen Christina of Sweden (r. 1632–1654), who brought René Descartes to Stockholm to provide the regulations for a new science academy, was an exception. When various scientific societies were founded, women were not admitted to membership. In that regard, there were virtually no social spaces that might have permitted women to pursue science easily.

Margaret Cavendish, who wrote widely on scientific subjects, was the most accomplished woman associated with the new science in seventeenth-century England.

ImageWorks/Mary Evans Picture Library Ltd.

What role did women play in the scientific revolution?

Yet a few isolated women from two different social settings did manage to engage in the new scientific activity—noblewomen and women from the artisan class. In both cases, they could do so only through their husbands or male relatives.

The social standing of certain noblewomen allowed them to command the attention of ambitious natural philosophers who were part of their husband's social circle. Margaret Cavendish (1623–1673) actually made significant contributions to the scientific literature of the day. As a girl she had been privately tutored and become widely read. Her marriage to the duke of Newcastle introduced her into a circle of natural philosophers. She understood the new science, quarreled with the ideas of Descartes and Hobbes, and criticized the Royal Society for being more interested in novel scientific instruments than in solving practical problems. She was the only woman in the seventeenth century to be allowed to visit a meeting of the Royal Society of London.

Women associated with artisan crafts actually achieved greater freedom to pursue the new sciences than did noblewomen. Traditionally, women had worked in artisan workshops, often with their husbands, and might take over the business when their spouse died. In Germany, much study of astronomy occurred in these settings, with women assisting their fathers or husbands. One German female astronomer, Maria Cunitz, published a book on astronomy that many people thought her husband had written until he added a preface supporting her sole authorship. Elisabetha and Johannes Hevelius constituted a wife-and-husband astronomical team, as did Maria Winkelmann and her husband Gottfried Kirch. Winkelmann had worked jointly with her husband who was the official astronomer of the Berlin Academy of Sciences and was responsible for an official calendar the academy published. When her husband died in 1710, Winkelmann applied for permission to continue the work, basing her application for the post on the guild's tradition of allowing women to continue their husbands' work, in this case the completion of observations required to create an accurate calendar. After much debate, the academy formally rejected her application on the grounds of her gender, although its members knew of her ability and previous accomplishments. Years later, she returned to the Berlin Academy as an assistant to her son, who had been appointed astronomer. Again, the academy insisted that she leave, forcing her to abandon astronomy. She died in 1720.

Such policies of exclusion, however, did not altogether prevent women from acquiring knowledge about scientific endeavors. Margaret Cavendish had composed a *Description of a New World, Called the Blazing World* (1666) to introduce women to the new science. Other examples of scientific writings for a female audience were Bernard de Fontenelle's *Conversations on the Plurality of Worlds* and Francesco Algarotti's *Newtonianism for Ladies* (1737). During the 1730s, Emilie du Châtelet (1706–1749) aided Voltaire in his composition of an important French popularization of Newton's science. Her knowledge of mathematics was more extensive than his and crucial to his completing his book. She also translated Newton's *Principia* into French, an accomplishment made possible only by her exceptional understanding of advanced mathematics.

Still, with few exceptions, women were barred from science and medicine until the late nineteenth century, and not until the twentieth century did they enter these fields in significant numbers.

QUICK REVIEW

Women and Science

- Significant obstacles stood in the way of women doing scientific work
- A few elite women, notably Margaret Cavendish, were allowed to make contributions
- Women from the artisan classes had more opportunities than other women

THE NEW SCIENCE AND RELIGIOUS FAITH

For many contemporaries, the new science posed a potential challenge to religion. Three major issues were at stake. First, certain theories and discoveries did not agree with biblical statements about the heavens. Second, who would decide conflicts between religion and science—church authorities or the natural philosophers? Finally, for many religious thinkers, the new science seemed to replace a universe of spiritual meaning and significance with a purely materialistic one.

WHAT EFFORTS were made to reconcile the new science and religion?

THE CASE OF GALILEO

The condemnation of Galileo by Roman Catholic authorities in 1633 is the single most famous incident of conflict between modern science and religious institutions. The condemnation of Copernicanism and of Galileo occurred at a particularly difficult moment in the history of the Roman Catholic Church. In response to Protestant emphasis on private interpretation of Scripture, the Council of Trent (1545–1563) had stated that only the church itself possessed the authority to interpret the Bible. Furthermore, after the Council, the Roman Catholic Church had adopted a more literalist mode of reading the Bible in response to the Protestant emphasis on the authority of Scripture. Galileo's championing of Copernicanism took place in this particular climate of opinion and practice when the Roman Catholic Church, on the one hand, could not surrender the interpretation of the Bible to a layman and, on the other, had difficulty moving beyond a literal reading of the Bible, lest the Protestants accuse it of abandoning Scripture.

Galileo Galilei.
© Bettmann/CORBIS

In a *Letter to the Grand Duchess Christina* (1615), Galileo, as a layman, had published his own views about how Scripture should be interpreted to accommodate the new science. To certain Roman Catholic authorities, his actions resembled those of a Protestant who looked to himself rather than the church to understand the Bible. In early 1616, the Roman Catholic Inquisition formally censured Copernicus's views, placing *On the Revolutions of the Heavenly Spheres* in the Index of Prohibited Books. The ground for the condemnation was Copernicus's disagreement with the literal word of the Bible and the biblical interpretations of the Church Fathers.

Galileo, who was not on trial in 1616, was formally informed of the condemnation of Copernicanism. Exactly what agreement he and the Roman Catholic authorities reached as to what he would be permitted to write about Copernicanism remains unclear. It appears that he agreed not to advocate that Copernican astronomy was actually physically true, but only to suggest that it could be true in theory.

In 1623, however, a Florentine acquaintance of Galileo's was elected as Pope Urban VIII. He gave Galileo permission to resume discussing the Copernican system, which he did in *Dialogue on the Two Chief World Systems* (1632). The book clearly was designed to defend the physical truthfulness of Copernicanism. Moreover, the voices in the dialogue favoring the older system appeared slow-witted—and those voices presented the views of Pope Urban. Feeling humiliated and betrayed, the pope ordered an investigation of Galileo's book. The actual issue in Galileo's trial of 1633 was whether he had disobeyed the mandate of 1616, and he was held to have done so even though the exact nature of that mandate was less than certain. Galileo was condemned, required to renounce his views, and placed under the equivalent of house arrest in his home near Florence for the last nine years of his life.

BLAISE PASCAL: REASON AND FAITH

Blaise Pascal (1623–1662), a French mathematician and a physical scientist who surrendered his wealth to pursue an austere, self-disciplined life, made one of the most influential efforts to reconcile faith and the new science. He aspired to write a work that would refute both dogmatism and skepticism. He never produced a definitive

Overview   Major Works of the Scientific Revolution

YEAR	WORK	AUTHOR
1543	*On the Revolutions of the Heavenly Spheres*	Copernicus
1605	*The Advancement of Learning*	Bacon
1609	*The New Astronomy*	Kepler
1610	*The Starry Messenger*	Galileo
1620	*Novum Organum*	Bacon
1632	*Dialogue on the Two Chief World Systems*	Galileo
1637	*Discourse on Method*	Descartes
1651	*Leviathan*	Hobbes
1687	*Principia Mathematica*	Newton
1689	*Letter Concerning Toleration*	Locke
1690	*An Essay Concerning Human Understanding*	Locke
1690	*Treatises of Government*	Locke

refutation of the two sides. Rather, he formulated his views on these matters in piecemeal fashion in a provocative collection of reflections on humankind and religion published posthumously under the title *Pensées (Thoughts)*.

Pascal believed that in religious matters, only the reasons of the heart and a "leap of faith" could prevail. For him, religion was not the domain of reason and science. He saw two essential truths in the Christian religion: A loving God exists, and human beings, because they are corrupt by nature, are utterly unworthy of God. He believed the atheists and the deists of his age had overestimated reason. To Pascal, reason itself was too weak to resolve the problems of human nature and destiny. Ultimately, reason should drive those who truly heeded it to faith in God and reliance on divine grace.

Pascal made a famous wager with the skeptics. It is a better bet, he argued, to believe God exists and to stake everything on his promised mercy than not to do so. This is because, if God does exist, the believer will gain everything, whereas, should God prove not to exist, comparatively little will have been lost by having believed in him.

Convinced that belief in God improved life psychologically and disciplined it morally (regardless of whether God proved in the end to exist), Pascal worked to strengthen traditional religious belief. He urged his contemporaries to seek self-understanding by "learned ignorance" and to discover humankind's greatness by recognizing its misery. He hoped thereby to counter what he believed to be the false optimism of the new rationalism and science.

QUICK REVIEW

Blaise Pascal (1623–1662)

- French mathematician and physical scientist
- His *Pensées (Thoughts)* was meant to refute both dogmatism and skepticism
- Believed reason could lead humans to religion, but that religion operated beyond reason

THE ENGLISH APPROACH TO SCIENCE AND RELIGION

Francis Bacon established a key framework for reconciling science and religion that long influenced the English-speaking world. He argued there were two books of divine revelation: the Bible and nature. Because both books of revelation shared the same author, they must be compatible. Whatever discord might first appear between science and religion must eventually be reconciled.

Later in the seventeenth century, with the work of Newton, the natural universe became a realm of law and regularity. Most natural philosophers were devout people who saw in the new picture of physical nature a new picture of God. The Creator of this rational, lawful nature must also be rational. To study nature was to come to a better understanding of that Creator. Science and religious faith were not only compatible, but also mutually supportive.

Finally, the new science and the technological and economic innovations associated with its culture came again, especially among English thinkers, to be interpreted as part of a divine plan. By the late seventeenth century, natural philosophy and its practical achievements had become associated in the public mind with consumption and the market economy. Scientific advance and economic enterprise came to be interpreted in the public mind as the fulfillment of God's plan: Human beings were meant to improve the world. This outlook provided a religious justification for the processes of economic improvement that would characterize much of eighteenth-century Western Europe.

CONTINUING SUPERSTITION

Despite the great optimism among certain European thinkers associated with the new ideas in science and philosophy, traditional beliefs and fears long retained their hold on Western culture.

WHAT EXPLAINS the witch hunts and panics of the sixteenth and seventeenth centuries?

WITCH HUNTS AND PANIC

Nowhere is the dark side of early modern thought and culture more strikingly visible than in the witch hunts and panics that erupted in almost every Western land. Between 1400 and 1700, courts sentenced an estimated 70,000 to 100,000 people to death for harmful magic (*maleficium*) and diabolical witchcraft.

Why did witch panics occur in the sixteenth and early seventeenth centuries? The disruptions created by religious division and warfare were major factors. (The peak years of the religious wars were also those of the witch hunts.) Some argue that the Reformation spurred the panics by taking away the traditional defenses against the devil and demons, thus compelling societies to protect themselves preemptively by searching out and executing witches. Political consolidation by secular governments and the papacy played an even greater role, as both aggressively conformed their respective realms in an attempt to eliminate competition for the loyalty of their subjects.

VILLAGE ORIGINS

The roots of belief in witches are found in both popular and elite culture. In village societies, feared and respected "cunning folk" helped people cope with natural disasters and disabilities by magical means. Those who were most in need of security and influence, particularly old, impoverished single or widowed women, often made claims to such magical powers. In village society witch beliefs may also have been a way to defy urban Christian society's attempts to impose its orthodox beliefs, laws, and institutions on the countryside. Under church persecution local fertility cults, whose semipagan practices were intended to ensure good harvests, acquired the features of diabolical witchcraft.

Three witches charged with practicing harmful magic are burned alive in Baden in southwest Germany. On the left, two of them are feasting with demons at a sabbat

Bildarchiv Preussicher Kulturbesitz

INFLUENCE OF THE CLERGY

Popular belief in magical power was the essential foundation of the witch hunts. Had ordinary people not believed that "gifted persons" could help or harm by magical means, and had they not been willing to accuse them, the hunts would never have occurred. However, the contribution of Christian theologians was equally great. In the late thirteenth century, the Church declared its magic to be the only true magic. Since such powers were not innate to humans, the theologians reasoned, they must come either from God or from the devil. Those from God were properly exercised within and by the church. Any who practiced magic outside and against the Church did so on behalf of the devil. From such reasoning grew allegations of "pacts" between nonpriestly magicians and Satan. Attacking accused witches became a way for the church to extend its spiritual hegemony.

WHO WERE THE WITCHES?

Roughly 80 percent of the victims of witch hunts were women, most single and aged over forty. Three groups of women appear especially to have drawn the witch-hunter's attention. The first was widows, who, living alone in the world after the deaths of their husbands, were often dependent on help from others, unhappy, and known to strike out. A second group was midwives, whose work made them unpopular when mothers and newborns died during childbirth. (See "Encountering the Past: Midwives.") Finally, there were women healers and herbalists, who were targeted because their work gave them a moral and spiritual authority over people whom the church wished to reserve for its priests.

END OF THE WITCH HUNTS

Several factors helped end the witch hunts. One was the emergence of a more scientific point of view. In the seventeenth century, mind and matter came to be viewed as two independent realities, making it harder to believe that thoughts in the mind or words on the lips could alter physical things. With advances in medicine, the rise of insurance companies, and the availability of lawyers, people gained greater physical security against the physical afflictions and natural calamities that drove the witch panics. Finally, the witch hunts began to get out of hand. Tortured witches, when asked whom they saw at witches' sabbats, sometimes alleged having seen leading townspeople there, and even the judges themselves! At this point the trials ceased to serve the interests of those conducting them, becoming dysfunctional and threatening anarchy as well.

baroque Naturalistic style associated with seventeenth-century painting, sculpture, and architecture that emphasized the emotional connection between art and the observer.

BAROQUE ART

HOW DID baroque art serve both religious and secular ends?

Art historians use the term *baroque* to denote the style associated with seventeenth-century painting, sculpture, and architecture. Baroque painters depicted their subjects in a thoroughly naturalistic, rather than an idealized, manner. This faithfulness to nature paralleled the interest in natural knowledge associated with the rise of the new science and the deeper understanding of human anatomy that was achieved during this period. These painters, the most famous of whom was Michelangelo Caravaggio (1573–1610), also were devoted to picturing sharp contrasts between light and darkness, which created dramatic scenes in their painting. Consequently, both baroque painting and sculpture have been seen as theatrical and intending to draw the observer into an emotional involvement with the subject that is being portrayed.

The work of baroque artists served both religious and secular ends. Baroque painters, especially in Roman Catholic countries, often portrayed scenes from the Bible and from the lives of saints intended to instruct the observer in religious truths. Artists used the same style of painting, however, to present objects and scenes of everyday life in new realistic detail. Such was the case with Dutch painters of still lifes who portrayed all manner of elaborate foodstuffs as well as with artists such Louis LeNain (1593–1648) who painted scenes of French peasant life.

Baroque art became associated, rightly or wrongly, with both Roman Catholicism and absolutist politics. The style first emerged in papal Rome, where Gian Lorenzo Bernini's great Tabernacle—situated under the dome of St. Peter's basilica, above the space where St. Peter is said to be buried—is the most famous example, along with the two vast colonnades outside the church. Bernini also created the dramatic sculpture of the Spanish mystic St. Teresa of Avila (1515–1582), depicting her in religious ecstasy.

The association of baroque art with Roman Catholicism had its counterpart in the secular world. Charles I (r. 1625–1649) of England employed the Roman Catholic

Bernini designed the elaborate Baldacchino that stands under the dome of St. Peter's Basilica. It is one of the major examples of baroque interior decoration.

Scala/Art Resource, NY

In what ways did baroque art reflect the values of seventeenth-century Catholicism?

ENCOUNTERING THE PAST

MIDWIVES

Although women were excluded from formal medical training until well into the nineteenth century, the delivery of children was largely left to professional women called midwives. Midwifery was a trade often pursued by elderly or widowed women of the lower social classes. They underwent years of apprenticeship but were not permitted to organize themselves into guilds. They were licensed by civil and church authorities who were invariably men. Sometimes upper-class women were appointed to supervise them.

A reputation for respectability and discretion was essential for a midwife, for she witnessed some of life's most private moments and was privy to the intimate affairs of families. Her character was also assumed to have an effect on the outcome of a birth. A bad character was said to produce stillbirths and imperfectly formed infants. Carelessness or incompetence could, of course, void her license.

Midwives had religious and civic duties associated with births. In emergencies they could baptize failing infants. They registered births, and they were required to report to the authorities any suspicion of abortion or infanticide. A trusted midwife might also be called on to testify to a child's legitimacy.

Male physicians began to replace midwives in the eighteenth century, and civil authorities increasingly required persons who assisted at births to have a formal medical training that was not available to women. Midwives, however, never ceased to serve the poor and rural populations of Europe.

Until well into the eighteenth century, midwives oversaw the delivery of most children in Europe.
CORBIS
Why were midwives viewed with suspicion by many physicians?

WHY WAS midwifery long considered a female activity? Why did men eventually take charge of supervising the birthing process?

Flemish artist Peter Paul Rubens (1577–1640) to decorate the ceiling of the Banqueting Hall at his palace in London with paintings commemorating his father James I (r. 1603–1625). Charles's employment of him fed Puritan suspicions that the king harbored Roman Catholic sympathies. Consequently, it was not by coincidence that Charles I was led to his execution in 1649 through the Rubens-decorated Banqueting Hall to his death on the scaffold erected outside.

The most elaborate baroque monument to political absolutism was Louis XIV's palace at Versailles. (See Chapter 13.) Room after room was decorated with vast, dramatic paintings and murals presenting Louis as the Sun King. Monarchs across Europe, Protestant as well as Catholic, who hoped to imitate Louis's absolutism in their own domains, erected similar, if smaller, palaces filled with elaborate decoration.

SUMMARY

WHAT WAS the scientific revolution?

The Scientific Revolution What we now call "science" emerged as a field of inquiry in the seventeenth century as "natural philosophy." Copernicus, hoping to simplify Ptolemy's geocentric system, had tentatively proposed in the sixteenth century that the sun might be the center of circular planetary motion. Brahe disagreed and performed extensive observations attempting to support the geocentric model. Brahe's assistant Kepler used Brahe's data to propose, in a 1609 book, that the sun was at the center of elliptical planetary orbits. Also in 1609, Galileo was the first to study astronomy through a telescope. Galileo became a strong advocate for the heliocentric universe and popularized the idea that the universe is rational and subject to the laws of mathematics. Finally, Newton combined mathematical modeling and scientific observation to derive his famous laws of motion and theory of universal gravitation. *page 348*

WHAT IMPACT did the new science have on philosophy?

Philosophy Responds to Changing Science Scientists of the seventeenth century were called natural philosophers, and there was some overlap between philosophers and natural philosophers. For this reason, and because of the challenges to traditional thinking posed by scientific work in this period, philosophers were profoundly influenced by the scientific revolution. Galileo's mathematical modeling of the physical world translated into a mechanistic worldview that was widespread among philosophers. Bacon, Descartes, Hobbes, and Locke all articulated philosophies that took aspects of the new science into account and also had implications for social and political organization. *page 351*

WHAT WAS the social and political context for scientific inquiry in the seventeenth century?

The New Institutions of Expanding Natural Knowledge Through the Reformation, most intellectuals had believed their task was to recover and elaborate on knowledge from the Classical/biblical period. The expansion of natural knowledge changed universities and existing centers of learning, and it led to the creation of new "institutions of sharing."

Scientific societies encouraged new kinds of social mingling and the cross-fertilization of ideas. *page 358*

WHAT ROLE did women play in the scientific revolution?

Women in the World of the Scientific Revolution European universities had offered little room for scholarship by women; the institutions of science soon turned out to be even more exclusionary. Two categories of women were occasionally able to work around these constraints: noblewomen and female artisans. Women did write important scientific works and popularizations. *page 359*

WHAT EFFORTS were made to reconcile the new science and religion?

The New Science and Religious Faith The new science challenged religion in three ways: Some scientific observations contradicted biblical descriptions (e.g., of the heavens); it was unclear who should resolve any potential conflicts between science and religion, natural philosophers or church authorities; and the new philosophy's materialism seemed to some to preclude spirituality. Most natural philosophers worked hard to reconcile their work with religious views, and they were generally successful. Galileo's condemnation by the church, however, was a dramatic exception to the general rule of accommodation between science and religion. *page 361*

WHAT EXPLAINS the witch hunts and panics of the sixteenth and seventeenth centuries?

Continuing Superstition Through the seventeenth century, most Europeans believed in some form of magic and in the power of demons. "Magic," in the form of transubstantiation, was indeed at the heart of Christian ritual. Although such beliefs had been present for centuries, witch hunts and panics soared in the late sixteenth and early seventeenth centuries. Possible explanations for this phenomenon include the impact of wars and upheaval, spiritual insecurity in the aftermath of the Reformation, and villagers' sublimated hostility toward urban leaders. There is also a variety of possible explanations for why witch hunts died out in the seventeenth century. *page 363*

HOW DID baroque art serve both religious and secular ends?

Baroque Art In the seventeenth century, styles of painting, sculpture, and architecture collectively known as *baroque* came to prominence across Europe. Baroque depictions were naturalistic rather than idealized and sought to involve the observer on an emotional level through dramatic portrayals and contrasts of light and darkness. Catholic baroque art and architecture aimed to instruct and impress. Secular artists depicted everyday life but also created grandiose monuments to political absolutism, such as Louis XIV's palace at Versailles. *page 364*

REVIEW QUESTIONS

1. What contributions to the scientific revolution were made by Copernicus, Brahe, Kepler, Galileo, and Newton? Was the scientific revolution truly a revolution? Which has a greater impact on history, political or intellectual revolution?

2. How do the political philosophies of Hobbes and Locke compare? How did each view human nature? Would you rather live under a government designed by Hobbes or by Locke? Why?

3. What prevented women from playing a greater role in the development of the new science? How did family connections enable some women to contribute to the advance of natural philosophy?

4. What things account for the Church's condemnation of Galileo? How did Pascal try to reconcile faith and reason? How do you explain the fact that witchcraft and witch hunts flourished during an age of scientific enlightenment?

5. What purposes and goals did baroque painting, sculpture, and architecture serve in the religious and secular spheres?

KEY TERMS

baroque (p. 364)
empiricism (p. 352)
Enlightenment (p. 359)

Ptolemaic system (p. 349)
scientific revolution (p. 348)

For additional learning resources related to this chapter, please go to **www.myhistorylab.com**

PEARSON
myhistorylab

15

Society and Economy Under the Old Regime in the Eighteenth Century

During the eighteenth century farm women normally worked in the home and performed such tasks as churning butter as well as caring for children. As time passed, tasks such as making butter were mechanized and women were displaced from such work.

Francis Wheatley (RA) (1747–1801), *Morning*, signed and dated 1799, oil on canvas, 17½ × 21½ in. (44.5 × 54.5 cm), Yale Center for British Art, Paul Mellon Collection, USA/Bridgeman Art Library (B1977.14.120)

What role did women play in the family economy?

Old Regime   Prerevolutionary era marked by absolutist monarchies, agrarian economies, tradition, hierarchy, and privilege.

*he French Revolution of 1789 was a turning point in European history. The era that led up to it—the ancien régime (**Old Regime**)—was characterized by absolutist monarchies and agrarian economies that suffered chronic scarcity of food. Tradition, hierarchy, corporateness, and privilege were dominant features of the era. Men and women saw themselves less as individuals than as members of groups. The social order seemed fixed and rigid, but there was some change. Population grew, and standards of living improved. As farming was slowly commercialized, food became more abundant, and as the Industrial Revolution took hold, consumer goods became more plentiful. The spirit of rationality that had fostered the scientific revolution of the seventeenth century thrived in the eighteenth, the "Age of Reason" or the "Enlightenment." In many ways, the Old Regime nourished the changes that terminated its way of life.* ▪

MAJOR FEATURES OF LIFE IN THE OLD REGIME

HOW DID tradition, hierarchy, and privilege shape life in the Old Regime?

Socially, prerevolutionary Europe was based on (1) aristocratic elites possessing a wide variety of inherited legal privileges; (2) established churches intimately related to the state and the aristocracy; (3) an urban labor force usually organized into guilds; and (4) a rural peasantry subject to high taxes and feudal dues.

MAINTENANCE OF TRADITION

During the eighteenth century, few persons outside the government bureaucracies, the expanding merchant groups, and the movement for reform called the Enlightenment (see Chapter 17) considered change or innovation desirable. This was especially true of social relationships. Both nobles and peasants, for different reasons, repeatedly called for the restoration of traditional, or customary, rights. The nobles asserted what they considered their ancient rights against the intrusion of the expanding monarchical bureaucracies. The peasants, through petitions and revolts, called for the revival or the maintenance of the customary manorial rights that allowed them access to particular lands, courts, or grievance procedures. Except for the early industrial development in Britain and the accompanying expansion of personal consumption, the eighteenth-century economy was also predominantly traditional.

HIERARCHY AND PRIVILEGE

Closely related to this traditional social and economic outlook was the hierarchical structure of the society. The medieval sense of rank and degree not only persisted but also became more rigid during the century.

Each state or society was considered a community composed of numerous smaller communities. The "community" might include the village, the municipality, the nobility, the church, the guild, a university, or the parish. In turn, each of these bodies enjoyed certain privileges, some great and some small. The privileges might involve exemption from taxation or from some especially humiliating punishment, the right to practice a trade or craft, the right of one's children to pursue a particular occupation, or, for the church, the right to collect the tithe.

THE ARISTOCRACY

WHAT WAS the foundation of the wealth and power for the eighteenth-century aristocracy?

The eighteenth century was the great age of the aristocracy. The nobility constituted approximately 1 to 5 percent of the population of any given country. Yet in every country, it was the single wealthiest sector of the population, had the widest degree of social, political, and economic power, and set the tone of polite society.

VARIETIES OF ARISTOCRATIC PRIVILEGE

To be an aristocrat was a matter of birth and legal privilege. This much the aristocracy had in common across the Continent. In almost every other respect, they differed markedly from country to country.

British Nobility The smallest, wealthiest, best defined, and most socially responsible aristocracy resided in Great Britain. It consisted of about four hundred families, and the eldest male members of each family sat in the House of Lords. Through the corruptions of the electoral system, these families also controlled many seats in the House of Commons. The nobles owned about one-fourth of all the arable land in the country. Increasingly, the British aristocracy invested its wealth in commerce, canals, urban real estate, mines, and even industrial ventures. They had few significant legal privileges, but their direct or indirect control of local government gave them immense political power and social influence.

The foundation of aristocratic life was the possession of land. English aristocrats and large landowners controlled local government as well as the English Parliament. This painting of Robert Andrews and his wife by Thomas Gainsborough (1728–1788) shows an aristocratic couple on their estate. The gun and the hunting dog in this portrait suggest the importance landowners assigned to the virtually exclusive hunting privileges they enjoyed on their land.

© National Gallery, London

What key characteristics of the English aristocracy did the artist include in this portrait?

French Nobility In France, the approximately 400,000 nobles were divided between nobles "of the sword," or those whose nobility was derived from military service, and those "of the robe," who had acquired their titles either by serving in the bureaucracy or by having purchased them.

The French nobles were also divided between those who held office or favor with the royal court at Versailles and those who did not. The court nobility reaped the immense wealth that could be gained from holding high office. The nobles' hold on such offices intensified during the century. Whereas these well-connected aristocrats were rich, the provincial nobility, called *hobereaux*, were often little better off than wealthy peasants.

Despite differences in rank, origin, and wealth, certain hereditary privileges set all French aristocrats apart from the rest of society. They were exempt from many taxes. The nobles were technically liable for payment of the *vingtième*, or the "twentieth," which resembled an income tax, but they rarely had to pay it in full. The nobles were not liable for the royal *corvées*, or forced labor on public works, which fell on the peasants. In addition to these exemptions, French nobles could collect feudal dues from their tenants and enjoyed exclusive hunting and fishing privileges.

Eastern European Nobilities East of the Elbe River, the character of the nobility became even more complicated and repressive. Throughout the area, the military traditions of the aristocracy remained important. In Poland, there were thousands of nobles, or *szlachta*, who were entirely exempt from taxes after 1741. Until 1768, these Polish aristocrats possessed the right of life and death over their serfs. Most of the Polish nobility were relatively poor. A few rich nobles who had immense estates exercised political power in the fragile Polish state.

In Austria and Hungary, the nobility continued to possess broad judicial powers over the peasantry through their manorial courts. They also enjoyed various degrees of exemption from taxation.

In Prussia, after the accession of Frederick the Great in 1740, the position of the Junker nobles became much stronger. Frederick drew his officers almost wholly from the Junker class. Nobles also increasingly made up the bureaucracy. As in other parts of eastern Europe, the Prussian nobles had extensive judicial authority over the serfs.

In Russia, Peter the Great's (r. 1682–1725) linking of state service and noble social status through the Table of Ranks (1722) established among Russian nobles a self-conscious class identity that had not previously existed. In 1785, in the Charter of the Nobility, Catherine the Great (r. 1762–1796) legally defined the rights and privileges of noble men and women in exchange for the assurance that the nobility would serve the state voluntarily. Noble privileges included the right of transmitting noble status to a nobleman's wife and children, the judicial protection of noble rights and property, considerable power over the serfs, and exemption from personal taxes.

ARISTOCRATIC RESURGENCE

aristocratic resurgence Eighteenth-century resurgence of nobles that maintained the exclusiveness of noble rank, made it difficult to obtain, reserved powerful posts to nobles, and protected nobles from taxation.

The Russian Charter of the Nobility constituted one aspect of the broader European-wide development termed the *aristocratic resurgence*. This was the nobility's reaction to the threat to their social position and privileges that they felt from the expanding power of the monarchies. This resurgence took several forms in the eighteenth century.

First, all nobilities tried to preserve their exclusiveness by making it more difficult to become a noble. Second, they pushed to reserve appointments to the officer corps of the armies, the senior posts in the bureaucracies and government ministries, and the upper ranks of the church exclusively for nobles. Third, the nobles attempted to use the authority of existing aristocratically controlled institutions against the power of the monarchies. These institutions included the British Parliament, the French courts, or *parlements*, and the local aristocratic estates and provincial diets in Germany and the Habsburg Empire. Finally, the nobility sought to improve its financial position by gaining further exemptions from taxation or by collecting higher rents or long-forgotten feudal dues from the peasantry. This aristocratic challenge to the monarchies was a fundamental political fact of the day and a potentially disruptive one.

THE LAND AND ITS TILLERS

HOW WERE peasants and serfs tied to the land in eighteenth-century Europe?

Land was the economic basis of eighteenth-century life. Well over three-fourths of all Europeans lived in the country. Except for the nobility and the wealthier nonaristocratic landowners, most people who dwelled on the land were poor, living in various states of economic and social dependency, exploitation, and vulnerability.

PEASANTS AND SERFS

Rural social dependency related directly to the land. The nature of the dependency differed sharply for free peasants, such as English tenants and most French cultivators, and for the serfs of Germany, Austria, and Russia, who were legally bound to a particular plot of land and a particular lord. Yet everywhere, the class that owned most of the land also controlled the local government and the courts.

Obligations of Peasants   The power of the landlord increased as one moved across Europe from west to east. Most French peasants owned some land, but there were a few serfs in eastern France. Nearly all French peasants were subject to certain feudal dues, called *banalités*. In Prussia and Austria, despite attempts by the monarchies late in the century to improve the lot of the serfs, the landlords continued to exercise almost complete control over them.

Serfs were worst off in Russia. Russian landlords, in effect, regarded serfs merely as economic commodities. They could demand as many as six days a week of labor, known as *barshchina*, from the serfs. Like Prussian and Austrian landlords, they enjoyed the right to punish their serfs. Serfs had no legal recourse against the orders and whims of their lords. There was little difference between Russian serfdom and slavery.

In southeastern Europe, where the Ottoman Empire held sway, peasants were free, though landlords tried to exert authority in every way. During the seventeenth and eighteenth centuries, disorder originating in Constantinople (now Istanbul), the capital, spilled over into the Balkan peninsula. In this climate, landlords increased their authority by offering their peasants protection from bandits or rebels. These landlords also owned all the housing and tools the peasants needed to work the land and also furnished their seed grain. Consequently, despite legal independence, Balkan peasants under the Ottoman Empire became largely dependent on the landlords, though never to the extent of serfs in eastern Europe or Russia.

Peasant Rebellions   Russia experienced vast peasant unrest, with well over fifty peasant revolts between 1762 and 1769. These culminated in Pugachev's Rebellion between 1773 and 1775, when Emelyan Pugachev (1726–1775) promised the serfs land of their own and freedom from their lords. All of southern Russia was in turmoil until the government brutally suppressed the rebellion.

Pugachev's was the largest peasant uprising of the eighteenth century, but smaller peasant revolts or disturbances took place in Bohemia in 1775, in Transylvania in 1784, in Moravia in 1786, and in Austria in 1789. There were almost no revolts in Western Europe, but England experienced many rural riots. The rebels usually sought to reassert traditional or customary rights against practices that they perceived as innovations. Peasant revolts were thus conservative in nature.

Emelyan Pugachev (1726–1775) led the largest peasant revolt in Russian history. In this contemporary propaganda picture he is shown in chains. An inscription in Russian and German was printed below the picture decrying the evils of revolution and insurrection.

Bildarchiv Preussischer Kulturbesitz

What factors contributed to peasant revolts in sixteenth-century Russia?

FAMILY STRUCTURES AND THE FAMILY ECONOMY

HOUSEHOLDS

Northwestern Europe   In northwestern Europe, the household almost invariably consisted of a married couple, their children through their early teenage years, and their servants. Except for the few wealthy people, households usually consisted of not more than five or six members. Furthermore, in these households, more than two generations of a family rarely lived under the same roof. The family structure of northwestern Europe was thus nuclear rather than extended.

Children lived with their parents only until their early teens. Then they normally left home, usually to enter the workforce of young servants who lived and worked in another household. A child of a skilled artisan might remain with his or her parents to learn a valuable skill, but only rarely would more than one child do so, because children earned more working outside the home.

Those young men and women who had left home would eventually marry and form their own independent households. Men were usually over twenty-six, and women over twenty-three when they married. The new couple usually had children as soon after marriage as possible. Frequently, the woman was already pregnant at marriage. Family and community pressure often compelled the man to marry her. In any case, premarital sexual relations were common. The new couple would soon employ a servant, who, together with their growing children, would undertake whatever form of livelihood the household used to support itself.

The word *servant* in this context does not refer to someone looking after the needs of wealthy people. Rather, in preindustrial Europe, a servant was a person—either male or female—who was hired, often under a clear contract, to work for the head of the household in exchange for room, board, and wages. The servant was usually young and by no means always socially inferior to his or her employer. Normally, the

WHAT ROLE did the family play in the economy of preindustrial Europe?

QUICK REVIEW

Eastern European Peasants

- Power of landlords increased across Europe from west to east
- Peasants in southeastern Europe became more dependent on landlords over the course of the seventeenth and eighteenth centuries
- Russian serfs endured the worst conditions

servant was an integral part of the household and ate with the family. Being a servant for several years—often as many as eight or ten years—allowed young people to acquire the productive skills and the monetary savings necessary to begin their own household.

Eastern Europe   As one moved eastward across the Continent, the structure of the household and the pattern of marriage changed. In eastern Europe, both men and women usually married before the age of twenty. Consequently, children were born to much younger parents. Often—especially among Russian serfs—wives were older than their husbands. Eastern European households were generally larger than those in the West. Frequently a rural Russian household consisted of more than nine, and possibly more than twenty, members, with three or perhaps even four generations of the same family living together. Early marriage made this situation more likely. In Russia, marrying involved not starting a new household, but remaining in and expanding one already established.

The landholding structure in eastern Europe accounts, at least in part, for these patterns of marriage and the family. The lords of the manor who owned land wanted to ensure that it would be cultivated, so they could receive their rents. Thus, in Poland, for example, landlords might forbid marriage between their own serfs and those from another estate and require widows and widowers to remarry quickly. Polish landlords also frowned on the hiring of free laborers—the equivalent of servants in the West—to help cultivate land. The landlords preferred to use other serfs. This practice inhibited the formation of independent households. In Russia, landlords ordered the families of young people in their villages to arrange marriages within a short set time. These lords discouraged single-generation family households because the death or serious illness of one person in such a household might mean the land assigned to it would go out of cultivation.

THE FAMILY ECONOMY

During the seventeenth century the French Le Nain brothers painted scenes of French peasant life. Although the images softened many of the harsh realities of peasant existence, the clothing and the interiors were based on actual models and convey the character of the life of better-off French peasants whose lives would have continued very much the same into the eighteenth century.

Erich Lessing/Art Resource, NY

What explains the fascination of early modern artists with peasant life?

Throughout Europe, most people worked within the family economy. That is to say, the household was the basic unit of production and consumption. Depending on their ages and skills, everyone in the household worked. The need to survive poor harvests or economic slumps meant that no one could be idle. Within this family economy, all goods and income produced went to the benefit of the household rather than to the individual family member. On a farm, much of the effort went directly into raising food or producing other agricultural goods that could be exchanged for food. Few Western Europeans, however, had enough land to support their household from farming alone. Thus, one or more family members might work elsewhere and send wages home; for example, the father and older children might work as harvesters, fishermen, or engage in other labor either in the neighborhood or farther from home. If the father was such a migrant worker, his wife and their younger children would have to work the family farm. This was not an uncommon pattern.

The family economy also dominated the life of skilled urban artisans. The father was usually the chief artisan. He normally employed one or more servants but would expect his children to work in the enterprise also. He usually trained his eldest child in the trade. His wife often sold his wares or opened a small shop of her own. Wives of merchants also frequently ran their husbands' businesses, especially when the husband traveled to purchase new goods.

In Western Europe, the death of a father often brought disaster to the household. The continuing economic life of the family usually depended on his land or skills. The widow might take on the farm or the business, or his children might do so. The widow usually sought to remarry quickly to restore the labor and skills of a male to the household and to prevent herself from becoming dependent on relatives or charity.

In Eastern Europe, the family economy functioned in the context of serfdom and landlord domination. Peasants clearly thought in terms of their families and expanding the land available for cultivation. The village structure may have mitigated the pressures of the family economy, as did the multigenerational family. Dependence on the available land was the chief fact of life. There were many fewer artisan and merchant households, and there was far less geographical mobility than in Western Europe.

WOMEN AND THE FAMILY ECONOMY

The family economy established many of the chief constraints on the lives and personal experiences of women in preindustrial society. Most of the historical research that has been undertaken on this subject relates to Western Europe. There, a woman's life experience was largely the function of her capacity to establish and maintain a household. For women, marriage was an economic necessity, as well as an institution that fulfilled sexual and psychological needs. Outside a household, a woman's life was vulnerable and precarious. Consequently, a woman devoted much of her life first to maintaining her parents' household and then to devising some means of getting her own household to live in as an adult. Bearing and rearing children were usually subordinate to these goals.

By the age of seven, a girl would have begun to help with the household work. The girl would remain in her parents' home as long as she made a real contribution to the family enterprise or as long as her labor elsewhere was not more remunerative to the family. An artisan's daughter might not leave home until marriage, because at home she could learn increasingly valuable skills associated with the trade. The situation was different for the much larger number of girls growing up on farms. Their parents and brothers could often do all the necessary farm work, and a girl's labor at home quickly became of little value to her family. She would then leave home, usually between the age of twelve and fourteen years. She might take up residence on another farm, but more likely she would migrate to a nearby town or city. She would then normally become a servant, once again living in a household, but this time in the household of an employer. Having left home, the young woman's chief goal was to accumulate enough capital for a dowry. Her savings would make her eligible for marriage, because they would allow her to make the necessary contribution to form a household with her husband. A young woman might well work for ten years or more to accumulate a dowry. This practice meant that marriage was usually postponed until her mid- to late twenties.

Within marriage, earning enough money or producing enough farm goods to ensure an adequate food supply dominated women's concerns. Domestic duties, childbearing, and child rearing were subordinate to economic pressures. Consequently, couples tried to limit the number of children they had, usually through the practice of *coitus interruptus*, the withdrawal of the male before ejaculation.

The work of married women differed markedly between city and country and was in many ways a function of their husbands' occupations. If the peasant household had enough land to support itself, the wife spent much of her time literally carrying things for her husband—water, food, seed, harvested grain, and the like. If the husband had to do work besides farming, such as fishing or migrant labor, the wife might actually be in charge of the farm and do the plowing, planting, and harvesting. In the city, the wife of an artisan or a merchant might be in charge of the household finances and help manage the business. When her husband died, she might take over the business and perhaps hire an artisan.

Despite all this economic activity, women found many occupations and professions closed to them because they were female. They labored with less education than men, because in such a society women at all levels of life consistently found fewer opportunities for education than did men. They often received lower wages than men for the same work.

QUICK REVIEW
Girlhood

- By age seven girls contributed to household work
- Most girls left home between the ages of twelve and fourteen
- A young woman's chief goal was to accumulate a dowry

CHILDREN AND THE WORLD OF THE FAMILY ECONOMY

For women of all social ranks, childbirth meant fear and vulnerability. Contagious diseases endangered both mother and child. Not all midwives were skillful practitioners. Furthermore, most mothers gave birth in conditions of immense poverty and wretched housing. Assuming both mother and child survived, the mother might nurse the infant, but often the child would be sent to a wet nurse. The wealthy may have done this for convenience, but economic necessity dictated it for the poor. The structures and customs of the family economy did not permit a woman to devote herself entirely to rearing a child.

The birth of a child was not always welcome. Through at least the end of the seventeenth century, unwanted or illegitimate births could lead to infanticide, especially among the poor. The late seventeenth and the early eighteenth centuries saw a new interest in preserving the lives of abandoned children. Although foundling hospitals established to care for abandoned children had existed before, their size and number expanded during these years. Such hospitals cared for thousands of children, and the demand for their services increased during the eighteenth century.

Sadness and tragedy surrounded abandoned children. Most of them were illegitimate infants from across the social spectrum. Many, however, were left with the foundling hospitals because their parents could not support them. Parents would sometimes leave personal tokens or saints' medals on the abandoned baby in the vain hope they might one day be able to reclaim the child. Few children were reclaimed. Leaving a child at a foundling hospital did not guarantee its survival. In Paris, only about 10 percent of all abandoned children lived to the age of ten.

Despite all these perils of early childhood, children did grow up and come of age across Europe. The world of the child may not have received the kind of attention it does today, but during the eighteenth century, the seeds of that modern sensibility were sown. Particularly among the upper classes, new interest arose in educating children. As economic skills became more demanding, literacy became more valuable, and literacy rates rose during the century. Yet most Europeans remained illiterate. Not until the late nineteenth century was the world of childhood inextricably linked to the process of education. Then children would be reared to become members of a national citizenry. In the Old Regime, they were reared to make their contribution to the economy of their parents' family and then to set up their own households.

THE REVOLUTION IN AGRICULTURE

WHAT LED to the agricultural revolution of the eighteenth century?

The main goal of traditional peasant society was a stability that would ensure the local food supply. Despite differences in rural customs across Europe, the tillers resisted changes that might endanger the sure supply of food, which they generally believed traditional methods of cultivation would provide. Failure of the harvest meant not only hardship, but also death from either outright starvation or malnutrition. Poor harvests also played havoc with prices. Even small increases in the cost of food could exert heavy pressure on peasant or artisan families.

Historians now believe that during the eighteenth century bread prices slowly but steadily rose, spurred largely by population growth. Prices rose faster than urban wages and brought no appreciable advantage to the small peasant producer. However, the rise in grain prices benefited landowners and those wealthier peasants who had surplus grain to sell. The rising grain prices gave landlords an opportunity to improve their incomes and lifestyle. To achieve those ends, landlords in Western Europe began a series of innovations in farm production that became known as the Agricultural Revolution. Landlords commercialized agriculture and thereby challenged the traditional peasant ways of production. Peasant revolts and disturbances often resulted. The governments of Europe, hungry for new taxes and dependent on the goodwill of the nobility, used their armies and militias to smash peasants who defended traditional practices.

NEW CROPS AND NEW METHODS

The drive to improve agricultural production began during the sixteenth and seventeenth centuries in the Low Countries, where the pressures of the growing population and the shortage of land required changes in cultivation. Dutch landlords and farmers devised better ways to build dikes and to drain land, so they could farm more land. They also experimented with new crops, such as clover and turnips, that would increase the supply of animal fodder and restore the soil.

This seed drill, devised by the English agricultural innovator Jethro Tull (1674–1741), increased wheat crops by planting seed deep in the soil rather than just casting it randomly on the surface.

Image Works/Mary Evans Picture Library Ltd.

How did technology contribute to the agricultural revolution?

English landlords provided the most striking examples of eighteenth-century agricultural improvement. They originated almost no genuinely new farming methods, but they popularized ideas developed in the previous century either in the Low Countries or in England. Some of these landlords and agricultural innovators became famous. For example, Jethro Tull (1674–1741) championed the use of iron plows to turn the earth more deeply and of planting wheat by a drill rather than by just casting seeds. His methods permitted land to be cultivated for longer periods without having to leave it fallow. Charles "Turnip" Townsend (1674–1738) instituted crop rotation, using wheat, turnips, barley, and clover. This new system of rotation replaced the fallow field with one sown with a crop that both restored nutrients to the soil and supplied animal fodder. The additional fodder meant that more livestock could be raised, increasing the quantity of manure available as fertilizer for the grain crops. Consequently, in the long run, both animals and human beings had more food. Finally, Robert Bakewell (1725–1795) pioneered new methods of animal breeding that produced more and better animals and more milk and meat.

Enclosure Replaces Open-Field Method   Many of the agricultural innovations, which were adopted only slowly, were incompatible with the existing organization of land in England. Small cultivators who lived in village communities still farmed most of the soil. Each farmer tilled an assortment of unconnected strips. The two- or three-field systems of rotation left large portions of land fallow and unproductive each year. Animals grazed on the common land in the summer and on the stubble of the harvest in the winter. Until at least the mid-eighteenth century, the whole community decided what crops to plant. The entire system discouraged improvement and favored the poorer farmers, who needed the common land and stubble fields for their animals.

In 1700, approximately half the arable land in England was farmed by this open-field method. By the second half of the century, the rising price of wheat encouraged landlords to consolidate or enclose their lands to increase production. The **enclosures** were intended to use land more rationally and to achieve greater commercial profits. The process involved the fencing of common lands, the reclamation of previously untilled waste, and the transformation of strips into block fields. These procedures brought turmoil to the economic and social life of the countryside. Riots often ensued.

Because many English farmers either owned their strips or rented them in a manner that amounted to ownership, the larger landlords usually resorted to parliamentary acts to legalize the enclosure of the land, which they owned but rented to the farmers. Because the large landowners controlled Parliament, such measures passed easily. Between 1761 and 1792, almost 500,000 acres were enclosed through acts of Parliament, compared with 75,000 acres between 1727 and 1760. In 1801, a general enclosure act streamlined the process.

enclosures   Process of land privatization and rationalization intended to produce greater commercial profits.

The enclosures permitted the extension of both farming and innovation, and thus increased food production on larger agricultural units. They also disrupted small traditional communities; they forced off the land independent farmers, who had needed the common pasturage, and poor cottage dwellers, who had lived on the reclaimed wasteland. The enclosures, however, did not depopulate the countryside. In some counties where the enclosures took place, the population increased. New soil had come into production, and services that supported farming also expanded.

The commercialization of agriculture, which spread from Britain slowly across the Continent during the next century, strained the paternal relationship between the governing and governed classes. Previously, landlords had often looked after the welfare of the lower orders through price controls or waivers of rent during hard times. As the landlords became increasingly concerned about profits, they began to leave the peasants to the mercy of the marketplace.

Limited Improvements in Eastern Europe   Improving agriculture tended to characterize farm production west of the Elbe River. (See "Compare & Connect: Two Eighteenth-Century Writers Contemplate the Effects of Different Economic Structures," pages 380–381.) In Prussia, Austria, Poland, and Russia, agricultural improvement was limited. Nothing in the relationship of the serfs to their lords encouraged innovation. In eastern Europe, the chief method of increasing production was to bring previously untilled lands under the plow. By extending tillage, the great landlords sought to squeeze more labor from their serfs, rather than greater productivity from the soil. The only significant nutritional gain they achieved was the introduction of maize and the potato.

EXPANSION OF THE POPULATION

The population explosion with which the entire world must contend today had its origins in the eighteenth century. Before that time, Europe's population had experienced dramatic increases, but plagues, wars, or famine had redressed the balance. Beginning in the second quarter of the eighteenth century, the population began to increase steadily. In 1700, Europe's population, excluding the European provinces of the Ottoman Empire, was probably between 100 million and 120 million people. By 1800, the figures had risen to almost 190 million and by 1850, to 260 million. Such extraordinary sustained growth put new demands on all resources and considerable pressure on the existing social organization.

The population expansion occurred across the Continent in both the country and the cities. Only a limited consensus exists among scholars about the causes of this growth. The death rate clearly declined. There were fewer wars and epidemics in the eighteenth century. Hygiene and sanitation also improved, but the most important factor may have been changes in the food supply.

Improved and expanding grain production made one contribution. Another and even more important change was the cultivation of the potato. This tuber was a product of the New World and came into widespread European production during the eighteenth century. On a single acre, a peasant family could grow enough potatoes to feed itself for an entire year.

The impact of the population explosion can hardly be overestimated. It created new demands for food, goods, jobs, and services. It provided a new pool of labor. Traditional modes of production and living had to be revised. More people lived in the countryside than could find employment there. Migration increased. There were also more people who might become socially and politically discontented. Because the population growth fed on itself, these pressures and demands continued to increase. The society and the social practices of the Old Regime literally outgrew their traditional bounds.

THE INDUSTRIAL REVOLUTION OF THE EIGHTEENTH CENTURY

The second half of the eighteenth century witnessed the beginning of the industrialization of the European economy. That achievement of sustained economic growth is known as the **Industrial Revolution**. At considerable social cost, industrialization made possible the production of more goods and services than ever before in human history. The new means of production demanded new kinds of skills, new discipline in work, and a large labor force. In the long run, industrialization raised the standard of living and overcame the poverty that most Europeans, who lived during the eighteenth century and earlier, had taken for granted. It gave human beings greater control over nature than they had ever known before, yet by the mid–nineteenth century, industrialism would also cause new and unanticipated problems with the environment.

WHY DID the Industrial Revolution begin in Britain?

Industrial Revolution Term coined by early-nineteenth-century observers to describe the changes that the spreading use of powered machinery made in society and economics.

A REVOLUTION IN CONSUMPTION

The inventions of the Industrial Revolution increased the supply of consumer goods as never before in history. The supply of goods was only one side of the economic equation, however. An unprecedented demand for the humble goods of everyday life created the supply. Those goods included clothing, buttons, toys, china, furniture, rugs, kitchen utensils, candlesticks, brassware, silverware, pewterware, glassware, watches, jewelry, soap, beer, wines, and foodstuffs. It was the ever-increasing demand for these goods that sparked the ingenuity of designers and inventors. Furthermore, consumer demand seemed unlimited.

Many social factors helped establish the markets for these consumer goods. During the seventeenth century, the Dutch had enjoyed enormous prosperity and had led the way in new forms of consumption. For reasons that are still not clear, during the eighteenth century, first the English and then the people on the Continent came to have more disposable income, allowing people to buy consumer goods that previous generations had inherited or did not possess. What is key to this change in consumption is that it depended primarily on expanding the various domestic markets in Europe.

This revolution, if that is not too strong a term, in consumption was not automatic. People became persuaded that they needed or wanted new consumer goods. Often, entrepreneurs caused it to happen by developing new methods of marketing. For example, the English porcelain manufacturer Josiah Wedgwood (1730–1795) first attempted to find customers among the royal family and the aristocracy. Once he had gained their business with luxury goods, then he produced a less expensive version of the chinaware for middle-class customers. He also used advertising, opened showrooms, and sent out salespeople with samples and catalogs of his wares. There seemed to be no limit to the markets for consumer goods that social emulation on the one hand and advertising on the other could stimulate. Manufacturers soon realized that by changing styles they could further increase demand, for the desire to have the latest in fashions and inventions prompted people to return to the market again and again.

This expansion of consumption quietly, but steadily, challenged the social assumptions of the day. Fashion publications made all levels of society aware of new styles. Clothing fashions could be copied. Servants could begin to dress well if not

Overview	Major Inventions in the Textile-Manufacturing Revolution
1733	James Kay's flying shuttle
1765	James Hargreaves's spinning jenny (patented 1770)
1769	James Watt's steam engine patent
1769	Richard Arkwright's water frame patent
1787	Edmund Cartwright's power loom

TWO EIGHTEENTH-CENTURY WRITERS CONTEMPLATE THE EFFECTS OF DIFFERENT ECONOMIC STRUCTURES

Among eighteenth-century public officials and commentators there existed a broad agreement that European economic life needed to be reorganized and stimulated to achieve greater productivity and wealth. These writers also understood that different modes of productive activity resulted in very different kinds of society. In these two documents a French writer bemoans problems of French agriculture and landholding while a Scottish writer praises the wealth and good society that flow from growing commerce and refinement of both mechanical and liberal arts.

QUESTIONS

1. Why does Turgot favor those farmers who can make investments in the land they rent from a proprietor?

2. What are the structures of the *métayer* system? Why did it lead to poor investments and lower harvests?

3. Why does Hume link industry and the arts?

4. How does he see a commercial, improving economy producing important intellectual outlooks and social skills?

5. What benefits to agriculture might Hume have assigned to prosperous cities, and what benefits might Turgot have seen agriculture contributing to urban life?

I. TURGOT DECRIES FRENCH LANDHOLDING

During the eighteenth century, many observers became keenly aware that different kinds of landholding led to different attitudes toward work and to different levels of production and wealth. Robert Jacques Turgot (1727–1781), who later became finance minister of France, analyzed these differences in an effort to reform French agriculture. He was especially concerned with arrangements that encouraged long-term investment. The métayer *system Turgot discusses was an arrangement whereby landowners had land farmed by peasants who received part of the harvest as payment for working the land, but the peasants had no long-term interest in improving the land. Virtually all observers regarded the system as inefficient.*

1. What really distinguishes the area of large-scale farming from the areas of small-scale production is that in the former areas the proprietors find farmers who provide them with a permanent revenue from the land and who buy from them the right to cultivate it for a certain number of years. These farmers undertake all the expenses of cultivation, the ploughing, the sowing and the stocking of the farm with cattle, animals and tools. They are really agricultural entrepreneurs, who possess, like the entrepreneurs in all other branches of commerce, considerable funds, which they employ in the cultivation of land. . . .

   They have not only the brawn but also the wealth to devote to agriculture. They have to work, but unlike workers, they do not have to earn their living by the sweat of their brow, but by the lucrative employment of their capital, just as the ship owners of Nantes and Bordeaux employ theirs in maritime commerce.

2. *Métayer System* The areas of small-scale farming, that is to say at least four-sevenths of the kingdom, are those where there are no agricultural entrepreneurs, where a proprietor who wishes to develop his land cannot find anyone to cultivate it except wretched peasants who have no resources other than their labor, where he is obliged to make, at his own expense, all the advances necessary for tillage, beasts, tools, sowing, even to the extent of advancing to his *métayer* the wherewithal to feed himself until the first harvest, where consequently a proprietor who did not have any property other than his estate would be obliged to allow it to lie fallow. After having deducted the costs of sowing and feudal dues with which the property is burdened, the proprietor shares with the *métayer* what remains of the profits, in accordance with the agreement they have concluded. The proprietor runs all the risks of harvest failure and any loss of cattle: he is the real entrepreneur. The *métayer* is

This is a detail of a 1739 map by Louis Bretez, a member of the Academy of Painting and Sculpture, showing an aerial view of the city of Paris. The primary function of the map was to reestablish Paris as the universal model of a capital city.

Library of Congress

What fueled the growth of Paris in the eighteenth century?

nothing more than a mere workman, a farm hand to whom the proprietor surrenders a share of his profits instead of paying wages. But in his work the proprietor enjoys none of the advantages of the farmer who, working on his own behalf, works carefully and diligently; the proprietor is obliged to entrust all his advances to a man who may be negligent or a scoundrel and is answerable for nothing.

This *métayer*, accustomed to the most miserable existence and without the hope and even the desire to obtain a better living for himself, cultivates badly and neglects to employ the land for valuable and profitable production; by preference he occupies himself in cultivating those things whose growth is less troublesome and which provide him with more foodstuffs, such as buckwheat and chestnuts which do not require any attention. He does not worry very much about his livelihood; he knows that if the harvest fails, his master will be obliged to feed him in order not to see his land neglected.

Source: From *Oeuvres, et documents les concernant*, by A. M. R. Turgot, ed. by F. Schelle, 5 vols. (Paris: F. Alcan, 1914), vol. II, pp. 448–450; *Documents of European Economic History*, as quoted and trans. by S. Pollard and C. Holmes, (London: Edward Arnold, 1968), pp. 38–39.

II. DAVID HUME PRAISES LUXURY AND THE REFINEMENT OF THE ARTS

David Hume (1711–1776) was a Scottish philosopher, historian, and economic commentator. He was deeply committed to the modernization of the Scottish and wider European economy through the growth of commerce and the fostering of improved means of mechanical production. In this essay published in 1752 he outlined the beneficial social consequence he saw resulting from commercial wealth and new mechanical inventions. He believed such economic activity not only increased riches but also produced a population capable of providing a national defense. He was quite concerned to demonstrate that luxury and the economy that fostered it would not lead to moral decay.

In times when industry and the arts flourish, men are kept in perpetual occupation, and enjoy, as their reward, the occupation itself, as well as those pleasures which are the fruit of their labour. The mind acquires new vigour; enlarges its powers and faculties; and by an assiduity in honest industry, both satisfies its natural appetites, and prevents the growth of unnatural ones, which commonly spring up, when nourished by ease and idleness. . . .

Another advantage of industry and of refinements in the mechanical arts, is, that they commonly produce some refinements in the liberal; nor can one be carried to perfection, without being accompanied, in some degree, with the other. . . .

The more these refined arts advance, the more sociable men become . . . They flock into cities; love to receive and communicate knowledge; to show their wit or their breeding; their taste in conversation or living, in clothes or furniture. Curiosity allures the wise; vanity the foolish, and pleasure both. Particular clubs and societies are everywhere formed: Both sexes meet in an easy and sociable manner: and the tempers of men, as well as their behaviour, refine apace. So that, beside the improvements which they receive from knowledge and the liberal arts, it is impossible but they must feel an encrease of humanity, from the very habit of conversing together, and contributing to each other's pleasure and entertainment. Thus *industry, knowledge,* and *humanity,* are linked together by an indissoluble chain, and are found, from experience as well as reason, to be peculiar to the more polished, and, what are commonly denominated, the more luxurious ages. . . .

But industry, knowledge, and humanity are not advantageous in private life alone: They diffuse their beneficial influence on the *public,* and render the government as great and flourishing as they make individuals happy and prosperous. The encrease and consumption of all the commodities . . . are advantageous to society; because . . . they are a kind of *storehouse* of labour, which, in the exigencies of state, may be turned to the public service. In a nation, where there is no demand for such superfluities, men sink into indolence, lose all enjoyment of life, and are useless to the public, which cannot maintain or support its fleets and armies, from the industry of such slothful members.

Source: David Hume, "Of Refinement in the Arts (1752)," in *Essays: Moral, Political and Literary* (Indianapolis, IN: Liberty Classics, 1985), pp. 270–272.

luxuriously. Changes in the consumption of food and drink demanded new kinds of dishware for the home. Tea and coffee became staples. The brewing industry became fully commercialized. Those developments entailed the need for new kinds of cups and mugs and many more of them.

There would always be critics of this consumer economy. Yet, the ever-increasing consumption and production of the goods of everyday life became a hallmark of modern Western society from the eighteenth century to our own day. It would be difficult to overestimate the importance of the desire for consumer goods and the higher standard of living that they made possible in Western history after the eighteenth century. The presence and accessibility of such goods became the hallmark of a nation's prosperity. It was the absence of such consumer goods, as well as of civil liberties, that during the 1980s led to such deep discontent with the communist regimes in Eastern Europe and the former Soviet Union.

INDUSTRIAL LEADERSHIP OF GREAT BRITAIN

Great Britain was the home of the Industrial Revolution and, until the middle of the nineteenth century, remained the industrial leader of Europe. Several factors contributed to the early start in Britain.

Great Britain took the lead in the consumer revolution that expanded the demand for goods that could be efficiently supplied. It seems to have been in Britain that a world of fashion first developed that led people to want to accumulate goods. In addition to the domestic consumer demand, the British economy benefited from demand from the colonies in North America.

Britain was also the single largest free-trade area in Europe. The British had good roads and waterways without internal tolls or other trade barriers. The country had rich deposits of coal and iron ore. Its political structure was stable, and property was absolutely secure. The sound systems of banking and public credit established a stable climate for investment. Taxation in Britain was heavy, but it was efficiently and fairly collected, largely from indirect taxes. Furthermore, British taxes received legal approval through Parliament, with all social classes and all regions of the nation paying the same taxes.

Finally, British society was mobile by the standards of the time. Persons who had money or could earn it could rise socially. The British aristocracy would receive into its ranks people who had amassed large fortunes. Even persons of wealth who did not join the aristocracy could enjoy their riches, receive social recognition, and exert political influence.

NEW METHODS OF TEXTILE PRODUCTION

The industry that pioneered the Industrial Revolution and met the growing consumer demand was the production of textiles for clothing. Textile production developed not in cities, but in the countryside. Although the eighteenth-century economy was primarily agricultural, manufacturing also permeated rural areas. The peasant family living in a one- or two-room cottage, rather than the factory, was the basic unit of production. The same peasants who tilled the land in spring and summer often spun thread or wove textiles in the winter.

Under what is termed the *domestic*, or putting-out, *system of textile production*, agents of urban textile merchants took wool or other unfinished fibers to the homes of peasants, who spun it into thread. The agent then transported the thread to other peasants, who wove it into the finished product. The merchant sold the wares.

By the mid–eighteenth century, however, production bottlenecks had developed within the domestic system. The demand for cotton textiles was growing more rapidly than production, especially in Britain, which had a large domestic and North American market for these goods. Inventors devised some of the most famous machines of the early Industrial Revolution to meet consumer demand for cotton textiles.

domestic system of textile production Means by which urban merchants obtained their wares. They bought wool or other unfinished fiber for distribution to peasant workers who took it home, spun it into thread, wove it into cloth, and returned the finished product to the merchants for sale.

The Spinning Jenny   Thanks to the invention of the flying shuttle in the 1730s, weavers had the technical capacity to produce enough cotton fabric to meet market demand. It was not until 1765, however, when James Hargreaves (d. 1778) invented the **spinning jenny**, that spinners began to be able to provide weavers with adequate supplies of thread. Hargreaves's machine spun 16 spindles of thread simultaneously. By the close of the century, capacity had increased to 120 spindles.

spinning jenny   Invented by James Hargreaves in 1765, this machine spun sixteen spindles of thread simultaneously.

The Water Frame   The spinning jenny broke the bottleneck between the productive capacity of the spinners and the weavers, but it was still a piece of machinery used in the cottage. The invention that took cotton textile manufacture out of the home and put it into the factory was Richard Arkwright's (1732–1792) **water frame**, patented in 1769. This was a water-powered device designed to permit the production of cotton fabric. From the 1780s onward, the cotton industry could meet an ever-expanding demand. Cotton output increased by 800 percent between 1780 and 1800. By 1815, cotton composed 40 percent of the value of British domestic exports and by 1830, just over 50 percent.

water frame   Invented in 1769 by Richard Arkwright, this water-powered device produced a cotton fabric and was suitable for use in factories.

The Industrial Revolution had commenced in earnest by the 1780s, but the full economic and social ramifications of this unleashing of human productive capacity were not really felt until the early nineteenth century. The expansion of industry and the incorporation of new inventions often occurred slowly. Nor did all the social ramifications of industrialism appear immediately. The first cotton mills used water power, were located in the country, and rarely employed more than two dozen workers. Not until the late-century application of the steam engine, perfected by James Watt (1736–1819) in 1769, to run textile machinery could factories easily be located in or near urban centers. The steam engine not only vastly increased and regularized the available energy but also made possible the combination of urbanization and industrialization.

THE STEAM ENGINE

More than any other invention, the steam engine permitted industrialization to grow on itself and to expand into one area of production after another. This machine provided for the first time in human history a steady and essentially unlimited source of inanimate power.

Thomas Newcomen had invented the first engine using steam power early in the eighteenth century. It was driven by injecting steam into a cylinder to push up a piston that fell back when the steam condensed. The machine was heavy and energy inefficient, but it was widely used in Britain to pump water out of coal and tin mines. During the 1760s, James Watt, a Scottish engineer, experimented with the Newcomen machine and achieved much greater efficiency by separating the condenser from the piston and the cylinder. His design, however, required precisely tooled metalwork, a technical liability that Matthew Boulton, a successful toy and button maker, and John Wilkinson, a cannon manufacturer, helped him overcome. In 1776, a Watt steam engine found its first commercial application: pumping water from mines in Cornwall.

By the early nineteenth century, the steam engine had become the prime mover for all industry. With its application to ships and then to wagons on iron rails, the steam engine also revolutionized transportation.

IRON PRODUCTION

The manufacture of high-quality iron has been basic to modern industrial development. Iron is the chief element of all heavy industry and of land or sea transport. During the early eighteenth century, British ironmakers produced somewhat less than 25,000 tons of iron annually. Three factors held back the production. First, charcoal rather than coke was used to smelt the ore. Charcoal, derived from wood, was becoming scarce as forests in Britain diminished, and it does not burn at as high a temperature as coke, derived from coal. Second, until the perfection of the steam engine, furnaces could not achieve high enough blasts. Finally, the demand for iron was limited. The elimination of the first two problems also eliminated the third.

Eventually, British ironmakers began to use coke, and the steam engine provided new power for the blast furnaces. Coke was an abundant fuel because of Britain's large coal deposits. The steam engine both improved iron production and increased the demand for iron.

In 1784, Henry Cort (1740–1800) introduced a new puddling process, that is, a new method for melting and stirring molten ore. Cort's process allowed the removal of more slag (the impurities that bubbled to the top of the molten metal) and thus the production of purer iron. Cort also developed a rolling mill that continuously shaped the still-molten metal into bars, rails, or other forms. Previously, the metal had to be pounded into these forms. All these innovations achieved a better, more versatile, cheaper product. The demand for iron consequently grew. By the early nineteenth century, the British produced over a million tons annually. The lower cost of iron, in turn, lowered the cost of steam engines and allowed them to be used more widely.

THE IMPACT OF THE AGRICULTURAL AND INDUSTRIAL REVOLUTIONS ON WORKING WOMEN

The transformation of agriculture and industry led to a series of seemingly modest changes that, taken collectively, diminished the importance and the role of those women already in the workforce.

Women had been an important part of traditional European agriculture. They worked in and often were permitted to glean the grain left over after the general harvest. Women also managed industries like milking and cheese production. However, primarily in Western Europe, increasing commercialization and mechanization eroded these traditional roles. Machinery operated by men displaced the work of women in the field and their skills in dairying and home industry, particularly in Britain. Even nonmechanized labor came to favor men. For example, during the late eighteenth century, heavy scythes wielded by men replaced the lighter sickles that women had used to harvest grain. Moreover, the drive to maximize profits led landlords to enclose lands and curtail customary rights like gleaning. This transformation of farming constricted women's ability to earn their living from the land.

A similar process took place in textile manufacturing, where mechanization deprived many women of one of their most traditional means of earning income. Before mechanization thousands of women worked at spinning wheels to produce thread that hand-loom weavers, who were often their husbands, then wove. The earlier, small spinning jennies did not immediately disrupt this situation because women could use them in the loft of a home, but the larger ones required a factory setting where men often ran the machinery. As a result, most women spinners were put out of work, and those women who did move into the factory labor force performed less skilled work than men.

Consumption of all forms of consumer goods increased greatly in the eighteenth century. This engraving illustrates a shop, probably in Paris. Here women, working apparently for a woman manager, are making dresses and hats to meet the demands of the fashion trade.

Bildarchiv Preussischer Kulturbesitz

Many working women, displaced from spinning thread or from farming, slowly turned to cottage industries, such as knitting, button making, straw plaiting, bonnet making, or glove stitching, that invariably earned them less than their former occupations had. The work and skills these occupations involved were considered inferior; and because it paid so poorly, women who did this work might become prostitutes or engage in other criminal activity. Consequently, the reputations and social standing of many working women suffered.

Among women who did not work in the cottage industries, thousands became domestic servants in the homes of landed or commercial families. During the nineteenth century, such domestic service became the largest area of female employment.

By the end of the eighteenth century, the work and workplaces of men and women were becoming increasingly separate and distinct. This shift in female employment produced several long-term results. First, women's work, whether in cottage industries or domestic service, became associated with the home rather than with places where men worked. Second, the laboring life of most women was removed from the new technologies in farming, transportation, and manufacturing. Woman's work thus appeared traditional, and people assumed women could do only such work. Third, during the nineteenth and early twentieth centuries, Europeans also assumed most women worked only to supplement a husband's income. Finally, because the work women did was considered marginal and only as supplementing a male income, men were paid much more than women. Most people associate the Industrial Revolution with factories, but for many working women, these revolutions led to a life located more in homes than ever before.

THE GROWTH OF CITIES

Remarkable changes occurred in the pattern of city growth between 1500 and 1800. In 1500, within Europe (excluding Hungary and Russia) 156 cities had a population greater than 10,000. Only four of those cities—Paris, Milan, Venice, and Naples—had populations larger than 100,000. By 1800, 363 cities had 10,000 or more inhabitants, and 17 of them had populations larger than 100,000. The percentage of the European population living in urban areas had risen from just over 5 percent to just over 9 percent. A major shift in urban concentration from southern, Mediterranean Europe to the north had also occurred.

WHAT PROBLEMS arose as a result of the growth of cities?

PATTERNS OF PREINDUSTRIAL URBANIZATION

The eighteenth century witnessed a considerable growth of towns. London grew from about 700,000 inhabitants in 1700 to almost 1 million in 1800. By the time of the French Revolution, Paris had more than 500,000 inhabitants. Berlin's population tripled during the century, reaching 170,000 in 1800. Warsaw had 30,000 inhabitants in 1730, but almost 120,000 in 1794. St. Petersburg, founded in 1703, numbered more than 250,000 inhabitants a century later. The number of smaller cities with 20,000 to 50,000 people also increased considerably. This urban growth must, however, be kept in perspective. Even in France and Great Britain, probably somewhat less than 20 percent of the population lived in cities. And the town of 10,000 inhabitants was much more common than the giant urban center.

Growth of Capitals and Ports   Between 1600 and 1750, the cities that grew most vigorously were capitals and ports. This situation reflects the success of monarchical state building during those years and the consequent burgeoning of bureaucracies, armies, courts, and other groups who lived in the capitals. The growth of port cities, in turn, reflects the expansion of European overseas trade—especially that of the Atlantic routes. Except for Manchester in England and Lyons in France, the new urban conglomerates were nonindustrial cities.

Furthermore, between 1600 and 1750, cities with populations of fewer than 40,000 inhabitants declined. These included older landlocked trading centers, medieval industrial cities, and ecclesiastical centers. They contributed less to the new political regimes, and the expansion of the putting-out system transferred production from medieval cities to the countryside because rural labor was cheaper than urban labor.

The Emergence of New Cities and the Growth of Small Towns   In the mid-eighteenth century, a new pattern emerged. The rate of growth of existing large cities declined, new cities emerged, and existing smaller cities grew. Several factors were at work in the process. First was the general overall population increase. Second, the early stages of the Industrial Revolution, particularly in Britain, occurred in the countryside and fostered the growth of smaller towns and cities located near factories. Factory organization itself led to new concentrations of population.

Cities also grew as a result of the new prosperity of European agriculture, even where there was little industrialization. Improved agricultural production promoted the growth of nearby market towns and other urban centers that served agriculture or allowed more prosperous farmers to have access to consumer goods and recreation. This new pattern of urban growth—new cities and the expansion of smaller existing ones—would continue into the nineteenth century.

URBAN CLASSES

Social divisions were as marked in eighteenth-century cities as they were in nineteenth-century industrial centers. The urban rich were often visibly segregated from the urban poor. Aristocrats and the upper middle class lived in fashionable town houses, often constructed around newly laid-out green squares. The poorest town dwellers usually congregated along the rivers. Small merchants and artisans lived above their shops. Whole families might live in a single room. Modern sanitary facilities were unknown. Pure water was rare. Cattle, pigs, goats, and other animals roamed the streets. All reports on the cities of Europe during this period emphasize both the striking grace and beauty of the dwellings of the wealthy and the dirt, filth, and stench that filled the streets. (See "Encountering the Past: Water, Washing, and Bathing.")

Poverty was not just an urban problem; it was usually worse in the countryside. In the city, however, poverty was more visible in the form of crime, prostitution, vagrancy, begging, and alcoholism. It did not require the Industrial Revolution and the urban factories to make the cities into hellholes for the poor and the dispossessed.

The Upper Classes   At the top of the urban social structure stood a generally small group of nobles, large merchants, bankers, financiers, clergy, and government officials. These upper-class men controlled the political and economic affairs of the town. Normally, they constituted a self-appointed and self-electing oligarchy that governed the city through its corporation or city council. In a few cities on the Continent, artisan guilds controlled the corporations, but generally, the local nobility and the wealthiest commercial people dominated the councils.

The Middle Class   Another group in the city was the prosperous, but not always immensely wealthy, merchants, trades people, bankers, and professional people. They were the most dynamic element of the urban population and made up the middle class, or bourgeoisie. The middle class itself was and would remain diverse and divided, with persons employed in the professions often resentful of those who drew their incomes from commerce. Less wealthy members of the middle class of whatever occupation resented wealthier members who might be connected to the nobility through social or business relationships.

The middle class had less wealth than most nobles, but more than urban artisans. Middle-class people lived in the cities and towns, and their sources of income had little or nothing to do with the land. In one way or another, they all benefited from expanding trade and commerce, whether as merchants, lawyers, or small-factory owners. They saw themselves as willing to put their capital and energy to work, whereas they portrayed the nobility as idle. The members of the middle class tended to be economically aggressive and socially ambitious. The middle class normally supported reform, change, and economic growth. They also wanted more rational regulations for trade and commerce, as did some progressive aristocrats.

The middle class was made up of people whose lives fostered the revolution in consumption. On one hand, as owners of factories and of wholesale and retail businesses, they produced and sold goods for the expanding consumer market; on the other hand, members of the middle class were among the chief consumers. They were also the people whose social values most fully embraced the commercial spirit. They might not enjoy the titles or privileges of the nobility, but they could enjoy material comfort

ENCOUNTERING THE PAST

WATER, WASHING, AND BATHING

Clear water was scarce in Europe until the end of the nineteenth century. Households that did not have wells drew their water from streams, rivers, and public wells or fountains. Governments did nothing to assure the purity of a resource whose importance was less appreciated than it is today. Where the average American now uses about 210 liters of water per day, an individual in the eighteenth century may have needed only about 7.5 liters.

Public bathhouses were common during the Middle Ages. Bodily cleanliness was associated with spiritual purity, and aristocrats and townspeople bathed frequently. In the late medieval period, however, physicians began to argue that bathing was unhealthy. They reasoned that it opened the pores of the skin and allowed *miasma* (bad air) to infect the body with disease. Until the end of the eighteenth century, medical texts advised people to wash only the parts of the body that are publicly visible (hands, face, neck, and feet). Clean clothing was, however, considered indispensable. A switch from wool to linen garments, which began in the sixteenth century, made laundering easier, and social mores of the Renaissance-Reformation era placed a great deal of emphasis on the quality and appearance of one's clothing. Consequently, garments were washed much more frequently than bodies.

Attitudes began to change again toward the middle of the eighteenth century. Bathing was once more seen as healthful (particularly as the germ theory of

In the eighteenth century, washing linen clothing by hand was a major task of women servants.

J. B. S. Chardin, *The Washerwoman.* Nationalmuseum med Prins Eugens Waldemarsudde. Photo: The National Museum of Fine Arts

Why was washing such a time-consuming task in the eighteenth century?

disease received acceptance). Public baths reappeared in the nineteenth century, and great engineering projects were undertaken to provide urban dwellers with sewage disposal and clean water (see Chapter 23).

WHAT CAUSED bathing customs to fluctuate from age to age?

---

and prosperity. It was this style of life that less well-off people could emulate as they sought to acquire consumer goods for themselves.

During the eighteenth century, the relationship between the middle class and the aristocracy was complicated. On one hand, the nobles, especially in England and France, increasingly embraced the commercial spirit associated with the middle class by improving their estates and investing in cities. On the other hand, wealthy members of the middle class often tried to imitate the lifestyle of the nobility by purchasing landed estates. The aspirations of the middle class for social mobility, however, conflicted with the determination of the nobles to maintain and reassert their own privileges and to protect their own wealth.

The bourgeoisie was not rising to challenge the nobility; rather, both were seeking to increase their existing political power and social prestige. The tensions that arose between the nobles and the middle class during the eighteenth century normally involved issues of power sharing or access to political influence, rather than clashes over values or goals associated with class.

The middle class in the cities also feared the lower urban classes as much as they envied the nobility. The lower orders were a potentially violent element in society, a threat to property, and, in their poverty, a drain on national resources. The lower classes, however, were much more varied than either the city aristocracy or the middle class cared to admit.

Artisans   Shopkeepers, artisans, and wage earners were the single largest group in any city. They were grocers, butchers, fishmongers, carpenters, cabinetmakers, smiths, printers, hand-loom weavers, and tailors, to give a few examples. They had their own culture, values, and institutions. Like the peasants, economic vulnerability made them, in many respects, conservative. These urban classes also contributed to the revolution in consumption, however. They could buy more goods than ever before, and, to the extent their incomes permitted, many of them sought to copy the domestic consumption of the middle class.

The lives of these artisans and shopkeepers centered on their work and their neighborhoods. They usually lived near or at their place of employment. Most of them worked in shops with fewer than a half dozen other artisans. Their primary institution had historically been the guild, but by the eighteenth century, the guilds rarely exercised the influence their predecessors had in medieval or early modern Europe.

Nevertheless, the guilds were not to be ignored. They played a conservative role. Rather than seeking economic growth or innovation, they tried to preserve the jobs and skills of their members. To lessen competition, they attempted to prevent too many people from learning a particular skill.

The guilds also provided a framework for social and economic advancement. At an early age, a boy might become an apprentice to learn a craft or trade. After several years, he would be made a journeyman. Still later, if successful and competent, he might become a master. The artisan could also receive social benefits from the guilds, including aid for his family during sickness or the promise of admission for his son. The guilds were the chief protection for artisans against the workings of the commercial market. They were particularly strong in central Europe.

THE URBAN RIOT

The artisan class, with its generally conservative outlook, maintained a rather fine sense of social and economic justice based largely on traditional practices. The most sensitive area was the price of bread, the staple food of the poor. If a baker or a grain merchant announced a price that was considered unjustly high, a riot might well ensue. Artisan leaders would confiscate the bread or grain and sell it for what the urban crowd considered a "just price." They would then give the money paid for the grain or bread to the baker or merchant. Thus, bread and food riots, which occurred throughout Europe, were not irrational acts of screaming, hungry people, but highly ritualized social phenomena of the Old Regime and its economy of scarcity.

Other kinds of riots also characterized eighteenth-century society and politics. The riot was a way in which people who were excluded in every other way from the political processes could make their will known. Sometimes religious bigotry led to urban riots. For example, in 1753, London Protestant mobs compelled the government to withdraw an act to legalize Jewish naturalization.

In these riots and in food riots, violence was normally directed against property rather than people. The rioters themselves were not disreputable people, but usually small shopkeepers, freeholders, artisans, and wage earners. They usually wanted only to restore a traditional right or practice that seemed endangered. Nevertheless, their actions could cause considerable turmoil and destruction.

During the last half of the century, urban riots increasingly involved political ends. Though often simultaneous with economic disturbances, the political riot always had nonartisan leadership or instigators. In fact, an eighteenth-century "crowd" was often the tool of the upper classes. Such outbursts indicate that the crowd or mob had entered the European political and social arena well before the revolution in France.

THE JEWISH POPULATION: THE AGE OF THE GHETTO

Although the small Jewish communities of Amsterdam and other Western European cities became famous for their intellectual life and financial institutions, the Jewish population of Europe was concentrated in Poland, Lithuania, and Ukraine, where no fewer than 3 million Jews dwelled. Perhaps 150,000 Jews lived in the Habsburg lands, primarily Bohemia, around 1760. Fewer than 100,000 Jews lived in Germany. France had approximately 40,000 Jews. England and Holland each had a Jewish population of fewer than 10,000. There were even smaller groups of Jews elsewhere.

Jews dwelled in most nations without enjoying the rights and privileges that other subjects had unless monarchs specifically granted them to Jews. Jews were regarded as a kind of resident alien whose residence might well be temporary or changed at the whim of rulers.

No matter where they dwelled, Old Regime Jews lived apart in separate communities from non-Jewish Europeans. These communities might be distinct districts of cities, known as **ghettos**, or in primarily Jewish villages in the countryside. Jews were also treated as a distinct people religiously and legally. In Poland for much of the century, they were virtually self-governing. In other areas, they lived under the burden of discriminatory legislation. Except in England, Jews could not and did not mix in the mainstream of the societies in which they dwelled. This period, which may be said to have begun with the expulsion of the Jews from Spain at the end of the fifteenth century, is known as the age of the ghetto, or separate community.

During the seventeenth century, a few Jews had helped finance the wars of major rulers. These financiers often became close to the rulers and were known as "court Jews." The court Jews and their financial abilities became famous. They tended to marry among themselves.

Most European Jews, however, lived in poverty. They occupied the most undesirable sections of cities or poor villages. Some were small-time moneylenders, but most worked at the lowest occupations. Their religious beliefs, rituals, and community set them apart. Virtually all laws and social institutions kept them socially inferior to and apart from their Christian neighbors.

Under the Old Regime, it is important to emphasize that this discrimination was based on religious separateness. Jews who converted to Christianity were welcomed, even if not always warmly, into the major political and social institutions of gentile European society. Until the last two decades of the eighteenth century, in every part of Europe, however, those Jews who remained loyal to their faith were subject to various religious, civil, and social disabilities. They could not pursue the professions freely, they often could not change residence without official permission, and they were excluded from the political structures of the nations in which they lived. Jews could be expelled from their homes, and their property could be confiscated. They could be required to listen to sermons that insulted their religion. Their children could be taken away from them and given Christian instruction. They knew their non-Jewish neighbors might suddenly turn against them and kill them.

In subsequent chapters, it will be shown how the end of the Old Regime brought major changes in the lives of European Jews and in their relationship to the larger culture.

HOW DID the suppression of Jews in European cities lead to the formation of ghettos?

ghettos   Separate districts in cities and entire villages in the countryside where Jews lived apart from Christians in eighteenth-century Europe.

During the Old Regime, European Jews were separated from non-Jews, typically in districts known as ghettos. Relegated to the least desirable section of a city or to rural villages, most lived in poverty. This watercolor painting depicts a street in Kazimlesz, the Jewish quarter of Cracow, Poland.

Judaica Collection, Max Berger, Vienna, Austria. Photograph © Erich Lessing/Art Resource, NY

What was life like for the majority of Europe's Jews during the Old Regime?

Summary

HOW DID tradition, hierarchy, and privilege shape life in the Old Regime?

Major Features of Life in the Old Regime Many aspects of life in the eighteenth century still followed traditional patterns. European economies were dominated by agriculture; nothing mattered more to most individuals—or their governments—than the grain harvest. Society was more oriented toward the past than the future. Rights accrued not to individuals, but to groups. *page 370*

WHAT WAS the foundation of the wealth and power for the eighteenth-century aristocracy?

The Aristocracy The aristocratic resurgence that took place across Europe was a noteworthy feature of eighteenth-century European social history. The nobility made up between 1 percent and 5 percent of the population in most European countries. They were wealthy and powerful; their income came largely from land ownership. In England especially, they also invested in various ventures, including industries. Other aristocratic characteristics varied from country to country, but nobles throughout Europe all tried to preserve noble exclusivity, to resist the growing power of the monarchies, and to improve their financial status. *page 370*

HOW WERE peasants and serfs tied to the land in eighteenth-century Europe?

The Land and Its Tillers Land was the basis of noble wealth, and its cultivation was the task of the huge class of peasants and serfs. Landowners controlled local government and the courts; continental Europe's tax burden fell on those who tilled the soil. Landowners' power increased the farther east one went in Europe. In Prussia, Austria, and Russia, a serf's life was nothing but a commodity to an aristocrat. Peasants revolted violently and repeatedly. *page 372*

WHAT ROLE did the family play in the economy of preindustrial Europe?

Family Structures and the Family Economy The "family economy" was the norm throughout Europe before the Industrial Revolution. In northwestern Europe, the "household" was generally a nuclear family and its servants. Premarital sex was common, and people married in their twenties, usually after spending several years earning wages. Eastern European "households" were larger, with more than nine members of three generations living together. Landowners in eastern Europe discouraged families from separating into multiple households. Everyone worked, who could, with the goal of supporting the family unit. The death of the father could easily spell disaster for the family. Women's economic contributions to the household were more important than their reproductive capacities. Women and babies experienced high mortality rates, and many infants were abandoned for economic reasons. *page 373*

WHAT LED to the agricultural revolution of the eighteenth century?

The Revolution in Agriculture Europe's population in 1750 was between 100 and 120 million people; by 1800, there were almost 190 million, and by 1850, there were 260 million. Historians have proposed many explanations for this population growth. One factor was the introduction of the potato from America. Increasing population led to increasing demand and prices for wheat and bread. This hurt peasants but helped larger landowners. Landlords began to treat crop cultivation as a commercial operation and introduced new techniques that increased crop yields. The economic and social organization of farming also changed: The enclosure movement in England rationalized the use of land and saw higher productivity. Governments sided with landowners, and serf revolts were suppressed. In eastern Europe, land ownership and social structures were less encouraging of agricultural innovation. *page 376*

WHY DID the Industrial Revolution begin in Britain?

The Industrial Revolution of the Eighteenth Century Europe's economy of scarcity was replaced by a demand-driven cycle of growth. Advertising and social emulation fueled consumer demand. In Great Britain political and economic factors were also favorable for innovation. The domestic system of textile production was the first area of industry to be transformed, through the invention of the spinning jenny in 1765, the water frame in 1769, and the power loom in the late 1780s. The 1769 steam engine was applied to industries ranging from mining to textiles to transportation. Iron became the backbone of industrial machinery. As work was reorganized to accommodate the new machines, labor was increasingly segregated by gender, and women's work was systematically devalued. *page 379*

WHAT PROBLEMS arose as a result of the growth of cities?

The Growth of Cities Many cities grew substantially between 1500 and 1800. Between 1600 and 1750, capital cities and ports grew most vigorously; most smaller cities actually lost population. After 1750, smaller cities began to grow more rapidly than larger ones, and entirely new cities emerged. City dwellers led radically different lives, depending on their social class. The upper classes lived quite comfortably and often controlled city government. The middle class had aspirations and fears that led them to support reform, change, and economic growth. Artisans, the largest group, were generally conservative. Bread riots were sparked by artisans who believed merchants were not charging "just" prices; other forms of riots could be fueled by religious prejudice or political agendas. *page 385*

HOW DID the suppression of Jews in European cities lead to the formation of ghettos?

The Jewish Population: The Age of the Ghetto Jews were segregated and discriminated against on religious grounds throughout Europe. The vast majority of Jews lived in eastern Europe, particularly Poland, Lithuania, and the Ukraine. In most countries Jews were treated as resident aliens, without political or civil rights and socially inferior; only in England was it possible for Jews to mingle with mainstream society. This was the age of the ghetto, or separate community, which were either distinct districts within cities or separate Jewish villages in rural areas. Most Jews were poor; one exceptional category was the so-called court Jews, who helped finance royal projects (usually wars). Jews, especially children, were sometimes forcibly converted to Christianity, and they were sometimes killed for their religious beliefs. *page 389*

REVIEW QUESTIONS

1. How did the situation of the English aristocracy differ from that of the French? What kind of privileges distinguished European aristocrats from other social groups?

2. What was the family economy? How did households in northwestern Europe differ from those in eastern Europe? In what ways were the lives of women constrained by the family economy?

3. What caused the Agricultural Revolution? To what extent did the English aristocracy contribute to it? What explains the growth of Europe's population in the eighteenth century? How did population growth change consumption?

4. What caused the Industrial Revolution of the eighteenth century? Why did Great Britain take the lead in the Industrial Revolution? What was city life like during the eighteenth century? How did the lifestyle of the upper class differ from that of the middle and lower classes? What were some of the causes of urban riots?

KEY TERMS

aristocratic resurgence (p. 372)
domestic system of textile production (p. 382)
enclosures (p. 377)
ghettos (p. 389)

Industrial Revolution (p. 379)
Old Regime (p. 370)
spinning jenny (p. 383)
water frame (p. 383)

For additional learning resources related to this chapter, please go to **www.myhistorylab.com**

PEARSON
myhistorylab

16

The Transatlantic Economy, Trade Wars, and Colonial Rebellion

General James Wolfe was mortally wounded during his victory over the French at Quebec in 1759. This painting by the American artist Benjamin West (1738–1820) became famous for portraying the dying Wolfe and the officers around him in poses modeled after classical statues.

Getty Images Inc.–Hulton Archive Photos

What does the presence of Native Americans at Wolfe's death suggest about their role in colonial conflicts?

*D*uring the eighteenth century, Europeans began to make wars on a global scale. Austria and Prussia struggled in central Europe, and Great Britain and France competed for colonies abroad. The result was a new balance of power on the Continent and on the high seas. Prussia became one of Europe's leading nations and Great Britain won a world empire. Wars forced European states to subordinate financial planning to military policy and led to economic decisions that had far-reaching political consequences. These included the American Revolution, the development of enlightened absolutist monarchies, a financial crisis for the French monarchy, and reform of Spain's American empire. ▪

PERIODS OF EUROPEAN OVERSEAS EMPIRES

HOW DID European contact with the rest of the world evolve in the centuries since the Renaissance?

Since the Renaissance, European contacts with the rest of the world have gone through four distinct stages. The first was that of the European discovery, exploration, initial conquest, and settlement of the New World. The second era—that of the mercantile empires, which are largely the concern of this chapter—was one of colonial trade rivalry among Spain, France, and Great Britain. The achievement of commercial goals, however, often sparked intense rivalry and conflict in key imperial trouble spots. As a result, the various imperial ventures led to the creation of large navies and a series of major naval wars at the midcentury—wars that in turn became linked to warfare on the European continent.

A fundamental element in these first two periods of European imperial ventures in the Americas was the presence of slavery. By the eighteenth century, the slave population of the New World consisted almost entirely of a black population that had either recently been forcibly imported from Africa or born to slaves whose forebearers had been forcibly imported from Africa. The Atlantic economy and the societies that arose in the Americas were, consequently, the creation of both Europeans and Africans while, as a result of the Spanish conquest, Native Americans were pressed toward the margins of those societies.

Finally, during the second period, both the British colonies of the North American seaboard and the Spanish colonies of Mexico and Central and South America emancipated themselves from European control. This same revolutionary era witnessed the beginning of the antislavery movement that extended through the third quarter of the nineteenth century.

The third stage of European contact with the non-European world occurred in the nineteenth century. During that period, European governments largely turned from their involvement in the Americas and carved out new formal empires involving the direct European administration of indigenous peoples in Africa and Asia.

The last period of the European empire occurred during the mid- and late twentieth century, with the decolonization of peoples who had previously lived under European colonial rule. (See Chapter 29.)

During the four-and-one-half centuries before decolonization, Europeans exerted political, military, and economic dominance over much of the rest of the world that was far disproportional to the geographical size or population of Europe. What allowed the Europeans initially to exert such influence and domination for so long over so much of the world was not any innate cultural superiority, but a technological supremacy related to naval power and gunpowder. Ships and guns allowed the Europeans to exercise their will almost wherever they chose.

MERCANTILE EMPIRES

Navies and merchant shipping were the keystones of the mercantile empires that were meant to bring profit to a nation rather than to provide areas for settlement. The Treaty of Utrecht (1713) established the boundaries of empire during the first half of the eighteenth century.

Except for Brazil, which Portugal governed, and Dutch Guiana, Spain controlled all of mainland South America. In North America, it ruled Florida, Mexico, California, and the Southwest. The Spanish also governed Central America and the islands of Cuba, Puerto Rico, Trinidad, and the eastern part of Hispaniola that is today the Dominican Republic. The British Empire consisted of the colonies along the North Atlantic seaboard, Nova Scotia, Newfoundland, Bermuda, Jamaica, and Barbados. Britain also possessed a few trading stations on the Indian subcontinent. The French domains covered the Saint Lawrence River valley and the Ohio and Mississippi River valleys. They included the West Indian islands of Saint Domingue (modern Haiti on the western part of Hispaniola), Guadeloupe, and Martinique, and also stations in India and on the West Coast of Africa. The Dutch controlled Surinam, or Dutch Guiana, in South America, Cape Colony in what is today South Africa, and trading stations in West Africa, Sri Lanka, and Bengal in India. Most importantly, they also controlled the trade with Java in what is now Indonesia.

MERCANTILIST GOALS

Critics have coined the term *mercantilism* to describe the economic theories that drove Europe's quest for empires. Mercantilists believed bullion was the measure of a country's wealth, and they advocated courses of action that encouraged its accumulation. The goal was to maintain an excess of exports over imports, for a favorable trade balance siphoned gold and silver away from trading partners. Mercantilists assumed the world's resources were limited and one nation's economy could grow only at the expense of others.

The economic well-being of the home country was the primary goal of the mercantilist system. It was taken for granted that a colony was the inferior partner in its relationship with its European sponsor. Colonies were established to provide markets and natural resources to support industries in the home country. The home country furnished its colonies with military security and political administration. Colonies were expected to remain subordinate and trade only with their homelands. Each country maintained monopolistic control of its colonies' commerce by means of navigation laws, tariffs, and regulations that prohibited trade with other colonies and European states.

Mercantilism worked better in theory than practice, for it was at odds with economic realities and human nature. Colonial and home markets failed to mesh. Spain could not produce sufficient goods for all of South America, and manufacturing in Britain's North American colonies competed with factories in England. It was also impossible to prevent trade among colonies belonging to different countries. English colonists, for instance, could buy sugar more cheaply from the French West Indies than from English suppliers, and efforts to prevent them simply encouraged smuggling and ultimately goaded them to rebel.

FRENCH–BRITISH RIVALRY

Major flash points existed between France and Britain in North America. Their colonists quarreled endlessly with each other over the coveted regions of the lower Saint Lawrence River valley, upper New England, and, later, the Ohio River valley. Other rivalries arose

WHAT WERE the characteristics of European mercantile empires?

mercantilism Economic theory in which governments heavily regulated economic activity and promoted empires in order to produce a positive balance of trade.

During the seventeenth and eighteenth centuries, European maritime nations established overseas empires and set up trading monopolies within them in an effort to magnify their economic strength. As this painting of the Old Custom House Quay in London suggests, trade from these empires and the tariffs imposed on it were expected to generate revenue for the home country. But behind many of the goods carried in the great sailing ships in the harbor and landed on these docks lay the labor of African slaves working on the plantations of North and South America.

Samuel Scott, *Old Custom House Quay* Collection. V & A Images, The Victoria and Albert Museum, London

How did eighteenth-century Europeans envision the relationship between European countries and their overseas colonies?

over fishing rights, the fur trade, and alliances with Native Americans. The heart of the eighteenth-century colonial rivalry in the Americas, however, lay in the West Indies. The West Indies plantations raised tobacco, cotton, indigo, coffee, and, above all, sugar, for which there existed huge markets in Europe. Only slave labor allowed the profitable cultivation of these products during the seventeenth and eighteenth centuries. (See "Encountering the Past: Sugar Enters the Western Diet," page 400.)

India was another area of French–British rivalry. In India, both France and Britain traded through privileged chartered companies that enjoyed a legal monopoly. The East India Company was the English institution; the French equivalent was the *Compagnie des Indes.* The original European footholds in India were trading posts called *factories.* They existed through privileges granted by various Indian governments that in theory were themselves subject to the decaying Mughal Empire, which exercised little effective authority.

Two circumstances in the mid–eighteenth century changed this situation in India. First, the administration and government of several Indian states had decayed. Second, to maintain their own security and to expand their privileges, each of the two companies began in effect to take over the government of some of the regions. Each group of Europeans hoped to checkmate the other.

The Dutch maintained their extensive commercial empire further to the east in what today is Indonesia. By the eighteenth century, the other European powers more or less acknowledged Dutch predominance in that region.

THE SPANISH COLONIAL SYSTEM

HOW DID Spanish colonial organization reflect its imperial goals?

Until the mid–eighteenth century, the primary purpose of the Spanish Empire was to supply Spain with the precious metals mined in the New World.

COLONIAL GOVERNMENT AND THE REGULATION OF TRADE

Because Queen Isabella of Castile (r. 1474–1504) had commissioned Columbus, the technical legal link between the New World and Spain was the crown of Castile. The Castilian monarch assigned the government of America to the Council of the Indies, which, with the monarch, nominated the viceroys of New Spain (Mexico) and Peru. These viceroys served as the chief executives in the New World and carried out the laws issued by the Council of the Indies. Virtually all power flowed from the top of this political structure downward; in effect, local initiative or self-government scarcely existed.

The colonial political structures functioned largely to support Spanish commercial self-interests. The *Casa de Contratación* (House of Trade) in Seville regulated all trade with the New World. A complicated system of trade and bullion fleets administered from Seville maintained Spain's trade monopoly. Each year, a fleet of commercial vessels (the *flota*), controlled by Seville merchants and escorted by warships, carried merchandise from Spain to a few specified ports in America. After selling their wares, the ships were loaded with silver and gold bullion and then sailed back to Spain. The *flota* system always worked imperfectly, but trade outside it was illegal.

COLONIAL REFORM UNDER THE SPANISH BOURBON MONARCHS

A crucial change occurred in the Spanish colonial system in the early eighteenth century. The War of the Spanish Succession (1701–1714) and the Treaty of Utrecht (1713) replaced the Spanish Habsburgs with the Bourbons of France on the Spanish throne. Philip V (r. 1700–1746) and his successors tried to use French administrative skills to reassert the imperial trade monopoly, which had decayed under the last Spanish Habsburgs, and thus to improve the domestic economy and revive Spanish power in Europe.

Under Philip V, Spanish coastal patrol vessels tried to suppress smuggling in American waters. An incident arising from this policy led to war with England in 1739, the year in which Philip established the viceroyalty of New Granada in the area that today includes Venezuela, Colombia, and Ecuador. The goal was to strengthen the royal government there.

The great midcentury wars exposed the vulnerability of the Spanish empire to naval attack and economic penetration. As an ally of France, Spain emerged as one of the defeated powers in 1763. Government circles then became convinced that the colonial system had to be reformed.

Charles III (r. 1759–1788) attempted to reassert Spain's control of the empire. Like his Bourbon predecessors, Charles emphasized royal ministers rather than councils. Thus, the role of both the Council of the Indies and the *Casa de Contratación* diminished. After 1765, Charles abolished the monopolies of Seville and Cádiz and permitted other Spanish cities to trade with America. He also opened more South American and Caribbean ports to trade and authorized commerce between Spanish ports in America. In 1776, he organized a fourth viceroyalty in the region of Río de la Plata, which included much of present-day Argentina, Uruguay, Paraguay, and Bolivia. (See Map 16–1, page 398.)

To increase the efficiency of tax collection and end bureaucratic corruption, Charles III introduced the institution of the *intendant* into the Spanish Empire. These loyal, royal bureaucrats were patterned on the domestic French *intendants* made so famous and effective as agents of French royal administration under the absolutism of Louis XIV.

The late-eighteenth-century Bourbon reforms did stimulate the imperial Spanish economy. Trade expanded and became more varied. These reforms, however, also brought the empire more fully under direct Spanish control. Many *peninsulares* (persons born in Spain) entered the New World to fill new posts, which were often the most profitable jobs in the region. As a result of these policies, the *creoles* (persons of European descent born in the Spanish colonies) came to feel they were second-class subjects. In time, their resentment would provide a major source of the discontent leading to the wars of independence in the early nineteenth century.

The Silver Mines of Potosi. Worked by conscripted Indian laborers under extremely harsh conditions, these mines provided Spain with a vast treasure in silver.

Hispanic Society of America

How did American silver shape the development of early modern Spain?

BLACK AFRICAN SLAVERY, THE PLANTATION SYSTEM, AND THE ATLANTIC ECONOMY

WHAT WERE the origins of slavery in the Americas?

Within various parts of Europe itself, slavery had existed since ancient times. Black slaves from Africa were not uncommon in various parts of the Mediterranean, and a few found their way into northern Europe. In the fifteenth century, they were typically used as personal servants or displayed because of the novelty of their color in royal courts or in wealthy homes.

Yet, from the sixteenth century onward, first within the West Indies and the Spanish and Portuguese settlements in South America and then in the British colonies on the South Atlantic seaboard of North America, slave labor became a fundamental social and economic factor. The development of those plantation economies based on slave labor led to unprecedented interaction between the peoples of Europe and Africa and between the European settlers in the Americas and Africa.

MAP EXPLORATION

Interactive map: To explore this map further, go to www.myhistorylab.com

DISPUTED BY
ENGLAND,
RUSSIA,
AND SPAIN

VICEROYALTY
OF
NEW SPAIN

Rio Grande

ATLANTIC

OCEAN

EFFECTIVE FRONTIER OF
SPANISH SETTLEMENT

Gulf of Mexico

Mexico
City
Veracruz

Santo Domingo

Caribbean Sea

Cartagena   Caracas
Portobelo

VICEROYALTY OF
NEW GRANADA
Separated From
Viceroyalty of
Peru,
1717, 1739

GUIANA

Bogotá

Quito

Amazon R.

VICEROYALTY
OF
PERU

VICEROYALTY
OF
BRAZIL

Pernambuco

Bahia

Lima

PACIFIC

Portosi

OCEAN

São Paulo

Rio de Janeiro

VICEROYALTY
OF
LA PLATA
Separated From the
Viceroyalty of Peru,
1776

Santiago

Buenos
Aires

AUDIENCIA
OF CHILE

Claimed but not
settled by Spain

MAP 16–1   Viceroyalties in Latin America in 1780   The late-eighteenth-century viceroyalites in Latin America display the effort of the Spanish Bourbon monarchy to establish more direct control of the colonies. They sought this control through the introduction of more royal officials and by establishing more governmental districts.

Given the size of the Spanish viceroyalties, how effective do you think Spain was in controlling its Latin American territories and trade?

From that point onward, Africa and Africans were drawn into the Western experience as never before in history.

THE AFRICAN PRESENCE IN THE AMERICAS

Once they had encountered and begun to settle the New World, the Spanish and Portuguese faced a severe shortage of labor. At first, they used Native Americans as laborers, but during the sixteenth century as well as afterward, disease killed hundreds of thousands of the native population. The Spanish and Portuguese then turned to the labor of imported African slaves. Settlers in the English colonies of North America during the seventeenth century turned more slowly to slavery, with the largest number coming to the Chesapeake Bay region of Virginia and Maryland and then later into the low country of the Carolinas.

The major sources for slaves were slave markets on the West African Coast from Senegambia to Angola. Slavery and an extensive slave trade had existed in West Africa for centuries. Just as particular social and economic conditions in Europe had led to the voyages of exploration and settlement, political and military conditions in Africa and warfare among various African nations similarly created a supply of slaves that certain African societies were willing to sell to Europeans.

The West Indies, Brazil, and Sugar   Although citizens of the United States mark the beginning of slavery in 1619 with the arrival of African slaves on a Dutch ship in Jamestown, Virginia, over a century of slave trading in the West Indies and South America had preceded that event. Indeed, by the late sixteenth century, Africans had become a major social presence in the West Indies and in the major cities of both Spanish and Portuguese South America. In these places, African slaves equaled or more generally surpassed the numbers of white European settlers in what soon constituted multiracial societies.

Within much of Spanish South America, the numbers of slaves declined during the late seventeenth century, and slavery became somewhat less fundamental there than elsewhere. Slavery continued to expand its influence, however, in Brazil and in the Caribbean through the spreading cultivation of sugar to meet the demand of the European market. By the close of the seventeenth century, the Caribbean islands were the world center for the production of sugar and the chief supplier for the ever-growing demand for it. The opening of new areas of cultivation and other economic enterprises required additional slaves during the eighteenth century, a period of major slave importation. A vast increase in the number of Africans brought as slaves to the Americas occurred during the eighteenth century, with most arriving in the Caribbean or Brazil.

Newly imported African slaves were needed because the fertility rate of the earlier slave population was low and the death rate high from disease, overwork, and malnutrition. Restocking through the slave trade meant the slave population of the West Indies and Brazil consisted of African-born persons rather than of persons of African descent. Consequently, one of the key factors in the social life of many of the areas of American slavery during the eighteenth century was the presence of persons newly arrived from Africa, carrying with them African languages, religion, culture, and local African ethnic identities that they would infuse into the already existing slave communities.

SLAVERY AND THE TRANSATLANTIC ECONOMY

Different nations dominated the slave trade in different periods. During the sixteenth century, the Portuguese and the Spanish were most involved. The Dutch supplanted them during most of the seventeenth century. Thereafter, during the late seventeenth and eighteenth centuries, the English were the chief slave traders. French traders also participated in the trade.

ENCOUNTERING THE PAST

SUGAR ENTERS THE WESTERN DIET

Sugarcane requires tropical temperatures and abundant rainfall. It could not be cultivated in Europe, and, prior to the discovery of the Americas, European consumers had to import it from Arab lands at great expense. It was a luxury item that few could afford.

Columbus quickly recognized the Caribbean's potential as a sugar-producing region, and he carried cane to the New World in 1493. Within a decade slaves were being used to grow it on Santo Domingo. Demand for sugar grew steadily until, by the eighteenth century, the small Caribbean islands that produced it (with slave labor) had become the most valuable real estate on earth. North American colonies imported large amounts of sugar to make rum, and it became Britain's largest colonial import. The market for it accelerated as Europeans acquired a taste for other tropical products—coffee, tea, and chocolate. Enormous quantities of these stimulants (all sweetened with sugar) were consumed in the seventeenth and eighteenth centuries.

As production increased, prices fell, but demand never slackened. The greater availability of a former luxury item persuaded people they were improving their living standards by consuming more and more of it. During the nineteenth century, the custom developed in Western countries to end meals with desserts—foods sweetened with sugar.

WHY DID demand for sugar steadily accelerate in Western societies from the sixteenth century to the present?

Sugar was both raised and processed on plantations such as this one in Brazil.
Library of Congress

Why were sugar production and African slavery so closely intertwined?

Slavery touched most of the economy of the transatlantic world. Colonial trade followed roughly a geographic triangle. European goods—often guns—were carried to Africa to be exchanged for slaves, who were then taken to the West Indies, where they were traded for sugar and other tropical products, which were then shipped to Europe. Another major trade pattern existed between New England and the West Indies with New England fish, rum, or lumber being traded for sugar. All the shippers who handled cotton, tobacco, and sugar depended on slavery, though they might not have had direct contact with the institution, as did all the manufacturers and merchants who produced finished products for the consumer market.

As had been the case during previous centuries, eighteenth-century political turmoil in Africa, such as the civil wars in the Kingdom of Kongo (modern Angola and Republic of Congo), increased the supply of slaves during that period. Similar political unrest and turmoil in the Gold Coast area (modern Ghana) during the eighteenth century increased the supply of African captives to be sold into American slavery. Consequently, warfare in West Africa, often far into the interior, and the economic development of the American Atlantic seaboard were closely related.

THE EXPERIENCE OF SLAVERY

The Portuguese, Spanish, Dutch, French, and English slave traders forcibly transported several million (perhaps more than 9 million; the exact numbers are disputed) Africans to the New World—the largest forced intercontinental migration in human history. The conditions of slaves' passage across the Atlantic were wretched. Many Africans died during the crossing. (See "Compare & Connect: The Atlantic Passage," pages 402–403.)

The newly arrived Africans were subjected to a process known as *seasoning*, during which they were prepared for the laborious discipline of slavery and made to understand that they were no longer free. The process might involve receiving new names, acquiring new work skills, and learning, to some extent, the local European language. Generally, North American plantation owners were only willing to purchase such recently arrived Africans seasoned in the West Indies.

Language and Culture   Within the sharply restricted confines of slavery, the recently arrived Africans were able, at least for a time, to sustain elements of their own culture and social structures. From the West Indies southward throughout the eighteenth century, there were more people whose first language was African rather than European. It would take more than two generations for the colonial language to dominate, and even then the result was often a dialect combining an African and a European language.

Through these languages, Africans on plantation estates could organize themselves into nations with similar, though not necessarily identical, ethnic ties to regions of West Africa. These nations that the plantation experience organized and sustained also became the basis for a wide variety of religious communities among African slaves who had roots in their African experience. In this manner, some Africans maintained a loyalty to the Islamic faith of their homeland. Many of the African nations on plantations, such as those of Brazil, organized lay religious brotherhoods that carried out various kinds of charitable work within the slave communities.

The shared language of a particular African nation in the Americas enabled the slaves to communicate among themselves during revolts such as those in South Carolina in 1739, in Jamaica in the early 1760s, and, most successfully, during the Haitian Revolution of the 1790s.

Daily Life   The life conditions of plantation slaves differed from colony to colony. Black slaves living in Portuguese areas had the fewest legal protections. In the Spanish colonies, the church attempted to provide some protection for black slaves but devoted more effort toward the welfare of Native Americans. Slave codes were developed in the British and the French colonies during the seventeenth century, but they provided only the most limited protection to slaves while assuring dominance to their owners.

"TO BE SOLD AS SLAVES."

This eighteenth-century print shows bound African captives being forced to a slaving port. It was largely African middlemen who captured slaves in the interior and marched them to the coast.
North Wind Picture Archives

Under what circumstances were most Africans enslaved?

THE ATLANTIC PASSAGE

Slavery lay at the core of the eighteenth-century transatlantic economy. At the heart of slavery lay the forced transportation in slave ships across the Atlantic of millions of Africans to the Americas. The frightening and horrific character of the Atlantic Passage became widely known through the memoirs of sailors and slave trade captains. Later the groups that after the mid-eighteenth century sought the abolition of slavery made known the inhumanity of the passage through published attacks on the slave trade and by providing illustrations of slave ships such as that of the *Brooks*.

QUESTIONS

1. Who are the various people described in this document who in one way or another were involved in or profited from the slave trade?

2. What dangers did the Africans face on the voyage?

3. What contemporary attitudes could have led this captain to treat and think of his human cargo simply as goods to be transported?

4. How might the publication of the interior compartments of a slave ship have served the cause of antislavery? How and why might this illustration of a slave ship have proved more persuasive in rousing antislavery sentiment than a prose description?

5. How would this illustration and the description of the Atlantic Passage have contrasted with contemporary illustrations and memoirs of victorious naval battles on the high seas?

I. A SLAVE TRADER DESCRIBES THE ATLANTIC PASSAGE

During 1693 and 1694, Captain Thomas Phillips carried slaves from Africa to Barbados on the ship Hannibal. *The financial backer of the voyage was the Royal African Company of London, which held an English crown monopoly on slave trading. Phillips sailed to the west coast of Africa, where he purchased the Africans who were sold into slavery by an African king. Then he set sail westward.*

Having bought my complement of 700 slaves, 480 men and 220 women, and finish'd all my business at Whidaw [on the Gold Coast of Africa], I took my leave of the old king and his *cappasheirs* [attendants], and parted, with many affectionate expressions on both sides, being forced to promise him that I would return again the next year, with several things he desired me to bring from England. . . . I set sail the 27th of July in the morning, accompany'd with the East-India Merchant, who had bought 650 slaves, for the Island of St. Thomas . . . from which we took our departure on August 25th and set sail for Barbadoes.

We spent in our passage from St. Thomas to Barbadoes two months eleven days, from the 25th of August to the 4th of November following: in which time there happened such sickness and mortality among my poor men and Negroes. Of the first we buried 14, and of the last 320, which was a great detriment to our voyage, the Royal African Company losing ten pounds by every slave that died, and the owners of the ship ten pounds ten shillings, being the freight agreed on to be paid by the charter-party for every Negro delivered alive ashore to the African Company's agents at Barbadoes. . . . The loss in all amounted to near 6500 pounds sterling.

The distemper which my men as well as the blacks mostly died of was the white flux, which was so violent and inveterate that no medicine would in the least check it, so that when any of our men were seized with it, we esteemed him a dead man, as he generally proved. . . .

The Negroes are so incident to [subject to] the small-pox that few ships that carry them escape without it, and sometimes it makes vast havoc and destruction among them. But tho' we had 100 at a time sick of it, and that it went thro' the ship, yet we lost not above a dozen by it. All the assistance we gave the diseased was only as much water as they desir'd to drink, and some palm-oil to annoint their sores, and they would generally recover without any other helps but what kind nature gave them. . . .

But what the smallpox spar'd, the flux swept off, to our great regret, after all our pains and care to give them their messes in due order and season, keeping their lodgings as clean and sweet as possible, and enduring so much misery and stench so long among a parcel of creatures nastier than swine, and after all our expectations to be defeated by their mortality. . . .

No gold-finders can endure so much noisome slavery as they do who carry Negroes; for those have some respite and satisfaction, but we endure twice the misery; and yet by their mortality our voyages are ruin'd, and we pine and fret ourselves to death, and take so much pains to so little purpose.

Source: From Thomas Phillips, "Journal," *A Collection of Voyages and Travels*, Vol. 6, ed. by Awnsham and John Churchill (London: Henry Linot, 1746), as quoted in Thomas Howard, ed., *Black Voyage: Eyewitness Accounts of the Atlantic Slave Trade* (Boston: Little, Brown and Company, 1971), pp. 85–87.

II. THE SLAVE SHIP *BROOKES*

This print records the main decks of the 320-ton slave ship *Brookes*.

The average space for each African destined for slavery in the Americas was 78 inches by 16 inches. The Africans were normally shackled to assure discipline and to prevent their injuring the crew. Iron shackles also prevented Africans from committing suicide on the voyage.

The ship measured 25 feet wide and 100 feet long.

Library of Congress

What does this image reveal about conditions aboard slave ships?

Through the most inhumane use of space efficiency, 609 slaves could be crammed onboard for the nightmarish passage to America. A Parliamentary inquiry in 1788 found that the ship had been designed to carry no more than approximately 450 persons.

Source: (See "*A Slave Trader Describes the Atlantic Passage.*")

Slaves on the plantations of the American South were the chattel property of their masters and their lives were grim. Some artists sought to disguise this harsh reality by depicting the lighter moments of slave society, as in this scene of slaves dancing.

Getty Images Inc.–Hulton Archive Photos

What elements of African culture are depicted in this painting?

Slave owners always feared a revolt, and legislation and other regulations were intended to prevent one. Slave masters were permitted to whip slaves and inflict other harsh corporal punishment. Furthermore, slaves were often forbidden to gather in large groups lest they plan a revolt. In most of these slave societies, the law did not recognize slave marriages. Legally, the children of slaves were slaves, and the owner of their parents owned them too. Owners could separate slave families, or their members could be sold separately after owners died. The slaves' welfare and their lives were sacrificed to the continuing expansion of the sugar, rice, and tobacco plantations that made their owners wealthy and that produced goods for European consumers.

Conversion to Christianity   Most African slaves transported to the Americas were, like the Native Americans, eventually converted to Christianity. Some African religious practices survived in muted forms, gradually separated from African religious belief. Although slaves did manage to mix Christianity with their previous African religions, their conversion to Christianity was nonetheless another example, like that of the Native Americans, of the crushing of a set of non-European cultural values in the context of the New World economies and social structures.

European Racial Attitudes   Many Europeans considered Africans to be savages or less than civilized. Still others looked down on them simply because they were slaves. In virtually all these plantation societies, race was an important element in keeping black slaves in subservience. Although racial thinking about slavery became important primarily in the nineteenth century, that slaves were black and masters were white was as fundamental to the system as that slaves were chattel property.

The plantations that stretched from the middle Atlantic colonies of North America through the West Indies and into Brazil constituted a vast corridor of slave societies in which social and economic subordination was based on both involuntary servitude and race. These societies had not existed before the European discovery and exploitation of the Americas. In its complete dependence on slave labor and racial differences, this kind of society was unique in both European and world history. To the present day, every society in which plantation slavery once existed still contends with the long-term effects of that institution.

QUICK REVIEW

Slaves' Lives

- Conditions on plantations varied from colony to colony
- Slave masters had all but unlimited power over slaves
- Race-based slavery in the Americas created a kind of society that was unique in world history

WHY DID mid-eighteenth-century European wars often involve both continental and global conflicts?

MID-EIGHTEENTH-CENTURY WARS

From the standpoint of international relations, the state system of the mid–eighteenth century was quite unstable and tended to lead the major states of Europe into prolonged warfare. The statesmen of the period generally assumed that warfare could further national interests. No forces or powers saw it in their interest to prevent war or maintain peace. Consequently, nations often viewed periods of peace at the conclusion of a war simply as opportunities to recoup their strength, so that they could start fighting again to seize another nation's territory or disrupt another empire's trading monopoly.

The two fundamental areas of great power rivalry were the overseas empires and central and eastern Europe. Conflict in one of these regions repeatedly overlapped with conflict in the other, and this interaction influenced strategy and the pattern of alliances among the great powers.

THE WAR OF JENKINS'S EAR

By the mid–eighteenth century, the West Indies had become a hotbed of trade rivalry and illegal smuggling. Much to British chagrin, the Spanish government took its own alleged trading monopoly seriously and maintained coastal patrols, which boarded and searched English vessels to look for contraband.

In 1731, during one such boarding operation, there was a fight, and the Spaniards cut off the ear of an English captain named Robert Jenkins. Thereafter he carried about his severed ear preserved in a jar of brandy. This incident was of little importance until 1738, when Jenkins appeared before the British Parliament, reportedly brandishing his ear as an example of Spanish atrocities to British merchants in the West Indies. The British merchant and West Indian planters lobbied Parliament to relieve Spanish intervention in their trade. Sir Robert Walpole (1676–1745), the British prime minister, could not resist these pressures. In late 1739, Britain went to war with Spain. This war might have been a relatively minor event, but because of developments in continental European politics, it became the opening encounter to a series of European wars fought across the world until 1815.

THE WAR OF THE AUSTRIAN SUCCESSION (1740–1748)

In December 1740, after being king of Prussia for less than seven months, Frederick II (r. 1740–1786) seized the Austrian province of Silesia in eastern Germany. The invasion shattered the provisions of the Pragmatic Sanction (see Chapter 13) and upset the continental balance of power.

Maria Theresa Preserves the Habsburg Empire The Prussian seizure of Silesia could have marked the opening of a general hunting season on Habsburg holdings and the beginning of revolts by Habsburg subjects. Instead, it led to new political allegiances. Maria Theresa's (r. 1740–1780) great achievement was not the reconquest of Silesia, which eluded her, but the preservation of the Habsburg Empire as a major political power. She won loyalty and support from her various subjects not merely through her heroism, but by granting new privileges to the nobility. Most significantly, the empress recognized Hungary as the most important of her crowns and promised the Magyar nobility local autonomy. She thus preserved the Habsburg state, but at considerable cost to the power of the central monarchy.

France Draws Great Britain into the War The war over the Austrian succession and the British–Spanish commercial conflict could have remained separate disputes. What united them was the role of France. Aggressive court aristocrats compelled the elderly Cardinal Fleury (1653–1743), first minister of Louis XV (r. 1715–1774), to abandon his planned naval attack on British trade and instead to support the Prussian aggression against Austria, the traditional enemy of France. This was among the more fateful decisions in French history.

In the first place, aid to Prussia consolidated a new and powerful state in Germany. That new power could, and indeed later did, endanger France. Second, the French move against Austria brought Great Britain into the continental war, as Britain sought to make sure the Low Countries remained in the friendly hands of Austria, not France. In 1744, the British–French conflict expanded beyond the Continent when France supported Spain against Britain in the New World. As a result, French military and economic resources were badly divided. The war ended in a stalemate in 1748 with the Treaty of Aix-la-Chapelle. Prussia retained Silesia, and Spain renewed Britain's privilege from the Treaty of Utrecht (1713) to import slaves into the Spanish colonies.

Overview Eighteenth-Century Conflicts

DATE	WAR	PARTICIPANTS	FACTORS
1739	The War of Jenkins's Ear	Great Britain vs. Spain	Sparked by British captain Robert Jenkins's account of atrocities inflicted on British merchants by Spaniards
1740–1748	The War of the Austrian Succession	Prussia and France vs. Austria and Great Britain	France and Great Britain were dragged into this war after Prussia seized an Austrian province
1756–1763	The Seven Years' War	France and Austria vs. Prussia	Prussia was aided financially by Great Britain in this war that continued in America between France and Britain
1776–1783	The American Revolution	Great Britain vs. Colonial America	Fought for American independence from Great Britain; France and Spain joined the colonists before war's end

THE "DIPLOMATIC REVOLUTION" OF 1756

Although the Treaty of Aix-la-Chapelle had brought peace in Europe, France and Great Britain continued to struggle unofficially in the Ohio River valley and in upper New England. These clashes were the prelude to what is known in American history as the French and Indian War, which formally erupted in the summer of 1755.

Before war commenced again in Europe, however, a dramatic shift of alliances took place, in part, as a result of the events in North America. The British king, George II (r. 1727–1760), who was also the Elector of Hanover in Germany, thought the French might attack Hanover in response to the conflict in America. In January 1756, Britain and Prussia signed the Convention of Westminster, a defensive alliance aimed at preventing the entry of foreign troops into the German states. Whereas George II feared a French attack on Hanover, Frederick II feared an alliance of Russia and Austria. The convention meant that Great Britain, the ally of Austria since the wars of Louis XIV, had now joined forces with Austria's major eighteenth-century enemy.

Maria Theresa was despondent over this development. It delighted her foreign minister, Prince Wenzel Anton Kaunitz (1711–1794), however. He had long hoped for an alliance with France to help dismember Prussia and, in May 1756, France and Austria signed a defensive alliance. France would now fight to restore Austrian supremacy in central Europe.

THE SEVEN YEARS' WAR (1756–1763)

Once again, however, Frederick II precipitated a European war that extended into a colonial theater.

Frederick the Great Opens Hostilities In August 1756, Frederick II opened what would become the Seven Years' War by invading Saxony. Frederick considered this to be a preemptive strike against a conspiracy by Saxony, Austria, and France to destroy Prussian power. The invasion itself, however, created the very destructive alliance that Frederick feared. In the spring of 1757, France and Austria made a new alliance dedicated to the destruction of Prussia. Sweden, Russia, and many of the smaller German states joined them.

Two factors saved Prussia. First, Britain furnished considerable financial aid. Second, in 1762, Empress Elizabeth of Russia (r. 1741–1762) died. Her successor, Tsar Peter III, immediately made peace with Prussia, thus relieving Frederick of one enemy and allowing him to hold off Austria and France. The Treaty of Hubertusburg of 1763 ended the continental conflict with no significant changes in prewar borders.

William Pitt's Strategy for Winning North America The survival of Prussia was less impressive to the rest of Europe than were the victories of Great Britain in every theater of conflict. The architect of these victories was William Pitt the Elder (1708–1778).

North America was the center of Pitt's real concern. Put simply, he wanted all of North America east of the Mississippi for Great Britain, and that was what he won. He sent more than 40,000 regular English and colonial troops against the French in Canada and achieved unprecedented cooperation with the American colonies, whose leaders realized they might finally defeat their French neighbors. The French government was unwilling and unable to direct similar resources against the English in America. In September 1759, on the Plains of Abraham, overlooking the valley of the Saint Lawrence River at Quebec City, the British army under James Wolfe defeated the French under Louis Joseph de Montcalm. The French Empire in Canada was ending.

Moreover, the major islands of the French West Indies fell to British fleets. Between 1755 and 1760, the value of the French colonial trade fell by more than 80 percent. In India, British victories opened the way for the eventual conquest of Bengal in northeast India and later of all of India by the British East India Company. (See Chapter 25.) Never had Great Britain or any other European power experienced such a complete worldwide military victory.

The Treaty of Paris of 1763 The Treaty of Paris of 1763 reflected somewhat less of a victory than Britain had won on the battlefield. Britain received all of Canada, the Ohio River valley, and the eastern half of the Mississippi River valley. Britain returned Pondicherry and Chandernagore in India and the West Indian sugar islands of Guadeloupe and Martinique to the French.

The Seven Years' War had been a vast worldwide conflict. At great internal sacrifice, Prussia had permanently wrested Silesia from Austria and had turned the Holy Roman Empire into an empty shell. France, though still having sources of colonial income, was no longer a great colonial power. The Spanish Empire remained largely intact, but the British were still determined to penetrate its markets. In India, the British East India Company continued to impose its own authority on the decaying indigenous governments. In North America, the British government faced the task of organizing its new territories. From this time until World War II, Great Britain was a world power, not just a European one.

The quarter century of warfare also caused a long series of domestic crises among the European powers. The financial burdens of the wars had astounded all contemporaries. Every power had to increase its revenues to pay its war debt and finance its preparation for the next combat. Nowhere did this search for revenue lead to more far-ranging consequences than in the British colonies in North America.

This scene, painted by artist Edward Penny, shows Robert Clive receiving a sum of money from Siraj-ud-daulah, the Mughal Nawab of Bengal, for injured officers and soldiers at Plassey. Clive's victory in 1757 at the Battle of Plassey brought English domination of the Indian subcontinent for almost two centuries. Clive had won the battle largely through bribing many of the Nawab's troops and potential allies.

Erich Lessing © The Trustees of the British Museum/Art Resource, NY

What role did private companies play in the British domination of India?

QUICK REVIEW
Treaty of Paris (1763)

◆ Ended the Seven Years' War

◆ Britain gave France generous terms

◆ War launched Britain as a global power

THE AMERICAN REVOLUTION AND EUROPE

WHAT WERE the
causes of the American
Revolution?

The revolt of the British colonies in North America marked the beginning of the end of European colonial domination of the American continents. The War of the American Revolution also continued the conflict between France and Great Britain. The French support of the Americans deepened the existing financial and administrative difficulties of the French monarchy.

MAP EXPLORATION

Interactive map: To explore this map further, go to www.myhistorylab.com

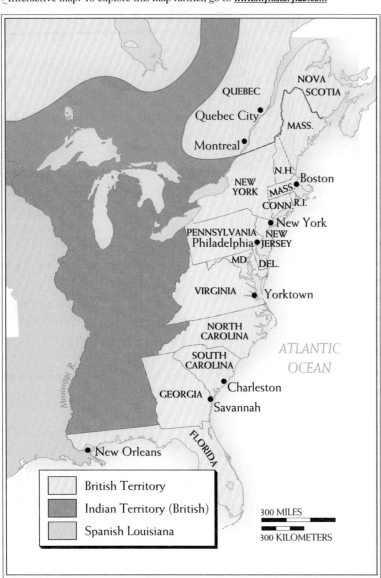

MAP 16–2 **North America in 1763** In the year of the victory over France, the English colonies lay along the Atlantic seaboard. The difficulties of organizing authority over the previous French territory in Canada and west of the Appalachian Mountains would contribute to the coming of the American Revolution.

How costly would it seem to conquer and control the territory encompassing the British colonies, former French Canada, and land east of the Mississippi River?

RESISTANCE TO THE IMPERIAL SEARCH FOR REVENUE

After the Treaty of Paris of 1763, the British government faced two imperial problems. The first was the sheer cost of maintaining their empire, which the British felt they could no longer carry alone. Since the American colonies had been the chief beneficiaries of the conflict, the British felt it was rational for the colonies henceforth to bear part of the cost of their protection and administration. The second problem was the vast expanse of new territory in North America that the British had to organize. This included all the land from the mouth of the Saint Lawrence River to the Mississippi River, with its French settlers and, more importantly, its Native Americans. (See Map 16–2.)

The British drive for revenue began in 1764 with the passage of the Sugar Act. The measure attempted to produce more revenue from imports into the colonies by the rigorous collection of what was actually a lower tax. The next year, Parliament passed the Stamp Act, which put a tax on legal documents and other items such as newspapers.

The Americans responded that they alone, through their colonial assemblies, had the right to tax themselves and that they were not represented in Parliament. Furthermore, they feared that if their colonial government was financed from outside, they would lose control over it. In October 1765, the Stamp Act Congress met in America and drew up a protest to the crown. The colonists agreed to refuse to import British goods. In 1766, Parliament repealed the Stamp Act, but through the Declaratory Act said it had the power to legislate for the colonies.

The Stamp Act crisis set the pattern for the next ten years. Parliament, under the leadership of a royal minister, would approve revenue or administrative legislation. The Americans would then resist by reasoned argument, economic pressure, and violence. Then the British would repeal the legislation, and the process would begin again. Each time, tempers on both sides became more frayed and positions more irreconcilable. With each clash, the Americans more fully developed their own thinking about political liberty.

THE CRISIS AND INDEPENDENCE

In 1767, Charles Townshend (1725–1767), as Chancellor of the Exchequer, the British finance minister, led Parliament to pass a series of revenue acts relating to colonial imports. The colonists again resisted. The ministry sent over its own customs agents to administer the laws. To protect these new officers, the British sent troops to Boston in 1768. The obvious tensions resulted. In March 1770, the Boston Massacre, in which British troops killed five citizens, took place. That same year, Parliament repealed all of the Townshend duties except the one on tea.

In May 1773, Parliament passed a new law relating to the sale of tea by the East India Company. The measure permitted the direct importation of tea into the American colonies. It actually lowered the price of tea while retaining the tax imposed without the colonists' consent. In some cities, the colonists refused to permit the unloading of the tea; in Boston, a shipload of tea was thrown into the harbor.

The British ministry of Lord North (1732–1792) was determined to assert the authority of Parliament over the colonies. During 1774, Parliament passed a series of laws known in American history as the **Intolerable Acts**. These measures closed the port of Boston, reorganized the government of Massachusetts, allowed troops to be quartered in private homes, and removed the trials of royal customs officials to England. The same year, the Quebec Act extended the boundaries of Quebec to include the Ohio River valley. The Americans regarded the Quebec Act as an attempt to prevent their mode of self-government from spreading beyond the Appalachian Mountains.

During these years, citizens critical of British policy had established committees of correspondence throughout the colonies. In September 1774, these committees organized the First Continental Congress in Philadelphia. This body hoped to persuade Parliament to restore self-government in the colonies and abandon its direct supervision of colonial affairs. Conciliation, however, was not forthcoming. By April 1775, the Battles of Lexington and Concord had been fought.

The Second Continental Congress gathered in May 1775. It still sought conciliation with Britain, but the pressure of events led it to begin to conduct the government of the colonies. By August 1775, George III had declared the colonies in rebellion. On July 4, 1776, the Continental Congress adopted the Declaration of Independence. Thereafter, the War of the American Revolution continued until 1781, when the forces of George Washington defeated those of Lord Cornwallis at Yorktown. Early in 1778, however, the war had widened into a European conflict when Benjamin Franklin (1706–1790) persuaded the French government to support the rebellion. In 1779, the Spanish also joined the war against Britain. The 1783 Treaty of Paris concluded the conflict, and the thirteen American colonies finally established their independence.

AMERICAN POLITICAL IDEAS

The American colonists looked to the English Revolution of 1688 as having established many of their own fundamental political liberties, as well as those of the English. Consequently, the colonists employed a theory that had developed to justify an aristocratic rebellion to support their own popular revolution. These Whig political ideas, largely derived from the writings of John Locke, were, however, only a part of the English ideological heritage that affected the Americans. Throughout the eighteenth century, they had become familiar with a series of British political writers called the Commonwealth-

The Bostonian's Paying the Excise-Man, or Tarring & Feathering
Plate I.

Many Americans fiercely objected to the British Parliament's attempts to tax the colonies. This print of a British tax collector being tarred and feathered warned officials of what could happen to them if they tried to collect these taxes.

Philip Dawe (c. 1750–c. 1785), *The Bostonians Paying the Excise-Man or Tarring & Feathering.* London, 1774. Colored Engraving. The Gilder Lehman Collection on deposit at the Pierpont Morgan Library. GL 4961.01. Photography: Joseph Zehavi. The Pierpont Morgan Library/Art Resource, NY

How did Americans evade, intimidate, and harass British officials?

Intolerable Acts Series of laws passed by Parliament in 1774 that closed the port of Boston, reorganized the government of Massachusetts, quartered soldiers in private homes, and transferred trials of customs officials accused of crimes to England.

men, who held republican political ideas that had their intellectual roots in the most radical thought of the Puritan revolution. During the early eighteenth century, these writers argued that the government of Sir Robert Walpole and his successors was corrupt and that it undermined liberty. They regarded much parliamentary taxation as simply a means of financing political corruption. They also considered standing armies instruments of tyranny. In Great Britain, this republican political tradition had only a marginal impact. Three thousand miles away, however, the policy of Great Britain toward America following the Treaty of Paris of 1763 and certain political events in Britain had made many colonists believe the worst fears of the Commonwealthmen were coming true. All these events coincided with the accession of George III to the throne.

EVENTS IN GREAT BRITAIN

George III believed that a few powerful Whig families and the ministries they controlled had bullied and dominated his two immediate royal predecessors. George III also believed he should have ministers of his own choice and Parliament should function under royal, rather than aristocratic, management. Between 1761 and 1770, George tried one minister after another, but each, in turn, failed to gain enough support from the various factions in the House of Commons. Finally, in 1770, he turned to Lord North, who remained the king's first minister until 1782. The Whig families and other political spokespersons claimed that George III was attempting to impose a tyranny. What they meant was that the king was attempting to curb the power of a particular group of the aristocracy.

The Challenge of John Wilkes   In 1763, the various factions that opposed the king coalesced around John Wilkes (1725–1797), a London political radical, member of Parliament, and publisher of a newspaper called *The North Briton*. Wilkes used his paper to attack Lord Bute, the king's first minister, for his handling of peace negotiations with France. Bute had him arrested, but Wilkes's privileges as a member of Parliament won his release. The courts ruled that the vague warrant by which he had been arrested was illegal. The House of Commons, however, convicted him of libel and expelled him. Wilkes fled the country and was outlawed, but many saw him as a victim of political persecution.

In 1768, Wilkes returned to England and was reelected to Parliament. The House of Commons, however, bowed to the wishes of the king and refused to seat him. Although he won three subsequent elections, the House ignored the verdict of the electorate and seated a rival government-supported candidate. Shopkeepers, artisans, and small property owners took to the streets to support Wilkes, and aristocrats who wanted to humiliate the king also backed him. Wilkes maintained that his was the cause of English liberty, and his supporters adopted the slogan, "Wilkes and Liberty." Wilkes became lord mayor of London and was finally seated by Parliament in 1774.

The American colonists followed these developments closely, for they seemed to confirm the colonists' suspicion that the king and Parliament were conspiring against English liberty. The Wilkes affair highlighted the arbitrary power of the monarch, the corruption of the House of Commons, and the contempt of both for the electorate. These aspects of tyranny seemed, to the colonists, to be at the heart of their struggles with England.

Movement for Parliamentary Reform   The political influences between America and Britain operated both ways. The colonial demand for no taxation without repre-

SIGNIFICANT DATES FROM THE EIGHTEENTH CENTURY

Year	Event
1713	Treaty of Utrecht
1739	War of Jenkins's Ear
1740–1748	War of the Austrian Succession
1756–1763	Seven Years' War
1763	John Wilkes challenges the British monarchy
1764	Sugar Act
1765	Stamp Act
1770	Boston Massacre
1773	Boston Tea Party
1774	First Continental Congress
1776–1783	War of the American Revolution

sentation and the criticism of the adequacy of the British system of representation struck at the core of the eighteenth-century British political structure. British subjects at home who were no more directly represented in the House of Commons than were the Americans could adopt the colonial arguments. The colonial questioning of the tax-levying authority of the House of Commons was related to the protest of John Wilkes. Both were protesting the power of a largely self-selected aristocratic political body. Moreover, both the colonial leaders and Wilkes appealed over the head of legally constituted political authorities to popular opinion and popular demonstrations.

The American colonists also demonstrated to Europe how a politically restive people in the Old Regime could fight tyranny and protect political liberty. They established revolutionary, but orderly, political bodies that could function outside the existing political framework. The legitimacy of these bodies lay not in existing law, but in the alleged consent of the governed.

The Yorkshire Association Movement   By the close of the 1770s, many in Britain resented the mismanagement of the American war, the high taxes, and Lord North's ministry. In northern England in 1778, Christopher Wyvil (1740–1822), a landowner and retired clergyman, organized the Yorkshire Association Movement. Its members intended that the association examine, and suggest reforms for, the entire government. The Association Movement was thus a popular attempt to establish an extra-legal institution to reform the government. The movement collapsed during the early 1780s because its supporters, unlike Wilkes and the American rebels, were not willing to appeal for broad popular support. Nonetheless, the agitation of the Association Movement provided many people with experience in political protest.

Parliament was, however, influenced by the Association Movement. In April 1780, the Commons advocated a reduction in the power of the crown. In 1782, Parliament implemented an "economical" reform, which abolished some sources of royal patronage, and in 1783, Parliament forced Lord North to form a ministry with Charles James Fox (1749–1806), a longtime critic of the king. In the same year, the king turned to William Pitt the Younger (1759–1806) for help in creating a more pliable House of Commons. During the election of 1784, Pitt used immense amounts of royal patronage to fill the House of Commons with men friendly to the king. Efforts to reform Parliament faded, and by the mid-1780s, the king's political dominance had been restored. Its resurgence was, however, short-lived. George III succumbed to mental illness, and the regency that had to be established to govern for him could not aggressively exercise royal authority.

BROADER IMPACT OF THE AMERICAN REVOLUTION

The Americans—through their state constitutions, the Articles of Confederation, and the federal Constitution adopted in 1788—had demonstrated to Europe the possibility of government without kings and hereditary nobilities. They had established the example of a nation in which written documents based on popular consent and popular sovereignty—rather than on divine law, natural law, tradition, or the will of kings—were the highest political and legal authority. The political novelty of these assertions should not be ignored.

Americans embraced democratic ideals, but they did not create a thoroughly democratic society. The equality of white male citizens—both before the law and in society—was endorsed. All white males were promised a chance to improve their social standing and economic lot by hard work and individual enterprise, and they alone were enfranchised. Slaves were not freed. Nor were the issues of women's rights and those of Native Americans addressed. Still, the American colonists of the eighteenth century produced a freer society than any the world had yet seen. Their revolution was a genuinely radical movement, whose influence would spread and inspire Europeans to question their traditional modes of government.

QUICK REVIEW

The Yorkshire Association Movement

◆ Started in 1778 by Christopher Wyvil

◆ Demanded moderate change in corrupt system of parliamentary elections

◆ Movement faded in the early 1780s

SUMMARY

HOW DID European contact with the rest of the world evolve in the centuries since the Renaissance?

Periods of European Overseas Empires There have been four stages in Europe's interactions with the rest of the world: (1) by the end of the seventeenth century, discovery and settlement of the New World, introduction of the transatlantic plantation economy, and market penetration of Southeast Asia; (2) by the 1820s, mercantile empires, with resulting competition among European powers, and independence in most of the Americas; (3) in the nineteenth century, formal empires ruled directly by Europe; and (4) by the late twentieth century, decolonization. Prior to colonial independence, Europeans generally treated indigenous peoples as inferior. Ships and guns gave Europeans insurmountable advantages. This chapter covers the mercantile period. *page 394*

WHAT WERE the characteristics of European mercantile empires?

Mercantile Empires Mercantilism, an economic theory based on the economy of scarcity, assumed the growth of one nation came at the expense of another. The goal of the mercantile system was for each European power to monopolize trade with its colonies, with the profits—in the form of gold and silver bullion—enriching each ruling country. Colonial rivalries could grow into conflicts between European nations. French–British rivalry was intense in the West Indies and in India. Dutch power in what is now Indonesia was acknowledged by other Europeans. *page 395*

HOW DID Spanish colonial organization reflect its imperial goals?

The Spanish Colonial System Spain attempted to impose control on trade with the colonies by restricting the American ports to which Spanish ships could sail. Smugglers, however, always found ways to carry out their work. The political system under which the Spanish colonies were administered concentrated power in the crown; local officials were appointed through royal patronage. In 1700, when the French Bourbon king Philip V took the Spanish throne, he tried to introduce effective French administrative techniques to Spain's empire. Spain was defeated in Europe's mid-eighteenth-century wars, and Charles III tried to

use imperial reform and colonial trade liberalization to bolster Spain's economy. He was successful initially, but he stoked resentments that would erupt into colonial rebellion. *page 396*

WHAT WERE the origins of slavery in the Americas?

Black African Slavery, the Plantation System, and the Atlantic Economy The transatlantic plantation economy created social, political, and production systems unlike any others in world history. Although slavery was practiced in many other times and places, the extent to which the plantation economy depended on slave labor made it unique. The racist element in the justification for the trade in black African human beings left a cultural legacy that is still with us. The sheer volume and economic impact of the slave trade itself, and the goods produced by slave labor, make slavery one of the most important elements in the history of the Americas, and an important factor in the histories of Europe and of Africa as well. *page 397*

WHY DID mid-eighteenth-century European wars often involve both continental and global conflicts?

Mid-Eighteenth-Century Wars The mid-eighteenth-century European state system encouraged warfare. Monarchs thought they could use war to further their own ends without risking the lives of their subjects or the stability of their societies. Overseas empires and central and eastern Europe saw repeated international rivalries. The 1739 British–Spanish conflict, the War of Jenkins's Ear, began a period of European warfare that lasted until 1815. Prussia, Austria, France, and other European nations fought wars that spilled over into colonial conflicts. Maria Theresa preserved the Habsburg Empire, at the cost of power sharing with the nobility and with the Hungarian Magyars. Frederick II saved Prussia, becoming "Frederick the Great." Britain's William Pitt the Elder set his country on the path to a global dominance it would enjoy for the next century and a half by deploying troops into colonial battlefields. *page 404*

WHAT WERE the causes of the American Revolution?

The American Revolution and Europe The Treaty of Paris of 1763 left Britain with the problems of financing its empire and administering vast new North

American territories. Starting in 1764, Britain passed a series of taxes on the American colonies that it intended to collect more aggressively. In each case, American resistance led Britain to rescind most of the legislation. Tensions increased. In 1776, the colonists' Continental Congress declared independence from Britain. France and Spain entered the war as American allies, and the Americans' victory was ratified by the 1783 Treaty of Paris. Through this period, Britain's King George III alienated Whigs and convinced radical political theorists that he wanted to impose tyranny. The writings and examples offered by John Wilkes in Britain, and the revolutionaries in America, provided a new vocabulary for advocates of liberty and new models for free sovereign government. *page 408*

REVIEW QUESTIONS

1. What were the main points of conflict between Britain and France in North America, the West Indies, and India? How was the Spanish colonial empire in the Americas organized and managed?

2. What was the nature of slavery in the Americas? How was it integrated into the economies of the Americas, Europe, and Africa? What was the plantation system?

3. What were the results of the Seven Years' War? Which countries emerged in a stronger position? Why?

4. To what extent were the colonists who began the American Revolution influenced by European ideas and political developments? What influence did their actions and arguments have on Europe?

KEY TERMS

Intolerable Acts (p. 409)   **mercantilism** (p. 395)

For additional learning resources related to this chapter, please go to **www.myhistorylab.com**

PEARSON
myhistorylab

17

The Age of Enlightenment:

Eighteenth-Century Thought

The salon of Madame Marie-Thérèse Geoffrin (1699–1777) was one of the most important Parisian gathering spots for Enlightenment writers during the middle of the eighteenth century. Well-connected women such as Madame Geoffrin were instrumental in helping the *philosophes* they patronized to bring their ideas to the attention of influential people in French society and politics.

Chateaux de Malmaison et Bois-Preau, Rueil-Malmaison. Bridgeman-Giraudon/Art Resource, NY

What does the importance of salons tell us about Enlightenment culture?

T he modern world's faith in the possibility and desirability of change is a key intellectual inheritance from the eighteenth century's self-proclaimed Enlightenment. The leaders of the movement were convinced that human reason could comprehend the processes of nature and manipulate them to create a better world. They believed the rational order that the scientific revolution had discovered in the physical universe should also exist in human societies. They insisted that all traditional beliefs and institutions be exposed to rational critique, which would inevitably inspire innovation and improvement. Some of the era's monarchs caught the spirit of the age and used the power of "enlightened absolutism" to implement rational plans for reordering their subjects' lives. ■

FORMATIVE INFLUENCES ON THE ENLIGHTENMENT

WHAT WAS the intellectual and social background of the Enlightenment?

The Newtonian worldview, the political stability and commercial prosperity of Great Britain after 1688, the need for administrative and economic reform in France after the wars of Louis XIV, and the consolidation of what is known as a *print culture* were the chief factors that fostered the ideas of the Enlightenment and the call for reform throughout Europe.

IDEAS OF NEWTON AND LOCKE

Isaac Newton (1642–1727) and John Locke (1632–1704) were the major intellectual forerunners of the Enlightenment. Newton's formulation of the law of universal gravitation exemplified the newly perceived power of the human mind. Newtonian physics had portrayed a pattern of mechanical and mathematical rationality in the physical world. During the eighteenth century, thinkers from a variety of backgrounds began to apply this insight to society. If nature was rational, they reasoned, society, too, should be organized rationally. Furthermore, Newton had encouraged natural philosophers to approach the study of nature directly and to avoid metaphysics and supernaturalism. He had insisted on the use of empirical experience to check rational speculation. This emphasis on concrete experience became a key feature of Enlightenment thought.

As explained in Chapter 14, Newton's success in physics had inspired his fellow countryman John Locke to explain human psychology in terms of experience. In *An Essay Concerning Human Understanding* (1690), Locke argued that all humans enter the world a **tabula rasa**, or blank page. Personality is the product of the sensations that impinge on an individual from the external world throughout his or her life. This essentially behaviorist theory implied that human nature is changeable and can be molded by modifying the surrounding physical and social environment. Locke's was thus a reformer's psychology that suggested the possibility of improving the human condition. Locke's psychology also, in effect, rejected the Christian doctrine that sin permanently flawed human beings.

tabula rasa   (a blank page) John Locke's *An Essay Concerning Human Understanding* (1690) theorized that at birth the human mind is a tabula rasa.

THE EXAMPLE OF BRITISH TOLERATION AND POLITICAL STABILITY

The domestic stability of Great Britain after the Revolution of 1688 furnished a living example of a society in which, to many contemporaries, enlightened reforms appeared to benefit everyone. England permitted religious toleration to all except Unitarians and Roman Catholics, and even they were not actively persecuted. Relative freedom of the press and free speech prevailed. The authority of the monarchy was limited, and political sovereignty resided in Parliament. The courts protected citizens from arbitrary government action. The army was small. Furthermore, the domestic economic life of Great Britain displayed far less regulation than that of France or other continental nations, and English commerce flourished. Many writers of the continental Enlightenment contrasted what they regarded as the wise, progressive features of English life with the absence of religious toleration, the extensive literary censorship, the possibility of arbitrary arrest, the overregulation of the economy, and the influence of aristocratic military values in their own nations and most particularly in France.

THE EMERGENCE OF A PRINT CULTURE

The Enlightenment flourished in a *print culture*, that is, a culture in which books, journals, newspapers, and pamphlets had achieved a status of their own. During the eighteenth century, the volume of printed material—books, journals, magazines, and daily newspapers—increased sharply throughout Europe, notably in Britain. One of the driving forces behind this expansion of printed materials was the increase in literacy that occurred across Europe.

A growing concern with everyday life and material concerns—with secular as opposed to religious issues—accompanied this expansion of printed forms. Toward the end of the seventeenth century, half the books published in Paris were religious; by the 1780s, only about 10 percent were. Prose came to be valued as highly as poetry, and the novel emerged as a distinct literary genre. Novels often came to provide the moral and social instruction that books of piety once furnished.

Books were not inexpensive in the eighteenth century, but they, and the ideas they conveyed, circulated in a variety of ways to reach a broad public. Private and public libraries grew in number, allowing single copies to reach many readers. Authors might also publish the same material in book form, in journals, and in newspapers.

Within both aristocratic and middle-class society, people were increasingly expected to be familiar with books and secular ideas. Popular publications fostered the value of polite conversation and the reading of books. Coffeehouses became centers for discussing writing and ideas. (See "Encountering the Past: Coffeehouses and Enlightenment," page 418.)

The expanding market for printed matter allowed writers to earn a living from their work for the first time, making authorship an occupation. Parisian ladies who hosted fashionable salons sought out popular writers. Some writers, notably Alexander Pope (1688–1744) in England and Voltaire in France, grew wealthy, providing an example for their young colleagues. In a challenge to older aristocratic values, status for authors in this new print culture was based on merit and commercial competition, not heredity and patronage.

Printing shops were the productive centers for the books and newspapers that spread the ideas of the Enlightenment.

The Granger Collection

How did printing help make the wide dissemination of Enlightenment ideas possible?

ENCOUNTERING THE PAST

COFFEEHOUSES AND ENLIGHTENMENT

Europe's first coffee imports came from the Ottoman Empire, where coffee drinking was encouraged by the Islamic prohibition of alcohol. Venice, which had close commercial ties with the Ottomans, opened the first European coffeehouse in the 1640s. By the middle of the eighteenth century, thousands of similar facilities were scattered across Europe.

Because no alcohol was served, behavior in a coffeehouse tended to be better than in a tavern, and coffeehouses provided social contexts for discussions of current events and serious issues. Proprietors of coffeehouses attracted customers by furnishing copies of newspapers and journals. Some even sponsored lectures on such topics as Newtonian physics or the relationship between science and religion. Respectable women did not frequent coffeehouses, but men of many different professional backgrounds and varying interests did. The coffeehouse provided a common meeting ground for persons interested in debating ideas and hearing the latest news and rumors from courts and governments. Although the discussion in such places often centered on issues of political liberty and freedom of thought, the great quantities of coffee and sugar their customers consumed were produced by the slaves who labored on Caribbean and Brazilian plantations.

Business, science, religion, and politics were discussed in London coffeehouses such as this.

© The Trustees of the British Museum/Art Resource, NY

Who went to coffeehouses? Why were they such popular meeting places?

HOW DID the coffeehouse work with the print culture to create an informed public?

A division, however, soon emerged between high and low literary culture. Successful authors of the Enlightenment addressed themselves to monarchs, nobles, the upper middle classes, and professional groups, and they were read and accepted in these upper levels of society. Other aspiring authors lived marginally, writing professionally for whatever newspaper or journal that would pay for their work. Many of these lesser writers grew resentful, blaming a corrupt society for their lack of success. From their anger, they often espoused radical ideas or took moderate Enlightenment ideas to radical extremes, transmitting them in this embittered form to their often lower-class audience.

An expanding literate public and the growing influence of secular printed materials created a new and increasingly influential social force called *public opinion*. This force—the collective effect on political and social life of views circulated in print and discussed in the home, the workplace, and centers of leisure—seems not to have existed before the middle of the eighteenth century. The emergence of public opinion changed the cultural and political climate in Europe. Governments could no longer operate wholly in secret or with disregard to the larger public sphere. They, as well as their critics, had to explain and discuss their views and policies openly. Government efforts to limit the freedom of the press underscored the challenge public opinion posed to traditional intellectual, social, and political authorities.

THE *PHILOSOPHES*

The writers and critics who flourished in the expanding print culture and who took the lead in forging the new attitudes favorable to change, championed reform, and advocated toleration were known as the *philosophes*.

A few of these *philosophes*, particularly those in Germany, were university professors. Most, however, were free agents who might be found in London coffeehouses, Edinburgh drinking spots, the salons of fashionable Parisian ladies, the country houses of reform-minded nobles, or the courts of the most powerful monarchs on the Continent. In eastern Europe, they were often royal bureaucrats. They were not an organized group; they disagreed on many issues and did not necessarily like or respect each other.

The *philosophes* drew the bulk of their readership from the prosperous commercial and professional urban classes. These people as well as forward-looking aristocrats discussed the reformers' writings and ideas in local philosophical societies, Freemason lodges, and clubs. Although the writers of the Enlightenment did not consciously champion the goals or causes of the middle class, they did provide an intellectual ferment and a major source of ideas that could be used to undermine existing social practices and political structures based on aristocratic privilege. Moreover, the *philosophes* generally supported the expansion of trade, the improvement of agriculture and transport, and the invention of new manufacturing machinery, events that were transforming the society and the economy of the eighteenth century and enlarging the business and commercial classes.

The chief bond among the *philosophes* was their common desire to reform religion, political thought, society, government, and the economy for the sake of human liberty. Though challenged over the last three centuries, no other single set of ideas has done so much to shape and define the modern Western world.

VOLTAIRE—FIRST AMONG THE *PHILOSOPHES*

By far the most influential of the philosophes was François-Marie Arouet, known to posterity by his pen name Voltaire (1694–1778). In 1726, to escape the wrath of a powerful aristocrat whom he had offended, Voltaire went into exile in England. In 1728, Voltaire returned to France and, in 1733, published *Letters on the English*, which appeared in French the next year. The book praised the virtues of the English, especially their religious liberty, and implicitly criticized the abuses of French society. Voltaire then moved to Cirey from which, if necessary, he could easily escape France into what was then the nearby independent duchy of Lorraine. In 1738, with the considerable help of Countess Emilie de Chatelet (1706–1749), he published *Elements of the Philosophy of Newton*, which more than any other single book popularized the thought of Isaac Newton across the continent.

Voltaire's most popular work is probably *Candide* (1759), an attack on war, religious persecution, and unwarranted (as he saw it) optimism about the human condition. Like most *philosophes*, Voltaire believed society could and should be improved, but he was not confident that reforms could be sustained. The Enlightenment is associated with optimistic attitudes, but its sunny outlook radiated more hopefulness than certainty.

Statue of Voltaire by Jean-Antoine Houdon (Theatre Français, Paris).

Musée Lambinet, Versailles/Giraudon/Art Resource, NY

Why is Voltaire thought by many to be the most important *philosophe*?

THE ENLIGHTENMENT AND RELIGION

HOW DID the *philosophes* challenge traditional religious ideas and institutions?

For many, but not all, *philosophes* of the eighteenth century, ecclesiastical institutions, especially in their frequently privileged position as official parts of the state, were the chief impediment to human improvement and happiness.

The critical *philosophes* complained that both established and nonestablished Christian churches hindered the pursuit of a rational life and the scientific study of humanity and nature. According to the doctrine of original sin—either Protestant or Catholic—meaningful improvement in human nature on earth was impossible. Religion thus turned attention away from this world to the world to come. Mired in conflicts over obscure doctrines, the churches promoted intolerance and bigotry, inciting torture, war, and other forms of human suffering. With this attack, the *philosophes* were challenging not only a set of ideas, but also some of Europe's most powerful institutions, as the churches were deeply enmeshed in the power structure of the Old Regime.

DEISM

deism The *philosophes'* theology. A rational religion, a faith without fanaticism and intolerance that acknowledged the sovereign authority of reason.

The *philosophes*, although critical of many religious institutions and frequently anticlerical, did not oppose all religion. What the *philosophes* sought, however, was religion without fanaticism and intolerance, a religious life that would largely substitute human reason for the authority of churches. The Newtonian worldview had convinced many writers that nature was rational. Therefore, the God who had created nature must also be rational, and the religion through which that God was worshipped should be rational. Most of them believed the life of religion and of reason could be combined, giving rise to a a broad set of ideas known as **deism**.

The deists' informal creed had two major points. The first was a belief in the existence of God, which they thought the contemplation of nature could empirically justify, and in this respect many Protestant and Roman Catholic writers fully agreed with them. Because nature provided evidence of a rational God, that deity must also favor rational morality. So the second point in the deists' creed was a belief in life after death, when rewards and punishments would be meted out according to the virtue of the lives people led on this earth.

Deism, Enlightenment writers urged, was empirical, tolerant, reasonable, and capable of encouraging virtuous living. Deists hoped that wide acceptance of their faith would end rivalry among the various Christian sects and with it religious fanaticism, conflict, and persecution. They also felt deism would remove the need for priests and ministers, who, in their view, were often responsible for fomenting religious differences and denominational hatred. Deistic thought led some contemporaries to believe God had revealed himself in different ways and that many religions might embody divine truth. There was never a formal or extensive deist movement, but deist ideas spread informally throughout the culture and provided for some people a framework for a non-dogmatic religious outlook.

TOLERATION

The *philosophes* presented religious toleration as a primary social condition for the virtuous life. Again Voltaire took the polemical lead in championing this cause. In 1762, the Roman Catholic political authorities in the city of Toulouse tortured and then executed a Huguenot named Jean Calas, who had been accused of murdering his son to prevent him from converting to Roman Catholicism. Voltaire made the dead man's cause his own, winning a reversal of the judicial decision against the unfortunate man in 1765. For Voltaire, the case illustrated the fruits of religious fanaticism and the need for rational reform of judicial processes. In 1779, the German playwright and critic Gotthold Lessing (1729–1781) wrote *Nathan the Wise*, a plea for toleration not only of different Christian groups, but also of religious faiths other than Christianity.

RADICAL ENLIGHTENMENT CRITICISM OF CHRISTIANITY

Some *philosophes* went beyond the formulation of a rational religious alternative to Christianity and the advocacy of toleration to attack the churches and the clergy with vehemence. The Scottish philosopher David Hume (1711–1776) argued in "Of Miracles," a chapter in his *Inquiry into Human Nature* (1748), that no empirical evidence supported the belief in divine miracles central to much of Christianity. Voltaire repeatedly questioned the truthfulness of priests and the morality of the Bible. In *The Decline and Fall of the Roman Empire* (1776), Edward Gibbon (1737–1794), the English historian, explained the rise of Christianity in terms of natural causes rather than the influence of miracles and piety. A few, but actually very few, *philosophes* went further than criticism. Most of the *philosophes*, however, sought not the abolition of religion, but its transformation into a humane force that would encourage virtuous living.

JEWISH THINKERS IN THE AGE OF ENLIGHTENMENT

Despite their emphasis on toleration, the *philosophes'* criticisms of traditional religion often reflected an implicit contempt not only for Christianity but also, and sometimes more vehemently, for Judaism and, as we see later, for Islam as well. The Enlightenment view of religion thus served in some ways to further stigmatize Jews and Judaism in the eyes of non-Jewish Europeans.

Enlightenment values also, however, allowed certain Jewish intellectuals to rethink the relationship of their communities to the wider European culture from which they had largely lived apart. Baruch Spinoza (1632–1677) set the example for a secularized version of Judaism, and Moses Mendelsohn (1729–1786) established the main outlines of an assimilationist position.

The new science of the mid–seventeenth century deeply influenced Spinoza, the son of a Jewish merchant of Amsterdam. Like his contemporaries, Hobbes and Descartes, he looked to the power of human reason to reconceptualize traditional thought. In that regard his thinking reflected the age of scientific revolution and looked toward the later Enlightenment. In his *Ethics*, the most famous of his works, Spinoza closely identified God and nature, or the spiritual and material worlds. In his *Theologico-Political Treatise* (1670), Spinoza directly anticipated much of the religious criticism of the Enlightenment and its attacks on the power of superstition in human life. Spinoza described the origins of religion in thoroughly naturalistic terms. Spinoza's extensive rational and historical criticism of the biblical narratives disturbed Christian and Jewish contemporaries who saw him as a writer seeking to lead people away from all religion. During his lifetime the controversial character of his writings led both Jews and Protestants to criticize him as an atheist.

Moses Mendelsohn, the leading Jewish philosopher of the eighteenth century, was known as the "Jewish Socrates." Writing almost a century after Spinoza, he also advocated the entry of Jews into modern European life. In contrast to Spinoza, however, Mendelsohn argued that a Jew could combine loyalty to Judaism with adherence to rational, Enlightenment values. Mendelsohn's most influential work was *Jerusalem, or, On Ecclesiastical Power and Judaism* (1783) in which he argued both for extensive religious toleration

Dutch Jewish philosopher Baruch Spinoza.
Library of Congress

Why did Spinoza face attack from both Christians and Jews?

and for maintaining the religious distinction of Jewish communities. Unlike Spinoza, Mendelsohn wished to advocate religious toleration while genuinely sustaining the traditional religious practices and faith of Judaism. Nevertheless, Mendelsohn believed Jewish communities should not have the right to excommunicate their members over differences in theological opinions or even if their members embraced modern secular ideas. He thus sought both toleration of Jews within European society and toleration by Jews of a wider spectrum of opinion within their own communities. His hope was that the rationalism of the Enlightenment would provide the foundation for both types of toleration.

ISLAM IN ENLIGHTENMENT THOUGHT

Islam continued to be seen as a rival to Christianity. European writers repeated what other Christian critics had said for centuries. They portrayed Islam as a false religion, Muhammad as an impostor and a false prophet, and attacked Islam as an exceptionally carnal or sexually promiscuous religion. European universities did endow professorships to study Arabic during the seventeenth century, but these university scholars generally agreed with theological critics that Islam too often embodied religious fanaticism.

Enlightenment *philosophes* spoke with two voices regarding Islam. Voltaire indicated his opinion along with that of many of his contemporaries in the title of his 1742 tragedy, *Fanaticism, or Mohammed the Prophet*. For Voltaire, Muhammad and Islam in general represented simply one more example of the religious fanaticism he had so often criticized among Christians. Some Enlightenment writers, however, spoke well of the Islamic faith. The deist John Toland, who opposed prejudice against both Jews and Muslims, contended that Islam derived from early Christian writings and was thus a form of Christianity. Other commentators approved of Islam's tolerance and the charitable work of Muslims.

One of the most positive commentators on eighteenth-century Islam was a woman. Between 1716 and 1718, Lady Mary Wortley Montagu (1689–1762) lived in Istanbul with her husband, the British ambassador to Turkey. She wrote a series of letters about her experiences there that was published the year after her death. In these *Turkish Embassy Letters*, she praised much about Ottoman society and urged the English to copy the Turkish practice of vaccination against smallpox. Nevertheless, the European voices demanding fairness and expressing empathy for Islam were rare throughout the eighteenth century.

Muslims were not curious about the Christian West. Only a handful of Muslims from the Ottoman Empire visited Western Europe in the eighteenth century, and no Islamic writers showed much interest in contemporary European authors. The *Ulema*, the Islamic religious establishment, reinforced these attitudes. They taught that God's revelations to Muhammad meant Islam had replaced Christianity as a religion and therefore there was little for Muslims to learn from Christian culture.

What role did images of the East play in the Enlightenment critique of European society and government?

QUICK REVIEW

Baruch Spinoza (1632–1677)

◆ Dutch Jewish thinker who was influenced by the scientific revolution

◆ Closely identified God and nature

◆ Recognized no reality beyond the natural order

QUICK REVIEW

Islam and the Enlightenment

◆ Eighteenth-century writers continued long-standing European hostility toward Islam

◆ *Philosophes* both damned and praised Islam

◆ Muslims showed little interest in Western Europe

HOW DID the *philosophes* apply Enlightenment ideas to social and economic problems?

THE ENLIGHTENMENT AND SOCIETY

THE *ENCYCLOPEDIA*: FREEDOM AND ECONOMIC IMPROVEMENT

The midcentury witnessed the publication of the *Encyclopedia*, one of the greatest monuments of the Enlightenment and its most monumental undertaking in the realm of print culture. Under the heroic leadership of Denis Diderot (1713–1784) and Jean

Le Rond d'Alembert (1717–1783), seventeen volumes appeared between 1751 and 1772. No other work of the Enlightenment so illustrated the movement's determination to probe life on earth rather than in the religious realm.

The *Encyclopedia* was the product of the collective effort of more than a hundred authors, and its editors had at one time or another solicited articles from all the major French *philosophes*. It included the most advanced critical ideas of the time on religion, government, and philosophy. The *Encyclopedia* also included numerous important articles and illustrations on manufacturing, canal building, ship construction, and improved agriculture, making it an important source of knowledge about eighteenth-century social and economic life.

The project had been designed to secularize learning and to undermine intellectual assumptions that lingered from the Middle Ages and the Reformation. The articles on politics, ethics, and society ignored divine law and concentrated on humanity and its immediate well-being. For the authors, the good life lay here and now and was to be achieved through the application of reason to human relationships. The publication of the *Encyclopedia* spread Enlightenment thought more fully over the Continent, penetrating German and Russian intellectual and political circles.

Denis Diderot was the heroic editor of the *Encylopedia*, published in seventeen volumes of text and eleven volumes of prints between 1751 and 1772. Through its pages many of the chief ideas of the Enlightenment reached a broad audience of readers.

Jean-Simon Berthelemy (1743-1811), "Denis Diderot" (1713–1784). Writer and Encyelopaedist. Oil on canvas, 55 x 46 cm. Inv.: P 2082. Photo: Bulloz. Musée de la Ville de Paris, Musée Carnavalet, Paris, France/Art Resource, NY

What topics were covered in the *Encyclopedia*? What were the editors' goals?

BECCARIA AND REFORM OF CRIMINAL LAW

Although the term did not appear until later, the idea of *social science* originated with the Enlightenment. *Philosophes* hoped to end human cruelty by discovering social laws and making people aware of them. These concerns are most evident in the *philosophes'* work on law and prisons.

In 1764, Marquis Cesare Beccaria (1738–1794), an Italian aristocrat and *philosophe*, published *On Crimes and Punishments*, in which he applied critical analysis to the problem of making punishments both effective and just. He thought the criminal justice system should ensure a speedy trial and certain punishment and the intent of punishment should be to deter further crime. The purpose of laws was not to impose the will of God or some other ideal of perfection, but to secure the greatest good or happiness for the greatest number of human beings. This utilitarian philosophy based on happiness in this life permeated most Enlightenment writing on practical reforms.

THE PHYSIOCRATS AND ECONOMIC FREEDOM

Economic policy was another area in which the *philosophes* saw existing legislation and administration preventing the operation of natural social laws. They believed mercantilist legislation (designed to protect a country's trade from external competition) and the regulation of labor by governments and guilds actually hampered the expansion of trade, manufacture, and agriculture. In France, these economic reformers were called the physiocrats. The physiocrats believed the primary role of government was to protect property and to permit its owners to use it freely.

ADAM SMITH ON ECONOMIC GROWTH AND SOCIAL PROGRESS

The most important economic work of the Enlightenment was Adam Smith's (1723–1790) *Inquiry into the Nature and Causes of the Wealth of Nations* (1776). Smith believed economic liberty was the foundation of a natural economic system. As a result, he urged that the mercantile system of England—including the navigation acts governing colonial trade, the bounties the government gave to favored merchants and industries, most tariffs, trading monopolies, and the domestic regulation of labor and manufacture—be abolished. The best way to encourage economic growth, he maintained, was to unleash individuals to pursue their own selfish economic interests.

Mercantilism assumed that the earth's resources were limited and scarce, so one nation could acquire wealth only at the expense of others. Smith's book challenged this assumption. He saw the resources of nature—water, air, soil, and minerals—as boundless. To him, they demanded exploitation for the enrichment and comfort of humankind. In effect, Smith was saying the nations and peoples of Europe need not be poor. Smith is usually regarded as the founder of **laissez-faire** economic thought and policy, which favors a limited role for the government in economic life. He was not opposed, however, to all government intervention in economic activity. The state, he believed, should provide schools, armies, navies, and roads, and it should fund commercial ventures that were desirable, but beyond the means of private enterprise.

Within *The Wealth of Nations*, Smith, like other Scottish thinkers of the day, embraced an important theory of human social and economic development, known as the *four-stage theory*. According to this theory, human societies move through four stages of development: the hunting and gathering stage, the pastoral or herding stage, the agricultural stage, and, finally, the commercial stage. Smith and other Scottish writers described the passage of human society through these stages as a movement from barbarism to civilization.

To Europeans, this outlook helped justify their economic and imperial domination of the world during the following century. They repeatedly portrayed themselves as bringing a higher level of civilization to people elsewhere who, according to the four-stage theory, lived in lower stages of human social and economic development. Europeans thus imbued with the spirit of the Enlightenment presented themselves as carrying out a civilizing mission to the rest of the world.

laissez-faire Policy of noninterference, especially the policy of government noninterference in economic affairs or business.

POLITICAL THOUGHT OF THE *PHILOSOPHES*

HOW DID the *philosophes* apply Enlightenment ideas to political issues?

Nowhere was the *philosophes*' reformist agenda, as well as tensions among themselves, so apparent as in their political thought. The most important political thought of the Enlightenment occurred in France. The French *philosophes*, however, were divided over how to solve their country's problems. Their proposed solutions spanned a wide political spectrum, from aristocratic reform to democracy to absolute monarchy.

MONTESQUIEU AND *SPIRIT OF THE LAWS*

Charles Louis de Secondat, baron de Montesquieu (1689–1755), was a lawyer, a noble of the robe, and a member of a provincial *parlement*. He also belonged to the Bordeaux Academy of Science, before which he presented papers on scientific topics. Although living comfortably within the bosom of French society, he saw the need for reform.

In his most enduring work, *Spirit of the Laws* (1748), Montesquieu pursued an empirical method, taking illustrative examples from the political experience of both ancient and modern nations. From these, he concluded that no single set of political laws could apply to all peoples at all times and in all places. Whether the best form of government for a country was a monarchy or a republic, for example, depended on that country's size, population, social and religious customs, economic structure, traditions, and climate. Only a careful examination and evaluation of these elements could reveal what mode of government would most benefit a particular people.

For France, Montesquieu favored a monarchical government tempered and limited by various intermediary institutions, including the aristocracy, the towns, and the other corporate bodies that enjoyed liberties the monarch had to respect. In France, he regarded the aristocratic courts, or *parlements*, as a major example of an intermediary association. Their role was to limit the power of the monarchy and thus to preserve the liberty of its subjects. In championing these aristocratic bodies and the general oppositional role of the aristocracy, Montesquieu was a political conservative. He adopted this conservatism in the hope of achieving reform, however, for he believed the oppressive and inefficient absolutism of the monarchy accounted for the degradation of French life.

One of Montesquieu's most influential ideas was that of the division of power in government. Executive, legislative, and judicial power should reside in separate branches of the government. He thought any two branches could check and balance the power of the other. Montesquieu's analysis illustrated his strong belief that monarchs should be subject to constitutional limits on their power and that a separate legislature, not the monarch, should formulate laws. For this reason, although he set out to defend the political privileges of the French aristocracy, Montesquieu's ideas have had a profound effect on the constitutional form of liberal democracies for more than two centuries.

Rousseau: A Radical Critique of Modern Society

Jean-Jacques Rousseau (1712–1778) held a different view of the exercise and reform of political power from Montesquieu's. Rousseau hated the world and the society in which he lived. It seemed to him impossible for human beings living according to the commercial values of his time to achieve moral, virtuous, or sincere lives. He contended that human beings in a primeval state of nature had been good, but that as they eventually formed social relations and then social institutions, they had lost that goodness. Society itself was the source of human evil for Rousseau, and one manifestation of that unnatural evil was unequal distribution of property.

Rousseau questioned the concepts of material and intellectual progress and the morality of a society in which commerce, industry, and the preservation of property rights were regarded as among the most important human activities. The other *philosophes* generally believed life would improve if people could enjoy more of the fruits of the earth or could produce more goods. Rousseau raised the more fundamental questions of what constitutes the good life and how can human society be reshaped to achieve that life.

Rousseau carried these same concerns into his political thought. His most extensive discussion of politics appeared in *The Social Contract* (1762). Rousseau suggested that society is more important than its individual members, because they are what they are only by virtue of their relationship to the larger community. Independent human beings living alone can achieve little. Through their relationship to the larger political community, they become moral creatures capable of significant action. The question then becomes: What kind of community allows people to behave morally?

Rousseau envisioned a society in which each person could maintain personal freedom while behaving as a loyal member of the larger community. Drawing on the traditions of Plato and Calvin, he defined freedom as obedience to law. In his case, the law to be obeyed was that created by the general will. In a society with virtuous customs and morals in which citizens have adequate information on important issues, the concept of the general will is normally equivalent to the will of a majority of voting citizens. Democratic participation in decision making would bind the individual citizen

Jean-Jacques Rousseau.
Library of Congress

Overview   Major Works of the Enlightenment and Their Publication Dates

DATE	WORK	AUTHOR
1670	*Theologico-Political Treatise*	Spinoza
1677	*Ethics*	Spinoza
1687	*Principia Mathematica*	Newton
1690	*An Essay Concerning Human Understanding*	Locke
1696	*Christianity Not Mysterious*	Toland
1721	*Persian Letters*	Montesquieu
1733	*Letters on the English*	Voltaire
1738	*Elements of the Philosophy of Newton*	Voltaire
1748	*Spirit of the Laws*	Montesquieu
1748	*Inquiry into Human Nature*	Hume
1750	*Discourse on the Moral Effects of the Arts and Sciences*	Rousseau
1751	*Encyclopedia* (Vol. 1)	Edited by Diderot
1755	*Discourse on the Origin of Inequality*	Rousseau
1759	*Candide*	Voltaire
1762	*The Social Contract and Émile*	Rousseau
1763	*Treatise on Tolerance*	Voltaire
1764	*Philosophical Dictionary*	Voltaire
1764	*On Crimes and Punishments*	Beccaria
1776	*The Decline and Fall of the Roman Empire*	Gibbon
1776	*The Wealth of Nations*	Smith
1779	*Nathan the Wise*	Lessing
1783	*Jerusalem, or, On Ecclesiastical Power and Judaism*	Mendelsohn
1792	*Vindication of the Rights of Woman*	Wollstonecraft
1793	*Religion Within the Limits of Reason Alone*	Kant

to the community. Rousseau believed the general will, thus understood, must always be right and that to obey the general will is to be free. This argument led him to the notorious conclusion that under certain circumstances some people must be forced to be free. Rousseau's politics thus constituted a justification for radical direct democracy and for collective action against individual citizens.

Rousseau had only a marginal impact on his own time. He proved, however, to be a figure to whom later generations returned. Leading figures in the French Revolution were familiar with his writing, and he influenced writers in the nineteenth and twentieth centuries who were critical of the general tenor and direction of Western culture.

ENLIGHTENED CRITICS OF EUROPEAN EMPIRES

Most European thinkers associated with the Enlightenment favored the extension of European empires across the world. A few Enlightenment voices, however, did criticize the European empires on moral grounds, especially the European conquest of the Americas, the treatment of Native Americans, and the enslavement of Africans on the two American continents. The most important of these critics were Denis Diderot and two German philosophers, Immanuel Kant and Johann Gottlieb Herder (1744–1803).

Three ideas in particular provided the grounds for this criticism. First, the Enlightenment critics of their empires argued for a form of shared humanity that the sixteenth-century European conquerors and their successors in the Americas and in other areas of imperial conquest had ignored. Kant, Diderot, and Herder rejected this dismissive outlook and the harsh policies that had flowed from it. A second of these critical ideas was the conviction that the people whom Europeans had encountered in the Americas had possessed cultures that should have been respected and understood rather than destroyed. For Herder, human beings living in different societies possessed the capacity as human beings to develop in culturally different fashions. He thus embraced an outlook later known as cultural relativism. A third idea, closely related to the second, was that human beings may develop distinct cultures possessing intrinsic values that cannot be compared, one to the detriment of another, because each culture possesses deep inner social and linguistic complexities that make any simple comparison impossible. Indeed, Diderot, Kant, and Herder argued that being a human includes the ability to develop a variety of distinctly different cultures.

WOMEN IN THE THOUGHT AND PRACTICE OF THE ENLIGHTENMENT

Women, especially in France, helped significantly to promote the careers of the *philosophes*. In Paris, the salons of women such as Marie-Thérèse Geoffrin (1699–1777), Julie de Lespinasse (1733–1776), and Claudine de Tencin (1689–1749) gave the *philosophes* access to useful social and political contacts and a receptive environment in which to circulate their ideas. Moreover, the women who organized the salons were well connected to political figures who could help protect the *philosophes* and secure royal pensions for them.

WHAT ROLE did women play in the Enlightenment?

Despite this help and support from the learned women of Paris, the *philosophes* were on the whole not strong feminists. Many urged better and broader education for women. They criticized the education women did receive as overly religious, and they tended to reject ascetic views of sexual relations. In general, however, they displayed traditional views toward women and advocated no radical changes in their social condition.

Montesquieu, for example, maintained, in general, that the status of women in a society was the result of climate, the political regime, culture, and women's physiology. He believed women were not naturally inferior to men and should have a wider role in society. Yet Montesquieu's willingness to consider social change for women in European life had limits. Although in the *Spirit of the Laws* he indicated a belief in the equality of the sexes, he still retained a traditional view of marriage and family and expected men to dominate those institutions. Furthermore, although he supported the right of women to divorce and opposed laws that oppressed them, he upheld the ideal of female chastity.

The views about women expressed in the *Encyclopedia* were less generous than those of Montesquieu. The *Encyclopedia* suggested ways to improve women's lives, but in general, it did not emphasize that the condition of women needed reform. Almost all the contributors were men, and the editors, Diderot and d'Alembert, evidently saw no need to include many articles by women. The Encyclopedists discussed women primarily within a family context—as daughters, wives, and mothers—and presented motherhood as a woman's most important occupation. On sexual behavior, the Encyclopedists upheld an unquestioned double standard.

M.ʳˢ WOLLSTONECRAFT.

Pg.16593 English Author & feminist.

Mary Wollstonecraft in *A Vindication of the Rights of Woman* defended equality of women with men on the grounds of men and women sharing the capacity of human reason.

CORBIS/Bettmann

How sympathetic were the *philosophes* as a group to the ideas of Mary Wollstonecraft?

One of the most surprising and influential analyses of the position of women came from Jean-Jacques Rousseau. This most radical of all Enlightenment political theorists urged a traditional and conservative role for women. In his novel *Émile* (1762) (discussed again in Chapter 19), he set forth a radical version of the view that men and women occupy separate spheres. Only men were to populate the world of citizenship, political action, and civic virtue. Women were relegated to the domestic sphere. Many of these attitudes were not new—some have roots as ancient as Roman law—but Rousseau's powerful presentation and the influence of his other writings gave them new life in the late eighteenth century. Rousseau deeply influenced many leaders of the French Revolution, who, as shall be seen in the next chapter, often incorporated his view on gender roles in their policies.

Paradoxically, Rousseau achieved a vast following among women in the eighteenth century. One explanation for this influence is that his writings, although they did not advocate liberating women or expanding their social or economic roles, did stress the importance of their emotions. He portrayed the domestic life and the role of wife and mother as a noble and fulfilling vocation, giving middle- and upper-class women a sense that their daily occupations had a purpose. He assigned them a degree of influence in the domestic sphere that they could not have competing with men outside it.

In 1792, in A *Vindication of the Rights of Woman*, Mary Wollstonecraft (1759–1797) brought Rousseau before the judgment of the rational Enlightenment ideal of progressive knowledge. The immediate incentive for this essay was her opposition to certain policies of the French Revolution, unfavorable to women, that Rousseau had inspired. Wollstonecraft accused Rousseau and others after him who upheld traditional roles for women of attempting to narrow women's vision and limit their experience. She argued that to confine women to the separate domestic sphere because of supposed limitations of their physiology was to make them the sensual slaves of men. Confined in this separate sphere, they were the victims of male tyranny, their obedience was blind, and they could never achieve their own moral or intellectual identity. Denying good education to women would impede the progress of all humanity. With these arguments, Wollstonecraft was demanding for women the kind of liberty that male writers of the Enlightenment had been championing for men for more than a century. In doing so, she placed herself among the *philosophes* and broadened the agenda of the Enlightenment to include the rights of women as well as those of men.

ROCOCO AND NEOCLASSICAL STYLES IN EIGHTEENTH-CENTURY ART

HOW DID rococo and neoclassicism reflect and contribute to the prevailing trends of the age?

rococo Style that embraced lavish, often lighthearted decoration with an emphasis on pastel colors and the play of light.

Two contrasting styles dominated eighteenth-century European art and architecture. The **rococo** style embraced lavish, often lighthearted decoration with an emphasis on pastel colors and the play of light. **Neoclassicism** embodied a return to figurative and architectural models drawn from the Renaissance and the ancient world.

Rococo architecture and decoration originated in early-eighteenth-century France. After Louis XIV's death in 1715, the Regent Philippe d'Orléans (1674–1723) and the French aristocracy spent less time at Versailles and began to enjoy the diversions of Paris. There, wealthy French aristocrats built houses known as *hôtels*. Their designers compensated for the relatively small scale and nondescript exteriors of these

The color, the light, and the elaborate decorative details associated with rococo style are splendidly exemplified in the Imperial Hall (*Kaisarsaal*) built in Würzburg, Bavaria, according to the design of Balthasar Neumann (1687–1753).

Art Resource, N.Y.

What values are reflected in rococo architecture?

neoclassicism   Style that embodied a return to figurative and architectural models drawn from the Renaissance and the ancient world.

mansions with interiors that were elaborately decorated and painted in light colors to make the rooms seem brighter and more spacious. Beyond such domestic and personally intimate settings in France, the rococo style spread across Europe and was adapted to many public buildings and churches.

The paintings associated with rococo art often portrayed the aristocracy, and particularly the French aristocracy, at play. The paintings showed not reality, but an idealized landscape with carefree men and women pursuing a life of leisure, romance, and seduction.

As the eighteenth century wore on, the way of life illustrated in rococo paintings and of more popular prints produced from them convinced many people in France that the monarchy, the court, and the aristocracy were frivolous and decadent. In reality, as seen in Chapter 15, many French and European aristocrats were hardworking and disciplined. Nonetheless, the lighthearted carelessness of rococo art increased hostility toward the political and social elites of the Old Regime.

Contemporaries, moreover, did not have to wait for the tumult of the French Revolution to view art that directly criticized the society rococo art portrayed. The mid–eighteenth century witnessed a new admiration for the art of the ancient world. Neoclassicism constituted a return to themes, topics, and styles drawn from antiquity itself and from the Renaissance appeal to antiquity.

Figures in neoclassical paintings rarely suggest movement and often seem to stand still in a kind of tableau illustrating a moral theme. These paintings were didactic rather than emotional or playful. Their subject matter was usually concerned with public life or public morals, rather than depicting intimate family life, daily routine, or the leisure activity favored by rococo painters.

Many neoclassical painters used scenes of heroism and self-sacrifice from ancient history to draw contemporary moral and political lessons. Such scenes provided a sharp moral contrast to rococo works in which lovers seek only pleasure and escape from care. Some neoclassical artists intended their paintings to be a form of direct political

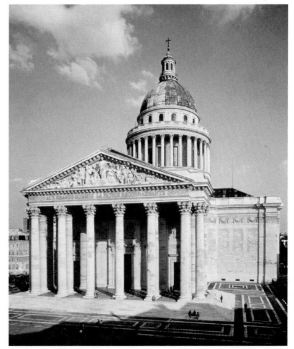

The Panthéon in Paris (construction commencing 1758) embodied the neoclassical style used for a Jesuit church. After the French Revolution it became a national monument where famous figures of the Enlightenment and Revolution were buried. The bodies of both Voltaire and Rousseau were transferred there during the 1790s.

Jacques Germain Soufflot (1713–1780), Facade of the Panthéon (formerly Church of Ste. Genevieve), 1757. Panthéon, Paris, France. © Bridgeman-Giraudon/Art Resource, NY

Why were so many eighteenth-century Europeans drawn to the neoclassical style?

criticism. Jacques-Louis David (1748–1825), the foremost French neoclassical painter, used ancient republican themes in the 1780s to emphasize the corruption of French monarchical government.

The *philosophes* themselves became the subjects of neoclassical artists. The French sculptor Jean-Antoine Houdon (1741–1828) produced numerous portraits in stone of leading *philosophes* including Voltaire and Rousseau as well as American admirers of the Enlightenment such as Benjamin Franklin (1706–1790) and Thomas Jefferson (1743–1826). Even religious structures built in the neoclassical style were, by the end of the century, transformed to monuments to the Enlightenment and Revolution. Modeled on its ancient pagan namesake in Rome, the Panthéon in Paris was begun in 1758 as a Jesuit church. During the French Revolution, the new government transformed it into a national monument where the remains of French heroes could be interred.

ENLIGHTENED ABSOLUTISM

WHAT WAS enlightened absolutism?

Most of the *philosophes* favored neither Montesquieu's reformed and revived aristocracy nor Rousseau's democracy as a solution to contemporary political problems. Like other thoughtful people of the day in other stations and occupations, they looked to the existing monarchies. Voltaire and other *philosophes*, such as Diderot, who visited Catherine II of Russia, and the physiocrats, some of whom were ministers to Louis XV and Louis XVI, did not wish to limit the power of monarchs. Rather, they sought to use that power to rationalize economic and political structures and liberate intellectual life.

During the last third of the century, some observers believed that several European rulers had embraced many of the reforms the *philosophes* advocated. Historians use the term *enlightened absolutism* for this form of monarchical government in which the central absolutist administration was strengthened and rationalized at the cost of other, lesser centers of political power, such as the aristocracy, the church, and the parliaments or diets that had survived from the Middle Ages. The monarchs most closely associated with it are Frederick II (r. 1740–1786) of Prussia, Joseph II of Austria (r. 1765–1790), and Catherine II (r. 1762–1796) of Russia.

The humanitarian and liberating zeal of the Enlightenment writers was, however, only part of what motivated the policies of these rulers. Frederick II, Joseph II, and Catherine II were also determined to play major diplomatic and military roles in Europe. In no small measure, they adopted Enlightenment policies favoring the rational economic and social integration of their realms because these policies also increased their military strength and political power.

FREDERICK THE GREAT OF PRUSSIA

More than any other ruler of the age, Frederick the Great of Prussia embodied enlightened absolutism. Drawing upon the accomplishments of his Hohenzollern forebearers, he forged a state that commanded the loyalty of the military, the Junker nobility, the Lutheran clergy, a growing bureaucracy recruited from an educated middle class, and university professors. Because the authority of the Prussian monarchy and the military were so strong and because the nobles, bureaucracy, clergy, and professors were so loyal, Frederick had the confidence to permit a more open discussion of Enlightenment ideas and to put into effect more Enlightenment values, such as extensive religious toleration, than any other continental ruler. Consequently, in marked contrast to France, Prussians sympathetic to the Enlightenment tended to support the state rather than criticize it.

Promotion Through Merit   Reflecting an important change in the European view of the ruler, Frederick frequently described himself as "the first servant of the State" contending that his own personal and dynastic interests should always be subordinate to the good of his subjects. Like earlier Hohenzollern rulers, he protected the local social and political interests of the Prussian nobility as well as their role in the army, but he also required nobles who sought positions in his well-paid bureaucracy to qualify for those jobs by merit. By 1770, a Prussian Civil Service Commission oversaw the education and examinations required for all major government appointments. Frederick thus made it clear that merit rather than privilege of birth would determine who served the Prussian state.

During his reign Frederick created few new nobles, and those persons whom he did ennoble earned their titles by merit, for having served the king and the state well. Because the Prussian state required academic training for appointment to positions of authority, nobles attended the universities. There they studied with middle-class Prussians who were training to serve the state either as Protestant clergy or bureaucrats. Consequently, nobles, clergy, and bureaucrats in Prussia shared a similar educational background that combined a moderate exposure to Enlightenment ideas with broadly shared religious values and loyalty to the state.

Frederick the Great of Prussia.
Library of Congress

Religious Toleration   No single policy so associated Frederick with the Enlightenment as that of full religious toleration. Continuing the Hohenzollern policy of toleration for foreign workers who brought important skills into Prussia, Frederick allowed Catholics and Jews to settle in his predominantly Lutheran country, and he protected the Catholics living in Silesia after he conquered that province from the Habsburgs in the 1740s. (See Chapter 13.) He even stated that he would be willing to build mosques for Turks should they move into his country. His religious toleration won the strong support of philosophers, such as Immanuel Kant and Moses Mendelsohn. Frederick nonetheless tended to appoint Protestants to most key positions in the bureaucracy and army.

Administrative and Economic Reforms   Frederick also ordered a new codification of Prussian law, which was completed after his death. His objective was to rationalize the existing legal system and make it more efficient, eliminating regional peculiarities, reducing aristocratic influence, abolishing torture, and limiting the number of capital crimes.

The midcentury wars had inflicted considerable economic damage on Prussia. Thereafter, Frederick used the power of the state to foster economic growth. He sought to develop Prussian agriculture. Under state supervision, swamps were drained, new crops introduced, and peasants encouraged and sometimes compelled to migrate where they were needed. Frederick also established a land-mortgage credit association to help landowners raise money for agricultural improvements. Despite these efforts, however, most Prussians did not prosper under Frederick's reign, and the burden of taxation, reflecting his protection of the interests of the nobles, fell disproportionately on peasants and townspeople.

JOSEPH II OF AUSTRIA

No eighteenth-century ruler so embodied rational, impersonal force as did the emperor Joseph II of Austria. He was the son of Maria Theresa and co-ruler with her from 1765 to 1780. Thereafter, he ruled alone until his death in 1790. Joseph II sincerely wished to improve the lot of his people. He was much less a political opportunist and cynic than either Frederick the Great of Prussia or Catherine the Great of Russia. Nonetheless, the ultimate result of his well-intentioned efforts was a series of aristocratic and peasant rebellions extending from Hungary to the Austrian Netherlands.

Centralization of Authority   As explained in Chapter 13, of all the rising states of the eighteenth century, Austria was the most diverse in its people and problems. The Habsburgs never succeeded in creating either a unified administrative structure or a strong aristocratic loyalty to the dynasty. To preserve the monarchy during the War of the Austrian Succession (1740–1748), Maria Theresa had guaranteed the aristocracy considerable independence, especially in Hungary.

Maria Theresa strengthened the power of the crown outside of Hungary by increasing the size of the empire's administrative bureaucracy. Her efficient tax agents collected from the clergy as well as the nobles in Austria and Bohemia. She appointed councils to handle various kinds of problems, and she brought education under state control to ensure her government a sufficient supply of trained officials. Her concern for schools extended to increasing opportunities for primary education at the local level. She also tried to protect peasants and serfs by using the royal bureaucracy to enforce limits on the amount of labor noble landowners could demand from their tenants. Her concern was not solely humanitarian. She wanted to preserve the pool of manpower from which she drew her soldiers.

Joseph II was more determined than his mother, and his projected reforms were more wide ranging. He sought to overcome the pluralism of the Habsburg holdings by imposing central authority on areas of political and social life in which Maria Theresa had wisely chosen not to interfere.

In particular, Joseph sought to reduce Hungarian autonomy. To avoid having to guarantee Hungary's existing privileges or extend new ones at the time of his coronation, he refused to have himself crowned king of Hungary and even had the Crown of Saint Stephen, symbol of the Hungarian state, sent to the Imperial Treasury in Vienna. He reorganized local government in Hungary to increase the authority of his own officials. He also required the use of German in all governmental matters.

Ecclesiastical Policies   Another target of Joseph's royal absolutism was the church. Maria Theresa was devout, but she had not allowed the church to limit her authority. Although she had attempted to discourage certain of the more extreme modes of Roman Catholic popular religious piety, such as public flagellation, she was adamantly opposed to religious toleration. (See "Compare & Conneect: Maria Theresa and Joseph II of Austria Debate Toleration," pages 434–435.)

Joseph II was also a practicing Catholic, but based on both Enlightenment values and pragmatic politics, he favored a policy of toleration. In October 1781, Joseph extended freedom of worship to Lutherans, Calvinists, and the Greek Orthodox. Joseph also granted the right of private worship to Jews and relaxed the financial and social burdens imposed on them, though he did not give Jews full equality with other Habsburg subjects.

Above all, Joseph sought to bring the Roman Catholic Church directly under royal control. He forbade the bishops of his realms to communicate directly with the pope. Since he considered religious orders that did not run schools or hospitals to be unproductive, he dissolved more than six hundred monasteries, confiscated their lands, and used some of their revenue to found new parishes in areas where there was a shortage of priests. He also reorganized the training of priests. In effect, Joseph's policies made Roman Catholic priests the employees of the state, ending the influence of the Roman Catholic Church as an independent institution in Habsburg lands.

Economic and Agrarian Reform   Like Frederick of Prussia, Joseph sought to improve the economic life of his domains. He abolished many internal tariffs, encouraged road building, and improved river transport. He personally inspected farms and manufacturing districts. Joseph also reconstructed the judicial system to make laws more uniform and rational and to lessen the influence of local landlords. All these improvements were expected to bring new unity to the state and more taxes into the imperial coffers in Vienna.

Joseph's policies toward serfdom and the land were a far-reaching extension of those Maria Theresa had initiated. During his reign, he introduced reforms that touched the very heart of the rural social structure. He did not abolish the authority of landlords over their peasants, but he did seek to make that authority more moderate and subject to the oversight of royal officials. He abolished serfdom as a legally sanctioned state of servitude. He granted peasants a wide array of personal freedoms, including the right to marry, to engage in skilled work, and to have their children learn a skill without having to secure the landlord's permission. Joseph reformed the procedures of the manorial courts and opened avenues of appeal to royal officials. He also encouraged landlords to change land leases, so that peasants could more easily inherit land or transfer it to other peasants. His goal in all these efforts to reduce traditional burdens on peasants was to make them more productive and industrious farmers.

Near the end of his reign, Joseph proposed a new and daring system of land taxation. He decreed in 1789 that all proprietors of the land were to be taxed regardless of social status. No longer were the peasants alone to bear the burden of taxation. He commuted *robot* (forced peasant labor) into a monetary tax, only part of which was to go to the landlord, the rest reverting to the state. Angry nobles blocked the implementation of this decree, and it died with Joseph in 1790. This and others of Joseph's earlier measures, however, brought turmoil throughout the Habsburg realms. Peasants revolted over disagreements with landlords about their newly granted rights. The nobles of the various Habsburg realms protested the taxation scheme. The Magyars resisted Joseph's centralization measures in Hungary and forced him to rescind them. Joseph was succeeded by his brother Leopold II (r. 1790–1792). Although sympathetic to Joseph's goals, Leopold was forced to repeal many of the most controversial decrees, such as that on taxation.

> **QUICK REVIEW**
>
> **Joseph II of Austria**
> **(r. 1765–1790)**
>
> ◆ Attempted widespread reforms based on Enlightenment principles
>
> ◆ Resistance forced Joseph to rescind most of his centralizing efforts
>
> ◆ Abolished serfdom and gave peasants more personal freedom

CATHERINE THE GREAT OF RUSSIA

Joseph II never grasped the practical necessity of forging political constituencies to support his policies. Catherine II, who had been born a German princess, but who became empress of Russia, understood only too well the fragility of the Romanov dynasty's base of power.

After the death of Peter the Great in 1725, the court nobles and the army repeatedly determined the Russian succession. Such had been the case for almost forty years when, in 1762, Peter III came to the throne. He was a weak ruler whom many contemporaries considered mad. He immediately exempted the nobles from compulsory military service and then rapidly made peace with Frederick the Great, for whom he held unbounded admiration. That decision probably saved Prussia from military defeat in the Seven Years' War. The one positive feature of this unbalanced creature's life was his marriage in 1745 to a young German princess born in the small duchy of Anhalt Zerbst. This was the future Catherine the Great.

MARIA THERESA AND JOSEPH II OF AUSTRIA DEBATE TOLERATION

The issue of religious toleration was widely debated throughout the age of Enlightenment. Many rulers feared that their domains would be overcome by religious turmoil and potential political unrest if their subjects could pursue religious freedom. The issue divided the Empress Maria Theresa and her son Joseph II who since 1765 had been co-rulers of the Austrian Empire. In 1777 they exchanged important letters setting forth their sharply differing views of the subject.

Joseph believed some religious toleration should be introduced into the Habsburg realms. Maria Theresa refused to consider toleration. The toleration of Protestants that is in dispute related only to Lutherans and Calvinists. Maria Theresa died in 1780; the next year Joseph issued an edict of toleration.

QUESTIONS

1. How does Joseph define toleration, and why does Maria Theresa believe it is the same as religious indifference?

2. Why does Maria Theresa fear that toleration will bring about political as well as religious turmoil?

3. Why does Maria Theresa think that Joseph's belief in toleration has come from Joseph's acquaintance with wicked books?

I. JOSEPH TO MARIA THERESA, JULY 20, 1777

It is only the word "toleration" which has caused the misunderstanding. You have taken it in quite a different meaning [from mine expressed in an earlier letter]. God preserve me from thinking it a matter of indifference whether the citizens turn Protestant or remain Catholic, still less, whether they cleave to, or at least observe, the cult which they have inherited from their fathers! I would give all I possess if all the Protestants of your states would go over to Catholicism.

The word "toleration," as I understand it, means only that I would employ any person, without distinction of religion, in purely temporal matters, allow them to own property, practice trades, be citizens, if they were qualified and if this would be of advantage to the State and its industry. Those who, unfortunately, adhere to a false faith, are far further from being converted if they remain in their own country than if they migrate into another, in which they can hear and see the convincing truths of the Catholic faith. Similarly, the undisturbed practice of their religion makes them far better subjects and causes them to avoid irreligion, which is a far greater danger to our Catholics than if one lets them see others practice their religion unimpeded.

II. MARIA THERESA TO JOSEPH, LATE JULY 1777

Without a dominant religion? Toleration, indifference are precisely the true means of undermining everything, taking away every foundation; we others will then be the greatest losers. . . . He is no friend of humanity, as the popular phrase is, who allows everyone his own thoughts. I am speaking only in the political sense, not as a Christian, nothing is so necessary and salutary as religion. Will you allow everyone to fashion his own religion as he pleases? No fixed cult, no subordination to the Church—what will then become of us? The result will not be quiet and content-

An eighteenth-century scroll of the biblical Book of Esther. According to the story, Queen Esther, who was married to King Ahasuerus of Persia, was responsible for thwarting a plan to annihilate all Jews in the Persian Empire.

What challenges did European Jews face in the eighteenth century?

ment; its outcome will be the rule of the stronger and more unhappy times like those which we have already seen. A manifesto by you to this effect can produce the utmost distress and make you responsible for many thousands of souls. And what are my own sufferings, when I see you entangled in opinions so erroneous? What is at stake is not only the welfare of the State but your own salvation. . . . Turning your eyes and ears everywhere, mingling your spirit of contradiction with the simultaneous desire to create something, you are ruining yourself and dragging the Monarchy down with you into the abyss. . . . I only wish to live so long as I can hope to descend to my ancestors with the consolation that my son will be as great, as religious as his forebearer, that he will return from his erroneous views, from those wicked books whose authors parade their cleverness at the expense of all that is most holy and most worthy of respect in the world, who want to introduce an imaginary freedom which can never exist and which degenerates into license and into complete revolution.

Source: As quoted in *The Habsburg and Hohenzollern Dynasties in the Seventeenth and Eighteenth Centuries* ed. by C. A. Macartney (New York: Walker, 1970), pp. 151–153. Reprinted by permission of Walker and Co.

For almost twenty years, Catherine lived in misery and frequent danger at the court. During that time, she befriended important nobles and read widely the books of the *philosophes*. A few months after his accession as tsar, Peter was deposed and murdered with Catherine's approval, if not her aid, and she was immediately proclaimed empress.

Catherine's familiarity with the Enlightenment and the general culture of Western Europe convinced her Russia was backward and that it needed major reforms to remain a great power. She understood that any significant reform must have a wide base of political and social support, especially since she had assumed the throne through a palace coup. In 1767, she summoned a legislative commission to advise her on revising the law and government of Russia. There were more than five hundred delegates, drawn from all sectors of Russian life.

Russian law, however, was not revised for more than half a century. In 1768, Catherine dismissed the commission before several of its key committees had reported. Yet the meeting had not been useless, for it had gathered a vast amount of information about the conditions of local administration and economic life throughout Russia. The inconclusive debates and the absence of programs from the delegates themselves suggested that most Russians saw no alternative to an autocratic monarchy, and Catherine had no intention of departing from absolutism.

Limited Administrative Reform   In 1767, Catherine formed a Legislative Commission and charged it with responsibility for proposing changes in Russian law and government. The empress provided her commissioners, who represented various sectors of Russian society, with a set of *Instructions* drawn from the political works of the *philosophes*. A year later, Catherine dismissed the commission before several of its key committees reported, but its members had not wasted their time. The commission had gathered vast amounts of information about local administration and economic life, and the upshot of discussions among the commissioners was that few Russians saw any alternative to autocratic monarchy. Their consensus provided support for Catherine's exercise of enlightened absolutism.

Economic Growth   Part of Catherine's program was to continue the economic development begun under Peter the Great. She attempted to suppress internal barriers to trade. Exports of grain, flax, furs, and naval stores grew dramatically. She also favored the expansion of the small Russian urban middle class that was so vital to trade.

Territorial Expansion   Catherine's limited administrative reforms and her policy of economic growth had a counterpart in the diplomatic sphere. The Russian drive for warm-water ports continued. (See Map 17–1.) This goal required warfare with the Turks. In 1769, as a result of a minor Russian incursion, the Ottoman Empire declared war on Russia. The Russians responded with a series of strikingly successful military moves, occupying the Ottoman provinces on the Danube River. The conflict dragged on until 1774, when the Treaty of Kuchuk-Kainardji gave Russia a direct outlet on the Black Sea, free navigation rights in its waters, and free access through the Bosporus. Crimea became an independent state, which Catherine painlessly annexed in 1783.

THE PARTITION OF POLAND

The Russian military successes increased Catherine's domestic political support, but they made the other states of eastern Europe uneasy. These anxieties were overcome by an extraordinary division of Polish territory known as the First Partition of Poland.

The Russian victories along the Danube River were most unwelcome to Austria, which also harbored ambitions of territorial expansion in that direction. At the same time, the Ottoman Empire was pressing Prussia for aid against Russia. Frederick the Great made a proposal to Russia and Austria that would give each something it wanted, prevent conflict among the powers, and save appearances. After long, complicated secret negotiations, Russia agreed to abandon the conquered Danubian provinces. In compensation, it received a large portion of Polish territory with almost 2 million inhabitants. As a reward for remaining neutral, Prussia annexed most of the territory between East Prussia and Prussia proper. This land allowed Frederick to unite two previously separate sections of his realm. Finally, Austria took Galicia in southern

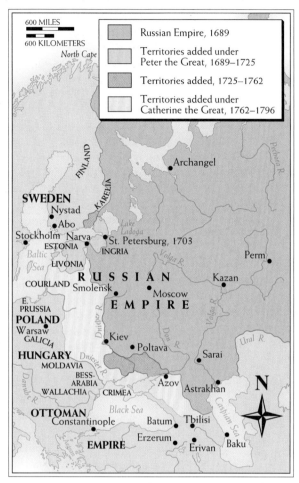

MAP EXPLORATION

To explore this interactive map, go to www.myhistorylab.com

MAP 17–1 **Expansion of Russia, 1689–1796** The overriding territorial aim of the two most powerful Russian monarchs of the eighteenth century, Peter the Great (in the first quarter of the century) and Catherine the Great (in the last half of the century), was to secure navigable outlets to the sea in both the north and the south for Russia's vast empire, hence Peter's push to the Baltic Sea and Catherine's to the Black Sea. Russia also expanded into Central Asia and Siberia during this time period.

Which empire came into direct conflict with Russian expansion?

Poland, with its important salt mines, and other Polish territory with more than 2.5 million inhabitants.

The partition of Poland clearly demonstrated that any nation without a strong monarchy, bureaucracy, and army could no longer compete within the European state system. It also demonstrated that the major powers in eastern Europe were prepared to settle their own rivalries at the expense of such a weak state. If Polish territory had not been available to ease tensions, international rivalries might have led to warfare among Russia, Austria, and Prussia.

THE END OF THE EIGHTEENTH CENTURY IN CENTRAL AND EASTERN EUROPE

During the last two decades of the eighteenth century, all three regimes based on enlightened absolutism became more conservative and politically repressive. In Prussia and Austria, the innovations of the rulers stirred resistance among the nobility. In Russia, fear of peasant unrest was the chief factor.

By the close of the century, fear of, and hostility to, change permeated the ruling classes of central and eastern Europe. This reaction had begun before 1789, but the events in France bolstered and sustained it for almost half a century. Paradoxically, nowhere did the humanity and liberalism of the Enlightenment encounter greater rejection than in those states that had been governed by "enlightened" rulers.

SUMMARY

WHAT WAS the intellectual and social background of the Enlightenment?

Formative Influences on the Enlightenment The ideas of the Enlightenment were based on the Newtonian worldview, Locke's psychology, Britain's wealth and stability, French reform, and the emerging print culture in Europe. The print culture facilitated increasing secularism, made writing an economically viable profession, and allowed the emergence of collective public opinion. Literary culture was generally divided between high and low. *page 416*

WHO WERE the *philosophes?*

The *Philosophes* The writers and critics of the eighteenth century who believed religion, politics, society, and the economy could be reformed to better support human liberty—the *philosophes*—included Montesquieu, Diderot, Rousseau, Hume, and Kant. Voltaire was the most influential, and his satire *Candide* reflects the *philosophes'* concerns and general attitudes. They were not an organized group, and they did not agree on all issues, but they all sought to use reason and common sense to improve institutions and social practices. The commercial and professional classes read and discussed the *philosophes'* works. *page 419*

HOW DID the *philosophes* challenge traditional religious ideas and institutions?

The Enlightenment and Religion Many eighteenth-century *philosophes* were hostile to the church and religious institutions in general. They did not, however, in general oppose religion itself. Deism was a movement that understood religion as something natural and rational, with God as the "divine watchmaker" who had created the universe, set it in motion according to certain laws, and then left it alone. Deists believed the existence of God could be proved empirically, and they believed in life after death, when virtue would be rewarded and sin punished. *Philosophes* valued religious toleration, although they did not always practice it. Jewish thinkers—particularly Spinoza and Mendelsohn—both contributed to, and responded to, the ideas of the Enlightenment. Enlightenment thinkers had less direct contact with Islam, and most sources of information about Islam available in the West were hostile. *page 420*

HOW DID the *philosophes* apply Enlightenment ideas to social and economic problems?

The Enlightenment and Society In an effort to secularize learning, *philosophes* compiled the *Encyclopedia*, a compendium of the views of most of France's leading *philosophes* on subjects ranging from religion to canal building. It helped spread Enlightenment ideas throughout Europe. The *philosophes* wanted to apply their ideas because they believed that human relationships obeyed rational laws through empirical examination and reason, that social laws could be learned, and that society could be improved. They criticized mercantilism and hoped to reform prisons and legal punishments. Many French economic reformers were physiocrats, who believed government's primary role was to provide only the protections necessary to allow owners to use their property to best advantage. Adam Smith's 1776 *Inquiry into the Nature and Causes of the Wealth of Nations* is described as the founding document for laissez-faire economic policy. One unsophisticated concept embedded in his work, the "four-stage theory" of social development, would have long-term consequences in relationships between the West and other cultures. *page 422*

HOW DID the *philosophes* apply Enlightenment ideas to political issues?

Political Thought of the *Philosophes* The French *philosophes* were the most discontented of a discontented lot. France's problems gave the *philosophes* more to criticize there than elsewhere in Europe at the time. The French *philosophes* proposed a wide array of reforms. Montesquieu and Rousseau both had a substantial influence on future political developments, and they represent two very different perspectives. Montesquieu believed that only empirical study could determine the best government for a given country. He advocated the division of political power. Rousseau was a radical, who raised the fundamental question of what constitutes the good life. He believed society was more important than the individual, because only within a properly functioning society could an individual live a moral life. A few thinkers criticized European treatment of and attitudes toward native peoples living in European empires, especially in the Americas, but such views would not gain significant public resonance until the end of the nineteenth century. *page 424*

WHAT ROLE did women play in the Enlightenment?

Women in the Thought and Practice of the Enlightenment The salons of French women were instrumental in spreading the ideas of the *philosophes*, but most of the *philosophes* were at best weak advocates of reforms that would help women. Some *philosophes* advocated improvements in education for women. But many *philosophes*—even the otherwise radical Rousseau!—had very traditional ideas about gender roles, and endorsed the double standard that frowned on female sexual expression. The beliefs that women were physiologically inferior to men and women's activities and aspirations should be limited to the domestic sphere were widely endorsed by *philosophes*. Late in the eighteenth century, Mary Wollstonecraft's *A Vindication of the Rights of Woman* placed women's rights within the Enlightenment agenda. *page 427*

HOW DID rococo and neoclassicism styles reflect and contribute to the prevailing trends of the age?

Rococo and neoclassical Styles in Eighteenth-Century Art In the early eighteenth century, the rococo style of art and architecture flourished in the private estates of monarchs and aristocrats and also in public buildings, both secular and religious. Rococo expressed frivolity, sensuality, and ornamentation that, by representing political and social elites of the Old Regime, eventually helped to increase popular hostility toward the decadence and corruption among the privileged strata of society. In the second half of the century, rococo gave way to neoclassicism, which embodied a didactic and disciplined attitude that hearkened back to the Renaissance and antiquity. Neoclassical works were concerned with public life and moral questions about civic virtue and self-sacrifice. Its works of art and architecture became identified with Enlightenment thought and criticism of the Old Regime and eventually with the French Revolution. *page 428*

WHAT WAS enlightened absolutism?

Enlightened Absolutism Many *philosophes* were fundamentally monarchists, although they believed monarchies should be reformed. In the last third of the eighteenth century, enlightened absolutism emerged under Frederick II of Prussia, Joseph II of Austria, and Catherine II of Russia. Frederick the Great tried to improve Prussian agriculture and the economy, with limited success. He widened religious toleration, codified Prussian law, and described himself as "the first servant of the State." Joseph II of Austria was unsuccessful in many of his reform efforts, and his successor repealed many of them. Catherine the Great empowered the local nobility and had some success in growing Russia's economy. She expanded Russian territory through various means including the partition of Poland. Late in the eighteenth century, all three of these regimes became increasingly conservative and politically repressive. After the French Revolution, central and eastern Europe's ruling classes began to resist change and oppose Enlightenment values. *page 430*

REVIEW QUESTIONS

1. What were the major formative influences on the *philosophes*? Why did the *philosophes* consider organized religion their greatest enemy? What were the basic tenets of deism? What were the attitudes of the *philosophes* toward women?

2. How did the arguments of the mercantilists differ from the theories developed by Adam Smith in *The Wealth of Nations*? How did each side in this debate view the earth's resources?

3. What political views were held by Montesquieu and Rousseau? Was Rousseau a child of the Enlightenment, or was he its opponent? Which did Rousseau value more, the individual or society?

4. What were the main Enlightenment attitudes about women? What was the significance of Mary Wollstonecraft?

5. How did the eighteenth-century styles of rococo and neoclassicism reflect and contribute to the prevailing political and social trends of the age?

6. Were the enlightened monarchs true believers in the ideals of the *philosophes* or was their "enlightenment" merely a pose or veneer? Was their power really absolute?

KEY TERMS

deism (p. 420)
laissez-faire (p. 424)
neoclassicism (p. 429)

rococo (p. 428)
tabula rasa (p. 416)

For additional learning resources related to this chapter, please go to **www.myhistorylab.com**

PEARSON
myhistörylab

18

The French Revolution

On July 14, 1789, crowds stormed the Bastille, a prison in Paris. This event, whose only practical effect was to free a few prisoners, marked the first time the populace of Paris redirected the course of the revolution.

What made the Bastille a target of popular anger and resentment?

*I*n 1789, the long-festering conflict between the French monarchy and aristocracy turned into a revolution that overturned the political and social order of France. Amidst the turmoil, small-town lawyers, artisans, and others of low birth exercised more control over events than kings and nobles. Neither France nor Europe would ever be the same. ■

THE CRISIS OF THE FRENCH MONARCHY

HOW DID the financial weakness of the French monarchy lay the foundations of revolution in 1789?

Although the French Revolution would shatter many of the political, social, and ecclesiastical structures of Europe, its origins lay in a much more mundane problem. By the late 1780s, the French royal government could not command sufficient taxes to finance itself.

THE MONARCHY SEEKS NEW TAXES

The French monarchy emerged from the Seven Years' War (1756–1763) defeated, deeply in debt, and unable thereafter to put its finances on a sound basis. French support of the American revolt against Great Britain further deepened the financial difficulties of the government. Given the economic vitality of France, the debt was neither overly large nor disproportionate to the debts of other European powers. The problem lay with the inability of the royal government to tap the nation's wealth through taxes to service and repay the debt.

The debt was symptomatic of the failure of the late-eighteenth-century French monarchy to come to terms with the political power of aristocratic institutions and, in particular, the *parlements*.

For twenty-five years after the Seven Years' War, a standoff occurred between the monarchy and the aristocracy, as one royal minister after another attempted to devise new tax schemes that would tap the wealth of the nobility, only to be confronted by opposition from both the *Parlement* of Paris and provincial *parlements*.

In 1770, Louis XV (r. 1715–1774) appointed René Maupeou (1714–1792) as chancellor. The new minister was determined to break the *parlements* and increase taxes on the nobility. He abolished the *parlements* and exiled their members to different parts of the country. He then began an ambitious program to make the administration more efficient. What ultimately doomed Maupeou's policy was less the resistance of the nobility than the unexpected death from smallpox of Louis XV in 1774. His successor, Louis XVI (r. 1774–1792), in an attempt to regain what he conceived to be popular support, dismissed Maupeou, restored all the *parlements*, and confirmed their old powers.

Although the *parlements* spoke for aristocratic interests, they appear to have enjoyed public support. By the second half of the eighteenth century, many French nobles shared with the wealthy professional and commercial classes similar economic interests and similar goals for administrative reforms that would support economic growth. Moreover, throughout these initial and later disputes with the monarchy, the *parlements*, though completely dominated by the aristocracy, used the language of liberty and reform to defend their cause.

The monarchy was unable to rally public opinion to its side because it had lost much of its moral authority. The sexually scandalous life of Louis XV was known throughout France, and the memory of his behavior lingered long after his death. Marie Antoinette (1755–1793), the wife of Louis XVI, also rightly or wrongly, gained a reputation for sexual misconduct and personal

Well meaning, but weak and vacillating, Louis XVI (r. 1774–1792) stumbled from concession to concession until he finally lost all power to save his throne.

Joseph Siffred Duplessis (1725–1802), *Louis XVI*. Versailles, France. Photograph copyright Bridgeman—Giraudon/Art Resource, NY

In what sense was Louis XVI a weak king? Could a stronger one have prevented the revolution?

extravagance. Furthermore, Louis XVI and his family continued to live at Versailles, rarely leaving its grounds to mix with his subjects and with the aristocracy, who now, unlike in the days of Louis XIV, often dwelled in Paris or on their estates. Hence, the French monarch stood at a distinct popular disadvantage in his clashes first with the *parlements* and later with other groupings of the aristocracy.

NECKER'S REPORT

France's successful intervention on behalf of the American colonists against the British only worsened the financial problems of Louis XVI's government. Nonetheless, the new royal director-general of finances, Jacques Necker (1732–1804), a Swiss banker, produced a public report in 1781 that suggested the situation was not as bad as had been feared. Necker's report also revealed that a large portion of royal expenditures went to pensions for aristocrats and other royal court favorites. This revelation angered court aristocratic circles, and Necker soon left office. His financial sleight of hand, nonetheless, made it more difficult for government officials to claim a real need to raise new taxes.

CALONNE'S REFORM PLAN AND THE ASSEMBLY OF NOTABLES

The monarchy hobbled along until 1786. By this time, Charles Alexandre de Calonne (1734–1802) was the minister of finance. Calonne proposed to encourage internal trade, to lower some taxes, such as the *gabelle* on salt, and to transform the *corvée*, peasants' labor services on public works, into money payments. He also sought to remove internal barriers to trade and reduce government regulation of the grain trade. More importantly, Calonne wanted to introduce a new land tax that all landowners would have to pay regardless of their social status. Calonne also intended to establish new local assemblies made up of landowners to approve land taxes; in these assemblies the voting power would have depended on the amount of land a person owned rather than on his social status. All these proposals would have undermined both the political and the social power of the French aristocracy.

Calonne needed public support for such bold new undertakings. In February 1787, he met with an Assembly of Notables, nominated by the royal ministry from the upper ranks of the aristocracy and the church, to seek support for his plan. The Assembly adamantly refused to give it and called for the reappointment of Necker, who they believed had left the country in sound fiscal condition. In addition, they claimed that only the Estates General of France, a medieval institution that had not met since 1614, could consent to new taxes. The notables believed that calling the Estates General, which had been traditionally organized to allow aristocratic and church dominance, would actually allow the nobility to have a direct role in governing the country alongside the monarchy.

DEADLOCK AND THE CALLING OF THE ESTATES GENERAL

Again, Louis XVI backed off. He replaced Calonne with Étienne Charles Loménie de Brienne (1727–1794), archbishop of Toulouse and the chief opponent of Calonne at the Assembly of Notables. Once in office, Brienne found, to his astonishment, that the financial situation was as bad as his predecessor had asserted. Brienne himself now sought to reform the land tax but received no more cooperation from the aristocracy than had his predecessors.

This late-eighteenth-century cartoon satirizes the French social structure. It shows a poor man in chains, who represents the vast majority of the population, supporting an aristocrat, a bishop, and a noble of the robe. The aristocrat is claiming feudal rights, the bishop holds papers associating the church with religious persecution and clerical privileges, and the noble of the robe holds a document listing the rights of the noble-dominated *parlements*.

CORBIS/Bettmann

What does this cartoon suggest about the relationship between the crown, the clergy, and the aristocracy in eighteenth-century France?

At the same time, local aristocratic *parlements* and estates in the provinces were making their own demands. They wanted to restore the privileges they had enjoyed during the early seventeenth century, before Richelieu and Louis XIV had crushed their independence. Furthermore, bringing the financial crisis to a new point of urgency, bankers refused in the summer of 1788 to extend necessary short-term credit to the government. Consequently, in July 1788, the king, through Brienne, agreed to convoke the Estates General the next year. Brienne resigned, and Necker replaced him.

THE REVOLUTION OF 1789

HOW DID the calling of the Estates General lead to revolution?

THE ESTATES GENERAL BECOMES THE NATIONAL ASSEMBLY

The Estates General had been called because of the political deadlock between the French monarchy and the vested interests of aristocratic institutions and the church. Almost immediately after it was summoned, however, the three groups, or estates, represented within it clashed with each other. The First Estate was the clergy, the Second Estate the nobility, and the **Third Estate** was, theoretically, everyone else in the kingdom, although its representatives were drawn primarily from wealthy members of the commercial and professional middle classes. All the representatives in the Estates General were men. During the widespread public discussions preceding the meeting of the Estates General, representatives of the Third Estate made it clear they would not permit the monarchy and the aristocracy to decide the future of the nation.

Third Estate Members of the commercial and professional middle classes, or everyone but the clergy (the First Estate) and the nobility (the Second Estate).

Debate over Organization and Voting Before the Estates General gathered, a public debate over its proper organization drew the lines of basic disagreement. The aristocracy made two important attempts to limit the influence of the Third Estate. First, a reconvened Assembly of Notables demanded that each estate have an equal number of representatives. Second, in September 1788, the *Parlement* of Paris ruled that voting in the Estates General should be conducted by order rather than by head—that is, each estate, or order, in the Estates General, rather than each individual member, should have one vote. This procedure would in all likelihood have ensured the aristocratically dominated First and Second Estates could always outvote the Third by a vote of two estates to one estate.

In many respects the interests of the aristocracy and the most prosperous and well-educated members of the Third Estates had converged during the eighteenth century. Yet a fundamental social distance separated the members of the two orders. Many aristocrats were much richer than members of the Third Estate, and noblemen had all but monopolized the high command in the army and navy. The Third Estate had also experienced various forms of political and social discrimination from the nobility. The resistance of the nobility to voting by head confirmed the suspicions and resentments of the members of the Third Estate.

Doubling the Third In the face of widespread public uproar over the aristocratic effort to dominate composition and procedures of the Estates General, the royal council eventually decided that strengthening the Third Estate would best serve the interests of the monarchy and the cause of fiscal reform. In December 1788, the council announced the Third Estate would elect twice as many representatives as either the nobles or the clergy. This so-called doubling of the Third Estate meant it could easily dominate the Estates General if voting proceeded by head rather than by order. The method of voting had not yet been decided when the Estates General gathered at Versailles in May 1789.

The *Cahiers de Doléances*   When the representatives came to the royal palace, they brought with them *cahiers de doléances*, or lists of grievances, registered by the local electors, to be presented to the king. The overwhelming demand of the *cahiers* was for equality of rights among the king's subjects. Yet it is also clear that the *cahiers* that originated among the nobility were not radically different from those of the Third Estate. There was broad agreement that the French government needed major reform, that greater equality in taxation and other matters was desirable, and that many aristocratic privileges must be abandoned. But that conflict among the estates, rather than cooperation, was to be the case became clear almost from the moment the Estates General opened.

The National Assembly and the Tennis Court Oath   The complaints, demands, and hopes for reform expressed in the *cahiers* could not, however, be discussed until the questions of the organization and voting in the Estates General had been decided. For several weeks there was a standoff. Then, on June 1, the Third Estate invited the clergy and the nobles to join them in organizing a new legislative body. A few priests did so. On June 17, that body declared itself the National Assembly, and on June 19 by a narrow margin, the Second Estate voted to join the Assembly.

At this point, Louis XVI hoped to reassert a role in the proceedings. He intended to call a "Royal Session" of the Estates General for June 23 and closed the room where the National Assembly had been gathering. On June 20, finding themselves thus unexpectedly locked out of their usual meeting place, the National Assembly moved to a nearby indoor tennis court. There, its members took an oath to continue to sit until they had given France a constitution. Louis XVI ordered the National Assembly to desist, but many clergy and nobles joined the Assembly in defiance of the royal command.

Overview   The Estates General Becomes the National Assembly

DEBATE OVER ORGANIZATION AND VOTING	• Public debate over proper organization • Spokespeople denounced the claims of the aristocracy • Resistance of nobility confirmed suspicions of Third Estate members
DOUBLING THE THIRD	• Council announces Third Estate would elect more representatives • Doubling meant Third Estate could dominate the Estates General • Liberal nobles and clergy supported the Third Estate
THE *CAHIERS DE DOLÉANCES*	• Lists of grievances brought to the royal palace by representatives • Documents recorded government waste, indirect taxes, and corruption • Demand was for equality of rights among the king's subjects
THE THIRD ESTATE CREATES THE NATIONAL ASSEMBLY	• Third Estate refused to sit as a separate order as the king desired • For several weeks there was a standoff • Clergy and nobles joined Third Estate, becoming National Assembly
THE TENNIS COURT OATH	• National Assembly took oath to sit until they gave France a constitution • The king eventually stipulated and requested the Estates to join them • Henceforth, monarchy could govern only in cooperation with Assembly

On June 27, the king, now having completely lost control of the events around him, capitulated and formally requested the First and Second Estates to meet with the National Assembly, where voting would occur by head rather than by order. The National Assembly, which renamed itself the National Constituent Assembly because of its intention to write a new constitution, was composed of a majority of members drawn from all three orders, who shared liberal goals for the administrative, constitutional, and economic reform of the country. The revolution in France against government by privileged hereditary orders, however, rapidly extended beyond events occurring at Versailles.

FALL OF THE BASTILLE

Two new forces soon intruded on the scene. First, Louis XVI again attempted to regain the political initiative by mustering royal troops near Versailles and Paris. On the advice of Queen Marie Antoinette, his brothers, and the most conservative aristocrats at court, he seemed to be contemplating the use of force against the National Constituent Assembly. On July 11, without consulting Assembly leaders, Louis abruptly dismissed Necker, his minister of finance. Louis's gathering troops and dismissal of Necker marked the beginning of a steady, but consistently poorly executed, royal attempt to undermine the Assembly and halt the revolution.

The second new factor to impose itself on the events at Versailles was the populace of Paris, which numbered more than 600,000 people. Those Parisians who had elected representatives to the Third Estate had continued to meet after the elections. By June they were organizing a citizen militia and collecting arms to protect the Assembly and the revolution it had begun.

On July 14, large crowds of Parisians, most of them small shopkeepers, tradespeople, artisans, and wage earners, marched to the Bastille to get weapons for the militia. Through miscalculations and ineptitude by the governor of the fortress, the troops in the Bastille fired into the crowd, killing ninety-eight people and wounding many others. Thereafter, the crowd stormed the fortress.

On July 15, the militia of Paris, by then called the National Guard, offered its command to a young liberal aristocrat, the Marquis de Lafayette (1757–1834). This hero of the American Revolution gave the guard a new insignia: the red and blue stripes from the colors of the coat of arms of Paris, separated by the white stripe of the royal flag. The emblem became the revolutionary *cockade* (badge) and eventually the tricolor flag of revolutionary France.

The attack on the Bastille marked the first of many crucial *journées*, days on which the populace of Paris redirected the course of the revolution. The fall of the fortress signaled that the National Constituent Assembly alone would not decide the political future of the nation. As the news of the taking of the Bastille spread, similar disturbances took place in provincial cities. A few days later, Louis XVI again bowed to the force of events and personally visited Paris, where he wore the revolutionary *cockade* and recognized the organized electors as the legitimate government of the city and the legitimacy of the National Guard.

THE "GREAT FEAR" AND THE NIGHT OF AUGUST 4

Simultaneous with the popular urban disturbances, a movement known as the "Great Fear" swept across much of the French countryside. Rumors that royal troops would be sent into the rural districts intensified the peasant disturbances that had begun during the spring. On the night of August 4, 1789, aristocrats in the National Constituent Assembly attempted to halt the spreading disorder in the countryside. By prearrangement, several liberal nobles and clerics rose in the Assembly and renounced their feudal rights, dues, and tithes. After the night of August 4, all French citizens were subject to the same and equal laws. This dramatic session of the Assembly effectively abolished the major social institutions of the Old Regime and created an unforeseen situation that required a vast legal and social reconstruction of the nation.

Both the attack on the Bastille and the Great Fear displayed characteristics of the urban and rural riots that had occurred often in eighteenth-century France. A deep economic downturn had struck France in 1787 and continued into 1788. The harvests for both years had been poor, and the food prices in 1789 were higher than at any time since 1703. Wages had not kept up with the rise in prices. Throughout the winter of 1788–1789, an unusually cold one, many people suffered from hunger. Wage and food riots had erupted in several cities. These economic problems fanned the fires of revolution.

THE DECLARATION OF THE RIGHTS OF MAN AND CITIZEN

On August 27, 1789, the Assembly issued the Declaration of the Rights of Man and Citizen. This declaration drew on the political language of the Enlightenment and the Declaration of Rights that the state of Virginia had adopted in June 1776.

The French declaration proclaimed that all men were "born and remain free and equal in rights." Governments existed to protect those rights. All political sovereignty resided in the nation and its representatives. All citizens were to be equal before the law and were to be "equally admissible to all public dignities, offices, and employments, according to their capacity, and with no other distinction than that of their virtues and talents." There were to be due process of law and presumption of innocence until proof of guilt. Freedom of religion was affirmed. Taxation was to be apportioned equally according to the capacity to pay. Property constituted "an inviolable and sacred right."

It was not accidental that the Declaration of the Rights of Man and Citizen specifically applied to men and not to women. As discussed in Chapter 17, much of the political language of the Enlightenment, and especially that associated with Rousseau, separated men and women into distinct gender spheres. According to this view, which influenced legislation during the revolution, men were suited for citizenship, women for motherhood and the domestic life. Nonetheless, in the charged atmosphere of the summer of 1789, many politically active and informed Frenchwomen hoped the guarantees of the declaration would be extended to them. Those hopes would be disappointed during the years of the revolution and for many decades thereafter.

Nonetheless, over the succeeding two centuries the universalist language of the Declaration of the Rights of Man and Citizen would provide an intellectual framework for bringing into the realm of active civic life many groups that were excluded in the late eighteenth century. (See "Compare & Connect: The Declaration of the Rights of Man and Citizen Opens the Door for Disadvantaged Groups to Demand Equal Civic Rights," pages 450–451.)

THE PARISIAN WOMEN'S MARCH ON VERSAILLES

Louis XVI stalled before ratifying both the Declaration of the Rights of Man and Citizen and the aristocratic renunciation of feudalism. His hesitations fueled suspicions that he might again try to resort to force. Moreover, bread remained scarce and expensive. On October 5, some 7,000 Parisian women armed with pikes, guns, swords, and knives marched to Versailles demanding more bread. Deeply suspicious of the monarch and believing that he must be kept under the watchful eye of the people, the Parisians

The July Column, which stands in the former location of the Bastille. The "Spirit of Liberty" is on top of the column.

James McConnachie © Rough Guides

The women of Paris marched to Versailles on October 5, 1789. The following day the royal family was forced to return to Paris with them. Henceforth, the French government would function under the constant threat of mob violence.

Anonymous, eighteenth century, *To Versailles, to Versailles.* The women of Paris going to Versailles, 7 October, 1789. French. Musée de la Ville de Paris, Musée Carnavalet, Paris, France. Photograph copyright Bridgeman—Giraudon/Art Resource, NY

What role did women play in Parisian politics during the revolution?

à Versaille à Versaille du 5 Octobre 1789.

demanded that Louis and his family return to Paris with them. The monarch had no real choice. On October 6, 1789, his carriage followed the crowd into the city, where he and his family settled in the old palace of the Tuileries in the heart of Paris.

The National Constituent Assembly also soon moved to Paris. Thereafter, both Paris and France remained relatively stable and peaceful until the summer of 1792. A decline in the price of bread in late 1789 helped to calm the atmosphere.

HOW DID the National Constituent Assembly reorganize France?

THE RECONSTRUCTION OF FRANCE

In Paris, the National Constituent Assembly set about reorganizing France. In government, it pursued a policy of constitutional monarchy; in administration, rationalism; in economics, unregulated freedom; and in religion, anticlericalism. Throughout its proceedings and following the principles of the Declaration of the Rights of Man and Citizen, the Assembly was determined to protect property in all its forms.

QUICK REVIEW

National Constituent Assembly Policies

◆ Determined to protect private property

◆ Forbid formation of workers' organizations

◆ Confiscated and sold church lands

POLITICAL REORGANIZATION

In the Constitution of 1791, the National Constituent Assembly established a constitutional monarchy. The major political authority of the nation would be a unicameral Legislative Assembly, in which all laws would originate. The monarch was allowed a suspensive veto that could delay, but not halt, legislation. The Assembly also had the power to make war and peace.

Active and Passive Citizens The constitution provided for an elaborate system of indirect elections to thwart direct popular pressure on the government. The citizens of France were divided into active and passive categories. Only active citizens—that is, men paying annual taxes equal to three days of local labor wages—could vote. They chose electors, who then, in turn, voted for the members of the legislature. Further property qualifications were required to serve as an elector or member of the legislature. Only about 50,000 citizens of a population of about 25 million could qualify as electors or members of the Legislative Assembly. Women could neither vote nor hold office. These constitutional arrangements effectively transferred political power from aristocratic wealth to all forms of propertied wealth in the nation.

Olympe de Gouges's Declaration of the Rights of Woman   The laws that excluded women from voting and holding office did not pass unnoticed. In 1791,
Olympe de Gouges (d. 1793), a butcher's daughter from Montauban in northwest
France who became a major revolutionary radical in Paris, composed a Declaration
of the Rights of Woman, which she ironically addressed to Queen Marie Antoinette.
Much of the document reprinted the Declaration of the Rights of Man and Citizen,
adding the word *woman* to the various original clauses. That strategy demanded that
women be regarded as citizens and not merely as daughters, sisters, wives, and mothers of citizens. Olympe de Gouges further outlined rights that would permit women
to own property and require men to recognize the paternity of their children. She
called for equality of the sexes in marriage and improved education for women. Her
declaration illustrated how the simple listing of rights in the Declaration of the
Rights of Man and Citizen created a structure of universal civic expectations even
for those it did not cover. (See "Compare & Connect: The Declaration of the Rights
of Man and Citizen Opens the Door for Disadvantaged Groups to Demand Equal
Civic Rights," pages 450–451.)

Departments Replace Provinces   In reconstructing the local and judicial administration, the National Constituent Assembly applied the rational spirit of the Enlightenment. It abolished the ancient French provinces, such as Burgundy and Brittany, and
established in their place eighty-three administrative units called departments, or
départements, of generally equal size named after rivers, mountains, and other geographical features. (See Map 18–1, page 452.)

   All the ancient judicial courts, including the seigneurial courts and the
parlements, were also abolished and replaced by uniform courts with elected judges and
prosecutors. Procedures were simplified, and the most degrading punishments, such as
branding, torture, and public flogging, were removed from the books.

ECONOMIC POLICY

In economic matters, the National Constituent Assembly suppressed the guilds and
liberated the grain trade. The Assembly established the metric system to provide the
nation with uniform weights and measures. (See "Encountering the Past: The Metric
System," page 453.)

Workers' Organizations Forbidden   The new policies of economic freedom and
uniformity disappointed both peasants and urban workers. In 1789, the Assembly
placed the burden of proof on the peasants to rid themselves of the residual feudal dues
for which compensation was to be paid. On June 14, 1791, the Assembly crushed the
attempts of urban workers to protect their wages by enacting the Chapelier Law, which
forbade workers' associations. Peasants and workers were henceforth to be left to the
freedom and mercy of the marketplace.

Confiscation of Church Lands   While these various reforms were being put into effect, the financial crisis that had occasioned the calling of the Estates General persisted. The continuing financial problem led the Assembly to take what may well have
been, for the future of French life and society, its most decisive action. The Assembly
decided to finance the debt by confiscating and then selling the land and property of
the Roman Catholic Church in France. The results were further inflation, religious
schism, and civil war. In effect, the National Constituent Assembly had opened a new
chapter in the relations of church and state in Europe.

THE DECLARATION OF THE RIGHTS OF MAN AND CITIZEN OPENS THE DOOR FOR DISADVANTAGED GROUPS TO DEMAND EQUAL CIVIC RIGHTS

The National Assembly passed the Declaration of the Rights of Man and Citizen on August 26, 1789. The principles of the declaration were very broad and in theory could be extended beyond the domestic male French citizens to whom it applied. Within months various civically disadvantaged groups stepped forward to demand inclusion within the newly proclaimed realm of civic rights. These included free persons of color from French Caribbean colony of St. Domingue and French women. It should be noted that during the same period French Jews also asked to have the principles of religious toleration proclaimed in the Declaration of the Rights of Man and Citizen extended to themselves.

QUESTIONS

1. How does Raymond portray himself as free but still clearly victimized by the Assembly in St. Domingue, composed only of white members?

2. How does Raymond invoke the principles of the Declaration of the Rights of Man and Citizen to apply pressure on the French National Assembly?

3. What are the specific parallels that de Gouges drew between the rights of man and the rights of woman?

4. How does her declaration suggest civic responsibilities for women as well as rights?

5. On what grounds might the same people who championed the Declaration of the Rights of Man and Citizen in 1789 deny the extension of those rights to the various groups that soon demanded inclusion under the ideals of the declaration?

I. A FREE PERSON OF COLOR FROM ST. DOMINGUE DEMANDS RECOGNITION OF HIS STATUS

In the spring of 1791, Julian Raymond, a free person of color from the French Caribbean colony of St. Domingue (Haiti), petitioned the French National Assembly to recognize persons such as himself as free citizens. The National Assembly did so in May 1791 but later rescinded the decree. Only in March, 1792 did the Assembly firmly recognize the civic equality of such persons. The background for the request and for the confusion of the French National Assembly over the matter was the eruption of the slave revolution in Haiti, which is discussed in Chapter 20.

Remaining to this day under the oppression of the white colonists, we dare hope that we do not ask the National Assembly in vain for the rights, which it has declared, belong to every man.

In our just protests, if the troubles, the calumnies that you have witnessed until today under the legislation of white colonists, and finally, if the truths which we had the honor of presenting yesterday to the bar of the Assembly do not overcome the unjust pretensions of the while colonial legislators who want to [proceed] without our participation, we beg the Assembly not to jeopardize the little remaining liberty we have, that of being able to abandon the ground soaked with the blood of our brothers and of permitting us to flee the sharp knife of the laws they will prepare against us.

If the Assembly has decided to pass a law which lets our fate depend on twenty-nine whites [in the colonial Assembly], our decided enemies, we demand to add an amendment to the decree which would be rendered in this situation, that free men of color can emigrate with their fortunes so that they can be neither disturbed nor hindered by the whites.

Mr. President, this is the last recourse which remains for us to escape the vengeance of the white colonists who menace us for not having given up our claims to the rights which the National Assembly has declared belong to every man.

Source: As quoted in Laura Mason and Tracey Rizzo, *The French Revolution: A Document Collection* (Boston: Houghton Mifflin Company, 1999), p. 109.

II. OLYMPE DE GOUGES ISSUES A DECLARATION OF THE RIGHTS OF WOMAN

In September 1791, Olympe de Gouges published a Declaration of the Rights of Woman that paralleled in many respects the Declaration of the Rights of Man and Citizen proclaimed two years earlier. A self-educated woman and butcher's daughter, she had written widely on a number of reform topics. Radical as she was, she remained loyal to the monarchy and was eventually executed by the revolutionary government in 1793.

Mothers, daughters, sisters [and] representatives of the nation demand to be constituted into a national assembly. . . . Consequently, the sex that is as superior in beauty as it is in courage during the sufferings of maternity recognizes and declares in the presence and under the auspices of the Supreme Being, the following Rights of Woman and of Female Citizens.

ARTICLE I

Woman is born free and lives equal to man in her rights. Social distinctions can be based only on the common utility.

ARTICLE II

The purpose of any political association is the conservation of the natural and imprescriptible rights of woman and man; these rights are liberty property, security, and especially resistance to oppression. . . .

ARTICLE IV

Liberty and justice consist of restoring all that belongs to others; thus, the only limits on the exercise of the natural rights of woman are perpetual male tyranny; these limits are to be reformed by the laws of nature and reason. . . .

ARTICLE VI

The law must be the expression of the general will; all female and male citizens must contribute either personally or through their representatives to its formation; it must be the same for all: male and female citizens, being equal in the eyes of the law, must be equally admitted to all honors, positions, and public employment according to their capacity and without other distinctions besides those of their virtues and talents. . . .

ARTICLE X

No one is to be disquieted for his very basic opinions; woman has the right to mount the scaffold; she must equally have the right to mount the rostrum, provided that her demonstrations do not disturb the legally established public order. . . .

ARTICLE XIII

For the support of the public force and the expenses of administration, the contributions of woman and man are equal; she shares all the duties and all the painful tasks; therefore, she must have the same share in the distribution of positions, employment, offices, honors, and jobs. . . .

ARTICLE XVII

Property belongs to both sexes whether united or separate; for each it is an inviolable and sacred right; no one can be deprived of it, since it is the true patrimony of nature, unless the legally determined public need obviously dictates it, and then only with a just and prior indemnity.

POSTSCRIPT

Woman, wake up; the tocsin of reason is being heard throughout the whole universe; discover your rights.

Source: As quoted in Darline Gay Levy, Harriet Branson Applewhite, and Mary Durham Johnson, eds., *Women in Revolutionary Paris, 1789–1795* (Urbana: University of Illinois Press, 1980), pp. 87–96.

This is an example of the French Revolution–era clothing worn by the *sans-culottes* or members of the poorer classes and their leaders.

Dorling Kindersley Media Library/Mark Hamilton © Dorling Kindersley

What political and social values are revealed by the clothes of the *sans-culottes*?

MAP EXPLORATION

Interactive map: To explore this map further, go to www.myhistorylab.com

MAP 18–1 French Provinces and the Republic In 1789, the National Constituent Assembly redrew the map of France. The ancient provinces (A) were replaced with a large number of new, smaller departments (B). This redrawing of the map was part of the Assembly's effort to impose greater administrative rationality in France. The borders of the republic (C) changed as the French army conquered new territory.

What do the revolutionary departments suggest about prevailing attitudes toward administrative governance after 1789?

ENCOUNTERING THE PAST

THE METRIC SYSTEM

France's revolutionaries hoped to realize the Enlightenment dream of dispelling superstition and obscurity by establishing the reign of science in all things. One of the revolution's lasting achievements was to simplify commercial transactions by eliminating the numerous local systems of weights and measures that had sprung up during the Middle Ages. There were political as well as economic motives for promoting the use of a common standard of measurement throughout the country. It symbolized France's existence as a single "indivisible" republic.

The metric (from *meter*) system, which the Assembly adopted (and is widely used today), was based on the work of astronomers. The revolutionaries wanted nature to establish the basic unit of measurement, and they chose the height of the arch of meridians (the highest point reached by the sun around the earth) in the latitude of Paris as their reference point. The meter was defined as one ten-millionth of one-quarter of that meridian. All other measurements of length were defined as decimal fractions or multiples of the meter. The gram, the standard for measuring weights, was decreed to be the weight of a cube of pure water measuring 0.01 meter on each side. Each measurement of weight was a decimal fraction or multiple of the gram.

Scientists quickly took to the new system, but the public resisted and clung to familiar weights and measures. Not until 1840 did political pressure, rationality, and convenience succeed in establishing use of the metric system throughout France. By the end of the nineteenth century, most of continental Europe had adopted it and it had been introduced to Latin America. It spread throughout Asia and Africa in the twentieth century. Today, English-speaking countries constitute the primary exceptions to its use. Scientists, engineers, and physicians employ it, but many people in the United States and Great Britain, despite encouragement, have declined to follow suit.

Jean-Baptiste Delambre (1749–1822) was one of the French astronomers whose measurements of the arch of meridians formed the basis for establishing the length of the meter.
Image Works/Mary Evans Picture Library Ltd.

How did Enlightenment ideas shape the French government's response to the fiscal crisis of the late eighteenth century?

HOW WAS the metric system consistent with the principles of the Enlightenment? Why has its use spread so widely?

The *Assignats* Having chosen to plunder the church, the Assembly authorized the issuance of *assignats*, or government bonds, in December 1789. Their value was guaranteed by the revenue to be generated from the sale of church property. Initially, a limit was set on the quantity of *assignats* to be issued. The bonds, however, proved so acceptable to the public that they began to circulate as currency. The Assembly decided to issue an ever-larger number of them to liquidate the national debt and to create a large body of new property owners with a direct stake in the revolution. Within a few months, however, the value of the *assignats* began to fall and inflation increased, putting new stress on the urban poor.

The *assignats* were government bonds that were backed by confiscated church lands. They circulated as money. When the government printed too many of them, inflation resulted and their value fell.

Bildarchiv Preussischer Kulturbesitz

How did fiscal problems undermine the Republican government in the early years of the revolution?

émigrés   French aristocrats and enemies of the revolution who fled to countries on France's borders and set up bases for counterrevolutionary activities.

THE CIVIL CONSTITUTION OF THE CLERGY

The confiscation of church lands required an ecclesiastical reconstruction. In July 1790, the National Constituent Assembly issued the Civil Constitution of the Clergy, which transformed the Roman Catholic Church in France into a branch of the secular state. The Assembly, which also dissolved all religious orders in France except those that cared for the sick or ran schools, consulted neither Pope Pius VI (r. 1775–1799) nor the French clergy about these sweeping changes.

The Civil Constitution of the Clergy was the major blunder of the National Constituent Assembly. The measure immediately created immense opposition within the French church, even from bishops who had long championed Gallican liberties over papal domination. In the face of this resistance, the Assembly unwisely ruled that all clergy must take an oath to support the Civil Constitution. Only seven bishops and a little less than half the lower clergy did so. In reprisal, the Assembly designated those clergy who had not taken the oath as "refractory" and removed them from their clerical functions.

Angry reactions were swift. Refractory priests celebrated Mass in defiance of the Assembly. In February 1791, Pope Pius condemned not only the Civil Constitution of the Clergy, but also the Declaration of the Rights of Man and Citizen. Within France itself, the pope's action created a crisis of conscience and political loyalty for all sincere Catholics. Religious devotion and revolutionary loyalty became incompatible for many people.

COUNTERREVOLUTIONARY ACTIVITY

The revolution had other enemies besides the pope and devout Catholics. As it became clear that the old political and social order was undergoing fundamental and probably permanent change, many aristocrats, eventually over 16,000, left France. Known as the *émigrés*, they settled in countries near the French border, where they sought to foment counterrevolution. Among the most important of their number was the king's younger brother, the count of Artois (1757–1836). In the summer of 1791, his agents and the queen persuaded Louis XVI to attempt to flee the country.

Flight to Varennes   On the night of June 20, 1791, Louis and his immediate family, disguised as servants, left Paris. They traveled as far as Varennes on their way to Metz in eastern France where a royalist military force was waiting for them. At Varennes the king was recognized, and his flight was halted. On June 24, a company of soldiers escorted the royal family back to Paris. It now seemed to many that the king was the chief counterrevolutionary in France and that the constitutional monarchy might not last long. Profound distrust dominated the political scene.

Declaration of Pillnitz   Two months later, on August 27, 1791, under pressure from the *émigrés*, Emperor Leopold II (r. 1790–1792) of Austria, who was the brother of Marie Antoinette, and King Frederick William II (r. 1786–1797) of Prussia issued the Declaration of Pillnitz. The two monarchs promised to intervene in France to protect the royal family and to preserve the monarchy if the other major European powers agreed. This provision rendered the declaration meaningless because, at the time, Great Britain would not have given its consent. The declaration was, however, taken seriously in France, where the revolutionaries saw the nation surrounded by aristocratic and monarchical foes seeking to undo all that had been accomplished since 1789.

THE END OF THE MONARCHY: A SECOND REVOLUTION

The National Constituent Assembly drew to a close in September 1791, having completed its task of reconstructing the government and the administration of France. The Assembly had passed a measure that forbade any of its own members to sit in the Legislative Assembly the new constitution established. That new Assembly filled with entirely new members met on October 1 and immediately had to confront the challenges flowing from the resistance to the Civil Constitution of the Clergy, the king's flight, and the Declaration of Pillnitz.

WHAT LED to the radicalization of the French Revolution?

EMERGENCE OF THE JACOBINS

Ever since the original gathering of the Estates General, deputies from the Third Estate had organized themselves into clubs composed of politically like-minded persons. The most famous and best organized of these clubs were the **Jacobins**. They had been the most advanced political group in the National Constituent Assembly and had pressed for a republic rather than a constitutional monarchy. They drew their political language from the most radical thought of the Enlightenment, most particularly Rousseau's emphasis on equality, popular sovereignty, and civic virtue.

Jacobins   The best organized of the political clubs, they embraced the most radical of the Enlightenment's political theories, and they wanted a republic, not a constitutional monarchy.

Factionalism plagued the Legislative Assembly throughout its short life (1791–1792). A group of Jacobins known as the *Girondists* assumed leadership of the Assembly. On April 20, 1792, the Girondists led the Legislative Assembly to declare war on Austria, by this time governed by Francis II (r. 1792–1835) and allied to Prussia. The Girondists believed the war would preserve the revolution from domestic enemies and bring the most advanced revolutionaries to power. Paradoxically, Louis XVI and other monarchists also favored the war. They thought the conflict would strengthen the executive power (the monarchy). The king also hoped that foreign armies might defeat French forces and restore the Old Regime. Both sides were playing a dangerously deluded political game. The war radicalized French politics and within months led to what is usually called the second revolution, which overthrew the constitutional monarchy and established a republic.

Initially, the war effort went poorly. In July 1792, the duke of Brunswick, commander of the Prussian forces, issued a manifesto threatening to destroy Paris if the French royal family were harmed. This statement stiffened support for the war and increased distrust of the king.

Late in July, under radical working-class pressure, the government of Paris passed from the elected council to a committee, or *commune*, of representatives from the sections (municipal wards) of the city. Thereafter the Paris commune became an independent political force casting itself in the role of the protector of the gains of the revolution against both internal and external enemies.

On August 10, 1792, a large crowd invaded the Tuileries palace and forced Louis XVI and Marie Antoinette to take refuge in the Legislative Assembly. The crowd fought with the royal Swiss guards. When Louis was finally able to call off the troops, several hundred of them and many Parisian citizens lay dead in the most extensive violence since the fall of the Bastille. Thereafter the royal family was imprisoned in comfortable quarters, but the king was allowed to perform none of his political functions.

THE CONVENTION AND THE ROLE OF THE *SANS-CULOTTES*

The September Massacres   Early in September, the Parisian crowd again made its will felt. During the first week of the month, in what are known as the **September Massacres**, the Paris Commune summarily executed or murdered about 1,200 people who

September Massacres   The execution ordered by the Paris Commune of approximately 1,200 aristocrats, priests, and common criminals who, because they were being held in city jails, were assumed to be counterrevolutionaries.

were in the city jails. Some of these people were aristocrats or priests, but most were simply common criminals. News of this event along with the massacre of the Swiss guards as well as the imprisonment of the royal family spread rapidly across Europe, rousing new hostility toward the revolutionary government.

The Paris Commune then compelled the Legislative Assembly to call for the election by universal male suffrage of still another new assembly to write a democratic constitution. That body, called the **Convention** after the American Constitutional Convention of 1787, met on September 21, 1792. The previous day, the French army filled with patriotic recruits willing to die for the revolution had halted the Prussian advance at the Battle of Valmy in eastern France. Victory on the battlefield had confirmed the victory of democratic forces at home. As its first act, the Convention declared France a republic—that is, a nation governed by an elected assembly without a monarch.

Convention The newly elected French body that met on September 21, 1792, whose first act was to declare France a republic—a nation governed by an elected assembly without a king.

Goals of the *Sans-culottes*

The second revolution had been the work of Jacobins more radical than the Girondists and of the people of Paris known as the *sans-culottes*. The *sans-culottes* were shopkeepers, artisans, wage earners, and, in a few cases, factory workers. The politics of the Old Regime had ignored them, and the policies of the National Constituent Assembly had left them victims of unregulated economic liberty. The government, however, required their labor and their lives if the war was to succeed. From the summer of 1792 until the summer of 1794, their attitudes, desires, and ideals were the primary factors in the internal development of the revolution.

sans-culottes Parisians (shopkeepers, artisans, wage earners, and factory workers who had been ignored by the Old Regime) who, along with radical Jacobins, began the second revolution in France.

The *sans-culottes* generally knew what they wanted. The Parisian tradespeople and artisans sought immediate relief from food shortages and rising prices through price controls. They believed all people have a right to subsistence, and they resented most forms of social inequality. This attitude made them intensely hostile to the aristocracy and the original leaders of the revolution of 1789 from the Third Estate, who, they believed, simply wanted to share political power, social prestige, and economic security with the aristocracy.

In politics they were antimonarchical, strongly republican, and suspicious even of representative government. They believed the people should make the decisions of government to an extent as great as possible. The Paris Commune organized the previous summer was their chief political vehicle and crowd action their chief instrument of action.

The Policies of the Jacobins

The goals of the *sans-culottes* were not wholly compatible with those of the Jacobins, republicans who sought representative government. Jacobin hatred of the aristocracy and hereditary privilege did not extend to a general suspicion of wealth. From the time of Louis XVI's flight to Varennes onward, however, the more extreme Jacobins began to cooperate with leaders of the Parisian *sans-culottes* and the Paris Commune to overthrow the monarchy. Once the Convention began to deliberate, these Jacobins, known as the *Mountain*, worked with the *sans-culottes* to carry the revolution forward and to win the war. This willingness to cooperate with the forces of the popular revolution separated the Mountain from the Girondists, who were also members of the Jacobin Club.

Execution of Louis XVI On January 21, 1793, the Convention executed Louis XVI.

18th century CE. "Execution of Louis XVI." Aquatint. French. Musée de la Ville de Paris, Musée Carnavalet, Paris, France. Copyright Bridgeman-Giraudon/Art Resource, NY

What events led to the radicalization of the revolution and the execution of Louis XVI?

Execution of Louis XVI

By the spring of 1793, several issues had brought the Mountain and its *sans-culottes* allies to dominate the Convention and the revolution. In December 1792, Louis XVI was put on trial as mere "Citizen Capet," the original medieval name of the royal family. An overwhelming majority convicted Louis of conspiring against the liberty of the people and the security of the state. Condemned to death by a smaller majority, he was beheaded on January 21, 1793.

The next month, the Convention declared war on Great Britain and Holland, and a month later on Spain. Soon thereafter, the Prussians renewed their offensive and drove the French out of Belgium. To make matters worse, General Dumouriez (1739–1823), the Girondist victor of Valmy, deserted to the enemy. Finally, in March 1793, a royalist revolt led by aristocratic officers and priests erupted in the Vendée in western France and roused much popular support. Thus, the revolution found itself at war with most of Europe and much of the French nation. The Girondists had led the country into the war but had been unable either to win it or to suppress the enemies of the revolution at home. The Mountain stood ready to take up the task.

EUROPE AT WAR WITH THE REVOLUTION

Initially, the rest of Europe had been ambivalent toward the revolutionary events in France. Those people who favored political reform regarded the revolution as wisely and rationally reorganizing a corrupt and inefficient government. The major foreign governments thought that the revolution meant France would cease to be an important factor in European affairs for years.

HOW DID Europe respond to the French Revolution?

EDMUND BURKE ATTACKS THE REVOLUTION

In 1790, however, the Irish-born writer and British statesman Edmund Burke (1729–1799) argued a different position in *Reflections on the Revolution in France*. Burke condemned the reconstruction of the French administration as the application of a blind rationalism that ignored the historical realities of political development and the concrete complexities of social relations. He also forecast further turmoil as people without political experience tried to govern France, predicted the possible deaths of Louis XVI and Marie Antoinette at the hands of the revolutionaries, and forecast that the revolution would end in military despotism. As the revolutionaries proceeded to attack the church, the monarchy, and finally the rest of Europe, Burke's ideas came to have many admirers. By the outbreak of the war with Austria in April 1792, the other European monarchies recognized, along with Burke, the danger of both the ideas and the aggression of revolutionary France. In response, one government after another turned to repressive domestic policies.

SUPPRESSION OF REFORM IN BRITAIN

In Great Britain, William Pitt the Younger (1759–1806), the prime minister, who had unsuccessfully supported moderate reform of Parliament during the 1780s, turned against both reform and popular movements. The government suppressed the London Corresponding Society, founded in 1792 as a working-class reform group. In Birmingham, the government sponsored mob action to drive Joseph Priestley (1733–1804), a famous chemist and a radical political thinker, out of the country. In early 1793, Pitt secured parliamentary approval for acts suspending *habeas corpus* and making the writing of certain ideas treasonable. With less success, Pitt also attempted to curb freedom of the press. All political groups who dared oppose the government faced being associated with sedition.

THE SECOND AND THIRD PARTITIONS OF POLAND, 1793, 1795

The final two partitions of Poland occurred as a direct result of fears by the eastern powers that the principles of the French Revolution were establishing themselves in Poland. After the first partition in 1772, Polish leaders had commenced reforms to provide for a stronger state. In 1791, a group of nobles known as the Polish Patriots actually issued a new constitution. Frederick William II of Prussia (r. 1786–1797) promised to defend the new Polish constitutional order because he believed that a stronger Poland was in Prussia's interest against the growing Russian power. Catherine the Great of Russia also understood that a reformed Polish state would diminish Russian influence in Poland and eastern Europe.

In April 1792, conservative Polish nobles who opposed the reforms invited Russia to restore the old order. In response to the Russian invasion, Frederick William II moved his troops from the west where they were confronting the French revolutionary army to his eastern frontier with Poland. However, rather than protecting Poland as he had promised, Frederick William reached an agreement with Catherine early in 1793 to carry out a second partition of Poland. The reformed constitution was abolished, and the new Polish government remained under the influence of Russia.

In the spring of 1794, Polish officers mutinied against efforts to unite their forces with the Russian army. As the rebellion expanded, the language and symbols of the French Revolution appeared in Polish cities. Before long, Prussia, Austria, and Russia sent troops into Poland. On November 4 in the single bloodiest day of combat in the decade, Russian troops killed well over 10,000 Poles outside Warsaw. Polish officers and troops who escaped Poland after the last partition later fought with the armies of the French Revolution and Napoleon against the forces of the partitioning powers.

THE REIGN OF TERROR

HOW DID war and ideology combine to create the Reign of Terror?

WAR WITH EUROPE

France's invasion and reorganization of the Austrian Netherlands roused the other European powers to hostile action, and heads of state were further alarmed, in November 1792, when the Convention announced it would aid all peoples everywhere who wanted to cast off the burdens of aristocracy and monarchy. The British, whose commerce was directly threatened, were on the point of declaring war on France when the Convention beat them to it (February 1793). By the time the Jacobins took charge of France's government in April 1793, France was at war with Austria, Prussia, Great Britain, Spain, Sardinia, and Holland.

This widening of the war in the winter and spring of 1792–1793 brought new, radical political actions within France as the revolutionary government mobilized itself and the nation for the conflict. Throughout France, there was the sense that a new kind of war had erupted. In this war the major issue was not protection of national borders as such, but rather the defense of the bold new republican political and social order that had emerged since 1789. The immediate need to protect the revolution from enemies, real or imagined, from across the spectrum of French political and social life was considered more important than the security of property or even of life. These actions to protect the revolution and silence dissent came to be known as the **Reign of Terror**.

THE REPUBLIC DEFENDED

To mobilize for war, the revolutionary government organized a collective executive in the form of powerful committees. These, in turn, sought to organize all French national life on a wartime footing. The result was an immense military effort dedicated both to protecting and promoting revolutionary ideals.

The Committee of Public Safety In April 1793, the Convention established a Committee of General Security and a Committee of Public Safety to carry out the executive duties of the government. The Committee of Public Safety eventually enjoyed almost dictatorial power. Its members saw their task as saving the revolution from mortal enemies at home and abroad.

Reign of Terror Extreme measures employed by the French government in an effort to protect the revolution.

The *Levée en Masse* The major problem for the Convention was to wage the war and at the same time to secure domestic support for the war effort. In early June 1793, the Parisian *sans-culottes* invaded the Convention and successfully demanded the expulsion of the Girondist members. That action further radicalized the Convention and gave the Mountain complete control. On August 23, Lazare Carnot (1753–1823), the member of the Committee of Public Safety in charge of the military, began a mobilization for victory by issuing a ***levée en masse***, a military requisition on the entire population, conscripting males into the army and directing economic production to military purposes.

Following the *levée en masse*, the Convention on September 29, 1793, established a ceiling on prices in accord with *sans-culotte* demands. During these same months, the armies of the revolution also successfully crushed many of the counterrevolutionary disturbances in the provinces. Never before had Europe seen a nation organized in this way, nor one defended by a citizen army, which, by late 1794, with over a million men, had become larger than any ever organized in European history.

Other events within France astounded Europeans even more. The Reign of Terror had begun. Those months of quasi-judicial executions and murders stretching from the autumn of 1793 to the midsummer of 1794 are probably the most famous or infamous period of the revolution. They can be understood only in the context of the war on one hand and the revolutionary expectations of the Convention and the *sans-culottes* on the other.

levée en masse Order for total military mobilization of both men and property.

THE "REPUBLIC OF VIRTUE" AND ROBESPIERRE'S JUSTIFICATION OF TERROR

The presence of armies closing in on the nation made it easy to dispense with legal due process. The people who sat in the Convention and those sitting on the Committee of Public Safety, however, did not see their actions simply in terms of expediency made necessary by war. They also believed they had created something new in world history, a "republic of virtue." In this republic, civic virtue largely understood in terms of Rousseau's *Social Contract*, the sacrifice of one's self and one's interest for the good of the republic, would replace selfish aristocratic and monarchical corruption. It was in the name of the public good that the Committee of Public Safety carried out the policies of the terror.

The person who embodied this republic of virtue defended by terror was Maximilien de Robespierre (1758–1794), who, by late 1793, had emerged as the dominant figure on the Committee of Public Safety. A shrewd and sensitive politician, Robespierre had opposed the war in 1792 because he feared it might aid the monarchy. He depended largely on the support of the *sans-culottes* of Paris, but he continued to dress as he had before the revolution in powdered wig and knee breeches. For him, the republic of virtue meant whole-hearted support of the republican government, the renunciation of selfish gains from political life, and the assault on foreign and domestic enemies of the revolution.

Maximilien Robespierre (1758–1794) emerged as the most powerful revolutionary figure in 1793 and 1794, dominating the Committee of Public Safety. He considered the Terror essential for the success of the revolution.

Musée des Beaux-Arts, Lille. Bridgeman—Giraudon/Art Resource, NY

What future did Robespierre imagine for France?

REPRESSION OF THE SOCIETY OF REVOLUTIONARY REPUBLICAN WOMEN

Revolutionary women established their own distinct institutions during these months. In May 1793, Pauline Léon and Claire Lacombe founded the Society of Revolutionary Republican Women. Its purpose was to fight the internal enemies of the revolution. Members of the society and other women filled the galleries of the Convention to hear the debates and cheer their favorite speakers. The society became increasingly radical, however. Its members sought stricter controls on the price of food and other commodities, worked to ferret out food hoarders, and brawled with working market women whom they thought to be insufficiently revolutionary. The women of the society also demanded the right to wear the revolutionary *cockade* that male citizens usually wore in their hats. By October 1793, the Jacobins in the Convention had begun to fear the turmoil the society was causing and banned all women's clubs and societies. The debates over these decrees show that the Jacobins believed the society opposed many of their economic policies, but the deputies used Rousseau's language of separate spheres for men and women to justify their exclusion of women from active political life.

There were other examples of repression of women in 1793. Olympe de Gouges, author of the Declaration of the Rights of Woman, opposed the Terror and accused Jacobins of corruption. She was guillotined in November 1793. The same year, women were formally excluded from serving in the French army and from the galleries of the Convention. The exclusion of women from public political life was part of the establishment of the Jacobin republic of virtue, because in such a republic men would be active citizens in the military and political sphere and women would be active only in the domestic sphere.

DE-CHRISTIANIZATION

The most dramatic step taken by the republic of virtue, and one that illustrates its imposition of political values to justify the Terror, was an the Convention's attempt to de-Christianize France. In November 1793, the Convention proclaimed a new calendar dating from the first day of the French Republic. There were twelve months of thirty days each, with names associated with the seasons and climate. Every tenth day, rather than every seventh, was a holiday. In November 1793, the Convention decreed the Cathedral of Notre Dame in Paris to be a "Temple of Reason."

The legislature then sent trusted members, known as deputies on mission, into the provinces to enforce de-Christianization by closing churches, persecuting clergy and believers (both Roman Catholic and Protestant), occasionally forcing priests to marry, and sometime simply by killing priests and nuns. Churches were desecrated, torn down, or used as barns or warehouses. This radical religious policy attacking both clergy and religious property roused enormous popular opposition and alienated parts of the French provinces from the revolutionary government in Paris.

REVOLUTIONARY TRIBUNALS

The Reign of Terror manifested itself in revolutionary tribunals that the Convention established during the summer of 1793. The mandate of these tribunals, the most prominent of which was in Paris, was to try the enemies of the republic, but the definition of who was an "enemy" shifted as the months passed. Those whom the tribunal condemned in Paris were beheaded on the guillotine, a recently invented instrument of efficient and supposedly humane execution. Other modes of execution, such as mass shootings and drowning, were used in the provinces.

The first victims of the Terror were Marie Antoinette, other members of the royal family, and aristocrats, who were executed in October 1793. Girondist politicians who had been prominent in the Legislative Assembly followed them. In early 1794, the Terror moved to the provinces, where the deputies on mission presided over the summary execution of thousands of people, most of whom were peasants, who had allegedly supported internal opposition to the revolution. One of the most infamous incidents occurred in Nantes on the west coast of France, where several hundred people, including many priests, were simply tied to rafts and drowned in the river Loire. The victims of the Terror were now coming from every social class, including the *sans-culottes.*

The Festival of the Supreme Being, which took place in June 1794, inaugurated Robespierre's new civic religion. Its climax occurred when a statue of Atheism was burned and another statue of Wisdom rose from the ashes.

Pierre-Antoine Demachy, *Festival of the Supreme Being at the Champ de Mars on June 8, 1794*. Musée de la Ville de Paris, Musée Carnavalet, Paris, France. Bridgeman—Giraudon/Art Resource, NY

Why did the French public fail to embrace the new revolutionary festivals and holidays?

THE END OF THE TERROR

Revolutionaries Turn Against Themselves In Paris during the late winter of 1794, Robespierre began to orchestrate the Terror against republican political figures of the left and right. On March 24, he secured the execution of certain extreme *sans-culottes* leaders known as the *enragés*. Robespierre then turned against other republicans in the Convention. Most prominent among them was Jacques Danton (1759–1794), who had provided heroic national leadership in the dark days of September 1792 and who had later served briefly on the Committee of Public Safety before Robespierre joined the group. Danton and others were accused of being insufficiently militant on the war, profiting monetarily from the revolution, and rejecting the link between politics and moral virtue. Danton was executed in April 1794. Robespierre thus exterminated the leadership of both groups that might have threatened his position.

Fall of Robespierre In May 1794, at the height of his power, Robespierre, considering the worship of "Reason" too abstract for most citizens, replaced it with the "Cult of the Supreme Being." This deistic cult reflected Rousseau's vision of a civic religion that would induce morality among citizens.

On July 26, Robespierre made an ill-tempered speech in the Convention, declaring that other leaders of the government were conspiring against him and the revolution. Similar accusations against unnamed persons had preceded his earlier attacks. No member of the Convention could now feel safe. On July 27—the Ninth of Thermidor on the revolutionary calendar—members of the Convention, by prearrangement, shouted him down when he rose to make another speech. That night Robespierre was arrested, and the next day he and approximately eighty of his supporters were executed.

THE THERMIDORIAN REACTION

The fall of Robespierre might simply have been one more shift in the turbulent politics of the revolution, but instead it proved to be a major turning point. The members of the Convention used the event to reassert their authority over the executive power of Committee of Public Safety. Within a short time, the Reign of Terror, which had claimed more than 25,000 victims, came to a close. It no longer seemed necessary since the war abroad was going well and the republican forces had crushed the provincial uprisings.

WHAT COURSE did the French Revolution take after 1794?

Thermidorian Reaction Tempering of revolutionary fervor that led to the establishment of a new constitutional regime.

This tempering of the revolution, called the **Thermidorian Reaction**, because of its association with the events of 9 Thermidore, consisted of the destruction of the machinery of terror and the establishment of a new constitutional regime. It resulted from a widespread feeling that the revolution had become too radical. The influence of generally wealthy middle-class and professional people soon replaced that of the *sans-culottes*.

In the weeks and months after Robespierre's execution, the Convention allowed the Girondists who had been in prison or hiding to return to their seats. A general amnesty freed political prisoners. Some, though by no means all, of the people responsible for the Terror were removed from public life. The Paris Commune was outlawed, and its leaders and deputies on mission were executed. The Paris Jacobin Club was closed, and Jacobin clubs in the provinces were forbidden to correspond with each other.

The executions of former terrorists marked the beginning of "the white terror." Throughout the country, people who had been involved in the Reign of Terror were attacked and often murdered. Jacobins were executed with little more due process than they had extended to their victims a few months earlier.

The Thermidorian Reaction also saw the repeal of legislation that had been passed in 1792 making divorce more equitable for women. As the passage of that measure suggests, the reaction did not extend women's rights or improve their education. The Thermidorians and their successors had seen enough attempts at political and social change. They sought to return family life to its status before the outbreak of the revolution. Political authorities and the church were determined to reestablish separate spheres for men and women and to reinforce traditional gender roles. As a result, Frenchwomen may have had less freedom after 1795 than before 1789.

THE FRENCH REVOLUTION

1789

May 5	The Estates General opens at Versailles
June 17	The National Assembly is declared
June 20	The Tennis Court Oath
July 14	Fall of the Bastille
August 4	Surrender of feudal rights
August 27	Declaration of the Rights of Man and Citizen
October 5	Parisian women march on Versailles

1790

July 14	Louis XVI accepts constitutional monarchy

1791

June 20	The royal family attempts to flee
October 1	Formation of the Legislative Assembly

1792

April 20	France declares war on Austria
September 2	The September Massacres
September 21	The Convention meets; monarchy is abolished

1793

January 21	Louis XVI is executed
February 1	France declares war on Great Britain
April	Formation of the Committee of Public Safety
June 22	Adoption of the Constitution of 1793
August 23	Levée en masse proclaimed
October 16	Marie Antoinette is executed
November 10	The Cult of Reason and the revolutionary calendar

1794

March 24	Execution of leaders of the *sans-culottes*
May 7	Cult of the Supreme Being proclaimed
June 10	The Law of 22 Prairial is adopted
July 27	Ninth of Thermidor; the fall of Robespierre

1795

August 22	Constitution of the Year III and the Directory

ESTABLISHMENT OF THE DIRECTORY

The Thermidorian Reaction led to still another new constitution. The Convention issued the Constitution of the Year III, which reflected the Thermidorian determination to reject *both* constitutional monarchy and democracy. In recognition of the danger of a legislature with only one chamber and unlimited authority, this new document provided for a legislature of two houses. The executive body was to be a five-person Directory, chosen from a list supplied by the legislature. Property

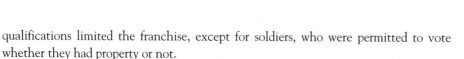

qualifications limited the franchise, except for soldiers, who were permitted to vote whether they had property or not.

Historically, the term *Thermidor* has come to be associated with political reaction. That association requires considerable qualification. By 1795, the political structure and society of the Old Regime in France based on rank and birth had given way permanently to a political system based on civic equality and social status based on property ownership. Representation was an established principle of politics. Henceforth, the question before France and eventually before all of Europe would be which new groups would be permitted representation. In the *levée en masse*, the French had demonstrated to Europe the power of the secular ideal of nationhood and of the willingness of citizen soldiers to embrace self-sacrifice.

The post-Thermidorian course of the French Revolution did not undo these stunning changes in the political and social contours of Europe. What triumphed in the Constitution of the Year III was the revolution of the holders of property. For this reason the French Revolution has often been considered a victory of the bourgeoisie, or middle class. The property that won the day, however, was not industrial wealth, but the wealth stemming from commerce, the professions, and land. The largest new propertied class to emerge from the revolutionary turmoil was the peasantry, who, as a result of the destruction of aristocratic privileges, now owned their own land.

REMOVAL OF THE *SANS-CULOTTES* FROM POLITICAL LIFE

The most decisively reactionary element in the Thermidorian Reaction and the new constitution was the removal of the *sans-culottes* from political life. With the war effort succeeding, the Convention severed its ties with the *sans-culottes*. True to their belief in an unregulated economy, the Thermidorians repealed the ceiling on prices. As a result, the winter of 1794–1795 brought the worst food shortages of the period. There were many food riots, which the Convention suppressed to prove that the era of the *sans-culottes journées* had come to a close. Royalist agents, who aimed to restore the monarchy, tried to take advantage of their discontent. On October 5, 1795—13 Vendémiaire—the sections of Paris led by the royalists rose up against the Convention. The government turned the artillery against the royalist rebels. A general named Napoleon Bonaparte (1769–1821) commanded the cannon, and with a "whiff of grapeshot," he dispersed the crowd.

By the Treaties of Basel in March and June 1795, the Convention concluded peace with Prussia and Spain. The legislators, however, feared a resurgence of both radical democrats and royalists in the upcoming elections. Consequently, the Convention ruled that at least two-thirds of the new legislature must have served in the Convention itself. The Two-Thirds Law, which sought to foster continuity but also clearly favored politicians already in office, quickly undermined public faith in the new constitutional order.

The suppression of the *sans-culottes*, the narrow franchise of the constitution, the Two-Thirds Law, and the Catholic royalist revival presented the Directory with challenges that it was never able to overcome. Because France remained at war with Austria and Great Britain, it needed a broader-based active loyalty than it was able to command. Instead, the Directory came to depend on the power of the army to govern France. All soldiers could vote. Moreover, within the army that the revolution had created and sustained were ambitious officers who were eager for power. As will be seen in the next chapter, the instability of the Directory, the growing role of the army, and the ambitions of its leaders held profound consequences not only for France but for the entire Western world.

SUMMARY

HOW DID the financial weakness of the French monarchy lay the foundations of revolution in 1789?

The Crisis of the French Monarchy
The cost of the Seven Years' War had caused a financial crisis for all Europe's monarchies. France's financial situation was exacerbated by the expenses incurred in joining the colonists' side in the American Revolutionary War. The government needed to raise new taxes; new taxes had to be approved by the nobility. France's noble class had been trying to reassert power ever since the end of Louis XIV's reign. The monarch's need for cash presented a perfect opportunity for the aristocrats to gain concessions from the king. Through various negotiations and standoffs, the aristocracy forced Louis XVI to reconvene the Estates General, which had not met since 1614. *page 442*

HOW DID the calling of the Estates General lead to revolution?

The Revolution of 1789 The 1789 calling of the Estates General and the events that followed have shaped the meanings of nation, state, and citizenship ever since. The royal council doubled the Third Estate, potentially strengthening the hand of the bourgeoisie and the nobility. On June 20, 1789, as delegates to the Estates General were attempting to resolve procedural questions, the Third Estate launched the National Assembly. On July 14, 1789, a mob stormed the Bastille and injected a populist, urban element into the political drama. In the countryside, the "Great Fear" intensified ongoing peasant disturbances aimed at limiting aristocratic privilege; on August 4, 1789, nobles and liberals in the National Constituent Assembly renounced their privileges. From then on, all French men were subject to the same laws. On August 27, 1789, the Assembly issued the Declaration of the Rights of Man and Citizen. Again, women were not portrayed as holding political rights. On October 5, 1789, Parisian women marched on Versailles and forced Louis XVI to move to Paris. *page 444*

HOW DID the National Constituent Assembly reorganize France?

The Reconstruction of France The National Constituent Assembly reorganized France as a constitutional monarchy, with a rational administration, an unregulated economy, and a state-controlled church. Property, in all its forms, was protected, and wealth—rather than bloodlines and titles—determined power. The Assembly divided the citizenry into "active" (propertied males) and "passive" (everyone else) elements. Olympe de Gouges protested with her Declaration of the Rights of Woman. Local and judicial administration was reorganized, and workers' organizations were banned. Most significantly in the long term, the Assembly confiscated all land and property of the Roman Catholic Church in France, in order to pay the royal debt. Under the Civil Constitution of the Clergy, the Roman Catholic Church was brought under the direct control of the French state. These moves against the church created massive opposition. The royal family attempted to flee France. The National Constituent Assembly closed in September 1791, having transformed the nation. The newly reconstructed nation was not stable, however. *page 448*

WHAT LED to the radicalization of the French Revolution?

The End of the Monarchy: A Second Revolution The short-lived (1791–1792) Legislative Assembly was factionalized. Jacobins had lobbied for a republic during the National Constituent Assembly. A faction within the Jacobin faction, the Girondists, took the leadership of the Legislative Assembly. On April 20, 1792, the Legislative Assembly declared war on Austria. The Girondists hoped war would suppress the counterrevolution within France; Louis XVI also supported war with Austria, hoping war would strengthen the monarchy. Instead, the *sans-culottes* seized control. In August 1792, a Parisian mob forced the royal family to take refuge in the Legislative Assembly; from then on, Louis XVI was unable to function as a monarch. The Paris Commune executed 1,200 prisoners in the September Massacres, and on September 21, 1792, the Convention met to write a democratic constitution for a French republic. Radical Jacobins within the Convention who collaborated with the *sans-culottes* constituted the "Mountain." In February 1793, the Convention declared war on Great Britain, Holland, and Spain; in March, the Vendée in France erupted in a royalist revolt. *page 455*

HOW DID Europe respond to the French Revolution?

Europe at War with the Revolution British statesman Edmund Burke, in his 1790 *Reflections on the Revolution in France,* was the first observer to articulate theoretical criticisms of the French Revolution and to predict further turmoil as a result of the revolution. European governments adopted repressive policies in response to France's ideas and military actions. In response to Polish reforms inspired by the revolution, Austria, Prussia, and Russia partitioned Poland out of existence. William Pitt the Younger suppressed political freedoms in Great Britain. By April 1793, the governments of all the countries with which France was at war—Austria, Prussia, Great Britain, Spain, Sardinia, and Holland—formed the First Coalition, an alliance to protect their social structures, political systems, and economic interests from the aggression of the revolution. *page 457*

HOW DID war and ideology combine to create the Reign of Terror?

The Reign of Terror In 1793, mobilization for war touched almost every aspect of French life. The Committee of General Security and the Committee of Public Safety were formed in April 1793 to facilitate the war effort. In August, the entire nation was requisitioned into national service; France had Europe's first citizen army. At about the same time, the Reign of Terror began. Robespierre and others in the Convention believed they were creating a "republic of virtue." The Convention established revolutionary tribunals in the summer of 1793; the Terror's first victims were Marie Antoinette and other members of the royal family. The Society of Revolutionary Women was among the first groups to be suppressed; Olympe de Gouges was guillotined in November 1793. Also in November 1793, the Convention attempted to de-Christianize France. Robespierre opposed this move, fearing it would lead to a backlash. In May 1794, he established the "Cult of the Supreme Being," a deistic cult over which he presided. Executions increased in 1794, as Robespierre turned on his political enemies, and a new law permitted convictions even in the absence of substantial evidence. Finally, on July 27, 1794, Robespierre himself was arrested. He was executed the next day, and the Terror died out soon thereafter. *page 458*

WHAT COURSE did the French Revolution take after 1794?

The Thermidorian Reaction The Thermidorian Reaction represented a tempering of the revolution. Propertied middle-class and professional people replaced the *sans-culottes* as the most influential group. The "white terror" turned violence against some of those responsible for the Terror. Catholicism revived throughout the country. Some progressive social legislation was repealed; women had, if anything, fewer rights than they had in 1789. The Constitution of the Year III created a bicameral legislature, under a five-man executive Directory, all limited to property-holding men. Voting was also limited to property holders and—significantly—soldiers. As the power of the *sans-culottes* waned, they and royalists revolted in Paris in October 1795. Napoleon Bonaparte was the general in charge of putting down their insurrection. The wars with Prussia and Spain ended in 1795, but France remained at war with Austria and Great Britain. In the absence of broad public support, the Directory came to rely on the army for stability. *page 461*

REVIEW QUESTIONS

1. How did the financial weaknesses of the French monarchy pave the way for the revolution of 1789? What role did Louis XVI play in the French Revolution? Would a constitutional monarchy have succeeded, or did the revolution ultimately have little to do with the competence of the monarch?

2. How was the Estates General transformed into the National Assembly? Which social and political values associated with the Enlightenment are reflected in the Declaration of the Rights of Man and Citizen? Why has the Civil Constitution of the Clergy been called the greatest blunder of the National Assembly?

3. Why were some political factions dissatisfied with the constitutional settlement of 1791? Who were the *sans-culottes*? How did they acquire political influence? What drew the *sans-culottes* and the Jacobins together? What ended their cooperation?

4. Why did France go to war with Austria in 1792? What were the benefits and drawbacks for France of fighting an external war while in the midst of a domestic political revolution? What were the causes of the Terror? In what ways did the French Revolution both live up to and betray its motto: "liberty, equality and fraternity"?

KEY TERMS

Convention (p. 456)
émigrés (p. 454)
Jacobins (p. 455)
levée en masse (p. 459)
Reign of Terror (p. 458)

sans-culottes (p. 456)
September Massacres (p. 455)
Thermidorian Reaction (p. 462)
Third Estate (p. 444)

For additional learning resources related to this chapter, please go to **www.myhistorylab.com**

myhistorylab

19

The Age of Napoleon and the Triumph of Romanticism

This portrait of Napoleon on his throne by Jean Ingres (1780–1867) shows him in the splendor of an imperial monarch who embodies the total power of the state.

Jean Auguste Dominique Ingres (1780-1867), *Napoleon on His Imperial Throne*, 1806. Oil on canvas, 259 162 cm. Musée des Beaux-Arts, Rennes. Photograph © Erich Lessing/Art Resource, NY

What does this painting tell us about the nature of Napoleon's rule?

467

By the late 1790s, many French people—especially property owners, who now included the peasantry—were longing for more political stability than the Directory seemed able to provide. The army, an institution associated with the values and successes of the revolution, offered the best hope for securing the nation. The most political of its generals was Napoleon Bonaparte. Once in power, he consolidated many of the achievements of the revolution. Ultimately, however, he overthrew the republic, declared himself emperor, and embarked on a mission of conquest that continued for over a decade. France's military offensive overturned Europe's old political and social order and fostered fierce nationalism among the French and the countries that allied to defeat Napoleon.

The Napoleonic period saw the flowering of the Romantic Era in European cultural history. Some Romantic ideas (nationalism, for example) sprang from the French Revolution, but the revolutionaries had opposed others (respect for history and religion most specifically). ▪

THE RISE OF NAPOLEON BONAPARTE

HOW DID Napoleon come to power in France?

The chief threat to the Directory came from royalists, who hoped to restore the Bourbon monarchy by legal means. Many of the *émigrés* had returned to France. Their plans for a restoration drew support from devout Catholics and from those citizens disgusted by the excesses of the revolution. The spring elections of 1797 replaced most incumbents with constitutional monarchists and their sympathizers, thus giving them a majority in the national legislature.

To preserve the republic and prevent a peaceful restoration of the Bourbons, the antimonarchist Directory staged a *coup d'état* on 18 Fructidor (September 4, 1797). They put their own supporters into the legislative seats their opponents had won. They then imposed censorship and exiled some of their enemies. At the request of the Directors, Napoleon Bonaparte, the general in charge of the French invasion of Italy, had sent a subordinate to Paris to guarantee the success of the coup. In 1797, as in 1795, the army and Bonaparte had saved the day for the government installed in the wake of the Thermidorian Reaction.

Napoleon Bonaparte was born in 1769 to a poor family of lesser nobles at Ajaccio, on the Mediterranean island of Corsica. He favored the revolution and was a fiery Jacobin. In 1793, he played a leading role in recovering the port of Toulon from the British. As a reward for his service, he was appointed a brigadier general. During the Thermidorian Reaction, his defense of the new regime on 13 Vendémiaire won him a command in Italy.

EARLY MILITARY VICTORIES

By 1795, French arms and diplomacy had shattered the enemy coalition, but France's annexation of Belgium guaranteed continued fighting with Britain and Austria. The invasion of Italy aimed to deprive Austria of its rich northern Italian province of Lombardy. In a series of lightning victories, Bonaparte crushed the Austrian and Sardinian armies. On his own initiative, and against the wishes of the government in Paris, he concluded the Treaty of Campo Formio in October 1797. The treaty took Austria out of the war and crowned Napoleon's campaign with success. Before long, France dominated all of Italy and Switzerland.

In November 1797, the triumphant Bonaparte returned to Paris as a hero and to confront France's only remaining enemy, Britain. He judged it impossible to cross the Channel and invade England at that time. Instead, he chose to attack British interests through the eastern Mediterranean by capturing Egypt from the Ottoman Empire. By this strategy, he hoped to drive the British fleet from the Mediterranean, cut off British communications with India, damage British trade, and threaten the British Empire.

Napoleon easily overran Egypt, but the invasion was a failure. Admiral Horatio Nelson (1758–1805) destroyed the French fleet at Abukir on August 1, 1798. The French army was cut off from France. To make matters worse, the situation in Europe was deteriorating. The invasion of Egypt had alarmed Russia, which had its own ambitions in the Near East. The Russians, the Austrians, and the Ottomans joined Britain to form the Second Coalition against France. In 1799, the Russian and Austrian armies defeated the French in Italy and Switzerland and threatened to invade France.

THE CONSTITUTION OF THE YEAR VIII

Economic troubles and the dangerous international situation eroded the Directory's fragile support. One of the Directors, the Abbé Siéyès (1748–1836), proposed a new constitution. The author of the pamphlet *What Is the Third Estate?* (1789) now wanted an executive body independent of the whims of electoral politics, a government based on the principle of "confidence from below, power from above." The change would require another *coup d'état* with military support. News of France's misfortunes had reached Napoleon in Egypt. Without orders and leaving his army behind, he returned to France in October 1799 to popular acclaim. Soon he joined Siéyès. On 19 Brumaire (November 10, 1799), his troops ensured the success of the coup.

Siéyès appears to have thought that Napoleon could be used and then dismissed, but he misjudged his man. Bonaparte quickly pushed Siéyès aside, and in December 1799, he issued the Constitution of the Year VIII. The new constitution established the rule of one man—the First Consul, Bonaparte.

In this early-nineteenth-century cartoon, England, personified by a caricature of William Pitt, and France, personified by a caricature of Napoleon, are carving out their areas of interest around the globe.

Bildarchiv Preussischer Kulturbesitz

How accurate a picture of international politics in the Napoleonic era does this cartoon draw?

THE CONSULATE IN FRANCE (1799–1804)

The **Consulate** in effect ended the revolution in France. The leading elements of the Third Estate—that is, officials, landowners, doctors, lawyers, and financiers—had achieved most of their goals by 1799. The newly established dominant classes had little or no desire to share their new privileges with the lower social orders. Bonaparte seemed just the person to give them security. When he submitted his constitution to the voters in a plebiscite, they overwhelmingly approved it.

HOW DID the Consulate end the revolution in France?

Consulate A republican facade for one-man government by Napoleon.

SUPPRESSING FOREIGN ENEMIES AND DOMESTIC OPPOSITION

Throughout much of the 1790s, the pressures of warfare, particularly conscription, had accounted for much French internal instability. Bonaparte justified the public's confidence in himself by making peace with France's enemies. Russia had already left the Second Coalition. The Treaty of Luneville early in 1801 took Austria out of the war. Britain was now alone and, in 1802, concluded the Treaty of Amiens, which brought peace to Europe.

Bonaparte also restored peace and order at home. He used generosity, flattery, and bribery to win over enemies. He issued a general amnesty and employed men from all political factions. He required only that they be loyal to him. Bonaparte, however, ruthlessly suppressed opposition. He established a highly centralized administration in which prefects responsible to the government in Paris managed all departments. He employed secret police. He stamped out the royalist rebellion in the west and made the rule of Paris effective in Brittany and the Vendée for the first time in years.

Napoleon also used and invented opportunities to destroy his enemies. A plot on his life in 1804 provided an excuse to attack the Jacobins, though it was the work of the royalists. Also in 1804, he violated the sovereignty of the German state of Baden to seize and execute the Bourbon duke of Enghien (1772–1804).

CONCORDAT WITH THE ROMAN CATHOLIC CHURCH

No single set of revolutionary policies had aroused so much domestic opposition as those regarding the French Catholic Church, nor were there any other policies to which fierce supporters of the revolution seemed so attached. In 1801, to the shock and dismay of his anticlerical supporters, Napoleon concluded a concordat with Pope Pius VII (r. 1800–1823). The concordat gave Napoleon what he most wanted. The agreement required both the refractory clergy and those who had accepted the revolution to resign. Their replacements received their spiritual investiture from the pope, but the state named the bishops and paid their salaries and the salary of one priest in each parish. In return, the church gave up its claims to its confiscated property.

The concordat declared, "Catholicism is the religion of the great majority of French citizens." This was merely a statement of fact and fell far short of what the pope had wanted: religious dominance for the Roman Catholic Church. The clergy had to swear an oath of loyalty to the state. The Organic Articles of 1802, which the government issued on its own authority without consulting the pope, established the supremacy of state over church. Similar laws were applied to the Protestant and Jewish communities, reducing still further the privileged position of the Catholic Church.

THE NAPOLEONIC CODE

In 1802, a plebiscite ratified Napoleon as consul for life, and he soon produced another constitution that granted him what amounted to full power. He thereafter set about reforming and codifying French law. The result was the Civil Code of 1804, usually known as the Napoleonic Code.

The Napoleonic Code safeguarded all forms of property and tried to secure French society against internal challenges. All the privileges based on birth that the revolution had overthrown remained abolished. The conservative attitudes toward labor and women that had emerged during the revolution also received full support. Workers' organizations remained forbidden, and workers had fewer rights than their employers. Fathers were granted extensive control over their children and husbands over their wives.

ESTABLISHING A DYNASTY

In 1804, a failed assassination attempt provided Napoleon with a rationale for ending the republic and establishing an empire. He argued that as emperor he could found a dynasty, and the hereditary rights of his descendants would guarantee continuity of government and make assassination pointless. This necessitated yet another constitution, which received overwhelming ratification by a plebiscite. Napoleon invited the pope to the cathedral of Notre Dame to witness his coronation, but not to crown him. Emperor Napoleon I placed the crown on his own head.

The coronation of Napoleon, December 2, 1804, as painted by Jacques-Louis David. Having first crowned himself, the emperor is shown about to place the crown on the head of Josephine. Napoleon instructed David to paint Pope Pius VII with his hand raised in blessing.

Jacques-Louis David (1748–1825), *Consecration of the Emperor Napoleon I and Coronation of Empress Josephine,* 1806–1807. Louvre, Paris. Bridgeman–Giraudon/Art Resource, NY

What role did Pope Pius VII play in the coronation of Napoleon? Why was his participation important to Napoleon?

NAPOLEON'S EMPIRE (1804–1814)

Between his coronation as emperor and his final defeat at Waterloo (1815), Napoleon conquered most of Europe. France's victories changed the map of the Continent. The wars put an end to the Old Regime and its feudal trappings throughout Western Europe and forced the eastern European states to reorganize themselves to resist Napoleon's armies.

HOW DID Napoleon build an empire?

CONQUERING AN EMPIRE

The Peace of Amiens (1802) between France and Great Britain was merely a truce. Napoleon's unlimited ambitions shattered any hope that it might last. He sent an army to restore the rebellious colony of Haiti to French rule. This move aroused British fears that he was planning a new French empire in America, because Spain had restored Louisiana to France in 1801. More serious were his interventions in the Dutch Republic, Italy, and Switzerland and his reorganization of Germany. The Treaty of Campo Formio had required a redistribution of territories along the Rhine River, and the petty princes of the region engaged in a scramble to enlarge their holdings. Among the results were the reduction of Austrian influence and the emergence of fewer, but larger, German states in the West, all dependent on Napoleon.

British Naval Supremacy   Alarmed by these developments, the British issued an ultimatum. When Napoleon ignored it, Britain declared war in May 1803. By August 1805, the British prime minister, William Pitt the Younger, had persuaded Russia and Austria to form a Third Coalition against France. On October 21, 1805, the British admiral Lord Nelson destroyed the combined French and Spanish fleets at the Battle of Trafalgar off the Spanish coast. Trafalgar ended all French hope of invading Britain and guaranteed British control of the sea for the rest of the war. (See "Encountering the Past: Sailors and Canned Food," page 472.)

Napoleonic Victories in Central Europe   On land the story was different. Even before Trafalgar, Napoleon had marched to the Danube River to attack his continental enemies. In mid-October he forced an Austrian army to surrender at Ulm and occupied Vienna. On December 2, 1805, in perhaps his greatest victory, Napoleon defeated the combined Austrian and Russian forces at Austerlitz. The Treaty of Pressburg that followed won major concessions from Austria. The Austrians withdrew from Italy and left Napoleon in control of everything north of Rome.

Overview   Napoleon and the Continental System

1806	Napoleon establishes the Continental System, prohibiting all trade with England
1807	The peace conference at Tilsit results in Russia joining the Continental System and becoming an ally of Napoleon
1809 and 1810	Napoleon at the peak of his power
1810	Russia withdraws from the Continental System and resumes relations with Britain; Napoleon plans to crush Russia militarily
1812	Napoleon invades Russia; the Russians adopt a scorched earth policy and burn Moscow; the thwarted Napoleon deserts his dwindling army and rushes back to Paris

ENCOUNTERING THE PAST

SAILORS AND CANNED FOOD

New technologies often emerge during wartime, and in 1803, Napoleon's navy carried out the first experiments with something that has become a staple of modern life: canned food. Earlier methods of food preservation (drying, salting, pickling, smoking, fermenting, or condensing) altered taste and destroyed nutrients. Navies were hampered by the fact that sailors who spent a long time at sea on a diet of bread and salted meat developed scurvy and other illnesses caused by malnutrition. If fleets were to undertake longer tours of duty at sea and armies campaign where they could not live off the land, some way had to be found to supply them with more healthy food.

In the 1790s, the French government offered a prize for anyone who could invent a superior method for preserving food. The challenge was met by Nicholas Appert, a Parisian chef, who invented canning. Appert did not know of the existence of the microbes that spoil food but he stumbled across a process that worked by destroying them. He sealed food in glass jars filled with water or sauce and cooked these jars in a hot water bath. The result was food that did not deteriorate and kept its taste and nutrients. Sailors on several of Napoleon's ships were the first (in 1803) to test Appert's new products.

In 1810, Appert published information about his process, and by 1813, an English company was canning food in tins (which were cheaper and more durable than glass jars). By the middle of the nineteenth century, canned goods had entered the diets of millions of people in western Europe and North America.

Nicholas Appert (1749–1841) invented canning as a way of preserving food nutritiously. Canned food could be transported over long distances without spoiling.

Private Collection/Bridgeman Art Library

Why was the French government so interested in discovering new ways of preserving food?

WHAT MOTIVATED the work that went into the discovery of the canning process?

Napoleon also made extensive political changes in Germany. In July 1806, he organized the Confederation of the Rhine, which included most of the western German princes. Their withdrawal from the Holy Roman Empire led Francis II to dissolve that ancient political body and henceforth to call himself Emperor Francis I of Austria.

At this point, Prussia, which had remained neutral, declared war on France, but Napoleon crushed the Prussians in famous encounters at Jena and Auerstädt (October 14, 1806). Two weeks later he entered Berlin. On June 13, 1807, he defeated the Russians at Friedland and moved on to Königsberg, the capital of East Prussia.

Treaty of Tilsit   Unable to fight another battle and unwilling to retreat into Russia, Tsar Alexander I (r. 1801–1825) was ready to make peace. On July 7, 1807, he signed the Treaty of Tilsit, which confirmed France's gains. Prussia lost half its territory. Only the support of Alexander saved it from extinction. Prussia openly and Russia secretly became allies of Napoleon.

Napoleon organized conquered Europe much like the estate of a Corsican family. The great French Empire was ruled directly by the head of the clan, Napoleon. On its borders lay satellite states ruled by members of his family. This establishment of the Napoleonic family as the collective sovereigns of Europe provoked political opposition that needed only encouragement and assistance to flare up into serious resistance.

THE CONTINENTAL SYSTEM

After the Treaty of Tilsit, such resistance could come only from Britain, and Napoleon knew he must defeat the British before he could feel safe. Unable to compete with the British navy, he planned to cut off all British trade with the European continent and thus to cripple British commercial and financial power. (See Map 19–1.)

Despite initial drops in exports and domestic unrest, the British economy survived. British control of the seas assured access to the growing markets of North and South America and of the eastern Mediterranean. At the same time, the Continental System badly hurt the European economies. Moreover, his tariff policies favored France, increased the resentment of foreign merchants, and made them less willing to enforce the system and more ready to engage in smuggling.

QUICK REVIEW

The Continental System

- Treaty of Tilsit left Britain as sole power opposing France
- Napoleon tried to cripple Britain's economy by closing continental ports to British commerce
- Policy created resentment in Europe

MAP 19–1   The Continental System, 1806–1810   Napoleon hoped to cut off all British trade with the European continent and thereby drive the British from the war. The areas in peach indicate the French Empire. These lands, along with the Grand Empire and Napoleon's allies (in blue), made up the Continental System.

Did the Continental System deprive Britain of all its overseas trade? Did it guarantee free trade within continental Europe?

EUROPEAN RESPONSE TO THE EMPIRE

WHY DID Napoleonic rule breed resentment in Europe?

Wherever Napoleon ruled, he imposed the Napoleonic Code and abolished hereditary social distinctions. Feudal privileges disappeared, and the peasants were freed from serfdom and manorial dues. In the towns, the guilds and the local oligarchies that had been dominant for centuries were dissolved or deprived of their power. The established churches lost their traditional independence and were made subordinate to the state. Toleration replaced monopoly of religion by an established church. Despite these reforms, however, it was always clear that Napoleon's policies were intended first for his own glory and that of France. Consequently, before long, the conquered states and peoples grew restive.

GERMAN NATIONALISM AND PRUSSIAN REFORM

At the beginning of the nineteenth century, the Romantic Movement had begun to take hold. One of its basic features in Germany was the emergence of nationalism, which went through two distinct stages there. Initially, nationalistic writers emphasized the unique and admirable qualities of German culture, which, they argued, arose from the history of the German people. Such cultural nationalism prevailed until Napoleon's humiliation of Prussia at Jena in 1806. At that point many German intellectuals began to urge resistance to Napoleon on the basis of German nationalism. The French conquest endangered the independence and achievements of all German-speaking people. Only a people united through its language and culture could resist the French onslaught. Henceforth, many Germans sought to solve their internal political problems by attempting to establish a unified German state, reformed to harness the energies of the entire people.

After Tilsit, only Prussia could arouse such patriotic feelings. Elsewhere German rulers were either under Napoleon's thumb or collaborating with him. Defeated, humiliated, and diminished, Prussia continued to resist, however feebly. To Prussia fled German nationalists from other states, calling for reforms and unification that King Frederick William III (r. 1797–1840) and the Junker nobility in fact feared and hated. Reforms came about despite such opposition because the defeat at Jena had shown that the Prussian state had to change to survive.

The Prussian administrative and social reforms were the work of Baron vom Stein (1757–1831) and Prince von Hardenberg (1750–1822). Neither of these reformers intended to reduce the autocratic power of the Prussian monarch or to end the dominance of the Junkers, who formed the bulwark of the state and of the officer corps. Their plan was to fight France by becoming what it had become—a democracy led by a strong monarchy.

Stein's reforms broke the Junker monopoly of landholding. Serfdom was abolished. However, unlike in the western German states where all remnants of serfdom simply disappeared, in Prussia the Junkers ensured that vestiges of the system survived. Military reforms sought to increase the supply of soldiers and to improve their quality. The Prussian reformers abolished inhumane military punishments, sought to inspire patriotic feelings in the soldiers, opened the officer corps to commoners, gave promotions on the basis of merit, and organized war colleges that developed new theories of strategy and tactics. These reforms soon enabled Prussia to regain its former power.

THE WARS OF LIBERATION

Spain France and Spain had been allies since 1796. In 1807, however, a French army came into the Iberian Peninsula to force Portugal to abandon its traditional alliance with Britain. The army stayed in Spain to protect lines of supply and communication. Napoleon used a revolt that broke out in Madrid in 1808 as a pretext to depose the Spanish Bourbons and to place his brother Joseph (1768–1844) on the Spanish throne.

QUICK REVIEW

German Nationalism

- After Tilsit, German nationalists fled to Prussia
- Nationalists called for German unification and reform
- Crisis situation forced Prussian leadership to accept reform

Attacks on the privileges of the church increased public outrage. Many members of the upper classes were prepared to collaborate with Napoleon, but the peasants, urged on by the lower clergy and the monks, rebelled.

In Spain, Napoleon faced a new kind of warfare. Guerrilla bands cut lines of communication, killed stragglers, destroyed isolated units, and then disappeared into the mountains. The British landed an army under Sir Arthur Wellesley (1769–1852), later the duke of Wellington, to support the Spanish insurgents. Thus began the long peninsular campaign that would drain French strength from elsewhere in Europe and hasten Napoleon's eventual defeat. (See "Compare & Connect: The Experience of War in the Napoleonic Age," pages 476–477.)

Austria   The French troubles in Spain encouraged the Austrians to renew the war in 1809. Since their defeat at Austerlitz, they had sought a war of revenge. The Austrians counted on Napoleon's distraction in Spain, French war weariness, and aid from other German princes. Napoleon was fully in command in France, however, and the German princes did not move. The French army marched swiftly into Austria and won the Battle of Wagram. The resulting Peace of Schönbrunn deprived Austria of much territory and 3.5 million subjects. Another spoil of victory was the Austrian archduchess Marie Louise (1791–1847), daughter of Emperor Francis I. Napoleon's wife, Josephine de Beauharnais (1763–1814), was forty-six and had borne him no children. His dynastic ambitions, as well as the desire for a royal marriage, led him to divorce Josephine and marry the eighteen-year-old Marie Louise.

THE INVASION OF RUSSIA

The Franco-Russian alliance concluded at Tilsit was shaky. Russian nobles disliked the alliance because of the liberal politics of France and because the Continental System prohibited timber sales to Britain. The organization of the Polish Duchy of Warsaw as a Napoleonic satellite on the Russian doorstep and its enlargement with Austrian territory in 1809 after the Battle of Wagram angered Alexander. Napoleon's annexation of Holland in violation of the Treaty of Tilsit, his recognition of the French marshal Bernadotte (1763–1844) as the future King Charles XIV of Sweden, and his marriage to Marie Louise further disturbed the tsar. At the end of 1810, Russia withdrew from the Continental System and began to prepare for war. (See Map 19–2, page 478.)

Napoleon was determined to end the Russian military threat. He amassed an army of more than 600,000 men. He intended the usual short campaign crowned by a decisive battle, but the Russians retreated before his advance, destroying all food and supplies as they went. The so-called Grand Army of Napoleon could not live off the country, and the expanse of Russia made supply lines too long to maintain. Napoleon's advisers urged him to abandon the venture, but he feared an unsuccessful campaign would undermine his position in the empire and in France. He pinned his faith on the Russians' unwillingness to abandon Moscow without a fight.

In September 1812, Russian public opinion forced the army to give Napoleon the battle he wanted. At Borodino, not far west of Moscow, the bloodiest battle of the Napoleonic era cost the French 30,000 casualties and the Russians almost twice as many. Yet the Russian army was not destroyed. Napoleon won nothing substantial, and the battle was regarded as a defeat for him.

Fires set by the Russians soon engulfed Moscow and left Napoleon far from home with a badly diminished army lacking adequate supplies as winter came to a vast and unfriendly country. By October, what was left of the Grand Army was forced to retreat. By December, Napoleon realized the Russian fiasco would encourage plots against him at home. He returned to Paris, leaving the remnants of his army to struggle westward. Perhaps only 100,000 of the original 600,000 survived their ordeal.

THE EXPERIENCE OF WAR IN THE NAPOLEONIC AGE

The Napoleonic Wars spread violence across Europe. Different participants, writers, and artists portrayed the experience of war differently. William Napier reported his own heroism in a quite matter-of-fact manner. The German poet and historian Ernest Moritz Arndt recalled moments of intense nationalistic patriotism. The Spanish painter Goya portrayed a moment of enormous brutality suffered by the Spanish at the hands of French troops.

QUESTIONS

1. What were Napier's expectations of his men? Of his officers? Of himself?

2. Why does Arndt claim each of these various groups wanted war?

3. How does Arndt suggest the possibility of a united nation that did not yet actually exist?

4. How does Goya portray Spaniards as victims of harsh, unmerciful military violence?

5. How do Napier's memoir, Arndt's call to arms, and Goya's painting illustrate different points of view and ways of interpreting the violence of modern warfare?

I. A COMMANDER RECALLS AN INCIDENT IN SPAIN

William Napier, a British officer during the Napoleonic Wars and later a distinguished leader in the British army, describes his experiences in a battle that took place in Spain during 1811.

I arrived [with two companies] just in time to save Captain Dobbs, 52nd, and two men who were cut off from their regiment. The French were gathering fast about us, we could scarcely retreat, and Dobbs agreed with me that boldness would be our best chance; so we called upon the men to follow, and, jumping over a wall which had given us cover, charged the enemy with a shout which sent the nearest back. . . .

Only the two men of the 52nd followed us, and we four arrived unsupported at a second wall, close to a considerable body of French, who rallied and began to close upon us. Their fire was very violent, but the wall gave cover. I was, however, stung by the backwardness of my men, and told Dobbs I would save him or lose my life by bringing up the two companies; he entreated me not, saying I could not make two paces from the wall and live. Yet I did go back to the first wall, escaped the fire, and, reproaching the men gave them the word again, and returned to Dobbs, who was now upon the point of being taken; but again I returned alone! The soldiers had indeed crossed the wall in their front, but kept edging away to the right to avoid the heavy fire. Being now maddened by this second failure, I made another attempt, but I had not made ten paces when a shot struck my spine, and the enemy very ungenerously continued to fire at me when I was down. I escaped death by dragging myself by my hands—for my lower extremities were paralyzed—towards a small heap of stones which was in the midst of the field, and thus covering my head and shoulders. . . . However, Captain Lloyd and my company, and some of the 52nd, came up at that moment, and the French were driven away.

Source: Quoted in H. A. Bruce, *Life of Sir William Napier* (London: John Murray, 1864), 1:55–57.

II. A GERMAN WRITER DESCRIBES THE WAR OF LIBERATION

The German resistance to Napoleon as his army retreated from Moscow in 1813 was the first time in modern German history that people from virtually all German-speaking lands cooperated together. Ernest Moritz Arndt (1769–1860) described the excitement of that moment in a passage frequently reprinted in German history textbooks for more than a century.

Fired with enthusiasm, the people rose, "with God for King and Fatherland." Among the Prussians there was only one voice, one feeling, one anger and one love, to save the Fatherland and to free Germany. . . . War, war, sounded the cry from the Carpathians to the Baltic, from the Niemen to the Elbe. War! cried the nobleman and landed proprietor who had become impoverished. War! that peasant who was driving his last horse to death. . . . War! the citizen who was growing exhausted from quartering soldiers and paying taxes. War! the widow who was sending her only son to the front. War! the young girl who, with tears of pride and pain, was leaving her betrothed. . . . Even young women, under all sorts of disguises, rushed to arms; all wanted to drill, arm themselves and fight and die for the Fatherland. . . .

The most beautiful thing about all this holy zeal and happy confusion was . . . that the one great feeling for the Fatherland, its freedom and honor, swallowed all other feelings, caused all other considerations and relationships to be forgotten.

Source: *Documents of German History*, trans. by Louis L. Snyder. Copyright © 1958 by Rutgers, the State University. Reprinted by permission of Rutgers University Press.

III. FRANCISCO GOYA, *THE THIRD OF MAY, 1808* (PAINTED 1814–1815)

Napoleon had begun to send troops into Spain in 1807 after the king of Spain had agreed to aid France against Portugal, which was assisting Britain. By early 1808 Spain had essentially become an occupied nation. On May 2, riots took place in Madrid between French troops, many of whom were Islamic soldiers whom Napoleon had recruited in Egypt, and Spanish civilians. In response to that resistance the French general Murat ordered the execution of numerous citizens of Madrid, which occurred the night of May 2 and 3. The events of these two days marked the opening of the Spanish effort to rid their peninsula of French rule.

After the restoration of the Spanish monarchy, Francisco Goya (1745–1828) depicted the savagery of those executions in the most memorable war painting of the Napoleonic era, The Third of May, 1808. There is one group of humble Spaniards who have already been shot, another in the process of execution, and a third group, some of whom are hiding their eyes, who will be the next victims.

The painting illustrates two forces of Napoleonic warfare confronting each other: the professional solider and the guerilla (a term coined during the Spanish resistance of this era). The guerilla must fight with what few resources he finds at his command and with few advanced weapons. By contrast, in this painting the soldiers, well disciplined and equipped with modern rifles, carry out the execution by the light of large technologically advanced lanterns fueled by either gas or oil with which Napoleon equipped his troops. Goya succeeds in making ordinary people and very poor clergy not only the victims, but also symbolic heroes of the national war of liberation.

Goya y Lucientes, Francisco de Goya, recorded Napoleon's troops executing Spanish guerrilla fighters who had rebelled against the French occupation in *The Third of May, 1808.*

Francisco de Goya, *Los fusilamientos del 3 de Mayo, 1808*. 1814. Oil on canvas, 8'6" × 11'4". © Museo Nacional del Prado, Madrid

What factors contributed to the rise of resistance movements in occupied countries?

MAP 19–2   Napoleonic Europe in Late 1812   By mid-1812 the areas shown in peach were incorporated into France, and most of the rest of Europe was directly controlled by or allied with Napoleon. But Russia had withdrawn from the failing Continental System, and the decline of Napoleon was about to begin.

Which areas in Europe were most problematic for Napoleon?

EUROPEAN COALITION

Even as the news of the disaster reached the West, the final defeat of Napoleon was far from certain. He was able to put down his opponents in Paris and raise another 350,000 men. Neither the Prussians nor the Austrians were eager to risk another contest with Napoleon, and even the Russians hesitated. The Austrian foreign minister, Prince Klemens von Metternich (1773–1859), would have been glad to make a negotiated peace that would leave Napoleon on the throne of a shrunken and chastened France rather than see Russia dominate Europe. Napoleon might have negotiated a reasonable settlement had he been willing to make concessions that would have split his jealous opponents. He would not consider that solution, however.

In 1813, patriotic pressure and national ambition brought together the last and most powerful coalition (Russia, Prussia, Austria, and Britain) against Napoleon. In October, the combined armies of the enemy decisively defeated him at Leipzig in what the Germans called the Battle of the Nations. In March 1814, the allied armies marched into Paris. A few days later, Napoleon abdicated and went into exile on the island of Elba, off the coast of central Italy.

QUICK REVIEW

Coalition of 1813

◆ Most powerful coalition created to oppose Napoleon

◆ Russia, Britain, Prussia, and Austria joined forces

◆ March 1814, allies defeat Napoleon at Leipzig

THE CONGRESS OF VIENNA AND THE EUROPEAN SETTLEMENT

Fear of Napoleon and hostility to his ambitions had held the victorious coalition together. As soon as he was removed, the allies pursued their separate ambitions. The key person in achieving eventual agreement among them was Robert Stewart, Viscount Castlereagh (1769–1822), the British foreign secretary. Even before the victorious armies had entered Paris, he brought about the signing of the Treaty of Chaumont on March 9, 1814. It provided for the restoration of the Bourbons to the French throne and the contraction of France to its frontiers of 1792. Even more importantly, Britain, Austria, Russia, and Prussia agreed to form a Quadruple Alliance for twenty years to preserve whatever settlement they agreed on. Remaining problems—and there were many—and final details were left for a conference to be held at Vienna.

WHAT WERE the consequences of the Congress of Vienna?

TERRITORIAL ADJUSTMENTS

The Congress of Vienna assembled in September 1814 but did not conclude its work until November 1815. The easiest problem the great powers faced was France. All the victors agreed that no single state should be allowed to dominate Europe, and all were determined to prevent France from doing so again. The restoration of the French Bourbon monarchy, which was temporarily popular, and a nonvindictive boundary settlement were designed to keep France calm and satisfied.

The powers also strengthened the states around France's borders to serve as barriers to renewed French expansion. They established the kingdom of the Netherlands in the north and added the important port of Genoa to strengthen Piedmont in the south. Prussia was given important new territories along the Rhine River to deter French aggression in the West. Austria gained full control of northern Italy to prevent a repetition of Napoleon's conquests there. As for the rest of Germany, most of Napoleon's territorial arrangements were left untouched and the Holy Roman Empire was not revived. In all these areas, the congress established the rule of legitimate monarchs and rejected any hint of the republican and democratic policies that had flowed from the French Revolution.

On these matters agreement was not difficult, but the settlement of eastern Europe sharply divided the victors. Alexander I of Russia wanted all of Poland under his rule. Prussia was willing to give it to him in return for all of Saxony, which had been allied with Napoleon. Austria, however, was unwilling to surrender its share of Poland or to see Prussian power grow or Russia penetrate deeper into central Europe. The Polish-Saxon question almost caused a new war among the victors, but defeated France provided a way out. The wily Talleyrand, now representing France at Vienna, suggested the weight of France added to that of Britain and Austria might bring Alexander to his senses. When news of a secret treaty among the three leaked out, the tsar agreed to become ruler of a smaller Poland, and Prussia settled for only part of Saxony. Thereafter, France was included as a fifth great power in all deliberations.

LE CONGRÈS.

In this political cartoon of the Congress of Vienna, Talleyrand simply watches which way the wind is blowing, Castlereagh hesitates, while the monarchs of Russia, Prussia, and Austria form the dance of the Holy Alliance. The king of Saxony holds on to his crown and the republic of Geneva pays homage to the kingdom of Sardinia.

Bildarchiv Preussischer Kulturbesitz

Who were the winners and losers at the Congress of Vienna?

THE HUNDRED DAYS AND THE QUADRUPLE ALLIANCE

Napoleon's escape from Elba on March 1, 1815, further united the victors. Once back in power, Napoleon promised a liberal constitution and a peaceful foreign policy. The allies were not convinced. They declared Napoleon an outlaw (a new device under international law) and sent their armies to crush him. Wellington, with the crucial help of

SIGNIFICANT DATES FROM THE ERA OF NAPOLEONIC EUROPE

1797	The Treaty of Campo Formio
1798	Nelson defeats the French navy
1799	The Consulate is established in France
1801	Concordat between France and the papacy
1802	Treaty of Amiens
1803	War renewed between France and Britain
1804	Execution of the Duke of Enghien
	Napoleonic Civil Code issued
	Napoleon crowned emperor
1805	Nelson wins at Trafalgar (October 21)
	Battle of Austerlitz (December 2)
1806	Battle of Jena
	Continental System imposed (November 21)
1807	Treaty of Tilsit
1808	Spain revolts against Napoleon
1809	Battle of Wagram
	Napoleon marries Marie Louise of Austria
1810	Russia leaves the Continental System
1812	Invasion of Russia; battle at Borodino
1813	Leipzig ("Battle of the Nations")
1814	Treaty of Chaumont and the Quadruple Alliance
	Congress of Vienna convenes (September)
1815	Napoleon returns from Elba (March 1)
	Battle of Waterloo (June 18)
	Holy Alliance formed (September 26)
	Quadruple Alliance renewed (November 20)
1821	Napoleon dies on Saint Helena

the Prussians under Field Marshal von Blücher (1742–1819), defeated Napoleon at Waterloo in Belgium on June 18, 1815. Napoleon again abdicated and was exiled on Saint Helena, a tiny Atlantic island off the coast of Africa, where he died in 1821.

The Hundred Days, as the period of Napoleon's return is called, frightened the great powers and made the peace settlement harsher for France. Alexander proposed a Holy Alliance, whereby the monarchs promised to act together in accordance with Christian principles. Austria and Prussia signed, but Castlereagh thought it absurd, and England abstained. The Holy Alliance soon became a symbol of extreme political reaction.

England, Austria, Prussia, and Russia renewed the Quadruple Alliance on November 20, 1815. Henceforth, it was as much a coalition for maintaining peace as for pursuing victory over France. A coalition for such a purpose had never existed in European diplomacy before. It represented an important new departure in European affairs. The leaders of Europe had learned that a treaty should secure not victory, but peace. The diplomats aimed to establish a framework for stability, rather than to punish France. The great powers sought to ensure that each of them would respect the Vienna settlement and not use force to change it.

The congress has been criticized for failing to recognize and provide for the great forces that would stir the nineteenth century—nationalism and democracy. Such criticism is inappropriate. At the time nationalist pressures were relatively rare; the general desire was for peace. The settlement, like all other such agreements, aimed to solve past ills, and in that it succeeded. The measure of the success of the Vienna settlement is that it remained essentially intact for almost half a century and prevented general war for a hundred years. (See Map 19–3.)

THE ROMANTIC MOVEMENT

WHY DID the Romantics reject much of the Enlightenment?

romanticism Reaction against the rationalism and scientism of the Enlightenment, insisting on the importance of human feelings, intuition, and imagination as supplements for reason in the human quest to understand the world.

While the French Revolution and Napoleon's reign were unfolding, an important new intellectual movement called **romanticism** spread throughout Europe. It was a reaction against the rationalism and scientism of the Enlightenment. Romantics insisted on the importance of human feelings, intuition, and imagination as supplements for reason in the human quest to understand the world. Many encouraged a revival of Christianity and of the art, literature, and architecture of Europe's Christian Middle Ages. They were fascinated by folklore, folk songs, and fairy tales, and they took dreams, hallucinations, and sleepwalking seriously as phenomena that pointed to a world that lay beyond the reach of empirical observation, sensory data, and discursive reasoning.

MAP 19–3 Europe 1815, After the Congress of Vienna The Congress of Vienna achieved the post-Napoleonic territorial adjustments shown on the map. The most notable arrangements dealt with areas along France's borders (the Netherlands, Prussia, Switzerland, and Piedmont) and in Poland and northern Italy.

In the European Settlement of 1815, did any single power dominate Europe?

ROMANTIC QUESTIONING OF THE SUPREMACY OF REASON

The romantic movement had roots in the individualism of the Renaissance, Protestant devotion and personal piety, sentimental novels of the eighteenth century, and dramatic German poetry of the *Sturm and Drang* (literally, "storm and stress") movement, which rejected the influence of French rationalism on German literature. However, two writers who were also closely related to the Enlightenment provided the immediate intellectual foundations for romanticism: Jean-Jacques Rousseau and Immanuel Kant.

Sturm and Drang ("Storm and Stress") Movement in German Romantic literature that emphasized feeling and emotion.

HOW DID Rousseau and Kant contribute to the development of romanticism?

Immanuel Kant.
Courtesy of the Library of Congress

ROUSSEAU AND EDUCATION

Rousseau's conviction that society and material prosperity had corrupted human nature profoundly influenced Romantic writers. Rousseau set forth his view on how the individual could develop to lead a good and happy life uncorrupted by society in his novel *Émile* (1762), a work that was for a long time far more influential than *The Social Contract*. In *Émile*, Rousseau stressed the difference between children and adults. He distinguished the stages of human maturation and urged that children be raised with maximum individual freedom. The parent or teacher would help most by providing the basic necessities of life and warding off what was manifestly harmful. Beyond that, the adult should stay completely out of the way. Rousseau thought that, because of their physical differences, men and women would naturally grow into social roles with different spheres of activity.

Rousseau also thought that adults should allow the child's sentiments, as well as its reason, to flourish. To Romantic writers, this concept of human development vindicated the rights of nature over those of artificial society. They thought such a form of open education would eventually lead to a natural society. Like Rousseau, the Romantics saw humankind, nature, and society as organically interrelated.

KANT AND REASON

Immanuel Kant (1724–1804) wrote the two greatest philosophical works of the late eighteenth century: *The Critique of Pure Reason* (1781) and *The Critique of Practical Reason* (1788). He sought to accept the rationalism of the Enlightenment and to still preserve a belief in human freedom, immortality, and the existence of God. For Kant, the human mind does not simply reflect the world around it like a passive mirror; rather, the mind actively imposes on the world of sensory experience "forms of sensibility" and "categories of understanding." The mind itself generates these categories. This meant that human perceptions are as much the product of the mind's own activity as of sensory experience.

Kant thought all human beings possess an innate sense of moral duty or an awareness of what he called a **categorical imperative**. This term refers to an inner command to act in every situation as one would have all other people always act in the same situation. Kant regarded the existence of this imperative of conscience as incontrovertible proof of humankind's natural freedom. On the basis of humankind's moral sense, Kant postulated the existence of God, eternal life, and future rewards and punishments.

To many Romantic writers, Kantian philosophy refuted the narrow rationality of the Enlightenment. Whether they called it "practical reason," "fancy," "imagination," "intuition," or simply "feeling," the Romantics believed that the human mind had the power to penetrate beyond the limits of largely passive human understanding as set forth by Hobbes, Locke, and Hume.

categorical imperative Kant's view that all human beings possess an innate sense of moral duty, an inner command to act in every situation as one would have other people act in that same situation.

ROMANTIC LITERATURE

HOW WERE the ideals of romanticism reflected in English and German literature?

The term *Romantic* appeared in English and French literature as early as the seventeenth century. Neoclassical writers then used the word to describe literature they considered unreal, sentimental, or excessively fanciful. In both England and Germany, the term came to be applied to all literature that did not observe classical forms and rules and gave free play to the imagination. As an alternative to such dependence on the classical forms, August Wilhelm von Schlegel (1767–1845) praised the "Romantic" literature of Dante, Petrarch, Boccaccio, Shakespeare, the Arthurian legends, Cervantes, and Calderón. According to Schlegel, Romantic literature was to classical literature what the organic and living were to the merely mechanical.

The romantic movement had peaked in Germany and England before it became a major force in France under the leadership of Madame de Staël (1766–1817) and Victor Hugo (1802–1885). So influential was the classical tradition in France that not until 1816 did a French writer openly declare himself a Romantic. That was Henri Beyle (1783–1842), who wrote under the pseudonym Stendhal.

THE ENGLISH ROMANTIC WRITERS

The English Romantics believed poetry was enhanced by freely following the creative impulses of the mind. In this belief, they directly opposed Lockean psychology, which regarded the mind as a passive receptor and poetry as a mechanical exercise of "wit" following prescribed rules.

Coleridge For Samuel Taylor Coleridge (1772–1834), the artist's imagination was God at work in the mind. As Coleridge expressed his views, the imagination was "a repetition in the finite mind of the eternal act of creation in the infinite I AM." Poetry thus could not be considered idle play. Rather, it was the highest of human acts, humankind's self-fulfillment in a transcendental world.

Wordsworth William Wordsworth (1770–1850) was Coleridge's closest friend. Together they published *Lyrical Ballads* in 1798 as a manifesto of a new poetry that rejected the rules of eighteenth-century criticism. Among Wordsworth's most important later poems is his "Ode on Intimations of Immortality" (1803), written in part to console Coleridge, who was suffering a deep personal crisis. Its subject is the loss of poetic vision, something Wordsworth also felt then in himself. Nature, which he had worshipped, no longer spoke freely to him, and he feared it might never speak to him again. He had lost what he believed all human beings lose in the necessary process of maturation: their childlike vision and closeness to spiritual reality.

Lord Byron A true rebel among the Romantic poets was Lord Byron (1788–1824). In Britain, even most of the other Romantic writers distrusted and disliked him. Outside England, however, Byron was regarded as the embodiment of the new person the French Revolution had created. He rejected the old traditions (he was divorced and famous for his many love affairs) and championed the cause of personal liberty. Byron was outrageously skeptical and mocking, even of his own beliefs. In *Childe Harold's Pilgrimage* (1812), he created a brooding, melancholy Romantic hero. In *Don Juan* (1819), he wrote with ribald humor, acknowledged nature's cruelty as well as its beauty, and even expressed admiration for urban life.

THE GERMAN ROMANTIC WRITERS

Much Romantic poetry was also written on the Continent, but almost all major German Romantics wrote at least one novel. Romantic novels often were highly sentimental and borrowed material from medieval romances. The characters of Romantic novels were treated as symbols of the larger truth of life. Purely realistic description was avoided.

Schlegel Friedrich Schlegel (1767–1845) wrote a progressive early Romantic novel, *Lucinde* (1799), that attacked prejudices against women as capable of being little more than lovers and domestics. Schlegel's novel reveals the ability of the Romantics to become involved in the social issues of their day. He depicted Lucinde as the perfect friend and companion, as well as the unsurpassed lover, of the hero. Like other early Romantic novels, the work shocked contemporary morals by frankly discussing sexual activity and by describing Lucinde as equal to the male hero.

Goethe Towering above all of these German writers stood Johann Wolfgang von Goethe (1749–1832). Perhaps the greatest German writer of modern times, Goethe defies easy classification. Part of his literary production fits into the Romantic mold, and part of it was a condemnation of Romantic excesses. The book that made his early reputation was *The Sorrows of Young Werther*, published in 1774. This novel, like many others in the eighteenth century, is a series of letters. The hero falls in love with Lotte, who is married to another man. The letters explore their relationship with the sentimentalism that was

Samuel Taylor Coleridge.
British Information Services

QUICK REVIEW
William Wordsworth (1770–1850)

- Rejected the rules of eighteenth-century literary criticism
- Believed that children existed in a more perfect spiritual state
- Believed that as people age they lose contact with natural and spiritual world

characteristic of the age. This novel became popular throughout Europe. Romantic authors admired its emphasis on feeling and on living outside the bounds of polite society.

Goethe's masterpiece is *Faust*, a long dramatic poem. In Part I (1808), Faust, a world-weary scholar, promises his soul to the devil in exchange for knowledge. Faust seduces and abandons a young woman named Gretchen. When she dies, disgraced on earth but judged worthy of heaven, he struggles with grief and guilt. In Part II of the poem (completed in the year of Goethe's death, 1832), Faust has strange adventures with witches and mythological beings, but in the end he finds peace, understanding, and salvation by dedicating his life to the improvement of humankind.

ROMANTIC ART

HOW DID Romantic artists portray nature?

The art of the Romantic Era, like its poetry and philosophy, stood largely in reaction to that of the eighteenth century. Whereas the Rococo artists had looked to Renaissance models and neoclassical painters to the art of the ancient world, Romantic painters often portrayed scenes from medieval life. For them, the Middle Ages represented the social stability and religious reverence that was disappearing from their own era.

THE CULT OF THE MIDDLE AGES AND NEO-GOTHICISM

Like many other early Romantic artists, the English landscape painter John Constable (1776–1837) was politically conservative. In *Salisbury Cathedral, from the Meadows*, he portrayed a stable world in which neither political turmoil nor industrial development challenged the traditional dominance of the church and the landed classes. Although the clouds and sky in the painting depict a severe storm, the works of both nature and humankind present a powerful sense of enduring order. The trees clearly have withstood this storm as they have withstood others for many years. The cathedral, built in the Middle Ages, has also stood majestically intact for centuries.

neo-Gothic Style of architecture in which Gothic motifs and forms are imitated.

Medieval structures not only appeared in Romantic painting. The **neo-Gothic** revival in architecture dotted the European landscape with modern imitations of them. Many medieval cathedrals were restored during this era, and new churches were designed to resemble their medieval forerunners. The British Houses of Parliament built in 1836–1837 were the most famous public buildings in the neo-Gothic style, but town halls, schools, and even railroad stations were designed to look like medieval buildings, while aristocratic country houses were rebuilt to resemble medieval castles.

NATURE AND THE SUBLIME

Beyond their attraction to history, Romantic artists also sought to portray nature in all of its majestic power as no previous generation of European artists had ever done. Their works often sought to portray what they and others termed *the sublime*—that is, subjects from nature that aroused strong emotions, such as fear, dread, and awe, and raised questions about whether and how much we control our lives.

Romantics saw nature as a set of infinite forces that overwhelmed the smallness of humankind. For example, in 1824, the German artist Caspar David Friedrich (1774–1840) in *The Polar Sea* painted the plight of a ship trapped and crushed by the force of a vast polar ice field. In direct contrast to eighteenth-century artists' portrayal of sunny Enlightenment, Friedrich also painted numerous scenes in which human beings stand shrouded in the mysterious darkness of night where moonlight and torches cast only fitful illumination.

Caspar David Friedrich's *The Polar Sea* illustrated the power of nature to diminish the creations of humankind as seen in the wrecked ship on the right of the painting.

Kunsthalle, Hamburg, Germany/A.K.G., Berlin/Super-Stock

What marks this as a Romantic painting?

An artist who similarly understood the power of nature but also depicted the forces of the new industrialism that was challenging them was Joseph Mallord William Turner (1775–1851) whose painting *Rain, Steam and Speed—The Great Western Railway* of 1844 illustrated the recently invented railway engine barreling through an enveloping storm. In this scene the new technology is both part of the natural world and strong enough to dominate it.

Friedrich's and Turner's paintings taken together symbolize the contradictory forces affecting Romantic artists—the sense of the power, awe, and mastery of nature coupled with the sense that the advance of industry represented a new kind of awesome human power that could challenge or even surpass the forces of nature itself.

RELIGION IN THE ROMANTIC PERIOD

Romantic religious thinkers sought the foundations of religion in the inner emotions of humankind. Reacting to the anticlericalism of both the Enlightenment and the French Revolution, these thinkers also saw religious faith, experience, and institutions as central to human life. Their forerunners were the mystics of Western Christianity. One of the first great examples of a religion characterized by romantic impulses—Methodism—arose in mid–eighteenth-century England during the Enlightenment itself and became one of the most powerful forces in transatlantic religion during the nineteenth century.

HOW DID Romantic religious thinkers view the religious experience?

METHODISM

Methodism originated in the middle of the eighteenth century as a revolt against deism and rationalism in the Church of England. The leader of the Methodist movement was John Wesley (1703–1791). While at Oxford University studying to be an Anglican priest, Wesley organized a religious group known as the Holy Club. He soon left England for missionary work in the new colony of Georgia in America, where he arrived in 1735. While he was crossing the Atlantic, a group of German Moravians on the ship deeply impressed him with their unshakable faith and confidence during a storm. Wesley, who had despaired of his life, concluded they knew far better than he the meaning of justification by faith. When he returned to England in 1738, Wesley began to worship with Moravians in London. There, in 1739, he underwent a conversion experience.

Wesley discovered he could not preach his version of Christian conversion and practical piety in Anglican church pulpits. Therefore, late in 1739, he began to preach in the open fields near the cities and towns of western England. Thousands of humble people responded to his message of repentance and good works. Soon he and his brother Charles (1707–1788), who became famous for his hymns, began to organize Methodist societies. By the late eighteenth century, the Methodists had become a separate church. They ordained their own clergy and sent missionaries to America, where they eventually achieved their greatest success and influence.

Methodism stressed inward, heartfelt religion and the possibility of Christian perfection in this life. Many people, weary of the dry rationalism that derived from deism, found Wesley's ideal relevant to their own lives. The Methodist preachers emphasized the role of enthusiastic, emotional experience as part of Christian conversion. After Wesley, religious revivals became highly emotional in style and content.

Methodism Movement begun in England by John Wesley, an Oxford-educated Anglican priest, the first major religion to embody romanticism. It emphasized religion as a "method" for living more than a set of doctrines.

NEW DIRECTIONS IN CONTINENTAL RELIGION

Similar religious developments based on feeling appeared on the Continent. After the Thermidorian Reaction, a strong Roman Catholic revival took place in France. Its followers disapproved of both the religious policy of the revolution and the anticlericalism of the Enlightenment. The most important book to express these sentiments was *The Genius of Christianity* (1802) by Viscount François René de Chateaubriand (1768–1848). In this work, which became known as the "bible of Romanticism," Chateaubriand argued that the essence of religion is "passion." The foundation of faith in the church was the emotion that its teachings and sacraments inspired in the heart of the Christian.

No one stated the Romantic religious ideal more eloquently or with greater impact on the modern world than Friedrich Schleiermacher (1768–1834). In 1799, he published *Speeches on Religion to Its Cultured Despisers*. According to Schleiermacher,

John Wesley (1703–1791) was the founder of Methodism. He emphasized the role of emotional experience in Christian conversion.

CORBIS/Bettmann

How did Methodism differ from older, more mainstream forms of Christianity?

religion was neither dogma nor a system of ethics. It was an intuition or feeling of absolute dependence on an infinite reality. Religious institutions, doctrines, and moral activity expressed that primal religious feeling only in a secondary, or indirect, way.

ROMANTIC VIEWS OF NATIONALISM AND HISTORY

WHAT WERE the Romantic views of history and national identity?

A distinctive feature of romanticism, especially in Germany, was its glorification of both the individual person and individual cultures. Behind these views lay the philosophy of German idealism, which understood the world as the creation of subjective egos. The world is as it is because especially strong persons conceive of it in a particular way and impose their wills on the world and other people. This philosophy has ever since served to justify the glorification of great persons and their actions in overriding all opposition to their will and desires.

HERDER AND CULTURE

In addition to this philosophy, the influence of new historical studies lay behind the German glorification of individual cultures. German Romantic writers went in search of their own past in reaction to the copying of French manners in eighteenth-century Germany, the impact of the French Revolution, and the imperialism of Napoleon. An early leader in this effort was Johann Gottfried Herder (1744–1803). Herder saw human beings and societies as developing organically, like plants, over time. Human beings were different at different times and places.

Herder revived German folk culture by urging the collection and preservation of distinctive German songs and sayings. His most important followers in this work were the Grimm brothers, Jakob (1785–1863) and Wilhelm (1786–1859), famous for their collection of fairy tales. Herder's writings led to a broad revival of interest in history and philosophy. Although initially directed toward identifying German origins, such work soon expanded to embrace other world cultures. Eventually the ability of the Romantic imagination to be at home in any age or culture spurred the study of non-Western religion, comparative literature, and philology.

HEGEL AND HISTORY

The most important philosopher of history in the Romantic period was the German, Georg Wilhelm Friedrich Hegel (1770–1831). Hegel believed ideas develop in an evolutionary fashion that involves conflict. At any given time, a predominant set of ideas, which he termed the thesis, holds sway. Conflicting ideas, which Hegel termed the antithesis, challenge the thesis. As these patterns of thought clash, a synthesis emerges that eventually becomes the new thesis. Then the process begins all over again. Periods of world history receive their character from the patterns of thought that predominate during them.

Several important philosophical conclusions followed from this analysis. One of the most significant was the belief that all periods of history have been of almost equal value because each was, by definition, necessary to the achievements of those that came later. Also, all cultures are valuable because each contributes to the necessary clash of values and ideas that allows humankind to develop.

ISLAM, THE MIDDLE EAST, AND ROMANTICISM

The new religious, literary, and historical sensibilities of the Romantic period modified the European understanding of both Islam and the Arab world while at the same time preserving long-standing attitudes.

The energized Christianity associated with Methodist-like forms of Protestantism, on the one hand, and Chateaubriand's emotional Roman Catholicism, on the other, renewed the traditional sense of necessary conflict between Christianity and Islam. Indeed, the medieval Crusades against Islam fired the Romantic imagination. The general nineteenth-century association of nationalistic aspirations with romanticism also cast the Ottoman Empire and with it Islam in an unfavorable political light. Romantic poets and intellectuals championed the cause of the Greek Revolution (see Chapter 20) and revived older charges of Ottoman despotism.

By contrast, other Romantic sensibilities induced Europeans to see the Muslim world in a more positive fashion. The Romantic emphasis on the value of literature drawn from different cultures and ages allowed many nineteenth-century European readers to enjoy the stories from *The Thousand and One Nights*, which first appeared in English in 1778 from a French translation. As poets across Europe rejected classicism in literature in favor of folk stories and fairy tales, they saw the *Arabian Nights* as mysterious and exotic. In 1859, Edward FitzGerald (1809–1883) published his highly popular translation of the *Rubáiyát of Omar Khayyám* of Nishapur, a Persian poet of the twelfth century.

Herder's and Hegel's concepts of history gave both the Arab peoples and Islam distinct roles in history. For Herder, Arab culture was one of the numerous communities that composed the human race and manifested the human spirit. For Hegel, Islam represented an important stage of the development of the world spirit. However, Hegel believed Islam had fulfilled its role in history and no longer had any significant part to play.

The British historian and social commentator Thomas Carlyle (1795–1881) attributed new, positive qualities to Muhammad himself. In his book *On Heroes and Hero-Worship* (1841), Carlyle presented Muhammad as the embodiment of the hero as prophet. To Carlyle, Muhammad was straightforward and sincere. Carlyle's understanding of religion was similar to Schleiermacher's, and thus in his pages, Muhammad appeared as a person who had experienced God subjectively and had communicated a sense of the divine to others. Although friendly to Muhammad from a historical standpoint, Carlyle nonetheless saw him as one of many great religious figures and not, as Muslims believed, as the last of the prophets through whom God had spoken.

The person whose actions in the long run did perhaps the most to reshape the idea of both Islam and the Middle East in the European imagination was Napoleon himself. With his Egyptian expedition of 1798, the first European military invasion of the Near East since the Crusades, the study of the Arab world became an important activity within French intellectual life. For his invasion of Egypt to succeed, Napoleon believed he must make it clear he had no intention of destroying Islam but rather sought to liberate Egypt from the military clique that governed the country in the name of the Ottoman Empire. To that end, he took with him scholars of Arabic and Islamic culture whom he urged to converse with the most educated people they could meet. Napoleon personally met with the local Islamic leaders and had all of his speeches and proclamations translated into classical Arabic. Such cultural sensitivity and the serious efforts of the French scholars to learn Arabic and study the Qur'an impressed Egyptian scholars. It was on this expedition that the famous Rosetta Stone was discovered. Now housed in the British Museum, it eventually led to the decipherment of ancient Egypt's hieroglyphic writing. Two cultural effects in the West of Napoleon's invasion were an increase in the number of European visitors to the Middle East and a demand for architecture based on ancient Egyptian models. Perhaps the most famous example of this fad is the Washington Monument in Washington, D.C., which is modeled after ancient Egyptian obelisks.

When Napoleon invaded Egypt in 1799, he met stiff resistance. On July 25, however, the French won a decisive victory. This painting of that battle by Baron Antoine Gros (1771–1835) emphasizes French heroism and Muslim defeat. Such an outlook was typical of European views of Arabs and the Islamic world.

Antoine Jean Gros (1771–1835). Detail, *Battle of Aboukir, July 25, 1799*, c. 1806. Oil on canvas. Chateaux de Versailles et de Trianon, Versailles, France. Bridgeman—Giraudon/Art Resource, NY

What differences were there, if any, between Enlightenment and Romantic views of Islam and the Middle East?

Summary

HOW DID Napoleon come to power in France?

The Rise of Napoleon Bonaparte In France in 1799, Napoleon Bonaparte made himself First Consul. He had taken advantage of the Directory's weaknesses, his own past military successes, and the naivete of politicians who thought Napoleon could be used as a figurehead, to grant himself powers comparable to those of Roman emperors. *page 468*

HOW DID the Consulate end the revolution in France?

The Consulate in France (1799–1804) The French Revolution ended with Napoleon's Consulate; the bourgeoisie and the peasants were satisfied. Napoleon seemed to offer stability, and the voters approved his constitution in a plebiscite. Napoleon signed treaties that brought peace to Europe and maneuvered to build coalitions and crush dissent at home. He concluded a concordat with the pope in 1801, which ratified the status quo but allowed Napoleon to replace clergy throughout France. Napoleon continued to increase his power and initiated codification of French law (the Napoleonic Code), which mostly endorsed changes that had been effected by the revolution while incrementally enhancing the state's power. By 1804, Napoleon was ready to crown himself emperor, making himself Napoleon I. *page 469*

HOW DID Napoleon build an empire?

Napoleon's Empire (1804–1814) Between 1804 and 1815, Napoleon conquered most of Europe, dismantling remnants of the Old Regime along the way. The revolution had mobilized France, and Napoleon took advantage of the fact that he could field more troops at once than any other military leader. Napoleon's greatest victory was probably his 1805 defeat of combined Austrian and Russian forces at Austerlitz. He occupied Vienna, reorganized Germany, caused the dissolution of the Holy Roman Empire, and reduced Prussia by half. Only Britain could compete with France. Napoleon's chief defeat had come in 1805 at the hands of Lord Nelson, at the Battle of Trafalgar. Napoleon attempted to weaken Britain through trade embargoes, but this turned out to hurt the Continental System more than it hurt Britain. *page 471*

WHY DID Napoleonic rule breed resentment in Europe?

European Response to the Empire Opposition to Napoleon fanned the flames of nationalism. Following his victory over the Prussians at Jena in 1806, nationalists called for Germany's unification. When he deposed the Bourbon monarchs of Spain in favor of his brother, the Spaniards rebelled. Austria's declaration of war on France gave him an opportunity to occupy Austrian territory, and in 1810, Russia's withdrawal from the Continental System prompted him to march on Moscow. The Russian winter forced him to retreat, and in October 1813, a powerful coalition defeated him. In the spring of 1814, he went into exile on the island of Elba. *page 474*

WHAT WERE the consequences of the Congress of Vienna?

The Congress of Vienna and the European Settlement In 1815 the Congress of Vienna broke new ground in international law by concluding treaties among states that prevented war in Europe for a century. France was reduced in size and its Bourbon dynasty restored. State boundaries were adjusted around France and in eastern Europe to enhance security. Napoleon attempted a comeback while the Congress was still debating these arrangements, but a British and Prussian force defeated him at Waterloo in June 1815, and he was exiled once again—this time to the island of Saint Helena. *page 479*

WHY DID the Romantics reject much of the Enlightenment?

The Romantic Movement Romanticism was an intellectual movement that emerged throughout Europe during the period of the French Revolution and Napoleonic rule. In a reaction against the Enlightenment, romanticism emphasized the value of intuition, spirituality, folklore, dreams, and other forms of human experience that lie beyond the realm of reason. *page 480*

HOW DID Rousseau and Kant contribute to the development of romanticism?

Romantic Questioning of the Supremacy of Reason Romanticism's intellectual foundations were laid largely by Jean-Jacques Rousseau and Immanuel Kant. Rousseau's belief that human nature is corrupted by society and by material prosperity, and his interest in childhood were reflected in the romantic movement's efforts to reform education and family life. Kant argued for the subjectivity of human knowledge. He theorized that because humans share an innate understanding of the categorical imperative, morality must be something independent of sensory experience. *page 481*

HOW WERE the ideals of romanticism reflected in English and German literature and in Romantic art at end of question?

Romantic Literature "Romantic literature" meant slightly different things in different countries and periods. In general, it meant literature that stressed the imaginative elements and was not bound by formal rules. Romantic literature peaked in England and Germany before France. English Romantics such as Coleridge and Wordsworth excelled in poetry that dealt with themes including morality, mortality, and creativity. German Romantics also wrote a great deal of poetry, but most of the major German Romantic authors wrote at least one novel. Goethe was the greatest German writer of the era, although he was a more complicated figure than the label "romantic" suggests. *Faust* was his seminal work. *page 481*

HOW DID Romantic artists portray nature?

Romantic Art The art of the romantic period, like its poetry and philosophy, reacted against the orderly, secular views of the Enlightenment that confidently sought to improve the world. Romantic artists looked to the Middle Ages for inspiration to capture the qualities of what they viewed as a more enduring order that emphasized social stability, religious reverence, the pastoral countryside, and nature in all its majestic and awesome force. The art of this era both feared and were impressed by the tremendous power of the industrializing world. *page 484*

HOW DID Romantic religious thinkers view the religious experience?

Religion in the Romantic Period Romanticism in religion stressed the individual's heartfelt response to the divine. Methodism developed in England in the eighteenth century as a reaction against deism and rationalism in the Church of England. Methodists believe in Christian perfectibility in this life; the enthusiastic emotional experience is part of Christian conversion. In France, Chateaubriand argued that passion is at the heart of religion. Schleiermacher described religion as a feeling of dependence on an infinite being. *page 485*

WHAT WERE the Romantic views of history and national identity?

Romantic Views of Nationalism and History Romanticism glorified both individuals and individual cultures. The German philosophy of idealism helped explain the relationship between the acts of strong individuals and the shaping of history. German Romantics also encouraged the study of folk culture. The German philosopher G. W. F. Hegel explained history in terms of the evolution of the prevailing ideas of a time and place. Europe's interest in the Arab world was revived by current events such as Napoleon's invasion of Egypt. The new European scholarship on Islam, however, perpetuated old Western stereotypes. *page 486*

REVIEW QUESTIONS

1. How did Napoleon rise to power? What were the stages by which he eventually made himself emperor? What were his major domestic achievements? Did his rule more nearly fulfill or betray the ideals of the French Revolution?

2. How did Napoleon acquire and rule his empire? Why did he invade Russia? Why did his campaign fail? Was he a military genius, or did his successes owe more to the ineptitude of his opponents?

3. Who were the principal personalities at the Congress of Vienna? What were the most significant problems they addressed? What was the long-term significance of the Congress?

4. How does the role Romantic writers assigned to feelings compare with the role Enlightenment writers claimed for reason? What questions did Rousseau and Kant raise about reason? How did the Romantic understanding of religion differ from Reformation Protestantism and Enlightenment deism? What was the importance of history to the Romantics? What inspired Romantic artists?

KEY TERMS

categorical imperative (p. 482)
Consulate (p. 469)
Methodism (p. 485)

neo-Gothic (p. 484)
romanticism (p. 480)
Sturm and Drang (p. 481)

For additional learning resources related to this chapter, please go to **www.myhistorylab.com**

PEARSON
myhistorylab

20

The Conservative Order and the Challenges of Reform (1815–1832)

In 1830, revolution again erupted in France as well as elsewhere on the Continent. Eugène Delacroix's *Liberty Leading the People* was the most famous image recalling that event. Note how Delacroix portrays persons from different social classes and occupations joining the revolution led by the figure of Liberty.

Eugène Delacroix (1798–1863), *Liberty Leading the People*, 1830. Oil on canvas, 260 × 325 cm—RF 129. Louvre/RMN Réunion des Musées Nationaux, France. Erich Lessing/Art Resource, NY

How did the French Revolution inspire movements for political change across Europe in the nineteenth century?

R eactionary movements that favored monarchy and aristocracy dominated European politics for the decade following the Congress of Vienna. However, nationalism and liberalism, two new ideologies, challenged the traditional understanding of the state as nothing more than a collection of properties belonging to a royal dynasty. Nationalists claimed that ethnicity was the true basis for statehood, and they wanted to redraw the map of Europe to reflect boundaries among ethnic groups. Liberals challenged the traditional order in a different way. They wanted governments to implement moderate political reforms and establish freer economic markets. ▪

THE CHALLENGES OF NATIONALISM AND LIBERALISM

HOW DID early-nineteenth-century nationalists define the nation?

Throughout the nineteenth-century Western world, secular ideologies began to take hold of the learned and popular imaginations in opposition to the political and social status quo. These included nationalism, liberalism, republicanism, socialism, and communism.

THE EMERGENCE OF NATIONALISM

nationalism The belief that the people who share an ethnic identity (language, culture, and history) should also be recognized as having a right to a government and political identity of their own.

Nationalism proved to be the single most powerful European political ideology of the nineteenth and early twentieth centuries. As a political outlook, nationalism was and is based on the relatively modern concept that a nation is composed of people who are joined together by the bonds of a common language, as well as common customs, culture, and history, and who, because of these bonds, should be administered by the same government. The idea came into its own during the late eighteenth and the early nineteenth centuries.

Opposition to the Vienna Settlement Early-nineteenth-century nationalism directly opposed the principle upheld at the Congress of Vienna that legitimate monarchies or dynasties, rather than ethnicity, provide the basis for political unity. Nationalists naturally protested multinational states such as the Austrian and Russian Empires. They also objected to peoples of the same ethnic group, such as Germans and Italians, dwelling in a political unit smaller than that of the ethnic nation. Consequently, nationalists challenged both the domestic and the international order of the Vienna settlement.

Behind the concept of nationalism usually, though not always, lay the idea of popular sovereignty, since the qualities of peoples, rather than their rulers, determine a national character. This aspect of nationalism, however, frequently led to confusion or conflict over the status of minorities in regions ruled by a different ethnic majority.

Creating Nations In fact, it was nationalists who actually created nations in the nineteenth century. During the first half of the century, a particular, usually small, group of nationalistically minded writers or other intellectual elites, using the printed word, spread a nationalistic concept of the nation. In effect, they gave a people a sense of their past and a literature of their own. These small groups of early nationalists established the cultural beliefs and political expectations on which the later mass-supported nationalism of the second half of the century would grow.

Which language to use in the schools and in government offices was always a point of contention for nationalists. In France and Italy, official versions of the national language were imposed in the schools and they replaced local dialects. In parts of Scandinavia and eastern Europe, nationalists attempted to resurrect from earlier times what they regarded as purer versions of the national language. This process of establishing national languages led to far more linguistic uniformity in European nations than had existed before the nineteenth century.

Language could become such an effective cornerstone in the foundation of nationalism thanks largely to the emergence of the print culture discussed in Chapter 17. The uniform language found in printed works could overcome regional spoken dialects and establish itself as dominant. In most countries, spoken and written proficiency in the official, printed language became a path to social and political advancement. The growth of a uniform language helped persuade people who had not thought of themselves as constituting a nation that in fact they were one.

Meaning of Nationhood   Nationalists used a variety of arguments and metaphors to express what they meant by *nationhood*. Some argued that gathering, for example, Italians into a unified Italy or Germans into a unified Germany, thus eliminating or at least federating the petty dynastic states that governed those regions, would promote economic and administrative efficiency. Adopting a tenet from political liberalism, certain nationalist writers suggested that nations determining their own destinies resembled individuals exploiting personal talents to determine their own careers. Some nationalists claimed that nations, like biological species in the natural world, were distinct creations of God. Other nationalists claimed a place for their nations in the divine order of things.

A significant difficulty for nationalism was, and is, determining which ethnic groups could be considered nations, with claims to territory and political autonomy. In theory, any of them could, but in reality, nationhood came to be associated with groups that were large enough to support a viable economy, that had a significant cultural history, that possessed a cultural elite that could nourish and spread the national language, and that had the military capacity to conquer other peoples or to establish and protect their own independence. (See "Compare & Connect: Mazzini and Lord Acton Debate the Political Principles of Nationalism," pages 494–495.)

Regions of Nationalistic Pressure   During the nineteenth century, nationalists challenged the political status quo in six major areas of Europe. England had brought Ireland under direct rule in 1800. Irish nationalists, however, wanted independence or at least larger measures of self-government. German nationalists sought political unity for all German-speaking peoples, challenging the multinational structure of the Austrian Empire and pitting Prussia and Austria against each other. Italian nationalists sought to unify Italian-speaking peoples on the Italian peninsula and to drive out the Austrians. Polish nationalists, targeting primarily their Russian rulers, struggled to restore Poland as an independent nation. In eastern Europe, a host of national groups, including Hungarians, Czechs, Slovenes, and others, sought either independence or formal recognition within the Austrian Empire. Finally, in southeastern Europe on the Balkan peninsula and eastward, national groups, including Serbs, Greeks, Albanians, Romanians, and Bulgarians, sought independence from Ottoman and Russian control.

EARLY-NINETEENTH-CENTURY POLITICAL LIBERALISM

The word *liberal*, as applied to political activity, entered the European and American vocabulary during the nineteenth century. Its meaning has varied over time, and the values and beliefs of nineteenth-century liberals bear little resemblance to the values and beliefs identified with liberalism in America today.

MAZZINI AND LORD ACTON DEBATE THE POLITICAL PRINCIPLES OF NATIONALISM

No political force in the nineteenth and twentieth centuries was stronger than nationalism. It eventually replaced loyalty to a dynasty with loyalty based on ethnic considerations. It received new standing after World War I when the self-determination of nations became one of the cornerstones of the Paris Peace Treaties. Still later, former European colonies embraced this powerful idea. Yet from the earliest enunciation of the principles of nationalism the concept confronted major critics who understood its potential destructiveness. In these two documents Mazzini, the great Italian nationalist, sets forth his understanding of nationalism, and Lord Acton, the distinguished nineteenth-century English historian, points to the dangers lurking behind the ideas and realities of politics based on nationalism.

QUESTIONS

1. What qualities of a people does Mazzini associate with nationalism?

2. How and why does Mazzini relate nationalism to divine purposes?

3. Why does Acton see the principle of nationality as dangerous to liberty?

4. Why does Acton see nationalism as a threat to minority groups and to democracy?

5. How might the connection that Mazzini draws between nationalism and divine will serve to justify the repression of minority rights that Acton feared?

I. MAZZINI DEFINES NATIONALITY

In 1835 the Italian nationalist and patriot Giuseppe Mazzini (1805–1872) explained his understanding of nationalism. Note how he combines a generally democratic view of politics with a religious concept of the divine destiny of nations. Once in power, however, nationalist states in Europe and the rest of the world were often not democratic states.

The essential characteristics of a nationality are common ideas, common principles and a common purpose. A nation is an association of those who are brought together by language, by given geographical conditions or by the role assigned them by history, who acknowledge the same principles and who march together to the conquest of a single definite goal under the rule of a uniform body of law.

The life of a nation consists in harmonious activity (that is, the employment of all individual abilities and energies comprised within the association) towards this single goal. . . .

But nationality means even more than this. Nationality also consists in the share of mankind's labors which God assigns to a people. This mission is the task which a people must perform to the end that the Divine Idea shall be realized in this world; it is the work which gives a people its rights as a member of Mankind; it is the baptismal rite which endows a people with its own character and its rank in the brotherhood of nations. . . .

Nationality depends for its very existence upon its sacredness within and beyond its borders.

If nationality is to be inviolable for all, friends and foes alike, it must be regarded inside a country as holy, like a religion, and outside a country as a grave mission. It is necessary too that the ideas arising within a country grow steadily, as part of the general law of Humanity which is the source of all nationality. It is necessary that these ideas be shown to other lands in their beauty and purity, free from any alien mixture, from any slavish fears, from any skeptical hesitancy, strong and active, embracing in their evolution every aspect and manifestation of the life of the nation. These ideas, a necessary component in the order of universal destiny, must retain their originality even as they enter harmoniously into mankind's general progress.

The people must be the basis of nationality; its logically derived and vigorously applied principles its means; the strength of all its strength; the improvement of the life of all and the happiness of the greatest possible number its results; and the accomplishment of the task assigned to it by God its goal. This is what we mean by nationality.

Source: From Herbert H. Rowen, ed., *From Absolutism to Revolution, 1648–1848*, 2nd ed. © 1969. Reprinted by permission of Prentice Hall, Inc., Upper Saddle River, NJ, pp. 277–280.

II. LORD ACTON CONDEMNS NATIONALISM

As well as being an historian, Lord Acton (1834–1902) was an important nineteenth-century commentator on contemporary religious and political events. He was deeply concerned with the character and preservation of liberty. In his essay "Nationality" of 1862, Lord Acton's became one of the earliest voices to warn that nationalism, or what he here terms "the modern theory of nationality," could endanger liberty of both individuals and people who found themselves to be an ethnic minority within a state dominated by a different ethnic or nationalist majority. Acton's words would prove prophetic with regard to the fate of ethnic minorities within Europe for the next century. Acton also pointed out that the pursuit of nationalist goals might mean that a government would ignore the economic well-being of its peoples.

The greatest adversary of the rights of nationality is the modern theory of nationality. By making the State and the nation commensurate with each other in theory, it reduces practically to a subject condition all other nationalities that may be within the boundary. It cannot admit them to an equality with the ruling nation which constitutes the State, because the State would then cease to be national, which would be a contradiction of the principle of its existence. According, therefore, to the degree of humanity and civilization in that dominant body which claims all the rights of the community, the inferior races are exterminated, or reduced to servitude, or outlawed, or put in a condition of dependence.

If we take the establishment of liberty for the realization of moral duties to be the end of civil society, we must conclude that those states are substantially the most perfect which, like the British and Austrian Empires, include various distinct nationalities without oppressing them. Those in which no mixture of races has occurred are imperfect; and those in which its effects have disappeared are decrepit. A State which is incompetent to satisfy different races condemns itself; a State which labors to neutralize, to absorb, or to expel them, destroys its own vitality; a State which does not include them is destitute of the chief basis of self-government. The theory of nationality, therefore, is a retrograde step in history. . . .

During the revolutionary months of 1848, Italian nationalists unfurled the tri-colored green, white and red Italian nationalist flag on St. Mark's Square in Venice to replace the flag of Austria, which then ruled the city. Austrian rule of Venice only ended in 1866.

Picture Desk Inc., Kobal Collection

What was the relationship between nationalism and militarism in the nineteenth century?

[N]ationality does not aim either at liberty or prosperity, both of which it sacrifices to the imperative necessity of making the nation the mold and measure of the State. Its course will be marked with material as well as moral ruin, in order that a new invention may prevail over the works of God and the interests of mankind. There is no principle of change, no phrase of political speculation conceivable, more comprehensive, more subversive, or more arbitrary than this. It is a confutation of democracy, because it sets limits to the exercise of the popular will, and substitutes for it a higher principle.

Source: From John Emerich Edward Dalbert-Acton, First Baron Acton, *Essays in the History of Liberty*, ed. by J. Rufus Fears (Indianapolis, IN: Liberty Classics, 1985), pp. 431–433.

Political Goals   Nineteenth-century liberals derived their political ideas from the writers of the Enlightenment, the example of English liberties, and the so-called principles of 1789 embodied in the French Declaration of the Rights of Man and Citizen. They sought to establish a political framework of legal equality, religious toleration, and freedom of the press. Their general goal was a political structure that would limit the arbitrary power of government against the persons and property of individual citizens. They generally believed the legitimacy of government emanated from the freely given consent of the governed. The popular basis of such government was to be expressed through elected representative, or parliamentary, bodies. Most importantly, free government required government ministers to be responsible to the representatives rather than to the monarch. Liberals sought to achieve these political arrangements through written constitutions. They wanted to see constitutionalism and constitutional governments installed across the Continent.

Those who espoused liberal political structures often were educated, relatively wealthy people, usually associated with the professions or commercial life, but who were excluded in one manner or another from the existing political processes. Although liberals wanted broader political participation, they did not advocate democracy. What they wanted was to extend representation to the propertied classes. Second only to their hostility to the privileged aristocracies was their contempt for the lower, unpropertied classes. Liberals transformed the eighteenth-century concept of aristocratic liberty into a new concept of privilege based on wealth and property rather than birth. By the middle of the century, this widely shared attitude meant that throughout Europe liberals had separated themselves from both the rural peasant and the urban working class, a division that was to have important consequences.

Economic Goals   The economic goals of nineteenth-century liberals also divided them from working people. Following the Enlightenment ideas of Adam Smith, they sought to abolish the economic restraints associated with mercantilism or the regulated economies of enlightened absolutists. They wanted to manufacture and sell goods freely. To that end, they favored the removal of international tariffs and internal barriers to trade. Economic liberals opposed the old paternalistic legislation that established wages and labor practices by government regulation or by guild privileges. They saw labor as simply one more commodity to be bought and sold freely.

Because the social and political circumstances of various countries differed, the specific programs of liberals also differed from one country to another. Great Britain and France already had many structures liberals favored. The problem for liberals in both countries was to protect civil liberties, define the respective powers of the monarch and the elected legislature, and expand the electorate moderately while avoiding democracy.

The complex political situation in German-speaking Europe was different from that in France or Britain, and German liberalism differed accordingly from its French and British counterparts. In the German states and Austria, monarchs and aristocrats offered stiffer resistance to liberal ideas, leaving German liberals with less access to direct political influence. Little or no precedent existed for middle-class participation in the government or the military, and there was no strong tradition of civil or individual liberty. Most German liberals favored a united Germany and looked either to Austria or to Prussia as the instrument of unification. As a result, they were more tolerant of a strong state and monarchical power than other liberals were.

Relationship of Nationalism to Liberalism   Nationalism could be, and often was, directly opposed to liberal political values. Some nationalists wanted their own particular ethnic group to dominate minority national or ethnic groups within a particular

QUICK REVIEW
Liberal Political Program

◆ Derived from principles embodied in the Declaration of the Rights of Man and Citizen
◆ Favored equality before the law, religious toleration, and freedom of the press
◆ Wanted to see constitutional governments established throughout Europe

QUICK REVIEW
Liberal Economics

◆ Embraced the theories of Adam Smith
◆ Wanted free markets with limited governmental interference
◆ Saw labor as a commodity to be bought and sold

region. Nationalists also often defined their own national group in opposition to other national groups whom they might regard as cultural inferiors or historical enemies. Furthermore, conservative nationalists might seek political autonomy for their own ethnic group but have no intention of establishing liberal political institutions thereafter. Nonetheless, although liberalism and nationalism were not identical, they were often compatible. By espousing representative government, civil liberties, and economic freedom, nationalist groups in one country could gain the support of liberals elsewhere in Europe who might not otherwise share their nationalist interests.

CONSERVATIVE GOVERNMENTS: THE DOMESTIC POLITICAL ORDER

Despite the challenges of liberalism and nationalism, the domestic political order that the restored conservative institutions of Europe established, particularly in Great Britain and eastern Europe, showed remarkable staying power. Not until World War I did their power and pervasive influence come to an end.

CONSERVATIVE OUTLOOKS

The major pillars of nineteenth-century **conservatism** were legitimate monarchies, landed aristocracies, and established churches. In the eighteenth century, these groups had often quarreled. Only the upheavals of the French Revolution and the Napoleonic era transformed them into natural, if sometimes reluctant, allies. In that sense, conservatism as an articulated outlook and set of cooperating institutions was as new a feature on the political landscape as nationalism and liberalism.

The more theoretical political and religious ideas of the conservative classes were associated with thinkers such as Edmund Burke (see Chapter 18) and Friedrich Hegel (see Chapter 19). Conservatives shared other, less formal attitudes forged by the revolutionary experience. The execution of Louis XVI at the hands of radical democrats convinced most monarchs they could trust only aristocratic governments or governments of aristocrats in alliance with the wealthiest middle-class and professional people. The European aristocracies believed that no form of genuinely representative government would protect their property and influence. The churches equally distrusted popular movements, except their own revivals. They also feared and hated most of the ideas associated with the Enlightenment.

All the nations of Europe in the years immediately after 1815 confronted problems arising directly from their entering an era of peace after a quarter century of armed conflict. The wartime footing had allowed all the belligerent governments to exercise firm control over their populations. War had fueled economies and had furnished vast areas of employment in armies, navies, military industries, and agriculture. The onset of peace meant citizens could raise new political issues and that economies were no longer geared to supplying military needs. Thus, the conservative statesmen who led every major government in 1815 confronted new pressures that would cause various degrees of domestic unrest and would lead them to resort to differing degrees of repression.

LIBERALISM AND NATIONALISM RESISTED IN AUSTRIA AND THE GERMANIES

The early-nineteenth-century statesman who, more than any other epitomized conservatism, was the Austrian prince Metternich (1773–1859). It was Metternich who seemed to exercise chief control over the forces of European reaction.

WHAT EXPLAINS the strength of conservatism in the early nineteenth century?

conservatism Form of political thought that, in mid-nineteenth-century Europe, promoted legitimate monarchies, landed aristocracies, and established churches.

Prince Klemens von Metternich (1773–1859) epitomized nineteenth-century conservatism.

Sir Thomas Lawrence (1769–1830), *Clemens Lothar Wenzel, Prince Metternich* (1773–1859), RCIN 404948, OM 905 WC 206. The Royal Collection © 2006, Her Majesty Queen Elizabeth II

Why was Metternich so hostile to liberalism and nationalism?

Dynastic Integrity of the Habsburg Empire   The Austrian government could make no serious compromises with the new political forces in Europe. To no other country were the programs of liberalism and nationalism potentially more dangerous. Germans and Hungarians, as well as Poles, Czechs, Slovaks, Slovenes, Italians, Croats, and other ethnic groups, peopled the Habsburg domains. Through client governments, Austria also dominated those parts of the Italian peninsula that it did not rule directly. For Metternich and other Austrian officials, the recognition of the political rights and aspirations of any of the various national groups would mean the probable dissolution of the empire. To safeguard dynastic integrity, Austria had to prevent the formation of a German national state that might absorb the German-speaking heart of the empire and exclude the other realms the Habsburgs governed.

Defeat of Prussian Reform   An important victory for this holding policy came in Prussia in the years immediately after the Congress of Vienna. In 1815, Frederick William III (r. 1797–1840) had promised some form of constitutional government. After stalling, he formally reneged on his pledge in 1817. Instead, he created a new Council of State, which, although it improved administrative efficiency, was responsible to him alone. In 1819, the king moved further from reform. After a major disagreement over the organization of the army, he replaced his reform-minded ministers with hardened conservatives. On their advice, in 1823, Frederick William III established eight provincial estates, or diets. These bodies were dominated by the Junkers and exercised only an advisory function. The old bonds linking monarchy, army, and landholders in Prussia had been reestablished.

Student Nationalism and the Carlsbad Decrees   Nonetheless, in the aftermath of the defeat of Napoleon, many young Germans continued to cherish nationalist and liberal expectations. University students who had grown up during the days of the reforms of Stein and Hardenberg and had read the writings of early German nationalists made up the most important of these groups. When they went to the universities, they continued to dream of a united Germany. They formed *Burschenschaften*, or student associations. Like student groups today, these clubs served numerous social functions, one of which was to replace old provincial attachments with loyalty to the concept of a united German state. It should also be noted that these clubs were often anti-Semitic. (See "Encountering the Past: Dueling in Germany.")

The activities of the *Burschenschaften* made the government uneasy. When, in early 1819, a student named Karl Sand, a *Burschenschaft* member, assassinated the conservative dramatist August von Kotzebue, Metternich used the incident to suppress institutions associated with liberalism. In July 1819, Metternich persuaded the major German states to issue the Carlsbad Decrees, which dissolved the *Burschenschaften*. The decrees also provided for university inspectors and press censors. The next year the German Confederation issued the Final Act, which limited the subjects that the constitutional chambers of Bavaria, Württemberg, and Baden could discuss. The measure also asserted the right of the monarchs to resist demands of constitutionalists. For many years thereafter, the secret police of the various German states harassed potential dissidents. In the opinion of the princes, these included almost anyone who sought even moderate social or political change.

In May 1820, Karl Sand, a German student and a member of a *Burschenschaft*, was executed for his murder of the conservative playwright August von Kotzebue the previous year. In the eyes of many young German nationalists, Sand was a political martyr.

Bildarchiv Preussischer Kulturbesitz

What role did universities play in the political upheavals of the first half of the nineteenth century?

POSTWAR REPRESSION IN GREAT BRITAIN

The years 1819 and 1820 marked a high tide for conservative influence and repression in western as well as eastern Europe. After 1815, Great Britain experienced two years of poor harvests. At the same time, discharged sailors and soldiers and out-of-work industrial workers swelled the ranks of the unemployed.

ENCOUNTERING THE PAST

DUELING IN GERMANY

Dueling clubs were prestigious student organizations in the German universities of the nineteenth century. Europe's aristocracy had deep roots in the military, and dueling had long been the preferred method for resolving disputes among "gentlemen" (members of the upper class). The injury and loss of life this occasioned had prompted most western European governments to outlaw dueling by the mid-nineteenth century, but the conservative aristocratic-military class that dominated Germany kept it alive. Dueling was technically against the law, but it was socially acceptable and considered a test of manhood that elevated the status of those who practiced it.

Duels were a part of aristocratic life, and respect for the aristocracy was so great in Germany that any man who fought a duel elevated his social standing. The universities, whose students were drawn from the upper middle class and the aristocracy, congregated men for whom dueling was considered a form of character building. Duels elsewhere were usually fought with pistols, but students fenced with sabers. They seldom killed one another, but their weapons inflicted facial wounds—producing scars that served a man as a badge of honor for a lifetime. The fad for dueling persisted into the era of World War I, but it faded following the defeat of Germany's militaristic establishment in 1918.

While fellow dueling-club members look on, a German student slashed in a duel is treated by a surgeon.

Image Works/Mary Evans Picture Library Ltd.

How would you explain the nineteenth-century German fad for dueling?

WHAT CAN you conclude about the politics of Germany in the nineteenth century from the fact that dueling became an avenue to social mobility?

Lord Liverpool's Ministry and Popular Unrest The Tory ministry of Lord Liverpool (1770–1828) was unprepared to deal with these problems of postwar dislocation. Instead, it sought to protect the interests of the landed and wealthy classes. In 1815, Parliament passed a Corn Law to maintain high prices for domestically produced grain (called "corn" in Britain) by levying import duties on foreign grain. The next year, Parliament replaced the income tax that only the wealthy paid with excise or sales taxes on consumer goods that both the wealthy and the poor paid. These laws continued a legislative trend that marked the abandonment by the British ruling class of its traditional role of paternalistic protector of the poor.

In light of these policies and the postwar economic downturn, it is hardly surprising that the lower social orders began to doubt the wisdom of their rulers and to demand political changes. Mass meetings called for the reform of Parliament. Reform clubs were organized. Radical newspapers demanded change. The government's answer to the discontent was repression.

"Peterloo" and the Six Acts This initial repression, in combination with improved harvests, calmed the political landscape for a time. By 1819, however, the people were restive again. In the industrial north, well-organized mass meetings demanded the reform of Parliament. The radical reform campaign culminated on August 16, 1819, with a meeting in the industrial city of Manchester at Saint Peter's Fields. Royal troops and the local militia were on hand to ensure order. As the speeches were about to begin, a local magistrate ordered the militia to move into the audience. The result was panic and death. At least eleven people in the crowd were killed; scores were injured. The event became known as the Peterloo Massacre, a phrase that drew a contemptuous comparison with Wellington's victory at Waterloo.

The Liverpool ministry decided to act once and for all to end these troubles. In December 1819, a few months after the German Carlsbad Decrees, Parliament passed a series of laws called the Six Acts, which (1) forbade large unauthorized, public meetings, (2) raised the fines for seditious libel, (3) speeded up the trials of political agitators, (4) increased newspaper taxes, (5) prohibited the training of armed groups, and (6) allowed local officials to search homes in certain disturbed counties. In effect, the Six Acts attempted to prevent radical leaders from agitating and to give the authorities new powers.

BOURBON RESTORATION IN FRANCE

The abdication of Napoleon in 1814 opened the way for a restoration of Bourbon rule. The new king, Louis XVIII (r. 1814–1824), understood he could not turn back the clock to 1789. France had undergone too many irreversible changes. Consequently, Louis XVIII agreed to become a constitutional monarch, but under a constitution of his own making called the Charter.

The Charter   The Charter provided for a hereditary monarchy and a bicameral legislature. The monarch appointed the upper house, the Chamber of Peers, modeled on the British House of Lords; a narrow franchise with a high property qualification elected the lower house, the Chamber of Deputies. The Charter guaranteed most of the rights the Declaration of the Rights of Man and Citizen had enumerated. The Charter also promised not to challenge the property rights of the current owners of land that had been confiscated from aristocrats and the church. With this provision, Louis XVIII hoped to reconcile to his regime those who had benefited from the revolution.

Ultraroyalism   This moderate spirit did not penetrate deeply into the ranks of royalist supporters whose families had suffered during the revolution. Rallying around Louis's brother and heir, the count of Artois (1757–1836), those people who were more royalist than the monarch now demanded their revenge. The ultraroyalist majority elected to the Chamber of Deputies in 1816 proved so dangerously reactionary that the king soon dissolved the chamber. The second election returned a more moderate majority. Several years of political give-and-take followed, with the king making mild accommodations to liberals.

In February 1820, however, the duke of Berri, son of Artois and heir to the throne after his father, was murdered by a lone assassin. The ultraroyalists persuaded Louis XVIII that the murder was the result of his ministers' cooperation with liberal politicians, and the king responded with repressive measures. By the early 1820s, the veneer of constitutionalism had worn away. Liberals were being driven out of politics and into a near illegal status.

THE CONSERVATIVE INTERNATIONAL ORDER

WHAT WERE the goals of the Concert of Europe?

At the Congress of Vienna, the major powers—Russia, Austria, Prussia, and Great Britain—had agreed to consult with each other from time to time on matters affecting Europe as a whole. The vehicle for this consultation was a series of postwar congresses, or conferences. Later, as differences arose among the powers, the consultations became more informal. This new arrangement for resolving mutual foreign policy issues was known as the *Concert of Europe*. It prevented one nation from taking a major action in international affairs without working in concert with and obtaining the assent of the others.

THE CONGRESS SYSTEM

The first congress took place in 1818 at Aix-la-Chapelle in Germany near the border of Belgium. As a result of this gathering, the four major powers removed their troops from France, which had paid its war reparations, and readmitted France to good standing among the European nations. Despite unanimity on these decisions, the conference was not without friction. Tsar Alexander I (r. 1801–1825) suggested that the Quadruple Alliance (see Chapter 19) agree to uphold the borders and the existing governments of all European countries. Viscount Castlereagh (1769–1822), representing Britain, flatly rejected the proposal. He contended the Quadruple Alliance was intended only to prevent future French aggression. These disagreements appeared somewhat academic until revolutions broke out in southern Europe.

THE SPANISH REVOLUTION OF 1820

When the Bourbon Ferdinand VII of Spain (r. 1814–1833) was placed on his throne after Napoleon's downfall, he had promised to govern according to a written constitution. Once in power, however, he ignored his pledge, dissolved the *Cortés* (the parliament), and ruled alone. In 1820, army officers who were about to be sent to suppress revolution in Spain's Latin American colonies rebelled. In March, Ferdinand once again announced he would abide by the provisions of the constitution. Almost at the same time, in July 1820, revolution erupted in Naples, where the king of the Two Sicilies quickly accepted a constitution. There were other, lesser revolts in Italy, but none of them succeeded.

Metternich wanted to intervene, for he feared that disturbances in Italy might spread into the Habsburg lands. Britain, however, opposed joint intervention by the major powers in either Italy or Spain. When the Congress of Troppau met in late October 1820, Tsar Alexander persuaded the members of the Holy Alliance (Austria and Prussia) to endorse the Protocol of Troppau—a declaration of the right of stable governments to intervene to restore order in countries threatened by revolution. The decision to authorize Austrian intervention in Italy was, however, delayed until the Congress of Laibach met in January 1821. Austrian troops then marched into Naples and restored monarchy and nonconstitutional government to the Two Sicilies.

The final postwar congress took place in October 1822 at Verona. Its primary purpose was to resolve the situation in Spain. Once again, Britain balked at joint action. At Verona, Britain, in effect, withdrew from continental affairs. Austria, Prussia, and Russia agreed to support French intervention in Spain. In April 1823, a French army crossed the Pyrenees and within a few months suppressed the Spanish revolution. French troops remained in Spain to prop up King Ferdinand until 1827. France did not, however, use its intervention as an excuse to aggrandize its power or increase its territory. The same had been true of all the other interventions under the congress system. The great powers authorized these interventions to preserve or restore conservative regimes, not to conquer territory for themselves. Their goal was to maintain the international order established at Vienna.

The Congress of Verona and the Spanish intervention had a second diplomatic result. The new British foreign minister, George Canning (1770–1827), was much more interested in British commerce and trade than Castlereagh had been. Thus Canning sought to prevent the extension of European reaction to Spain's colonies in Latin America, which were then in revolt (see page 503). He intended to exploit these South American revolutions to break Spain's old trading monopoly with its colonies and gain access for Britain to Latin American trade. Britain soon recognized the Spanish colonies as independent states. Through the rest of the century, British commercial interests dominated Latin America.

An English poet appears as an Albanian. The famous English poet George Gordon, Lord Byron (1788–1824), was one of many European liberals who went to Greece to aid the cause of its independence. He died there of fever in 1824.

The Granger Collection, NY

Why were European liberals attracted to the cause of Greek independence?

REVOLT AGAINST OTTOMAN RULE IN THE BALKANS

The Greek Revolution of 1821   While the powers were plotting conservative interventions in Italy and Spain, a third Mediterranean revolt erupted—in Greece. Ottoman weakness and instability troubled European diplomacy throughout the nineteenth century, raising what was known as "the Eastern Question": What should the European powers do about the Ottoman inability to assure political and administrative stability in its possessions in and around the eastern Mediterranean? Most of the major powers had a keen interest in those territories. Russia and Austria coveted land in the Balkans. France and Britain were concerned with the empire's commerce and with control of key naval positions in the eastern Mediterranean. Also at issue was the treatment of the Christian inhabitants of the empire and access to the Christian shrines in the Holy Land. The goals of the great powers often conflicted with the desire for independence of the many national groups in the Ottoman Empire. Yet, because the powers had little desire to strengthen the empire, they were often more sympathetic to nationalistic aspirations there than elsewhere in Europe.

These conflicting interests, as well as mutual distrust, prevented any direct intervention in Greek affairs for several years. Eventually, however, Britain, France, and Russia concluded that an independent Greece would benefit their strategic interests and would not threaten their domestic security. In 1827, they signed the Treaty of London, demanding Turkish recognition of Greek independence, and sent a joint fleet to support the Greek revolt. In 1828, Russia sent troops into the Ottoman holdings in what is today Romania, ultimately gaining control of that territory in 1829 with the Treaty of Adrianople. The treaty also stipulated the Turks would allow Britain, France, and Russia to decide the future of Greece. In 1830, a second Treaty of London declared Greece an independent kingdom.

Serbian Independence   Since the late eighteenth century, Serbia had sought independence from the Ottoman Empire. During the Napoleonic wars, its fate had been linked to Russian policy and Russian relations with the Ottoman Empire. Between 1804 and 1813, a remarkable Serbian leader, Kara George (1762–1817), had led a guerrilla war against the Ottomans. This ultimately unsuccessful revolution helped build national self-identity and attracted the interest of the great powers.

In 1815 and 1816, a new leader, Milos Obrenovitch (1780–1860), succeeded in negotiating greater administrative autonomy for some Serbian territory, but most Serbs lived outside the borders of this new entity. In 1830, the Ottoman sultan formally granted independence to Serbia, and by the late 1830s, the major powers granted it diplomatic recognition.

Serbia's political structure, however, remained in doubt for many years. In 1833, Milos, now a hereditary prince, pressured the Ottoman authorities to extend the borders of Serbia, which they did. These new boundaries persisted until 1878. Serbian leaders continued to seek additional territory, however, creating tensions with Austria. The status of minorities, particularly Muslims, within Serbian territory, was also a problem. In the mid-1820s, Russia, which like Serbia was a Slav state and Eastern Orthodox in religion, became Serbia's formal protector. In 1856, Serbia came under the collective protection of the great powers, but the special relationship between Russia and Serbia would continue until the First World War and would play a decisive role in the outbreak of that conflict.

THE WARS OF INDEPENDENCE IN LATIN AMERICA

The wars of the French Revolution and, more particularly, those of Napoleon sparked movements for independence from European domination throughout Latin America. In less than two decades, between 1804 and 1824, France was driven from Haiti, Portugal lost control of Brazil, and Spain was forced to withdraw from all of its American empire except Cuba and Puerto Rico.

WHAT SPARKED the wars of independence in Latin America?

REVOLUTION IN HAITI

Between 1791 and 1804, the French colony of Haiti achieved independence. This event was of key importance for two reasons. First, it was sparked by policies of the French Revolution overflowing into its New World Empire. Second, the Haitian Revolution demonstrated that slaves of African origins could lead a revolt against white masters and mulatto freemen. The example of the Haitian Revolution for years thereafter terrified slaveholders throughout the Americas.

Once the French Revolution had broken out in France, the French National Assembly in 1791 decreed that free property-owning mulattos on Haiti should enjoy the same rights as white plantation owners. The Colonial Assembly in Haiti resisted the orders from France. In the same year, a full-fledged slave rebellion shook Haiti. It arose as a result of a secret conspiracy among the slaves. François-Dominique Toussaint L'Ouverture (1743–1803), himself a former slave, quickly emerged as its leader. Although the slave rebellion collapsed, mulattos and free black people on Haiti, who hoped to gain the rights the French National Assembly had promised, then took up arms against the white colonial masters. French officials sent by the revolutionary government in Paris soon backed them. Slaves now came to the aid of an invading French force, and in early 1793, the French abolished slavery in Haiti.

By this time both Spain and Great Britain were attempting to intervene in Haitian events to expand their own influence in the Caribbean. Both were opposed to the end of slavery and both coveted Haiti's rich sugar-producing lands. Toussaint L'Ouverture and his force of ex-slaves again supported the French against the Spanish and the British. By 1800, his army had achieved dominance throughout the island of Hispanola.

The French government under Napoleon distrusted L'Ouverture and feared that his example would undermine French authority elsewhere in the Caribbean and North America. In 1802, Napoleon sent an army to Haiti and eventually captured L'Ouverture, who was sent back to France where he died in prison in 1803. Other Haitian military leaders of slave origin, the most important of whom was Jean-Jacques Dessalines (1758–1806), continued to resist. When Napoleon found himself again at war with Britain in 1803, he decided to abandon his American empire, selling Louisiana to the United States and withdrawing his forces from Haiti. Thus, the Haitian slave-led rebellion became the first successful assault on colonial government in Latin America. France formally recognized Haitian independence in 1804.

Toussaint L'Ouverture (1743–1803) began the revolt that led to Haitian independence in 1804.

Library of Congress

How did revolution in France contribute to revolution in Haiti?

WARS OF INDEPENDENCE ON THE SOUTH AMERICAN CONTINENT

Haiti's revolution, which involved the popular uprising of a repressed social group, proved to be the great exception in the Latin American drive for liberty from European masters. Generally speaking, on the South American continent, the **Creole** elite— merchants, landowners, and professional people of Spanish descent—led the movements against Spain and Portugal. The Creoles were determined that any drive for political independence from Spain and Portugal should not cause social disruption or the loss of their own privileges.

Creole   Person of European, usually Spanish, descent born in the Americas.

Overview The Wars of Independence in Latin America

DATE	NATION	LEADER/S
1804	Haiti	Toussaint L'Ouverture and Jean-Jacques Dessalines
1820	Peru	José de San Martín
1821	New Spain	Miguel Hidalgo and José María Morelos
1821	Venezuela	Simón Bolívar

Creole Discontent   Creole discontent with Spanish colonial government had many sources. (The Brazilian situation will be discussed separately. See page 505.) Latin American merchants wanted to trade more freely within the region and with North American and European markets. They wanted commercial regulations that would benefit them rather than Spain. They had also resented increases in taxation by the Spanish crown. Finally, Creoles resented Spanish policies that favored *peninsulares*—white people born in Spain—for political patronage, including appointments in the colonial government, church, and army.

Discontent was transformed into rebellion when, in 1807, Napoleon invaded Portugal and made his own brother king of Spain in 1808. The Portuguese royal family fled to Brazil and established its government there, but the Bourbon monarchy of Spain had, for the time being, been overthrown. That situation created an imperial political vacuum throughout Spanish Latin America and gave Creole leaders both the opportunity and the necessity to act.

The Creole elite feared a liberal Napoleonic monarchy in Spain would attempt to impose reforms in Latin America that would harm their economic and social interests. They also feared a French-controlled Spain would try to drain the region of the wealth and resources Napoleon needed for his wars. To protect their interests and to seize the opportunity to direct their own political destiny, between 1808 and 1810 Creole *juntas*, or political committees, claimed the right to govern different regions of Latin America. After the establishment of these local *juntas*, Spain never effectively reestablished its authority in South America. The establishment of the *juntas* also ended the privileges of the *peninsulares*, whose welfare had always depended on the favors of the Spanish crown. Creoles now took over positions in the government and army.

San Martín in Río de la Plata   The vast size of Latin America, its geographical barriers, its distinct regional differences, and the absence of an even marginally integrated economy meant there would be several different paths to independence. The first region to assert itself was the Río de la Plata, or modern Argentina. In 1810, the *junta* in Buenos Aires not only thrust off Spanish authority, but also sent forces into Paraguay and Uruguay to liberate them from Spain. These armies were defeated, but Spain nevertheless lost control of both areas. Paraguay asserted its own independence. Brazil took over Uruguay.

These early defeats did not discourage the Buenos Aires government, which determined to liberate Peru, the stronghold of royalist power and loyalty on the continent. By 1817, José de San Martín (1778–1850), the leading general of the Río de la Plata forces, led an army in a daring march over the Andes Mountains and occupied Santiago in Chile, where the Chilean independence leader Bernardo O'Higgins (1778–1842) was established as the supreme dictator. From Santiago, San Martín organized a fleet that, in 1820, carried his army by sea to Peru. The next year, San Martín drove royalist forces from Lima and became Protector of Peru.

Simon Bolívar's Liberation of Venezuela   While the army of San Martín had been liberating the southern portion of the continent, Simón Bolívar (1783–1830) had been pursuing a similar task in the north. Bolívar had been involved in the organization of a liberating *junta* in Caracas, Venezuela, in 1810. He was a firm advocate of both independence and a republic. Between 1811 and 1814, civil war broke out throughout Venezuela. Bolívar had to go into exile first in Colombia and then in Jamaica. In 1816, with help from Haiti, he returned to the continent. By the summer of 1821, Bolívar's forces captured Caracas, and he was named president.

A year later, in July 1822, the armies of Bolívar and San Martín joined as they moved to liberate Quito, the capital of what is today Ecuador. At a famous meeting in Guayaquil, the two liberators sharply disagreed about the future political structure of Latin America. San Martín believed the peoples of the region required monarchies; Bolívar maintained his republicanism. Not long after the meeting, San Martín quietly retired from public life and went into exile in Europe. Meanwhile, Bolívar deliberately allowed the political situation in Peru to fall into confusion, and in 1823, he sent in troops to establish his control. On December 9, 1824, at the Battle of Ayacucho, the liberating army crushed the main Spanish royalist forces, ending Spain's effort to retain its South American empire.

Simón Bolívar was the liberator of much of Latin America. He inclined toward a policy of political liberalism.

© Christie's Images/CORBIS

Why did liberalism fail to take hold in the independent states of Latin America?

INDEPENDENCE IN NEW SPAIN

The drive for independence in New Spain, which included present-day Mexico as well as Texas, California, and the rest of the southwest United States, illustrates better than in any other region the socially conservative outcome of the Latin American colonial revolutions. As elsewhere, a local governing *junta* was organized in 1808. Before it had undertaken any significant measures, however, a Creole priest, Miguel Hidalgo y Costilla (1753–1811), in 1810, issued a call for rebellion to the Indians in his parish. Father Hidalgo set forth a program of social reform, including hints of changes in landholding. Soon he stood at the head of a loosely organized group of 80,000 followers, who captured several major cities and then marched on Mexico City. In July 1811, the revolutionary priest was captured and executed. Leadership of his movement then fell to José María Morelos y Pavón (1765–1815), a mestizo priest. Far more radical than Hidalgo, he called for an end to forced labor and for substantial land reforms. He was executed in 1815, ending five years of popular uprising.

The uprising and its demand for fundamental social reforms united all conservative political groups in Mexico, both Creole and Spanish. These groups opposed any kind of reform that might diminish their privileges. In 1820 the revolution in Spain had forced Ferdinand VII to accept a liberal constitution. Conservative Mexicans feared the new liberal monarchy would attempt to impose liberal reforms on Mexico. Therefore, for the most conservative of reasons, they rallied behind a former royalist general, Augustín de Iturbide (1783–1824), who declared Mexico independent of Spain in 1821. Shortly thereafter, Iturbide was declared emperor.

BRAZILIAN INDEPENDENCE

Brazilian independence, in contrast to that of Spanish Latin America, came relatively simply and peacefully. As already noted, the Portuguese royal family, along with several thousand government officials and members of the court, fled to Brazil in 1807. The prince regent João addressed many of the local complaints, equivalent to those of the Spanish Creoles, by, for example, taking measures that expanded trade. In 1815, he made Brazil a kingdom, which meant it was no longer to be regarded merely as a colony of Portugal. Then, in 1820, a revolution occurred in Portugal, and its leaders demanded João's return to Lisbon. They also demanded the return of Brazil to colonial status. João, who had become King João VI in 1816 (r. 1816–1826), returned to Portugal but

MAP EXPLORATION

Interactive map: To explore this map further, go to www.myhistorylab.com

MAP 20–1 **Latin America In 1830** By 1830 most of Latin America had been liberated from Europe. This map shows the initial borders of the states of the region with the dates of their independence. The United Provinces of La Plata formed the nucleus of what later became Argentina.

What caused the spread of independence throughout Latin America in the first quarter of the nineteenth century?

left his son Dom Pedro as regent in Brazil and encouraged him to be sympathetic to the political aspirations of the Brazilians. In September 1822, Dom Pedro embraced the cause of Brazilian independence against the recolonizing efforts of Portugal. By the end of the year, he had become emperor of an independent Brazil. Thus, in contrast to virtually all other nations of Latin America, Brazil achieved independence in a way that left no real dispute as to where the center of political authority lay.

Two other factors aided the peaceful transition to independence in Brazil. First, the political and social elite of Brazil wanted to avoid the destruction that the wars of independence had unleashed in the Spanish American Empire. Second, these leaders had every intention of preserving slavery. The wars of independence elsewhere had generally led to the abolition of slavery or moved the new states closer to abolishing it. Warfare in Brazil might have caused social turmoil with similar consequences.

THE CONSERVATIVE ORDER SHAKEN IN EUROPE

Beginning in the mid-1820s, the conservative governments of Russia, France, and Great Britain faced new political discontent. (See Map 20–2.) In Russia the result was suppression, in France revolution, and in Britain, accommodation. Belgium emerged as a newly independent state.

HOW DID Russia, France, and Britain respond to challenges to the conservative order?

RUSSIA: THE DECEMBRIST REVOLT OF 1825

Tsar Alexander I had come to the throne in 1801 after a palace coup against his father, Tsar Paul (r. 1796–1801). After flirting with Enlightenment ideas, Alexander turned permanently away from reform. Both at home and abroad, he took the lead in suppressing liberalism and nationalism. There would be no significant challenge to tsarist autocracy until his death.

Unrest in the Army As Russian forces drove Napoleon's army across Europe and then occupied defeated France, many Russian officers were exposed to the ideas of the French Revolution and the Enlightenment and some developed reformist sympathies. Unable to express themselves openly because of Alexander's repressive policies, they formed secret societies. Sometime during 1825, two such societies, the Southern Society and the Northern Society, apparently decided to carry out a *coup d'état* in 1826.

Dynastic Crisis In late November 1825, Tsar Alexander I died unexpectedly. His death created two crises. The first was dynastic. Alexander had no direct heir. Through a series of secret instructions made public only after his death, Alexander had named his younger brother, Nicholas (r. 1825–1855), as the new tsar. Once Alexander was dead, the legality of these instructions became uncertain. The tsar's brother Constantine acknowledged Nicholas as tsar, and Nicholas acknowledged Constantine. Then, in early December, the army command told Nicholas about a conspiracy among certain officers. Able to wait no longer, Nicholas had himself declared tsar.

The second crisis then unfolded. On December 26, 1825, the army was to take the oath of allegiance to Nicholas, who was less popular than Constantine and regarded as more conservative. Most regiments took the oath, but the Moscow regiment, whose chief officers, surprisingly, were not secret society members, marched into the Senate Square in Saint Petersburg and refused to swear allegiance. Late in the afternoon, Nicholas ordered the cavalry and the artillery to attack the insurgents. More than sixty people were killed. Early in 1826, Nicholas himself presided over the commission that investigated the Decembrist Revolt and the secret army societies. Five of the plotters were executed, and more than a hundred others were exiled to Siberia.

The Autocracy of Nicholas I Although Nicholas was neither an ignorant nor a bigoted reactionary, he came to symbolize the most

MAP EXPLORATION

Interactive map: To explore this map further, go to www.myhistorylab.com

MAP 20–2 Centers of Revolution, 1820–1831 The conservative order imposed by the great powers in post-Napoleonic Europe was challenged by various uprisings and revolutions, beginning in 1820–1821 in Spain, Naples, and Greece and spreading to Russia, Poland, France, and Belgium later in the decade.

Which countries were spared uprisings in this period?

When the Moscow regiment refused to swear allegiance to Nicholas, he ordered the cavalry and artillery to attack them. Although a total failure, the Decembrist Revolt came to symbolize the yearnings of all Russian liberals in the nineteenth century for a constitutional government.

The Insurrection of the Decembrists at Senate Square, St. Petersburg on 14th December, 1825 (w/c on paper) by Russian School (nineteenth century). Private Collection/Archives Charmet/Bridgeman Art Library

What pressures and tensions led to the Decembrist Revolt?

extreme form of nineteenth-century autocracy. He knew economic growth and social improvement in Russia required reform, but he was afraid of change. To remove serfdom would necessarily, in his view, have undermined the nobles' support of the tsar. So Nicholas turned his back on this and practically all other reforms. Literary and political censorship and a widespread system of surveillance by secret police flourished throughout his reign.

Official Nationality In place of reform, Nicholas and his closest advisers embraced a program called Official Nationality. Its slogan, published repeatedly in government documents, newspapers, journals, and schoolbooks, was "Orthodoxy, Autocracy, and Nationalism." The Russian Orthodox church was to provide the basis for morality, education, and intellectual life. The church, which, since the days of Peter the Great, had been an arm of the secular government, controlled the schools and universities. Autocracy meant the unrestrained power of the tsar as the only authority that could hold the vast expanse of Russia and its peoples together. Through the glorification of Russian nationality, Russians were urged to see their religion, language, and customs as a source of perennial wisdom that separated them from the moral corruption and political turmoil of the West. This program alienated serious Russian intellectuals from the tsarist government.

Revolt and Repression in Poland Nicholas I was also extremely conservative in foreign affairs, as became apparent in Poland in the 1830s. Most of Poland, which had been partitioned in the late eighteenth century and ceased to exist as an independent state, remained under Russian domination after the Congress of Vienna but was granted a constitutional government with a parliament, called the diet, that had limited powers. Under this arrangement, the tsar also reigned as king of Poland. Although both Alexander and Nicholas frequently infringed on the constitution and quarreled with the Polish diet, this arrangement held through the 1820s.

In late November 1830, after news of the French and Belgian revolutions of that summer had reached Poland, a small insurrection of soldiers and students broke out in Warsaw. Disturbances soon spread throughout the country. The tsar sent troops into the country and suppressed the revolt. In February 1832, Nicholas issued the Organic Statute, declaring Poland to be an integral part of the Russian Empire. The Polish uprising had confirmed the tsar's worst fears. Henceforth Russia and Nicholas became the gendarme of Europe, ever ready to provide troops to suppress liberal and nationalist movements.

REVOLUTION IN FRANCE (1830)

The Polish revolt was the most distant of several disturbances that flowed from the overthrow of the Bourbon dynasty in France during July 1830. When Louis XVIII had died in 1824, his brother, the count of Artois, the leader of the ultraroyalist faction, succeeded him as Charles X (r. 1824–1830).

The Reactionary Policies of Charles X Charles X's first action was to have the Chamber of Deputies in 1824 and 1825 indemnify aristocrats who had lost their lands in the revolution. He did this by lowering the interest rates on government bonds to create a fund to pay an annual sum to the survivors of the *émigrés* who had forfeited land. Middle-class bondholders, who lost income, resented this measure. Charles also restored the rule of primogeniture, whereby only the eldest son of an aristocrat inherited the family domains. To support the Roman Catholic Church, he enacted a law that punished sacrilege with imprisonment or death.

In the elections of 1827, the liberals gained enough seats in the Chamber of Deputies to compel the king to compromise. Liberals, however, wanted a genuinely constitutional regime and remained unsatisfied. In 1829, the king replaced his moderate ministry with an ultraroyalist cabinet headed by the Prince de Polignac (1780–1847). The opposition, in desperation, opened negotiations with the liberal Orléans branch of the royal family.

The July Revolution   In 1830, Charles X called for new elections, in which the liberals scored a stunning victory. Instead of accepting the new Chamber of Deputies, the king and his ministers decided to attempt a royalist seizure of power. In June and July 1830, Polignac sent a naval expedition against Algiers. News of the capture of Algiers and the founding of a French Empire in North Africa reached Paris on July 9. Taking advantage of the euphoria this victory created, Charles issued the Four Ordinances on July 25, 1830, staging what amounted to a royal *coup d'état*. These ordinances restricted freedom of the press, dissolved the recently elected Chamber of Deputies, limited the franchise to the wealthiest people in the country, and called for new elections.

This engraving captures one of the confrontations between workers and the king's forces in Paris on July 28, 1830.

Picture Desk, Inc./Kobal Collection

How does this depiction of the revolutionary events of 1830 in France differ from Delacroix's depiction of these same events in *Liberty Leading the People* on page 490?

The Four Ordinances provoked swift and decisive popular reaction. Liberal newspapers called on the nation to reject the monarch's actions. The workers of Paris, burdened since 1827 by an economic downturn, erected barricades in the streets. The king called out troops, and although more than 1,800 people died during the ensuing battles, the army was not able to gain control of Paris. On August 2, Charles X abdicated and went into exile in England. The Chamber of Deputies named a new ministry composed of constitutional monarchists. In an act that finally ended the rule of the Bourbon dynasty, it also proclaimed Louis Philippe (r. 1830–1848), the duke d'Orléans, the new king.

Had the liberals, who favored a constitutional monarchy, not acted quickly, the workers and shopkeepers of Paris might have attempted to form a republic. By seizing the moment, the middle class, the bureaucrats, and the moderate aristocratic liberals overthrew the restoration monarchy and still avoided a republic. These liberals feared a new popular revolution such as the one that had swept France in 1792. A fundamental political and social tension thus underlay the new monarchy. The revolution had succeeded thanks to a temporary alliance between hard-pressed laborers and the prosperous middle class, but these two groups soon realized that their basic goals were different.

Monarchy under Louis Philippe   Politically, the July Monarchy, as the new regime was called, was more liberal than the restoration government. Socially, however, the Revolution of 1830 proved conservative. The hereditary peerage was abolished in 1831, but the everyday economic, political, and social influence of the landed oligarchy continued. Money was the path to power and influence in the government. There was much corruption.

Most importantly, the liberal monarchy displayed little or no sympathy for the lower and working classes. In 1830, the workers of Paris had called for the protection of jobs, better wages, and the preservation of the traditional crafts, rather than for the usual goals of political liberalism. The government of Louis Philippe ignored their demands and their plight. In late 1831, troops suppressed a workers' revolt in Lyons. In July 1832, an uprising occurred in Paris during the funeral of a popular Napoleonic general. Again the government called out troops, and more than eight hundred people were killed or wounded. In 1834, a large strike by silk workers in Lyons was crushed. Such discontent might be smothered for a time, but unless the government addressed the social and economic conditions that created it, new turmoil would eventually erupt.

The new French government of 1830 was only too happy to retain the control of the city of Algiers that Charles X had achieved less than a month before his overthrow. The occupation of Algeria gave French merchants in Marseilles new economic ties to North Africa. By the 1850s, the French had extended their rule, after constant warfare

Beginning in the 1820s Daniel O'Connell revolutionized the organization of Irish politics. He created a grass-roots organization and collected funds to finance Irish nationalist activities. He was also known as one of the great public speakers of his generation.

© Chris Hellier/CORBIS. All Rights Reserved.

How did nineteenth-century Irish opposition to English occupation differ from earlier efforts to expel the English?

against Muslim tribesmen, as far as the northern Sahara desert. France now had a vast new empire, and French citizens and other Europeans also began to settle in Algeria in large numbers, especially in the cities. In the second half of the nineteenth century, the French government came to regard Algeria, despite its overwhelmingly Muslim population, as not a colony but an integral part of France itself.

BELGIUM BECOMES INDEPENDENT (1830)

The July Revolution in Paris sent sparks to other political tinder on the Continent. The revolutionary fires first flared in neighboring Belgium. The former Austrian Netherlands, Belgium had been merged with the kingdom of Holland in 1815. The two countries differed in language, religion, and economy, however, and the Belgian upper classes never reconciled themselves to Dutch rule.

On August 25, 1830, disturbances broke out in Brussels after the performance of an opera about a rebellion in Naples against Spanish rule. To end the rioting, the municipal authorities and people from the propertied classes formed a provisional national government. When compromise between the Belgians and the Dutch failed, King William I of Holland (r. 1815–1840) sent troops and ships against Belgium. By November 10, 1830, the Dutch had been defeated. A national congress then wrote a liberal Belgian constitution, which was issued in 1831.

Although the major powers saw the revolution in Belgium as upsetting the boundaries the Congress of Vienna had established, they were not inclined to intervene to reverse it. Russia, Prussia, and Austria were preoccupied with uprisings of their own and France under Louis Philippe hoped to dominate an independent Belgium. Britain could tolerate a liberal Belgium, as long as it was free of foreign domination.

In December 1830, Lord Palmerston (1784–1865), the British foreign minister, persuaded representatives of the powers in London to recognize Belgium as an independent and neutral state. In July 1831, Prince Leopold of Saxe-Coburg (r. 1831–1865), who had connections to the British royal family and was the husband of the daughter of Louis Philippe, became king of the Belgians.

THE GREAT REFORM BILL IN BRITAIN (1832)

In Great Britain, the revolutionary year of 1830 saw the election of a House of Commons that debated the first major bill to reform Parliament. The passage of the Great Reform Bill, which became law in 1832, was the result of a series of events different from those that occurred on the Continent. In Britain, the forces of conservatism and reform accommodated each other.

Political and Economic Reform   Several factors contributed to this spirit of compromise. First, the commercial and industrial class was larger in Britain than in other countries. No government, could ignore their economic interests without damaging British prosperity. Second, Britain's liberal Whig aristocrats, who regarded themselves as the protectors of constitutional liberty, had a long tradition of favoring moderate reforms that would make revolutionary changes unnecessary. Finally, British law, tradition, and public opinion all showed a strong respect for civil liberties.

Catholic Emancipation Act   English determination to maintain the union with Ireland brought about another key reform. In 1800, fearful that Irish nationalists might again rebel as they had in 1798 and perhaps turn Ireland into a base for a French invasion, William Pitt the Younger had persuaded Parliament to pass the Act of Union between Ireland and England. Ireland now sent a hundred members to the House of Commons. Only Protestant Irishmen, however, could be elected to represent their overwhelmingly Roman Catholic nation.

During the 1820s, under the leadership of Daniel O'Connell (1775–1847), Irish nationalists organized the Catholic Association to agitate for Catholic emancipation. In 1828, O'Connell secured his own election to Parliament, where he could not legally take his seat. The duke of Wellington, who was now prime minister, realized that henceforth Ireland might elect an overwhelmingly Catholic delegation. If they were not seated, civil war might erupt across the Irish Sea. Consequently, in 1829, Wellington and Robert Peel steered the Catholic Emancipation Act through Parliament. Roman Catholics could now become members of Parliament. This measure, together with the repeal in 1828 of restrictions against Protestant nonconformists, ended the Anglican monopoly on British political life.

Catholic emancipation was a liberal measure passed for a conservative purpose: the preservation of order in Ireland. It alienated many of Wellington's Anglican Tory supporters and split the Tory Party. When an election in 1830 seated a Parliament disposed to reform, Wellington's ministry fell, and King William IV asked Earl Grey (1764–1845), leader of the Whigs, to form the next government.

Legislating Change   The Whig ministry presented the House of Commons with a major reform bill that had two broad goals. The first was to replace "rotten boroughs," or boroughs that had few voters, with representatives for the previously unrepresented manufacturing districts and cities. Second, the number of voters in England and Wales was to be increased by about 50 percent through a series of new franchises. In 1831, the House of Commons narrowly defeated the bill. Grey called for a new election and won a majority in favor of the bill. The House of Commons passed the reform bill, but the House of Lords rejected it. Mass meetings were held throughout the country. Riots broke out in several cities. Finally, William IV agreed to create enough new peers to give a third reform bill a majority in the House of Lords. Under this pressure, the measure became law in 1832.

The Great Reform Bill expanded the size of the English electorate, but it was not a democratic measure. It increased the number of voters by more than 200,000, or almost 50 percent, but it kept a property qualification for the franchise. Some members of the working class actually lost the right to vote because certain old franchise rights were abolished. New urban boroughs were created to allow the growing cities to have a voice in the House of Commons. Yet the passage of the reform act did not, as was once thought, constitute the triumph of middle-class interests in England: For every new urban electoral district, a new rural district was also drawn, and the aristocracy was expected to dominate rural elections. What the bill permitted was a wider variety of property to be represented in the House of Commons.

The success of the reform bill reconciled previously unrepresented property owners and economic interests to the political institutions of the country. The act laid the groundwork for further orderly reforms of the church, municipal government, and commercial policy. By admitting into the political forum people who sought change and giving them access to the legislative process, it made revolution in Britain unnecessary. Great Britain thus maintained its traditional institutions of government while allowing an increasingly diverse group of people to influence them.

SIGNIFICANT DATES FROM THE ERA OF POLITICAL REACTION AND REFORM

1814	Louis XVIII, Bourbon monarchy restored in France
1815	Holy Alliance (Russia, Austria, and Prussia); Quadruple Alliance (Russia, Austria, Prussia, and Britain)
1819	Carlsbad Decrees, Peterloo Massacre; The Six Acts passed in Great Britain
1820	Spanish revolution
1821	Greek revolution
1823	France intervenes to crush the Spanish revolution
1824	Charles X becomes king in France
1825	Decembrist Revolt in Russia
1829	Catholic Emancipation Act passed in Great Britain
1830	Charles X abdicates; Louis Philippe proclaimed king; Belgian revolution; Polish revolt
1832	Great Reform Bill passed in Great Britain

Summary

HOW DID early-nineteenth-century nationalists define the nation?

The Challenges of Nationalism and Liberalism Secular ideologies including nationalism, liberalism, republicanism, socialism, and communism gained currency in nineteenth-century Europe. Nationalists opposed multinational states that were held together only by the legitimacy of their rulers, such as the Austrian and Russian Empires. The widespread existence of minority enclaves presented a practical problem for nineteenth-century nationalists. Nations were often created in the nineteenth century through the work of intellectual elites who used the print culture and schools to standardize a language and narrate a shared history. Nationalism was particularly fervent, and often politically disruptive, in nineteenth-century Ireland, Germany, Italy, Poland, eastern Europe, and the Balkans. Liberalism sought a political framework that institutionalized the "principles of 1789." Liberals were generally well educated and relatively wealthy; they did not trust the working class and did not want full democracy. They believed free trade would facilitate material progress. As a practical matter, nationalism and liberalism were often linked, although in some situations the goals of nationalists and liberals were directly contradictory. *page 492*

WHAT EXPLAINS the strength of conservatism in the early nineteenth century?

Conservative Governments: The Domestic Political Order Conservatism established itself as a coherent political program in Europe in response to nationalism and liberalism. Throughout Europe, the peace after 1815 presented problems. In Austria, Prince Metternich was the Continent's mastermind of conservatism. Austria found nationalism and liberalism particularly threatening. In Great Britain, popular unrest was suppressed. The Bourbon king Louis XVIII ascended the French throne. He was aware of the balancing act that his position required. Louis XVIII's moderation came to an end in 1820, however, when an heir to the throne was assassinated and ultraroyalists persuaded the king to break with liberal politicians. *page 497*

WHAT WERE the goals of the Concert of Europe?

The Conservative International Order The Concert of Europe was a device created at the Congress of Vienna whereby the major powers would meet from time to time to attempt to maintain international peace. It was unprecedented and surprisingly successful. The Spanish revolution of 1820 was consequential for Latin America, and, coupled with revolts in Italy, led Metternich to lobby the other powers for more active intervention in troubled regions. Greece and Serbia successfully revolted against the Ottoman Empire early in the nineteenth century. Independence movements throughout Latin America took various forms but had similar results. *page 500*

WHAT SPARKED the wars of independence in Latin America?

The Wars of Independence in Latin America The Napoleonic era marked the end of Europe's long domination of Latin America. A slave revolt, begun in 1794, won Haiti its independence. The Haitian slave revolt haunted the Creoles, who were growing discontented. Between 1808 and 1810, various Creole *juntas* governed different parts of Latin America, and Spain was never able to restore its authority over the continent. Different parts of Latin American took different paths toward independence. José de San Martín assembled an army and liberated Peru. In the north, Simón Bolívar began the fight that led to a republican Venezuela. Miguel Hidalgo y Costilla and José María Morelos y Pavón, both priests, were involved in early attempts for an independent New Spain but failed. Brazil's independence came relatively simply and peacefully. The prince regent, João, addressed local grievances and in 1815 declared Brazil a kingdom independent of Portugal. Latin America emerged from its wars for independence economically exhausted and politically unstable. *page 503*

HOW DID Russia, France, and Britain respond to challenges to the conservative order?

The Conservative Order Shaken in Europe Starting in the mid-1920s, political discontent led to suppression in Russia, revolution in France, independence in Belgium, and accommodation in Britain. The death of Tsar Alexander I in 1825 sparked a succession crisis, which led to the Decembrist Revolt of reform-minded army officers. Nicholas I feared reform at home and revolt abroad, so he ruled autocratically. In France, the Bourbon dynasty was overthrown in July 1830, after Charles X had attempted to concentrate political power in the monarchy. Louis Philippe's July Monarchy was politically liberal and socially conservative. Belgium revolted against the Dutch in 1830 and became a constitutional monarchy. In Britain, the Great Reform Bill widened the franchise and gave a broader section of Britain's population a stake in the existing political system. *page 507*

REVIEW QUESTIONS

1. What is nationalism? What parts of Europe saw significant nationalist movements between 1815 and 1830? Which of these movements succeeded and which failed?

2. Which institutions and groups supported the conservative governments in Europe? What were the main threats to these governments?

3. What were the tenets of liberalism? What effects did liberalism have on political developments during the early nineteenth century? What relationship does liberalism have to nationalism?

4. What political changes took place in Latin America between 1804 and 1824? What were the main reasons for Creole discontent with Spanish rule? To what extent were Creole leaders influenced by Enlightenment political philosophy? Who were the major leaders in the fight for Latin American independence? Why did they succeed?

5. What kind of constitution was decreed for the restored monarchy in France? What were the causes of the Revolution of 1830? How do you explain the fact that although prior to 1820 Britain was moving down the same reactionary road as the other major European powers, events arrived at a different outcome in Britain?

KEY TERMS

conservatism (p. 497)   nationalism (p. 492)
Creole (p. 503)

For additional learning resources related to this chapter, please go to **www.myhistorylab.com**

PEARSON
myhistorylab

21

Economic Advance and Social Unrest (1830–1850)

In 1848 Ana Ipatescu helped to lead Transylvanian revolutionaries against Russian rule. Transylvania is part of present-day Romania. The revolutions of 1848 in eastern Europe were primarily uprisings of nationalist groups. Although generally repressed in the revolutions of that year, subject nationalities would prove a source of political upheaval and unrest in the region throughout the rest of the century, ultimately providing the spark for the outbreak of World War I.

The Art Archive/Picture Desk, Inc./Kobal Collection

Why was nationalism a particular problem in Eastern Europe?

516   **PART 4**   ENLIGHTENMENT AND REVOLUTION, 1700–

By 1830, Great Britain had become an industrialized nation, and the rest of Europe was also soon to resound with the pounding of machinery and the grinding of railway engines. Between 1825 and 1850, while the groups that opposed industrialism made their final protests, intellectuals articulated major creeds that both supported and criticized the emerging society. These were years of uncertainty, a period of self-conscious transition leading to an unknown future. They culminated in 1848 with a continent-wide outbreak of revolution. ▪

TOWARD AN INDUSTRIAL SOCIETY

HOW DID industrialization spread across Europe?

The Industrial Revolution had begun in eighteenth-century Great Britain with the advances in textile production described in Chapter 15. Natural resources, adequate capital, native technological skills, a growing food supply, a social structure that allowed considerable mobility, and strong foreign and domestic demand for goods had given Britain an edge in achieving a vast new capacity for production in manufacturing. Also, the French Revolution and the wars of Napoleon had finally destroyed the French Atlantic trade and thus disrupted continental economic life for two decades. The Latin American wars of independence opened the markets of South America to British goods. In North America, both the United States and Canada demanded British products. Through its control of India, Britain commanded the markets of southern Asia. British banks similarly dominated the international financial markets.

The wealth that Britain gained through textile production and its other industries of iron making, shipbuilding, china production, and the manufacture of other finished goods was invested all over the world, but especially in the United States and Latin America. This enormous activity provided the economic foundation for British dominance of the world scene throughout the nineteenth century.

Despite their economic lag, the continental nations were beginning to make material progress. By the 1830s, Belgium, France, and Germany had begun to imitate Britain. Industrial areas on the Continent were generally less concentrated than in Britain, nor did the Continent have large manufacturing districts, such as the British Midlands. Major pockets of production did exist in Western Europe, but most continental manufacturing still took place in the countryside. The slow pace of continental imitation of the British example meant that, at midcentury, peasants and urban artisans remained more important politically than industrial factory workers.

POPULATION AND MIGRATION

While the process of industrialization spread, the population of Europe continued to grow on the base of the eighteenth-century population explosion. The number of people in France rose from 32.5 million in 1831 to 35.8 million in 1851. During approximately the same period, the population of Germany rose from 26.5 million to 33.5 million and that of Britain from 16.3 million to 20.8 million. More and more of the people of Europe lived in cities. By midcentury, one-half of the population of England and Wales and one-quarter of the population of France and Germany had become town dwellers. Eastern Europe, by contrast, remained overwhelmingly rural, with little industrial manufacturing.

The sheer numbers of human beings put considerable pressure on the physical resources of the cities. Existing housing, water, sewers, food supplies, and lighting were completely inadequate. Slums with indescribable filth grew, and disease, especially cholera, ravaged the population. Crime increased and became a way of life for those who could make a living in no other manner.

QUICK REVIEW
Britain's Advantages

- Natural resources, investment capital, technology, and an adequate food supply
- Relatively mobile society
- Strong foreign and domestic markets

London's Crystal Palace during the International Exhibition of 1851.
Victoria & Albert Museum, London, Great Britain/Art Resource, NY

Who visited the International Exhibition? What was the exhibition meant to say about the future of British society?

The situation in the countryside was scarcely better. The enclosures of the late eighteenth century, the land redistribution of the French Revolution, and the emancipation of serfs in Prussia and later in Austria (1848) and Russia (1861) commercialized landholding. Liberal reformers had hoped the legal revolution in ownership would transform peasants into progressive, industrious farmers. Instead, most peasants became conservative landholders without enough land to make agricultural innovations or, oftentimes, even to support themselves. It is important to note the differing dates of rural emancipation across Europe. From Germany eastward, the pace of industrialization was much slower, in part because of the absence of a fluid market for free labor moving to the cities.

The specter of poor harvests still haunted Europe. The worst such experience of the century was the Irish famine of 1845 to 1848. (See "Encountering the Past: The Potato and the Great Hunger in Ireland.") By midcentury, the revolution in landholding led to greater agricultural production. It also resulted in a vast uprooting of people from the countryside into cities and from Europe into the rest of the world.

George Stephenson (1781–1848) invented the locomotive in 1814, but the "Rocket," his improved design shown here, did not win out over other competitors until 1829. In the following two decades the spread of railways transformed the economy of western Europe.

Image Works/Mary Evans Picture Library Ltd.

How did railways tie British communities together?

ENCOUNTERING THE PAST

THE POTATO AND THE GREAT HUNGER IN IRELAND

The potato was introduced to Europe from South America in the seventeenth century. It grew better than grain in parts of Europe that had cool, wet climates, and in these places it became the staple crop. On less than an acre of land, an Irish peasant could raise enough potatoes to feed eleven people for a year—and pay his rent (few owned their land). Reliance on a single food source is risky, however, for if that source fails, starvation threatens.

In 1845, a mysterious fungus blighted potato fields across Ireland, and half the crop was lost. In 1846, it reappeared and destroyed the entire harvest. The situation improved in 1847, but the blight struck again with devastating effects in 1848. The failure of the Irish potato crop was the worst natural disaster to strike Europe in the nineteenth century, and it created social catastrophe. Landlords drove peasants who could not pay their rent from the land, and the British government, which ruled Ireland, provided little aid.

Tens of thousands died, and many other thousands sought to escape "The Great Hunger" by emigrating to the United States and Britain. As a result, the population of Ireland began to fall. It stood at 8,197,000 in 1841. By 1901, it had declined to 4,459,000, and today Ireland is the only European country to have fewer inhabitants than it had in the nineteenth century.

Painter George Frederick Watts's 1850 depiction of a scene set during the Irish Potato Famine. So many people starved during the famine that workhouses could not shelter them all.

© Trustees of the Watts Gallery, Compton, Surrey, UK/The Bridgeman Art Library International

What did Watts want to convey about the victims of the famine with this painting?

WHY WAS the failure of a single crop such a disaster for Ireland? What long-range effect did it have on Ireland?

MAP EXPLORATION

Interactive map: To explore this map further, go to **www.myhistorylab.com**

MAP 21–1 European Railroads in 1850 At midcentury Britain had the most extensive rail network and the most industrialized economy in Europe, but rail lines were expanding rapidly in France, the German states, and Austria. Southern and eastern Europe had few railways and the Ottoman Empire had none.

What effect did railroads have on the European workforce?

RAILWAYS

Industrial advance itself had also contributed to this migration. The 1830s and 1840s opened the first great age of railway building. At midcentury, Britain had 9,797 kilometers of railway, France 2,915, and Germany 5,856. (See Map 21–1, page 518.) The railroads, plus canals and improved regular roads, meant people could leave the place of their birth more easily than ever before.

Railways epitomized the character of the industrial economy during the second quarter of the century. They represented investment in capital goods rather than in consumer goods. Consequently, there was a shortage of consumer goods at cheap prices. The railways in and of themselves also brought about still more industrialization. Embodying the most dramatic application of the steam engine, they sharply increased demand for iron and steel and then for a more skilled labor force. The new iron and steel capacity soon permitted the construction of ironclad ships and iron machinery rather than ships and machinery made of wood. These new capital industries led to the formation of vast industrial fortunes that would be invested in still newer enterprises. Industrialism had begun to grow on itself.

THE LABOR FORCE

The composition and experience of the early-nineteenth-century labor force was varied. Some of the workforce was reasonably well off and enjoyed steady employment and decent wages. Other workers were the "laboring poor," who held jobs but earned little more than subsistence wages. Furthermore, the conditions of workers varied from decade to decade and from industry to industry within any particular decade.

Only the textile-manufacturing industry became thoroughly mechanized and moved into the factory setting during the first half of the century. Far more of the nonrural, nonagricultural workforce consisted of skilled artisans living in cities or small towns. They were attempting to maintain the value of their skills and control over their trades in the face of changing features of production.

THE EMERGENCE OF A WAGE-LABOR FORCE

During the nineteenth century, artisans as well as factory workers eventually came to participate in a wage-labor force in which their labor became a commodity of the labor marketplace. This process has often been termed *proletarianization*. In the process of becoming wage laborers, artisans gradually lost both significant ownership of the means of production, such as tools and equipment, and of control over the conduct of their own trades. The process occurred most rapidly wherever the factory system arose displacing previous skilled labor.

Factory workers also had to submit to various kinds of factory discipline that were virtually always unpopular and difficult to impose. Closing of factory gates to late workers, fines for such lateness, dismissal for drunkenness, and public scolding of faulty laborers were attempts to create human discipline that would match the mechanical regularity of the cables, wheels, and pistons. (See "Compare & Connect: Andrew Ure and John Ruskin Debate the Conditions of Factory Production," pages 520–521.)

Urban artisans in the nineteenth century entered the wage-labor force more slowly than factory workers, and machinery had little to do with the process. The emergence of factories in and of itself did not harm urban artisans. Where the urban artisans encountered difficulty and where they found their skills and livelihood threatened was in the organization of production.

In the eighteenth century, a European town or city workplace had usually consisted of a few artisans laboring for a master. They labored first as apprentices, then as journeymen, and eventually as masters in their own right, according to established guild regulations and practices. This guild system had allowed workers to exercise a considerable degree of control over labor recruitment and training, the pace of production, the quality of the product, and its price. In the nineteenth century, it became increasingly difficult for artisans to exercise corporate or guild direction and control over their trades. The legislation of the French Revolution had outlawed such organizations in France. Across Europe, political and economic liberals disapproved of labor and guild organizations and attempted to ban them.

Other destructive forces were also at work. The masters often found themselves under increased competitive pressure from larger, more heavily capitalized establishments or from the introduction of machine production into a previously craft-dominated industry. In many workshops masters began to follow a practice, known in France as *confection*, whereby goods, such as shoes, clothing, and furniture, were produced in standard sizes and styles rather than by special orders for individual customers.

This practice increased the division of labor in the workshop. Each artisan produced a smaller part of the more-or-less uniform final product. Thus, less skill was required of each artisan, and the particular skills a worker possessed became less valuable. To increase production and reduce costs, masters also tried to lower the wages

HOW DID industrialization change the European labor force?

ANDREW URE AND JOHN RUSKIN DEBATE THE CONDITIONS OF FACTORY PRODUCTION

The factory was itself as much an invention of the Industrial Revolution as were the new machines the factory often housed. The factory required a new organization of labor. It also made possible the production of vast new quantities of manufactured goods. From its inception the factory system provoked both praise and criticism. Andrew Ure saw much positive good arising from factory production whereas John Ruskin became a vehement critic.

QUESTIONS

1. Why does Ure emphasize the willingness of workers to be employed in factories?

2. How does Ure portray the factory system as creating the possibility of new abundance?

3. How does Ruskin see the use of machinery reducing workers to a machine?

4. Is Ruskin's criticism of the division of labor a correct analysis or simply a well-crafted metaphorical criticism?

5. How might Andrew Ure have replied to Ruskin?

I. ANDREW URE PRAISES THE FACTORY SYSTEM

Andrew Ure (1778–1857) was a Scottisch physician and a great proponent of the benefits of the factory system. In 1835 he published The Philosophy of Manufactures, *which went through many editions from then until late in the century. He saw factories as not only increasing productivity but also providing a healthier environment than agricultural work or mining.*

Power looms used in the mass production of textiles during the Industrial Revolution.

Dorling Kindersley Medial Library/David Lyons © Dorling Kindersley. Courtesy of the Boott Cotton Mills Museum, Lowell, Massachusetts

How did the advent of factories change the relationship between work and home?

The term Factory, in technology, designates the combined operation of many orders of work—people, adult and young, in tending with assiduous skill a system of productive machines continuously impelled by a central power. This definition includes such organizations as cotton-mills, flax-mills, silk-mills, woolen-mills, and certain engineering works. . . . I conceive that this title, in its strictest sense, involves the idea of a vast automaton, composed of various mechanical and intellectual organs, acting in uninterrupted concert for the production of a common object, all of them being subordinated to a self-regulated moving force. . . .

In its precise acceptation, the Factory system is of recent origin, and may claim England for its birthplace. . . .

When the first water-frames for spinning cotton were erected at Cromford, in the romantic valley of the Derwent, about sixty years ago, mankind were little aware of the mighty revolution which the new system of labor was destined by Providence to achieve, not only in the structure of British society, but in the fortunes of the world at large.

Arkwright alone had the sagacity to discern, and the boldness to predict in glowing language, how vastly productive human industry would become, when no longer proportioned in its results to muscular effort, which is by its nature fitful and capricious, but when made to consist in the task of guiding the work of mechanical fingers and arms, regularly impelled with great velocity by some indefatigable physical power. . . .

In my recent tour, continued during several months, through the manufacturing districts, I have seen tens of thousands of old, young, and middle-aged of both sexes, many of them too feeble to get their daily bread by any of the former modes of industry, earning abundant food, raiment, and domestic accommodation, without perspiring at a single pore, screened meanwhile from the summer's sun and the winter's frost, in apartments more airy and salubrious than those of the metropolis, in which our legislative and fashionable aristocracies assemble. In those spacious halls the benignant power of steam summons around him his myriads of willing menials, and assigns to each the regulated task, substituting for painful muscular effort on their part, the energies of his own gigantic arm, and demanding in return only attention and dexterity to correct such little aberrations as casually occur in his workmanship. . . . Such is the factory system, replete with prodigies in mechanics and political economy, which promises, in its future growth, to become the great minister of civilization to the terraqueous globe, enabling this country, as its heart, to diffuse along with its commerce, the life-blood of science and religion to myriads of people still lying "in the region and shadow of death."

Source: Andrew Ure, *The Philosophy of Manufactures; or, An Exposition of the Scientific, Moral, and Commercial Economy of the Factory System* (London: Chas Knight, 1835), pp. 13 ff., as quoted in *Metternich's Europe*, ed. by Mack Walker (New York: Walker and Company, 1968), pp. 275–276, 278–279.

II. JOHN RUSKIN DECRIES THE IMPACT OF INDUSTRIAL PRODUCTION ON WORKERS

The Englishman John Ruskin (1819–1900) was the foremost mid-nineteenth-century critic of art and architecture. He commenced his career interested primarily in painting and then moved to architecture. In the course of that transition he became increasingly sensitive to the working conditions of the craftsmen who constructed the buildings he studied. Over time he became a major social critic of the new industrial order. His earliest statement of social criticism occurred in a chapter entitled "The Nature of Gothic" in his book of 1851 entitled The Stones of Venice. *Here Ruskin passionately attacked the mechanical routine of work associated with industrial machinery. He also attacked the concept of increasing work through the division of labor, which had been conceptualized by Adam Smith in* The Wealth of Nations *(1776). Smith had illustrated the division of labor by describing a pin factory. Ruskin here responds to Smith's analysis.*

You must either make a tool of the creature, or a man of him. You cannot make both. Men were not intended to work with the accuracy of tools, to be precise and perfect in all their actions. If you will have that precision out of them, and make their fingers measure degrees like cog-wheels, and their arms strike curves like compasses, you must unhumanize them. All the energy of their spirits must be given to make cogs and compasses of themselves. All their attention and strength must go to the accomplishment of the mean act . . . On the other hand, if you will make a man of the working creature, you cannot make a tool. Let him but begin to imagine, to think to try to do anything worth doing; and the engine-turned precision is lost at once. Out come all his roughness, all his dulness, all his incapability; shame upon shame, failure upon failure, pause after pause: but out comes the whole majesty of him also; . . .

It is verily this degradation of the operative into a machine, which, more than any other evil of the times, is leading the mass of the nations everywhere into vain, incoherent, destructive struggling for a freedom of which they cannot explain the nature to themselves. . . . It is not that men are ill read, but that they have no pleasure in the work by which they make their bread, and therefore look to wealth as the only means of pleasure. . . .

It is not, truly speaking, the labour that is divided; but the men:—Divided into mere segments of men—broken into small fragments and crumbs of life; so that all the little piece of intelligence that is left in a man is not enough to make a pin, or a nail, but exhausts itself in making the point of a pin or the head of a nail . . . . And all the evil to which that cry is urging our myriads can be met only in one way: not by teaching nor preaching, for to teach them is but to show them their misery, and to preach to them, if we do nothing more than preach, is to mock at it. It can be met only by a right understanding, on the part of all classes, of what kinds of labour are good for men, raising them, and making them happy; by a determined sacrifice of such convenience, or beauty, or cheapness as is to be got only by the degradation of the workman; and by equally determined demand for the products and results of healthy and ennobling labour.

Source: J. Ruskin, *Stones of Venice* (New York: Lovell, Coryell, and Co., n.d.), 2, pp. 162, 164, 165–166.

Chartism Political movement associated with the London Working Men's Association's 1838 proposal for political reform.

they paid for piecework. Those attempts often led to work stoppages or strikes. Migrants from the countryside or small towns into the cities created, in some cases, a surplus of relatively unskilled workers. They were willing to work for lower wages or under less favorable and protected conditions than traditional artisans. This situation made it much more difficult for urban journeymen ever to hope to become masters in charge of their own workshops. Increasingly, these artisans became lifetime wage laborers whose skills were simply bought and sold in the marketplace.

WORKING-CLASS POLITICAL ACTION: THE EXAMPLE OF BRITISH CHARTISM

By midcentury, such artisans, proud of their skills and frustrated in their social and economic expectations, became the most radical political element in the European working class. From at least the 1830s onward, these artisans took the lead in one country after another in attempting to formulate new ways to protect their social and economic interests.

By the late 1830s, many British workers linked the solution of their economic plight to a program of political reform known as **Chartism**. In 1836, William Lovett (1800–1877) and other London radical artisans formed the London Working Men's Association. In 1838, the group issued the Charter, demanding six specific reforms. The Six Points of the Charter included universal male suffrage, annual election of the House of Commons, the secret ballot, equal electoral districts, and the abolition of property qualifications for and the payment of salaries to members of the House of Commons.

For more than a decade, the Chartists fought for the adoption of their program. On three occasions the Charter was presented to Parliament. Petitions with millions of signatures were sent to the House of Commons. Strikes were called, and a newspaper, *The Northern Star*, was published—all to no avail.

The Chartists had more success dealing with local governments, but Chartism failed to cohere as a national movement. It split between those who favored violence and those who wanted to use peaceful tactics to enact reform. Rising prosperity in the wake of a depression in the late 1830s and early 1840s also led many working people to lose interest in the issues Chartism advocated. Nevertheless, as the first large-scale political movement organized by the working class, Chartism provided an inspiration and organizational model for workers throughout Europe who wanted to improve their situation.

FAMILY STRUCTURES AND THE INDUSTRIAL REVOLUTION

HOW DID industrialization affect European families?

It is more difficult to generalize about the European working-class family structure in the age of early industrialism than under the Old Regime. Industrialism developed at different rates across the Continent, and the impact of industrialism cannot be separated from that of migration and urbanization. More is known about the relationships of the new industry to the family in Great Britain than elsewhere, and many British developments foreshadowed those in other countries.

THE FAMILY IN THE EARLY FACTORY SYSTEM

Before the late-eighteenth-century revolution in textile production in England, the individual family involved in textiles was the chief unit of production. The mechanization of weaving led to a major change. The father who became a machine weaver was then employed in a factory. His work was thus separated from his home. Nonetheless, the structure of early English factories allowed the father to preserve certain of his traditional family roles as they had existed before the factory system.

In the domestic system of the family economy, the father and mother had worked with their children in textile production as a family unit. Early factory owners and supervisors permitted the father to employ his wife and children as his assistants. Thus, parental training and discipline could be transferred from the home into the early factory. Despite those accommodations to family life, family members still had to face the new work discipline of the factory setting. Moreover, women assisting their husbands in the factory often did less skilled work than they had in their homes.

A major shift in this family and factory structure began in the mid-1820s in England and had been more or less completed by the mid-1830s. As spinning and weaving were put under one roof, the size of factories and of the machinery grew. These newer machines required fewer skilled operators, but many relatively unskilled attendants. This became the work of unmarried women and children, who would accept lower wages and were less likely than adult men to try to form worker organizations or unions.

Factory wages for the more skilled adult males, however, became sufficiently high to allow some fathers to remove their children from the factory and send them to school. The wives of the skilled operatives also usually no longer worked in the factories. So the original links of the family in the British textile factory that had existed for well over a quarter century largely disappeared.

Concern for Child Labor   At this point in the 1830s, workers became concerned about the plight of child laborers because parents were no longer exercising discipline over their own children in the factories. The English Factory Act of 1833 forbade the employment of children under age nine, limited the workday of children aged nine to thirteen to nine hours a day, and required the factory owner to pay for two hours of education a day for these children. The effect was further to divide work and home life.

By the mid-1840s, in the lives of industrial workers, the roles of men as breadwinners and as fathers and husbands had become distinct in the British textile industry. Furthermore, reformers' concerns about the working conditions of women in factories and in mines arose in part from the relatively new view that the place of women was in the home rather than in an industrial or even agrarian workplace.

Changing Economic Role for the Family   By the middle of the 1840s, men of the working class in the British textile industry had evolved distinct roles as breadwinners, fathers, and husbands. What took place in Britain was paralleled elsewhere as industrial capitalism and public education spread. The European family ceased to be a unit of production and consumption and became only a consumer. The family did not stop performing as an economic unit, but its members shared wages from different sources rather than work in a home or factory. Sharing wages rather than labor affected the strength of family bonds. Children could find work far from home, for wages could be sent over long distances.

WOMEN IN THE EARLY INDUSTRIAL REVOLUTION

The industrial economy eventually took most productive work out of the home and allowed many families to live on the wages of the male spouse. That transformation prepared the way for a new concept of gender-determined roles in the home and in domestic life generally. Women came to be associated with domestic duties or with poorly paid, largely unskilled cottage industries. Men came to be associated almost exclusively with supporting the family. Children were raised to conform to these expected gender patterns.

WHAT ROLE did women play in the Industrial Revolution?

As textile production became increasingly automated in the nineteenth century, textile factories required fewer skilled workers and more unskilled attendants. To fill these unskilled positions, factory owners turned increasingly to unmarried women and widows who worked for lower wages than men and were less likely to form labor organizations.

Courtesy of the Library of Congress

How would you explain the fact that all of the workers depicted in this image of factory life are young and female?

OPPORTUNITIES AND EXPLOITATION IN EMPLOYMENT

Because the early Industrial Revolution had begun in textile production, women and their labor were deeply involved from the start. Women usually worked in all stages of textile production and hand spinning was virtually always a woman's task. At first, when spinning was moved into factories and involved large machines, men often displaced women.

Women in Factories   With the next generation of machines in the 1820s, however, unmarried women rapidly became employed in the factories, where they often constituted the majority of workers. Their new jobs, however, often demanded fewer skills than those they had previously exercised in the home production of textiles. There was thus a certain paradox in the impact of the factory on women: It opened many new jobs to them but lowered the level of skills they needed to have.

Moreover, almost always, the women in the factories were young, single women or widows. Upon marriage or perhaps after the birth of the first child, young women usually found their husbands earned enough money for them to leave the factory. Widows might return to factory work because they lacked their husbands' former income.

Work on the Land and in the Home   In Britain and elsewhere by midcentury, industrial factory work still accounted for less than half of all employment for women. The largest group of employed women in France continued to work on the land. In England, they were domestic servants. Throughout Western Europe, domestic cottage industries, such as lace making, glove making, garment making, and other kinds of needlework, employed many women. It cannot be overemphasized that all work by women commanded low wages and involved low skills. They had virtually no effective modes to protect themselves from exploitation.

The low wages of female workers in all areas of employment sometimes led them to become prostitutes to supplement their wage income. Such sexual exploitation of women was hardly new to European society, but the particular pressures of the transformation of the economy from one of skilled artisans to that of unskilled factory workers made many women especially vulnerable.

CHANGING EXPECTATIONS IN THE WORKING-CLASS MARRIAGE

Moving to cities and entering the wage economy gave women wider opportunities for marriage. Cohabitation before marriage was not uncommon. Parents had less to do with arranging marriages than in the past. Marriage now usually meant a woman would leave the workforce to live on her husband's earnings. Despite these changes, many of the traditional practices associated with the family economy survived into the industrial era. As a young woman came of age, both family needs and her desire to marry still directed what she would do with her life. As in the past, as a young woman she would try to earn enough in wages to give herself a dowry, so she might marry and set up her own household.

Marriage in the wage industrial economy was different in certain respects from marriage in earlier times. Marriage was less an economic partnership. The husband's wages might well be able to support the entire family. The wage economy and the industrialization separating workplace from home made it difficult for women to combine domestic duties with work. More often than not, the children rather than the wife were sent to work. This may help explain the increase in the number of births within marriages, as children in the wage economy usually were an economic asset. Married women worked outside the home only when family needs, illness, or widowhood forced them to.

In the home, working-class women were by no means idle. Wives were concerned primarily with food and cooking, but they were also often in charge of the family's finances. The role of the mother expanded when the children still living at home became wage earners. She was now providing home support for her entire wage-earning family. The longer period of home life of working children may also have increased and strengthened familial bonds of affection between those children and their hard-working homebound mothers. In all these respects, the culture of the working-class marriage and family tended to imitate the family patterns of the middle and upper classes, whose members had often accepted the view of separate gender spheres set forth by Rousseau and popularized in hundreds of novels, journals, and newspapers.

QUICK REVIEW
Modern Police

- First appeared in early nineteenth century
- Their creation reflected elite fears and anxieties about disorder
- Came to be seen by most Europeans as a positive force

PROBLEMS OF CRIME AND ORDER

Throughout the nineteenth century, the political and economic elite in Europe were profoundly concerned about social order. The revolutions of the late eighteenth and early nineteenth centuries made them fearful of future disorder and threats to life and property, at the same time as industrialization and urbanization upset traditional social patterns. Throughout the first sixty years of the nineteenth century, crime appears to have increased slowly but steadily before more or less reaching a plateau.

HOW DID the establishment of police forces and the reform of prisons change society?

NEW POLICE FORCES

From the propertied, elite classes, two major views about containing crime and criminals emerged during the nineteenth century: better systems of police and prison reform. The result of these efforts was the triumph in Europe of the idea of a policed society in which a paid, professionally trained group of law-enforcement officers keeps order, protects property and lives, investigates crime, and apprehends offenders. Professional police forces did not really exist until the early nineteenth century. They differed from one country to another in both authority and organization, but their creation proved crucial to the emergence of an orderly European society.

Professional police forces appeared in Paris in 1828. The next year, the British Parliament passed legislation sponsored by Sir Robert Peel (1788–1850) that placed police on London streets. Berlin deployed similar police departments after the Revolution of 1848. Although citizens sometimes viewed police with suspicion, by the end of the century, most Europeans regarded the police as their protectors.

PRISON REFORM

Before the nineteenth century, European prisons were local jails or state prisons, such as the Bastille. In prisons, inmates lived under wretched conditions. Men, women, and children were housed together. Persons guilty of minor offenses were left in the same room with those guilty of the most serious offenses.

Beginning in the late eighteenth century, the British government sentenced persons convicted of the most serious offenses to transportation. Transportation to the colony of New South Wales in Australia was regarded as an alternative to capital punishment, and the British used it until the mid–nineteenth century, when the colonies began to object. Thereafter, the British government housed long-term prisoners in public works prisons in Britain.

London Policeman Professional police forces did not exist before the early nineteenth century. The London police force was created in 1828.

Peter Newark's Pictures

What urban problems were police forces created to address?

Overview   Major Works of Economic and Political Commentary

YEAR	WORK	AUTHOR
1776	*The Wealth of Nations*	Adam Smith
1798	*Essay on the Principle of Population*	Thomas Malthus
1817	*Principles of Political Economy*	David Ricardo
1839	*The Organization of Labor*	Louis Blanc
1845	*The Condition of the Working Class in England*	Friedrich Engels
1848	*The Communist Manifesto*	Karl Marx and Friedrich Engels

By the close of the eighteenth century and in the early nineteenth century, reformers, such as John Howard (1726–1790) and Elizabeth Fry (1780–1845) in England and Charles Lucas (1803–1889) in France, exposed the horrendous conditions in prisons and demanded change. Reform came slowly because of the expense of constructing new prisons and a lack of sympathy for criminals. In the 1840s, however, both the French and the English undertook several bold efforts at prison reform. These efforts would appear to indicate a shift in opinion whereby crime was seen not as an assault on order or on authority but as a mark of a character fault in the criminal. Thereafter, part of the goal of imprisonment was to rehabilitate or transform the prisoner.

Europeans used various prison models originally established in the United States. All these experiments depended on separating prisoners from each other. The chief characteristics of these systems were an individual cell for each prisoner and long periods of separation and silence among prisoners. The point of the system was to induce self-reflection in which the prisoners would think about their crimes and eventually decide to repudiate their criminal tendencies. As time passed, the system became more relaxed because the intense isolation often led to mental collapse.

These attempts to create a police force and to reform prisons illustrate the concern about order and stability by European political and social elites that developed after the French Revolution. On the whole, their efforts succeeded. By the end of the century, an orderly society had been established, and the new police and prisons had no small role in that development.

CLASSICAL ECONOMICS

WHAT WERE the key assumptions of classical economic theory?

Economists whose thought derived largely from Adam Smith's *The Wealth of Nations* (1776) dominated private and public discussions of industrial and commercial policy. Their ideas are often associated with the phrase *laissez-faire* (a French phrase that means roughly "let people do as they please"). Although they thought the government should perform many important functions, they believed the mechanism of the marketplace should govern most economic decisions.

MALTHUS ON POPULATION

The classical economists had complicated and pessimistic ideas about the working class. Thomas Malthus (1766–1834) and David Ricardo (1772–1823), probably the most influential of all these writers, suggested, in effect, that nothing could improve the condition of the working class. Malthus contended that population must eventually outstrip the food supply. Although the human population grows geometrically, the food supply can expand only arithmetically. There was little hope of averting the disaster, in Malthus's opinion, except through late marriage, chastity, and contraception, the last of which he considered a vice.

RICARDO ON WAGES

In his *Principles of Political Economy* (1817), David Ricardo transformed the concepts of Malthus into the "iron law of wages." If wages were raised, parents would have more children. They, in turn, would enter the labor market, thus expanding the number of workers and lowering wages. As wages fell, working people would produce fewer children. Wages would then rise, and the process would start all over again. Consequently, in the long run, wages would always tend toward a minimum level. These arguments simply supported employers in their natural reluctance to raise wages and also provided strong theoretical support for opposing labor unions.

GOVERNMENT POLICIES BASED ON CLASSICAL ECONOMICS

The working classes of France and Great Britain, needless to say, resented the attitudes of the economists, but the governments embraced them. Louis Philippe (1773–1850) and his minister François Guizot (1787–1874) told the French to go forth and enrich themselves. The July Monarchy (1830–1848) saw the construction of major capital-intensive projects, such as roads, canals, and railways. Little, however, was done about the poverty in the cities and the countryside.

After the Napoleonic wars, Prussian reformers had seen the desirability of abolishing internal tariffs that impeded economic growth. In 1834, all the major German states, except Austria, formed the *Zollverein*, or free trading union. Classical economics had less influence in Germany because of the tradition dating from the enlightened absolutism of state direction of economic development.

Britain was the home of the major classical economists, and their policies were widely accepted. The utilitarian thought of Jeremy Bentham (1748–1832) increased their influence. Although **utilitarianism** did not originate with him, Bentham sought to create codes of scientific law that were founded on the principle of utility, that is, the greatest happiness for the greatest number. The application of reason and utility would remove the legal clutter that prevented justice from being realized. He believed the principle of utility could be applied to other areas of government administration.

Bentham gathered round him political disciples who combined his ideas with those of classical economics. In 1834, the reformed House of Commons passed a new Poor Law that followers of Bentham had prepared. This measure established a Poor Law Commission that set out to make poverty the most undesirable of all social situations. Government poor relief was to be disbursed only in workhouses. Life in the workhouse was consciously designed to be more unpleasant than life outside. The law and its administration presupposed that people would not work because they were lazy. The laboring class, not unjustly, regarded the workhouses as new "bastilles."

The second British monument to applied classical economics was the repeal of the Corn Laws in 1846. The Anti-Corn Law League, organized by manufacturers, had sought this goal for more than six years. The League wanted to abolish the tariffs protecting the domestic price of grain. That change would lead to lower food prices, which would then allow lower wages at no real cost to the workers. In turn, the prices on British manufactured goods could also be lowered to strengthen their competitive position in the world market. The actual reason for Sir Robert Peel's repeal of the Corn Laws in 1846 was the Irish famine. Peel had to open British ports to foreign grain to feed the starving Irish.

EARLY SOCIALISM

The early socialists generally applauded the new productive capacity of industrialism. They denied, however, that the free market could adequately produce and distribute goods the way the classical economists claimed. Moreover, the socialists thought human society should be organized as a community, rather than merely as a conglomerate of atomistic, selfish individuals.

Thomas Malthus.
Courtesy of the Library of Congress

utilitarianism Maintained that people should always pursue the course that promotes the greatest happiness for the greatest number.

HOW DID socialism challenge classical economics?

UTOPIAN SOCIALISM

utopian socialists Early critics of industrialism whose visionary programs often involved plans to establish ideal societies based on noncapitalistic values.

Among the earliest people to define the social question were a group of writers whom their critics called the **utopian socialists.** They were considered utopian because their ideas were often visionary and because they frequently advocated the creation of ideal communities. They were called socialists because they questioned the structures and values of the existing capitalistic framework. In some cases, they actually deserved neither description.

Saint-Simonianism   Count Claude Henri de Saint-Simon (1760–1825) was the earliest of the socialist pioneers. Above all else, Saint-Simon believed modern society would require rational management. Private wealth, property, and enterprise should be subject to an administration other than that of its owners. His ideal government would have consisted of a large board of directors organizing and coordinating the activity of individuals and groups to achieve social harmony. Not the *redistribution* of wealth, but its *management* by experts, would alleviate the poverty and social dislocation of the age.

When Saint-Simon died in 1825, he had persuaded only a handful of people his ideas were correct. Nonetheless, Saint-Simonian societies were always centers for lively discussion of advanced social ideals. Some of the earliest debates in France over feminism took place within these societies.

Owenism   The major British contributor to the early socialist tradition was Robert Owen (1771–1858), a self-made cotton manufacturer. In his early twenties, Owen became a partner in one of the largest cotton factories in Britain at New Lanark, Scotland. Owen was a firm believer in the environmentalist psychology of the Enlightenment that had flowed from the thought of John Locke. If human beings were placed in the correct surroundings, they and their character could be improved. Moreover, Owen saw no incompatibility between creating a humane industrial environment and making a good profit.

At New Lanark, he put his ideas into practice. Workers were provided with good quarters. Recreational possibilities abounded, and the children received an education. There were several churches, although Owen himself was a notorious freethinker on matters of religion and sex. In the factory itself, rewards were given for good work. His plant made a fine profit. Visitors flocked from all over Europe to see what Owen had done through enlightened management.

During the 1820s, Owen sold his New Lanark factory and then went to the United States, where he established the community of New Harmony, Indiana. When quarrels among the members led to the community's failure, he refused to give up his reformist causes. He returned to Britain, where he became the moving force behind the organization of the Grand National Union, an attempt to draw all British trade unions into a single body. It collapsed along with other labor organizations during the early 1830s.

Mr OWEN'S INSTITUTION, NEW LANARK.
(Quadrille Dancing.)

Robert Owen, the Scottish industrialist and early socialist, created an ideal industrial community at New Lanark, Scotland. He believed deeply in the power of education and saw that the children of workmen received sound educations.

Eileen Tweedy/Picture Desk, Inc./Kobal Collection

What light does this image shed on Owen's ideas about social order and harmony?

Fourierism   Charles Fourier (1772–1837) was Owen's French intellectual counterpart. Fourier believed the industrial order ignored the passionate side of human nature. Social discipline ignored all the pleasures that human beings naturally seek. Fourier advocated the construction of communities, called *phalanxes*, in which liberated living would replace the boredom and dullness of industrial existence. Agrarian rather than industrial production would predominate in these communities. Sexual activity would be relatively free, and marriage was to be reserved only for later life. Fourier also urged that no person be required to perform the same kind of work for the entire day. People would be both happier and more productive if they moved from one task to another. Through his emphasis on the problem of boredom, Fourier isolated one of the key difficulties of modern economic life.

Saint-Simon, Owen, and Fourier failed to confront the political difficulties their envisioned social transformations would arouse. Other figures paid more attention to the politics of the situation. In 1839, Louis Blanc (1811–1882) published *The Organization of Labor*. Blanc called for political reform that would give the vote to the working class. Once so empowered, workers could use the vote to turn the political processes to their own economic advantage. A state controlled by a working-class electorate would finance workshops to employ the poor. In time, such workshops might replace private enterprise, and industry would be organized to ensure jobs. The state itself could become the great employer of labor.

ANARCHISM

Other writers and activists of the 1840s, however, rejected both industry and the dominance of government. These were the **anarchists**. They are usually included in the socialist tradition, although they do not exactly fit there. Some favored programs of violence and terrorism; others were peaceful. Auguste Blanqui (1805–1881) was a major spokesperson for terror. Seeking to abolish both capitalism and the state, Blanqui urged the development of a professional revolutionary vanguard to attack capitalist society.

Pierre-Joseph Proudhon (1809–1865) represented the other strain of anarchism. He believed that society should be organized on the basis of mutualism, which amounted to a system of small businesses and other cooperative enterprises among which there would be peaceful cooperation and exchanges of goods based on mutual recognition of the labor each area of production required. With such a social system, the state as the protector of property would be unnecessary. Proudhon's ideas later influenced the French labor movement, which was generally less directly political in its activities than the labor movements in Britain and Germany.

MARXISM

The mode of socialist thought that eventually exerted more influence over modern European history than any other was **Marxism**. At midcentury, the ideas of Karl Marx were simply one more contribution to a heady mixture of concepts and programs criticizing the emerging industrial capitalist society. Marxism differed from its competitors in its claims to scientific accuracy, its rejection of liberal reform, its harsh criticism of other contemporary socialist platforms, and its call for revolution, though the character of that revolution was not well defined. Furthermore, Marx set the emergence of the industrial workforce in the context of a world historical development from which he drew sweeping political conclusions.

Karl Marx (1818–1883) was born in Germany in the Prussian Rhineland. Marx's middle-class parents sent him to the University of Berlin, where he became deeply involved in Hegelian philosophy and radical politics. Soon the Prussian authorities drove him from his native land. He lived as an exile, first in Paris, then in Brussels, and finally, after 1849, in London.

Partnership with Engels   In 1844, Marx met Friedrich Engels (1820–1895), another young middle-class German, whose father owned a textile factory in Manchester, England. The next year Engels published *The Condition of the Working Class in England*, which presented a devastating picture of industrial life. Late in 1847, they were asked

QUICK REVIEW

Charles Fourier (1772–1837)

◆ Believed that industrial order ignored the emotional side of human nature

◆ Advocated the construction of communities called *phalanxes*

◆ Envisioned agrarian production as the basis of *phalanxes*

anarchists   Those who opposed any cooperation with industry or government.

Marxism   Socialist movement begun by Karl Marx in the mid–nineteenth century that differed from competing socialist views primarily in its claim to a scientific foundation and in its insistence on reform through revolution.

Karl Marx's socialist philosophy eventually triumphed over most alternative versions of socialism in Europe, but his monumental work became subject to varying interpretations, criticism, and revisions that continue to this day.
Library of Congress

Should Marx be considered a utopian thinker?

to write a pamphlet for a newly organized and ultimately short-lived secret Communist League. *The Communist Manifesto*, published in German, appeared early in 1848.

Sources of Marx's Ideas   Marx derived the major ideas of the *Manifesto* and of his later work, including *Capital* (vol. 1, 1867), from German Hegelianism, French utopian socialism, and British classical economics. Marx applied to concrete historical, social, and economic developments Hegel's abstract philosophical concept that thought develops from the clash of thesis and antithesis into a new intellectual synthesis. For Marx, the conflict between dominant and subordinate social groups led to the emergence of a new dominant social group. These new social relationships, in turn, generated new discontent, conflict, and development. The French utopian socialists had depicted the problems of capitalist society and had raised the issue of property redistribution. Both Hegel and Saint-Simon led Marx to see society and economic conditions as developing through historical stages. The classical economists had produced the analytical tools for an empirical, scientific examination of the industrial capitalist society. Using the intellectual tools of Hegel, the French utopian socialists, and the British classical economists provided, Marx fashioned a philosophy that gave a special role or function to the new industrial workforce as the single most important driving force of contemporary history.

Revolution Through Class Conflict   In *The Communist Manifesto*, Marx and Engels contended that human history must be understood rationally and as a whole. History is the record of humankind's coming to grips with physical nature to produce the goods necessary for survival. That basic productive process determines the structures, values, and ideas of a society. Historically, the organization of the means of production has always involved conflict between the classes that owned and controlled the means of production and the classes that worked for them. That necessary conflict has provided the engine for historical development; it is not an accidental by-product of mismanagement or bad intentions. Thus, piecemeal reforms cannot eliminate the social and economic evils inherent in the very structures of production. To achieve that, a radical social transformation is required. The development of capitalism will make such a revolution inevitable.

In Marx's and Engels's eyes, the class conflict that had characterized previous Western history had become simplified during the early nineteenth century into a struggle between the bourgeoisie and the proletariat, or between the middle class associated with industry and commerce, on the one hand, and the workers, on the other. The character of capitalism itself ensured the sharpening of the struggle. Capitalist production and competition would steadily increase the size of the unpropertied proletariat, at the same time as it resulted in fewer, but larger, capitalist firms. As this ever-expanding body of workers suffered increasingly from the competition among the ever-enlarging firms, Marx contended, they would eventually begin to foment revolution. Finally, they would overthrow the few remaining owners of the means of production. For a time, the workers would organize the means of production through a dictatorship of the proletariat. This would eventually give way to a propertyless and classless communist society. This victory of the proletariat over the bourgeoisie would represent the culmination of human history. For the first time in human history, one group of people would not be oppressing another.

The economic environment of the 1840s had conditioned Marx's analysis. The decade had seen much unemployment and deprivation. During the later part of the century, however, European and American capitalism did not collapse as he had predicted, nor did the middle class become proletarianized. Rather, the industrial system benefited more and more people. Nonetheless, within a generation of the publication of *The Communist Manifesto*, Marxism had captured the imagination of many socialists, especially in Germany, and large segments of the working class. Marxist doctrines appeared to be based on the empirical evidence of hard economic fact. Marxism's scientific claim helped spread the ideology as science became more influential during the second half of the century. At its core, however, the attraction of the ideology was its utopian vision of ultimate human liberation, no matter how illiberal or authoritarian the governments that embraced the Marxist vision in the twentieth century were.

1848: YEAR OF REVOLUTIONS

In 1848, a series of liberal and nationalistic revolutions erupted across the Continent. (See Map 21–2, page 532.) No single factor caused this general revolutionary groundswell; rather, similar conditions existed in several countries. Severe food shortages had prevailed since 1846. The commercial and industrial economy was also depressed. Unemployment was widespread. Systems of poor relief were overburdened. These difficulties, added to the wretched living conditions in the cities, heightened the frustration and discontent of the urban artisan and laboring classes.

WHY DID a series of revolutions erupt across Europe in 1848?

The dynamic force for change in 1848 originated, however, not with the working classes, but with the political liberals, who were generally drawn from the middle classes. Throughout the Continent, liberals were pushing for their program of a more representative government, civil liberty, and unregulated economic life. To put additional pressure on their governments, they began to appeal for the support of the urban working classes. The latter, however, wanted improved working and economic conditions, rather than a more liberal government. Moreover, their tactics were frequently violent rather than peaceful. The temporary alliance of liberals and workers in several states overthrew or severely shook the old order; then the allies began to fight each other.

Finally, outside France, nationalism was an important common factor in the uprisings. Germans, Hungarians, Italians, Czechs, and smaller national groups in eastern Europe sought to create national states that would reorganize or replace existing political entities. At the same time, various national groups clashed with each other during these revolutions.

The immediate results of the 1848 revolutions were stunning. Yet, without exception, the revolutions failed to establish genuinely liberal or national states. The conservative order proved stronger and more resilient than anyone had expected. The liberals refused to follow political revolution with social reform and thus isolated themselves from the working classes. Once separated from potential mass support, the liberal revolutions became an easy prey for the armies of the reactionary classes.

FRANCE: THE SECOND REPUBLIC AND LOUIS NAPOLEON

As had happened twice before, the revolutionary tinder first blazed in Paris. The liberal political opponents of the corrupt regime of Louis Philippe and his minister Guizot organized a series of political banquets. They used these occasions to criticize the government and demand further admission for them and their middle-class supporters to the political process. The poor harvests of 1846 and 1847 and the resulting high food prices and unemployment brought working-class support to the liberal campaign. On February 21, 1848, the government forbade further banquets. On February 22, disgruntled Parisian workers paraded through the streets demanding reform and Guizot's ouster. The next morning the crowds grew, and by afternoon, Guizot had resigned. The crowds erected barricades, and numerous clashes occurred between the citizenry and the municipal guard. On February 24, 1848, Louis Philippe abdicated and fled to England.

MAP 21–2   **Centers of Revolution in 1848–1849**   The revolution that toppled the July Monarchy in Paris in 1848 soon spread to Austria and many of the German and Italian states. Yet by the end of 1849, most of these uprisings had been suppressed.

Why would Austria and Germany have provided fertile grounds for the spread of a revolutionary movement that began in France?

The National Assembly and Paris Workers   The liberal opposition, led by the poet Alphonse de Lamartine (1790–1869), organized a provisional government. The liberals intended to call an election for an assembly that would write a republican constitution. The various working-class groups in Paris, however, had other ideas: They wanted a social as well as a political revolution. Led by Louis Blanc, they demanded representation in the cabinet. Blanc and two other radical leaders became ministers. Under their pressure, the provisional government organized national workshops to provide work and relief for thousands of unemployed workers.

On Sunday, April 23, an election based on universal male suffrage chose the new National Assembly. The result was a legislature dominated by moderates and conservatives. In the French provinces, many people resented the Paris radicals and were frightened by their ideas. The new conservative National Assembly had little sympathy for the expensive national workshops, which they incorrectly perceived to be socialistic.

Throughout May, government troops and the unemployed workers and artisans of Paris clashed. As a result, the assembly closed the workshops to new entrants and planned to eject many enrolled workers. By late June, barricades again appeared in Paris. On June 24, under orders from the government, General Louis Cavaignac (1802–1857), with troops drawn largely from the conservative countryside, moved to destroy the barricades and quell disturbances. During the next two days, more than four hundred people were killed. Thereafter, troops hunted down another 3,000 persons in street fighting. The drive for social revolution had ended.

Emergence of Louis Napoleon   The so-called June Days confirmed the political predominance of conservative property holders in French life. They wanted a state that was safe for small property. Late in 1848, the election for president confirmed this search for social order. The new president was Louis Napoleon Bonaparte (1808–1873), a nephew of the great emperor. After the corruption of Louis Philippe and the turmoil of the early months of the Second Republic, the voters turned to the name of Bonaparte as a source of stability and greatness.

The election of the "Little Napoleon" doomed the Second Republic. Louis Napoleon was dedicated to his own fame rather than to republican institutions. In 1851, the assembly refused to amend the constitution to allow the president to run for reelection. Consequently, on December 2, 1851, the anniversary of the great Napoleon's victory at Austerlitz, Louis Napoleon seized power. Troops dispersed the assembly, and the president called for new elections. More than two hundred people died resisting the coup, and more than 26,000 persons were arrested throughout the country. Almost 10,000 persons who opposed the coup were transported to Algeria.

Yet, in the plebiscite of December 21, 1851, more than 7.5 million voters supported the actions of Louis Napoleon and approved a new constitution that consolidated his power. Only about 600,000 citizens dared to vote against him. A year later, in December 1852, an empire was proclaimed, and Louis Napoleon became Emperor Napoleon III. Again a plebiscite approved the action.

Frenchwomen in 1848   The years between the February Revolution of 1848 and the Napoleonic coup of 1851 saw major feminist activity by Frenchwomen. Especially in Paris, women seized the opportunity of the collapse of the July Monarchy to voice demands for reform of their social conditions. They joined the wide variety of political clubs that emerged in the wake of the revolution. Some of these clubs emphasized women's rights. Some women even tried unsuccessfully to vote in the elections of 1848. Both middle-class and working-class women were involved in these activities. The most radical group, the Vesuvians, demanded full domestic household equality between men and women, the right of women to serve in the military, and similarity in dress for both sexes. They also conducted street demonstrations. The radical character of their demands and actions lost them the support of more moderate women.

Certain Parisian women quickly attempted to use for their own cause the liberal freedoms that suddenly had become available. They organized the *Voix des femmes* (*The Women's Voice*), a daily newspaper that addressed issues of concern to women. The newspaper insisted that improving the lot of men would not necessarily improve the condition of women. They soon organized a society with the same name as the newspaper. Members of the *Voix des femmes* group were relatively conservative feminists. They cooperated with male political groups, and they urged the integrity of the family and fidelity in marriage. They furthermore warmly embraced the maternal role for women but tried to use it to raise the importance of women in society. The emphasis on family and motherhood represented, in part, a defensive strategy to prevent conservative women and men from accusing the advocates of women's rights of seeking to destroy the family and traditional marriage.

The fate of French feminists in 1848 was similar to that of the radical workers. Once the elections were held that spring, the new government expressed no sympathy for their causes. The closing of the national workshops adversely affected women workers as well as men and blocked one outlet that women had used to make their needs known. The conservative crackdown on political clubs closed another arena in which women had participated. Women were soon specifically forbidden to participate in political clubs either by themselves or with men. By 1852, the entire feminist movement that had sprung up in 1848 had been eradicated.

THE HABSBURG EMPIRE: NATIONALISM RESISTED

The events of February 1848 in Paris immediately reverberated throughout the Habsburg domains. The empire was susceptible to revolutionary challenge on every score. Its government rejected liberal institutions. Its borders cut across national lines. Its society perpetuated serfdom. In 1848, the regime confronted rebellions in Vienna, Prague, Hungary, and Italy. The disturbances that broke out in Germany also threatened Habsburg predominance.

The Vienna Uprising   The Habsburg troubles began on March 3, 1848, when Louis Kossuth (1802–1894), a Magyar nationalist and member of the Hungarian diet, attacked Austrian domination, called for the independence of Hungary, and demanded a responsible ministry under the Habsburg dynasty. Ten days later, inspired by Kossuth's speeches, students led a series of disturbances in Vienna. The army failed to restore order. Metternich resigned and fled the country. The feeble-minded Emperor Ferdinand (r. 1835–1848) promised a moderately liberal constitution. Unsatisfied, the radical students then formed democratic clubs to press the revolution further. On May 17, the emperor and the imperial court fled to Innsbruck.

What the Habsburg government most feared was not the urban rebellions, but an uprising of the serfs in the countryside. Consequently, almost immediately after the Vienna uprising, the imperial government emancipated the serfs in much of Austria. The Hungarian diet also abolished serfdom in March 1848. These actions smothered the most serious potential threat to order in the empire.

The Magyar Revolt   The Vienna revolt had emboldened the Hungarians. The Magyar leaders of the Hungarian March Revolution were primarily liberals supported by nobles who wanted their aristocratic liberties guaranteed against the central government in Vienna. The Hungarian Diet passed the March Laws, which mandated equality of religion, jury trials, the election of the lower chamber of the Diet, a relatively free press, and payment of taxes by the nobility. Emperor Ferdinand approved these measures because in the spring of 1848 he could do little else.

The Magyars also hoped to establish a separate Hungarian state within the Habsburg domains. As part of this scheme for a partially independent state, the Hungarians attempted to annex Transylvania, Croatia, and other eastern territories of the Habsburg Empire. That annexation would have brought Romanians, Croatians, and Serbs under Magyar government. These national groups resisted the drive toward Magyarization, especially the imposition on them, for the purposes of the government and administration, of the Hungarian language. The national groups whom the Hungarians were now repressing believed the Habsburgs offered them a better chance to preserve their national or ethnic identity, their languages, and their economic self-interest. In late March, the Vienna government sent Count Joseph Jellachich (1801–1859) to aid the national groups who were rebelling against the rebellious Hungarians. By early September 1848, he was invading Hungary with the support of the national groups who were resisting Magyarization.

Louis Kossuth, a Magyar nationalist, shown here seeking to raise troops to fight for Hungarian independence during the revolutionary disturbances of 1848.

Bildarchiv Preussischer Kulturbesitz

Who were the leaders of the Magyar revolt? What did they want?

Czech Nationalism   In mid-March 1848, with Vienna and Budapest in revolt, Czech nationalists demanded that the Czech provinces of Bohemia and Moravia be permitted to constitute an autonomous Slavic state within the empire similar to that just enacted in Hungary. Conflict immediately developed, however, between the Czechs and the Germans living in these regions. The Czechs summoned a congress of Slavs, including Poles, Ruthenians, Czechs, Slovaks, Croats, Slovenes, and Serbs, which met in Prague in early June. Under the leadership of Francis Palacky (1798–1876), this first Pan-Slavic Congress called for the national equality of Slavs within the Habsburg Empire. The manifesto also protested the repression of all Slavic peoples under Habsburg, Hungarian, German, and Ottoman domination.

On June 12, the day the Pan-Slavic Congress closed, a radical insurrection broke out in Prague. General Prince Alfred Windischgraetz (1787–1862), whose wife had been killed by a stray bullet, moved his troops against the uprising. The Prague middle class was happy to see the radicals suppressed, which was finalized by June 17. The Germans in the area approved the smothering of Czech nationalism. The policy of "divide and conquer" had succeeded.

Rebellion in Northern Italy   While repelling the Hungarian and Czech bids for autonomy, the Habsburg government also faced war in northern Italy. A revolt against Habsburg domination began in Milan on March 18. King Charles Albert of Piedmont (r. 1831–1849), who wanted to annex Lombardy (the province of which Milan is the capital), aided the rebels. The Austrian forces fared badly until July, when Austrian reinforcements arrived, defeated Piedmont, and suppressed the revolt. For the time being, Austria held its position in northern Italy.

Vienna and Hungary remained to be recaptured. In midsummer, the emperor returned to the capital and the imperial government decided to reassert its control. When a new insurrection occurred in October, the imperial army bombarded Vienna and crushed the revolt. On December 2, Emperor Ferdinand, clearly too feeble to govern, abdicated in favor of his young nephew Francis Joseph (r. 1848–1916). Real power now lay with Prince Felix Schwarzenberg (1800–1852), who intended to use the army with full force.

On January 5, 1849, troops occupied Budapest. By March the triumphant Austrian forces had imposed military rule over Hungary, and the new emperor repudiated the recent constitution. The Magyar nobles attempted one last revolt. In August, Austrian troops, reinforced by 200,000 soldiers that Tsar Nicholas I of Russia (r. 1825–1855) happily furnished, finally crushed the Hungarians. Croatians and other nationalities that had resisted Magyarization welcomed the collapse of the revolt. The imperial Habsburg government survived its gravest internal challenge because of the divisions among its enemies and its own willingness to use military force with a vengeance.

ITALY: REPUBLICANISM DEFEATED

The brief war between Piedmont and Austria in 1848 marked only the first stage of the Italian revolution. Many Italians hoped King Charles Albert of Piedmont would drive Austria from the peninsula and thus prepare the way for Italian unification. Liberal and nationalist hopes then shifted to Pope Pius IX (r. 1846–1878) who had a liberal reputation. Nationalists believed a united Italian state might emerge under his leadership.

In Rome, however, as in other cities, political radicalism was on the rise. On November 15, 1848, a democratic radical assassinated Count Pelligrino Rossi (r. 1787–1848), the liberal minister of the Papal States. The next day, popular demonstrations forced the pope to appoint a radical ministry. Shortly thereafter, Pius IX fled to Naples for refuge. In February 1849, the radicals proclaimed the Roman Republic. Republican nationalists from all over Italy, including Giuseppe Mazzini (1805–1872) and Giuseppe Garibaldi (1807–1882), two of the most prominent, flocked to Rome. They hoped to use the new republic as a base of operations to unite the rest of Italy under a republican government.

In March 1849, radicals in Piedmont forced Charles Albert to renew the patriotic war against Austria. After the almost immediate defeat of Piedmont at the Battle of Novara, the king abdicated in favor of his son, Victor Emmanuel II (r. 1849–1878). The defeat meant the Roman Republic must defend itself alone. The troops that attacked Rome and restored the pope came from France. The French wanted to prevent the rise of a strong, unified state on their southern border. By the end of the June, the French were victorious and the Roman Republic had dissolved.

GERMANY: LIBERALISM FRUSTRATED

The revolutionary contagion had also spread rapidly through the German states. The most important of these revolutions occurred in Prussia.

Revolution in Prussia   By March 15, 1848, large popular disturbances had erupted in Berlin. Frederick William IV (r. 1840–1861) refused to turn his troops on the Berliners and even announced limited reforms. Nevertheless, on March 18, several citizens were killed when troops cleared a square near the palace.

The king called for a Prussian constituent assembly to write a constitution. The next day, as angry Berliners crowded around the palace, Frederick William IV appeared on the balcony to salute the corpses of his slain subjects. He made further concessions and implied that henceforth Prussia would help unify Germany. For all practical purposes, the Prussian monarchy had capitulated.

Frederick William IV appointed a cabinet headed by David Hansemann (1790–1864), a widely respected moderate liberal. The Prussian constituent assembly, however, proved to be radical and democratic. As time passed, the king and his conservative supporters decided to ignore the assembly. The liberal ministry resigned and a conservative one replaced it. In April 1849, the assembly was dissolved, and the monarch proclaimed his own constitution. One of its key elements was a system of three-class voting which gave the wealthy disproportionate political power. In the revised Prussian constitution of 1850, the ministry was responsible to the king alone. Moreover, the Prussian army and officer corps swore loyalty directly to the monarch.

The Frankfurt Parliament While Prussia was moving from revolution to reaction, other events were unfolding in Germany as a whole. On May 18, 1848, representatives from all the German states gathered in Saint Paul's Church in Frankfurt to revise the organization of the German Confederation. The Frankfurt Parliament intended to write a moderately liberal constitution for a united Germany. The liberal character of the Frankfurt Parliament alienated both German conservatives and the German working class. The very existence of the parliament, representing as it did a challenge to the existing political order, offended the conservatives. The liberals were too attached to the concept of a free labor market to offer meaningful legislation to workers. This failure marked the beginning of a profound split between German liberals and the German working class. For the rest of the century, German conservatives would be able to play on that division.

The Frankfurt Parliament also floundered on the issue of unification. Members differed over whether to include Austria in a united Germany. The "large German [*grossdeutsch*] solution" favored Austria's inclusion, whereas the "small German [*kleindeutsch*] solution" advocated its exclusion. The latter formula prevailed because Austria rejected the whole notion of German unification. Consequently, the Frankfurt Parliament looked to Prussian, rather than Austrian, leadership.

On March 27, 1849, the parliament produced its constitution. Shortly thereafter, its delegates offered the crown of a united Germany to Frederick William IV of Prussia. He rejected the offer, asserting that kings ruled by the grace of God rather than by the permission of man-made constitutions. On his refusal, the Frankfurt Parliament began to dissolve. Not long afterward, troops drove off the remaining members. German liberals never fully recovered from this defeat.

THE REVOLUTIONARY CRISIS OF 1848 TO 1851

1848

February 22–24	Abdication of Louis Philippe
March 3	Kossuth demands freedom for Hungary
March 13	Revolution in Vienna
March 15	Habsburg emperor accepts the March Laws
March 18	Frederick William IV promises a constitution; revolution in Milan
March 22	Piedmont declares war on Austria
April 23	Election of the French National Assembly
May 17	Emperor Ferdinand flees Vienna
May 18	Frankfurt Parliament gathers
June 2	Pan-Slavic Congress convenes in Prague
July 24	Austria defeats Piedmont
September 17	General Jellachich invades Hungary
October 31	General Windischgraetz pacifies Vienna
November 16	Revolution in Rome
November 25	Pope Pius IX flees Rome
December 2	Francis Joseph becomes Habsburg emperor
December 10	Louis Napoleon and the Second French Republic

1849

January 5	General Windischgraetz occupies Budapest
February 2	The Roman Republic proclaimed
March 12	War resumes between Piedmont and Austria
March 23	Piedmont is defeated; Victor Emmanuel II crowned
March 28	German crown offered to Frederick William IV
June 18	Frankfurt Parliament dispersed
July 3	Collapse of the Roman Republic
August 9–13	Austria defeats Hungarian forces

1851

December 2	Coup d'état of Louis Napoleon

SUMMARY

HOW DID industrialization spread across Europe?

Toward an Industrial Society Multiple factors helped make Britain the early leader in the Industrial Revolution. Textiles were the first industrialized industry. Belgium, France, and Germany were industrializing rapidly by the 1830s. Population growth and urbanization continued; many cities were unable to accommodate the new influx of residents, so slums grew and crime increased. Most peasants had become landowners, but many lacked the capital to use their land effectively. The ease with which people could leave rural land varied, with migration generally more difficult in eastern parts of Europe. Railroads, canals, and improved roads facilitated movement. Many railways were built in the 1830s and 1840s, reflecting this period's emphasis on capital production rather than consumer production. *page 516*

HOW DID industrialization change the European labor force?

The Labor Force The labor experience varied, according to industry and location. In the first half of the nineteenth century, only textile manufacture was fully mechanized and factory based. Skilled artisans made up far more of the nonagricultural workforce than factory workers. Both, however, were proletarianized. Textile workers who resisted factory production were slowly impoverished. Urban artisans were slowly proletarianized, as labor and guild organizations were suppressed for political reasons, and craftwork was standardized for economic reasons. British Chartists provided a model for a large-scale working-class political movement. *page 519*

HOW DID industrialization affect European families?

Family Structures and the Industrial Revolution Industrialization transformed the family from being the chief unit of both production and consumption, to being the chief unit of consumption alone. This occurred slowly and was not completed throughout Europe before the end of the nineteenth century. By the 1830s, work associated with textile machinery had largely been split into skilled work, performed by men who were relatively well paid, and unskilled work, performed by poorly paid unmarried women and the children of poor weavers. Child labor and education laws improved children's working conditions but further separated them from their families. *page 522*

WHAT ROLE did women play in the Industrial Revolution?

Women in the Early Industrial Revolution With industrialization, the gender division of labor spread to the working class. In the 1820s, factory work for women became more widely available but paid less. Wages for men in factories were often enough to support a family; in families where that was not the case, children were more likely to enter the workforce than were wives. Therefore, the women who worked in factories were generally young and single, or widowed. Domestic cottage industries employed many women throughout Europe. In virtually all cases, however, women were poorly paid. Marriage and family life changed too, although slowly. Women's domestic work became more sharply defined. *page 523*

HOW DID the establishment of police forces and the reform of prisons change society?

Problems of Crime and Order Revolutions, industrialization, and urbanization all contributed to a fear of crime. In cities, crime did increase in the early to mid–nineteenth century. To assuage the fears of the propertied elite, prisons were reformed, and police systems were instituted or improved. The existence of a paid, professional, nonpolitical group of law enforcement officers, distinct from the army, was a new development in nineteenth-century Europe. By the end of the century, most Europeans of all classes viewed police favorably. Experimental prisons based on models used in the United States, in which prisoners were separated from each other, were tried in England and France. *page 525*

WHAT WERE the key assumptions of classical economic theory?

Classical Economics Laissez-faire economic theories predominated in this period. Classical economists believed competitive free enterprise was the best path to economic growth. Malthus argued that food supply could not grow as quickly as population; if working-class wages were raised, working-class families would have more children, worsening the situation. Ricardo postulated the "iron law of wages," linking wages and fertility in an even more deterministic and pessimistic way than Malthus. The governments of France, Germany, and Britain all enacted policies based on classical economic theory. *page 526*

HOW DID socialism challenge classical economics?

Early Socialism Socialists believed society could and should be organized as a community. They rejected the classical economists' claim that the free market was the best system. Saint-Simon in France advocated rational management. Owen combined a wholesome environment for employees with a healthy profit for himself at his factory. In the 1840s, anarchists rejected industry and government. Marx believed revolution, not reform, was inevitable. Although some of his predictions had already been disproved by the mid-nineteenth century, his theories proved themselves to be enormously appealing and influential. *page 527*

WHY DID a series of revolutions erupt across Europe in 1848?

1848: Year of Revolutions Revolutions occurred throughout Europe in 1848. All essentially ended in failure. During the revolutions, middle-class liberals, who wanted more representative government, civil liberty, and minimal economic regulations, joined forces with the urban working class, which sought improved working and economic conditions. Nationalists generally hoped to use the revolutions to further their own ends. Conservatives fought back, however, and the middle-class/working-class alliance faltered after the political liberals got what they wanted and refused to support working-class social demands. In France, King Louis Philippe abdicated in February 1848; in the new National Assembly, moderates and conservatives quickly displaced Paris radicals. Napoleon's nephew, Louis Napoleon Bonaparte, was elected president in December, and in 1852 he proclaimed himself emperor. In the Habsburg Empire, Hungary called for independence in March 1848. Serfs were emancipated in Austria and Hungary. The Slavs held their first Pan-Slavic Congress in the summer. Northern Italy revolted against the Habsburgs but was quickly suppressed. In late 1848 and early 1849, revolt spread throughout Italy, and the French sent troops to protect the pope until 1870. In Prussia, Frederick William IV went along with liberal demands at first, then imposed his own reforms on the state. In Germany, attempts to revise the German Confederation failed and led to a long-standing division between German liberals and the working class. *page 531*

REVIEW QUESTIONS

1. What inventions were particularly important in the development of industrialism? What changes did industrialism make in society? What is meant by "the proletarianization of workers"? In what ways did the industrial economy change the working-class family?

2. How did the police change in the nineteenth century? Why were new systems of enforcement instituted? In what ways were prisons improved? How do you account for the reform movement that led to the improvements?

3. How would you define *socialism*? Were Karl Marx's ideas different from those of the socialists?

4. Why did revolutions break out in so many places in 1848? Were circumstances essentially the same or were they different in the various countries? Why did the revolutions fail? What roles did liberals and nationalists play in them? Did they always agree?

KEY TERMS

anarchists (p. 529)
Chartism (p. 522)
Marxism (p. 529)

utilitarianism (p. 527)
utopian socialists (p. 528)

For additional learning resources related to this chapter, please go to **www.myhistorylab.com**

PEARSON
myhistorylab

22

The Age of Nation-States

Giuseppe Garibaldi, the charismatic leader, can be seen on the right urging on his troops in the rout of Neapolitan forces at Calatafimi, Sicily, in 1860.

Bildarchiv Preussischer Kulturbesitz

How did Garibaldi's vision of a united Italy differ from that of Cavour?

541

A
lthough the revolutions of 1848 collapsed and authoritarian regimes spread across Europe in the early 1850s, many of the objectives of early-nineteenth-century liberals and nationalists had been achieved by 1875. Italy and Germany were each unified under constitutional monarchies. The Habsburg emperor accepted a constitution that recognized the liberties of the Magyars of Hungary. Russia's tsar emancipated the serfs. France again became a republic. Liberalism (even democracy) flourished in Great Britain, and the Ottoman Empire attempted major reforms. Paradoxically, most of this liberal agenda was enacted while conservatives were in power. ■

WHY WAS the
Crimean War fought?

THE CRIMEAN WAR (1853–1856)

As has so often been true in modern European history, the impetus for change originated in war. The Crimean War (1853–1856) was rooted in the long-standing desire of Russia to extend its influence over the Ottoman Empire. Two disputes led to the conflict. First, as noted in Chapter 17, the Russians had, since the time of Catherine the Great (r. 1762–1796), been given protective oversight of Orthodox Christians in the Empire, and France had similar oversight of Roman Catholics. In 1851, yielding to French pressure, the Ottoman sultan had assigned care of certain holy places in Palestine to Roman Catholics, angering Russia. Second, in the summer of 1853, the Russians used their right to protect Orthodox Christians in the Ottoman Empire as the pretext to occupy the Ottoman provinces of Moldavia and Wallachia. Shortly thereafter, the Ottoman Empire declared war on Russia.

The Russian government envisioned the eventual breakup of the empire and hoped to extend its influence at Ottoman expense. Both France and Britain, though recognizing the difficulties of the Ottoman government and using it to their own advantage when the opportunity presented itself, opposed Russian expansion in the eastern Mediterranean, where they had extensive naval and commercial interests. On March 28, 1854, France and Britain declared war on Russia in alliance with the Ottomans.

Both sides conducted the conflict ineptly, a fact that became widely known in Western Europe because the Crimean War was the first to be covered by war correspondents and photographers. The ill-equipped and poorly commanded armies became bogged down along the Crimean coast of the Black Sea. In September 1855, after a long siege, the Russian fortress of Sevastopol finally fell to the French and British. Thereafter, both sides moved to end the war.

This painting by Elizabeth Thompson, Lady Butler, portrays the comradeship and suffering of ordinary troops. Completed in 1874 and purchased by Queen Victoria, Butler's work reflects the public's awareness of the horrors of war and the mismanagement by discredited aristocratic army officers.

Lady Elizabeth Thompson Butler (1846–1933), *The Roll Call: Calling the Roll after an Engagement, Crimea* (unframed). The Royal Collection © 2003, Her Majesty Queen Elizabeth II. Photo by SC

How did widespread print reporting change public perceptions of war in the second half of the nineteenth century?

Overview   Reforms and Attempts at Reform in the Ottoman Empire

YEAR	REFORM	INTENTION OF REFORM
1839	*Hatt-i Sharif of Gülhane*	A decree calling for reform measures.
1856	*Hatt-i Hümayun*	Rights of non-Muslims were spelled out. It put Jews and Christians on equal footing with Muslims for military service, school admission, and political offices.
1908	*Young Turks*	A military revolution brought up this group of reformist officers. Their decision to ally the empire with the Central Powers led to its defeat.

PEACE SETTLEMENT AND LONG-TERM RESULTS

In March 1856, a conference in Paris concluded the Treaty of Paris. This treaty required a series of concession from Russia and the image of an invincible Russia that had prevailed across Europe since the close of the Napoleonic Wars was shattered. Also shattered was the Concert of Europe, as a means of dealing with international relations on the Continent. Following the successful repression of the 1848 uprisings, the great powers feared revolution less than they had earlier in the century, and, consequently, they displayed much less reverence for the Vienna settlement. As a result, for about twenty-five years after the Crimean War, European affairs were unstable, producing a period of adventurism in foreign policy. While these events reshaped Western Europe, however, the Ottoman Empire over whose fate the Crimean War had been fought undertook reforms.

REFORMS IN THE OTTOMAN EMPIRE

The short-lived Napoleonic invasion of the Ottoman province of Egypt in 1798–1799 (see Chapter 19) sparked a drive for change in the Ottoman Empire. In 1839, the sultan issued a decree, called the *Hatt-i Sharif of Gülhane*, that attempted to reorganize the empire's administration and military along European lines. This decree opened what became known as the *Tanzimat* (meaning "reorganization") era of the Ottoman Empire, lasting from 1839 to 1876. The reforms liberalized the economy, ended the practice of tax farming, and sought to eliminate corruption. The *Hatt-i Sharif* was particularly remarkable for extending civic equality to Ottoman subjects regardless of their religion. Muslims, Christians, and Jews were now equal before the law. The empire also made it much easier for Muslims to enter into commercial agreements with non-Muslims, both within the empire and from abroad.

HOW DID the Ottoman Empire attempt to reform itself?

Another reform decree isssued in 1856, called the *Hatti-i Hümayun*, spelled out the rights of non-Muslims more explicitly, giving them equal obligations with Muslims for military service and equal opportunity for state employment and admission to state schools. The decree also abolished torture and allowed foreigners to acquire some forms of property. The imperial government took these steps to gain the loyalty of its Christian subjects at a time when nationalism was making increasing inroads among them.

However, putting these reforms into practice proved difficult. In some regions of the empire, especially in Egypt and Tunis, local rulers were virtually independent of Istanbul. They carried out their own modernizing reforms, often working closely with European powers. In the capital itself, power struggles developed between proponents and opponents of reform. Because of these tensions, as well as growing nationalism in various regions, the Ottoman Empire failed to achieve genuine political strength and stability.

The Balkan wars of the late 1870s, which resulted in either the independence of, or Russian or Austrian dominance over, most of the empire's European holdings, demonstrated the inability of the Ottoman Empire to master its own destiny. (See Chapter 26.) The response to these foreign defeats resulted in greater efforts to modernize the army and the economy and to build railways and telegraphs. In 1876, reformers persuaded the sultan to proclaim an Ottoman constitution. The constitution called for a parliament consisting of an elected chamber of deputies and an appointed senate (these met for the first time in 1877) but left the sultan's power mostly intact. Nonetheless, a new sultan soon rejected even these limited steps toward constitutionalism and dismissed the parliament. In 1908, military officers carried out a revolution against the authority, though not the person, of the sultan. Another group of reformist officers, known as the *Young Turks*, came to the fore with another program to modernize the empire. They were still in charge when World War I broke out, and their decision to enter the war on the side of the Central Powers in November 1914 led to the empire's defeat and collapse. (See Chapter 26.)

ITALIAN UNIFICATION

HOW DID Italy achieve unification?

Nationalists had long wanted to unite Italy into a single state. During the first half of the century, however, opinion differed about how to achieve unification.

ROMANTIC REPUBLICANS

After the Congress of Vienna, secret romantic republican societies were founded throughout Italy, the most famous of which was the Carbonari ("charcoal burners"). They were ineffective and, after the failure of nationalist uprisings in Italy in 1831, the leadership of romantic republican nationalism passed to Giuseppe Mazzini (1805–1872). In 1831, he founded the Young Italy Society to drive Austria from the peninsula and establish an Italian republic. During the 1830s and 1840s, Mazzini and his fellow republican Giuseppe Garibaldi (1807–1882) led insurrections. Both were involved in the ill-fated Roman Republic of 1849. Throughout the 1850s, they continued to conduct what amounted to guerrilla warfare.

At midcentury, "Italy" remained a geographical expression rather than a political entity. Yet by 1860, the Italian peninsula was transformed into a nation-state under a constitutional monarchy. Count Camillo Cavour (1810–1861), the prime minister of Piedmont—no friend of romantic republicanism—made this possible. His method was a force of arms tied to secret diplomacy.

QUICK REVIEW

Romantic Republicans

- Giuseppe Mazzini (1805–1872)
- Giuseppe Garibaldi (1807–1882)
- Campaigned for Italian unification in the 1830s, 40s, and 50s

CAVOUR'S POLICY

Piedmont (officially styled the Kingdom of Sardinia), in northwestern Italy, was the most independent state on the peninsula. The Congress of Vienna had restored the kingdom as a buffer between French and Austrian ambitions. As has been seen, during 1848 and 1849, King Charles Albert of Piedmont twice unsuccessfully fought Austria. After the second defeat, he abdicated in favor of his son, Victor Emmanuel I (r. 1849–1878). In 1852, the new monarch chose Cavour as his prime minister.

A cunning statesman, Cavour had begun political life as a conservative but had gradually moved toward a moderately liberal position. He was deeply imbued with the ideas of the Enlightenment, classical economics, and utilitarianism. Cavour was a nationalist of a new breed who had no respect for Mazzini's ideals. A strong monarchist, Cavour rejected republicanism. Economic and material progress, not romantic ideals, required a large, unified state on the Italian peninsula. The prime minister also believed only French intervention could defeat Austria and unite Italy. The accession of Napoleon III in France seemed to open the way for such aid.

French Sympathies   Cavour used the Crimean War to bring Italy into European politics. Piedmont's small but significant participation in the war allowed Cavour to raise the Italian question at the Paris conference. During the rest of the decade, he achieved further international respectability for Piedmont by opposing Mazzini, who was still attempting to lead nationalist uprisings. By 1858, Cavour represented a moderate liberal, monarchist alternative to both republicanism and reactionary absolutism in Italy.

In January 1858, an Italian named Felice Orsini attempted to assassinate Napoleon III. The incident heightened the emperor's interest in the Italian issue. He also saw Piedmont as a potential ally against Austria. In July 1858, Cavour and Napoleon III met at Plombières in southern France. The two men plotted to provoke a war in Italy that would permit them to defeat Austria.

War with Austria   In early 1859, tension grew between Austria and Piedmont as Piedmont mobilized its army. On April 22, Austria demanded that Piedmont demobilize. That allowed Piedmont to claim that Austria was provoking a war. France intervened to aid its ally. On June 4, the Austrians were defeated at Magenta, and on June 24 at Solferino. Meanwhile, revolutions had broken out across northern Italy.

With the Austrians in retreat and the new revolutionary regimes calling for union with Piedmont, Napoleon III feared too extensive a Piedmontese victory. On July 11, he concluded peace with Austria at Villafranca. Piedmont received Lombardy, but Venetia remained under Austrian control. Later that summer, Parma, Modena, Tuscany, and the Romagna voted to unite with Piedmont. (See Map 22–1, page 546.)

Garibaldi's Campaign   At this point, the forces of romantic republican nationalism compelled Cavour to pursue the complete unification of northern and southern Italy. In May 1860, Garibaldi landed in Sicily, captured Palermo, and prepared to attack the mainland. By September he controlled the city and kingdom of Naples. For more than two decades Garibaldi had hoped to form a republican Italy, but Cavour forestalled him. He rushed Piedmontese troops south to confront Garibaldi. On the way, they conquered the rest of the Papal States except the area around Rome, which French troops saved for the pope. Garibaldi's nationalism won out over his republicanism, and he accepted Piedmontese domination. In late 1860, Naples and Sicily voted to join the Italian kingdom. (See "Compare & Connect: Nineteenth-Century Nationalism: Two Sides" pages 548–549.)

THE NEW ITALIAN STATE

In March 1861, Victor Emmanuel II was proclaimed king of Italy. Three months later Cavour died. The new state more than ever needed his skills, because Piedmont had, in effect, not so much united Italy as conquered it. The republicans resented the treatment of Garibaldi. The clericals were appalled at the conquest of the Papal States. In the south, armed resistance against the imposition of Piedmontese-style administration continued until 1866. The economies and societies of north and south Italy were incompatible. The south was rural, poor, and backward. The north was industrializing, and its economy was increasingly linked to that of the rest of Europe.

The political framework of the united Italy could not overcome these problems. The constitution, which was that promulgated for Piedmont in 1848, provided for a conservative constitutional monarchy. Parliament consisted of two houses: a senate

MAP 22–1   The Unification of Italy   Beginning with the association of Sardinia and Piedmont by the Congress of Vienna in 1815, unification was achieved through the expansion of Piedmont between 1859 and 1870. Both Cavour's statesmanship and the campaigns of ardent nationalists played large roles.

Why was it so difficult to unify Italy?

appointed by the king and a chamber of deputies elected on a narrow franchise. Ministers were responsible to the monarch, not to Parliament. These arrangements did not foster vigorous parliamentary life and Italian politics became a byword for corruption.

Many Italians believed other territories should be added to their nation. The most important of these were Venetia and Rome. The former was gained in 1866 in return for Italy's alliance with Prussia in the Austro-Prussian War. French troops continued to guard Rome and the papacy until the troops were withdrawn during the Franco-Prussian War of 1870. The Italian state then annexed Rome and made it the capital.

GERMAN UNIFICATION

German unification was the most important political development in Europe between 1848 and 1914. (See Map 22–2.) It transformed the balance of economic, military, and international power.

During the 1850s, German unification seemed remote. The political structure of the German-speaking lands was the German Confederation, which had been established at the Congress of Vienna. It was a loose federation of thirty-nine states, the two strongest of which

HOW DID Bismarck use war as a tool for achieving German unification?

MAP 22–2 **The Unification of Germany** Under Bismarck's leadership, and with the strong support of its royal house, Prussia used diplomatic and military means, on both the German and international stages, to forcibly unify the German states into a strong national entity.

Which neighboring countries were most directly affected by German unification?

NINETEENTH-CENTURY NATIONALISM: TWO SIDES

The second quarter of the nineteenth century witnessed the unification first of Italy and then of Germany. Both processes involved warfare. The Kingdom of Sardinia conquered and united northern Italy, and then Garibaldi led his "Red Shirts" to conquer the south. Prussia united Germany in a series of wars against Denmark, Austria, and France. These two documents illustrate different justifications for the call to military action for unifying each nation. Garibaldi presents his forces as liberators against tyranny. Treitschke makes an argument for the German annexation of Alsace and Lorraine on the grounds of national security and history.

QUESTIONS

1. How does Garibaldi's manifesto turn the war for unification in southern Italy into a popular campaign?

2. How does Garibaldi portray the struggle for unification as a battle against tyranny?

3. On what grounds does Treitschke base the German claim to Alsace and Lorraine?

4. Why does Treitschke contend it is proper to ignore the wishes of the people involved?

5. How could one nationalist, Garibaldi, see his goal as one of popular liberation while another, Treitschke, see his as reclaiming lost regions of a national homeland? Are these two views compatible or distinctly different?

I. GARIBALDI CALLS ITALIANS TO ACT TO UNIFY THEIR NATION

General Giuseppe Garibaldi (1807–1882)

Getty Images, Inc.—Hulton Archive Photos/Museum of the City of New York/Hulton Archive

How might Garibaldi have defined "nation"?

Garibaldi was the most charismatic figure in the drive to Italian unification. He was the leader of guerrilla military forces known as the Red Shirts. In May 1860, after northern Italy had been united under the Kingdom of Sardinia whose monarch was Victor Emmanuel, Garibaldi landed his force of about a thousand men in Sicily and from there they crossed into southern Italy to conquer the kingdom of Naples and make it part of a united Italian state. Garibaldi was himself a republican, but he reconciled himself to supporting Victor Emmanuel. Before leaving Sicily for the mainland, Garibaldi issued this call to arms demanding that the Italians of southern Italy rise against the kingdom of Naples. The various geographical areas he mentions were located from the south northward to Rome. The Tincino River lay in northern Italy and Garibaldi is recalling the participation of his troops in the war that unified the north.

Italians! The Sicilians are fighting against the enemies of Italy and for Italy. To help them with money, arms, and especially men, is the duty of every Italian.

Let the Marches, Umbria, Sabine, the Roman Compagne, and the Neapolitan territory rise, so as to drive the enemy's forces.

If the cities do not offer a sufficient basis for insurrection, let the more resolute throw themselves into the open country. A brave man can always find a weapon. In the name of Heaven, hearken not to the voice of those who cram themselves at well-served tables. Let us arm. Let us fight for our brothers; tomorrow we can fight for ourselves.

A handful of brave men, who have followed me in battles for our country, are advancing with me to the rescue. Italy knows them; they always appear at the hour of danger. Brave and generous companions, they have devoted their lives to their country; they will shed their last drop of blood for it, seeking no other reward than that of a pure conscience.

"Italy and Victor Emmanuel!"—that was our battle-cry when we crossed the Tincino; it will resound into the very depths of Aetna [the volcanic mountain]. As this prophetic battle-cry re-echoes from the hills of Italy to the Tarpeian Mount, the tottering thrones of tyranny will fall to pieces, and the whole country will rise like one man.

Source: "History," *The Annual Register . . . l860* (London: F. and J. Rivington, 1861), p. 221 as quoted in Raymond Phineas Stearns, *Pageant of Europe: Sources and Selections from the Renaissance to the Present Day* (New York: Harcourt, Brace and Company, 1948), pp. 583–584.

II. HEINRICH VON TREITSCHKE DEMANDS THE ANNEXATION OF ALSACE AND LORRAINE

The Franco-Prussian War witnessed outbursts of extreme nationalistic rhetoric on both sides. One such voice was that of the German historian Heinrich von Treitschke (1834–1896). In a newspaper article, he demanded the annexation of Alsace and Lorraine from France. He did so even though the population of Alsace wished to remain part of France and German was not the dominant language in the region. He appealed to an earlier time when the region had been German in language and culture, and he asserted that "might makes right" to assure German domination.

The sense of justice to Germany demands the lessening of France. . . .

What is demanded by justice is, at the same time, absolutely necessary for our security. . . .

Every State must seek the guarantees of its own security in itself alone. . . .

In view of our obligation to secure the peace of the world, who will venture to object that the people of Alsace and Lorraine do not want to belong to us? The doctrine of the right of all the branches of the German race to decide on their own destinies, the plausible solution of demagogues without a fatherland, shiver to pieces in presence of the sacred necessity of these great days. These territories are ours by the right of the sword, and we shall dispose of them in virtue of a higher right—the right of the German nation, which will not permit its lost children to remain strangers to the German Empire. We Germans, who know Germany and France, know better than these unfortunates themselves what is good for the people of Alsace. . . . Against their will we shall restore them to their true selves. We have seen with joyful wonder the undying power of the moral forces of history, manifested far too frequently in the immense changes of these days, to place much confidence in the value of a mere popular disinclination. The spirit of a nation lays hold, not only of the generation which lives beside it, but of those who are before and behind it. We appeal from the mistaken wishes of the men who are there today to the wishes of those who were there before them. We appeal to all those strong German men who once stamped the seal of our German nature on the language and manners, the art and the social life of the Upper Rhine. Before the nineteenth century closes, the world will recognize that . . . we were only obeying the dictates of national honor when we made little account of the preferences of the people who live in Alsace today. . . .

At all times the subjection of a German race to France has been an unhealthy thing; today it is an offense against the reason of History—a vassalship of free men to half-educated barbarians. . . .

There is no perfect identity between the political and national frontier of any European country. Not one of the great Powers, and Germany no more than the rest of them, can ever subscribe to the principle that "language alone decides the formation of States." It would be impossible to carry that principle into effect. . . .

The German territory which we demand is ours by nature and by history. . . . In the tempests of the great Revolution the people of Alsace, like all the citizens of France, learned to forget their past. . . .

Most assuredly, the task of reuniting there the broken links between the ages is one of the heaviest that has ever been imposed upon the political forces of our nation. . . .

The people of Alsace are already beginning to doubt the invincibility of their nation, and at all events to divine the mighty growth of the German Empire. Perverse obstinacy, and a thousand French intrigues creeping in the dark, will make every step on the newly conquered soil difficult for us: but our ultimate success is certain, for on our side fights what is stronger than the lying artifices of the stranger—nature herself and the voice of common blood.

Source: From Heinrich von Treitschke, "What We Demand from France" (1870), in Heinrich von Treitschke, *Germany, France, Russia and Islam* (New York: G. P. Putnam's Sons, 1915), pp. 100, 102, 106, 109, 120, 122, 134–135, 153, 158.

by far were Austria and Prussia. Frederick William IV of Prussia had given up thoughts of unification under Prussian leadership. Austria continued to oppose any union that might lessen its influence. Liberal nationalists had not recovered from the humiliations of 1848 and 1849, so they could do little or nothing for unification. What quickly overturned this static situation was a series of domestic political changes and problems within Prussia.

In 1858, Frederick William IV was adjudged insane, and his brother William assumed the regency. William I (r. 1861–1888), who became king in his own right in 1861, was less idealistic than his brother and more of a Prussian patriot. In 1860, his war minister and chief of staff, in an effort to enhance Prussia's military power, proposed to enlarge the army, to increase the number of officers, and to extend the period of conscription from two to three years. The Prussian Parliament, created by the Constitution of 1850, refused to approve the necessary taxes. The liberals, who dominated the body, sought to avoid placing additional power in the hands of the monarchy. For two years, monarch and Parliament were deadlocked.

BISMARCK

In September 1862, William I turned for help to the person who, more than any other single individual, shaped the next thirty years of European history: Otto von Bismarck (1815–1898). Bismarck opposed parliamentary government, but not a constitutionalism that preserved a strong monarchy. He understood that Prussia—and later, Germany—must have a strong industrial base. In politics, he was a pragmatist who put more trust in power and action than in ideas.

Upon becoming prime minister in 1862, Bismarck immediately moved against the liberal Parliament. He contended that even without new financial levies, the Prussian constitution permitted the government to carry out its functions on the basis of previously granted taxes. Therefore, taxes could be collected and spent despite the parliamentary refusal to vote them. The army and most of the bureaucracy supported this interpretation of the constitution. In 1863, however, new elections sustained the liberal majority in the Parliament. Bismarck had to find a way to attract popular support away from the liberals and toward the monarchy and the army. He, therefore, set about uniting Germany through the conservative institutions of Prussia. In effect, Bismarck embraced the cause of German nationalism as a strategy to enable Prussian conservatives to outflank Prussian liberals.

The Danish War (1864)   Bismarck's vision of a united Germany did not include all German-speaking lands. He intended to exclude Austria from any future united German state. This goal required complex diplomacy.

The Schleswig-Holstein problem gave Bismarck the handle for his policy. The kings of Denmark had longed ruled these two northern duchies, which had never actually become part of Denmark itself. Their populations were a mixture of Germans and Danes. Holstein, where Germans predominated, belonged to the German Confederation. In 1863, the Danish Parliament moved to incorporate both duchies into Denmark. The smaller states of the German Confederation proposed an all-German war to halt this move. Bismarck, however, wanted Prussia to act alone or only in cooperation with Austria. Together, the two large states easily defeated Denmark in 1864.

The Danish defeat increased Bismarck's personal prestige and strengthened his political hand. Over the next two years, he managed to maneuver Austria into war with Prussia. In August 1865, the two powers negotiated the Convention of Gastein, which put Austria in charge of Holstein and Prussia in charge of Schleswig. Bismarck then mended other diplomatic fences. He had gained Russian sympathy in 1863 by supporting Russia's suppression of a Polish revolt, and he persuaded Napoleon III to promise neutrality in an Austro-Prussian conflict. In April 1866, Bismarck promised Italy Venetia if it attacked Austria in support of Prussia when war broke out. Now Bismarck had to provoke his war.

The Austro-Prussian War (1866)   Constant Austro-Prussian tensions had arisen over the administration of Schleswig and Holstein. Bismarck ordered the Prussian forces to be as obnoxious as possible to the Austrians. On June 1, 1866, Austria appealed to the German Confederation to intervene in the dispute. Bismarck claimed that this request violated the 1864 alliance and the Convention of Gastein. The Seven Weeks' War, which resulted in the summer of 1866, led to the decisive defeat of Austria. The Treaty of Prague, which ended the conflict on August 23, was lenient toward Austria, which lost only Venetia, but permanently excluded the Austrian Habsburgs from German affairs. Prussia had thus established itself as the only major power among the German states.

The North German Confederation   In 1867, Prussia annexed the German states that had supported Austria during the war and deposed their rulers. Under Prussian leadership, all Germany north of the Main River now formed the North German Confederation. Each state retained its own local government, but all military forces were under federal control. The president of the federation was the king of Prussia, represented by his chancellor, Bismarck. A legislature consisted of two houses: a federal council, or *Bundesrat*, composed of members appointed by the governments of the states, and a lower house, or *Reichstag*, chosen by universal male suffrage.

Bismarck embraced a democratic franchise because he sensed that the peasants would vote for conservatives. Moreover, the *Reichstag* had little real power. The constitution of the North German Confederation, which, after 1871, became the constitution of the German Empire, possessed some of the appearances, but none of the substance, of liberalism. Germany was, in effect, a military monarchy.

Bismarck's spectacular successes overwhelmed the liberal opposition in the Prussian Parliament. The liberals were split between those who prized liberalism and those who supported unification. In the end, nationalism proved more attractive. Bismarck had crushed the Prussian liberals by making the monarchy and the army the most popular institutions in the country.

THE FRANCO-PRUSSIAN WAR AND THE GERMAN EMPIRE (1870–1871)

Bismarck now wanted to complete unification by bringing the states of southern Germany into the newly established confederation. Spain gave him the excuse. In 1868, a military coup deposed the corrupt Bourbon queen of Spain, Isabella II (r. 1833–1868). To replace her, the Spaniards chose Prince Leopold of Hohenzollern-Sigmaringen, a Catholic cousin of William I of Prussia. On June 19, 1870, Leopold accepted the Spanish crown with Prussian blessings. Bismarck knew that France would object strongly to a Hohenzollern Spain. On July 12, Leopold's father renounced his son's candidacy for the Spanish throne, fearing the issue would cause war between Prussia and France.

There the matter might have rested had it not been for the impetuosity of the French and the guile of Bismarck. On July 13, the French government instructed their ambassador to Prussia to ask William for assurances he would tolerate no future Spanish candidacy for Leopold. The king refused but said he might take the question under further consideration. Later that day he sent Bismarck, who was in Berlin, a telegram

The proclamation of the German Empire in the Hall of Mirrors at Versailles, January 18, 1871, after the defeat of France in the Franco-Prussian War. Kaiser Wilhelm I is standing at the top of the steps under the flags. Bismarck is in the center in a white uniform.

Bildarchiv Preussischer Kulturbesitz

What was the symbolic importance of holding this ceremony in Versailles?

QUICK REVIEW

Keys to German Unification

- Victory in the Danish War (1864)
- Victory in the Austro-Prussian War (1866)
- Creation of the North German Federation (1867)
- Victory in the Franco-Prussian War (1870–1871)

reporting the substance of the meeting. The peaceful resolution of the controversy had disappointed the chancellor, who desperately wanted a war with France to complete unification. The king's telegram gave him a new opportunity to provoke war. Bismarck released an edited version of the dispatch that made it appear that William had insulted the French ambassador. The idea was to goad France into declaring war.

The French government fell for Bismarck's bait and declared war on July 19. Once the conflict erupted, the southern German states, honoring treaties of 1866, joined Prussia against France, whose defeat was not long in coming. France's defeat was capped with the capitulation of Paris on January 28, 1871.

Ten days earlier, in the Hall of Mirrors at the Palace of Versailles, the German Empire had been proclaimed. The German princes requested William to accept the title of German emperor. The princes remained heads of their respective states within the new empire. Through the peace settlement with France, Germany annexed Alsace and part of Lorraine and forced the French to pay a large indemnity.

Both the fact and the manner of German unification produced long-range effects in Europe. A powerful new state had been created in north central Europe. It was rich in natural resources and talented citizens. Militarily and economically, the German Empire would be far stronger than Prussia had been alone. The unification of Germany was also a blow to European liberalism, because the new state was a conservative creation.

FRANCE: FROM LIBERAL EMPIRE TO THE THIRD REPUBLIC

WHAT EVENTS led to the establishment of a Third Republic in France?

Historians divide the reign of Napoleon III (r. 1852–1870) into the years of the authoritarian empire and those of the liberal empire. The year of division is 1860. After the coup in December 1851, Napoleon III had controlled the legislature, censored the press, and harassed political dissidents. From the late 1850s onward, Napoleon III began to modify his policy. In 1860, he concluded a free-trade treaty with Britain and permitted freer debate in the legislature. By the late 1860s, he had relaxed the press laws and permitted labor unions. In 1870, he allowed the leaders of the moderates in the legislature to form a ministry, and he also agreed to a liberal constitution that made the ministers responsible to the legislature.

Napoleon III's liberal concessions sought to shore up domestic support to compensate for his failures in foreign policy. By 1860, he had lost control of the diplomacy of Italian unification. Between 1861 and 1867, he had supported a disastrous military expedition against Mexico. In 1866, France had watched passively while Bismarck and Prussia reorganized German affairs. The war of 1870 against Germany had been the French government's last and most disastrous attempt to shore up its foreign policy and secure domestic popularity.

The Second Empire, but not the war, came to an inglorious end with the Battle of Sedan in September 1870. The emperor was captured and then allowed to go to England, where he died in 1873. Shortly after news of Sedan reached Paris, a republic was proclaimed and a government of national defense established. Paris itself was soon under Prussian siege, and the government moved to Bordeaux. Paris finally surrendered in January 1871, but France had been ready to sue for peace long before.

THE PARIS COMMUNE

The division between the provinces and Paris became sharper after the fighting with Germany stopped. Monarchists dominated the new National Assembly elected in February. For the time being, the assembly gave executive power to Adolphe Thiers (1797–1877) who negotiated a settlement with Prussia (the Treaty of Frankfurt).

Many Parisians felt betrayed by the monarchist National Assembly. They elected a new municipal government, called the *Paris Commune*, which was formally proclaimed on March 28, 1871. The Commune intended to administer Paris separately from the rest of France. Radicals and socialists of all stripes participated in the Commune. In April, the National Assembly surrounded Paris with an army. On May 8, this army bombarded the city. On May 21, it broke through the city's defenses. During the next seven days, the troops killed about 20,000 inhabitants while the communards shot scores of hostages.

THE THIRD REPUBLIC

The National Assembly backed into a republican form of government against its will. Its monarchist majority was divided in loyalty between the House of Bourbon and the House of Orléans. While the monarchists quarreled among themselves, events marched on. By September 1873, the indemnity had been paid, and the Prussian occupation troops had withdrawn. Thiers was ousted from office and replaced with a president more sympathetic to the monarchist cause, Marshal Patrice MacMahon (1808–1893). In 1875, the National Assembly, still monarchist in sentiment, but unable to find a king, decided to regularize the political system. It adopted a law that provided for a Chamber of Deputies elected by universal male suffrage, a Senate chosen indirectly, and a president elected by the two legislative houses. This rather simple republican system had resulted from the bickering and frustration of the monarchists.

THE DREYFUS AFFAIR

The greatest trauma of the Third Republic occurred over what became known as the *Dreyfus affair*. On December 22, 1894, a French military court found Captain Alfred Dreyfus (1859–1935) guilty of passing secret information to the German army. The evidence against him was flimsy and was later revealed to have been forged. Someone in the officer corps had been passing documents to the Germans, and it suited the army investigators to accuse Dreyfus, who was Jewish. After Dreyfus had been sent to Devil's Island, a notorious prison in French Guiana, however, secrets continued to flow to the German army. In 1896, a new head of French counterintelligence reexamined the Dreyfus file and found evidence of forgery. A different officer was implicated, but a military court acquitted him of all charges.

By then the affair had provoked near-hysterical public debate. The army, the French Catholic Church, political conservatives, and vehemently anti-Semitic newspapers contended that Dreyfus was guilty. In 1898, however, the novelist Émile Zola (1840–1902) published a newspaper article entitled "*J'accuse*" ("I

The prosecution of Captain Alfred Dreyfus, who is shown here standing on the right at his military trial, provoked the most serious crisis of the Third Republic.

© Bettman/CORBIS

Why was the Dreyfus case so divisive? What were its long-term political repercussions?

accuse"), in which he contended that the army had denied due process to Dreyfus and had suppressed or forged evidence. Zola was convicted of libel and fled to England to avoid serving a one-year prison sentence.

Zola was only one of numerous liberals, radicals, and socialists who had begun to demand a new trial for Dreyfus. In August 1898, further evidence of forged material came to light. The officer responsible for those forgeries committed suicide in jail, but a new military trial again convicted Dreyfus. The president of France immediately pardoned him, however, and eventually, in 1906, a civilian court set aside the results of both military trials.

The Dreyfus case divided France as no issue had done since the Paris Commune. By its conclusion, the conservatives were on the defensive. They had allowed themselves to persecute an innocent person and to manufacture false evidence against him to protect themselves from disclosure. They had also embraced violent anti-Semitism. On the political left, radicals, republicans, and socialists developed an informal alliance, which outlived the Dreyfus case itself. These groups realized that the political left had to support republican institutions to achieve its goals. Nonetheless, the political, religious, and racial divisions and suspicions growing out of the Dreyfus affair continued to divide the Third Republic until France's defeat by Germany in 1940.

QUICK REVIEW

Captain Alfred Dreyfus (1859–1935)

- December 22, 1894: found guilty of espionage
- Conviction stirred near-hysterical public debate
- 1906: civilian court voids his conviction

WHY WAS nationalism such a threat to the Habsburg Empire?

THE HABSBURG EMPIRE

In the age of national states, liberal institutions, and industrialism, the Habsburg domains remained primarily dynastic, absolutist, and agrarian. The Habsburg response to the revolts of 1848–1849 had been to reassert absolutism. During the 1850s, Emperor Francis Joseph's (r. 1848–1916) ministers attempted to impose a centralized administration on the empire. The system amounted to a military and bureaucratic regime dominated by German-speaking Austrians. Although this system provoked resentment, it eventually floundered because of setbacks in foreign affairs.

Austrian refusal to support Russia during the Crimean War meant the new tsar Alexander II (r. 1855–1881) would no longer help preserve Habsburg rule in Hungary, as Nicholas I had done in 1849. The Austrian defeat in 1859 at the hands of France and Piedmont and the subsequent loss of territory in Italy confirmed the necessity for a new domestic policy. For seven years the emperor, the civil servants, the aristocrats, and the politicians tried to construct a viable system of government.

FORMATION OF THE DUAL MONARCHY

In 1860, Francis Joseph issued the October Diploma, which created a federation among the states and provinces of the empire. There were to be local diets dominated by the landed classes and a single imperial parliament. The Magyar nobility of Hungary, however, rejected the plan.

Consequently, in 1861, the emperor issued the February Patent, which set up an entirely different form of government. It established a bicameral imperial parliament, or *Reichsrat*, with an upper chamber appointed by the emperor and an indirectly elected lower chamber. Again, the Magyars refused to cooperate in a system designed to give political dominance in the empire to German-speaking Austrians. Nevertheless, for six years, the February Patent governed the empire, and it prevailed in Austria proper until 1918. Ministers were responsible to the emperor, not the *Reichsrat*, and civil liberties were not guaranteed. Armies could be levied and taxes raised without parliamentary consent. When the *Reichsrat* was not in session, the emperor could simply rule by decree.

Meanwhile, secret negotiations between the emperor and the Magyars produced no concrete result until the Prussian defeat of Austria in the summer of 1866. Francis

Joseph now had to come to terms with the Magyars. The subsequent Ausgleich, or Compromise, of 1867 transformed the Habsburg Empire into a dual monarchy known as Austria-Hungary. Francis Joseph was crowned king of Hungary in Budapest in 1867. Except for the common monarch, army, and foreign relations, Austria and Hungary became almost wholly separate states. The Compromise reconciled the Magyars to Habsburg rule. They had achieved the free hand they had long wanted in Hungary.

UNREST OF NATIONALITIES

The Compromise of 1867 introduced two different principles of political legitimacy into the two sections of the Habsburg Empire. In Hungary, political loyalty was based on nationality because Hungary had been recognized as a distinct part of the monarchy on the basis of nationalism. In the rest of the Habsburg domains, the principle of legitimacy meant dynastic loyalty to the emperor. Many of the other nationalities wished to achieve the same type of settlement that the Hungarians had won, or to govern themselves, or as time went on, to unite with fellow nationals who lived outside the empire. (See Map 22–3.)

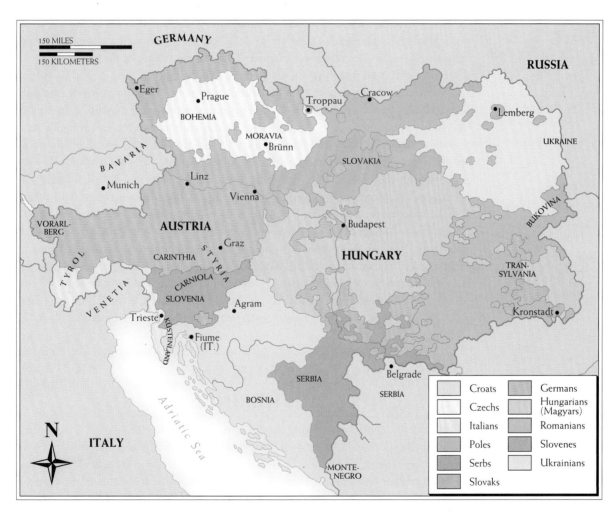

MAP 22–3 Nationalities within the Habsburg Empire The patchwork appearance reflects the unusual problem of the numerous ethnic groups that the Habsburgs could not, of course, meld into a modern national state. Only the Magyars were recognized in 1867, leaving nationalist Czechs, Slovaks, and the others chronically dissatisfied.

Why was ethnic diversity in the Habsburg Empire an impediment to building a strong national state?

Many of these other national groups—including the Czechs, the Ruthenians, the Romanians, and the Croatians—opposed the Compromise of 1867 that, in effect, had permitted the German-speaking Austrians and the Hungarian Magyars to dominate all other nationalities within the empire. The most vocal critics were the Czechs of Bohemia. They favored a policy of "trialism," or triple monarchy, in which the Czechs would have a position similar to that of the Hungarians. In 1871, Francis Joseph was willing to accept this concept. The Magyars, however, vetoed it.

For more than twenty years, generous patronage and posts in the bureaucracy placated the Czechs. By the 1890s, however, Czech nationalism again became more strident. In 1897, Francis Joseph gave the Czechs and the Germans equality of language in various localities. Thereafter, the Germans in the Austrian *Reichsrat* opposed these measures by disrupting Parliament. The Czechs replied in kind. By the turn of the century, this obstructionism had paralyzed parliamentary life. The emperor ruled by imperial decree through the bureaucracy. In effect, by 1914, constitutionalism was a dead letter in Austria.

There is reason to believe nationalism became stronger during the last quarter of the nineteenth century. Language became the single most important factor in defining a nation. The expansion of education made this possible. Furthermore, during these same years, as will be seen in Chapter 24, racial thinking became important in Europe. Once language and race became the ways to define an ethnic or national group, the lines between such groups became much more sharply drawn.

The unrest of the various nationalities within the Habsburg Empire not only caused internal political difficulties; it also became a major source of political instability for all of central and eastern Europe. Each of the nationality problems normally had ramifications for both foreign and domestic policy. Both the Croats and the Poles wanted an independent state in union with their fellow nationals who lived outside the empire—and in the case of the Poles, with fellow nationals in the Russian Empire and Germany. Other national groups, such as Ukrainians, Romanians, Italians, and Bosnians, saw themselves as potentially linked to Russia, Romania, Serbia, Italy, or a yet-to-be established south Slavic, or Yugoslav, state. Many of these nationalities looked to Russia to protect their interests or influence the government in Vienna. The Romanians were also concerned about the Romanian minority in Hungary. Serbia sought to expand its borders to include Serbs who lived within Habsburg or Ottoman territory. Out of these Balkan tensions emerged much of the turmoil that would spark the First World War. Many of the same ethnic tensions account for warfare in the former Yugoslavia.

RUSSIA: EMANCIPATION AND REVOLUTIONARY STIRRINGS

WHY DID reform in Russia fail to produce political stability?

Russia changed remarkably during the last half of the nineteenth century. The government finally addressed the long-standing problem of serfdom and undertook a broad range of administrative reforms. During the same period, however, radical revolutionary groups began to organize. These groups tried to draw the peasants into revolutionary activity and assassinated government officials, including the tsar. The government's response was renewed repression.

REFORMS OF ALEXANDER II

Russia's defeat in the Crimean War and its humiliation in the Treaty of Paris compelled the government to reconsider its domestic policies. The debacle of the war had made reform both necessary and possible. Alexander II (r. 1855–1881) took advantage of this turn of events to institute the most extensive restructuring of Russian society and administration since Peter the Great. Like Peter, Alexander imposed his reforms from the top.

Abolition of Serfdom   In Russia, serfdom had changed little since the eighteenth century, although every other nation on the Continent had abandoned it. In March 1856, at the conclusion of the Crimean War, Alexander II announced his intention to abolish serfdom. He had decided that its abolition was necessary if Russia was to remain a great power. For five years, government commissions wrestled over how to implement the tsar's desire. Finally, in February 1861, despite opposition from the nobility and the landlords, Alexander II ended serfdom.

The actual emancipation law was a disappointment, however, because land did not accompany freedom. Serfs immediately received the personal right to marry without their landlord's permission, as well as the rights to buy and sell property, to sue in court, and to pursue trades. What they did not receive was free title to their land. They had to pay for their land over a period of forty-nine years and would not receive title to the land until the debt was paid. The redemption payments led to almost unending difficulty. Poor harvests made it impossible for many peasants to keep up with the payments, and they fell increasingly behind in their debt. The situation was not remedied until 1906, when, during the widespread revolutionary unrest following the Japanese defeat of Russia in 1905, the government grudgingly completed the process of emancipation by canceling the remaining debts.

Reform of Local Government and the Judicial System   The abolition of serfdom required the reorganization of local government and the judicial system. The authority of village communes replaced that of the landlord over the peasant. The nobility were given a larger role in local administration through a system of provincial and county *zemstvos*, or councils, organized in 1864. These councils were to oversee local matters, such as bridge and road repair, education, and agricultural improvement. The *zemstvos*, however, were underfunded, and many of them remained ineffective.

In 1864, Alexander II issued a new statute on the judiciary that for the first time introduced Western European legal principles into Russia. These included equality before the law, impartial hearings, uniform procedures, judicial independence, and trial by jury. The new system was far from perfect. The judges were not genuinely independent, and the tsar could increase as well as reduce sentences. Certain offenses, such as those involving the press, were not tried before a jury. Nonetheless, the new courts were both more efficient and less corrupt than the old system.

Military Reform   The government also reformed the army. Russia possessed the largest army on the Continent, but it had floundered badly in the Crimean War. In the 1860s, the army lowered the period of service from twenty-five to fifteen years and relaxed discipline slightly. In 1874, the enlistment period was lowered to six years of active duty and nine years in the reserves. All males were subject to military service after the age of twenty.

Repression in Poland   Alexander's reforms became more measured shortly after the Polish Rebellion of 1863. As in 1830, Polish nationalists attempted to overthrow Russian dominance. Once again the Russian army suppressed the rebellion. Alexander II then moved to Russify Poland. Russian law, language, and administration were imposed on all areas of Polish life. Henceforth, until the close of World War I, Poland was treated as merely another Russian province.

As the Polish suppression demonstrated, Alexander II was a reformer only within the limits of his own autocracy. His changes in Russian life failed to create new loyalty to, or gratitude for, the government among his subjects. Consequently, although

Tsar Alexander II (r. 1855–1881) was assassinated on March 1, 1881. The assassins first threw a bomb that wounded several Imperial guards. When the tsar stopped his carriage to see the wounded, the assassins threw a second bomb that killed him.

Bildarchiv Preussischer Kulturbesitz

How did the event depicted here alter the course of Russian history?

Alexander II became known as the Tsar Liberator, he was never popular. After an attempt was made on his life in 1866, Russia increasingly became a police state. This new repression fueled the activity of radical groups within Russia. Their actions, in turn, made the autocracy more reactionary.

REVOLUTIONARIES

The initial reforms of Alexander II had raised great hopes among Russian students and intellectuals, but they soon became discontented with the limited character of the reforms. These students formed a revolutionary movement known as *populism*. They sought a social revolution based on the communal life of the Russian peasants. The chief radical society was called *Land and Freedom*.

In the early 1870s, hundreds of young Russian men and women took their revolutionary message into the countryside. They intended to live with the peasants, to gain their trust, and to teach them about the peasant's role in the coming revolution. The bewildered and distrustful peasants turned most of the youths over to the police. In the winter of 1877–1878, almost two hundred students were tried. Most were acquitted or given light sentences, because they had been held for months in preventive detention and because the court believed a display of mercy might lessen public sympathy for the young revolutionaries. The court even suggested the tsar might wish to pardon those students given heavier sentences. The tsar refused and let it be known he favored heavy penalties for all persons involved in revolutionary activity. Thereafter, the revolutionaries decided the tsarist regime must be attacked directly. They adopted a policy of terrorism.

In 1879, Land and Freedom split into two groups. One advocated educating the peasants, and it soon dissolved. The other, known as *The People's Will*, was dedicated to the overthrow of the autocracy. On March 1, 1881, a bomb hurled by a member of The People's Will killed Alexander II. Four men and two women were sentenced to death for the deed. The emergence of such dedicated revolutionary opposition was as much a part of the reign of Alexander II as were his reforms. The limited character of those reforms convinced many Russians that the autocracy could never truly redirect Russian society.

The reign of Alexander III (r. 1881–1894) strengthened that pessimism. Some slight improvements were made to conditions in Russian factories, but Alexander III sought primarily to roll back his father's reforms. In effect, he confirmed all the evils that the revolutionaries saw as inherent in autocratic government. His son, Nicholas II (r. 1894–1917), would discover that autocracy could not survive the pressures of the twentieth century.

GREAT BRITAIN: TOWARD DEMOCRACY

WHAT FORCES led to the expansion of democracy in Great Britain?

While the continental nations became unified and struggled toward internal political restructuring, Great Britain symbolized the confident liberal state. Britain was not without its difficulties and domestic conflicts, but it seemed able to deal with them through its existing political institutions. (See "Encountering the Past: The Arrival of Penny Postage.")

ENCOUNTERING THE PAST

THE ARRIVAL OF PENNY POSTAGE

Communication systems help draw nations together and are essential to the functioning of popular government. Thus, the inexpensive postal system was one of the nineteenth century's more significant innovations, and the British government led the way in its development.

Early postal systems charged by weight and distance to delivery, and the receiver, not the sender, was liable for the cost of delivery. High postage made newspapers expensive and encouraged inventive strategies for avoiding payment. In 1837, an English reformer, Rowland Hill (1795–1879), proposed a simple new system. He suggested low uniform rates for each category of mail (letters, newspapers, etc.) regardless of distance and charged the sender with paying the postage. A system known as the Uniform Penny Post was launched in 1840 and became an instant success. By 1849, it was delivering 329 million items annually. Low cost meant almost everyone could afford to send letters, and the postal service provided a huge number of new jobs in the public sector. In 1874, an international treaty, the Universal Postal Union, guaranteed that postage paid in a sender's nation would assure delivery anywhere in the world.

Hill also proposed the self-adhesive postage stamp—a small receipt pasted to the cover of an item to indicate that delivery costs had been paid. The first stamp bore only the simple legend, "Postage One

With the new British postal system, the volume of mail vastly increased as did the number of postal workers involved in sorting and delivering it.

Image Works/Mary Evans Picture Library Ltd.

How did the development of an inexpensive postal system help bind British communities together?

Penny." Governments soon began to print more elaborate stamps from engraved plates and frequently to alter their design to frustrate forgers. As the number of stamps and postal systems multiplied, the hobby of stamp collecting was born.

WHAT POSTAGE innovations did Rowland Hill introduce? What were their effects on society?

THE SECOND REFORM ACT (1867)

By the early 1860s, most observers realized the franchise would again have to be expanded. In 1866, Lord Russell's Liberal ministry introduced a reform bill that a coalition of traditional Conservatives and antidemocratic Liberals defeated. Russell resigned, and the Conservative Lord Derby (1799–1869) replaced him. A surprise then occurred. The Conservative ministry, led in the House of Commons by Benjamin Disraeli (1804–1881), introduced its own reform bill in 1867. As the debate proceeded, Disraeli accepted one amendment after another and expanded the electorate well beyond the limits the Liberals had earlier proposed. The final measure increased the number of voters from approximately 1,430,000 to 2,470,000. Britain had taken a major step toward democracy.

Disraeli hoped the Conservatives would receive the gratitude of the new voters. Because reform was inevitable, it was best for the Conservatives to enjoy the credit for it. The immediate election of 1868, however, dashed Disraeli's hopes. William Gladstone (1809–1898) became the new prime minister.

In a House of Commons debate, William Ewart Gladstone, standing on the right, is attacking Benjamin Disraeli, who sits with legs crossed and arms folded. Gladstone served in the British Parliament from the 1830s through the 1890s. Four times the Liberal Party prime minister, he was responsible for guiding major reforms through Parliament. Disraeli, regarded as the founder of modern British conservatism, served as prime minister from 1874 to 1880.

Image Works/Mary Evans Picture Library Ltd.

What were the most important political differences between Gladstone and Disraeli?

GLADSTONE'S GREAT MINISTRY (1868–1874)

Gladstone's ministry of 1868 to 1874 witnessed the culmination of classical British liberalism. Those institutions that remained the preserve of the aristocracy and the Anglican church were opened to people from other classes and religious denominations. In 1870, competitive examinations for the civil service replaced patronage. In 1871, the purchase of officers' commissions in the army was abolished. The same year, Anglican religious requirements for the faculties of Oxford and Cambridge universities were removed. The Ballot Act of 1872 introduced voting by secret ballot. The most momentous measure of Gladstone's first ministry was the Education Act of 1870. For the first time in British history, the government assumed the responsibility for establishing and running elementary schools.

These reforms were typically liberal. They sought to remove abuses without destroying institutions and to permit all able citizens to compete on the grounds of ability and merit. They tried to avoid the potential danger to a democratic state of an illiterate citizenry. These reforms were also a mode of state building, because they reinforced loyalty to the nation by abolishing sources of discontent.

DISRAELI IN OFFICE (1874–1880)

The liberal policy of creating popular support for the nation by extending political liberties and reforming abuses had its conservative counterpart in concern for social reform. Disraeli succeeded Gladstone as prime minister in 1874, when the election produced sharp divisions among Liberal Party voters over religion, education, and the sale of alcohol.

Disraeli believed in paternalistic legislation to protect the weak and ease class antagonisms, but he had few specific programs or ideas. The significant social legislation of his ministry stemmed primarily from the efforts of his home secretary, Richard Cross (1823–1914). The Public Health Act of 1875 consolidated previous legislation on sanitation and reaffirmed the duty of the state to interfere with private property to protect health and physical well-being. Through the Artisan Dwelling Act of 1875, the government became actively involved in providing housing for the working class. That same year, in an important symbolic gesture, the Conservative majority in Parliament gave new protection to British trade unions and allowed them to raise picket lines.

THE IRISH QUESTION

In 1880, a second Gladstone ministry took office after an agricultural depression and an unpopular foreign policy undermined the Conservative government. In 1884, with Conservative cooperation, a third reform act gave the vote to most male farm workers. The major issue of the decade, however, was Ireland. From the late 1860s onward, Irish nationalists had sought to achieve **home rule** for Ireland, by which they meant Irish control of local government.

During his first ministry, Gladstone addressed the Irish question through two major pieces of legislation. In 1869, he disestablished the Church of Ireland, the Irish branch of the Anglican church. Henceforth, Irish Roman Catholics would not pay taxes to support the hated Protestant church, to which few of the Irish belonged. Second, in 1870, the Liberal ministry sponsored a land act that provided compensation to those Irish tenant farmers who were evicted and loans for those

home rule   Government of a country or locality by its own citizens.

who wished to purchase their land. Throughout the 1870s, the Irish question continued to fester. Land remained the center of the agitation. The organization of the Irish Land League in the late 1870s led to intense agitation and intimidation of landlords, who were often Protestants of English descent. The leader of the Irish movement for a just land settlement and for home rule was Charles Stewart Parnell (1846–1891). In 1881, the second Gladstone ministry passed another Irish land act that strengthened tenant rights. It was accompanied, however, by a Coercion Act to restore law and order to Ireland.

By 1885, Parnell had organized eighty-five Irish members of the House of Commons into a tightly disciplined party. In the election of 1885, the Irish Party emerged holding the balance of power between the English Liberals and Conservatives. In December 1885, Gladstone announced his support of home rule for Ireland. Parnell gave his votes to a Liberal ministry. The home rule issue then split the Liberal Party. In 1886, a group known as the Liberal Unionists joined with the Conservatives to defeat home rule. Gladstone called for a new election, but the Liberals were defeated. They remained divided, and Ireland remained firmly under English administration.

The new Conservative ministry of Lord Salisbury (1830–1903) attempted to reconcile the Irish to British rule through public works and administrative reform. The policy, which was tied to further coercion, had only marginal success. In 1892, Gladstone returned to power. A second Home Rule Bill passed the House of Commons but was defeated in the House of Lords. There the Irish question stood until after the turn of the century. The Conservatives sponsored a land act in 1903 that carried out the final transfer of land to tenant ownership. Ireland became a country of small farms. In 1912, a Liberal ministry passed the third Home Rule Bill. Under the provisions of the House of Lords Act of 1911, which curbed the power of the Lords, the bill had to pass the Commons three times over the Lords' veto to become law. The third passage occurred in the summer of 1914, but the implementation of home rule was suspended for the duration of World War I.

Normal British domestic issues could not be resolved because of the political divisions Ireland created. The split of the Liberal Party proved especially harmful to the cause of further social and political reform. People who could agree about reform could not agree about Ireland, and the Irish problem seemed more important. Because the two traditional parties failed to deal with the social questions by the turn of the century, a newly organized Labour Party began to fill the vacuum.

CONSOLIDATION OF STATES (1854–1900)

1854–1856	The Crimean War
1855	Alexander II becomes tsar
1859	Piedmont and France fight Austria
1860	Garibaldi invades southern Italy
1861	Austria issues the February Patent; Proclamation of the Kingdom of Italy (March 17); Russia abolishes serfdom
1862	Bismarck becomes prime minister of Prussia
1863	Russia suppresses the Polish Rebellion
1864	Danish-Prussian War
1866	Austro-Prussian War; Venetia ceded to Italy
1867	North German Confederation formed; formation of the Dual Monarchy; Hungary and Austria; Britain's Second Reform Act
1868	Gladstone becomes prime minister of Britain
1870	Franco-Prussian War begins (July 19); Third Republic proclaimed in France (September 4); Italian state annexes Rome (October 2)
1871	The German Empire proclaimed (January 18); Paris Commune (March 28–May 28); Treaty of Frankfurt between France and Germany (May 1)
1872	Introduction of the secret ballot in Britain
1874	Disraeli becomes prime minister of Britain
1880	Gladstone's second ministry
1881	Alexander II assassinated; Alexander III succeeds
1884	Britain's Third Reform Act
1886	Lord Salisbury becomes prime minister of Britain
1892	Gladstone's third ministry
1894	Nicholas II becomes tsar

SUMMARY

WHY WAS the Crimean War faught?

The Crimean War (1853–1856) Russia's attempts to expand its influence over the Ottoman Empire resulted in the Crimean War. France and Britain were hardly natural allies of the Ottomans, but because they did not want Russian power to grow in a region where they had extensive naval and commercial interest, they declared war on Russia in March 1854. The war was a debacle for all parties, made all the more embarrassing by the presence of journalists and photographers who recorded the ineptness on all sides. The Russian mistakes were worse than the British and French mistakes, and the March 1856 Treaty of Paris required Russia to give up territories and claims. Russia lost the image of invincibility that the nation had earned by defeating Napoleon. The Concert of Europe, too, was a casualty of the war. *page 542*

HOW DID the Ottoman Empire attempt to reform itself?

Reforms in the Ottoman Empire During the Tanzimat era, the Ottoman Empire underwent significant reforms. Under the *Hatt-i Sharif*, in 1839, and the *Hatt-i Hümayun*, in 1856, the economy was liberalized, corruption reduced, and all Ottoman subjects were granted civic equality regardless of religion. The rights of non-Muslims and foreigners were spelled out. Christian missionaries opened schools and operated printing presses. The imperial government sought to copy European legal and military institutions and the secular values of liberalism. Local leaders undertook their own reforms while tension and opposition prevented the Ottoman Empire from gaining strength and stability. In the late 1870s, the Ottoman Empire lost most of its European holdings in the Balkan wars. In 1876, reformers took even bolder steps, but a backlash set in. The empire collapsed after entering World War I on the side of the Central Powers. *page 543*

HOW DID Italy achieve unification?

Italian Unification Nationalists of various persuasions wanted to unify Italy. The romantic republicans started with secret societies after the Congress of Vienna. Later, Mazzini and Garibaldi publicized the republican cause and mounted guerrilla campaigns. They were opposed by moderate Italians. Count Camillo Cavour rejected republicanism and embraced Enlightenment ideals. He was a monarchist who believed economic ties would foster Italian desire for unification. In 1859, French and Piedmontese forces defeated the Austrians in most of northern Italy; soon thereafter, a large group of Italian provinces united with Piedmont. Meanwhile, Garibaldi was uniting southern Italy by force. The Italian kingdom was created in 1860, under Piedmontese rule. *page 544*

HOW DID Bismarck use war as a tool for achieving German unification?

German Unification Germany was unified under Prussia, and specifically under the conservative guidance of prime minister Otto von Bismarck. Through complex diplomacy, Bismarck joined Austria in war against Denmark in 1864, then turned against Austria in 1866. Prussia won both conflicts, and in the process cut the Habsburgs out of German affairs. In 1867, the North German Confederation was organized under a constitution that looked liberal but kept real power in the hands of the Prussian monarchy. Another complex round of diplomacy and warfare, this time involving the Spanish monarchy and French pride, resulted in an important German victory at the Battle of Sedan in September 1870, and the proclamation of the German Empire in January 1871. *page 547*

WHAT EVENT led to the establishment of a Third Republic in France?

France: From Liberal Empire to the Third Republic Napoleon III began his rule in 1851 as an authoritarian. Around 1860, his rule entered a liberal phase, in which he endorsed free trade, loosened political controls and, in 1870, agreed to a liberal constitution. Although these measures widened his domestic support, his foreign policy continued to be disastrous. The Second Empire ended at the Battle of Sedan in September 1870, when Napoleon III was captured by the Germans. France declared the Third Republic and was ready to sue, but Paris continued to resist Prussian siege until January 1871. The National Assembly was dominated by monarchists, although they could not agree on a monarch. Paris, meanwhile, attempted to govern itself independently under the Paris Commune, but the army surrounded the city in April and invaded in late May. In 1875, the National Assembly created a republican legislative system. The Dreyfus affair in the 1890s presented the Third Republic with its greatest trauma. *page 552*

WHY WAS nationalism such a threat to the Habsburg Empire?

The Habsburg Empire From 1848 until it collapsed, the Habsburg Empire caused problems. Francis Joseph used various mechanisms to attempt to preserve the empire, but in the end he failed. When Austria failed to assist Russia in the Crimean War, it lost a valuable ally. In 1859, Austria was defeated by France and Piedmont. In 1860 and 1861, Francis Joseph attempted to organize the empire's government, but the Magyars resisted. The February Patent of 1861 was the basis of government in Austria proper until World War I. In 1866, Austria was defeated by the Prussians, and in 1867, Francis Joseph compromised with the Magyars to create the dual monarchy, Austria-Hungary. But the Compromise of 1867 fed the hopes of other nationalists, at a time when language and race were being used to draw the boundaries of national and ethnic groups more sharply than ever before. *page 554*

WHY DID reform in Russia fail to produce political stability?

Russia: Emancipation and Revolutionary Stirrings When Alexander II took the throne in Russia in 1855, he set out to impose reforms from the top. He abolished serfdom, but the mechanisms he used for emancipation were a huge disappointment. Local government, the judicial system, and the military were more satisfactorily reformed. But as his reforms failed to earn him new loyalty, and after Polish nationalists rebelled in 1863, Alexander turned increasingly to repression. In the 1870s, students started a revolutionary movement called populism. In 1881, a member of the radical society The People's Will assassinated Alexander II. His son Alexander III ruled more repressively until 1894, when Nicholas II took the throne. *page 556*

WHAT FORCES led to the expansion of democracy in Great Britain?

Great Britain: Toward Democracy Great Britain experienced difficulties and domestic conflicts during this period but was able to deal with them through the political institutions of the liberal state. Conservative Benjamin Disraeli shepherded the Second Reform Act in 1867. William Gladstone was elected prime minister in 1868, and over the next six years access to government institutions was widened to include members of all classes and religions. The paternalistic Disraeli returned to the prime minister's office in 1874 and instituted public health measures, among others. The largest question of the 1880s was Irish home rule. Home rule passed the House of Commons repeatedly but was only able to overcome the veto of the House of Lords in 1914. *page 558*

REVIEW QUESTIONS

1. Why was it so difficult to unify Italy? What were Garibaldi's contributions to Italian unification? What was Otto von Bismarck's plan for unifying Germany? What effect did the unification of Germany have on the rest of Europe?

2. How did France's Second Empire (under Napoleon III) become its Third Republic? What made the Paris Commune a legend throughout Europe? What effect did the Dreyfus affair have on the politics of the Third Republic?

3. What reforms did Tsar Alexander II institute? Can he accurately be called a "visionary" reformer?

4. How did the politics of the British Liberal and Conservative Parties evolve in the period from 1860 to 1890? How did British politicians handle the "Irish question"? Are there similarities between England's situation with Ireland and the Austrian Empire's struggles with its nationalities?

KEY TERMS

home rule (p. 560)

For additional learning resources related to this chapter, please go to **www.myhistorylab.com**

PEARSON
myhistorylab

23

The Building of European Supremacy: Society and Politics to World War I

Women Laundry Workers Although new opportunities opened to them in the late nineteenth century, many working-class women, like these women ironing in a laundry, remained in traditional occupations. As the wine bottle suggests, alcoholism was a problem for women as well as men engaged in tedious work. The painting is by Edgar Degas (1834–1917).

Réunion des Musées Nationaux/Art Resource, NY

How did artists' and writers' depictions of working-class life change in the late nineteenth century?

he growth of industrialism between 1860 and 1914 increased Europe's productive capacity to unprecedented levels. As goods and capital flowed out of Europe and across the globe, Europe's political, economic, and social institutions assumed many of their current characteristics. Nation-states with centralized bureaucracies, large electorates, and competing political parties appeared. Huge corporate structures dominated the business world. Labor organized trade unions. The number of white-collar workers increased. Urban life predominated. Socialism became a major political force. Foundations were laid for welfare states and for vast military establishments—and tax burdens increased to support them.

Europeans, confident in their prosperity, failed to realize how dependent they were on the resources and markets of the wider world. Their assumption that European supremacy was natural and enduring was challenged as the twentieth century unfolded. ■

POPULATION TRENDS AND MIGRATION

WHY WERE so many Europeans on the move in the late nineteenth century?

The number of Europeans rose from approximately 266 million in 1850 to 401 million in 1900 and to 447 million in 1910. Thereafter, birth and death rates declined or stabilized in Europe and other developed regions, and population growth began to slow in those areas but not elsewhere. The result has been a persistent demographic differential between the developed and undeveloped world—stable or slowly growing populations in developed countries and large, rapidly growing populations in undeveloped regions—that contributes to the world's present food and resource crisis.

Europe's peoples were on the move in the latter half of the century as never before (see Map 23–1). The midcentury emancipation of peasants lessened the authority of landlords and made legal movement and migration easier. Railways, steamships, and better roads increased mobility. Cheap land and better wages accompanied economic development in Europe, North America, Latin America, and Australia, enticing people to move from regions where they had little prospect of improving their lives to regions that held or seemed to hold opportunity. In Europe itself the main migration continued to be from the countryside into urban areas. Between 1846 and 1932, more than 50 million Europeans left their homelands. The major areas to benefit from this movement were the United States, Canada, Australia, South Africa, Brazil, Algeria, and Argentina. At midcentury, most of the emigrants were from Great Britain (especially Ireland), Germany, and Scandinavia. After 1885, migration from southern and eastern Europe rose. This exodus helped relieve the social and population pressures on the Continent. The outward movement of peoples, in conjunction with Europe's economic and technological superiority, contributed heavily to the Europeanization of the world.

THE SECOND INDUSTRIAL REVOLUTION

HOW DID the second Industrial Revolution transform European life?

During the third quarter of the nineteenth century, the gap that had long existed between British and continental economic development closed. (See Map 23–2, page 568.) In particular, the growth of the German industry was stunning. German steel production surpassed Britain's in 1893 and was nearly twice that of Britain by the outbreak of World War I. This emergence of an industrial Germany was the major fact of European economic and political life at the turn of the century.

NEW INDUSTRIES

Initially, the economic expansion of the third quarter of the century involved the spread of industries similar to those pioneered earlier in Great Britain. In particular, the expansion of railway systems on the Continent spurred economic growth. Thereafter, however, wholly

MAP 23–1 Patterns of Global Migration, 1840–1900 Emigration was a global process by the late nineteenth century, but more immigrants went to the United States than to all other nations combined.

What changes enabled the migration of millions of people in the late nineteenth century?

new industries emerged. This latter development is usually termed the *second Industrial Revolution*. The first Industrial Revolution was associated with textiles, steam, and iron; by contrast, the second was associated with steel, chemicals, electricity, and oil.

In the 1850s, Henry Bessemer (1830–1898), an English engineer, discovered a new process, named after him, for manufacturing steel cheaply in large quantities. In 1860, Great Britain, Belgium, France, and Germany combined produced 125,000 tons of steel. By 1913, the figure had risen to over 32 million tons.

second Industrial Revolution
Started after 1850, it expanded the production of steel, chemicals, electricity, and oil.

MAP EXPLORATION

Interactive map: To explore this map further, go to www.myhistorylab.com

Industrialization in 1860
Level of Industrial Output
Per Capita (100 = UK in 1900)

0 – 5	
16 – 30	
60 – 75	

Industrialization in 1913
Level of Industrial Output
Per Capita (100 = UK in 1900)

0 – 5	61 – 75
16 – 30	76 – 90
31 – 45	91 – 115
46 – 60	

MAP 23–2   European Industrialization, 1860–1913   In 1860, Britain was far more industrialized than other European countries. But in the following half century, industrial output rose significantly, if unevenly, across much of western Europe, especially in the new German Empire. The Balkan states and the Ottoman Empire, however, remained economically backward.

Why did Britain and Germany take the lead in the second Industrial Revolution?

The invention and commercialization of automobiles soon led to auto races in Europe and North America. Here Henri Fournier, the winner of the 1901 Paris to Berlin Motor Car Race, sits in his winning racing car manufactured by the Paris-based auto firm of Emile and Louis Mors.

Getty Images Inc.— Hulton Archive Photos

What made the widespread availability of automobiles possible?

The chemical industry also came of age during this period. Formal scientific research played an important role in this growth of the chemical industry, marking the beginning of a direct link between science and industrial development. As in so many other aspects of the second Industrial Revolution, Germany was a leader in forging this link, fostering scientific research and education.

The most significant change for industry and, eventually, for everyday life involved the application of electrical energy to production. The first major public power plant was constructed in 1881 in Great Britain. Soon electric poles, lines, and generating stations dotted the European landscape. Homes began to use electric lights. Streetcar and subway systems were electrified.

The internal combustion automobile was invented by the German engineer Gottlieb Daimler (1834–1900) in 1889. France initially took the lead in auto manufacturing, but it was the American, Henry Ford (1863–1947), who later made the automobile accessible to the masses. The automobile industry created a vast new demand for steel and the materials that went into other auto parts and established an ever-growing demand for petroleum products that continues to this day.

ECONOMIC DIFFICULTIES

Despite the multiplication of new industries, the second half of the nineteenth century was not a period of uninterrupted or smooth economic growth. In the last quarter of the century, economic advance slowed. Bad weather and foreign competition put grave pressures on European agriculture and caused many European peasants to emigrate to other parts of the world.

unemployment

As new farming regions developed in the United States, Canada, Argentina, Australia, and New Zealand, products from those areas challenged the market for home-produced European agricultural goods. Refrigerated ships could bring meat and dairy products to Europe from all over the world. Grain could be grown more economically on the plains of North America, Argentina, and Ukraine than it could in Western Europe, and railways and steamships made it easy and cheap to ship it across continents and oceans.

Several large banks failed in 1873, and the rate of capital investment slowed. Some industries then entered a two-decade-long period of stagnation that many contemporaries regarded as a depression. Overall, however, the general standard of living in the industrialized nations improved in the second half of the nineteenth century. Yet many workers still lived and labored in abysmal conditions. There were pockets of *unemployment* (a word that was coined during this period), and strikes and other forms of labor unrest were common. These economic difficulties fed the growth of trade unions and socialist political parties.

The new industries produced consumer goods, and expansion in consumer demand brought the economy out of stagnation by the end of the century. (See "Encountering the Past: Bicycles: Transportation, Freedom, and Sport," page 570.) Lower food prices eventually allowed all classes to spend more on consumer goods. Urbanization naturally created larger markets. New forms of retailing and marketing appeared—department stores, chain stores, mail-order catalogs, and advertising—simultaneously stimulating and feeding consumer demand. Imperialism also opened new markets overseas for European consumer goods.

THE MIDDLE CLASSES IN ASCENDANCY

The sixty years before World War I were the age of the middle classes. The middle classes became the arbiter of consumer taste and ceased to be a revolutionary group.

WHAT EXPLAINS the prominence of the middle class in late-nineteenth-century Europe?

SOCIAL DISTINCTIONS WITHIN THE MIDDLE CLASSES

The middle classes, never perfectly homogeneous, grew increasingly diverse. Their most prosperous members—the owners and managers of great businesses and banks—lived in splendor that rivaled, and sometimes exceeded, that of the aristocracy. Beneath them were the comfortable small entrepreneurs and professional people. Also in this group were the shopkeepers, schoolteachers, librarians, and others who had either a bit of property or a skill derived from education that provided respectable nonmanual employment. Finally, there was a wholly new element—"white-collar workers"—who formed the lower middle class, or ***petite bourgeoisie***. They included secretaries, retail clerks, and lower-level bureaucrats in business and government. They often had working-class origins and might even belong to unions, but they had middle-class aspirations and consciously sought to distance themselves from a lower-class lifestyle.

Significant tensions and social anxieties marked relations among the various middle-class groups. Small shopkeepers resented the power of the great capitalists, with their department stores and mail-order catalogs. There is some evidence that the professions

petite bourgeoisie New lower middle class made up of white-collar workers such as secretaries, retail clerks, and lower-level bureaucrats.

ENCOUNTERING THE PAST

BICYCLES: TRANSPORTATION, FREEDOM, AND SPORT

Bicycles, the first mass-produced affordable machines for individual travel, took Western nations by storm between 1880 and 1900. The unprecedented freedom to travel that they gave men and (significantly) women had an immense impact on society.

The bicycle was invented in Germany about 1817, but the early models were clumsy, dangerous, and uncomfortable. They were made of wood, had to be pushed, and riders could not control their speed. Metal frames, solid rubber tires, and chain drives did not appear until the 1870s. In the 1880s, John Boyd Dunlop, an Irish physician, invented the pneumatic tire and France's Michelin brothers the inner tube. By the 1890s, the modern "safety bicycle" was in mass production.

Bicycles enabled people to commute from homes located farther from their workplaces, and bicycles provided new opportunities for recreation and sport. Special clothing was designed for cyclists. "Bloomers," ample trousers worn under skirts, preserved the modesty of female riders. (Feminists hailed the mobility the bicycle provided as a major contribution to women's liberation.) Cycling clubs appeared in the early twentieth century, and the first travel guides were published for cycling tourists. The Michelin tire company's famous series of *Guides Michelin* was initiated in 1900 to promote cycling—and consumption of tires. Bicycle racing soon became

a competitive sport. It was featured in the first modern Olympic Games in 1896, and in 1903, the first Tour de France was held.

The bicycle helped liberate women's lives, but as this poster suggests, it was also associated with glamour and fashion.

© Archivo Iconografico, S.A./CORBIS

Who rode bicycles? What needs did they meet?

WHAT EXPLAINS the bicycle's huge popularity in the late nineteenth century?

---

were becoming overcrowded. People who had only recently attained a middle-class lifestyle feared losing it in bad economic times. Nonetheless, in the decades immediately before World War I, the middle classes set the values and goals for most of society.

LATE-NINETEENTH-CENTURY URBAN LIFE

WHAT FORCES shaped the development of European cities?

Europe became more urbanized than ever in the latter half of the nineteenth century as migration to the cities continued. The rural migrants to the cities often faced poor housing, social anonymity, and, because they rarely possessed the right kinds of skills, unemployment. People from different ethnic backgrounds found themselves in proximity to one another and had difficulty mixing socially. Competition for jobs generated new varieties of political and social discontent, such as the anti-Semitism directed at the thousands of Russian Jews who had migrated to Western Europe. Indeed, much of the political anti-Semitism of the latter part of the century had its roots in the problems urban migration generated.

THE REDESIGN OF CITIES

The inward urban migration placed new social and economic demands on already strained city resources and gradually transformed the patterns of urban living. National and municipal governments redesigned the central portions of many large European cities during the second half of the century.

The New Paris   The most famous and extensive transformation of a major city occurred in Paris. Like so many other European cities, Paris had expanded from the Middle Ages onward with little or no design or planning. Great public buildings and squalid hovels stood near each other. The Seine River was an open sewer. The streets were narrow, crooked, and crowded. Of more concern to the government of Napoleon III (r. 1852–1870), the city's streets had for sixty years provided battlegrounds for urban insurrections that had threatened or toppled French governments on numerous occasions, most recently in 1848.

Napoleon III personally determined to redesign Paris. He appointed Baron Georges Haussmann (1809–1891), who, as prefect of the Seine from 1853 to 1870, oversaw a vast urban reconstruction program. Whole districts were destroyed to open the way for the broad boulevards and streets that became the hallmark of modern Paris. Much, though by no means all, of the purpose of this street planning was political. The wide vistas not only were beautiful, but they also allowed for the quick deployment of troops to put down riots. The eradication of the many small streets and alleys removed areas where barricades could be, and had been, erected. Urban reconstruction was also political in another sense. It created thousands of government and private sector jobs.

Further rebuilding and redesign occurred under the Third Republic after the destruction that accompanied the suppression of the Commune in 1871. Many department stores, office complexes, and largely middle-class apartment buildings were constructed. The public transportation network was expanded to include mechanical trams, a subway system, and new railroad stations linking the city and the suburbs.

Development of Suburbs   Commercial development, railway construction, and slum clearance displaced many city dwellers and raised urban land values and rents. Consequently, both the middle classes and the working class began to seek housing elsewhere. The middle classes looked for neighborhoods removed from urban congestion. The working class looked for affordable housing. The result, in virtually all countries, was the

EVENTS IN THE FORMATION OF THE EARLY TWENTIETH CENTURY

1848	Britain's Public Health Act
1851	France's Melun Act
1857	Bessemer steel manufacturing process invented
1864	Meeting of the First International
1869	John Stuart Mill publishes *The Subjection of Women*
1875	German Social Democratic Party founded
1876	Telephone invented
1879	Electric light bulb invented
1882	England's Married Woman's Property Act
1884	Britain's Fabian Society founded
1887	Automobile invented
1889	Establishment of the Second International
1895	Invention of wireless telegraphy
1900	Lenin leaves Russia
1902	Formation of the British Labour Party
1903	British Women's Social and Political Union founded; Lenin creates the Bolsheviks; the Wright brothers begin the age of aviation
1904–1905	Russo-Japanese War
1905	Saint Petersburg's Bloody Sunday; Russia's October Manifesto
1907	Norway, first nation to grant women the vote
1909	Henry Ford begins mass production of automobiles
1910	British suffragettes adopt radical tactics
1911	Stolypin assassinated
1914	World War I begins
1918	Some British women acquire the vote
1918	Constitution of the Weimar Republic gives women the vote
1928	British women acquire same voting rights as men

Overview   Growth of Major European Cities (Figures in Thousands)

	1850	1880	1910
BERLIN	419	1,122	2,071
BIRMINGHAM	233	437	840
FRANKFURT	65	137	415
LONDON	2,685	4,470	7,256
MADRID	281	398	600
MOSCOW	365	748	1,533
PARIS	1,053	2,269	2,888
ROME	175	300	542
SAINT PETERSBURG	485	877	1,962
VIENNA	444	1,104	2,031
WARSAW	160	339	872

development of suburbs surrounding the city proper. These suburbs housed families whose breadwinners worked in the central city or in a factory located within the city limits.

The expansion of railways with cheap workday fares and the introduction of mechanical and, later, electric tramways, as well as subways, allowed tens of thousands of workers from all classes to move daily between the city and the outlying suburbs. For hundreds of thousands of Europeans, home and work became more physically separated than ever before.

URBAN SANITATION

The efforts of governments and of the increasingly conservative middle classes to maintain public order after 1848 led to a growing concern with the problems of public health and housing for the poor. A widespread feeling arose that only when the health and housing of the working class were improved would middle-class health also be secure and the political order stable.

Impact of Cholera   Concerns with health and housing first manifested themselves as a result of the great cholera epidemics of the 1830s and 1840s. Unlike many other common deadly diseases of the day that touched only the poor, cholera struck all classes, and the middle class demanded a solution. Physicians and sanitary reformers believed that miasmas in the air spread the infections that led to cholera and other diseases. These miasmas, which could be detected by their foul odors, were believed to arise from filth. The way to get rid of the dangerous, foul-smelling air was to clean up the cities.

During the 1840s, many physicians and some government officials began to publicize the dangerous unsanitary conditions associated with overcrowding in cities and with businesses, such as basement slaughterhouses. They closely linked the issues of wretched living conditions and public health. They also argued that sanitary reform would remove the dangers.

New Water and Sewer Systems   The proposed solution to the health hazard was cleanliness, to be achieved through new water and sewer systems. These facilities were constructed slowly, usually first in capital cities and then much later in provincial centers. The building of such systems was one of the major health and engineering achievements of the second half of the nineteenth century. Wherever these sanitary facilities were installed, the mortality rate dropped considerably—not because they prevented miasmas, but because they disposed of human waste and provided clean water free of harmful bacteria for people to drink, cook with, and bathe in.

Expanded Government Involvement in Public Health   The concern with public health led to an expansion of governmental power on various levels. In Britain the Public Health Act of 1848, in France the Melun Act of 1851, and various laws in the still-disunited German states, as well as later legislation, introduced new restraints on private life and enterprise. This legislation allowed medical officers and building inspectors to enter homes and businesses in the name of public health. The state could condemn private property for posing health hazards. Private land could be excavated to construct the sewers and water mains required to protect the public. New building regulations restrained the activities of private contractors.

Full acceptance at the close of the century of the bacterial theory of disease associated with the discoveries of Louis Pasteur (1822–1895) in France, Robert Koch (1843–1910) in Germany, and Joseph Lister (1827–1912) in Britain increased public concern about cleanliness. Throughout Europe, issues related to the maintenance of public health and the physical well-being of the population repeatedly opened the way for new modes of government intervention in the lives of citizens.

A major feature of the reconstruction of mid-nineteenth-century Paris under the Emperor Napoleon III was a vast new sewer system to provide for drainage in the city. Sewer workmen could travel the length of the structure on small rail cars. Even today tourists still may visit parts of the midcity Paris sewer system.

Nadar/Getty Images

What were the motives behind the reconstruction of Paris?

QUICK REVIEW

Improved Conditions in Cities

- Cholera epidemics spurred action
- New awareness of the value of modern water and sewer systems
- Expanded involvement of government in public health

HOUSING REFORM AND MIDDLE-CLASS VALUES

The information about working-class living conditions the sanitary reformers revealed also led to heated debates over the housing problem. The wretched dwellings of the poor were themselves a cause of poor sanitation and thus became a newly perceived health hazard. Furthermore, the domestic arrangements of the poor, whose large families might live in a single room without any personal privacy, shocked middle-class reformers and bureaucrats. After the revolutions of 1848, the overcrowding in housing and the social discontent that it generated were also seen to pose a political danger. Middle-class reformers thus turned to housing reform to solve the medical, moral, and political dangers slums posed. Decent housing would foster a good home life, in turn leading to a healthy, moral, and politically stable population.

Private philanthropy made the first attack on the housing problem. Companies operating on low profit margins or making low-interest loans encouraged housing for the poor. Firms such as the German Krupp Armaments concern that sought to ensure a contented, healthy, and stable workforce constructed model housing projects and industrial communities.

By the mid-1880s, the migration into cities had made housing a political issue. Legislation in England in 1885 lowered the interest rates to construct cheap housing, and soon thereafter local governments began public housing projects. In Germany, action on housing came later in the century through the initiative of local municipalities. In 1894, France made inexpensive credit available to construct housing for the poor.

VARIETIES OF LATE-NINETEENTH-CENTURY WOMEN'S EXPERIENCES

WHAT WAS life like for women in late-nineteenth-century Europe?

Late-nineteenth-century women and men led lives that reflected their social rank. Yet, within each rank, the experience of women was distinct from that of men. Women remained, generally speaking, economically dependent and legally inferior, whatever their social class.

WOMEN'S SOCIAL DISABILITIES

In the mid–nineteenth century, virtually all European women faced social and legal disabilities in three areas: property rights, family law, and education. By the close of the century, there had been some improvement in each area.

Women and Property   Until the last quarter of the century in most European countries, married women could not own property in their own names, no matter what their social class. Their legal identities were subsumed in their husbands' identities, and they had no independent standing before the law. Because private property and wage earning were the bases of European society, these disabilities put married women at a great disadvantage, limiting their freedom to work, to save, and to move from one location to another.

Reform of women's property rights came slowly. By 1882, Great Britain had passed the Married Woman's Property Act, which allowed married women to own property in their own right. In France, however, a married woman could not even open a savings account in her own name until 1895, and married French women did not gain possession of the wages they earned until 1907. In 1900, Germany allowed women to take jobs without their husbands' permission, but except for her wages, a German husband retained control of most of his wife's property.

Family Law   European family law also disadvantaged women. The Napoleonic Code and the remnants of Roman law still in effect made women legal minors throughout Europe. Divorce was difficult everywhere for most of the century. Most nations did not permit divorce by mutual consent. Thereafter, the majority of nations recognized a legal cause for divorce—cruelty or injury—which had to be proved in court. Across Europe, some version of the double standard prevailed whereby husbands' extramarital sexual relations were tolerated to a much greater degree than those of wives. Everywhere, divorce required hearings in court and the presentation of legal proof, making the process expensive and more difficult for women, who did not control their own property.

The authority of husbands also extended to children. A husband could take children away from their mother and give them to someone else to rear. Only a father, in most countries, could permit his daughter to marry. In some countries, he could virtually force his daughter to marry the man of his choice. In cases of divorce and separation, courts normally awarded the husband authority over, and custody of, children, no matter how he had treated them previously.

Until well into the twentieth century, both contraception and abortion were illegal. The law surrounding rape normally worked to the disadvantage of women. Wherever they turned with their problems—whether to physicians or lawyers—women confronted an official or legal world that men almost wholly populated and controlled.

Educational Barriers   Throughout the nineteenth century, women had less access to education than men had and what was available to them was inferior to that available to men. Not surprisingly, there were many more illiterate women than men.

QUICK REVIEW
Family Law

- European family law disadvantaged women
- Divorce was difficult for most of the century
- Husbands were given considerable authority over wives and children
- Contraception and abortion were illegal

Women only gradually gained access to secondary and university education during the second half of the nineteenth century and the early twentieth century. Young women on their way to school, the subject of this 1880 English painting, would thus have been a new sight when it was painted.

Sir George Clausen (RA) (1852–1944), *Schoolgirls, Haverstock Hill,* signed and dated 1880, oil on canvas, 20 1/2 X 30 3/8 in. (52 × 77.2 cm), Yale Center for British Art/Paul Mellon Collection, USA/Bridgeman Art Library (B1985.10.1). Courtesy of the Estate of Sir George Clausen

Why do you think the artist included the older working-class woman in the street in this painting?

University and professional education remained reserved for men until at least the third quarter of the century. Moreover, the absence of a system of private or public secondary education for women prevented most of them from gaining the qualifications they needed to enter a university whether or not the university prohibited them. Evidence suggests that educated, professional men feared that admitting women would overcrowd their professions. Women who attended universities and medical schools were sometimes labeled political radicals.

By the turn of the century, some men in the educated elites feared the challenge educated women posed to traditional gender roles in the home and workplace. Restricting women's access to secondary and university education helped bar them from social and economic advancement. Women would benefit only marginally from the expansion of professional employment that occurred during the late nineteenth and early twentieth centuries. Some women did enter the professions, particularly medicine, but their number remained few. Most nations refused to allow women to become lawyers until after World War I.

The few women who pioneered in the professions and on government commissions and school boards or who dispersed birth control information faced social obstacles, humiliation, and often outright bigotry. These women and their male supporters were challenging that clear separation into male and female spheres that had emerged in middle-class European social life during the nineteenth century. Women themselves were often hesitant to support feminist causes or expanded opportunities for females because they had been so thoroughly acculturated into the recently stereotyped roles. Many women, as well as men, saw a real conflict between family responsibilities and feminism.

NEW EMPLOYMENT PATTERNS FOR WOMEN

During the second Industrial Revolution, two major developments affected the economic lives of women. The first was the large-scale expansion in the variety of jobs available to women outside the better-paying learned professions. The second was the withdrawal of many married women from the workforce.

Availability of New Jobs   The expansion of governmental bureaucracies, the emergence of corporations and other large businesses, and the vast growth of retail stores opened many new employment opportunities for women. The need for elementary school teachers, usually women, grew as governments adopted compulsory education laws. Women by the thousands became secretaries and clerks for governments and private businesses. Thousands more became shop assistants.

Although these jobs did open new and often better employment opportunities for women, they nonetheless required low-level skills and involved minimal training. They were occupied primarily by unmarried women or widows. Women rarely occupied more prominent positions.

Employers continued to pay women low wages, because they assumed, although they often knew better, that a woman did not need to live on what she herself earned but could expect additional financial support from her father or her husband. Consequently, a woman who did need to support herself independently could seldom find a job that paid an adequate income—or a position that paid as well as one a man who was supporting himself held.

Withdrawal from the Labor Force   Most of the women filling the new service positions were young and unmarried. Upon marriage, or certainly after the birth of her first child, a woman normally withdrew from the labor force. This pattern was not new, but it had become significantly more common by the end of the nineteenth century. The kinds of industrial occupations that women had filled in the mid–nineteenth century, especially textile and garment making, were shrinking. Employers in offices and retail stores preferred young, unmarried women whose family responsibilities would not interfere with their work.

The real wages paid to male workers increased during this period, so families had a somewhat reduced need for a second income. Also, thanks to improving health conditions, men lived longer than before, so the death of their husbands was less likely to thrust wives into the workforce. The smaller size of families also lowered the need for

Shown are women working in the London Central Telephone Exchange. The invention of the telephone opened new employment opportunities for women.

Image Works/Mary Evans Picture Library Ltd.

How did technology change women's employment opportunities in the late nineteenth century?

supplementary wages. Working children stayed at home longer and continued to contribute to the family's wage pool.

Finally, the cultural dominance of the middle class established a pattern of social expectations, especially for wives. The more prosperous a working-class family became, the less involved in employment its women were supposed to be. Indeed, the less income-producing work a wife did, the more prosperous and stable the family was considered.

Yet behind these generalities stands the enormous variety of social and economic experiences late-nineteenth-century women actually encountered. As might be expected, the chief determinant of these individual experiences was social class.

WORKING-CLASS WOMEN

Although the textile industry and garment making were much less dominant than earlier in the century, they continued to employ many women. The German clothing-making trade illustrates the kind of vulnerable economic situation that women could encounter as a result of their limited skills and the way the trade was organized. A major manufacturer would produce clothing through what was called a *putting-out system*. The manufacturer would purchase the material and then put it out for tailoring. Usually, numerous independently owned, small sweatshops or workers in their homes made the clothing.

In Berlin in 1896, this system employed more than 80,000 garment workers. When business was good and demand strong, employment for these women was high. As the seasons shifted or business slackened, however, less and less work was put out, idling many of them. In effect, the workers who actually sewed the clothing carried much of the risk of the enterprise. Some women did work in clothing factories, but they, too, were subject to layoffs. Furthermore, women in the clothing trade were nearly always in positions less skilled than those of the male tailors or the middlemen who owned the workshops.

The expectation of separate social and economic spheres for men and women and the definition of women's chief work as pertaining to the home contributed mightily to the exploitation of women workers outside the home. Because their wages were regarded merely as supplementing their husbands' wages, they became particularly vulnerable to economic exploitation. Women were nearly always treated as casual workers everywhere in Europe.

POVERTY AND PROSTITUTION

The economic vulnerability of women and the consequent poverty many of them faced were among the chief causes of prostitution. Every major late-nineteenth-century European city had thousands of prostitutes. Prostitution was, of course, not new. It had always been one way for poor women to find income. In the late nineteenth century, however, it was closely related to the difficulty encountered by indigent women who were trying to make their way in an overcrowded female labor force. On the Continent, prostitution was generally legalized and subject to governmental and municipal regulations that male legislatures and councils passed and male police and physicians enforced. In Britain, prostitution received only minimal regulation.

The most recent studies of prostitution in England emphasize that most prostitutes were active on the streets for only a few years, from their late teens to about age twenty-five. Certain cities—those with large army garrisons or naval bases or those, like London, with large transient populations—attracted prostitutes. Far fewer prostitutes worked in manufacturing towns, where there were more opportunities for steady employment and community life was more stable.

QUICK REVIEW

Women's Work

- Opportunities in factories diminished
- Expansion of governmental bureaucracies, large-scale business organizations, and retail stores increased demand for women workers
- Many married women left workforce

Department stores, such as Bon Marché in Paris, sold wide selections of consumer goods under one roof. These modern stores increased the economic pressure on small traditional merchants who specialized in selling only one kind of good.

Image Works/Mary Evans Picture Library Ltd.

How did department stores embody middle-class values and aspirations?

Women who became prostitutes usually came from families of unskilled workers and had minimal skills and education themselves. Many had been servants. They also often were orphans or came from broken homes. The customers of poor working-class prostitutes were primarily working-class men.

WOMEN OF THE MIDDLE CLASS

A vast social gap separated poor working-class women from their middle-class counterparts. As their fathers' and husbands' incomes permitted, middle-class women participated in the vast expansion of consumerism and domestic comfort that marked the late nineteenth and the early twentieth centuries.

The Cult of Domesticity   Middle-class women, if at all possible, did not work. More than any other women, they became limited to the roles of wife and mother. As a result, they might enjoy great domestic luxury and comfort, but their lives, talents, ambitions, and opportunities for applying their intelligence were sharply circumscribed.

Middle-class women became, in large measure, the product of a particular understanding of social life. Home life was to be different from the life of business and the marketplace. The home was to be a private place of refuge, a view scores of women's journals across Europe set forth. For middle-class women, the home came to be seen as the center of virtue, children, and the respectable life. Marriages were usually arranged to benefit the family economically. The first child was often born within the first year. Rearing and nurturing her children was a woman's chief task. Her only experience or training was for the role of dutiful daughter, wife, and mother.

Within the home, a middle-class woman largely directed the household. She oversaw virtually all domestic management and child care. She was in charge of the home as a unit of consumption, which is why so much advertising was directed toward women. All this domestic activity, however, occurred within the bounds of the approved middle-class lifestyle that set strict limits on a woman's initiative. In her conspicuous position within the home and family, a woman symbolized first her father's and then her husband's worldly success.

Religious and Charitable Activities   The cult of domesticity in France and elsewhere assigned firm religious duties to women, which the Roman Catholic Church strongly supported. Women were expected to attend Mass frequently and assure the religious instruction of their children. They were charged with observing meatless Fridays and participating in religious observances. Prayer was a major part of their daily lives. They internalized those portions of the Christian religion that stressed meekness and passivity. In other countries, religion and religious activities also became part of the expected work of women. This close association between religion and a strict domestic life for women was one reason for later tension between feminism and religious authorities.

Another important role for middle-class women was the administration of charity. Women were considered especially qualified for this work because of their presumed innate spirituality and their capacity to instill domestic and personal discipline. Women were supposed to be particularly interested in the problems of poor women, their families, and their children. By the end of the century, middle-class women seeking to expand their spheres of activity became social workers for the church, for private charities, or for the government. These vocations were a natural extension of the roles society assigned to them.

Sexuality and Family Size   Historians have come to realize that the world of the middle-class wife and her family was much more complicated than they once thought. Neither all wives nor their families conformed to the stereotypes. Recent studies suggest that the middle classes of the nineteenth century enjoyed sexual relations within marriage far more than was once thought. Much of the inhibition about sexuality stemmed from the dangers of childbirth, which, in an age of limited sanitation and anesthesia, were widely and rightly feared, rather than from any dislike or disapproval of sex itself.

One of the major changes in this regard during the second half of the century was the acceptance of a small family size among the middle classes. During the last decades of the century, new contraceptive devices became available, which middle-class couples used. One of the chief reasons for the apparently conscious decision of couples to limit their family size was to maintain a relatively high level of material consumption. Fewer children probably meant more attention for each of them, possibly increasing the emotional bonds between mothers and their children.

THE RISE OF POLITICAL FEMINISM

Plainly, liberal society and its values had neither automatically nor inevitably improved the lot of women. In particular, they did not give women the vote or access to political activity.

Obstacles to Achieving Equality   Women were often reluctant to support feminist causes. Political issues relating to gender were only one of several priorities for many women. Some were sensitive to their class and economic interests. Others subordinated feminist political issues to national unity and patriotism. Still others would not support particular feminist organizations because they objected to their tactics. The various social and tactical differences among women often led to sharp divisions within the feminists' own ranks. There were other disagreements about which goals were most important for improving women's legal and social conditions.

Although liberal society and law presented women with many obstacles, they also provided feminists with many of their intellectual and political tools. As early as 1792 in Britain, Mary Wollstonecraft (1759–1797), in *The Vindication of the Rights of Woman*, had applied the revolutionary doctrines of the rights of man to the predicament of the members of her own sex. (See Chapter 17.) John Stuart Mill (1806–1873), together with his wife, Harriet Taylor (1804–1858), extended the logic of liberal freedom to the position of women in *The Subjection of Women* (1869). The arguments for utility and efficiency so dear to middle-class liberals could be used to expose the human and social waste implicit in the inferior role assigned to women.

Furthermore, the socialist criticism of capitalist society often, though by no means always, included a harsh indictment of the social and economic position to which women had been relegated. The earliest statements in support of feminism arose from critics of the existing order who were often people who had unorthodox opinions about sexuality, family life, and property. This hardened resistance to the feminist message, especially on the Continent.

These difficulties prevented continental feminists from raising the massive public support or mounting the large demonstrations that feminists in Britain and the United States could. Everywhere in Europe, however, including Britain, the feminist cause was badly divided over both goals and tactics.

Votes for Women in Britain   Europe's most advanced women's movement was in Britain. There, Millicent Fawcett (1847–1929) led the moderate National Union of Women's Suffrage Societies. She believed Parliament would grant women the vote only if it were convinced they would be respectable and responsible in their political activity. Her tactics were those of English liberals.

Emmeline Pankhurst (1858–1928) led a much more radical branch of British feminists. In 1903, Pankhurst and her daughters, Christabel and Sylvia, founded the Women's Social and Political Union. For years they and their followers, known derisively as **suffragettes**, lobbied publicly and privately for extending the vote to women. By 1910, having failed to move the government, they turned to the violent tactics of arson, breaking windows, and sabotage of postal boxes. They marched en masse on Parliament. The Liberal government of Prime Minister Herbert Asquith (1852–1928) imprisoned demonstrators and force-fed those who went on hunger strikes in jail. The government refused to extend the franchise. Only in 1918, and then as a result of their contribution to the war effort in World War I, did British women over age thirty receive the vote. (Men could vote at age twenty-one.)

Political Feminism on the Continent   The contrast between the women's movement in Britain and those in France and Germany shows how advanced the British women's movement was. In France, when Hubertine Auclert (1848–1914) began campaigning for the vote in the 1880s, she stood virtually alone. During the 1890s, several women's organizations emerged. In 1901, the National Council of French Women (CNFF) was organized among upper-middle-class women, but it did not support the vote for women for several years. French Roman Catholic feminists such as Marie Mauguet (1844–1928) supported the franchise. Almost all French feminists, however, rejected violence. Nor were they ever able to organize mass rallies. In 1919, the French Chamber of Deputies passed a bill granting the vote to women, but in 1922, the French Senate defeated the bill. French women did not receive the right to vote until after World War II.

In Germany, feminist awareness and action were even more underdeveloped. In 1894, the Union of German Women's Organizations (BDFK) was founded. By 1902, it

suffragettes   Derisive name for members of the Women's Social and Political Union, who lobbied for votes for women.

was supporting the right to vote. But its main concern was improving women's social conditions, increasing their access to education, and extending their right to other protections. The BDKF also tried to gain women's admittance to political or civic activity on the municipal level. Its work usually included education, child welfare, charity, and public health. The German Social Democratic Party supported women's suffrage, but the German authorities and German Roman Catholics so disdained the socialists that its support only made suffrage more suspect in their eyes. Women received the vote in Germany only in 1919, under the constitution of the Weimar Republic after the German defeat in war and revolution at home.

JEWISH EMANCIPATION

The emancipation of European Jews from the narrow life of the ghetto into a world of equal or nearly equal citizenship and social status was a major accomplishment of political liberalism and had an enduring impact on European life. Emancipation, slow and never fully completed, began in the late eighteenth century and continued throughout the nineteenth. It moved at different paces in different countries.

HOW DID Jewish life in Europe change in the late nineteenth century?

DIFFERING DEGREES OF CITIZENSHIP

In 1782, Joseph II, the Habsburg emperor, issued a decree that placed the Jews of his empire under more or less the same laws as Christians. In France, the National Assembly recognized Jews as French citizens in 1789. These steps toward political emancipation were always uncertain and were frequently limited or abrogated when rulers or governments changed. Even countries that had given Jews political rights did not permit them to own land and often subjected them to discriminatory taxes. Nonetheless, during the first half of the century, Jews in Western Europe, and to a much lesser extent in central and eastern Europe, began to gain equal or more nearly equal citizenship.

In Russia, and in Poland under Russian rule, the traditional modes of prejudice and discrimination continued unabated until World War I. Russian rule treated Jews as aliens. The government undermined Jewish community life, limited the publication of Jewish books, restricted areas where Jews could live, required Jews to have internal passports to move about the country, banned Jews from many forms of state service, and excluded Jews from many institutions of higher education. The state allowed the police and right-wing nationalist groups to conduct *pogroms*—organized riots—against Jewish neighborhoods and villages.

BROADENED OPPORTUNITIES

After the revolutions of 1848, European Jews saw a general improvement in their situation that lasted for several decades. Indeed, from about 1850 to 1880, relatively little organized or overt prejudice was expressed against Jews in Western Europe. They entered the professions and other occupations once closed to them. They participated fully in literary and cultural life. They were active in the arts and music. They became leaders in science and education. Jews intermarried freely with non-Jews as legal, secular prohibitions against such marriages were repealed during the last quarter of the century. Outside of Russia, Jewish politicians entered cabinets and served in the highest offices of the state. In Western Europe, including England, France, Italy, Germany, and the Low Countries, the legalized persecution and discrimination that had so haunted Jews in the past seemed to have ended.

Because many major financial institutions of nineteenth-century Europe were owned by wealthy Jewish families, anti-Semitic political figures often blamed them for economic hard times. The most famous such family was the Rothschilds, who controlled banks in several countries. The head of the London branch was Lionel Rothschild (1808–1879). He was elected to Parliament several times but was not seated because he would not take the required Christian oath. After the requirement of that oath was abolished in 1858, he sat in Parliament from 1858 to 1874.

Getty Images Inc.— Hulton Archive Photos

What was life like for the majority of European Jews?

That newfound security began to erode during the last two decades of the nineteenth century. Anti-Semitic voices began to be heard in the 1870s, attributing the economic stagnation of the decade to Jewish bankers and financial interests. In the 1880s, organized **anti-Semitism** erupted in Germany, as it did in France at the time of the Dreyfus affair. Most Jewish leaders believed the attacks on Jewish life were merely temporary recurrences of older forms of prejudice; they felt their communities would remain safe under the liberal legal protections that had been extended during the century. That analysis would be proved disastrously wrong in the 1930s and 1940s.

anti-Semitism Hostility toward or prejudice against Jews.

LABOR, SOCIALISM, AND POLITICS TO WORLD WAR I

WHAT ROLE did the socialist and labor movements play in late-nineteenth-century politics?

The late-century industrial expansion further changed the life of the labor force. In all industrializing continental countries, the numbers of the urban proletariat rose. The proportion of artisans and highly skilled workers declined, and for the first time, factory wage earners predominated. The number of unskilled workers in shipping, transportation, and building also grew.

After 1848, European workers stopped rioting in the streets to voice their grievances. They also stopped trying to revive the old paternal guilds and similar institutions. Instead, they turned to new institutions and ideologies. Chief among these were trade unions, democratic political parties, and socialism.

TRADE UNIONISM

Trade unionism came of age when governments extended legal protections to unions during the second half of the century. Unions became fully legal in Great Britain in 1871. In France, the Third French Republic fully legalized unions in 1884. In Germany, unions were permitted to function with little disturbance after 1890. Union participation in the political process was at first marginal. As long as the representatives of the traditional governing classes looked after labor interests, members of the working class rarely sought office themselves. Unions directed their midcentury organizational efforts toward skilled workers and the immediate improvement of wages and working conditions. By the close of the century, industrial unions for unskilled workers were being organized. Employers intensely opposed these large unions of thousands of workers. Unions frequently had to engage in long strikes to convince employers to accept their demands. Despite union advances, however, and the growth of union membership, most of Europe's labor force was never unionized in this period. What the unions did represent for workers was a new collective form of association to confront economic difficulties and improve security.

Trade unions continued to grow in late-century Great Britain. The effort to curb the unions eventually led to the formation of the Labour Party. The British unions often had quite elaborate membership certificates, such as this one for the National Union of Gas Workers and General Labourers of Great Britain and Ireland.

The Granger Collection

What role did unions play in late nineteenth-century British politics?

DEMOCRACY AND POLITICAL PARTIES

Except for Russia, all the major European states adopted broad-based, if not perfectly democratic, electoral systems in the late nineteenth century. Great Britain passed its second voting reform act in 1867 and its third in 1884. Bismarck brought universal male suffrage to the German Empire in 1871. The French Chamber of Deputies was democratically elected. The broadened franchise meant politicians could no longer ignore workers, and discontented groups could now voice their grievances and advocate their programs within the institutions of government rather than from the outside.

The advent of democracy brought organized mass political parties like those already in existence in the United States to Europe for the first time. The expansion of the electorate brought into the political process many people whose level of political consciousness, awareness, and interest was low. This electorate had to be organized and taught about power and influence in the liberal democratic state. The organized political party—with its workers, newspapers, offices, social life, and discipline—was the vehicle that mobilized the new voters. The democratization of politics presented the socialists with opportunities and required the traditional ruling classes to vie with the socialists for the support of the new working-class voters.

The major question for late-century socialist parties throughout Europe was whether revolution or democratic reform would improve the life of the working class. This question sharply divided all socialist parties and especially those whose leadership adhered to the intellectual legacy of Karl Marx. The dispute over whether to achieve socialism through revolution or reform sharply shaped socialist thought, party programs, and political behavior and influenced not only socialism but the larger European political arena as well.

KARL MARX AND THE FIRST INTERNATIONAL

In 1864, a group of British and French trade unionists founded the International Working Men's Association. Known as the First International, its membership encompassed a vast array of radical political types, including socialists, anarchists, and Polish nationalists. In the inaugural address for the First International, Karl Marx approved workers' and trade unions' efforts to reform the conditions of labor within the existing political and economic processes. In his private writings he often criticized such reformist activity, but these writings were not made public until near the end of the century, years after his death.

The violence involved in the rise and suppression of the Paris Commune (see Chapter 22), which Marx had declared a genuine proletarian uprising, cast a pall over socialism throughout Europe. British trade unionists, who received legal protections in 1871, wanted no connection with the events in Paris. The French authorities used the uprising to suppress socialist activity. Under these pressures, the First International held its last European congress in 1873. It soon transferred its offices to the United States, where it was dissolved in 1876.

The short-lived First International had a disproportionately great impact on the future of European socialism. Throughout the late 1860s, the organization gathered statistics, kept labor groups informed of mutual problems, provided a forum to debate socialist doctrine, and extravagantly proclaimed (and overstated) its own influence over contemporary events. From these debates and activities, Marxism emerged as the single most important strand of socialism. Marx's thought deeply impressed German socialists, who were to establish the most powerful socialist party in Europe, and became the chief vehicle for preserving and developing it. The full development of German socialism, however, also involved the influence of non-Marxist socialists in Great Britain.

GREAT BRITAIN: FABIANISM AND EARLY WELFARE PROGRAMS

Neither Marxism nor any other form of socialism made significant progress in Great Britain, the most advanced industrial society of the day. There trade unions grew steadily, and their members normally supported Liberal Party candidates. Until 1901, labor's general political activity remained limited. In that year, however, the House of Lords, which also acts as Britain's highest court, through the Taff Vale decision, removed the legal protection previously accorded union funds. The Trades Union Congress responded by launching the Labour Party. In the election of 1906, the fledgling party sent twenty-nine members to Parliament. Their goals as trade unionists, however, did not yet include socialism. In this same period, the British labor movement became more militant. In scores of strikes before the war, workers fought for wages to meet the rising cost of living. The government took a larger role than ever before in mediating these strikes.

British socialism itself remained primarily the preserve of non-Marxist intellectuals. The Fabian Society, founded in 1884, was Britain's most influential socialist group. Many Fabians were civil servants who believed the problems of industry, the expansion of ownership, and the state direction of production could be solved and achieved gradually, peacefully, and democratically. They sought to educate the country about the rational wisdom of socialism. They were particularly interested in modes of collective ownership on the municipal level, the so-called gas-and-water socialism.

The British government and the Liberal and Conservative parties responded slowly to these pressures. In 1903, Joseph Chamberlain (1836–1914) launched his unsuccessful campaign to match foreign tariffs and to finance social reform through higher import duties. The campaign split the Conservative Party. After 1906, the Liberal Party, led by Sir Henry Campbell-Bannerman (1836–1908) and, after 1908, by Herbert Asquith, pursued a two-pronged policy. Fearful of losing seats in Parliament to the new Labour Party, they restored the former protection of the unions. Then, after 1909, with Chancellor of the Exchequer David Lloyd George (1863–1945) as its guiding light, the Liberal ministry undertook a broad program of social legislation that included establishing labor exchanges, regulating certain trades, and passing the National Insurance Act of 1911, which provided unemployment benefits and health care.

The new taxes and social programs meant that in Britain, the home of nineteenth-century liberalism, the state was taking on an expanded role in the life of its citizens. The early welfare legislation was only marginally satisfactory to labor, many of whose members still thought they could gain more from the direct action of strikes.

FRANCE: "OPPORTUNISM" REJECTED

French socialism was a less united and more politically factionalized movement than socialism in other countries. At the turn of the century, Jean Jaurès (1859–1914) and Jules Guesde (1845–1922) led the two major factions of French socialists. Jaurès believed socialists should cooperate with middle-class Radical ministries to ensure the enactment of needed social legislation. Guesde opposed this policy, arguing that socialists could not, with integrity, support a bourgeois cabinet they were theoretically dedicated to overthrowing. The government's response to the Dreyfus affair brought the quarrel to a head. In 1899, seeking to unite all supporters of Dreyfus, Prime Minister René Waldeck-Rousseau (1846–1904) appointed the socialist Alexander Millerand (1859–1943) to the cabinet.

The Second International had been founded in 1889 in a new effort to unify the various national socialist parties and trade unions. By 1904, the Amsterdam Congress of the Second International debated the issue of *opportunism*, as such participation by socialists in cabinets was termed. The Congress condemned opportunism in France and ordered French socialists to form a single party. Jaurès accepted the decision. Thereafter French socialists began to work together, and by 1914, the recently united Socialist Party had become the second largest group in the Chamber of Deputies.

The French labor movement, with deep roots in anarchism, was uninterested in either politics or socialism. French workers usually voted socialist, but the unions themselves, unlike those in Britain, avoided active political participation. The main labor union, Confédération Générale du Travail, founded in 1895, regarded itself as a rival to the socialist parties. Its leaders sought to improve the workers' conditions through direct action, such as general strikes. The strike tactic often conflicted with the socialist belief in aiding labor through state action. Strikes were common in France between 1905 and 1914, and the middle-class Radical ministry used troops to suppress them on more than one occasion.

GERMANY: SOCIAL DEMOCRATS AND REVISIONISM

The German Social Democratic Party, or SPD, was founded in 1875. From the beginning, the SPD was divided between those who advocated reform and those who advocated revolution.

Bismarck's Repression of the SPD   Twelve years of persecution under Bismarck forged the character of the SPD. The so-called Iron Chancellor used an assassination attempt on Emperor William I (r. 1861–1888) in 1878, in which the socialists were not involved, to steer antisocialist laws through the *Reichstag*. The measures suppressed the organization, meetings, newspapers, and other public activities of the SPD. Thereafter, to remain a socialist meant to remove oneself from the mainstream of respectable German life and possibly to lose one's job. Nonetheless, from the early 1880s onward, the SPD steadily polled more and more votes in elections to the *Reichstag*.

As simple repression failed to wean German workers from socialist loyalties, Bismarck undertook a program of social welfare legislation. In 1883, the German Empire adopted a health insurance measure. The next year the *Reichstag* enacted accident insurance legislation. Finally, in 1889, Bismarck sponsored a plan for old age and disability pensions. These programs, to which both workers and employers contributed, represented a paternalistic, conservative alternative to socialism.

The Erfurt Program   After forcing Bismarck's resignation mainly because of differences over foreign policy, Emperor William II (r. 1888–1918) allowed the antisocialist legislation to expire, hoping to build new political support among the working class. Even under the repressive laws, members of the SPD could sit in the *Reichstag*. With the repressive measures lifted, the party needed to decide what attitude to assume toward the German Empire.

The answer came in the Erfurt Program of 1891. In good Marxist fashion, the program declared the imminent doom of capitalism and the necessity of socialist ownership of the means of production. The party intended to pursue these goals through legal political participation rather than by revolutionary activity. So, although in theory the SPD was vehemently hostile to the German Empire, in practice the party functioned within its institutions.

The Debate over Revisionism   The dilemma of the SPD, however, generated the most important challenge within the socialist movement to the orthodox Marxist analysis of capitalism and the socialist revolution. The author of this socialist heresy, Eduard Bernstein (1850–1932), had lived in Britain and was familiar with the Fabians. In *Evolutionary Socialism* (1899), he questioned whether Marx and his later orthodox followers had been correct in their pessimistic appraisal of capitalism and the necessity of revolution. For Bernstein, social reform through democratic institutions replaced revolution as the path to a humane socialist society. (See "Compare & Connect: Bernstein and Lenin Debate the Character of Tactics of European Socialism," pages, 590–591.)

Bernstein's doctrines, known as Revisionism, generated heated debate among German socialists, who finally condemned them. Nonetheless, while still calling for revolution, the SPD pursued a course of action similar to what Bernstein advocated. Its trade union members, prospering within the German economy, did not want revolution. Its grassroots members wanted to be patriotic Germans as well as good socialists. Its leaders feared anything that might renew the persecution they had experienced under Bismarck. Consequently, the SPD worked for electoral gains, expansion of its membership, and short-term political and social reform. It prospered and became one of the most important institutions of imperial Germany. Even middle-class Germans voted for it to oppose the illiberal institutions of the empire.

RUSSIA: INDUSTRIAL DEVELOPMENT AND THE BIRTH OF BOLSHEVISM

In the 1890s, Russia entered the industrial age and confronted many of the problems that the more advanced nations of the Continent had experienced fifty or seventy-five years earlier. Unlike those other countries, Russia had to deal with political discontent and economic development simultaneously. Russian socialism reflected that peculiar situation.

Witte's Program for Industrial Growth   Tsar Alexander III (r. 1881–1894) and, after him, Nicholas II (r. 1894–1917) were determined that Russia should become an industrial power. Only by doing so, they believed, could the country maintain its position as a great power. Count Sergei Witte (1849–1915) led Russia into the industrial age. After a career in railways and other private business, he was appointed first minister of communications and then finance minister in 1892. Witte pursued a policy of planned economic development, protective tariffs, high taxes, putting Russia's currency on the gold standard, and efficiency in government and business.

Witte favored heavy industries. Between 1890 and 1904, the Russian railway system grew from 30,596 to 59,616 kilometers. Coal, pig-iron, and steel output rose rapidly. Textile manufacturing continued to expand and was still the single largest industry. The factory system spread extensively.

Industrialism, however, also brought social discontent to Russia, as it had elsewhere. Landowners felt that foreign capitalists were earning too much of the profit. The peasants saw their grain exports and tax payments finance development that did not measurably improve their lives. A small, but significant, industrial proletariat emerged. In 1900, Russia had approximately 3 million factory workers, working and living in poor conditions, with little or no state protection.

Similar social and economic problems arose in the countryside. Russian agriculture had not prospered after the emancipation of the serfs in 1861. The peasants remained burdened with redemption payments for the land they farmed, local taxes, excessive national taxes, and falling grain prices. Peasants did not own their land as individuals, but communally through the *mir*, or village. They farmed the land inefficiently through strip farming or by tilling small plots. Many free peasants with too little land to support their families had to work on large estates owned by nobles or for more prosperous peasant farmers, known as *kulaks*. Between 1860 and 1914, the population of European Russia rose from about 50 million to around 103 million people. Land hunger and discontent spread among the peasants and sparked frequent uprisings in the countryside.

New political developments accompanied economic changes. The Social Revolutionary Party, founded in 1901, opposed industrialism and looked to the communal life of rural Russia as a model for the future. In 1903, the Constitutional Democratic Party, or Cadets, was formed. Modeling themselves on the liberal parties of Western

How did Lenin change communist theory to fit Russian circumstances?

Europe, the Cadets wanted a constitutional monarchy under a parliamentary regime with civil liberties and economic progress.

Lenin's Early Thought and Career   The situation of Russian socialists differed radically from that of socialists in other major European countries. Russia had no representative institutions and only a small working class. The compromises and accommodations achieved elsewhere were meaningless in Russia, where socialists believed that in both theory and practice they must be revolutionary. The repressive policies of the tsarist regime required the Russian Social Democratic Party, founded in 1898, to function in exile. The party members greatly admired the German Social Democratic Party and adopted its Marxist ideology.

The future leader of the communist revolution, Vladimir Ilyich Ulyanov (1870–1924), who later took the name of Lenin, was the son of a high bureaucrat. In 1893, Lenin moved to Saint Petersburg, where he studied law and was soon drawn to the revolutionary groups among the factory workers. He was arrested in 1895 and exiled to Siberia. In 1900, after his release, Lenin left Russia for the West. He spent most of the next seventeen years in Switzerland.

There, Lenin became deeply involved in the disputes of the exiled Russian Social Democrats. Unlike the backward-looking Social Revolutionaries, the Social Democrats were modernizers who favored industrial development. Looking to Karl Marx's writings, most Russian Social Democrats believed Russia must develop a large proletariat before the Marxist revolution could come. They also hoped to build a mass political party like the German SPD.

Lenin dissented from both these ideas. In *What Is to Be Done?* (1902), he condemned any accommodations, such as those the German SPD practiced. He also criticized trade unionism that settled for short-term reformist gains and rejected the concept of a mass democratic party composed of workers. Instead, he declared that revolutionary consciousness would not arise spontaneously from the working class. Only a small, tightly organized, elite party could possess the proper dedication to revolution and resist penetration by police spies. Lenin thus rejected both the view that revolution was inevitable and that democratic means could achieve revolutionary goals. Lenin substituted the small, professional, nondemocratic revolutionary party for Marx's proletariat as the instrument of revolutionary change. (See ""Compare & Connect: Bernstein and Lenin Debate the Character of Tactics of European Socialism," pages 590–591.)

In 1903, at the London Congress of the Russian Social Democratic Party, Lenin forced a split in the party ranks. He and his followers lost many votes on questions put before the congress, but near its close they mustered a slim majority. Thereafter Lenin's faction assumed the name **Bolsheviks**, meaning "majority," and the other, more moderate, democratic revolutionary faction came to be known as the **Mensheviks**, or "minority."

A fundamental organizational difference had existed between what in 1903 were the two chief factions of the Russian Social Democratic Party. The Mensheviks wanted a party with a mass membership, similar to the German SDP and other Western European socialist parties, which would function democratically. The Bolsheviks intended the party to consist of elite professional revolutionaries who would provide centralized leadership for the working class.

In 1905, Lenin complemented his organizational theory with a program for revolution in Russia. In *Two Tactics of Social Democracy in the Bourgeois-Democratic Revolution*, he urged the socialist revolution to unite the proletariat and the peasantry. Lenin grasped better than any other revolutionary the profound discontent in the Russian countryside. He believed the tsarist government probably could not suppress an alliance of workers and peasants in rebellion.

The Revolution of 1905 and Its Aftermath   The quarrels among the exiled Russian socialists and Lenin's doctrines had no immediate influence on events in Russia. Industrialization continued to stir resentment. In 1903, Nicholas II dismissed Witte, hoping to quell the criticism. The next year, in response to conflicts over Manchuria and Korea, Russia went to war against Japan, partly in hopes the conflict would rally public opinion to the tsar. Instead, the Russians lost the war, and the government faced an internal political crisis. The Japanese captured Port Arthur, Russia's naval base on the coast of China, early in 1905. A few days later, on January 22, a Russian Orthodox priest named Father George Gapon led several hundred workers to present a petition to the tsar to improve industrial conditions. As they approached the Winter Palace, troops opened fire, killing approximately forty people and wounding hundreds of others. As word of this massacre spread, and large, angry crowds gathered elsewhere in the city, the military shot more people. The final death toll was approximately two hundred killed and eight hundred wounded. The day, soon known as Bloody Sunday, marked a turning point. Vast numbers of ordinary Russians came to believe they could no longer trust the tsar or his government.

During the next ten months, revolutionary disturbances spread throughout Russia. In early October 1905, strikes broke out in Saint Petersburg, and for all practical purposes, worker groups, called soviets, controlled the city. Nicholas II, who had recalled Witte, issued the October Manifesto, which promised Russia a constitutional government. Early in 1906, Nicholas II announced the creation of a representative body, the Duma, with two chambers. He reserved to himself, however, ministerial appointments, financial policy, and military and foreign affairs. The April elections returned a highly radical group of representatives. The tsar then replaced Witte with P. A. Stolypin (1862–1911), who had little sympathy for parliamentary government. Stolypin persuaded Nicholas to dissolve the Duma. A second assembly was elected in February 1907. Again, cooperation proved impossible, and the tsar dissolved that Duma in June. A third Duma, elected in late 1907 on the basis of a more conservative

Bolsheviks ("majority") Lenin's turn-of-the-century socialist Russian faction favoring a party of elite professionals who would provide the working class with centralized leadership.

Mensheviks ("minority") Turn-of-the-century socialist Russian faction that wanted to create a party with a large mass membership (like Germany's SPD).

On Bloody Sunday, January 22, 1905, troops of Tsar Nicholas II fired on a peaceful procession of workers who sought to present a petition for better working and living conditions at the Winter Palace in St. Petersburg. This event all but destroyed any chance of reconciliation between the tsarist government and the Russian working class.

Bildarchiv Preussischer Kulturbesitz

How did defeat in the Russo-Japanese war contribute to domestic political unrest in Russia?

franchise, proved sufficiently pliable for the tsar and his minister. Thus, within two years of the 1905 Revolution, Nicholas II had recaptured much of the ground he had conceded.

Stolypin set about repressing rebellion, removing some causes of the revolt, and rallying property owners behind the tsarist regime. Early in 1907, special field courts-martial condemned almost seven hundred rebellious peasants to death. Before undertaking this repression, Stolypin, in November 1906, had canceled any redemptive payments that the peasants still owed the government from the emancipation of the serfs in 1861. He took this step to encourage peasants to assume individual proprietorship of the land they farmed and to abandon the communal system of the *mirs*. Combined with a program to instruct peasants on how to farm more efficiently, this policy improved agricultural production. However, many peasant small-holders sold their land and joined the industrial labor force.

The moderate liberals who sat in the Duma approved of the new land measures. They liked the idea of competition and individual property ownership. The Constitutional Democrats wanted a more genuinely parliamentary mode of government, but they compromised out of fear of new revolutionary disturbances. Hatred of Stolypin was still widespread, however, among the country's older conservative groups, and industrial workers remained antagonistic to the tsar. In 1911, Stolypin was assassinated by a Social Revolutionary, who may have been a police agent in the pay of conservatives. Nicholas II found no worthy successor. His government simply muddled along.

Meanwhile, at court, the monk Grigory Efimovich Rasputin (1871?–1916) gained ascendancy with the tsar and his wife because of his alleged power to heal the tsar's hemophilic son Alexis, the heir to the throne, when medicine proved unable to help the boy. The undue influence of this strange, uncouth man, as well as continued social discontent and conservative resistance to any further liberal reforms, undermined the position of the tsar and his government after 1911. Once again, as in 1904, he and his ministers thought that some bold move in foreign policy might bring the regime the popular support it desperately needed.

BERNSTEIN AND LENIN DEBATE THE CHARACTER OF TACTICS OF EUROPEAN SOCIALISM

By the close of the nineteenth century, the European Socialist movement found itself sharply divided over its future goals and tactics. On the one side, some socialists, here represented by Eduard Bernstein, came to reject many of the ideas of Karl Marx, particularly that of a proletarian revolution, and embraced democratic politics as the best way to realize their goals of the improvement of the life of the working class. Others, a minority at the time, represented here by Lenin, rejected democracy and embraced the concept of violent revolution achieved by a small professional elite rather than by a spontaneous proletarian uprising. In the twentieth century after the 1917 Bolshevik Revolution in Russia, those divisions would play themselves out in an enormously hostile conflict between democratic socialist parties in Western Europe and Communists in the Soviet Union and Communist parties in Western Europe dominated by the Soviet Union. (See Chapters 26 and 27.)

QUESTIONS

1. According to Bernstein, what specific predictions in The *Communist Manifesto* failed to materialize?

2. Why is the advance of democracy important to Bernstein's argument? Why does he renounce the concept of a "dictatorship of the proletariat"?

3. What does Lenin mean by "professional revolutionaries"? Why does Russia need such revolutionaries?

4. How does Lenin reconcile his antidemocratic views to the goal of aiding the working class?

5. How could the ideas of both Bernstein and Lenin be seen as departures from Marx's own thinking?

I. EDUARD BERNSTEIN URGES SOCIALISTS TO EMBRACE DEMOCRACY

Eduard Bernstein was responsible for the emergence of Revisionism within the German Social Democratic Party. He was a dedicated socialist who recognized that Marx's Communist Manifesto *(1848) had not predicted the actual future of the European working classes. Bernstein believed the capitalist system would not suddenly collapse and that socialists should change their tactics to achieve democratic political rights and pursue reform instead of revolution.*

Social conditions have not developed to such an acute opposition of things and classes as is depicted in the [*Communist*] *Manifesto.* . . . The number of members of the possessing classes is today not smaller but larger. The enormous increase of social wealth is not accompanied by a decreasing number of large capitalists but by an increasing number of capitalists of all degrees. . . .

In all advanced countries we see the privileges of the capitalist bourgeoisie yielding step by step to democratic organizations. . . .

The conquest of political power by the working classes, the expropriation of capitalists, are not ends in themselves but only means for the accomplishment of certain aims and endeavours. . . .

Democracy is in principle the suppression of class government, though it is not yet the actual suppression of classes. . . . The right to vote in a democracy makes its members virtually partners in the community, and this virtual partnership must in the end lead to real partnership. . . .

Universal franchise is, from two sides, the alternative to a violent revolution. But universal suffrage is only a part of democracy, although a part which in time must draw the other parts after it as the magnet attracts to itself the scattered portions of iron. It certainly proceeds more slowly than many would wish, but in spite of that it is at work. And social democracy cannot further this work better than by taking its stand unreserved only the theory of democracy—on the ground of universal suffrage with all the consequences resulting therefrom to its tactics. . . .

Is there any sense . . . in maintaining the phrase of the 'dictatorship of the proletariot' at a time when in all possible places representatives of social democracy have placed themselves practically in the arena of Parliamentary work, have declared for the proportional representation of the people, and for direct legislation—all of which is inconsistent with a dictatorship.

The phrase is to-day so antiquated that is is only to be reconciled with reality by stripping the word dictatorship of its actual meaning and attaching to it some kind of weakened interpretation. The whole practical activity of social democracy is directed towards creating circumstances and condition which shall render possible and secure a transition (free from convulsive outbursts) of the modern social order to a higher one.

Source: From Eduard Bernstein, *Evolutionary Socialism: A Criticism and Affirmation, 1899* (New York: Schocken Books, 1961), pp. xxiv–xxv, xxix, 143–146.

II. LENIN ARGUES FOR THE NECESSITY OF A SECRET AND ELITE PARTY OF PROFESSIONAL REVOLUTIONARIES

Social democratic parties in Western Europe had mass memberships and were generally democratic organizations. In this passage from What Is to Be Done? *(1902), Lenin explains why the autocratic political conditions of Russia demanded a different kind of organization for the Russian Social Democratic Party. Lenin's ideas became the guiding principles of Bolshevik organization. Lenin departed from Marx's own thought by urging the necessity of fulminating revolution rather than waiting for it to occur as a necessary result of the collapse of capitalism.*

By the close of the nineteenth century, European socialists had come to doubt whether the industrial proletariat around the world, such as these workers in the United States, would or could actually bring about a revolution as predicted by Marx. Eduard Bernstein thought democratic social change would improve the lot of workers. Lenin believed an elite revolutionary party would produce such radical change.

Courtesy of the Library of Congress

Did late nineteenth-century industrial workers see themselves as a unified political force capable of and committed to bringing about the kind of revolutionary change that socialists advocated?

I assert that it is far more difficult [for government police] to unearth a dozen wise men than a hundred fools. This position I will defend, no matter how much you instigate the masses against me for my "anti-democratic" views, etc. As I have stated repeatedly, by "wise men," in connection with organization, I mean professional revolutionaries, irrespective of whether they have developed from among students or working men. I assert: (1) that no revolutionary movement can endure without a stable organization of leaders maintaining continuity; (2) that the broader the popular mass drawn spontaneously into the struggle, which forms the basis of the movement and participates in it, the more urgent the need for such an organization, and the more solid this organization must be . . .; (3) that such an organization must consist chiefly of people professionally engaged in revolutionary activity; (4) that in an autocratic state [such as Russia], the more we confine the membership of such an organization to people who are professionally engaged in revolutionary activity and who have been professionally trained in the art of combating the political police, the more difficult will it be to unearth the organization; and (5) the greater will be the number of people from the working class and from other social classes who will be able to join the movement and perform active work in it. . . .

The only serious organization principle for the active workers of our movement should be the strictest secrecy, the strictest selection of members, and the training of professional revolutionaries.

Source: From *Socialist Thought: A Documentary History*, ed. by Albert Fried and Ronald Sanders (Garden City, NY: Anchor Doubleday, 1964), pp. 460, 468.

SUMMARY

WHY WERE so many Europeans on the move in the late nineteenth century?

Population Trends and Migration
Europeans made up approximately 20 percent of the world's population around 1900. Soon thereafter, birth and death rates stabilized or declined in developed regions but continued to increase elsewhere. In the second half of the nineteenth century, Europeans emigrated in huge numbers. Many went to the Americas, Australia, and South Africa. At midcentury, most of them came from Great Britain, Germany, and Scandinavia; after 1885, more came from southern and eastern Europe. *page 566*

HOW DID the second Industrial Revolution transform European life?

The Second Industrial Revolution
The second Industrial Revolution was dominated by Germany. At the turn of the century, the emergence of an industrial Germany was the most significant aspect of political and economic life in Europe. The steel industry produced over 32 million tons of steel by 1913. The chemical industry depended on scientific research, and Germany was the first country to attempt to facilitate the flow of information between research and industry. Electrical energy was widely applied, and the automobile had been invented. Economic advances slowed in the final quarter of the century, although the standard of living in most industrial nations continued to grow slowly. Unemployment and poverty contributed to the appeal of trade unions and socialist political parties. Consumer goods were an important aspect of the urban lifestyle. *page 566*

WHAT EXPLAINS the prominence of the middle class in late-nineteenth-century Europe?

The Middle Classes in Ascendancy
The middle classes set the values and goals for most of society between the middle of the nineteenth century and World War I. In reaction to the 1848 revolutions, the middle classes put aside revolution in favor of preserving their status and possessions. The middle classes diversified: A few families gained wealth exceeding that of the aristocracy; small entrepreneurs and professionals earned enough to purchase private homes, education for their children, and vacations; secretaries, retail workers, and low-level bureaucrats made up the white-collar workers (the *petite bourgeoisie*), who were close to the working class but deliberately

adopted middle-class behaviors and consumption patterns. Tensions existed among these middle-class groups. *page 569*

WHAT FORCES shaped the development of European cities?

Late-Nineteenth-Century Urban Life
Urbanization increased in the late nineteenth century. Between 1850 and 1910, the population of many major European cities doubled or tripled. There were social, political, economic, environmental, and health consequences of this growth. Governments led the redesign of the central portions of many cities. Parisian streets were widened, for aesthetic and practical reasons. Public works projects created many jobs. Displaced city dwellers often moved to suburbs. Health and housing for the poor came to be seen as prerequisites for safety and security for the middle classes. The cholera epidemics of the early nineteenth century led to concerns in public health and sanitation. Governments gained new powers to intervene in citizens' lives in the name of public health. Working-class housing conditions also became a subject of medical, moral, and political concern to middle-class reformers and bureaucrats. Philanthropies, businesses, and government offered economic incentives to build housing for the poor, trying to create working-class homes and facilitate middle-class family life. *page 570*

WHAT WAS life like for women in late-nineteenth-century Europe?

Varieties of Late-Nineteenth-Century Women's Experiences Like men, women's experiences reflected their class, but women of all ranks faced disabilities in property rights, family law, and education. The degree of disability diminished in the late nineteenth century. Men controlled their wives' property in Europe until late in the century. Family law often required a woman's obedience to her husband; sexual double standards prevailed; divorce was difficult; and contraception and abortion were illegal. Women's education was minimal and inferior. Teaching was one of the few career paths open to women. The second Industrial Revolution opened more jobs to women, but the jobs were often low skilled and almost inevitably low paying. Working-class women often labored in sweatshops that lacked job security; some became prostitutes. Middle-class women were usually wives and mothers and discouraged from employment. The "cult of domesticity" made women and their roles within the home a symbol of the success of their father or husband. Women in Britain ("suffragettes"), France, Germany, and elsewhere lobbied for the right to vote, but nowhere did they gain it until after the turn of the century. *page 574*

HOW DID Jewish life in Europe change in the late nineteenth century?

Jewish Emancipation Political liberalism facilitated the emancipation of European Jews, to varying degrees and at various speeds in different nations. In the late eighteenth century and the first half of the nineteenth century, Jews gained rights approximating those of other citizens in most western European states. In Russia, traditional discrimination persisted. After the revolutions of 1848, the situation for most European Jews improved, with further political and citizenship rights being granted to Jews in most of western Europe. Even Jews in Austria-Hungary gained full legal rights in 1867. Institutionalized prejudice seemed to have dissipated in western Europe, although certainly not in Russia and only sporadically in eastern Europe. Anti-Semitism grew in the 1870s and 1880s, though, largely as a by-product of economic stagnation. Jewish leaders had faith in liberal government structures to protect their rights. *page 581*

WHAT ROLE did the socialist and labor movements play in late-nineteenth-century politics?

Labor, Socialism, and Politics to World War I With industrial expansion, the size of the urban proletariat grew. New institutions and ideologies had replaced riots as the way by which workers expressed their will. Unions grew in the second half of the century, but most workers were still not unionized. Broader-based political systems everywhere except Russia brought with them organized mass political parties. Socialist parties divided on whether change would come through reform or revolution. Marx publicly endorsed reform. In Great Britain, trade unionism was allied with the Liberal Party and then the Labour Party. The Fabian Society was Britain's most significant socialist group, and it was gradualist and non-Marxist. In France, socialist parties quarreled among themselves; labor unions favored strikes over political participation. The German Social Democratic Party kept Marxist socialism alive through the turn of the century. In Russia, socialism was almost by definition revolutionary. In 1903, Lenin forced a split in the Russian Social Democratic Party over whether the party should strive for mass membership (the "Menshevik" position) or be limited to elite professional revolutionaries (Lenin's "Bolshevik" position). In 1905, Lenin wrote that the proletariat and the peasantry should unite in revolution in Russia. His formula would prove successful in 1917. Meanwhile, the Bloody Sunday massacre of January 1905 led to upheaval. By October 1905, worker groups called soviets controlled Saint Petersburg, and tsar Nicholas II promised constitutional government. By 1907, however, Nicholas II had dissolved two sessions of the Duma, the new representative legislature, and had taken back most of his powers. *page 582*

REVIEW QUESTIONS

1. How was European society transformed by the second Industrial Revolution? What were living conditions like in European cities during the late nineteenth century? Why were European cities redesigned during this period? How were they redesigned?

2. What was the status of European women in the second half of the nineteenth century? Why did they grow discontented with their lot? What tactics did they use in effecting change? What forms did the emancipation of Jews take in the nineteenth century?

3. What was the status of the proletariat in 1860? Had it improved by 1914? What caused the growth in trade unions and organized mass political parties? What were the differences among socialist parties?

4. How important was industrialism in Russia? Were the tsars wise to attempt to modernize their country? How did Lenin's view of socialism differ from that of the socialists in western Europe?

KEY TERMS

anti-Semitism (p. 582)
Bolsheviks (p. 588)
Mensheviks (p. 588)
petite bourgeoisie (p. 569)

second Industrial Revolution (p. 567)
suffragettes (p. 580)

For additional learning resources related to this chapter, please go to **www.myhistorylab.com**

myhistorylab

24

The Birth of Modern European Thought

Darwin's theories about the evolution of humankind from the higher primates aroused enormous controversy. This caricature shows him with a monkey's body holding a mirror to an apelike creature.

National History Museum, London, UK/Bridgeman Art Library

What groups felt most threatened by Darwin's theories? Why?

he political systems, industrialized economies, and middle-class lifestyles that emerged in the late nineteenth century were accompanied by intellectual developments that shaped a "modern" mind. The new intellectual orientation was rooted in the Enlightenment (which contributed confidence in reason and science and a tolerant, cosmopolitan outlook) and the romantic movement (which fostered respect for feeling, imagination, artistic insight, and the value of individuals). Most of the West's traditional assumptions about nature, religion, and social life were subjected to radical reexamination. As a result, at the turn of the century European intellectuals were more daring than ever before but less certain about where their work might lead. Fading confidence in the reliability of traditional points of view helped some disadvantaged groups, such as women, win liberating social reforms. ▪

THE NEW READING PUBLIC

WHAT EFFECT did state-financed education have on literacy in late-nineteenth-century Europe?

The social context of intellectual life changed in the latter part of the nineteenth century. For the first time in Europe, a mass reading public came into existence as more people than ever before became drawn into the world of print culture.

ADVANCES IN PRIMARY EDUCATION

Literacy on the Continent improved steadily from the 1860s onward as governments financed education. By 1900, in Britain, France, Belgium, the Netherlands, Germany, and Scandinavia, approximately 85 percent or more of the people could read, but Italy, Spain, Russia, Austria-Hungary, and the Balkans still had illiteracy rates of between 30 and 60 percent.

The new primary education in the basic skills of reading, writing, and elementary arithmetic reflected and generated social change. Both liberals and conservatives regarded such minimal training as necessary for orderly political behavior by the newly enfranchised voters. They also hoped that literacy would create a more productive labor force.

Literacy and its extension, however, soon became a force in its own right. The school-teaching profession grew rapidly in numbers and prestige and, as noted in Chapter 23, became a major area for the employment of women. Having created systems of primary education, the major nations had to give further attention to secondary education by the time of World War I. In another generation, the question would become one of democratic university instruction.

READING MATERIAL FOR THE MASS AUDIENCE

The expanding literate population created a vast market for new reading material. The number of newspapers, books, magazines, mail-order catalogs, and libraries grew rapidly. Cheap mass-circulation newspapers enjoyed their first heyday. Such newspapers carried advertising that alerted readers to the new consumer products available through the Second Industrial Revolution. Other publishers produced newspapers with specialized political or religious viewpoints. Probably more people with different ideas could get into print in the late nineteenth century than ever before in European history. In addition, more people could read their ideas than ever before.

Because many of the new readers were only marginally literate and still ignorant about many subjects, the books and journals catering to them were often mediocre. The cheap newspapers prospered on stories of sensational crimes and political scandal and on pages of adver-

Public education became widespread in Europe during the second half of the nineteenth century and women came to dominate the profession of schoolteaching, especially at the elementary level. This 1905 photograph shows English school-children going through morning drills.

© Hulton-Deutsch Collection/CORBIS

How did public education affect home life for working-class families?

Overview Development in Science, Psychology, Sociology, and Fiction

DISCIPLINE	YEAR	DEVELOPMENT
SCIENCE	1830s	Comte's positivism says all knowledge should be knowledge common to the physical sciences
	1859	Darwin's theory of evolution by natural selection disputes creationism
	1895	Roentgen announces the discovery of X-rays
PSYCHOLOGY	1900	Freud, the founder of psychoanalysis, publishes *The Interpretation of Dreams*
	early 1900s	Jung, student of Freud, theorizes that the subconscious is inherited from ancestors
	mid-1900s	Horney and Klein attempt to establish a psychoanalytic basis for feminism
SOCIOLOGY	1850s	Gobineau presents first arguments that race is the major determinant of human history
	1870s	Nationalism becomes a well-organized mass movement equating nationality with race
	1900	Weber traces capitalism to religious doctrines of Puritanism
FICTION	1856	*Madame Bovary* by Flaubert signals the advent of realism
	1870	Verne modernizes popular science fiction
	1920s	Woolf becomes a chief proponent of modernism

tising. Religious journals depended on denominational rivalry. A brisk market existed for pornography. Newspapers with editorials on the front page became major factors in the emerging mass politics. The news could be managed, but in central Europe more often by the government censor than by the publisher.

SCIENCE AT MIDCENTURY

In about 1850, the basic Newtonian picture of physical nature still prevailed. At midcentury, learned persons regarded the physical world as rational, mechanical, and dependable. Experiment and observation could reveal its laws objectively. Scientific theory purportedly described physical nature as it really existed. Moreover, by 1850, science had a strong institutional life in French and German universities and in new professional societies. (See "Encountering the Past: The Birth of Science Fiction," page 598.)

COMTE, POSITIVISM, AND THE PRESTIGE OF SCIENCE

During the early nineteenth century, science had continued to establish itself as the model for all human knowledge. The French philosopher Auguste Comte (1798–1857) developed **positivism**, a philosophy of human intellectual development that culminated in science. In *The Positive Philosophy* (1830–1842), Comte argued that human thought had developed in three stages. In the first, or theological, stage, physical nature was explained in terms of the action of divinities or spirits. In the second, or metaphysical, stage, abstract principles were regarded as the operative agencies of nature. In the final, or positive stage, explanations of nature became matters of exact description of phenomena, without recourse to an unobservable operative principle. Physical science had, in Comte's view, entered the positive stage, and similar thinking should penetrate other areas of analysis, including social behavior. He is, thus, generally regarded as the father

WHAT ROLE did science play in the second half of the nineteenth century?

father of modern sociology

positivism Comte's philosophy that all knowledge should be the kind of knowledge common to the physical sciences.

ENCOUNTERING THE PAST

THE BIRTH OF SCIENCE FICTION

During the Renaissance, Europe's fantasy writers set their stories in exotic foreign lands. In the seventeenth century, the moon became a favorite locale, and during the nineteenth century, authors turned to outer space and the earth's unexplored deep seas and interior. Modern popular science fiction begins with the work of Jules Verne (1828–1905), who wrote serialized stories for magazines. Verne prided himself on scientific accuracy, and he set his tales in his own age—giving his readers a sense of experiencing real adventures. His most enduring novel is Twenty Thousand Leagues under the Sea *(1870), the story of Captain Nemo's submarine Nautilus. English author H. G. Wells (1866–1946) helped establish many of the conventions of science fiction.* The Time Machine *(1895) explored the conundrum of time travel.* The Island of Dr. Moreau *(1896) described the consequences of inhuman medical experimentation, and* The War of the Worlds *(1898) raised the possibility of invasion from outer space.*

The stories of Verne and Wells appeared in cheap illustrated magazines with mass circulation and helped establish science fiction as a fixture of popular culture. As new entertainment media appeared (radio, movies, and then television), their works were repeatedly dramatized. A radio play by Orson Wells (1915–1985) in 1938 based on Wells's *The War of the Worlds* was so realistic that many Americans mistook it for a news report of a Martian landing in New Jersey.

Captain Nemo's submarine confronts a giant octopus in Verne's *Twenty Thousand Leagues under the Sea.*
© Bettman/CORBIS

What sort of future did nineteenth-century science fiction writers imagine?

WHY DID science fiction suddenly become popular with the masses in the late nineteenth century? What is the reason for its enduring popularity?

of sociology. Works like Comte's helped convince learned Europeans that all knowledge must resemble scientific knowledge.

From the mid–nineteenth century onward, the links of science to the technology of the Second Industrial Revolution made the general European public aware of science and technology as never before. Writers spoke of a religion of science that would explain all nature without resorting to supernaturalism. Popularizers, such as Thomas Henry Huxley (1825–1895) in Britain and Ernst Haeckel (1834–1919) in Germany, worked to gain government support of scientific research and to include science in the schools and universities.

DARWIN'S THEORY OF NATURAL SELECTION

In 1859, Charles Darwin (1809–1882) published *On the Origin of Species*, which carried the mechanical interpretation of physical nature into the world of living things. Darwin did not originate the concept of evolution, which had been discussed widely before he wrote. What he and Alfred Russel Wallace (1823–1913) did, working independently, was to formulate the principle of natural selection, which explained how species had changed or evolved over time. Earlier writers had believed evolution might occur; Darwin and Wallace explained how it could occur.

(deistic)

Drawing on Malthus, the two scientists contended that more living organisms come into existence than can survive in their environment. Those organisms with a marginal advantage in the struggle for existence live long enough to propagate. This principle of survival of the fittest Darwin called **natural selection**. Darwin and Wallace's theory represented the triumph of naturalistic explanation, which removed the idea of purpose from organic nature. Eyes were not made for seeing according to the rational wisdom and purpose of God but had developed mechanistically over time. Thus, the theory of evolution through natural selection not only contradicted the biblical narrative of the Creation but also undermined both the deistic argument for the existence of God from the design of the universe and the whole concept of fixity in nature or the universe at large. The world was a realm of flux. The idea that physical and organic nature might be constantly changing allowed people to believe that society, values, customs, and beliefs should also change.

In 1871, in *The Descent of Man*, Darwin applied the principle of evolution by natural selection to human beings. Darwin contended that humankind's moral nature and religious sentiments, as well as its physical frame, had developed naturalistically largely in response to the requirements of survival. Neither the origin nor the character of humankind, in Darwin's view, required the existence of a god for their explanation.

natural selection Darwin and Wallace's theory that those species with a unique trait that gives them a marginal advantage in the struggle for existence change the nature of their species by reproducing more successfully than their competitors; the fittest survive to pass on their unique characteristics.

SCIENCE AND ETHICS—SOCIAL DARWINISM

One area in which science came to have a new significance was social thought and ethics. Philosophers applied the concept of the struggle for survival to human social relationships. The phrase "survival of the fittest" predated Darwin and reflected the competitive outlook of classical economics. Darwin's use of the phrase gave it the prestige associated with advanced science.

The most famous advocate of evolutionary ethics was Herbert Spencer (1820–1903), a British philosopher. Spencer, a strong individualist, believed human society progresses through competition. If the weak receive too much protection, the rest of humankind is the loser. The concept could be applied to justify not aiding the poor and the working class or to justify the domination of colonial peoples or to advocate aggressive competition among nations. Evolutionary ethics and similar concepts, all of which are usually termed *social Darwinism*, often came close to saying that "might makes right."

One of the chief opponents of such thinking was Thomas Henry Huxley, the great defender of Darwin. In 1893, Huxley declared that the physical process of evolution was at odds with human ethical development. The struggle in nature only showed how human beings should not behave. (See "Compare & Connect: The Debate over Social Darwinism," pages 600–601.) Despite Huxley's arguments, the ideas of social Darwinism continued to influence thought and public policy on both sides of the Atlantic.

social Darwinism Darwin and Wallace's theory that those species with a unique trait that gives them a marginal advantage in the struggle for existence change the nature of their species by reproducing more successfully than their competitors; the fittest survive to pass on their unique characteristics.

CHRISTIANITY AND THE CHURCH UNDER SIEGE

The nineteenth century was one of the most difficult periods in the history of the organized Christian churches. Many European intellectuals left the faith. The secular, liberal nation-states attacked the influence of the church. The expansion of population and the growth of cities challenged its organizational capacity. Yet during all of this

WHAT CHALLENGES did European Christianity face in the late nineteenth century?

THE DEBATE OVER SOCIAL DARWINISM

During the late nineteenth and early twentieth centuries, scientists as well as other social commentators debated the question of whether the concept of "survival of the fittest" on which Charles Darwin had based his concept of evolution by natural selection should apply to human society and the competition between nations. Some commentators, such as Herbert Spencer, had advocated generally unbridled economic competition with little or no help to the poor and others who fared badly as a result of such competition. In 1893, T. H. Huxley rejected that view. However, a few years later, Karl Pearson, another distinguished British scientist who supported the idea of evolution, argued that social Darwinism should and did govern the relationships among nations.

QUESTIONS

1. Why does Huxley equate "social progress" with the "ethical process"?

2. In this passage, does Huxley present human society as part of nature or as something that may be separate from nature?

3. How does Pearson connect Darwin's ideas to the concept of human progress?

4. How might Pearson's ideas justify imperial expansion, which will be considered in the next chapter? How could these arguments foster a climate of international violence?

5. How might Huxley's ideas be used to support broadly beneficial social welfare programs enacted to produce national populations healthy enough to compete in the international rivalry envisioned by Pearson?

I. T. H. HUXLEY CRITICIZES EVOLUTIONARY ETHICS

T. H. Huxley (1825–1895) was a British scientist who had been among Darwin's strongest defenders. Huxley, however, became a major critic of social Darwinism, which attempted to deduce ethical principles from evolutionary processes involving struggle in nature. Drawing a strong distinction between the cosmic process of evolution and the social process of ethical development, he argued in Evolution and Ethics *(1893) that human ethical progress occurs through combating the cosmic process.*

Men in society are undoubtedly subject to the cosmic process. As among other animals, multiplication goes on without cessation, and involves severe competition for the means of support. The struggle for existence tends to eliminate those less fitted to adapt themselves to the circumstances of their existence. The strongest, the most self-assertive, tend to tread down the weaker. But the influence of the cosmic process on the evolution of society is the greater the more rudimentary its civilization. Social progress means a checking of the cosmic process at every step and the substitution for it of another, which may be called the ethical process; the end of which is not the survival of those who may happen to be the fittest, in respect of the whole of the conditions which obtain, but of those who are ethically the best.

As I have already urged, the practice of that which is ethically best—what we call goodness or virtue—involves a course of conduct which, in all respects, is opposed to that which leads to success in the cosmic struggle for existence. In place of ruthless self-assertion it demands self-restraint; in place of thrusting aside, or treading down, all competitors, it requires that the individual shall not merely respect, but shall help his fellows; its influence is directed, not so much to the survival of the fittest, as to the fitting of as many as possible to survive. It repudiates the gladiatorial theory of existence.

It is from neglect of these plain considerations that the fanatical individualism of our time attempts to apply the analogy of cosmic nature to society. . . .

The first step towards lightening

"The White Man's Burden"

is through teaching the virtues of cleanliness.

Pears' Soap

is a potent factor in brightening the dark corners of the earth as civilization advances, while amongst the cultured of all nations it holds the highest place—it is the ideal toilet soap.

All sorts of people use it, all sorts of stores sell it.

Racism was often a by-product of social Darwinist theory. At the turn of the twentieth century, racism permeated many facets of popular life. This ad for Pears' Soap caters to the racist attitudes held by many whites during this time.

Library of Congress/*Colliers*, October 4, 1899

What relationship did this advertisement posit between race and hygiene?

Let us understand, once for all, that the ethical progress of society depends, not on imitating the cosmic process, still less in running away from it, but in combating it.

Source: From T. H. Huxley, *Evolution and Ethics* (London: Macmillan & Co., 1893), as quoted in Franklin L. Baumer, *Main Currents of Western Thought: Readings in Western European Intellectual History from the Middle Ages to the Present*, 3rd ed., rev. (New York: Alfred A. Knopf, 1970), pp. 561–562.

II. SOCIAL DARWINISM AND IMPERIALISM

T. H. Huxley's assault did not end the influence of social Darwinism. Debates about competition among nations for trade, military superiority, and empire dominated much turn-of-the-twentieth-century political thought. The idea of biological competition became applied to nations and races and produced substantial impact on public opinion and among policymakers. In the selection that follows, Karl Pearson (1857–1936), an English scientist, attempts to connect concepts from evolutionary theory—the struggle for survival and the survival of the fittest—to the development of human societies.

History shows me one way, and one way only, in which a state of civilisation has been produced, namely, the struggle of race with race, and the survival of the physically and mentally fitter race. This dependence of progress on the survival of the fitter race, terribly black as it may seem to some of you, gives the struggle for existence its redeeming features; it is the fiery crucible out of which comes the finer metal. You may hope for a time when the sword shall be turned into the ploughshare, when American and German and English traders shall no longer compete in the markets of the world for raw materials, for their food supply, when the white man and the dark shall share the soil between them, and each till it as he lists. But, believe me, when that day comes mankind will no longer progress; there will be nothing to check the fertility of inferior stock; the relentless law of heredity will not be controlled and guided by natural selection. Man will stagnate. . . . The path of progress is strewn with the wreck of nations; traces are everywhere to be seen of the hecatombs of inferior races, and of victims who found not the narrow way to the greater perfection. Yet these dead peoples are, in very truth, the stepping stones on which mankind has arisen to the higher intellectual and deeper emotional life of today.

Source: From Karl Pearson, *National Life from the Standpoint of Science*, 2nd ed. (Cambridge: Cambridge University Press, 1907), pp. 21, 26–27, 64.

turmoil, the Protestant and Catholic churches continued to draw much popular support and personal religious devotion. Nonetheless, what would in the twentieth century become the overwhelmingly secular character of European society, a development that now largely distinguishes Europe from the United States, had its roots in the changes that commenced in the late nineteenth century.

INTELLECTUAL SKEPTICISM

The intellectual attack on Christianity challenged its historical credibility, its scientific accuracy, and its morality.

History   In 1835, David Friedrich Strauss (1808–1874) published *The Life of Jesus*, in which he questioned whether the Bible provides any genuine historical evidence about Jesus. Strauss argued the story of Jesus is a myth that arose from the particular social and intellectual conditions of first-century Palestine. Other authors also published skeptical examinations of the life of Jesus. During the second half of the century, scholars such as Julius Wellhausen (1844–1918) in Germany, Ernst Renan (1823–1892) in France, and Matthew Arnold (1822–1888) in Great Britain contended that human authors had written and revised the books of the Bible with the problems of Jewish society and politics in mind. This questioning of the historical validity of the Bible caused more literate men and women to lose faith in Christianity than any other single cause.

Science   Science also undermined Christianity and faith in the validity of biblical narratives. The geology of Charles Lyell (1797–1875) suggested the earth is much older than the biblical records contend. By looking to natural causes to explain floods, mountains, and valleys, Lyell removed the miraculous hand of God from the physical development of the earth. Darwin's theory cast doubt on the Creation. His ideas and those of other writers suggested that the moral nature of humankind can be explained without appeal to God. Finally, anthropologists, psychologists, and sociologists proposed that religious sentiments are just one more set of natural phenomena.

Morality   Other intellectuals questioned the morality of Christianity. The morality of the Old Testament God, his cruelty and unpredictability, did not fit well with the tolerant, rational values of liberals. They also wondered about the morality of the New Testament God, who would sacrifice for his own satisfaction the only perfect being ever to walk the earth. Many of the clergy began to wonder if they could preach doctrines they felt to be immoral. From another direction, writers like Friedrich Nietzsche (1844–1900) in Germany portrayed Christianity as a religion that glorified weakness rather than the strength life required. These skeptical currents created a climate in which Christianity lost much of its intellectual respectability.

The secularism of everyday life proved as harmful to the faith as the direct attacks. This situation was especially prevalent in the cities, which were growing faster than the capacity of the churches to meet the challenge. Whole generations of the urban poor grew up with little or no experience of the church as an institution or of Christianity as a religious faith.

CONFLICT BETWEEN CHURCH AND STATE

The secular states of late-nineteenth-century Europe clashed with both the Protestant and the Roman Catholic churches. The primary area of conflict between the state and the churches was education. Previously, most education in Europe had taken place in church schools. The churches feared that future generations would emerge from the new state-financed schools without any religious teaching. From 1870 through the turn of the century, all the major countries debated religious education.

Great Britain   In Great Britain, the Education Act of 1870 provided for state-supported schools run by elected school boards, whereas earlier the government had given small grants to religious schools. The new schools were to be built in areas where the religious denominations did not provide satisfactory education. There was rivalry both between the Anglican church and the state and between the Anglican church and the Nonconformist denominations—that is, those Protestant denominations that were not part of the Church of England. All the churches opposed improvements in education because these increased the costs of church schools. In the Education Act of 1902, the government provided state support for both religious and nonreligious schools but imposed the same educational standards on each.

France   The British conflict was calm compared with that in France, which had a dual system of Catholic and public schools. The conservative French Catholic Church and the Third French Republic loathed each other. Between 1878 and 1886, a series of educational laws sponsored by Jules Ferry (1832–1893) replaced religious instruction in the public schools with civic training. The number of public schools was expanded, and members of religious orders could no longer teach in them. After the Dreyfus affair, the French Catholic Church again paid a price for its reactionary politics. The Radical government of Pierre Waldeck-Rousseau (1846–1904), drawn from pro-Dreyfus groups, suppressed the religious orders. In 1905, the Napoleonic Concordat was terminated, and church and state were separated.

Germany and the _Kulturkampf_   The most extreme and violent church-state conflict occurred in Germany during the 1870s. At unification, the German Catholic hierarchy wanted freedom for the churches guaranteed in the constitution. Bismarck left the matter to the federal states, but he soon felt the Roman Catholic Church and the Catholic Center Party threatened the unity of the German Empire. In 1870 and 1871, he removed the clergy from overseeing local education in Prussia and set education under state direction. This secularization of education represented the beginning of a concerted attack on the Catholic Church in Germany.

The "May Laws" of 1873, which applied to Prussia, but not to the entire German Empire, required priests to be educated in German schools and universities and to pass state examinations. The state could veto the appointments of priests. The legislation abolished the disciplinary power of the pope and the church over the clergy and transferred it to the state. Many of the clergy refused to obey these laws, and by 1876, Bismarck had either arrested or expelled all Catholic bishops from Prussia. In the end, Bismarck's _Kulturkampf_ ("cultural struggle") against the Catholic Church failed. By the end of the 1870s, he abandoned his attack. He had gained state control of education and civil laws governing marriage only at the price of provoking Catholic resentment against the German state.

AREAS OF RELIGIOUS REVIVAL

The German Catholic resistance to the intrusions of the secular state illustrates the continuing vitality of Christianity during this period of intellectual and political hardship for the church. Across Europe, Christianity showed signs of revival and growth. In effect, the last half of the nineteenth century witnessed the final great effort to Christianize Europe. It was well organized, well led, and well financed. It failed only because

Zwischen Berlin und Rom.

The conflict between church and state disrupted German politics during the 1870s. This cartoon shows Bismarck and Pope Pius IX attempting to checkmate each other in a game of chess.

Bildarchiv Preussischer Kulturbesitz

Why did Bismarck see the Catholic Church as a threat to the German state?

Kulturkampf   ("cultural struggle") An extreme church-state conflict waged by Bismarck in Germany during the 1870s in response to a perceived threat to German political unity from the Roman Catholic Church.

QUICK REVIEW
Sites of Conflict

◆ Britain: quality of education provided by schools sponsored by religious institutions

◆ France: increasing hostility between conservative clergy and the state

◆ Germany: Bismarck's _Kulturkampf_

the population of Europe had outstripped the resources of the churches. The vitality of the churches accounts, in part, for the intense hostility of their enemies.

THE ROMAN CATHOLIC CHURCH AND THE MODERN WORLD

The most striking feature of Christian religious revival was the resilience of the papacy. In 1864, Pope Pius IX (r. 1846–1878) issued the *Syllabus of Errors*, which set the Catholic Church squarely against contemporary science, philosophy, and politics. In 1869, the pope summoned the First Vatican Council. The next year, through the political manipulations of the pontiff and against opposition from many bishops, the council promulgated the dogma of **papal infallibility** when speaking officially on matters of faith and morals. No earlier pope had asserted such centralized authority within the church. Pius IX and many other Roman Catholics believed the Catholic Church could sustain itself in the modern world of nation-states with large electorates only by centering the authority of the church in the papacy itself.

papal infallibility   Assertion that the pope's pronouncements on matters of faith and morals could not be questioned.

Pius IX was succeeded by Leo XIII (r. 1878–1903) who tried to be more accommodating to the modern age. Leo's most important pronouncement on public issues was the encyclical *Rerum Novarum* (1891). In that document, he defended private property, religious education, and religious control of the marriage laws, and he condemned socialism and Marxism, but he also declared that employers should treat their employees justly, pay them proper wages, and permit them to organize labor unions. The pope supported laws to protect workers and urged that modern society be organized in corporate groups that would include people from various classes who would cooperate according to Christian principles. On the basis of Leo XIII's pronouncements, democratic Catholic political parties and Catholic trade unions were founded throughout Europe.

His successor Pius X (r. 1903–1914) hoped to resist modern thought and restore traditional devotional life. Between 1903 and 1907, he condemned Catholic modernism, a movement of modern biblical criticism within the church, and in 1910 he required all priests to take an anti-Modernist oath. The struggle between Catholicism and modern thought was resumed.

ISLAM AND LATE-NINETEENTH-CENTURY EUROPEAN THOUGHT

The few European thinkers who wrote about Islam in the late nineteenth century discussed it using the same scientific and naturalistic scholarly methods they applied to Christianity and Judaism. In the works of scholars such as the influential French writer Ernest Renan, Islam was, like Judaism, a manifestation of the ancient Semitic mentality, which had given rise to a powerful monotheistic vision. Renan, and sociologists such as Max Weber, also dismissed Islam as a religion and culture incapable of developing science and closed to new ideas.

The European racial and cultural outlooks that denigrated nonwhite peoples and their civilizations were also directed toward the Arab world. European authors who championed white racial superiority looked to India and the Aryan civilization that was supposed to have risen there and later influenced northern European life as the source of Europe's cultural superiority.

Christian missionaries reinforced these anti-Islamic attitudes. They blamed Islam for Arab economic backwardness, for mistreating women, and for condoning slavery. They founded schools and hospitals, hoping these Christian foundations would eventually lead some Muslims to Christianity. Few Muslims converted, but these institutions did educate young Arabs in Western science and medicine, and many of their students became leaders in the Middle East.

Within the Islamic world, and especially in the decaying Ottoman Empire, as political leaders continued to champion Western scientific education and technology, they confronted a variety of responses from religious thinkers. Some of these thinkers sought to combine modern thought with Islam. For example, the Salafi, or the salafiyya movement, believed there was no inherent contradiction between science and Islam. Other Islamic religious leaders simply rejected the West and modern thought. They included the Mahdist movement in Sudan, the Sanussiya in Libya, and the Wahhabi movement in the Arabian peninsula.

TOWARD A TWENTIETH-CENTURY FRAME OF MIND

The last quarter of the nineteenth century and the first decade of the twentieth century were the crucible of modern Western thought. New concepts challenged the major presuppositions of mid-nineteenth-century science, rationalism, liberalism, and bourgeois morality.

HOW DID developments in art, psychology, and science reflect a profound shift in Western thought?

SCIENCE: THE REVOLUTION IN PHYSICS

The changes in the scientific worldview originated within the scientific community itself. By the late 1870s, discontent existed over the excessive realism of midcentury science. In 1883, Ernst Mach (1838–1916) published *The Science of Mechanics*, in which he urged that scientists consider their concepts descriptive not of the physical world, but of the sensations the scientific observer experiences. In line with Mach, the French scientist Henri Poincaré (1854–1912) urged that the theories of scientists be regarded as hypothetical constructs of the human mind rather than as true descriptions of nature. By World War I, few scientists believed they could portray the "truth" about physical reality. Rather, they saw themselves as recording the observations of instruments and as offering useful hypothetical or symbolic models of nature.

X-Rays and Radiation   Discoveries in the laboratory paralleled the philosophical challenge to nineteenth-century science. In December 1895, Wilhelm Roentgen (1845–1923) published a paper on his discovery of X-rays, a form of energy that penetrated various opaque materials. In 1896, Henri Becquerel (1852–1908) discovered that uranium emitted a similar form of energy. The next year, J. J. Thomson (1856–1940), at Cambridge University, formulated the theory of the electron. The interior world of the atom had become a new area for human exploration. In 1902, Ernest Rutherford (1871–1937) explained the cause of radiation through the disintegration of the atoms of radioactive materials. Shortly thereafter, he speculated on the immense store of energy present in the atom.

Theories of Quantum Energy, Relativity, and Uncertainty   The discovery of radioactivity and discontent with the existing mechanical models led to revolutionary theories in physics. In 1900, Max Planck (1858–1947) pioneered the articulation of the quantum theory of energy, according to which energy is a series of discrete quantities, or packets, rather than a continuous stream. In 1905, Albert Einstein (1879–1955) published his first epoch-making papers on relativity in which he

Marie Curie (1869–1934) and Pierre Curie (1859–1906) were two of the most important figures in the advance of physics and chemistry. Marie was born in Poland but worked in France for most of her life. She is credited with the discovery of radium, for which she was awarded the Nobel Prize in Chemistry in 1911.

The Granger Collection, New York.

How did the Curies contribute to the revolution in physics?

contended that time and space exist not separately, but rather as a combined continuum. Moreover, the measurement of time and space depends on the observer as well as on the entities being measured. In 1927, Werner Heisenberg (1901–1976) set forth his uncertainty principle, according to which the behavior of subatomic particles is a matter of statistical probability rather than of exactly determinable cause and effect. The mathematical complexity of twentieth-century physics meant science would rarely again be successfully popularized. At the same time, science, through research, medicine, and technological change, has affected modern life more significantly than any other intellectual activity.

LITERATURE: REALISM AND NATURALISM

Between 1850 and 1914, the moral certainties of middle-class Europeans changed no less radically than their concepts of the physical universe. The realist movement in literature portrayed the hypocrisy, brutality, and the dullness that underlay bourgeois life. The **realist** and **naturalist** writers brought scientific objectivity and observation to their work. The major figures of late-century realism examined the dreary and unseemly side of life without being certain whether a better life was possible. In good Darwinian fashion, they portrayed human beings as subject to the passions, the materialistic determinism, and the pressures of the environment like any other animals. Most of them, however, also saw society itself as perpetuating evil.

Flaubert and Zola   Critics have often considered Gustave Flaubert's (1821–1880) *Madame Bovary* (1857), with its story of colorless provincial life and a woman's hapless search for love in and outside of marriage, as the first genuinely realistic novel. The work portrayed life without heroism, purpose, or even civility.

The author who turned realism into a movement, however, was Émile Zola (1840–1902). He believed absolute physical and psychological determinism ruled human events in the way it did the physical world. Between 1871 and 1893, Zola published twenty novels exploring subjects normally untouched by writers: alcoholism, prostitution, adultery, labor strife. Nothing in his purview received the light of hope or the aura of romance. Although critics faulted his taste and moralists condemned his subject matter, Zola enjoyed a worldwide following. As noted in Chapter 22, he took a leading role in the defense of Captain Dreyfus.

Ibsen and Shaw   The Norwegian playwright Henrik Ibsen (1828–1906) carried realism into the dramatic presentation of domestic life. He sought to strip away the illusory mask of middle-class morality. His most famous play is *A Doll's House* (1879). Its chief character, Nora, has a narrow-minded husband who cannot tolerate independence of character or thought on her part. Ibsen's works were controversial. He dared to attack sentimentality, the ideal of the female "angel of the house," and the cloak of respectability that hung so insecurely over the middle-class family. One of Ibsen's greatest champions was the Irish writer George Bernard Shaw (1856–1950), who spent most of his life in England. Shaw defended Ibsen's work and made his own realistic onslaught against romanticism and false respectability.

Realist writers believed it their duty to portray reality and the commonplace. By presenting their audiences with unmentionable subjects, they sought to remove the veneer of hypocrisy that had forbidden such discussion. They hoped to destroy illusions and compel the public to face reality. Few of the realist writers who raised these problems posed solutions to them. They often left their readers unable to sustain old values and uncertain about where to find new ones.

---

realists   Authors who tried to describe human behavior with scientific objectivity, rejecting the romantic idealization of nature, poverty, love, and polite society, and portraying the hypocrisy, physical and psychic brutality, and the dullness that underlay bourgeois life.

naturalists   Authors who tried to portray nature and human life without sentimentality.

QUICK REVIEW

Leading Realists

- Gustave Flaubert (1821–1880)
- Émile Zola (1840–1902)
- Henrik Ibsen (1828–1906)
- George Bernard Shaw (1856–1950)

MODERNISM IN LITERATURE

From the 1870s onward throughout Europe, a new multifaceted movement, usually called **modernism**, touched all the arts. Like realism, modernism was critical of middle-class society and morality. Modernism, however, was not deeply concerned with social issues. What drove the modernists was a concern for the aesthetic or the beautiful. Across the spectrum of the arts, modernists tried to break the received forms and to create new forms.

Among the chief proponents of modernism in England were the members of the Bloomsbury Group, including authors Virginia Woolf (1882–1941) and Leonard Woolf (1880–1969), artists Vanessa Bell (1879–1961) and Duncan Grant (1885–1978), the historian and literary critic Lytton Strachey (1880–1932), and the economist John Maynard Keynes (1883–1946). In both personal practice and theory, the Bloomsbury Group rejected what they regarded as the repressive sexual morality of their parents' generation.

On the Continent, one of the major practitioners of modernism in literature was Marcel Proust (1871–1922). In his seven-volume novel *In Search of Time Past* (*À la Recherche du Temps Perdu*), published between 1913 and 1927, he adopted a stream-of-consciousness format that allowed him to explore his memories. In Germany, Thomas Mann (1875–1955), through a long series of novels, the most famous of which were *Buddenbrooks* (1901) and *The Magic Mountain* (1924), explored both the social experience of middle-class Germans and how they dealt with the intellectual heritage of the nineteenth century. In *Ulysses* (1922), James Joyce (1882–1941), who was born in Ireland but spent much of his life on the Continent, transformed not only the novel, but also the structure of the paragraph.

modernism Movement of the 1870s criticizing middle-class society and traditional morality.

THE COMING OF MODERN ART

The last quarter of the nineteenth century witnessed a series of new departures in Western art that transformed painting and later sculpture in a revolutionary manner that has continued to the present day.

Impressionism   Impressionism in European painting arose primarily in Paris. Two major characteristics marked this new style of painting. First, instead of portraying religious, mythological, and historical themes, painters began to depict modern life itself, focusing on the social life and leisure activities of the urban middle and lower-middle classes. Second, many of these artists were fascinated with light, color, and the representation through painting itself of momentary, largely unfocused, visual experience whether of social life or of landscape.

The new paintings of modern life by the impressionists, including Édouard Manet (1837–1883), Claude Monet (1840–1926), Camille Pissaro (1830–1903), Pierre-Auguste Renoir (1841–1919), and Edgar Degas (1834–1917), recorded Parisians attending cafés, dance halls, concerts, picnics, horse races, boating excursions, and beach parties. The backdrop for these works was Paris as it had been reconstructed under Napoleon III (r. 1852–1870) into a city of wide boulevards, parks, and places for middle-class leisure.

The sites included in these paintings allowed people from different classes to mix socially while pursuing a leisure activity. One such meeting place was the Folies-Bergère, a café/concert hall where patrons could enjoy a variety of popular entertainment, including singers, musicians, dancers, gymnasts, and

impressionism Focuses on social life and leisured activities of the urban middle and lower-middle classes, a fascination with light, color, and representation of momentary experience of social life or of landscape.

Édouard Manet (1832–1883), *A Bar at the Folies-Bergère*, 1882

Oil on canvas, 96 X 130 cm. Signed dated. Courtauld gift 1932. Courtauld Institute Gallery, London

What does this painting suggest about the commercialization of late-nineteenth-century life?

A Sunday on La Grande Jatte, 1884, by Georges Seurat implicitly includes social commentary.

Georges Seurat (French 1859-1891), *A Sunday Afternoon on the Island of La Grande Jatte.* 1884–86. Oil on Canvas. 81 3/4 X 121 1/4 in. (207.5 X 308.1 cm). Helen Birch Bartlett Memorial Collection. 1926.224. Reproduction, The Art Institute of Chicago. Photograph © The Art Institute of Chicago. All Rights Reserved.

What comment was Seurat making on the social life of the Parisian middle class?

postimpressionism   Focuses more on form and structure to bring painting of modern life back in touch with earlier artistic traditions.

cubism   Autonomous realm of art with no purpose beyond itself. Includes as many different perspectives, angles, or views of the object as possible.

animal shows. Paris had many such establishments, but the Folies-Bergère was one of the largest and most expensive.

Postimpressionism   By the 1880s, the impressionists had had an enormous impact on contemporary art. Their work was followed by that of younger artists who drew upon their techniques but also attempted often to relate the achievement of impressionism to earlier artistic traditions. Form and structure rather than the effort to record the impression of the moment played a major role in their work. This later group of artists has been described as *postimpressionists*. The chief figures associated with postimpressionism are Georges Seurat, Paul Cezanne, Vincent van Gogh, and Paul Gauguin.

Georges Seurat (1859–1891) was a young French painter who read extensively in contemporary scientific works about light, color, and vision. These studies led him to a technique of painting known as pointillism whereby the artist applied small dots or points of paint to the canvas. Through this laborious process he hoped to decompose colors into their basic units leaving it to the eye of the viewer to mix those dots into the desired color or shade of color. Seurat is counted among the first postimpressionists because he saw himself bringing the new painting of modern life back into touch with earlier artistic traditions.

Seurat's work implicitly included social commentary, as in his 1884 painting *A Sunday on La Grande Jatte*, situated on the Grande Jatte, an island in the Seine where Parisians would gather on Sundays. A boatman indicates a brooding working-class presence amid the largely middle-class figures, all of whom resemble mechanical mannequins who stand bored and perhaps puzzled by their situation of comfort, leisure, and ease.

In reaction to the impressionists' fascination with light, Paul Cezanne (1839–1906), working largely in isolation, attempted to bring form and solidity back into his paintings of still life and of the landscape of Provence. Displaying a new sensitivity to non-Western peoples and their art, Paul Gauguin (1848–1903) produced works portraying peoples living in the South Pacific. Other artists collected African masks or studied such objects in the anthropological museum in Paris. The art of Africa and of the Pacific gave artists examples of remarkable works that had no relationship to the long-standing Western artistic tradition.

Cubism   The single most important new departure in early-twentieth-century Western art was *cubism*, a term first coined to describe the paintings of Pablo Picasso (1881–1973) and Georges Braque (1882–1963).

Beginning in 1907, Picasso and Braque rejected the idea of a painting as constituting a window onto the real world. Rather, they saw painting as an autonomous realm of art itself with no purpose beyond itself. Echoing the art of ancient Egypt, medieval primitives, and Africa, Picasso and Braque represented only two dimensions in their painting. They attempted to include at one time on a single surface as many different perspectives, angles, or views of the object painted as possible. "Reality" was the construction of their experience of multiple perceptions.

Braque's still life *Violin and Palette* (1909 and 1910) represents the cubist determination to present "a new, completely non-illusionistic and non-imitative method of depicting the visual world." Various shapes seem to flow into other shapes. Portions of the violin and of the palette are recognizable, but as shapes, not as objects in and of themselves. The violin appears at one moment from a host of perspectives, but the violin has interest only in its relationship to the other shapes of color in the painting. Throughout the painting Braque is literally taking apart the violin and other objects, so that he and the viewer can analyze them. The elements of the palette, the violin, and the notes of a musical score floating on folded paper tents hold interest and meaning in this painting only because they are in the painting, not because they are imitations of a violin, a palette, or a musical score.

FRIEDRICH NIETZSCHE AND THE REVOLT AGAINST REASON

During the second half of the century, philosophers began to question the adequacy of rational thinking to address the human situation. No writer better exemplified this new attitude than the German philosopher Friedrich Nietzsche (1844–1900). He was wholly at odds with the values of the age and attacked Christianity, democracy, nationalism, rationality, science, and progress. He sought less to change values than to probe their sources in the human character. He wanted not only to tear away the masks of respectable life, but also to explore how human beings made such masks.

His first important work was *The Birth of Tragedy* (1872) in which he urged that the nonrational aspects of human nature are as important and noble as the rational characteristics. He insisted on the positive function of instinct and ecstasy in human life. In Nietzsche's view, the strength for the heroic life and the highest artistic achievement arises from sources beyond rationality.

In later works, such as the prose poem *Thus Spake Zarathustra* (1883), Nietzsche criticized democracy and Christianity. Both would lead only to the mediocrity of sheepish masses. He announced the death of God and proclaimed the coming of the *Overman* (Übermensch), who would embody heroism and greatness. The term was frequently interpreted as some mode of superman or super race, but such was not Nietzsche's intention. He sought a return to the heroism that he associated with Greek life in the Homeric age.

Two of Nietzsche's most profound works are *Beyond Good and Evil* (1886) and *The Genealogy of Morals* (1887). Nietzsche sought to discover not what is good and what is evil, but the social and psychological sources of the judgment of good and evil. In Nietzsche's view, morality was a human convention that had no independent existence. Christianity, utilitarianism, and middle-class respectability could, in good conscience, be abandoned. Human beings could create a new moral order that would glorify pride, assertiveness, and strength rather than meekness, humility, and weakness.

In his appeal to feelings and emotions and in his questioning of the adequacy of rationalism, Nietzsche drew on the romantic tradition. The kind of creative impulse that earlier romantics had considered the gift of artists Nietzsche saw as the burden of all human beings. The character of the human situation that this philosophy urged on its contemporaries was that of an ever-changing flux in which nothing but change itself was permanent. Human beings had to forge from their own will and determination the values that were to exist in the world.

THE BIRTH OF PSYCHOANALYSIS

A determination to probe beneath the surface or public appearance united the major figures of late-nineteenth-century science, art, and philosophy. As a result of their theories and discoveries, educated Europeans could never again view the surface of life with complacency or even with much confidence. No intellectual development more exemplified this trend than psychoanalysis through the work of Sigmund Freud (1856–1939).

Georges Braque, *Violin and Palette* (*Violon et Palette*), 1909–1910, is representative of the autonomous realm of art itself.

What were the goals of the cubist painters?

Development of Freud's Early Theories   Freud was born into an Austrian Jewish family that settled in Vienna. In 1886, he opened his medical practice in Vienna, where he lived until the Nazis drove him out in 1938. Freud conducted all his research and writing from the base of his medical practice. His earliest medical interests had been psychic disorders, to which he sought to apply the critical method of science. In late 1885, he studied in Paris with Jean-Martin Charcot (1825–1893), who used hypnosis to treat hysteria.

In the mid-1890s, Freud abandoned hypnosis and allowed his patients to talk freely and spontaneously about themselves. He found that they associated their particular neurotic symptoms with experiences related to earlier experiences, going back to childhood. He also noted that sexual matters were significant in his patients' problems. By 1897, Freud had formulated a theory of infantile sexuality, according to which sexual drives and energy already exist in infants and do not simply emerge at puberty. For Freud, human beings are sexual creatures from birth through adulthood. He also portrayed the little acknowledged matter of sexuality as one of the bases of mental order and disorder.

Freud's Concern with Dreams   During the same decade, Freud also examined the psychic phenomena of dreams. Freud believed the seemingly irrational content of dreams must have a reasonable, scientific explanation. His research led him to reconsider the general nature of the human mind. He concluded that dreams allow unconscious wishes, desires, and drives that had been excluded from everyday conscious life to enjoy freer play in the mind. During the waking hours, the mind represses or censors certain wishes, which are as important to the individual's psychological makeup as conscious thought is. In fact, Freud argued, unconscious drives and desires contribute to conscious behavior. Freud developed these concepts and related them to his idea of infantile sexuality in his most important book *The Interpretation of Dreams*, published in 1900.

Freud's Later Thought   In later books and essays, Freud developed a new model of the internal organization of the mind as an arena of struggle and conflict among three entities: the id, the superego, and the ego. The **id** consists of amoral, irrational, driving instincts for sexual gratification, aggression, and general physical and sensual pleasure. The **superego** embodies the external moral imperatives and expectations imposed on the personality by society and culture. The **ego** mediates between the impulses of the id and the asceticism of the superego and allows the personality to cope with the inner and outer demands of its existence. Consequently, everyday behavior displays the activity of the personality as its inner drives are partially repressed through the ego's coping with external moral expectations, as interpreted by the superego.

It has been a grave misreading of Freud to see him as urging humankind to thrust off all repression. He did indeed believe that excessive repression could lead to a mental disorder, but he also believed civilization and the survival of humankind required some repression of sexuality and aggression. Freud thought the sacrifice and struggle were worthwhile, but he understood the immense sacrifice of instinctual drives required for rational civilized behavior and was pessimistic about the future of civilization in the West.

Divisions in the Psychoanalytic Movement   By 1910, Freud had gathered around him a small, but able, group of disciples. Several of his early followers soon moved toward theories of which the master disapproved. The most important of these dissenters was Carl Jung (1875–1961). Jung questioned the primacy of sexual drives in forming personality and in contributing to mental disorder. He also put less faith in reason.

id   Among Freud's three entities of the mind, the *id* consists of innate, amoral, irrational drives for sexual gratification, aggression, and sensual pleasure.

superego   Among Freud's three entities of the mind, the *superego* internalizes the moral imperatives that society and culture impose on the personality.

ego   Among Freud's three entities of the mind, the *ego* mediates between the impulsive id and the self-denying superego.

Jung believed the human subconscious contains inherited memories from previous generations. These collective memories, as well as the personal experience of an individual, constitute his or her soul. Jung regarded human beings in the twentieth century as alienated from these useful collective memories. In *Modern Man in Search of a Soul* (1933) and other works, Jung tended toward mysticism and saw positive values in religion. Freud was highly critical of most of Jung's work. If Freud's thought derived primarily from the Enlightenment, Jung's was more dependent on romanticism.

RETREAT FROM RATIONALISM IN POLITICS

Nineteenth-century liberals and socialists agreed that rational analysis could discern the problems of society and prepare solutions. These thinkers felt that, once given the vote, individuals would behave according to their rational political self-interest. Education would improve the human condition. By 1900, these views had come under attack. Political scientists and sociologists painted politics as frequently irrational. Racial theorists questioned whether rationality and education could affect human society at all.

In 1909 Freud and his then-devoted disciple Carl Jung visited Clark University in Worcester, Massachusetts, during Freud's only trip to the United States. Here Freud sits on the right holding a cane; Jung is sitting on the far left.

Archives of the History of American Psychology—The University of Akron. Courtesy Clark University, Special Collections

How did Freud see the relationship between the individual and civilization?

Weber During this period, however, one major social theorist was impressed by the role of reason in human society. The German sociologist Max Weber (1864–1920) regarded the emergence of rationalism throughout society as the major development of human history. Such rationalization displayed itself in the rise of both scientific knowledge and bureaucratic organization.

Weber saw bureaucratization as the basic feature of modern social life. He used this view to oppose Marx's concept of the development of capitalism as the driving force in modern society. Bureaucratization involved the division of labor as each individual fit into a particular role in much larger organizations. Furthermore, Weber believed that in modern society people derive their own self-images and sense of personal worth from their positions in these organizations. Weber also contended—again, in contrast to Marx—that noneconomic factors might account for major developments in human history. For example, in his best known essay *The Protestant Ethic and the Spirit of Capitalism* (1905), Weber traced much of the rational character of capitalist enterprise to the ascetic religious doctrines of Puritanism.

Theorists of Collective Behavior In his emphasis on the individual and on the dominant role of rationality, Weber differed from many contemporary social scientists, such as Gustave LeBon (1841–1931), Emile Durkheim (1858–1917), and Georges Sorel (1847–1922) in France, Vilfredo Pareto (1848–1923) in Italy, and Graham Wallas (1858–1932) in England. LeBon was a psychologist who explored the activity of crowds and mobs. He believed that crowds behave irrationally. In *Reflections on Violence* (1908), Sorel argued that people do not pursue rationally perceived goals but are led to action by collectively shared ideals. Durkheim and Wallas became deeply interested in the necessity of shared values and activities in a society. Besides playing down the function of reason in society, all these theorists emphasized the role of collective groups in politics rather than that of the individual, formerly championed by liberals.

racism   Belief that some peoples are innately superior to others.

RACISM

The same tendencies to question or even to deny the constructive activity of reason in human affairs and to sacrifice the individual to the group manifested themselves in theories of race. **Racism** had long existed in Europe. What transformed racial thinking at the end of the century was its association with the biological sciences. The prestige associated with biology and science in general became transferred to racial thinking, whose advocates now claimed to possess a materialistic, scientific basis for their thought.

Gobineau   Count Arthur de Gobineau (1816–1882), a reactionary French diplomat, enunciated the first important theory of race as the major determinant of human history. In his four-volume *Essay on the Inequality of the Human Races* (1853–1854), Gobineau claimed the white Aryan race had unwisely intermarried with the inferior yellow and black races, thus diluting the greatness and ability that originally existed in its blood. Gobineau saw no way to reverse this degeneration.

Chamberlain   At the close of the century, Houston Stewart Chamberlain (1855–1927), an Englishman who settled in Germany, championed the concept of biological determinism through race but believed that through genetics the human race could be improved and even that a superior race could be developed. Chamberlain was anti-Semitic. He pointed to the Jews as the major enemy of European racial regeneration.

Late-Century Nationalism   Racial thinking was one part of a wider late-century movement toward more aggressive nationalism. Previously, nationalism had in general been a movement among European literary figures and liberals. From the 1870s onward, however, nationalism became a movement with mass support, well-financed organizations, and political parties. Nationalists often redefined nationality in terms of race and blood. The new nationalism opposed the internationalism of both liberalism and socialism. The ideal of nationality was used to overcome the pluralism of class, religion, and geography. The nation replaced religion for many secularized people. It sometimes became a secular religion in the hands of state schoolteachers, who were replacing the clergy as the instructors of youth. Nationalism of this aggressive, racist variety became the most powerful ideology of the early twentieth century and would reemerge after the collapse of communism in the 1990s.

Some Europeans also used racial theory to support harsh, condescending treatment of colonial peoples in the late nineteenth and early twentieth centuries. They were convinced that white Europeans were racially superior to the peoples of color whom they governed and that these peoples would always be inferior to them. Similar racial theory also informed attitudes toward peoples of color in the West itself as was the case with the inferiority ascribed to African Americans and Native Americans in the United States.

ANTI-SEMITISM AND THE BIRTH OF ZIONISM

Political and racial anti-Semitism, which cast such dark shadows across the twentieth century, developed, in part, from the prevailing atmosphere of racial thought and the retreat from rationality in politics. Since the French Revolution, West European Jews had gradually gained entry into civil life. Popular anti-Semitism, however, survived, with the Jewish community being identified with money and banking interests. During the last third of the century, as finance capitalism changed the economic structure of Europe, many non-Jewish Europeans threatened by the changes became hostile toward the Jewish community.

Anti-Semitic Politics   In Vienna, Mayor Karl Lueger (1844–1910) used anti-Semitism as a major attraction for his Christian Socialist Party. In Germany, the ultraconservative Lutheran chaplain Adolf Stoecker (1835–1909) revived anti-Semitism. The Dreyfus affair in France focused a new hatred toward the Jews.

To this ugly atmosphere, racial thought contributed the belief that no matter to what extent Jews assimilated themselves into the culture of their country, their Jewishness—and thus their alleged danger to society—would remain. For racial thinkers, the problem of race was not in the character, but in the blood of the Jew. An important Jewish response to this new, rabid outbreak of anti-Semitism was the launching in 1896 of the **Zionism** movement to found a separate Jewish state. Its founder was the Austro-Hungarian Theodor Herzl (1860–1904).

Herzl's Response   Herzl was convinced that liberal politics and the institutions of the liberal state could not protect the Jews in Europe or ensure that they would be treated justly. In 1896, Herzl published *The Jewish State*, in which he called for a separate state in which all Jews might be assured of those rights and liberties that they should be enjoying in the liberal states of Europe. Furthermore, Herzl followed the tactics of late-century mass democratic politics by directing his appeal particularly to the poor Jews who lived in the ghettos of Eastern Europe and the slums of Western Europe. The original call to Zionism thus combined a rejection of the anti-Semitism of Europe and a desire to realize some of the ideals of both liberalism and socialism in a state outside Europe.

Zionism   Movement based on the theory that if Jews were unacceptable as citizens of European nations, their only safety lay in establishing a nation of their own.

WOMEN AND MODERN THOUGHT

The ideas that so shook Europe from the publication of *The Origin of Species* through the opening of World War I produced, at best, mixed results for women. Within the often radically new ways of thinking about the world, views of women and their roles in society often remained remarkably unchanged.

HOW DID women challenge gender stereotypes in the late nineteenth and early twentieth centuries?

ANTIFEMINISM IN LATE-CENTURY THOUGHT

The influence of biology on the thinking of intellectuals during the late nineteenth century and their own interest in the nonrational side of human behavior led many of them to sustain what had become stereotyped views of women. The emphasis on biology, evolution, and reproduction led intellectuals to concentrate on women's mothering role. Their interest in the nonrational led them to reassert the traditional view that feeling and the nurturing instinct are basic to women's nature. Many late-century thinkers and writers of fiction also often displayed fear and hostility toward women, portraying them as creatures susceptible to overwhelming and often destructive feelings and instincts. A genuinely misogynist strain emerged in late-century fiction and painting.

This conservative and hostile perception of women manifested itself in several ways within the scientific community. In London in 1860, the Ethnological Society excluded women from its discussions on the grounds that the subject matter of the customs of primitive peoples was unfit for women and that women were amateurs whose presence would lower the level of the discussion. T. H. Huxley, in public lectures, claimed to have found scientific evidence of the inferiority of women to men. Karl Vogt (1817–1895), a leading German anthropologist, held similar views about the character of women. Darwin would repeat the ideas of both Huxley and Vogt in his *Descent of Man*. Late-Victorian anthropologists tended likewise to assign women, as well as nonwhite races, an inferior place in the human family.

The position of women in Freud's thought is controversial. Critics have claimed that Freud portrayed women as incomplete human beings who might be inevitably destined to unhappy mental lives. He saw the natural destiny of women as motherhood and the rearing of sons as their greatest fulfillment. The first psychoanalysts were trained as medical doctors, and their views of women reflected contemporary medical education, which, like much of the scientific establishment, tended to portray women as inferior. Distinguished women psychoanalysts, such as Karen Horney (1885–1952) and Melanie Klein (1882–1960), would later challenge Freud's views on women, and other writers would try to establish a psychoanalytic basis for feminism. Nonetheless, the psychoanalytic profession would remain dominated by men, as would academic psychology.

The social sciences of the late nineteenth and early twentieth centuries similarly reinforced traditional gender roles. Most major theorists believed that women's role in reproduction and child rearing demanded a social position inferior to men. Virtually all the early sociologists took a conservative view of marriage, the family, child rearing, and divorce.

NEW DIRECTIONS IN FEMINISM

The close of the century witnessed a revival of feminist thought in Europe that would grow in the twentieth century. Many women's organizations, as seen in Chapter 23, concentrated on achieving the vote for women, but feminist writers and activists raised other questions as well.

Sexual Morality and the Family   In various nations, middle-class women began to challenge the double standard of sexual morality and the traditional male-dominated family. This often meant challenging laws about prostitution.

Between 1864 and 1886, English prostitutes were subject to the Contagious Diseases Acts. The police in certain cities with naval or military bases could require any woman identified as, or suspected of being, a prostitute to undergo an immediate internal medical examination for venereal disease. Those found to have a disease could be confined for months to locked hospitals (women's hospitals for the treatment of venereal diseases) without legal recourse. The law took no action against their male customers.

These laws angered English middle-class women who believed the harsh working conditions and the poverty imposed on so many working-class women were the true causes of prostitution. They framed the issue in the context of their own efforts to prove that women are as human and rational as men and thus properly subject to equal treatment. The Contagious Diseases Acts assumed that women were inferior to men and treated them as less than rational human beings. The laws literally put women's bodies under the control of male customers, male physicians, and male law-enforcement personnel. They denied to poor women the freedoms that all men enjoyed in English society. By 1869, the Ladies' National Association for the Repeal of the Contagious Diseases Acts, a distinctly middle-class organization led by Josephine Butler (1828–1906), began actively to oppose those laws. The group achieved the suspension of the acts in 1883 and their repeal in 1886. Government and police regulation of prostitution roused similar movements in other nations, which adopted the English movement as a model.

The feminist groups that demanded the abolition of laws that punished prostitutes without questioning the behavior of their customers were challenging the double standard and, by extension, the traditional relationship of men and women in marriage. In their view, marriage should be a free union of equals with men and women sharing responsibility for their children. In Germany, the Mothers' Protection League (*Bund für Mutterschutz*) contended that both married and unmarried mothers required the help of the state, including leaves for pregnancy and child care. This radical group emphasized the need to rethink all sexual morality. In Sweden, Ellen Key (1849–1926), in *The Century of the Child* (1900) and *The Renaissance of Motherhood* (1914), maintained that motherhood is so crucial to society that the government, rather than husbands, should support mothers and their children.

Virtually all turn-of-the-century feminists in one way or another supported wider sexual freedom for women, often claiming it would benefit society as well as improve women's lives. Many of the early advocates of contraception had also been influenced by social Darwinism. They hoped that limiting the number of children would allow more healthy and intelligent children to survive.

Women Defining Their Own Lives   For many continental feminists, achieving legal and social equality for women would be one step toward transforming Europe from a male-dominated society to one in which both men and women could control their own destinies. Increasingly, feminists would concentrate on freeing and developing women's personalities through better education and government financial support for women engaged in traditional social roles, whether or not they had gained the vote.

Some women also became active within socialist circles. There they argued that the socialist transformation of society should include major reforms for women. Socialist parties usually had all-male leadership. By the close of the century, most male socialist leaders, including Lenin and later Stalin, were intolerant of demands for changes in the family or greater sexual freedom for either men or women. Nonetheless, socialist writings began to include calls for improvements in the economic situation of women that were compatible with more advanced feminist ideals.

It was within literary circles, however, that feminist writers often most clearly articulated the problems that they now understood themselves to face. Virginia Woolf's *A Room of One's Own* (1929) became one of the fundamental texts of twentieth-century feminist literature. In it, she meditated first on the difficulties that women of both brilliance and social standing encountered in being taken seriously as writers and intellectuals. She concluded that a woman who wishes to write requires both a room of her own, meaning a space not dominated by male institutions, and an adequate independent income. Woolf was concerned with more than asserting the right of women to participate in intellectual life, however. Establishing a new stance for feminist writers, she asked whether women, as writers, must imitate men or whether they should bring to their endeavors the separate intellectual and psychological qualities they possessed as women. As she had challenged some of the literary conventions of the traditional novel in her fiction, she challenged some of the accepted notions of feminist thought in *A Room of One's Own* and concluded that male and female writers must actually be able to think as both men and women and share the sensibilities of each. In this sense, she sought to open the whole question of gender definition.

By World War I, feminism in Europe, fairly or not, had become associated in the popular imagination with challenges to traditional gender roles and sexual morality and with either socialism or political radicalism. So when extremely conservative political movements arose between the world wars, their leaders often emphasized traditional roles for women and traditional ideas about sexual morality. (See Chapter 27.)

Virginia Woolf, a member of the Bloomsbury Group whose members were the chief proponents of modernism in England.

Hulton Archive Photos/Getty Images, Inc.

What were the goals of the modernist writers?

SUMMARY

WHAT EFFECT did state-financed education have on literacy in late-nineteenth-century Europe?

The New Reading Public Governments started funding education in the late 1860s. Liberals and conservatives shared the Enlightenment belief that new voters needed more information to exercise their rights properly and thus maintain the political order. By 1900, 85 percent or more of the population of Britain, France, Belgium, the Netherlands, Germany, and Scandinavia could read. (Literacy rates in Italy, Spain, Russia, Austria-Hungary, and the Balkans were about 40 to 70 percent.) This created a mass reading public. New reading material proliferated. Much of it was of low quality, but the sheer numbers of readers allowed an unprecedented popularization of knowledge. *page 596*

WHAT ROLE did science play in the second half of the nineteenth century?

Science at Midcentury In the mid–nineteenth century, many considered science the model for all forms of human understanding. Educated people believed the physical world was rational, mechanical, and predictable and that science described nature as it really was. Comte developed positivism. Sociology is based on his belief that positive knowledge, the kind obtained by physical science, is possible in other areas, including social behavior. Darwin proposed natural selection as the mechanism for evolution. Darwin explained humans as products of the struggle for survival. Philosophers and economists also applied the idea of survival of the fittest to their fields. Spencer wrote of competition as an ethical imperative. Huxley countered that evolution determines only physical development, not moral behavior. *page 597*

WHAT CHALLENGES did European Christianity face in the late nineteenth century?

Christianity and the Church under Siege Protestant and Catholic churches remained popular, despite urban growth that outstripped their capacity, attacks on church influence by the secular nation-state, and a rejection of faith by many European intellectuals. Nineteenth-century historical scholarship challenged the validity of the Bible. Science and moral reasoning also posed challenges to Christian faith. The secular state and the church clashed over many issues, particularly education. In Great Britain, France, and Germany, the government limited religious roles in education. But Christian churches were still strong enough to fight back. Different popes had different ideas about the Catholic Church's best response to modernism, but all aggressively engaged it. The small group of scholars of Islam in Europe applied scientific and naturalistic forms of inquiry to the Islamic faith and the Qur'an. In the Ottoman Empire, political leaders called for Westernized scientific education and technology, but religious leaders had more varied responses to Western ideas. *page 599*

HOW DID developments in art, psychology, and science reflect a profound shift in Western thought?

Toward a Twentieth-Century Frame of Mind At the turn of the century, new ideas of physical reality, human nature, and society challenged the beliefs of earlier science, rationalism, liberalism, and bourgeois morality. New scientific discoveries pointed to the inadequacy of the mechanistic models of the physical world. Einstein's theories of relativity and Heisenberg's uncertainty principle opened the doors to new ways of understanding the material world. Middle-class morality was also thrown into disarray; realist and naturalist authors adopted objective, "scientific" stances. Modernism was critical of bourgeois morality but endorsed an aesthetic ideal of beauty and experimentation with form. In literature and art, modernism was interested in artistic experience for its own sake. Freud's psychoanalysis explored areas of the human mind that had not yet been imagined. He used romanticism and Enlightenment rationality. Weber built a model of social behavior that emphasized noneconomic factors in social development. Racism was used to explain the history and characteristics of large groups. Racial thinking and biological determinism linked with anti-Semitism and aggressive nationalism in a poisonous strand of political theory. The Zionist movement was an important Jewish response to anti-Semitism. *page 605*

HOW DID women challenge gender streotypes in the late nineteenth and early twentieth centuries?

Women and Modern Thought Women's social roles remained largely static. A distinct strain of misogyny became evident in fiction and painting at the end of the nineteenth century. The scientific community, too, held a conservative and hostile view of women. Racial thinking often placed women on a lower plane than men of the same race. Biological thinking led social scientists to reinforce so-called traditional roles for women. Feminist groups worked to gain voting rights for women. They also questioned the double standard of sexual morality and the male domination of the family. Often they approached these issues through challenges to prostitution laws, which punished female prostitutes but not their customers. Some advocated contraception. Others argued that women should be free to develop their personalities; still others joined socialist movements and worked to incorporate a change for the role of women into the socialist agenda. Virginia Woolf articulated a vision of men and women both becoming aware of the full range of identities within each individual. *page 613*

REVIEW QUESTIONS

1. What were some of the major changes in scientific outlook that occurred between 1850 and 1914? What advances took place in physics? What was the theory of natural selection proposed by Darwin and Wallace? Why did Christianity come under attack in the late nineteenth century? What form did the attack take?

2. How were changes in society reflected in the literature of the late nineteenth century? What was the significance of the explosion of literacy and literary material? What was literary *realism*? How did literary *modernism* differ from realism?

3. How did Nietzsche and Freud challenge traditional middle-class and religious morality? How do you account for the fear and hostility many late-nineteenth-century intellectuals displayed toward women? What were some of the social and political issues that especially affected women in the late nineteenth and early twentieth centuries? What new directions did feminism take?

4. What forms did racism take in the late nineteenth century? How did it become associated with anti-Semitism? What was Zionism? Why did Herzl develop it?

KEY TERMS

cubism (p. 608)
ego (p. 610)
id (p. 610)
Impressionism (p. 607)
Kulturkampf (p. 603)
modernism (p. 607)
naturalists (p. 606)
natural selection (p. 599)

papal infallibility (p. 604)
positivism (p. 597)
postimpressionism (p. 608)
racism (p. 612)
realists (p. 606)
social Darwinism (p. 599)
superego (p. 610)
Zionism (p. 613)

For additional learning resources related to this chapter, please go to **www.myhistorylab.com**

myhistorylab

25

The Age of Western Imperialism

The British Dominions Beyond the Seas:
Natives of the Greatest Empire the World
has ever Known.

SPECIALLY PAINTED FOR "THE ILLUSTRATED LONDON NEWS"

(For Details, see the Key on the Opposite Page and the Appendix.)

The global British Empire dominated the nineteenth-century European imperial experience. The empire was popularized in newspapers, books, and novels, as well as in thousands of illustrations and photographs. This illustration seeks to portray the worldwide reach of the British Empire and the varied peoples whom it governed abroad and, at the same time, as seen in the caption, how Great Britain sought to build domestic pride in the imperial achievement. Similar illustrations could be found portraying the empires of France, German, the Netherlands, Belgium, and Russia.

"Citizens of the British Empire, the Greatest Empire the world has ever known . . ." 1911, London Illustrated News. © Mary Evans Picture Library

What relationship did white Britons see between themselves and the peoples of the empire?

New Imperialism The extension in the late nineteenth and early twentieth centuries of Western political and economic dominance to Asia, the Middle East, and Africa.

The half-century between the opening of the American Revolution and the end of the Latin American Wars of Independence (1775–1830) marked the end of the early modern era of European interaction with the wider world that had begun in the late fifteenth century. The second and third quarters of the nineteenth century witnessed the high age of the British Empire. During that time other European nations had fewer interests in the non-Western world. For a variety of reasons, this situation began to change in the 1870s, however, with the dawn of the period historians call the **New Imperialism**. For the next half-century, until the outbreak of World War I in 1914, European powers brought much of the world under their dominance and direct control. During this period the United States and Japan also first appeared as major players on the world stage. ■

THE CLOSE OF THE AGE OF EARLY MODERN COLONIZATION

HOW DID early modern colonization differ from nineteenth-century Western imperialism?

The era of early modern European expansion that lasted from the late fifteenth to the late eighteenth centuries had witnessed the encounter, conquest, settlement, and exploitation of the American continents by the Spanish, Portuguese, French, and English, the establishment of modest trading posts by European countries in Africa and Asia, Dutch dominance in the East Indies (modern Indonesia), and British domination of India.

Early European colonial rivalry had occurred primarily within the transatlantic world. By the early eighteenth century, the following patterns of European domination prevailed in the Americas. The Spanish Empire extended from California and Texas to Argentina. The Spanish also claimed Florida. Portugal controlled Brazil. The Dutch, French, Spanish, and British exploited the rich sugar islands of the Caribbean. France loosely controlled the Saint Lawrence and Mississippi River Valleys and the upper Atlantic coast. The British had settled the Atlantic coast from Maine to Georgia.

Between the mid–eighteenth and the early nineteenth centuries, a vast political transformation occurred in these regions. The French lost their North American empire to the British. The American Revolution drove the British from their Atlantic coastal colonies, which became the United States. But thousands of American loyalists fled to Canada, which developed a closer relationship with Britain. Warfare shifted the ownership of the Caribbean islands from one country to another with Haiti by 1804 establishing its independence from France. (See Chapter 20.) In 1803, Napoleon sold the vast Louisiana Territory to the United States. In the 1820s Latin America shook off Spanish and Portuguese control. Except for Canada, the Caribbean islands, and a few toeholds on the coasts of Central and South America, European rule in the Americas had ended. The Monroe Doctrine, which the United States announced in 1823 and the British navy enforced, closed the Americas to European colonialism. The most striking result of these events was the collapse of Spain, Portugal, and France as significant colonial powers.

 In contrast to early modern European empires, slavery was absent from those of the nineteenth century. In 1807 Britain had banned the slave trade and had abolished slavery itself in its own colonies in 1833–1834. Thereafter, the British navy worked to close down the slave trade of other nations. Consequently, although economic inequality and forced labor were common in the European empires of the late nineteenth century, the institution of slavery, which had been the chief characteristic of the earlier imperial transatlantic plantation economies, had disappeared.

Roman Catholicism had been the driving religious influence among the early modern transatlantic empires. Almost from the moment Europeans first reached the Americas in the 1490s, Catholic priests, friars, and nuns had worked relentlessly to convert the indigenous peoples of the Caribbean, Latin America, and French Canada. These regions remain overwhelming Catholic. The largely Protestant settlers of the British colonies had been religiously zealous, but their missionary impulse was less strong, and there were fewer indigenous people along the Atlantic seaboard for them to convert. By contrast, during the nineteenth century, evangelical Protestants from Britain and the societies that backed them set the pace for missionary enterprises that other Western nations imitated, including those that sponsored Roman Catholic missions.

THE AGE OF BRITISH IMPERIAL DOMINANCE

During the first half of the nineteenth century, no one doubted that Great Britain was the single power that could exert its influence virtually around the world. However, until the 1860s and 1870s, except in India and western Canada, Britain did not seek additional territory. Rather, it extended its influence through what historians call the **Imperialism of Free Trade**.

HOW DID Britain use its economic might to extend its influence around the world?

THE IMPERIALISM OF FREE TRADE

Nineteenth-century British imperial economic ideas differed sharply from the mercantilist doctrines that had dominated previous centuries. Mercantile economic doctrine had asserted that a nation measured its wealth in terms of the amount of gold and silver it amassed and that the amount of trade was finite: If one nation's trade increased, another nation's trade had to decrease. But in the 1770s, economic thinkers such as Adam Smith (see Chapter 17) argued that empires would best prosper by abandoning closed imperial systems in favor of free trade, that is, by fostering the exchange of goods across borders and oceans with minimal government regulation and tariff barriers. Free traders argued that this would allow trade to grow upon itself—that the amount of trade was potentially infinite—and would assure consumers the lowest prices.

As a result of the productive energies that the Industrial Revolution of the late eighteenth and early nineteenth centuries unleashed, Britain became "the workshop of the world." It could and did produce more manufactured goods than its population could absorb on its own. Britain was also able to produce those goods, especially consumer goods such as textiles, more cheaply than anyone else. To dominate a foreign market, British merchants needed only the ability to trade without government interference in the form of tariffs, subsidies, or price controls. Until at least the 1870s, free trade alone allowed Britain to dominate economically one region of the world after another without the need to establish a formal colonial administration.

Free trade could and did lead to warfare. The most important example of this concerned the opium trade between British merchants operating out of India and their potential Chinese customers. Europeans and Americans wanted to import Chinese goods, especially tea, silk, and porcelain, in large quantities. With the Chinese uninterested in buying Western manufactured goods, British merchants looked for another product to sell to the Chinese market. They found it in the opium produced in India. The Chinese government resisted the import of opium to prevent addiction among its people.

Between 1839 and 1842 and again between 1856 and 1860, the British went to war to impose a free trade in opium on China. At the conclusion of the first of these Opium Wars, the British gained control of Hong Kong, and forced the Chinese to allow Christian missionaries to operate in China, to open various ports to

Imperialism of Free Trade The advance of European economic and political interests in the nineteenth century by demanding that non-European nations allow European nations, most particularly Great Britain, to introduce their manufactured goods freely into all nations or to introduce other goods, such as opium into China, that allowed those nations to establish economic influence and to determine the terms of trade.

Armed Chinese junks were no match for British warships during the first Opium War. The war ended in 1842 with the Treaty of Nanjing.

Picture Desk, Inc./Kobal Collection

Why were the British so determined to import opium into China?

British merchants who remained subject to British rather than Chinese law, and to pay substantial reparations. During the Second Opium War, Britain in alliance with France forced the Chinese to allow foreign envoys to establish embassies in Beijing, to open more ports and areas to foreign trade, and to permit Christian missionaries to operate even more freely in China.

BRITISH SETTLER COLONIES

During the early nineteenth century, Britain oversaw the settlement and economic development of three regions that had come under its domination in the eighteenth century: Canada, Australia, and New Zealand. The settlement of these lands, which attracted millions of immigrants from Britain and other European nations, resembled the westward movement in the United States during the same period, including conflicts with native peoples.

The British assumed that eventually these regions would have some form of self-government and be a market for British goods. And in fact during the nineteenth century, each of these colonies did establish responsible self-government based on British law and political institutions. The British system of self-government based on an increasingly inclusive franchise was thus transferred to large parts of the world.

INDIA—THE JEWEL IN THE CROWN OF THE BRITISH EMPIRE

WHY WAS India such an important part of the British empire?

Except for Canada, nineteenth-century British colonial interest shifted from the Atlantic world to Asia and the Indian and Pacific Oceans. During the same years that Britain had lost its North American colonies (1775–1783), it had established itself as the ruler of India. The protection of the commercial and military routes to India would be the chief concern of British imperial strategy during the nineteenth century.

In theory until 1857, India was still ruled by the Mughal Empire, which had governed the region since the 1500s. But that empire was only a shadow of its former self. Local rulers, called nawabs or maharajahs, paid little attention to the Mughal emperor who still resided in Delhi, the old imperial capital.

MAP 25–1 **British India, 1820 and 1856.**

What were the key factors in British expansion in India between 1820 and 1856?

Initially the British achieved their domination of India through the East India Company, which was a private company of merchants chartered by Parliament in 1600. In the late eighteenth and early nineteenth centuries, the company expanded its authority across India by warfare and negotiation. By the 1830s, British control over India was essentially complete. The willingness of Indians to defer to British authority rather than accept the dominance of other Indians made British rule possible. Like the Romans, the British had perfected the imperial art of dividing and conquering (see Map 25–1).

The rationale for British rule in India changed over time. The East India Company essentially saw India as a place to make money through economic exploitation. By the early nineteenth century, while still hoping to make India profitable, the British saw themselves as bringing wise administration to a subcontinent where local authority was in disarray. In 1813, Parliament permitted British Christian missionaries to work in India. Their presence meant that for the first time Britons would challenge the religious customs of Indian Hindus and Muslims. Some British administrators began to cooperate with missionaries to bring the "enlightenment" of Western values to India. These and other intrusions suggested that British administrators believed they could raise India to what they considered to be a higher rung on the ladder of civilization.

In 1857, however, India witnessed the most extensive resistance against any European power that occurred in the nineteenth century. The sepoy rebellion or mutiny (Indian troops were called sepoys) was all the more frightening to the British because it occurred within the Indian Army itself. The precipitating cause of the mutiny was the company's introduction of new cartridges for its soldiers' muskets that the sepoys believed (falsely, the cartridges were in fact coated with vegetable oil) were lubricated with pork or beef fat. Soldiers had to bite off the end of the cartridge to use it. This would have offended both Muslims, for whom the pig was unclean, and Hindus, to

The mutinous sepoy cavalry attacking a British infantry division at the Battle of Cawnpore in 1857. Although the uprising was suppressed, it was not easily forgotten. In its aftermath the British reorganized the government of India.

The Granger Collection, New York

What importance might be attached to the contrast between the orderly ranks of British soldiers on the right and the relative disorder of the sepoys on the left?

whom the cow was sacred. There was also simmering anger over the way the company treated native rulers and with the company's policy of paying British troops more than it paid Indians.

With support from native rulers, the British harshly suppressed the rebels. Their tactics became even more ruthless after sepoys massacred British women and children. Tens of thousands of Indians and more than 10,000 Britons were killed. By June 1858, the British were firmly back in control.

The immediate British political response to the mutiny was passage of the Government of India Act in 1858, which transferred political authority from the East India Company to the British Crown. The British also restrained their efforts to change India or to move it "toward civilization." Instead, the British administration sought to refrain from interfering with Indian religion and became distrustful of missionary efforts to convert Indians to Christianity. The British also worked more closely with Indian rulers. One-third of India remained under the rule of Indian princes who swore allegiance to the British Crown and were "advised" by British officials. More British troops were also stationed in India, and Indian troops were not allowed artillery. Finally in 1877, Prime Minister Benjamin Disraeli pushed through an Act of Parliament that declared Queen Victoria (r. 1837–1901) to be Empress of India.

But India remained restive. In 1885, Hindus founded the Indian National Congress with the goals of modernizing Indian life and liberalizing British policy. Muslims organized the Muslim League in 1887, which for a time cooperated with the National Congress but eventually sought an independent Muslim state.

THE "NEW IMPERIALISM," 1870–1914

WHAT WAS new about the "New Imperialism"?

Whereas in the first three quarters of the nineteenth century Britain had largely dominated the world stage, between 1870 and 1914 other Western powers undertook colonial ventures with remarkable results. During this half-century, Western nations including the United States and Japan, which had industrialized and modernized its government and armed forces along Western lines between the 1860s and the 1880s, achieved unprecedented influence and control over the rest of the world and provoked intense colonial rivalries with each other. During this period, imperial expansion went forward with great speed, and empire was regarded as necessary for a great power. Contemporaries at the time and historians have regarded this era as constituting a "New Imperialism" that was different from the imperialism of the early nineteenth century.

Why were the imperial encounters of this era perceived to be "new"? First, they were more intentionally imperial and involved direct political and administrative control of non-Westerners by the Western powers. In a **protectorate** a Western nation placed officials in a foreign state to oversee its government without formally assuming responsibility for administration. In other instances, a European state, the United States, or Japan established "**spheres of influence**" in which it received special commercial and legal privileges in part of an Asian or African state without direct political involvement.

Second, the New Imperialism occurred over a relatively brief period and involved an unprecedented number of nations. In addition to the older imperial powers—Britain, France, Russia, the Netherlands, Spain, and Portugal—the newly united Germany and Italy and the Belgian monarchy, which had only existed since 1830, sought to achieve empires as did the United States and Japan.

protectorate A non-Western territory administered by a Western nation without formal conquest or annexation, usually a de facto colony.

spheres of influence A region, city, or territory where a non-Western nation exercised informal administrative influence through economic, diplomatic, or military advisors.

Third, virtually none of the numerous imperial ventures of this era involved significant numbers of immigrants as settlers. Rather in one way or another over a few decades, Westerners came to govern directly or indirectly vast numbers of non-European peoples. Fourth, during these decades Europeans at home and in colonial settings exhibited a cultural confidence and racial arrogance that marked a departure from previous eras when many persons associated with European empires esteemed indigenous cultures or assumed that these cultures could be raised on the ladder of civilization. Fifth, despite its worldwide scope and especially the establishment of French rule in Indochina, the New Imperialism focused to an unprecedented degree on Africa with the European powers partitioning Africa among themselves. The boundaries they established still determine Africa's political divisions.

Two other points should be noted about the New Imperialism. First, the actual number of Westerners involved in carrying it out was relatively small. Except for soldiers and sailors, only a few thousand administrators, merchants, and missionaries were associated with empire. Second, the empires created by the New Imperialism were short-lived. In most places they lasted less than a century, much shorter than the earlier European empires, which had endured for more than three centuries.

MOTIVES FOR THE NEW IMPERIALISM

Until the mid–twentieth century, the predominant interpretation of the motives for the New Imperialism was economic. This view originated in a book entitled *Imperialism: A Study* published in 1902 by the English economist and journalist J. A. Hobson (1858–1940). According to Hobson, capitalist economies overproduced, which caused manufacturers, bankers, and financiers, to press governments into imperial ventures to provide new markets for their excess goods and capital. Hobson, who was a radical, but not a Marxist critic of capitalism, believed that European economies should be restructured to make imperialism as he understood it unnecessary.

WHAT ROLE did economic motives play in nineteenth-century imperialism?

In 1916 Lenin adopted and modified Hobson's ideas in his book *Imperialism: The Highest Stage of Capitalism.* Lenin argued that competition inevitably eliminates inefficient capitalists and therefore leads to monopoly. Powerful industrial and financial capitalists soon run out of profitable investments in their own countries and persuade their governments to gain colonies in "less developed" countries. Here they can find higher profits, new markets for their products, and safe sources of raw materials. For Lenin, as we saw in Chapter 23, capitalism could not be reformed. Revolution was needed.

The history of the Western imperial advance, as we will see in subsequent sections of this chapter, does not support the theories of Hobson and Lenin. European powers did invest considerable capital abroad and did seek markets, but not in a way that fits the Hobson-Lenin model. Britain, for example, made heavier investments abroad before 1875, when it was not actively acquiring new colonies than during the next two decades when it was expanding its empire. Only a small percentage of British and European overseas investments, moreover, went to their new colonies. Most capital went into other European countries or to older, well-established states like the United States and Argentina and to the settler colonies of Canada, Australia, and New Zealand. Even when Western countries did invest in new colonies, they often did not invest in their own colonies.

The facts are equally discouraging for those who try to explain the New Imperialism by emphasizing the need for markets and raw materials. While some European businesspeople and politicians hoped that colonial expansion would cure the great depression of 1873 to 1896, few colonies were important markets for the great imperial nations. All these states were forced to rely on areas that they did not control as sources of vital raw materials. It is not even clear that control of the new colonies was particularly profitable, though Britain, to be sure, benefited greatly from its rule of India, a rule, however, established long before the New Imperialism. Economics certainly played a part, but a full understanding of the New Imperialism requires a search for other motives.

It is now clear that many motives beyond economic ones influenced the imperial policies of each of the major European nations. Three stand out.

First, after 1870, many political leaders came to believe that the possession of colonies or of imperial influence was an important and even necessary characteristic of a great European power. Here they were clearly following the British example. By the 1880s French politicians believed that colonies could compensate for France's loss of prestige and territory in the Franco-Prussian War of 1870–1871. Similar motives drove Russia's advance into Asia following its defeat in the Crimean War (1854–1856). As a result, vast French and Russian empires were created. Two newly created European states also embraced imperial ventures: Italy believed it must secure colonies to prove that it was a great power, but did so with only modest success; Germany created a more significant, if short-lived, empire. The United States at the time of the Spanish-American War in 1898 also came to believe that possession of colonies was essential to its world status. So did Japan, which became a major imperial power in Asia, acquiring Taiwan in 1895 after defeating China and annexing the independent kingdom of Korea in 1910.

Second, much of the territorial acquisitions associated with the New Imperialism as well as subsequent Western involvement in the Middle East arose in direct response to the power vacuums that the decay of the Ottoman Empire created (see Chapter 22). Throughout the nineteenth century, the Ottoman government in Istanbul slowly but steadily lost province after province to Western powers or nationalist revolts. Ottoman decay gave rise to grave and long-lasting problems. The demise of Ottoman authority in the Balkans created the conflicts that provided the immediate cause for the outbreak of World War I, and the turmoil that has characterized much of the Middle East since 1945 originated in the collapse of Ottoman power in that area. The painfully slow collapse of the Ottoman Empire also brought the West into an unprecedented encounter with Islam.

Third, the geopolitical assumptions of European statesmen led them to deeper and deeper involvements from the eastern Mediterranean to Africa. European powers often intruded into other regions of the world to protect what they regarded as their strategic interest and then had to decide what to do with those regions when faced with the necessity of administering them.

THE PARTITION OF AFRICA

HOW DID European politics contribute to the "Scramble for Africa"?

For almost fifty years inter-European rivalries played out in regions far away from Europe itself and nowhere more intensely than in Africa. During the so-called "Scramble for Africa," which occurred between the late 1870s and about 1912, the European powers sought to maximize their strategic control of African territory, markets, and raw materials. Motivated by intense competition, the imperial powers eventually divided almost all the continent among themselves (see Maps 25–2 and 25–3, on page 630).

The European partition of Africa was not based on a universal policy, and each power acquired and administered its new possessions in different ways. Their goals, however, were the same: to gain control, or at least dominance, through diplomacy or force and then either to place Europeans directly in charge of administering the territories or to compel local rulers to accept European "advisors" who would exercise real authority.

MAP EXPLORATION

Interactive map: To explore this map further, go to www.myhistorylab.com

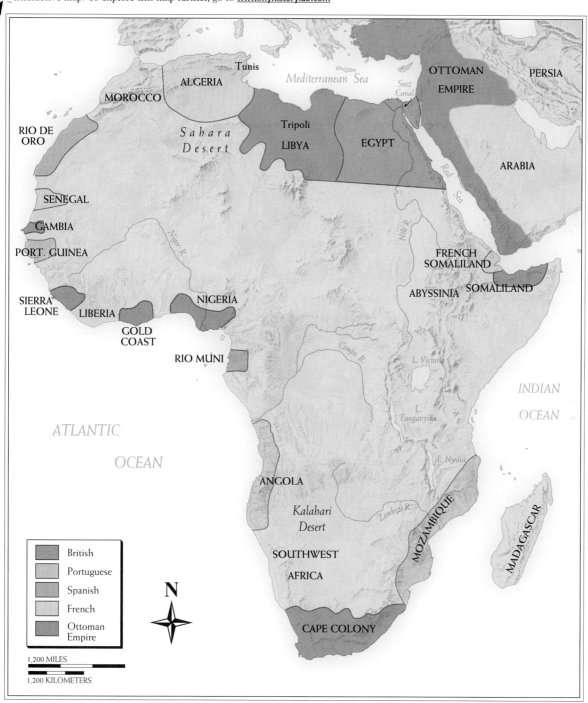

	British
	Portuguese
	Spanish
	French
	Ottoman Empire

1,200 MILES

1,200 KILOMETERS

MAP 25–2 Imperial Expansion in Africa to 1880 Until the 1880s, few European countries held colonies in Africa, mostly on its fringes.

For what purposes did European countries control parts of Africa before 1880?

TWO VIEWS OF TURN-OF-THE-TWENTIETH-CENTURY IMPERIAL EXPANSION

Throughout the age of the most active European expansion, political and popular opinion was divided over whether imperialism was desirable and morally right for the major European powers. Gustav Schmoller, a German political economist, sets forth the argument in favor of imperial expansion about 1900; four years later, the French socialist novelist Anatole France attacked imperialism.

QUESTIONS

1. What are the characteristics that Schmoller ascribes to other contemporary imperial powers?

2. What are the benefits Schmoller sees arising from colonies?

3. Why does France equate imperialism with barbarism?

4. Why does France believe that virtually no benefits result from imperialism?

5. How could writers looking at the European imperial enterprise come to such different conclusions about it? What values inform the views of each writer?

I. GUSTAV SCHMOLLER MAKES THE CASE FOR GERMAN IMPERIAL EXPANSION

Gustav Schmoller (1838–1917) was a highly respected German economist and active political figure who served in the Prussian Privy Council and as a member of the Upper Chamber in the Prussian Diet. He was a strong German nationalist. In this lecture from around the turn of the century Schmoller presents Germany as surrounded on the world scene by aggressive imperial powers. He argues that Germany must imitate them and create its own strong navy and overseas empire. Note the importance he attached to the victory of the United States in the Spanish-American War and the manner in which he portrays Spain as an unsuccessful imperial power.

In various States, arrogant, reckless, cold-blooded daring bullies, men who possess the morals of a captain of pirates. . . push themselves more and more forward into the Government. . . . We must not forget that it is in the freest States, England and North America, where the tendencies of conquest, Imperial schemes, and hatred against new economic competitors are growing up amongst the masses. The leaders of these agitations are great speculators, who have the morals of a pirate, and who are at the same time party leaders and Ministers of State. . . . The conquest of Cuba and the Philippines by the United States alters their political and economical basis. Their tendency to exclude Europe from the North and South American markets must needs lead to new great conflicts. . . . These bullies, these pirates and speculators *à la* Cecil Rhodes, act like poison within their State. They buy the press, corrupt ministers and the aristocracy, and bring on wars for the benefit of a bankrupt company or for the gain of filthy lucre. . . . We mean to extend our trade and industries far enough to enable us to live and sustain a growing population. We mean to defend our colonies, and, if possible, to acquire somewhere agricultural colonies. We mean to prevent extravagant mercantilism everywhere, and to prevent the division of the earth among the three world powers, which would exclude all other countries and destroy their trade. In order to attain this modest gain we require to-day so badly a large fleet. The German Empire must become the centre of a coalition of States, chiefly in order to be able to hold the balance in the death-struggle between Russia and England, but that is only possible if we possess a stronger fleet than that of today. . . . We must wish that at any price a German country, peopled by twenty to thirty7 million Germans, should grow up in Southern Brazil. Without the possibility of energetic proceedings on the part of Germany our future over there is threatened. . . . We do not mean to press for an economic alliance with Holland, but if the Dutch are wise, if they do not want to lose their colonies someday, as Spain did, they will hasten to seek our alliance.

Source: Gustav Schmoller lecture of about 1900, quoted in J. Ellis Barker, *Modern Germany: Her Political and Economic Problems, Her Foreign and Domestic Policy, Her Ambitions, and the Causes of Her Success*, 2nd ed. (London: Smith, Elder, & Co., 1907), pp. 139–140.

II. ANATOLE FRANCE DENOUNCES IMPERIALISM

Arrival in Saigon of Paul Beau (1857–1927), governor general of Indo-China 1902–1907, from "Le Petit Journal," November 1902.

Private Collection/The Bridgeman Art Library International

Does the encounter depicted in this illustration seem friendly or hostile? Why?

Anatole France (1844–1924) was a famous late-century French novelist who was also active in the French socialist movement. Many socialists across Europe criticized the imperial ventures of their governments. In this passage France provides both a moral and a utilitarian critique of French imperialism around the world. He associates it with ambitious military figures, greedy businessmen, and corrupt politicians. He also contends that it brings nothing of value to France. Critiques of similar character appeared among other liberal, socialist, and radical politicians and political commentators across Europe and also in the United State. Criticism of imperialism of this character would continue until the close of the colonial age during the last quarter of the twentieth century. Notice that like Schmoller, France see imperialism as something now characterizing all the major powers.

Imperialism is the most recent form of barbarism, the end of the line for civilization. I do not distinguish between the two terms—imperialism and barbarism—for they mean the same thing.

We Frenchmen, a thrifty people, who see to it that we have no more children than we are able to support easily, careful of adventuring into foreign lands, we Frenchmen who hardly ever leave our own gardens, for what in the world do we need colonies? What can we do with them? What are the benefits for us? It has cost Franc much in lives and money so that the Congo, Cochinchina, Annam, Tonkin, Guinea, and Madagascar may be able to buy cotton from Manchester, liquors from Danzig, and wine from Hamburg. For the last seventy years France has attacked and persecuted the Arabs so that Algeria might be inhabited by Italians and Spaniards!

The French people get nothing from the colonial lands of Africa and Asia. But their government finds it profitable. Through colonial conquest the military people get promotions, pensions, and awards, in addition to the glory gained by quelling the natives. Shipowners, army contractors, and shady politicians prosper. The ignorant mob is flattered because it believes that an overseas empire will make the British and Germans green with envy.

Will this colonial madness never end? I know well that nations are not reasonable. Considering their composition, it would be strange, indeed, if they were. But sometimes they know instinctively what is bad for them. Through long and bitter experience they will come to see the mistakes they have made. And, one day, they will realize that colonies bring only danger and ruin.

Source: Anatole France, "The Colonial Folly," (1904), as quoted in Louis L. Snyder, *The Imperialism Reader: Documents and Readings on Modern Expansionism* (New York: D. Van Nostrand Company, Inc., 1962), pp. 155–156.

MAP EXPLORATION

Interactive map: To explore this map further, go to www.myhistorylab.com

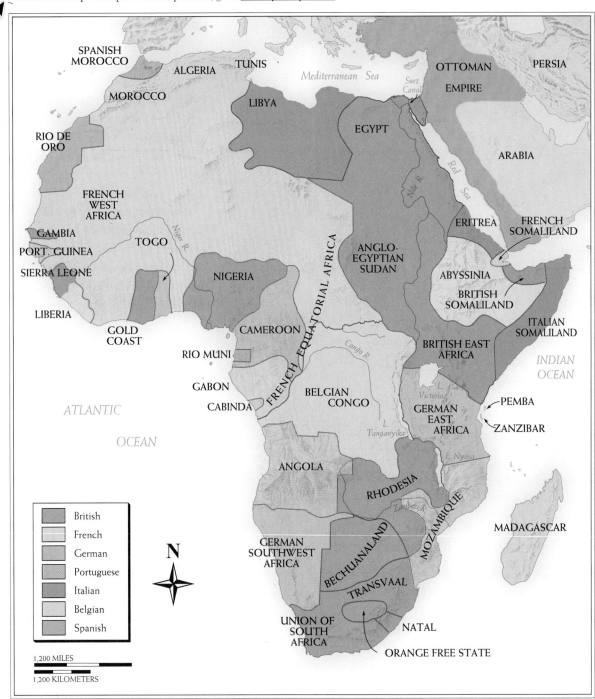

MAP 25–3   **Partition of Africa, 1880–1914**   Before 1880, the European presence in Africa was largely the remains of early exploration by old imperialists and did not penetrate the heart of the continent. By 1914, the occupying powers included most large European states; only Liberia and Abyssinia remained independent.

Which European country had the most African colonies?

ALGERIA, TUNISIA, MOROCCO, AND LIBYA

France left the Congress of Vienna in 1815 with only a few small colonies and trading posts. For a time French popular opinion seems to have resisted further colonial ventures. Then in 1830, as we saw in Chapter 20, the government of Charles X (r. 1824–1830) literally in its last days launched a military expedition against Algiers. Following the Revolution of 1830, which deposed Charles, France did not pull back from Algeria. French governments saw Algeria's fertile coastal regions as providing the land for a settler colony. By 1871 more than 275, 000 French settlers were living there. Over the decades, France pushed beyond the coast into the Sahara Desert where its forces established their authority over various nomadic Muslim peoples. The French came to regard Algeria as an integral part of France.

In 1881–1882, the French also established a protectorate over Tunisia, which was nominally a province of the Ottoman Empire, and then between 1901 and 1912, set up another protectorate in Morocco. In both Tunisia and Morocco, the French retained the local rulers as puppet monarchs.

Italy, having failed to conquer Ethiopia in 1896, seized Libya from Turkey in 1911–1912, establishing its most important colony. These French and Italian colonial advances in North Africa demonstrated the profound weakness of the Ottoman Empire. Thus by the outbreak of World War I, all of North Africa lay under some form of European control. In each of these cases a Western power dominated a largely Muslim population.

EGYPT AND BRITISH STRATEGIC CONCERN ABOUT THE UPPER NILE

Egypt, the richest and most populous region of North Africa, came under European domination as a result of political stagnation and economic collapse. Like Tunisia, Egypt was a semi-independent province of the Ottoman Empire under the hereditary rule of a Muslim dynasty. After the failed Napoleonic invasion in 1798, the Khedives, as these rulers were titled, had tried to modernize Egypt by building new harbors, roads, and a modern army. Egypt also sought to expand its rule into the Sudan. To pay for these projects, the Khedives borrowed money from European creditors. To earn the money to repay these loans, they forced farmers to plant cash crops, particularly cotton, which could be sold on the international market. The Egyptian economy and government revenue rose and fell with the price of cotton. Ultimately, the Egyptian government became utterly dependent on European creditors for new loans at exorbitant rates of interest. The construction of the Suez Canal was the final blow to Egypt's finances.

The Suez Canal was opened in 1869. Built by French engineers with European capital, it was one of the most remarkable engineering feats of the day. The canal

Linking Asia and Europe, the Suez Canal, opened in 1869, was a major engineering achievement. It also became a major international waterway benefiting all maritime states by reducing the distance from London to Bombay by half.

Bibliothèque des Arts Decoratifs, Paris, France/The Bridgeman Art Library International

What benefits, if any, did the people of Egypt get from the opening of the Suez Canal?

connected the Mediterranean to the Red Sea, which meant that ships from Europe no longer had to sail around Africa to reach Asia. The canal increased the speed of international contacts and, by reducing shipping costs, made many goods on the world market more affordable. Yet the tangible benefits to Egypt itself were not immediately clear. By 1875, the Khedive was bankrupt. Egypt's European creditors were taking more than 50 percent of Egyptian revenue each year to repay their loans, and they forced the Egyptian government to increase taxes to raise more revenue. This provoked a nationalist rebellion, and in 1881, the Egyptian army took over the government to defend Egypt from foreign exploitation. In 1882 Britain sent a fleet and army to Egypt that easily defeated the Egyptians and established seventy years of British supremacy in the country.

Egypt was never an official part of the British Empire. The Khedives continued to reign, but a small number of British officials dominated the Egyptian administration. Britain's primary goal in Egypt was political and military stability. Egypt had to repay its debts, and Britain was to retain control of the Suez Canal. The British built a naval base at Alexandria and installed a large garrison in Cairo. They established municipal governments that were responsible for taxation and public services and further expanded cotton cultivation. They also prevented the Egyptians from establishing a textile industry that would compete with Britain's own mills.

Economically, this meant that while the Egyptian economy grew and tax revenues increased, per capita income actually declined among Egyptians, most of whom were peasants who owned little or no land. Politically, it led to the growth of Egyptian nationalism, to Islamic militancy, and to demands that the British leave Egypt.

The British occupation of Egypt quickly drew Britain even deeper into Africa along the Nile. Control of the upper Nile had been understood to be essential to the security of Egypt since ancient times. The collapse of the Khedive's authority in Cairo in 1881 had led to a similar collapse of Egyptian authority in the Sudan. The Sudan remained in turmoil until 1898 when an Anglo-Egyptian army under General Sir Herbert, later Lord, Kitchener (1850–1916) conquered it in a remarkably violent campaign during which 11,000 Sudanese troops were killed and 16,000 wounded by modern weaponry in a single battle at Omdurman. The British lost only 48 men in the battle.

The British determination to secure the upper Nile and the Sudan led to one of the major crises of the imperial age. Although the French had refused to participate when British forces invaded Egypt in 1882, they retained large investments there and still hoped to influence Egyptian affairs by controlling the upper Nile. In the summer of

The battle of Omdurman, fought on September 2, 1898, demonstrated the capacity of European forces armed with the most modern weapons—in this case, a British army composed of British, Egyptian, and Sudanese troops, commanded by Major General Sir Horatio Kitchener, to decimate a vast Sudanese force armed with less advanced weapons. In the battle, which occurred near Khartoum, the British encircled the Sudanese forces. Approximately 10,000 African warriors were killed, while British losses numbered 48 men. Contrary to the image on this contemporary print, the British forces wore khaki rather than red uniforms.

Picture Desk, Inc./Kobal Collection

How did this battle demonstrate the power of Western military technology?

1898, a small French military force from West Africa reached the upper Nile at an unimportant location called Fashoda. As Kitchener's forces moved south, he confronted the French. War seemed possible until Paris ordered the French to withdraw. Instead of fighting, France and Britain eventually resolved their imperial rivalries. France acquiesced in Britain's domination of Egypt, and Britain agreed to support French ambitions in Morocco. The peaceful resolution of the Fashoda incident and other imperial disputes was essential to the formation of the loose alliance called the Anglo-French Entente in 1904 and to the two countries fighting as allies in World War I.

WEST AFRICA

France could surrender hope of dominating Egypt because it already controlled much of sub-Saharan Africa. West Africa, in particular, was a key area for French imperialism. In 1895 French West Africa included 12 million inhabitants and was eight times larger than France itself.

The British had four West African colonies: Sierra Leone, which was originally a home for freed slaves, Gambia, the Gold Coast (now Ghana), and Nigeria, the largest and most populous black African colony that any European power possessed. British slavers had worked on the Nigerian coast during the eighteenth century, and Britain had moved steadily into the Nigerian interior since the 1840s seeking to establish trade and acquire tropical products, especially palm oil and cotton. Over time the British established protectorates over the Muslim emirates in northern Nigeria and direct control over other areas. In 1914, they combined all these territories into a single administrative unit, which they called the colony of Nigeria. To prevent indigenous resistance, British officials ran the country through local rulers, a policy known as indirect rule.

THE BELGIAN CONGO

Perhaps the most remarkable story in the European Scramble for Africa was the acquisition of the Belgian Congo. As a young monarch, King Leopold II of Belgium (r. 1865–1909) had become determined that Belgium, despite its small territory, must acquire colonies. The Belgian government, however, had no interest in colonies. So despite being a constitutional monarch, Leopold used his own wealth and political guile to realize his colonial ambitions. He did so under the guise of humanitarian concern for Africans. In 1876, he gathered explorers, geographers, and antislavery reformers in Brussels and formed the International African Association. He then recruited the English-born journalist and explorer Henry Morton Stanley (1841–1904) to undertake an expedition into the Congo. Between 1879 and 1884, he explored the Congo and on Leopold's behalf made "treaties" with African rulers who had no idea what they were signing. Leopold then won diplomatic recognition for those treaties and for his own allegedly humanitarian efforts in the region. Leopold, thus, personally became the ruler of an African domain that was over seventy times the size of Belgium.

Although Leopold cultivated the image of a humanitarian ruler by sponsoring antislavery conferences and manipulating public relations, his goal in the Congo was brutal economic exploitation. Leopold's administrators used slave labor, intimidation, torture, mutilation, and mass murder to extract rubber and ivory from what became known as the Congo Free State. Eventually, Leopold's crimes were exposed, and he formally turned the Congo over to Belgium in 1908, the year before he died.

GERMAN EMPIRE IN AFRICA

The German chancellor Otto von Bismarck appears to have pursued an imperial policy, however briefly, from coldly political motives and with only modest enthusiasm. In 1884 and 1885, Germany declared protectorates over South-West Africa (today the country of Namibia), Togoland, and the Cameroons in West Africa, and Tanganyika in East Africa. Bismarck acquired colonies chiefly to improve Germany's diplomatic position in Europe and to divert France into colonial expansion and away from hostility to Germany. He also used German colonial activities in Africa to pressure the British to be reasonable about European affairs.

Bismarck had used Leopold II's efforts in the Congo to call the Berlin Conference in 1884 (not to be confused with the Congress of Berlin, which sought to settle the Eastern Question in 1879). At the Berlin Conference the major European powers decided on what amounted to the formal partition of Africa. By 1890 almost all the continent had been parceled out.

Germany's proved to be the shortest lived of any of the European colonial ventures. German imperialism involved few Germans and produced no significant economic returns. At the end of World War I, the Allies stripped Germany of its colonial holdings. This meant that Germany was the only major West European state not drawn into the struggles of decolonization after World War II. But the German entry into the arena of imperial competition did contribute to the tensions that led to World War I (see Chapter 26).

Genocide in South-West Africa   The German Empire lasted for only about three decades, but in that time German administrators carried out a major atrocity against indigenous peoples in German South-West Africa. In 1904 the Herero people in the colony revolted, and the Germans decided to take severe action. They announced that the Hereros had to leave their land, and the German commander General Lothar von Trotha authorized the killing of all male Hereros and driving their women and children into the desert. Herero prisoners were placed in concentration camps where the death rates from disease were high although the Germans ran the camps with meticulous bureaucratic attention to detail. A United Nations report in 1985 concluded that by the time the Germans suppressed the revolt in 1908, 80 percent of the Herero population had died.

Great Trek   The migration by Boer (Dutch) farmers during the 1830s and 1840s from regions around Cape Town into the eastern and northeastern regions of South Africa that ultimately resulted in the founding of the Orange Free State and Transvaal.

SOUTHERN AFRICA

Except for coastal Algeria, only South Africa had attracted large numbers of European settlers. The Dutch had begun to settle there in the mid-1600s. By 1800, Cape Town had become an important port for ships on their way to Asia. During the Napoleonic Wars the British captured Cape Town from the Dutch. Soon thereafter, British settlers began to arrive, and British economic and cultural influence soon predominated on the Cape.

Not surprisingly, the Dutch resented British control. During the 1830s and 1840s, the Boers or Afrikaners, as the descendants of the Dutch were known, undertook the **Great Trek** during which they moved north and east of the Cape. This migration became the key moment in the forging of Afrikaner national consciousness. They founded states outside British control that would become Natal, Transvaal, and the Orange Free State.

In 1886 gold was discovered in the Transvaal, and 50,000 miners rushed to Johannesburg. There were now more non-Boer white settlers in the

Diamond mining in South Africa took off in the late 1860s. By 1880 Kimberly, the biggest mine in the region, had 30,000 people, second only to Cape Town. Whites, such as these diamond sorters, monopolized the well-paid, skilled jobs.

National Archives of South Africa

How did the discovery of gold and gems in South Africa lead to conflict in the region?

Transvaal than Boers, but the government refused to allow non-Boers the right to vote. Tensions mounted between Britain and the Boers over the region and, in 1899, war broke out. Although the British finally won this Boer War in 1902, they were surprised by the strength of Boer resistance. When the Boers resorted to guerilla tactics, the British gathered Boer women and children into what they called **concentration camps** where many died from disease and exposure.

In 1910, the British combined the colonies in South Africa into a confederation whose constitution guaranteed the rule of the European minority over the majority black and nonwhite population. Africans and people of mixed race whom the British referred to as "colored" were forbidden to own land, denied the right to vote, and excluded from positions of power. To preserve their political power and economic privileges, the white elite of South Africa eventually enforced a policy of racial **apartheid**—"separateness"—that turned the country into a totally segregated land until the 1990s. The result was decades of oppression, racial tensions, and economic exploitation.

concentration camps Camps first established by Great Britain in South Africa during the Boer War to incarcerate noncombatant civilians; later camps established for political prisoners and other persons deemed dangerous to the state in the Soviet Union and Nazi Germany. The term is now primarily associated with the camps established by the Nazis during the Holocaust.

apartheid (a-PAR-tid) An official policy of segregation, assignment of peoples to distinct regions, and other forms of social, political, and economic discrimination based on race associated primarily with South Africa.

RUSSIAN EXPANSION IN MAINLAND ASIA

The British presence in India was intimately related to Russian expansion across mainland Asia in the nineteenth century, which eventually brought huge territories and millions of people of a variety of ethnicities and religions under tsarist rule.

During the early eighteenth century, the tsars had consolidated their control around the Baltic Sea. Catherine the Great (r. 1762–1796) had gained much of southern Ukraine and opened the regions around the Black Sea to Russian control at the cost of Ottoman influence. The partitions of Poland had extended Russian authority toward the west (see Chapter 17). During the nineteenth century the Russian government would look to the east where no major state could oppose its advance and where the weakness of the Ottoman Empire and China worked to Russian advantage.

Even during the eighteenth century, the tsarist government had ruled extremely diverse groups of people who were not Russian by language, religion, or cultural heritage. The Russians had generally approached these peoples in a pragmatic way, tolerating their religions and recognizing their social elites. What the Russian government sought was those elites' loyalty to the tsar rather than conformity to Russian language, the Orthodox Church, or Russian culture.

Beginning in the late eighteenth century, however, the tsarist government began to regard the nomadic societies or communities who lived in the mountainous regions to the south and east as *inorodtsy*, meaning "foreign." Moreover, the government drew upon the Enlightenment four-stage theory of social development, discussed in Chapter 17, to distinguish sedentary peoples as superior to those who lived as hunters, gatherers, fishermen, or nomads. One of the purposes thereafter of Russian expansion was, like that of early Victorian British administrators in India, to raise these people

HOW DID Russia come to control a vast and diverse Asian empire?

EXPANSION OF EUROPEAN POWER AND THE NEW IMPERIALISM

1869	Suez Canal completed
1875	Britain gains control of the Suez Canal
1879–1884	Leopold II establishes his personal rule in the Congo
1882	France controls Tunisia
1880s	Britain establishes protectorate over Egypt
1884–1885	Germany establishes protectorate over Southwest Africa (Namibia), Togoland, the Cameroons, and East Africa (Tanzania)
1895	Japan seizes Taiwan from China
1898	Spanish-American War: United States acquires Puerto Rico, Philippines, and Guam, annexes Hawaiian Islands, and establishes virtual protectorate over Cuba
1899	United States proposes Open Door Policy in Far East
1899–1902	Boer War in South Africa
1908	Belgium takes over the Congo from Leopold II
1905–1912	France establishes protectorate over Morocco
1910	Japan annexes Korea
1912	Italy conquers Libya from Turkey

Though the Russians largely subdued the Caucasus region by the 1860s—with a Muslim separatist movement led by Imam Shamil put down only after decades of struggle—the many ethnic groups of this rugged mountain region remained largely autonomous until well into the twentieth century. This photograph, most likely taken around 1890, shows a group of chain-clad warriors from the Khevsureti region of Georgia (which had been incorporated into the Russian Empire early in the nineteenth century). With their primitive firearms, swords, and shields, these fighting men may appear like no match for mechanized firepower, but in reality the people of this region remained largely free of governmental authority until well into the twentieth century.

Courtesy of the Library of Congress

What challenges did Russia's ethnic diversity pose for the Russian Empire?

on the ladder of civilization. Russian governors would henceforth rarely, if ever, consider conquered peoples to be their social or cultural equals.

The nineteenth century saw Russia extend its authority in three distinct areas of mainland Asia. The first was in the Transcaucasus. This expansion came at the cost of Persia and the Ottoman Empire, both of which by nineteenth-century standards had become weak states. But Russia never securely incorporated these regions into the Russian Empire because their aristocratic elites were not willing to be co-opted. By the late nineteenth century, nationalistic unrest was rising among Georgians, Armenians, and Azerbaijainis. The Russians were also only modestly successful in subjugating the Muslim peoples living in the Caucasus regions of Chechnya, Dagestan, and Circassia.

The second prong of Russian imperial advance occurred in the vast steppes of Central Asia where various nomadic peoples lived. The most important of these were Kazakhs who remained nomadic even under Russian rule until Stalin forced them onto collective farms in the 1930s (see Chapter 27).

The final area of Russian imperial conquest occurred in southern Middle Asia from the 1860s to the 1880s. This is the region of present-day Uzbekistan, Turkistan, and the areas bordering Afghanistan, all of which are primarily Muslim. Expansion in this area followed Russia's defeat in the Crimean War and sought to demonstrate that Russia could still exert imperial influence in Asia and counter the British presence in India. The Russian-British rivalry over these regions sometimes brought Russia and Britain to the edge of war until the early twentieth century when both powers became concerned about German influence in the Ottoman Empire. The Anglo-Russian Convention of 1907 ended their Central Asian rivalry and gave each power spheres of influence in Persia. Like the settlement of colonial claims between Britain and France, the end of this particular imperial contest also opened the way for Britain and Russia to become allies against Germany during World War I.

WESTERN POWERS IN ASIA

WHAT DEVELOPMENTS facilitated Western penetration and control of Asia?

FRANCE IN ASIA

While merchants had established the British interest in India and South Asia, French interest in Indochina arose because of the activity of Roman Catholic missionaries. French missionaries gained ground in Indochina and elsewhere in Asia in the 1830s and 1840s. Persecution soon followed. In 1856, Napoleon III (r. 1852–1870) sent forces to Vietnam to protect the missionaries and give France a base from which the French navy could operate in the Far East and French commerce could expand in Asia. By the 1880s, France controlled all of Vietnam and had made Cambodia a protectorate. In 1896, Laos also became a French protectorate. Missionary work continued throughout Indochina, especially in Vietnam where Catholics became and remain a significant minority.

THE UNITED STATES ACTIONS IN ASIA AND THE PACIFIC

In 1853, a United States naval squadron under Commodore Matthew C. Perry (1794–1858) arrived in Japanese waters to open Japanese markets to American goods. In 1867, American interest in the Pacific again manifested itself when the United States bought Alaska from Russia. For the next twenty-five years, the United States assumed a fairly passive role in foreign affairs, but it had established its presence in the Pacific.

Cuba's revolt against Spain in the 1890s ended this passivity and provided the impetus for the creation of an American Empire. Sympathy for the Cuban cause, investments on the island, the desire for Cuban sugar, and concern over Cuba's strategic importance all helped drive the United States to fight Spain.

Victory in the brief Spanish-American War of 1898 brought the United States an informal protectorate over Cuba, and the annexation of Puerto Rico ended four hundred years of Spanish rule in the Western Hemisphere. The United States also forced Spain to sell it the Philippines and Guam, while Germany bought the other Spanish islands in the Pacific. The United States and Germany divided Samoa between them. In 1898 the United States also annexed Hawaii, five years after an American-backed coup had overthrown the native Hawaiian monarchy. This burst of activity made the United States an imperial power.

THE BOXER REBELLION

By the close of the nineteenth century, the Qing Dynasty, which had ruled China since 1644, was in a state of near collapse, and its decay both enabled Western penetration and was exacerbated by it. The United States feared that the European powers and Japan would soon carve up China and close its lucrative markets and investment opportunities to American interests. In 1899, to prevent this, the United States proposed the Open Door Policy, which was designed to prevent formal foreign annexations of Chinese territory and to allow businesspeople from all nations to

In 1900 an international force composed of troops drawn from Austria-Hungary, the French Third Republic, the German Empire, Italy, Japan, Russia, Great Britain, and the United States invaded China to put down the Boxer Rebellion, which had endangered Western missionaries and Western interests in China. In August 1900 these forces occupied Beijing. This contemporary print presents the image of a romanticized heroic assault by these foreign troops.

Courtesy of the Library of Congress

Who were the Boxers and what did they want?

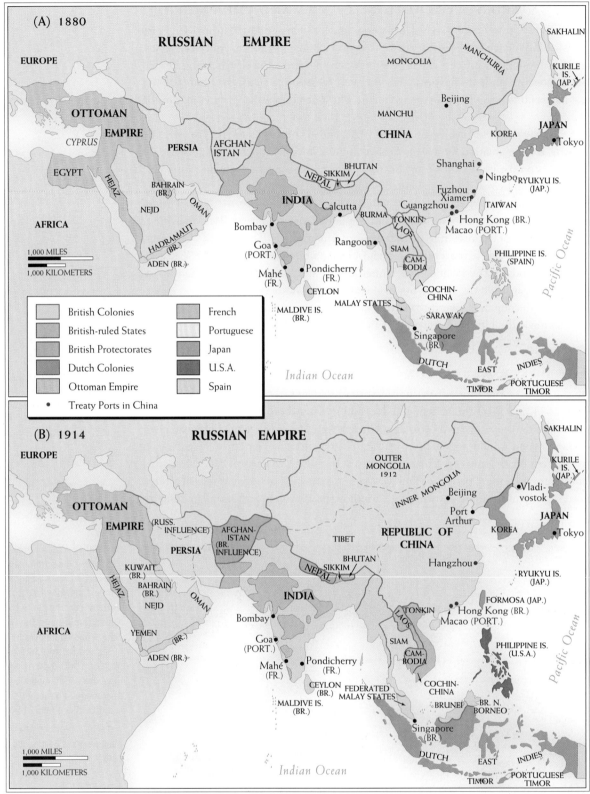

MAP 25–4   Asia, 1880–1914   As in Africa, the decades before World War I saw imperialism spread widely and rapidly in Asia. Two new powers, Japan and the United States, joined the British, French, and Dutch in extending control both to islands and to the mainland and in exploiting an enfeebled China.

Why did the emergence of Japan as a great power frighten European nations?

trade in China on equal terms. Although all the powers except Russia eventually agreed to this policy in principle, they nonetheless carved out spheres of influence in China, and France, Britain, Germany, and Russia established naval bases on the Chinese coast (see Map 25–4).

Although the Qing government was too feeble to resist Western bullying, hatred of foreigners and resentment at their presence were strong. From late 1899 through the autumn of 1901, a Chinese group called The Righteous and Harmonious Society of Fists, better known in the West as the Boxers, attempted to resist the Western incursions. The Boxers, who were supported by a faction at the Qing court, hated missionaries whom they saw as agents of the imperial powers and killed thousands of their Chinese converts.

For the imperial powers, the key moment in the Boxer Rebellion was the attacks on the foreign diplomatic missions in Beijing, which lasted off and on for three months in 1900 until an international army occupied the Chinese capital in August 1900. For the second time in less than half a century, Western troops had seized Beijing. In September 1901, the Chinese government agreed to execute officials who had helped the Boxers and pay large reparations to the Western powers and Japan.

TOOLS OF IMPERIALISM

The domination that Europe and peoples of European descent came to exert over the entire globe by 1900 was based on distinct and temporary technological advantages, what one historian called the "tools of empire." These tools gave Westerners the capacity to conquer and dominate vast areas of the world. (See "Encountering the Past: Submarine Cables," page 640.)

HOW DID technological innovations make nineteenth-century imperialism possible?

STEAMBOATS

Robert Fulton, an American, had invented the steamboat in 1807. By the 1830s, steam power enabled warships to penetrate the inland rivers and shallow coastal waters of Asia and Africa, giving rise to the projection of Western power that became known as "gunboat diplomacy." By the late 1820s, steamboats were being constructed of iron. In the nineteenth century, such boats carried European goods and European arms to assure trade in those goods up rivers around the world. It was almost impossible for local rulers and officials to defend themselves against iron warships.

Western steamboats were particularly effective along the vast rivers of Asia. The presence of gunboats on a river beside a city usually assured European merchants, and especially for many decades British merchants, access to the local markets. Iron steamboats, including some of the largest built to that date, assured British success against China in the first Opium War.

CONQUEST OF TROPICAL DISEASES

Tropical diseases often proved more of an obstacle to European conquest than African or Asian armed forces. For centuries diseases, especially malaria, had prevented Europeans from penetrating deep into the forests of sub-Saharan Africa. To move inland and increase their profits from commerce, especially after the formal end of the slave trade in the early nineteenth century, Europeans had to find a way around the malaria problem. The solution was quinine. Quinine pills made possible the rapid exploration and eventual partition of Africa. Moreover, the demand for quinine transformed its area of production. Originally cinchona bark had been grown in Peru. By the late

ENCOUNTERING THE PAST

SUBMARINE CABLES

Underwater telegraphic cables were among the important inventions of the mid–nineteenth century utilizing the then new electrical technology. Submarine cables amazed people of that era and the early twentieth century much as the Internet does today. These cables also allowed for unprecedented international communication.

The first submarine cable was laid between Great Britain and France in 1850, and the first transatlantic cable was installed successfully in 1866. Thereafter, to a remarkable extent, made evident by the accompanying world map of the early twentieth century, the imperial strategic, military concerns of the British government determined the pattern of the installation of these cables of the Eastern Associated Telegraph Companies founded in 1872. It was a case of imperial expansion determining the application of an exciting new technology using electricity. The route of the original Eastern cable of 1872 traced the coast of Western Europe, then across the Mediterranean through the Red Sea into the Indian Ocean to India, then overland in India, then eastward underwater to northern Australia and Hong Kong. By 1922, as seen in the map, cables linked all the areas of the British Empire acquired in the previous half-century as well as the important markets for British trade in Latin America. The company oversaw approximately 130,000 miles of cable. These submarine cables thus reflected late-nineteenth-century British imperial expansion and also provided essential communication allowing the empire to function economically, politically, and militarily.

In 1922 the Eastern Associated Telegraph Companies of Great Britain published a celebratory fifti-eth-anniversary volume. It opened by declaring, "On the world's oceans, surrounded by forests of vegetation, faintly reflected in the waving seaweeds of shallow shores, amidst the haunts of creatures which never see the light of the sun, where the skeletons of the wrecked ships of today and yesterday loom like phantom far and near, lie the great submarine ropes with which man has encircled the earth. Through the dark underworld of the sea, across submerged continents, and over valleys, plains and mountains, trodden in an ageless past by the forerunners of mankind, these electrified ropes carry the messages of man to man." Eastern Associated Telegraph described its cables as "the nervous system of the civilized world" and boasted, "There is hardly any spot in the more developed parts of the British Empire and of the world which cannot speedily be reached by a message marked 'via Eastern.'"

Fifty Years of "Via Eastern": A Souvenir and Record of the Celebrations in Connection with the Jubilee of the Eastern Associated Telegraph Companies MXMXII (privately printed, 1922), pp. 13, 16.

The Eastern and Associated Telegraph Companies' Cable System. "Via Eastern" "Via Eastern" (Indicated in Red) 1922

HOW DID the deployment of undersea telegraph cables facilitate the imperial campaign?

Overview The Tools of Imperialism

STEAMBOATS	• Steam power enabled warships to penetrate inland rivers and shallow coastal waters of Asia and Africa • Advent of ironclad warships gave rise to "gunboat diplomacy" • Steamboats particularly effective along the vast rivers of Asia
CONQUEST OF TROPICAL DISEASES	• Tropical diseases often an obstacle to European conquest • Malaria prevented exploitation of inland sub-Saharan Africa • Use of quinine to prevent malaria made the "Scramble for Africa" possible
FIREARMS	• Improved firearms gave Europeans an overwhelming military advantage over non-Western peoples • Advances were made in weapons, bullets, and gunpowder • Technological advances culminated in the invention of the machine gun

nineteenth century, its chief regions of cultivation were Dutch plantations in the East Indies and British plantations in India.

FIREARMS

During the nineteenth century, vast and momentous changes occurred in the technology of Western firearms. These changes gave Western nations an overwhelming advantage over non-Western peoples.

The rifle was improved, so that bullets would spin more rapidly and move in a straighter direction. Early in the century, Thomas Shaw invented the percussion cap for bullets. Unlike the earlier flintlock rifles, the percussion caps could easily be used in wet weather. The design of bullets themselves changed to allow greater speed and precision. By the mid-1850s, the British had adopted the Enfield rifle, which incorporated all the new technologies and was manufactured with interchangeable parts. The invention of the breechloader in the 1860s brought still greater distance and precision in firepower for both rifles and artillery. Later in the century, smokeless gunpowder and repeating mechanisms further enhanced accuracy and firepower.

All these technological changes were incorporated into the development of the machine gun. By 1900, the machine gun had become arguably the single most important weapon in colonial warfare and accounted for the deaths of tens of thousands of non-European peoples. Europeans also used dum-dum bullets, which exploded inside a wound, against native peoples when they would not use them against other Europeans.

THE MISSIONARY FACTOR

The modern Western missionary movement, which continues to the present day, originated in Great Britain in the late eighteenth century as a direct outgrowth of the rise of evangelical Christianity. Evangelicalism, which influenced Protestant communities from Central Europe to the United States, emphasized the authority of the Bible, the importance of a personal conversion experience, and the duty to spread the Gospel. By

WHAT WAS the relationship between missionaries and their home governments?

Women played a prominent role as teachers in the Western foreign missionary effort. Miss Emily Hartwell was a turn-of-the-century, American-born Protestant missionary to the Foochow Mission in Fuzhou Shi, China. Here, in a photo from the missionary magazine *Light and Life*, she is pictured with one of her Bible classes composed of Chinese women. Her letters home spoke of the disadvantages of women in Chinese culture.

Courtesy of the Library of Congress

What explains the surge of missionary activity in the late nineteenth century?

the close of the eighteenth century, small groups of Evangelicals began to be active in the non-Western world. Roman Catholics later copied these early Protestant missionary efforts. The result of this widespread nineteenth-century missionary campaign was the establishment of large Christian communities in Africa and Asia, which today thrive and continue to expand.

EVANGELICAL PROTESTANT MISSIONARIES

The chief moving forces in the British missionary movement were the Baptist Missionary Society, the London Missionary Society, the Edinburgh and Glasgow Missionary Societies, and the Church [of England] Missionary Society, all founded in the 1790s. American Protestant missionary societies soon followed. Initially the missionary societies, who often competed with each other along denominational lines, floundered and attracted little support, but by the mid-1820s, they were firmly established and growing enterprises. By 1900, British missionary societies employed approximately 10,000 missionaries.

German Protestants also embraced the missionary impulse. The earliest German societies such as the Leipzig Mission, founded in 1836, devoted their efforts to India. The Rhenish Missionary Society, founded 1828, established itself in East Africa and supported German colonial claims there in the 1880s. As early as 1833, the Berlin Missionary Society sent missionaries to South Africa; by 1869, it was also working to China.

ROMAN CATHOLIC MISSIONARY ADVANCE

The nineteenth-century French Roman Catholic missionary effort was also enormous. It reflected the resurgence of the Catholic Church in France in the decades following the French Revolution and Napoleon. The Society for the Propagation of the Faith, the largest French missionary society, was founded in 1822. By the 1860s, it had over a million members. Its earliest missionaries went to China and Vietnam. Over time, however, French Catholic missionaries worked on every continent, including the islands of the Pacific.

TENSIONS BETWEEN MISSIONARIES AND IMPERIAL ADMINISTRATORS

The mission societies and their missionaries had a complex relationship with their home governments. Missionary work did not necessarily support imperial missions. Missionaries from both Europe and America often settled in regions their governments did not control, and missionary societies often employed missionaries who came from a country other than the one sponsoring their mission. Nonetheless, the missionaries did develop many links with Western governments. The British missionary movement often saw the expansion of the British Empire as opening the way for the spread of the Gospel. They saw the spread of Western commerce as both financially beneficial for missions and as opening up new areas for the missionary enterprise. Missionaries and advocates of free trade imperialism thus could have a mutually supportive relationship. This relationship softened toward the close of the century when the missionary societies defined themselves more strictly in terms of the spiritual mission of bearing witness to the Gospel.

Colonial administrators frequently resisted the introduction of missionaries into their territories for fear the missionaries would prove a destabilizing force as they challenged traditional religions and cultural values. Missionaries might defend the rights of native peoples against official imperial policy or commercial interests' efforts to increase their profits. In the settlement colonies missionaries often clashed with the settlers who wanted to prevent native peoples from gaining the skills that would enable them to compete with whites. Colonial officials were also concerned about conflicts between Christian converts from different denominations. Some missionaries also tried to change the modes of worship that an earlier generation of missionaries had introduced and persecuted converts who refused to conform. Furthermore, missionaries frequently educated persons from the lower levels of society who might resent colonial rule and the authority of native elites. The Christian vision of equality before God could, though it did not always, undermine the hierarchies of colonial authority.

But even when colonial officials disliked them, missionaries nonetheless provided much of the educational infrastructure of imperialism particularly in India. At the village level their schools provided instruction in the local languages and English. Missionaries also established institutions of higher education. Later in the century, missionaries founded women's colleges. These colleges trained primarily members of the Indian elite, both Hindu and Muslim. As missionary groups became more directly associated with education, the number of women missionaries in India grew, and by the early twentieth century, most missionaries there were women.

The relationship of French Roman Catholic missionaries to imperialism was complicated because the governments of the Third Republic in France were usually anticlerical after the 1870s. Yet although the republican government often clashed with the Catholic Church in France, it frequently supported missionary activity abroad as a way of extending French national interests. In some cases the government in Paris or local colonial administrators encouraged French missionary activity to make native peoples sympathetic to French rule or to block the advance of other European powers. By teaching the French language, French missionaries also made it easier for French commercial interests to operate in a territory.

By 1900, approximately 58,000 French priests, religious brothers, and nuns were involved in the missionary enterprise. Like their British and German counterparts, French missionaries also often experienced tense relations with colonial administrators. Sometimes the colonial government pressed the **civilizing mission** through secular physicians, teachers, and agricultural consultants to counter the religious influence of missionaries. At the same time, however, the success of the French Catholic missionary effort meant that colonial officials in Vietnam and parts of Africa and the

civilizing mission The concept that Western nations could bring advanced science and economic development to non-Western parts of the world that justified imperial administration.

Pacific had to deal with large numbers of native Roman Catholics who supported and admired the missionaries. Yet by the early twentieth century, French missionaries increasingly saw their role as not only winning converts, but as also molding native cultures in the image of France.

However sympathetic missionaries might become to indigenous peoples, they remained spokespersons for Western civilization. Because missionaries wished to convert indigenous peoples to Western Christianity, they implicitly shared with colonial officials the general cultural assumption of the superiority of things Western. Even when missionaries were not formal agents of empire, they introduced Western cultural values, manners, and outlooks. While colonial governments might be associated with more advanced military and transportation technology, missionaries might be associated with more advanced medicine or agriculture in the hospitals and mission stations they ran. And missionaries, like colonial officials, generally assumed that native peoples were inferior to Westerners. While a few missionaries by 1900 believed that Christians and persons of other religions could learn from each other, most missionaries, regarded non-Christians simply as heathens. That outlook, like the attitudes of secular administrators, generated its own sets of reactions.

MISSIONARIES AND INDIGENOUS RELIGIOUS MOVEMENTS

Just as the presence of colonial administrations during the nineteenth century gave rise to various nationalist movements or movements that promoted the rights and interests of native peoples, the missionary activities gave rise to Asian and African religious movements that challenged the dominance of Western missionaries. The founding of new African and Asian Christian churches occurred as a result of the rejection of the racial and cultural assumptions of Western missionaries and as a means of reconciling Christianity with long-standing cultural practices, such as polygamy in Africa. The most important fact about the independent churches of Africa was that their leaders were African. For example, in 1888 David Brown Vincent established the Native Baptist Church in Lagos, Nigeria, after leaving the American-founded Baptist Church there. Not long thereafter, in South Africa Mangena Makone broke with the Methodists to found the Ethiopian Church. In Kenya, Christian members of the Kikuyu tribe split with the Church of Scotland Mission. In the early twentieth century, Christian Pentecostal groups arose among African Christians, as did other churches associated with gifts of healing or prophecy.

In summary, how may one describe the interrelationship of the missionary movement and colonialism? First, it was dynamic and changed during the nineteenth century as missionary goals and sensibilities changed from one generation to another. Second, the missionary movement spawned an enormous amount of printed publicity in the form of newspaper and journal articles, missionary society publications, and missionary narratives and autobiographies. These materials publicized the vision of empire and raised interest in the West about the non-Western world. They also strongly influenced popular culture at a time when the churches were more influential than they are today, especially in Europe. Third, the missionary societies and the churches with which they were associated became skilled at pressuring their governments. Initially they directed their efforts toward permitting and protecting missionary activities. By the early twentieth century, however, many missionaries were supporting native peoples in their opposition to colonial authorities. Fourth, the religious effects of the missions were a two-way street. While Westerners brought Christianity to Africa and Asia, by 1900, non-Western Christians were beginning to move Christianity away from its dominance by Europeans and Americans. This

QUICK REVIEW

The Missionary Movement

- Changed over the course of the nineteenth century
- Helped publicize the vision of empire and stirred interest in non-Western peoples and places
- Missionary societies and associated churches were skilled at pressuring governments
- Had an impact on Christianity in both the Western and non-Western worlds
- Made Christianity a true world religion for the first time

process is still going on today. Finally, the missionary movement of the nineteenth century made Christianity a genuinely worldwide religion for the first time. The spread of Christianity like the development of self-government in the British settler colonies was thus one of the major elements of the extension of Western civilization around the globe.

SCIENCE AND IMPERIALISM

HOW DID science help imperialism capture the imagination of domestic audiences in Europe?

The early modern European encounter with the non-Western world from the fifteenth-century voyages of discovery onward had been associated with the expansion of natural knowledge. The same would be true of Western imperialism in the nineteenth and early twentieth centuries. Geography was an expanding scientific discipline in the nineteenth century. Explorers wrote of their discoveries and adventures in Africa and Asia. Some explorers, such as the Scottish Presbyterian David Livingstone (1813–1873) and the French Jesuit Armand David (1829–1900), were also missionaries. Explorers portrayed themselves as pioneers who opened wild and savage spaces for commerce, religion, and ultimately civilization. Consequently, scientific and geographical societies generally supported their nations' imperialist goals and saw their research as benefiting from it.

Four areas of scientific research deserve particular mention because they demonstrate how imperialism could filter into the wider European culture and capture the imagination of domestic audiences who never set foot outside Europe. These are botany, zoology, medicine, and anthropology.

BOTANY

Botany was the nineteenth-century colonial science par excellence, reflecting and nurturing the vast expansion of agriculture around the globe. This expansion brought millions of acres of new land under cultivation in the Americas, Australia, New Zealand, and Algeria. Colonial officials and Western investors also forced or induced colonial peoples, mainly in the tropics, to grow cash crops, such as coffee, sugar, tea, rubber, jute, cotton, bananas, and cocoa, for export to Europe.

European botanists were intensely interested in the plants they might discover abroad. Their interest ranged from the discovery of previously unknown specimens through the development of new crops that would improve agriculture. Changes in taste like the spread of tea and coffee drinking and in technology like the demand for rubber for bicycle and motorcar tires could create demands for colonial agricultural products.

Gardens such as the Royal Botanical Garden at Kew, near London, and the *Jardin des Plantes* at Paris also allowed the general public to encounter a soft and inviting side of empire. Visitors could experience different parts of the empire in a pleasant setting as they strolled along flowerbeds, under trees, or through greenhouses. These gardens and the new products and foods that Europeans and Americans consumed persuaded them that empire was part of the general progress of the age, which they associated with science.

The gardens with their research staffs also were devices for transforming economies. The same spirit of agricultural improvement that had begun in Britain in the eighteenth century was carried throughout the empire. Botanists worked as economic innovators to achieve intercontinental transfers of plants to secure products for their home countries and to develop colonial economies.

As plant commodities fell in value in one part of the British Empire, British administrators and merchants would contact Kew Garden for suggestions of other profitable crops. The botanists thus profited from empire by establishing themselves as the experts for the economic development of colonies after they had been annexed or after the crops that had once supported them were no longer profitable. Planters associations in the European colonies also established their own experimental stations to improve existing crops or develop new ones for cultivation.

ZOOLOGY

In the eighteenth century, some European monarchs, such as the Habsburg emperors in Vienna and the French kings in Paris, had established collections of exotic animals. In the nineteenth century, zoos and zoological gardens were founded in major European and American cities. These zoos displayed animals from around the world that expeditions acquired from the regions that European imperialism was penetrating.

Other scientists would collect specimens of animals, particularly birds, which they killed and brought back from the colonies to Europe to be placed in natural history museums. These museums became increasingly popular in the late nineteenth century.

MEDICINE

Medical science was an integral part of the imperial enterprise on several different levels. As already noted, Westerners had to overcome various tropical diseases, especially malaria, that prevented them from surviving in the tropics. But Western medicine also became a fundamental feature of the civilizing mission of colonial administrators and missionaries, many of whom were physicians. The spread of Western medicine justified colonial rule and helped win converts. The primary diseases that Western doctors sought to battle in the tropical colonies were yellow fever, sleeping sickness, small pox, hookworms, and leprosy.

Missionaries had pioneered the introduction of Western medicine into the colonial setting. Some missionaries thought they could convert native peoples to Christianity by first demonstrating the power of Western medicine. Physicians and medical researchers sought to win government financial support by demonstrating that modern medicine could cure the endemic diseases that ravaged colonial peoples. Among the most influential colonial medical institutions were the Pasteur Institutes, named after Louis Pasteur (1822–1895), the French scientist who had found a cure for rabies and other diseases.

In general in the colonial world, Western science became a vehicle for what is often termed *cultural imperialism*. Medical advances allowed Western penetration of the tropics and then underpinned Western cultural and political domination. European medical institutions controlled research in the colonies. Westerners seldom had respect for Asian and African medical personnel no matter how well they were trained. Yet there is no question that Western medicine either eradicated or lessened the impact of diseases that had ravaged the non-Western world for centuries and, especially in the twentieth century, extended the life span and physical well-being of colonial or former colonial peoples.

ANTHROPOLOGY

In the late nineteenth century, the study of non-Western peoples became associated with the science of anthropology. Anthropological societies were founded in Paris (1859), London (1863), and Berlin (1870). The leaders of these new societies were convinced of the multiple origins of the races of humankind (a theory termed *polygenesis*) and of the inherent inequality of races. Polygenesis was one of many scientific theories that supported a hierarchy of unequal races at the top of which Westerners always placed the white races.

Peoples from colonized nations were transported to various world's fairs and similar exhibitions during the late nineteenth and early twentieth centuries. They constituted living exhibitions, where they were expected to portray "native customs" or the like. Here at the St. Louis World's Fair of 1904, African Pygmies demonstrated beheading. In this and other similar examples, native peoples were frequently presented in demeaning roles that filled the expectations of spectators to see "exotic" behavior. Such performances and exhibitions served to convince the Western spectators of the superiority of their civilization over that of the peoples living in the colonized world.

Courtesy of the Library of Congress

What light does this image shed on late nineteenth-century views of non-Western peoples?

Many anthropologists believed that such factors as skull type determined human character. Paul Broca (1824–1880), a French physician who specialized in the brain, measured the skulls of human beings from different races and assigned them intellectual capacity on the basis of brain size. Other European and American scientists followed his lead. Anthropologists who studied colonial societies carried these ideas with them.

Anthropology as a social science infused with racial thinking (see Chapter 24) had become organized in Western Europe on the eve of the Scramble for Africa. Anthropologists from then through the Second World War rode the wave of imperial enthusiasm. In fact, however, colonial officials rarely sought anthropologists' advice. Instead, anthropologists influenced imperial policies through their books, lectures, and university classes. European and American readers and students were invariably told that non-Western peoples were inferior, that their economies were underdeveloped, that their societies were corrupt, decadent, or primitive, and that their religions were dangerous and false. All this proved the need for Western administration and control.

Many of these same attitudes informed the creation of the great anthropological museums in Europe and the United States. These museums, which were very popular, often presented artifacts of African and Asian culture that explorers or other travelers or researchers had brought home. These exhibitions, like the botanical gardens, zoos, and museums of natural history, introduced Western audiences to what they considered to be the exotic features and otherness of non-Western peoples and cultures.

The idea of museums or zoos to display exotic creatures was also extended to human beings in both Europe and the United States. Showmen such as the American P. T. Barnum would exhibit Africans, Asians, and Native Americans. Carl Hagenbeck, a German, brought Polynesians, Sudanese, and Inuits from Canada to live in "native villages" in the Hamburg Zoo. In the thirty years before World War I, the Paris zoo staged over twenty-five such exhibitions. At World's Fairs, millions of Europeans and Americans paid to view native peoples.

QUICK REVIEW

Anthropology and Imperialism

♦ Study of non-Western peoples became associated with the science of anthropology

♦ Racial thinking shaped much of anthropology

♦ Anthropological museums reflected racial thinking and reinforced its place in the popular imagination

SUMMARY

HOW DID early modern colonization differ from nineteenth-century Western imperialism?

The Close of the Age of Early Modern Colonization The era of early modern European expansion lasted from the late fifteenth to the late eighteenth centuries. Between the mid–eighteenth and the early nineteenth centuries, a vast political transformation occurred in the colonized transatlantic world. The French lost their North American empire and the British were driven from their Atlantic coastal colonies. In the 1820s Latin America shook off Spanish and Portuguese control. The most striking result of these events was the collapse of Spain, Portugal, and France as significant colonial powers. *page 620*

HOW DID Britain use its economic might to extend its influence around the world?

The Age of British Imperial Dominance Until at least the 1870s, free trade alone allowed Britain to dominate economically one region of the world after another without the need to establish a formal colonial administration. Free trade could and did lead to warfare, the most important example being the Opium Wars between Britain and China. During the early nineteenth century, Britain oversaw the settlement and economic development of Canada, Australia, and New Zealand. *page 621*

WHY WAS India such an important part of the British Empire?

India—The Jewel in the Crown of the British Empire Initially the British achieved their domination of India through the East India Company. By the 1830s, British control over India was essentially complete. The sepoy rebellion or mutiny of 1857 precipitated the passage of the Government of India Act in 1858, which transferred political authority from the East India Company to the British Crown. The late nineteenth century saw the formation of the Indian National Congress and the Muslim League. *page 622*

WHAT WAS new about the "New Imperialism"?

The "New Imperialism," 1870–1914 Between 1870 and 1914, Western nations including the United States and Japan achieved unprecedented influence and control over the rest of the world and provoked intense colonial rivalries with each other. The "New Imperialism" involved direct political and administrative control of non-Westerners by the Western powers, occurred over a relatively brief period and involved an unprecedented number of nations, did not involve significant numbers of immigrants as settlers, exhibited a new cultural confidence and racial arrogance, and focused to an unprecedented degree on Africa. *page 624*

WHAT ROLE did economic motives play in nineteenth-century imperialism?

Motives for the New Imperialism Until the mid–twentieth century, the predominant interpretation of the motives for the New Imperialism was economic. However, many motives beyond economic ones influenced the imperial policies of each of the major European nations. First, after 1870, many political leaders came to believe that the possession of colonies or of imperial influence was an important and even necessary characteristic of a great European power. Second, much of the territorial acquisitions associated with the New Imperialism arose in direct response to the power vacuums that the decay of the Ottoman Empire created. Third, the geopolitical assumptions of European statesmen led them to deeper and deeper involvements from the eastern Mediterranean to Africa. *page 625*

HOW DID European politics contribute to the "Scramble for Africa"?

The Partition of Africa During the so-called "Scramble for Africa," which occurred between the late 1870s and about 1912, the European powers sought to maximize their strategic control of African territory, markets, and raw materials, eventually dividing almost all the continent among themselves. France came to see Algeria as part of France and controlled much of sub-Saharan Africa. Political stagnation and economic collapse paved the way for British domination of Egypt. King Leopold II of Belgium's rule of the Congo was one of brutal economic exploitation. German imperialism in Africa was motivated primarily by European diplomatic concerns. The British and the Boers competed for control of South Africa. *page 626*

HOW DID Russia come to control a vast and diverse Asian empire?

Russian Expansion in Mainland Asia Russian expansion across mainland Asia in the nineteenth century brought huge territories and millions of people of a variety of ethnicities and religions under tsarist rule. Beginning in the late eighteenth century, the tsarist government began to regard the nomadic societies or communities under its domination as foreign and inferior. The nineteenth century saw Russia extend its authority in the Transcaucasus, the steppes of Central Asia, and southern Middle Asia. *page 635*

WHAT DEVELOPMENTS facilitated Western penetration and control of Asia?

Western Powers in Asia Roman Catholic missionaries spearheaded French involvement in Indonesia. The United States established its interest in the Pacific and gained an empire as a result of victory in the Spanish-American war. By the close of the nineteenth century, the Qing Dynasty of China was in a state of near collapse. The Open Door policy of the United States was meant to prevent China's partition by European powers. Resentment of Western interference and domination led to the Boxer Rebellion. *page 636*

HOW DID technological innovations make nineteenth-century imperialism possible?

Tools of Imperialism The domination that Europe and peoples of European descent came to exert over the entire globe by 1900 was based on distinct and temporary technological advantages. Key among them were ironclad steam-powered warships, advances in the prevention of tropical diseases, and superior firearms. *page 639*

WHAT WAS the relationship between missionaries and their home government?

The Missionary Factor The modern Western missionary movement originated in Great Britain in the late eighteenth century as a direct outgrowth of the rise of evangelical Christianity. Roman Catholics later copied Protestant missionary efforts. The mission societies and their missionaries had a complex relationship with their home governments and tensions sometimes arose. Missionaries provided much of the educational infrastructure of imperialism. Missionaries shared with colonial officials the general cultural assumption of the superiority of things Western. Missionary activities gave rise to Asian and African religious movements that challenged the dominance of Western missionaries. *page 641*

HOW DID science help imperialism capture the imagination of domestic audiences in Europe?

Science and Imperialism Western imperialism in the nineteenth and early twentieth centuries was associated with the expansion of natural knowledge. Developments in botany, zoology, medicine, and anthropology demonstrate how imperialism could filter into the wider European culture and capture the imagination of domestic audiences. *page 645*

REVIEW QUESTIONS

1. How did European imperial interests shift geographically in the nineteenth century? How was free trade related to the expansion of European influence around the globe?
2. What was the New Imperialism? How was it different from free-trade imperialism? Why was Britain the dominant world power until the late nineteenth century? What were the Opium Wars?
3. How did the British come to dominate India? What were the causes of the Indian rebellion of 1857? How did British rule in India change after the rebellion? Why was India so important to Britain?
4. Why was Algeria the most important part of the French Empire? What parts of the Ottoman Empire fell under European rule between the 1880s and 1914? Why did Britain come to dominate Egypt? Why did Germany and Italy acquire colonies? Why did Leopold II build an empire in the Congo? What was the "Scramble for Africa"?
5. What were the "tools of imperialism"? Why was quinine so important for the spread of empires? What technological improvements enabled Western powers to dominate so much of the non-Western world? Why were the new colonial empires so short lived?
6. Why did Western missionary efforts expand in the nineteenth century? Why was the relationship between Western missionaries and colonial officials so complicated? Why did Africans want to found their own churches? How has the spread of Christianity in the non-Western world affected the Christian churches?
7. How did Westerners justify imperialism? What was the civilizing mission? What sciences were most associated with the New Imperialism? What role did racism play in the New Imperialism?

KEY TERMS

apartheid (p. 635)
civilizing mission (p. 643)
concentration camps (p. 635)
Great Trek (p. 634)
Imperialism of Free Trade (p. 621)

New Imperialism (p. 620)
protectorate (p. 324)
spheres of influence (p. 624)

For additional learning resources related to this chapter, please go to **www.myhistorylab.com**

PEARSON
myhistorylab

26

Alliances, War, and a Troubled Peace

World War I produced unprecedented destruction and loss of life. Rather than a war of rapid movement, much combat occurred along stationary trenches dug in both western and eastern Europe. Here, Austro-Hungarian troops fight from trenches on the eastern front wearing gas masks. The use of poison gas was one of the innovations of the war and was generally condemned after the war.

National Archives and Records Administration

How did the reality of combat during World War I differ from public expectations at the beginning of the war?

*D*uring the second half of the nineteenth century, Europe wielded unprecedented worldwide influence. Europe's dominance created a single world economy that might have increased general prosperity, but competition among the great powers led instead to a terrible war that undermined Europe's strength and global influence. The peace settlement that followed humiliated Germany and provoked its desire for revenge. The United States also made the fateful decision to withdraw into disdainful isolation from world affairs. ■

EMERGENCE OF THE GERMAN EMPIRE AND THE ALLIANCE SYSTEMS (1873–1890)

WHY DID the alliance system fail?

Prussia's victories over Austria and France and its creation of a large, powerful German Empire in 1871 revolutionized European diplomacy. A vast new political unit had united the majority of Germans to form a nation of great and growing population, wealth, industrial capacity, and military power. Its sudden appearance created new problems and upset the balance of power that the Congress of Vienna had forged. Britain and Russia retained their positions, although the Crimean War had weakened the latter. Austria, however, had been severely weakened, and the forces of nationalism threatened it with disintegration. The Franco-Prussian War and the German annexation of Alsace-Lorraine badly damaged French power and prestige.

BISMARCK'S LEADERSHIP

Until 1890, Bismarck continued to guide German policy. After 1871, he insisted Germany was a satisfied power and wanted no further territorial gains, and he meant it. He tried to assuage French resentment by pursuing friendly relations and by supporting French colonial aspirations. He also prepared for the worst. If France could not be conciliated, it must be isolated. Bismarck sought to prevent an alliance between France and any other European power—especially Austria or Russia—that would threaten Germany with a war on two fronts.

War in the Balkans   Bismarck's first move was to establish the Three Emperors' League in 1873, which brought together Germany, Austria, and Russia. The league soon collapsed over Austro-Russian rivalry in the Balkans that arose from the Russo-Turkish War that broke out in 1877. Ottoman weakness encouraged Serbia and Montenegro to come to the aid of their fellow Slavs in Bosnia and Herzegovina when they revolted against Turkish rule. Soon the rebellion spread to Bulgaria.

Then Russia entered the fray and turned it into a major international crisis. The Russians hoped to pursue their traditional policy of expansion at Ottoman expense and especially to achieve their most cherished goal: control of Constantinople and the Dardanelles. Russian intervention also reflected the influence of the Pan-Slavic movement, which sought to unite all the Slavic peoples, even those under Austrian or Ottoman rule, under the protection of Holy Mother Russia.

Bismarck and the young Kaiser William II meet in 1888. The two disagreed over many issues, and in 1890 William dismissed the aged chancellor.

German Information Center

How did the dismissal of Bismarck contribute to heightened international tension?

The Ottoman Empire was soon forced to sue for peace. Under the Treaty of San Stefano of March 1878, the Slavic states in the Balkans were freed of Ottoman rule, and Russia itself obtained territory and a large monetary indemnity. The settlement, however, alarmed the other great powers. Austria feared that the Slavic victory and the increase in Russian influence in the Balkans would threaten its own Balkan provinces. The British were alarmed both by the effect of the Russian victory on the European balance of power and by the possibility of Russian control of the Dardanelles, which would make Russia a Mediterranean power and threaten Britain's control of the Suez Canal.

The Congress of Berlin   Britain and Austria forced Russia to agree to an international conference at which the other great powers would review the provisions of San Stefano. The resulting Congress of Berlin met in June and July 1878 under the presidency of Bismarck. The choice of site and presiding officer was a clear recognition of Germany's new importance and of Bismarck's claim that Germany wanted no new territory and sought to preserve the peace.

The decisions of the congress were a blow to Russian ambitions. Bulgaria, a Russian client, was reduced in size by two-thirds and deprived of access to the Aegean Sea. Austria-Hungary was given Bosnia and Herzegovina to "occupy and administer," although those provinces remained formally under Ottoman rule. Britain received Cyprus, and France was encouraged to occupy Tunisia. These territories were compensation for the gains that Russia was permitted to keep. Germany asked for nothing but still earned Russian resentment. The Three Emperors' League was dead. Moreover, the south Slavic states of Serbia and Montenegro resented the Austrian occupation of Bosnia and Herzegovina, as did many of the natives of those provinces. The south Slavic question, no less than the estrangement between Russia and Germany, was a threat to the peace of Europe.

German Alliances with Russia and Austria   With Russia alienated, Bismarck concluded a secret treaty with Austria in 1879. This Dual Alliance provided that Germany and Austria would come to each other's aid if Russia attacked either of them. If another country attacked one of them, each promised at least to maintain neutrality.

Bismarck believed that monarchical, reactionary Russia would not seek an alliance either with republican, revolutionary France or with increasingly democratic Britain. In fact, he expected the Austro-German negotiations to frighten Russia into seeking closer relations with Germany, and he was right. By 1881, he had renewed the Three Emperors' League on a firmer basis.

The Triple Alliance   In 1882, Italy, ambitious for colonial expansion and angered by the French occupation of Tunisia, asked to join the Dual Alliance. Bismarck's policy was now a complete success. He was allied with three of the great powers and friendly with the other, Great Britain, which held aloof from all alliances. France was isolated and no threat. Bismarck's diplomacy was a great achievement, but an even greater challenge was to maintain this complicated system of secret alliances in the face of the continuing rivalries among Germany's allies. Despite a war in 1885 between Serbia and Bulgaria that again estranged Austria and Russia, Bismarck succeeded.

Although the Three Emperors' League lapsed, the Triple Alliance (Germany, Austria, and Italy) was renewed for another five years. To restore German relations with Russia, Bismarck negotiated the Reinsurance Treaty of 1887, in which both powers promised to remain neutral if either was attacked. All seemed smooth, but a change in the German monarchy upset Bismarck's arrangements. In 1888, William II

QUICK REVIEW
Congress of Berlin (1878)

- Convened to review the terms of the Treaty of San Stefano between Russia and the Ottoman Empire
- Bismarck acted as the impartial arbiter
- Russian concessions created animosity in Russia against Germany

(r. 1888–1918) came to the German throne. He was twenty-nine years old, ambitious, and impetuous. Like many Germans of his generation, William II was filled with a sense of Germany's destiny as the leading power of Europe. He wanted recognition of at least equality with Britain. To achieve a "place in the sun," he and his contemporaries wanted a navy and colonies like Britain's. These aims, of course, ran counter to Bismarck's limited continental policy. In 1890, William used a disagreement over domestic policy to dismiss Bismarck.

FORGING THE TRIPLE ENTENTE (1890–1907)

Franco-Russian Alliance   Almost immediately after Bismarck's retirement, his system of alliances collapsed. His successor, General Leo von Caprivi (1831–1899), refused the Russian request to renew the Reinsurance Treaty, in part because he felt incompetent to continue Bismarck's complicated policy and in part because he wished to draw Germany closer to Britain, but Britain remained aloof, and Russia was alienated.

Political isolation and the need for foreign capital drove the Russians toward France. The French, who were even more isolated, encouraged their investors to pour capital into Russia if such investment would help produce security against Germany. In 1894, France and Russia signed a defensive alliance against Germany.

Britain and Germany   Britain now became the key to the international situation. Colonial rivalries pitted the British against the Russians in Central Asia and against the French in Africa. (See Chapter 25.) Traditionally, Britain had also opposed Russian control of Constantinople and the Dardanelles and French control of the Low Countries. There was no reason to think Britain would soon become friendly to its traditional rivals or abandon its accustomed friendliness toward the Germans. Yet within a decade of William II's accession, Germany had become the enemy in British minds.

William II admired Britain's colonial empire and mighty fleet. At first, Germany tried to win the British over to the Triple Alliance, but when Britain clung to its "splendid isolation," German policy changed. The idea was to demonstrate Germany's worth as an ally by withdrawing support and even making trouble for Britain. In Africa, the Germans blocked British attempts to build a railroad from Cape Town to Cairo. They also openly sympathized with the Boers of South Africa in their resistance to British expansion. In 1896, William congratulated Paul Kruger (1825–1904), president of the Boer Transvaal Republic, for repulsing a British raid "without having to appeal to friendly powers [i.e., Germany] for assistance." (See Chapter 25.)

In 1898, William began to realize his dream of a German navy with the passage of a naval law providing for the construction of nineteen battleships. In 1900, a second law doubled that figure. The architect of the new navy was Admiral Alfred von Tirpitz (1849–1930), who openly proclaimed that Germany's naval policy was aimed at Britain. The naval policy was a failure. Its main results were to waste German resources and to begin a great naval race with Britain. Eventually, the threat the German navy posed so antagonized and alarmed British opinion that the British abandoned their traditional policies of avoiding alliances.

The Entente Cordiale   The first breach in Britain's isolation came in 1902, when it concluded an alliance with Japan to defend British interests in the Far East against Russia. Next, Britain abandoned its traditional antagonism toward France and in 1904 concluded a series of agreements with the French, collectively called the Entente Cordiale. It was not a formal treaty and had no military provisions, but it settled all outstanding colonial differences between the two nations. In particular, Britain gave France a free hand in Morocco in return for French recognition of British control over Egypt. The Entente Cordiale was a long step toward aligning the British with Germany's great potential enemy.

Britain's new relationship with France was surprising, but in 1904, hardly anyone believed the British whale and the Russian bear would ever come together. The Russo-Japanese War of 1904–1905 made such a development seem even less likely, because Britain was allied with Russia's enemy, but Britain had behaved with restraint, and their unexpected defeat, which also led to the Russian Revolution of 1905, humiliated the Russians. Although the revolution was put down, it weakened Russia and reduced British apprehensions about Russian power. The British also became concerned that Russia might again drift into the German orbit.

The First Moroccan Crisis   At this point, Germany decided to test the new under-standing between Britain and France. In March 1905, Emperor William II landed at Tangier, made a speech in favor of Moroccan independence, and by implication assert-ed Germany's right to participate in Morocco's destiny. This speech was a challenge to France.

The Germans demanded an international conference to show their power more dramatically. The conference met in 1906 at Algeciras in Spain. Austria sided with its German ally, but Spain, which also had claims in Morocco, Italy, Russia, and the Unit-ed States, voted with Britain and France. The Germans had overplayed their hand, re-ceiving trivial concessions, and the French position in Morocco was confirmed. German bullying had, moreover, driven Britain and France closer together. By 1914, French and British military and naval plans were so mutually dependent that the two countries were effectively, if not formally, allies.

British Agreement with Russia   Britain's fear of Germany's growing naval power, its concern over German ambitions in the Near East, and its closer relations with France made it desirable for Britain to become more friendly with France's ally, Russia. With French support, in 1907 the British concluded an agreement with Russia much like the Entente Cordiale with France. It settled Russo-British quarrels in Central Asia and opened the door for wider cooperation. The Triple Entente, an informal, but powerful, association of Britain, France, and Russia, was now ranged against the Triple Alliance. Italy was an unreliable ally, however, which meant two great land powers and Great Britain encircled Germany and Austria-Hungary.

William II and his ministers had turned Bismarck's nightmare of the prospect of a two-front war with France and Russia into a reality. They had made it more horrible by adding Britain to their foes. The equilibrium that Bismarck had worked so hard to achieve was destroyed. Britain would no longer support Austria in restraining Russian ambitions in the Balkans. Germany, increasingly alarmed by a sense of being encircled, was less willing to restrain the Austrians for fear of alienating them, too.

Bismarck had built his alliance system to maintain peace, but the new alliance increased the risk of war and made the Balkans a likely spot for it to break out. Bis-marck's diplomacy had left France isolated and impotent. The new arrangement associ-ated France with the two greatest powers in Europe besides Germany. The Germans could rely only on Austria, and Austria's troubles made it less likely to provide aid than to need it.

QUICK REVIEW

First Moroccan Crisis

- March 1905: William II implies Germany has a role in furthering Moroccan independence
- Germany hoped to weaken relationship between France and Great Britain
- 1906: Conference in Algeciras confirms France's claims in Morocco

WORLD WAR I

HOW DID conflict in the Balkans lead to the outbreak of general war in Europe?

THE ROAD TO WAR (1908–1914)

The weak Ottoman Empire still controlled the central strip of the Balkan Peninsula running west from Constantinople to the Adriatic. North and south of it were the independent states of Romania, Serbia, Montenegro, and Greece, as well as Bulgaria, technically still part of the empire, but legally autonomous and practically independent. The Austro-Hungarian Empire included Croatia and Slovenia and, since 1878, had "occupied and administered" Bosnia and Herzegovina.

Except for the Greeks and the Romanians, most of the inhabitants of the Balkans spoke variants of the same Slavic language and felt a cultural and historical kinship with one another. For centuries Austrians, Hungarians, or Turks had ruled them, and the nationalism that characterized late-nineteenth-century Europe made many of them eager for independence. The more radical among them longed for a union of the south Slavic, or Yugoslav, peoples in a single nation with Serbia at its center.

In 1908, a group of modernizing reformers called the Young Turks seized power in the Ottoman Empire. Their actions threatened to breathe new life into the empire and to interfere with the plans of the European jackals to pounce on the Ottoman corpse. These events brought on the first of a series of Balkan crises that would eventually lead to war.

The Bosnian Crisis   In 1908, the Austrian and Russian governments decided to act quickly before Turkey became strong enough to resist. They struck a bargain in which Russia agreed to support the Austrian annexation of Bosnia and Herzegovina in return for Austrian backing for opening the Dardanelles to Russian warships.

Austria, however, declared the annexation before the Russians could act. The British and French, eager for the favor of the Young Turks, refused to agree to the Russian demand to open the Dardanelles. The Russians were humiliated and furious, but too weak to do anything but protest. The Austrian annexation of Bosnia enraged Russia's "little brothers," the Serbs.

Germany had not been warned in advance of Austria's plans and was unhappy because the action threatened its relations with Russia and Turkey. Germany felt so dependent on the Dual Alliance, however, that it nevertheless assured Austria of its support. It was a dangerous precedent. Also, the failure of Britain and France to support Russia strained the Triple Entente. This made it harder for them to oppose Russian interests in the future if they were to keep Russian friendship.

The Second Moroccan Crisis   The second Moroccan crisis, in 1911, emphasized the French and British need for mutual support. When France sent an army to Morocco, Germany took the opportunity to "protect German interests" there as a means to extort colonial concessions in the French Congo. To add force to their demands, the Germans sent the gunboat *Panther* to the Moroccan port of Agadir, purportedly to protect German citizens there. Once again, as in 1905, the Germans went too far. The *Panther*'s visit to Agadir provoked a strong reaction in Britain. For some time Anglo-German relations had been growing worse, chiefly because the naval race had intensified. The British wrongly believed the Germans meant to turn Agadir into a naval base on the Atlantic. The crisis passed, but Britain drew closer to France. The British made plans to send an expeditionary force to defend France in case Germany attacked, and the British and French navies agreed to cooperate. Without any formal treaty, the German naval construction and the Agadir crisis had turned the Entente Cordiale into a de facto alliance.

QUICK REVIEW

Second Moroccan Crisis

- 1911: France sends an army to Morocco and Germany sends gunboat to Moroccan port of Agadir
- British overreaction leads to naval arms race between Germany and Britain
- Chief effects of the crisis were to increase suspicion between Germany and Britain and to draw France and Britain closer together

War in the Balkans   The second Moroccan crisis also provoked another crisis in the Balkans. Italy sought to gain colonies and to take its place among the great powers. It wanted Libya and feared that the recognition of the French protectorate in Morocco would encourage France to move into Libya also. So, in 1911, Italy attacked the Ottoman Empire to preempt the French and forced Turkey to cede Libya and the Dodecanese Islands in the Aegean. The Italian victory encouraged the Balkan states to try their luck. In 1912, Bulgaria, Greece, Montenegro, and Serbia jointly attacked the Ottoman Empire and won easily. After this First Balkan War, the victors fell out among themselves over the division of Macedonia, and in 1913 a Second Balkan War erupted. This time, Turkey and Romania joined Serbia and Greece against Bulgaria and stripped away much of what the Bulgarians had gained in 1878 and 1912.

After the First Balkan War, the alarmed Austrians were determined to limit Serbian gains and especially to prevent the Serbs from gaining a port on the Adriatic. This policy meant keeping Serbia out of Albania, but the Russians backed the Serbs, and tensions mounted. An international conference sponsored by Britain in early 1913 resolved the dispute in Austria's favor and called for an independent principality of Albania. The Serbs, however, defied the powers and continued to occupy parts of Albania. Finally, in October 1913, Austria issued an ultimatum, and Serbia withdrew its forces from Albania.

The lessons learned from this crisis of 1913 influenced behavior in the final crisis in 1914. As in 1908, the Russians had been embarrassed by their passivity; and their allies were more reluctant to restrain them again. The Austrians were embarrassed by the results of accepting an international conference and were determined not to do it again. They had gotten better results from threatening to use force; they and their German allies did not miss the lesson.

The Austrian archduke Francis Ferdinand and his wife photographed in Sarajevo on June 28, 1914. Later in the day the royal couple were assassinated by young revolutionaries trained and supplied in Serbia, igniting the crisis that led to World War I.
Brown Brothers

What made the archduke Francis Ferdinand a target for a terrorist attack?

SARAJEVO AND THE OUTBREAK OF WAR (JUNE–AUGUST 1914)

The Assassination   On June 28, 1914, a nineteen-year-old Serbian nationalist shot and killed Archduke Francis Ferdinand, heir to the Austrian throne, and his wife as they drove in an open car through the Bosnian capital of Sarajevo. The chief of intelligence of the Serbian army's general staff had helped plan and prepare the crime. Though his role was not known at the time, it was generally believed throughout Europe that Serbian officials were involved.

Moments after the assassination the Austrian police captured one of the assassins.
Brown Brothers

Who were the archduke Francis Ferdinand's assassins and what did they hope to achieve?

Germany and Austria's Response   News of the assassination produced outrage everywhere in Europe except in Serbia. To those Austrians who had long favored an attack on Serbia, the opportunity seemed irresistible. Count Leopold von Berchtold (1863–1942), the Austro-Hungarian foreign minister, felt the need for strong action, but he knew German support would be required in the likely event that Russia should intervene to protect Serbia. Moreover, only German support could persuade the Hungarians to accept a war. The question of peace or war against Serbia, therefore, had to be answered in Berlin.

William II and Chancellor Theobald von Bethmann-Hollweg (1856–1921) readily promised German support for an attack on Serbia. It has often been said that they gave the Austrians a "blank check," but their message was more specific than that. They urged the Austrians to move swiftly while the other powers were still angry at Serbia. They also made the Austrians feel they would view a failure to act as evidence of Austria-Hungary's weakness and uselessness as an ally. Therefore, the Austrians never wavered in their determination to make war on Serbia. They hoped, with the protection of Germany, to fight Serbia alone, but they were prepared to risk a general European conflict. The Germans also knew they risked a general war, but they too hoped to "localize" the fight between Austria and Serbia.

Unfortunately, the calculations proved to be incorrect. Bethmann-Hollweg hoped the Austrians would strike swiftly and present the powers with a fait accompli while the outrage of the assassination was still fresh, and he hoped German support would deter Russia. Failing that, he was prepared for a continental war against France and Russia. This policy, though, depended on British neutrality, and the German chancellor convinced himself the British would stand aloof.

The Austrians, however, were slow to act. They did not even deliver their deliberately unacceptable ultimatum to Serbia until July 23, when the general hostility toward Serbia had begun to subside. Serbia further embarrassed the Austrians by returning so soft and conciliatory an answer that even the mercurial German emperor thought it removed all reason for war, but the Austrians were determined not to turn back. (See "Compare & Connect: The Outbreak of World War I," pages 660–661.) On July 28, they declared war on Serbia, even though the army would not be ready to attack until mid-August.

The Triple Entente's Response   The Russians, previously so often forced to back off, responded angrily to the Austrian demands on Serbia and ordered partial mobilization, against Austria only. This policy was militarily impossible, but its intention was to put diplomatic pressure on Austria to refrain from attacking Serbia. Mobilization of any kind, however, was a dangerous weapon because it was generally understood to be equivalent to an act of war. In fact, only Germany's war plan made mobilization the first and irrevocable start of a war. It required a quick victory in the west before the Russians were ready to act. Even partial Russian mobilization seemed to jeopardize this plan and put Germany in great danger. From this point on, the general staff pressed for German mobilization and war. Their claim of military necessity soon became irresistible.

France and Britain were not eager for war. France's president and prime minister were on their way back from a long-planned state visit to Russia when the crisis flared on July 23. In their absence and without consulting his government, the French ambassador to Russia gave the Russians the same assurances of support that Germany had given Austria. The British worked hard to resolve the crisis by traditional means: a conference of the powers. Austria, still smarting from its humiliation after the London Conference of 1913, would not hear of it. The Germans privately supported the Austrians but publicly took on a conciliatory tone to placate the British.

On July 30, Austria ordered mobilization against Russia. Bethmann-Hollweg resisted the enormous pressure to mobilize, not because he hoped to avoid war, but because he wanted Russia to mobilize against Germany first and appear to be the aggressor. Only in that way could he win the support of the German nation for war, especially the backing of pacifist Social Democrats. His luck was good for a change. The news of Russian general mobilization came only minutes before Germany would have mobilized in any case. Germany then declared war on Russia on August 1. The Schlieffen Plan went into effect. The Germans occupied Luxembourg on August 2 and invaded Belgium, which resisted, on August 3—the same day Germany declared war on France. The invasion of Belgium violated the treaty of 1839 in which the British had joined the other

Overview   Relative Strengths of Combatants in World War I

	POPULATION (TOTAL)	SOLDIERS POTENTIALLY AVAILABLE	MILITARY EXPENDITURES (1913–1914)
GREAT BRITAIN	45,000,000	711,000	$250,000,000
FRANCE	40,000,000	1,250,000	$185,000,000
ITALY	35,000,000	750,000	$50,000,000
RUSSIA	164,000,000	1,200,000	$335,000,000
BELGIUM	7,500,000	180,000	$13,750,000
ROMANIA	7,500,000	420,000	$15,000,000
GREECE	5,000,000	120,000	$3,750,000
SERBIA	5,000,000	195,000	$5,250,000
MONTENEGRO	500,000		
UNITED STATES	92,000,000	150,000	$150,000,000
GERMANY	65,000,000	2,200,000	$300,000,000
AUSTRIA-HUNGARY	50,000,000	810,000	$110,000,000
OTTOMAN EMPIRE	20,000,000	360,000	$40,000,000
BULGARIA	4,500,000	340,000	$5,500,000

powers in guaranteeing Belgian neutrality. This factor undermined sentiment in Britain for neutrality and united the nation against Germany, which then invaded France. On August 4, Britain declared war on Germany. The Great War had begun.

STRATEGIES AND STALEMATE: 1914–1917

Throughout Europe, jubilation greeted the outbreak of war. After years of crises and resentments, war came as a release of tension. The popular press had increased public awareness of, and interest in, foreign affairs and had fanned the flames of patriotism.

Both sides expected to take the offensive, force a battle on favorable ground, and win a quick victory. The Triple Entente powers—or the Allies, as they called themselves—held superiority in numbers and financial resources, as well as command of the sea. Germany and Austria, the Central Powers, had the advantages of possessing internal lines of communication and having launched their attack first.

Germany's war plan was based on ideas developed by Count Alfred von Schlieffen (1833–1913), chief of the German general staff from 1891 to 1906. It aimed to outflank the French frontier defenses by sweeping through Belgium to the Channel and then wheeling to the south and east to envelop the French and crush them against the German

THE OUTBREAK OF WORLD WAR I

In the century between the Congress of Vienna and the events at Sarajevo, Europe had overcome one crisis after another without recourse to a major war. Yet the assassination of the Archduke Francis Ferdinand, heir to the Austro-Hungarian Empire, in a Bosnian town on June 28, 1914, produced a crisis that led to a general and catastrophic war. It is interesting to focus attention on the crisis of July 1914 and to trace the steps that turned a Balkan incident into a major disaster. Austria's ultimatum to Serbia and the answer of the Serbians were critical events in bringing on the war.

QUESTIONS

1. Which of the demands were the most difficult for the Serbians to meet?

2. Why did the Austrians fix so short a time for response?

3. Which demands did the Serbians fail to grant? Why?

4. Was the Austrian immediate declaration of war justified?

I. THE AUSTRIAN ULTIMATUM

On the afternoon of July 23, after an investigation of the assassination of the Archduke Franz Ferdinand at Sarajevo, the Austrians presented a list of demands to Serbia, and the Serbs were given forty-eight hours to reply. The Austrian ambassador to Belgrade was instructed to leave the country and break off diplomatic relations unless the demands were met without reservations. The Serbians knew that some officials of the Serbian government took part in the plot.

THE RESULTS BROUGHT OUT by the inquiry no longer permit the Imperial and Royal Government to maintain the attitude of patient tolerance which it has observed for years toward those agitations which center at Belgrade and are spread thence into the territories of the Monarchy. Instead, these results impose upon the Imperial and Royal Government the obligation to put an end to those intrigues, which constitute a standing menace to the peace of the Monarchy.

In order to attain this end, the Imperial and Royal Government finds itself compelled to demand that the Serbian Government give official assurance that it will condemn the propaganda directed against Austria-Hungary, that is to say, the whole body of the efforts whose ultimate object it is to separate from the Monarchy territories that belong to it; and that it will obligate itself to suppress with all the means at its command this criminal and terroristic propaganda. . . .

1. to suppress every publication which shall incite to hatred and contempt the Monarchy, and the general tendency of which shall be directed against the territorial integrity of the latter;

2. to proceed at once to the dissolution of the Narodna Odbrana, [a Serbian nationalist propaganda and paramilitary organization] confiscate all of its means of propaganda, and in the same manner to proceed against the other unions and associations in Serbia which occupy themselves with propaganda against Austria-Hungary; the Royal Government will take such measures as are necessary to make sure that the dissolved associations may not continue their activities under other names in other forms;

This ethnographic map of the Balkan peninsula, made by a Serbian nationalist named Jovan Cvijić in 1918, served as inspiration for the campaign of ethnic cleansing that would devastate the region once known as Yugoslavia.
Library of Congress

Why were the Balkans a focal point of international conflict?

3. to eliminate without delay from public instruction in Serbia, everything, whether connected with the teaching corps or with the methods of teaching, that serves or may serve to nourish the propaganda against Austria-Hungary;
4. to remove from the military and administrative service in general all officers and officials who have been guilty of carrying on the propaganda against Austria-Hungary, whose names the Imperial and Royal Government reserve the right to make known to the Royal Government . . . ;
5. to agree to the cooperation in Serbia of the organs of the Imperial Royal Government in the suppression of the subversive movement directed against the integrity of the Monarchy;
6. to institute a judicial inquiry against every participant in the conspiracy of the twenty-eighth of June who may be found in Serbian territory; the organs of the Imperial and Royal Government delegated for this purpose will take part in the proceedings held for this purpose;
7. to undertake with all haste the arrest of Major Voislav Tankositch and of one Milan Ciganovitch, a Serbian official, who have been compromised the results of the inquiry; . . .
10. to inform the Imperial and Royal Government without delay of the execution of the measures comprised in the foregoing points.

The Imperial and Royal Government awaits the reply of the Royal Government by Saturday, the twenty-fifth instant, at 6 P.M., at the latest.

Source: "The Austrian Ultimatum," in *Outbreak of the World War; German Documents Collected by Karl Kautsky* and ed. by *Max Montgelas and Walther Schucking*, trans. by the Carnegie Endowment for International Peace. Division of International Law, Supplement I (1924). (New York: Oxford University Press, 1924), pp. 604–605.

II. THE SERBIAN RESPONSE

The reply of the Serbians was remarkably reasonable. In his first reaction to it, the German Kaiser said: "AFTER READING OVER THE SERBIAN REPLY, which I received this morning, I am convinced that on the whole the wishes of the Danube Monarchy have been acceded to. The few reservations that Serbia makes in regard to individual points could, according to my opinion, be settled by negotiation. But it contains the announcement orbi et urbi of a capitulation of the most humiliating kind, and as a result, every cause for war falls to the ground." But it was not unconditional acceptance of the ultimatum.

THE ROYAL SERVIAN GOVERNMENT have received the communication of the Imperial and Royal Government of the 10th instant, and are convinced that their reply will remove any misunderstanding which may threaten to impair the good neighbourly relations between the Austro-Hungarian Monarchy and the Kingdom of Servia. . . .

The Royal Government have been pained and surprised at the statements, according to which members of the Kingdom of Servia are supposed to have participated in the preparations for the crime committed at Serajevo; the Royal Government expected to be invited to collaborate in an investigation of all that concerns this crime, and they were ready, in order to prove the entire correctness of their attitude, to take measures against any persons concerning whom representations were made to them. Falling in, therefore, with the desire of the Imperial and Royal Government, they are prepared to hand over for trial any Servian subject, without regard to his situation or rank, of whose complicity in the crime of Serajevo proofs are forthcoming, and more especially they undertake to cause to be published on the first page of the "Journal officiel," on the date of the 13th (26th) July, the following declaration:—

The Royal Government of Servia condemn all propaganda which may be directed against Austria-Hungary, that is to say, all such tendencies as aim at ultimately detaching from the Austro-Hungarian Monarchy territories which form part thereof and they sincerely deplore the baneful consequences of these criminal movements. The Royal Government regret that, according to the communication from the Imperial and Royal Government, certain Servian officers and officials should have taken part in the above-mentioned propaganda and thus compromised the good neighbourly relations to which the Royal Servian Government was solemnly engaged by the declaration of the 31st March, 1909, which

(continued)

declaration disapproves and repudiates all idea or attempt at interference with the destiny of the inhabitants of any part whatsoever of Austria-Hungary, and they consider it their duty formally to warn the officers, officials, and entire population of the kingdom that henceforth they will take the most rigorous steps against all such persons as are guilty of such acts, to prevent and to repress which they will use their utmost endeavour. . . .

The Royal Government further undertake:—

1. To introduce at the first regular convocation of the Skuptchina a provision into the press law providing for the most severe punishment of incitement to hatred or contempt of the Austro-Hungarian Monarchy, and for taking action against any publication the general tendency of which is directed against the territorial integrity of Austria-Hungary. . . .

2. The Royal Government will accept the demand of the Imperial and Royal Government, and will dissolve the "Narodna Odbrana" Society and every other society which may be directing its efforts against Austria-Hungary.

3. The Royal Servian Government undertake to remove without delay from their public educational establishments in Servia all that serves or could serve to foment propaganda against Austria-Hungary, whenever the Imperial and Royal Government furnish them with facts and proofs of this propaganda.

4. The Royal Government also agree to remove from military service all such persons as the judicial enquiry may have proved to be guilty of acts directed against the integrity of the territory of the Austro-Hungarian Monarchy, and they expect the Imperial and Royal Government to communicate to them at a later date the names and the acts of these officers and officials for the purposes of the proceedings which are to be taken against them.

5. The Royal Government must confess that they do not clearly grasp the meaning or the scope of the demand made by the Imperial and Royal Government that Servia shall undertake to accept the collaboration of the organs of the Imperial and Royal Government upon their territory, but they declare that they will admit such collaboration as agrees with the principle of international law, with criminal procedure, and with good neighbourly relations.

6. It goes without saying that the Royal Government consider it their duty to open an enquiry against all such persons as are, or eventually may be, implicated in the plot of the 15th June, and who happen to be within the territory of the kingdom. As regards the participation in this enquiry of Austro-Hungarian agents or authorities appointed for this purpose by the Imperial and Royal Government, the Royal Government cannot accept such an arrangement, as it would be a violation of the Constitution and of the law of criminal procedure; nevertheless, in concrete cases communications as to the results of the investigation in question might be given to the Austro-Hungarian agents.

7. The Royal Government proceeded, on the very evening of the delivery of the note, to arrest Commandant Voislav Tankossitch. As regards Milan Ziganovitch, who is a subject of the Austro-Hungarian Monarchy and who, up to the 15th June was employed (on probation) by the directorate of railways, it has not yet been possible to arrest him. . . .

10. The Royal Government will inform the Imperial and Royal Government the execution of the measures comprised under the above heads, in so far as this has not already been done by the present note, as soon as each measure has been ordered and carried out.

If the Imperial and Royal Government are not satisfied with this reply, the Servian Government, considering that it is not to the common interest to precipitate the solution of this question, are ready, as always, to accept a pacific understanding, either by referring this question to the decision of the International Tribunal of The Hague, or to the Great Powers which took part in the drawing up of the declaration made by the Servian Government on the 18th (31st) March 1909.

Belgrade, July 12 (25), 1914

Source: "Serbia's Answer to Ultimatum," from *British Diplomatic Correspondence in Collected Diplomatic Documents Relating to the Outbreak of the European War*, No. 39 (H. M. Stationary Off: 1915), pp. 31–37.

fortresses in Lorraine. In the east, the Germans planned to stand on the defensive against Russia until France had been crushed, a task they thought would take only six weeks.

The apparent risk, besides the violation of Belgian neutrality and the consequent alienation of Britain, lay in weakening the German defenses against a direct attack across the frontier. The true danger was that the German striking force on the right through Belgium would not be powerful enough to make the swift progress vital to success. In the end, for reasons still debated, the plan failed by a narrow margin.

The War in the West   The French had also put their faith in the offensive, but with less reason than the Germans. They underestimated the numbers and effectiveness of the German reserves and overestimated what the courage and spirit of their own troops could achieve. The French offensive on Germany's western frontier failed totally. This defeat probably was preferable to a partial success, because it released troops for use against the main German army. As a result, the French and the British were able to stop the German advance on Paris at the Battle of the Marne in September 1914. (See Map 26–1 and Map 26–2, page 664.)

MAP 26–1   **World War I in Europe**   Despite the importance of military action in the Far East, in the Arab world, and at sea, the main theaters of activity in World War I were in the European areas.

Which European countries saw the most military action in World War I?

MAP EXPLORATION

Interactive map: To explore this map further, go to
www.myhistorylab.com

MEUSE–ARGONNE MAJOR AMERICAN DRIVES CUT THE GERMAN SUPPLY LINE AT SEDAN AND END THE WAR, NOV. 11, 1918.

100 MILES
100 KILOMETERS

① Farthest German Advance, Sept., 1914
② Nivelle's Offensive, Spring, 1917
③ Hindenburg Line (Stabilized Line) 1917–1918
④ German Gains, March–July, 1918
⑤ Major American Drives, Nov. 11, 1918
⑥ Armistice Line, Nov. 11, 1918

MAP 26–2   The Western Front, 1914–1918   This map shows the crucial western front in detail.

What factors made the war on the western front one of position rather than of movement?

Thereafter, the nature of the war in the west became one of position instead of movement. Both sides dug in behind a wall of trenches protected by barbed wire that stretched from the North Sea to Switzerland. Strategically placed machine-gun nests made assaults difficult and dangerous. Both sides, nonetheless, attempted massive attacks preceded by artillery bombardments of unprecedented and horrible force and duration. Still, the defense was always able to recover and to bring up reserves fast enough to prevent a breakthrough.

Assaults that cost hundreds of thousands of lives produced advances of only hundreds of yards. Even poison gas proved ineffective. In 1916, the British introduced the tank, which eventually proved to be the answer to the machine gun. The Allied command was slow to understand this, however, and until the end of the war, defense was supreme. For three years after its establishment, the western front moved only a few miles in either direction.

The War in the East   In the east, the war began auspiciously for the Allies. The Russians advanced into Austrian territory and inflicted heavy casualties, but Russian incompetence and German energy soon reversed the situation. In 1915, the Central Powers pressed their advantage in the east and drove into the Baltic states and Russian Poland, inflicting more than 2 million casualties in a single year.

As the battle lines hardened, both sides sought new allies. Turkey (because of its hostility to Russia) and Bulgaria (the enemy of Serbia) joined the Central Powers. Both sides bid for Italian support with promises of the spoils of victory. Because the Austrians held what the Italians wanted most, the Allies could promise more. In a secret treaty of 1915, they agreed to deliver to Italy after victory most of *Italia irredenta* (i.e., the South Tyrol, Trieste, and some of the Dalmatian Islands), plus colonies in Africa and a share of the Turkish Empire. By the spring of 1915, Italy was engaging Austrian armies. Romania joined the Allies in 1916 but was quickly defeated and driven from the war.

In the Far East, Japan honored its alliance with Britain and entered the war. The Japanese quickly overran the German colonies in China and the Pacific and used the opportunity to put pressure on China. Both sides also appealed to nationalistic sentiment in areas the enemy held. The Germans supported nationalist movements among the Irish, the Flemings in Belgium, and the Poles and Ukrainians under Russian rule. They even tried to persuade the Turks to lead a Muslim uprising against the British in Egypt and India, and against the French and Italians in North Africa. The Allies made the same appeals with greater success. They sponsored movements of national autonomy for the Czechs, the Slovaks, the south Slavs, and againt the Poles who were under Austrian rule. They also favored a movement of Arab independence from Turkey.

In 1915, the Allies tried to break the deadlock on the western front by going around it. The idea came chiefly from Winston Churchill (1874–1965), first lord of the British admiralty. He proposed to attack the Dardanelles and capture Constantinople. This policy supposedly would knock Turkey from the war, bring help to the Balkan front, and ease communications with Russia. The success of Churchill's plan depended on timing, speed, and daring leadership, but all of these were lacking. Worse, the execution of the attack was inept and overly cautious. Before the campaign was abandoned, the Allies lost almost 150,000 men and diverted three times that number from more useful occupations.

British tanks moving toward the Battle of Cambrai in Flanders late in 1917. Tanks were impervious to machine-gun fire. Had they been used in great numbers, they might have broken the stalemate in the west.

Bildarchiv Preussischer Kulturbesitz

How did tanks change the nature of the fighting on the western front?

Return to the West   Both sides turned back to the west in 1916. General Erich von Falkenhayn (1861–1922), who had succeeded Moltke in September 1914, attacked the French stronghold of Verdun. The French held Verdun with comparatively few men and inflicted almost as many casualties as they suffered. The commander of Verdun, Henri Pétain (1856–1951), became a national hero, and "They shall not pass" became a slogan of national defiance.

The Allies tried to end the impasse by launching a major offensive along the River Somme in July. Aided by a Russian attack in the east that drew off some German strength and by an enormous artillery bombardment, they hoped at last to break through. Once again, the defense was superior. Enormous casualties on both sides brought no result. The war on land dragged on with no end in sight.

The War at Sea   As the war continued, control of the sea became more important. The British imposed a strict blockade meant to starve out the enemy. The Germans responded with submarine warfare meant to destroy British shipping and starve the British. They declared the waters around the British Isles a war zone, where even neutral ships would not be safe. Both policies were unwelcome to neutrals, and especially to the United States, which conducted extensive trade in the Atlantic. Yet the sinking of neutral ships by German submarines was both more dramatic and more offensive than the British blockade.

In May 1915, a German submarine torpedoed the British liner *Lusitania*. Among the 1,200 who drowned were 118 Americans. President Woodrow Wilson (1856–1924) warned Germany that a repetition would have grave consequences; the Germans desisted for the time being, rather than further anger the United States.

America Enters the War   In December 1916, President Woodrow Wilson intervened to try to bring about a negotiated peace. Neither side, however, was willing to renounce war aims that its opponent found acceptable. The war seemed likely to continue until one or both sides reached exhaustion. Two events early in 1917 changed the situation radically. First, on February 1, the Germans announced the resumption of unrestricted submarine warfare, which led the United States to break off diplomatic relations and to declare war on Germany on April 6. Second, in March 1917 a revolution in Russia overthrew the tsarist government.

The use of poison gas (by both sides) during the First World War and its dreadful effects—blinding, asphyxiation, burned lungs—came to symbolize the horrors of modern war. This painting shows a group of British soldiers being guided to the rear after they were blinded by mustard gas on the western front.

John Singer Sargent, *Gassed*, 1918–1919. Imperial War Museum, London

How did the horrors of World War I shape political opinion in the post-war era?

THE RUSSIAN REVOLUTION

WHAT FACTORS made the rise of the Bolsheviks to power in Russia possible?

No political faction planned or led the March 1917 Revolution in Russia. It was the result of the collapse of the monarchy's ability to govern. Nicholas II was weak and incompetent and suspected of being under the domination of his German wife and the insidious peasant faith healer Rasputin, whom a group of Russian noblemen assassinated in 1916. Military and domestic failures produced massive casualties, widespread hunger, strikes by workers, and disorganization in the army. The peasant discontent that had plagued the countryside before 1914 did not subside during the conflict. In 1915, the tsar took personal command of the armies on the German front, which kept him away from the capital. In his absence, corrupt and incompetent ministers increasingly discredited the government even in the eyes of conservative monarchists. All political factions in the Duma, Russia's parliament, were discontented.

THE PROVISIONAL GOVERNMENT

In early March 1917, strikes and worker demonstrations erupted in Petrograd, as Saint Petersburg had been renamed. The ill-disciplined troops in the city refused to fire on the demonstrators. The tsar abdicated on March 15. The government of Russia fell into the hands of members of the Duma, who soon formed a provisional government composed chiefly of Constitutional Democrats (Cadets) with Western sympathies.

At the same time, the various socialist groups, including both Social Revolutionaries and Social Democrats of the Menshevik wing, began to organize soviets, councils of workers and soldiers. Initially, they allowed the provisional government to function without actually supporting it, but they became estranged when the Cadets failed to control the army or to purge "reactionaries" from the government.

In this climate, the provisional government decided to remain loyal to Russia's alliances and continue the war. The provisional government thus accepted tsarist foreign

What was the relationship between World War I and political upheaval in Russia?

policy and associated itself with the main source of domestic suffering and discontent. The collapse of the last Russian offensive in the summer of 1917 sealed its fate. Disillusionment with the war, shortages of food and other necessities at home, and the peasants' demands for land reform undermined the government. This occurred even after the moderate socialist Alexander Kerensky (1881–1970) became prime minister. Moreover, discipline in the army had disintegrated.

LENIN AND THE BOLSHEVIKS

Ever since April, the Bolshevik wing of the Social Democratic Party had been working against the provisional government. The Germans, in their most successful attempt at subversion, had rushed the brilliant Bolshevik leader V. I. Lenin (1870–1924) in a sealed train from his exile in Switzerland across Germany to Petrograd. They hoped he would cause trouble for the revolutionary government.

Lenin saw the opportunity to achieve the political alliance of workers and peasants he had discussed before the war. In speech after speech, he hammered away on the theme of peace, bread, and land. The Bolsheviks demanded that all political power go to the soviets, which they controlled. The failure of the summer offensive encouraged them to attempt a coup, but the effort was a failure. Lenin fled to Finland, and his chief collaborator, Leon Trotsky (1879–1940), was imprisoned.

The failure of a right-wing countercoup gave the Bolsheviks another chance. Trotsky, released from prison, led the powerful Petrograd soviet. Lenin returned in October and insisted to his doubting colleagues that the time was ripe to take power. Trotsky organized the coup that took place on November 6 and concluded with an armed assault on the provisional government. The Bolsheviks, almost as much to their own astonishment as to that of the rest of the world, had come to rule Russia.

THE COMMUNIST DICTATORSHIP

The victors moved to fulfill their promises and to assure their own security. The provisional government had decreed an election for late November to select a Constituent Assembly. The Social Revolutionaries won a large majority over the Bolsheviks. When the assembly gathered in January, it met for only a day before the Red Army, controlled by the Bolsheviks, dispersed it. In November and January, the Bolshevik government nationalized the land and turned it over to its peasant proprietors. Factory workers were put in charge of their plants. The state seized banks and repudiated the debt of the tsarist government. Property of the church reverted to the state.

The Bolshevik government also took Russia out of the war, which they believed benefited only capitalism. They signed an armistice with Germany in December 1917 and in March 1918 accepted the Treaty of Brest-Litovsk, by which Russia yielded Poland, Finland, the Baltic states, and Ukraine. Some territory in the Transcaucasus region went to Turkey. The Bolsheviks also agreed to pay a heavy war indemnity. These terms were a high price to pay for peace, but Lenin had no choice. Russia was incapable of renewing the war effort, and the Bolsheviks needed time to impose their rule.

The new Bolshevik government met major domestic resistance. Civil war erupted between Red Russians, who supported the revolution, and White Russians, who opposed it. In the summer of 1918, the Bolsheviks murdered the tsar and his family. Loyal army officers continued to fight the revolution and received aid from Allied armies. Under the leadership of Trotsky, however, the Red Army eventually overcame the domestic opposition. By 1921, Lenin and his supporters were in firm control.

THE END OF WORLD WAR I

WHAT WERE the immediate consequences of the end of World War I?

The collapse of Russia and the Treaty of Brest-Litovsk were the zenith of German success. The Germans controlled eastern Europe and its resources, especially food, and by 1918 they were free to concentrate their forces on the western front. These developments would probably have been decisive without American intervention. Still, American troops would not arrive in significant numbers for about a year, and both sides tried to win the war in 1917.

An Allied attempt to break through in the west failed disastrously. The Austrians, supported by the Germans, defeated the Italians at Caporetto and threatened to overrun northern Italy, until they were checked with the aid of Allied troops. The deadlock continued, but time was running out for the Central Powers.

GERMANY'S LAST OFFENSIVE

In March 1918, the Germans decided to gamble everything on one last offensive. The German army reached the Marne again but got no farther. They had no more reserves, and the entire nation was exhausted. In contrast, the arrival of American troops in ever-increasing numbers bolstered the Allies. An Allied counteroffensive proved irresistible. As the exhausted Austrians collapsed in Italy, and Bulgaria and Turkey dropped out of the war, the German high command knew the end was imminent.

Ludendorff was determined to make peace before the German army was thoroughly defeated in the field and to make civilians responsible for ending the war. For some time, he had been the effective ruler of Germany under the aegis of the emperor. He now allowed a new government to be established on democratic principles and to seek peace immediately. The new government, under Prince Max of Baden, asked for peace on the basis of the **Fourteen Points** that President Wilson had declared as the American war aims. These were idealistic principles, including self-determination for nationalities, open diplomacy, freedom of the seas, disarmament, and the establishment of the League of Nations to keep the peace.

Fourteen Points President Woodrow Wilson's idealistic principles articulated as America's goals in World War I, including self-determination for nationalities, open diplomacy, freedom of the seas, disarmament, and establishment of the League of Nations to keep the peace.

Women Munitions Workers in England. World War I demanded more from the civilian populations than had previous wars, resulting in important social changes. The demands of the munitions industries and a shortage of men (so many of whom were in uniform) brought many women out of traditional roles at home and into factories and other war-related work.

Getty Images Inc.—Hulton Archive Photos

What were the consequences of World War I for British society?

THE ARMISTICE

The disintegration of the German army forced William II to abdicate on November 9, 1918. The majority branch of the Social Democratic Party proclaimed a republic to prevent their radical Leninist wing from setting up a soviet government. Two days later, this republican, socialist-led government signed the armistice that ended the war by accepting German defeat. The German people were, in general, unaware their army had been defeated and was crumbling. Many of them came to believe Germany had not been defeated but had been tricked by the enemy and betrayed—even stabbed in the back—by republicans and socialists at home.

The Great War, as contemporaries called it, lasted more than four years, doing terrible damage. Battle casualties alone counted more than 4 million dead and 8.3 million wounded among the Central Powers and 5.4 million dead and 7 million wounded from their opponents, and millions of civilians died from the war and causes arising from it. Among the casualties also were the German, Austro-Hungarian, Russian, and Turkish Empires. The American intervention in 1917 thrust the United States into European affairs with a vengeance, and the collapse of the Russian autocracy brought the Bolshevik revolution and the reality of a great communist state. Disappointment, resentment, and economic dislocations caused by the war brought various forms of fascism to Italy, Germany, and other countries. The comfortable nineteenth-century assumptions of inevitable progress based on reason, science and technology, individual freedom, democracy, and free enterprise gave way in many places to cynicism, nihilism, dictatorship, statism, official racism, and class warfare. It is widely agreed that the First World War was the mother of the Second and to most of the horrors of the rest of the century.

These kinds of changes affected the colonial peoples the European powers ruled, and overseas empires would never again be as secure as they had seemed before the war. Europe was no longer the center of the world, free to interfere when it wished or to ignore the rest of the world if it chose. The memory of that war lived on to shake the nerve of the victorious Western powers as they faced the new conditions of the postwar world.

SIGNIFICANT DATES FROM THE ERA CULMINATING IN WORLD WAR I

1871	Creation of the German Empire
1873	The Three Emperors' League
1875	The Russo-Turkish War
1879	The Dual Alliance (Germany and Austria)
1882	The Triple Alliance (Germany, Austria, and Italy)
1888	William II becomes the German emperor (kaiser)
1890	Bismarck is dismissed
1894	The Franco-Russian alliance
1898	Germany begins to build a battleship navy
1899–1902	Boer War
1902	The British alliance with Japan
1904	The Entente Cordiale (Britain and France)
1904–1905	The Russo-Japanese War
1905	The first Moroccan crisis
1908–1909	The Bosnian crisis
1911	The second Moroccan crisis
1912–1913	The First and Second Balkan Wars
1914	(August) Germans attack in the West; (August–September) First Battle of the Marne; (September) Battles of Tannenberg and the Masurian Lakes
1915	(April) Dardanelles campaign; (May) Germans sink British ship *Lusitania*
1916	(February) Germans attack Verdun; (May–June) Battle of Jutland
1917	(February) Germans declare unrestricted submarine warfare; (March) Russian Revolution; (April) United States enters war; (November) Bolsheviks seize power
1918	(March) Treaty of Brest-Litovsk; German offensive in the West; (November) Armistice

THE END OF THE OTTOMAN EMPIRE

At the outbreak of World War I in August 1914, the Ottoman Empire was neutral, but many military officers, the so-called Young Turks who had taken control of the Ottoman government in 1909, were pro-German. After hesitating for three months, the Turks decided to enter the war on the German side in November 1914. This decision ultimately brought about the end of the Ottoman Empire. Early victories gave way to defeat after defeat at the hands of the Russians and the British. By October 30, 1918, Turkey was out of the war. In November, an Allied fleet sailed into the harbor of Constantinople and landed troops who occupied the city.

The peace treaty signed in Paris in 1920 between Turkey and the Allies dismembered the Ottoman Empire, placing large parts of it, particularly the areas Arabs inhabited, under the control of Britain and France. In Mesopotamia the British created the state of Iraq, which, along with Palestine, became British mandates. Syria and Lebanon became French mandates. (**Mandates** were territories that were legally administered under the auspices of the League of Nations, but were in effect ruled as colonies.) A Greek invasion of the Turkish homeland in Anatolia in 1919 provoked a nationalist reaction, bringing the young general Mustafa Kemal (1881–1938), who later took the name Ataturk, meaning "Father of the Turks," to power. He drove the Greeks out of Anatolia and compelled the victorious powers to make a new arrangement sealed by the treaty of Lausanne in 1923. Ataturk abolished the Ottoman sultanate and deposed the last caliph. The new Republic of Turkey abandoned most of the old Ottoman Empire but became fully independent of control by the European powers and sovereign in its Anatolian homeland. Under Ataturk and his successors, Turkey, although its population was overwhelmingly Muslim, became a secular state and a force for stability in the region.

mandates Territories under the aegis of the League of Nations but actually ruled as a colonies.

The Arab portions of the old empire, however, were a different story. Divided into a collection of artificial states that had no historical reality, governed or dominated as client regimes by the British and French, they were relatively quiet during the 1920s and 1930s. The weakening of Britain and France during and after the Second World War, however, and their subsequent abandonment of control in the Middle East would create problems in the latter part of the century.

THE SETTLEMENT AT PARIS

WHAT WERE the key weaknesses of the Paris peace settlement?

The representatives of the victorious states gathered at Versailles and other Parisian suburbs in the first half of 1919. Wilson speaking for the United States, David Lloyd George (1863–1945) for Britain, Georges Clemenceau (1841–1929) for France, and Vittorio Emanuele Orlando (1860–1952) for Italy made up the Big Four. Japan also had an important part in the discussions.

OBSTACLES THE PEACEMAKERS FACED

The negotiators at Paris in 1919 represented constitutional, generally democratic governments, and public opinion had become a mighty force. Though there were secret sessions, the conference often worked in the full glare of publicity. Nationalism had become almost a secular religion, and Europe's many ethnic groups could not be relied on to remain quiet while the great powers distributed them on the map. Moreover, propaganda and especially the intervention of Woodrow Wilson had transformed World War I into a moral crusade to achieve a peace that would be just as well as secure. (See "Encountering the Past: War Propaganda and the Movies," page 672) The Fourteen Points set forth the right of nationalities to self-determination as an absolute value, but in fact no one could draw the map of Europe to match ethnic groups perfectly with their homelands. All these elements made compromise difficult. Wilson's idealism, moreover, came into conflict with the more practical war aims of the victorious powers and with many of the secret treaties that had been made before and during the war.

The continuing national goals of the victors presented further obstacles to an idealistic "peace without victors." France was painfully conscious of its numerical inferiority to Germany and of the low birthrate that would keep it inferior. So France was naturally eager to weaken Germany permanently and preserve French superiority. Italy continued to seek *Italia irredenta*, Britain looked to its imperial interests, and Japan pursued its own advantage in Asia. The United States insisted on freedom of the seas, which favored American commerce, and on its right to maintain the Monroe Doctrine.

Finally, the peacemakers of 1919 faced a world still in turmoil. The greatest immediate threat appeared to be the spread of Bolshevism. While civil war distracted Lenin and his colleagues, the Allies landed small armies in Russia to help overthrow the Bolshevik regime. The revolution seemed likely to spread as communist governments were established in Bavaria and Hungary. A communist uprising led by the "Spartacus group" had to be suppressed in Berlin. The worried Allies even allowed an army of German volunteers to fight the Bolsheviks in the Baltic states.

THE PEACE

The Paris settlement consisted of five separate treaties between the victors and the defeated powers. Formal sessions began on January 18, 1919, and the last treaty

The Allies promoted Arab efforts to secure independence from Turkey in an effort to remove Turkey from the war. Delegates to the peace conference of 1919 in Paris included British colonel T. E. Lawrence, who helped lead the rebellion, and representatives from the Middle Eastern region. Prince Feisal, the third son of King Hussein, stands in the foreground of this picture; Colonel T. E. Lawrence is in the middle row, second from the right; and Brigadier General Nuri Pasha Said of Baghdad is second from the left.

CORBIS/Bettmann

How did the settlements reached after World War I contribute to future unrest in the Middle East?

"The Big Four" attending the Paris peace conference in 1919: Vittorio Orlande, premier of Italy; David Lloyd George, prime minister of Great Britain; Georges Clemenceau, premier of France, and Woodrow Wilson, president of the United States (l. to r.).

National Archives and Records Administration

What were the goals of the "Big Four" at the peace conference that followed World War I?

ENCOUNTERING THE PAST

WAR PROPAGANDA AND THE MOVIES—CHARLIE CHAPLIN

The huge expenditure of life and treasure required to conduct the war would not have been tolerated by the masses had governments on both sides not used propaganda to convince their people of its necessity. Propagandists demonized opponents and represented the homefront as totally committed to a noble, even holy, cause. The propagandists of World War I initially relied on newspaper articles and pamphlets to get their message across, but they soon developed powerful visual media—posters, cartoons, caricatures, and (by the middle war years) films. These were equally effective with persons of every age, class, and level of education, and they had great emotional impact.

Movies graphically represented the enemy as horrible or ridiculous and one's own people as noble, brave, and self-sacrificing. Both sides in the Great War produced films that were immensely popular with their people. The Germans considered films so important as morale boosters that they issued special rations of scarce fuel to theaters to keep them functioning through the brutal winter of 1917–1918. Germany did not, however, produce an actor of the status of the British-American comedian Charlie Chaplin (1889–1977). Chaplin came to America in 1914 to work in vaudeville, and he was a noted film star by the time the war broke out. His most famous character was a tragi-comic tramp figure who had many adventures in many movies. Chaplin's major wartime success was *Shoulder Arms* (1918), a farce in which a lone American soldier single-handedly captures a unit of bumbling Germans and the kaiser himself.

Charlie Chaplin in *Shoulder Arms.*
© Sunset Boulevard/ Corbis Sygma

What new forms of propaganda were used during World War I?

WHAT IS the purpose of military propaganda? Can films hurt as well as help war efforts?

was signed on August 10, 1920. (See Map 26–3.) Wilson arrived in Europe to unprecedented popular acclaim. Liberals and idealists expected a new kind of international order achieved in a new and better way, but they were soon disillusioned. "Open covenants openly arrived at" soon gave way to closed sessions in which Wilson, Clemenceau, and Lloyd George made arrangements that seemed cynical to outsiders.

The notion of "a peace without victors" became a mockery when the Soviet Union (as Russia was now called) and Germany were excluded from the peace conference. The principle of national self-determination was violated many times and was unavoidable. Still, their exclusion from decisions angered the diplomats from the small nations. The undeserved adulation accorded Wilson on his arrival gradually turned into equally undeserved scorn. He had not abandoned his ideals lightly but had merely given way to the irresistible force of reality.

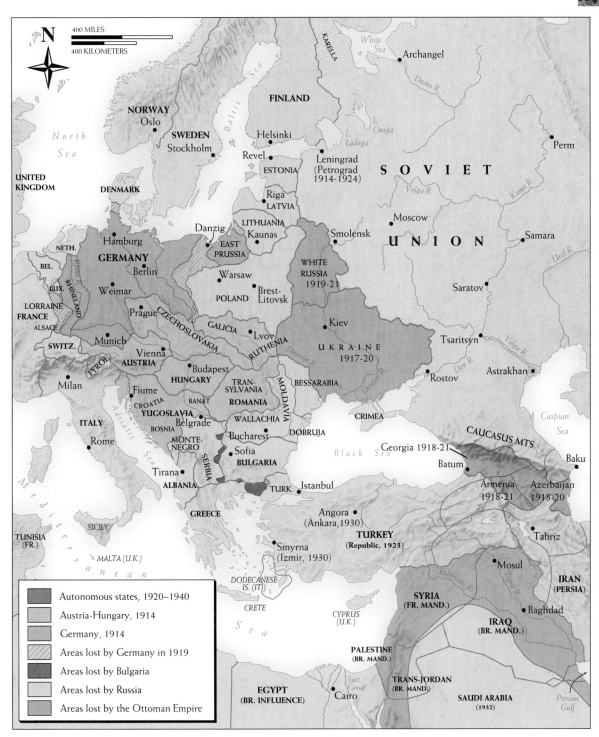

MAP 26–3   World War I Peace Settlement in Europe and the Middle East   The map of central and eastern Europe, as well as that of the Middle East, underwent drastic revision after World War I. The enormous territorial losses suffered by Germany, Austria-Hungary, the Ottoman Empire, Bulgaria, and Russia were the other side of the coin represented by gains for France, Italy, Greece, and Romania and by the appearance or reappearance of at least eight new independent states from Finland in the north to Yugoslavia in the south. The mandate system for former Ottoman territories outside Turkey proper laid foundations for several new, mostly Arab, states in the Middle East. In Africa, the mandate system placed the former German colonies under British, French, and South African rule.

How did the peace settlement affect the territorial makeup of Europe?

The League of Nations   Wilson could make unpalatable concessions without abandoning his ideals because he put great faith in a new instrument for peace and justice: the League of Nations. Its covenant was an essential part of the peace treaty. The league was to be not an international government, but a body of sovereign states that agreed to pursue common policies and to consult in the common interest, especially when war threatened. The members promised to submit differences among themselves to arbitration, an international court, or the League Council. (The league was unlikely to be effective, however, because it had no armed forces at its disposal.) Furthermore, any action required the unanimous consent of its council, consisting permanently of Britain, France, Italy, the United States, and Japan, as well as four other states that had temporary seats. The Covenant of the League bound its members to "respect and preserve" the territorial integrity of all its members; this was generally seen as a device to ensure the security of the victorious powers. (The exclusion of Germany and the Soviet Union from the League Assembly further undermined its claim to evenhandedness.)

Germany   In the West, the main territorial issue was the fate of Germany. The French wanted to set the Rhineland up as a separate buffer state, but Lloyd George and Wilson would not permit it. Still, they could not ignore France's need for protection against a resurgent Germany. France received Alsace-Lorraine and the right to work the coal mines of the Saar for fifteen years. Germany west of the Rhine and fifty kilometers east of it was to be a demilitarized zone. Allied troops could stay on the west bank for fifteen years. The treaty also provided that Britain and the United States would help France if Germany attacked it. Such an attack was made more unlikely by the permanent disarmament of Germany. As long as these provisions were observed, France would be safe.

The East   The settlement in the East reflected the collapse of the great defeated empires that had ruled it for centuries. Germany lost part of Silesia, and East Prussia was cut off from the rest of Germany by a corridor carved out to give the revived state of Poland access to the sea. The Austro-Hungarian Empire disappeared entirely, giving way to five small successor states. Most of its German-speaking people were gathered in the Republic of Austria, cut off from the Germans of Bohemia and forbidden to unite with Germany.

The Magyars were left with the much reduced kingdom of Hungary. The Czechs of Bohemia and Moravia joined with the Slovaks and Ruthenians to the east to form Czechoslovakia, and this new state included several million unhappy Germans plus Poles, Magyars, and Ukrainians. The southern Slavs were united in the Kingdom of Serbs, Croats, and Slovenes, or Yugoslavia. Italy gained Trentino, which included tens of thousands of German speakers, and the port of Trieste. Romania was enlarged by receiving Transylvania from Hungary and Bessarabia from Russia. Bulgaria lost territory to Greece and Yugoslavia. Russia lost vast territories in the west. Finland, Estonia, Latvia, and Lithuania became independent states, and most of Poland was carved out of formerly Russian soil.

Reparations   (Perhaps the most debated part of the peace settlement dealt with reparations for the damage Germany did during the war. Before the armistice, the Germans promised to pay compensation "for all damages done to the civilian population of the Allies and their property." The Americans judged the amount would be between $15 billion and $25 billion and that Germany would be able to pay that amount. France and Britain, however, who worried about repaying their war debts to the United States, were eager to have Germany pay the full cost of the war, including pensions to survivors and dependents.)

There was general agreement that Germany could not afford to pay such a huge sum, whatever it might be, and the conference did not specify an amount. In the meantime, Germany was to pay $5 billion annually until 1921. At that time, a final figure would be set, which Germany would have to pay in thirty years.

To justify these huge reparation payments, the Allies inserted the notorious war guilt clause (Clause 231) into the treaty in which German aggression was identified as the sole cause of the war. The Germans, of course, did not believe they were solely responsible for the war and bitterly resented the charge. They had lost territories containing badly needed natural resources. Yet they were presented with an astronomical and apparently unlimited reparations bill. To add insult to injury, they were required to admit to a war guilt they did not feel.

Finally, to heap insult upon insult, they were required to accept the entire treaty as the victors wrote it, without negotiation. There was no choice. The Social Democrats and the Catholic Center Party formed a new government, and their representatives signed the treaty. These parties formed the backbone of the Weimar government that ruled Germany until 1933. They never overcame the stigma of having accepted the Treaty of Versailles.

WORLD WAR I AND COLONIAL EMPIRES

The First World War and the peace settlement introduced numerous changes and transformations into the European colonial world.

Redistribution of Colonies into Mandates   The rivalries over empire that had predated the outbreak of the war and that had contributed so mightily to prewar tensions continued throughout the conflict. The war opened the possibility for whoever won it to expand their empires at the cost of the defeated powers. As a result, the single most important imperial consequence of World War I was Germany being stripped of its colonies and the Ottoman Empire of regions it had formerly governed.

The Covenant of the League of Nations established mandates within these former colonies and regions. These mandates located in the Middle East, Africa, and the Pacific were placed under the "tutelage" of one of the great powers under League of Nations supervision and encouraged to advance toward independence. Britain and France became the chief mandate administrators and were consequently drawn more deeply into new regions of the world, most particularly, the Middle East. In effect, the mandates became colonies of the administering powers. Some mandates, most notably Iraq, became independent between the wars. Other mandates became independent often with considerable conflict from the closing years of World War II through the third quarter of the twentieth century. These latter mandates included Palestine, Syria, Lebanon, Transjordan, Tanganyka, Kamerun, Southwest Africa, and German New Guinea to mention only some of the major areas.

Colonial Participation   Colonial peoples themselves had played a significant role in the First World War. Germany itself did not call upon troops from its colonies. The war led Britain and France, however, to view their empires in new ways as sources of military as well as economic support. The French government recruited tens of thousands of Algerians into its armed forces and over 150,000 West Africans. It is estimated that more than 2.5 million British colonial troops participated in the war. The presence of so many non-European troops on the European continent even before the arrival of U.S. troops was one of the factors that made the war a genuinely world conflict.

What Europeans had learned from the wartime experience was the value of their colonies in terms of troops to be recruited and natural resources to be devoted to the war effort, and they tended to seek ways to draw them into closer relations. In this respect, the years after the war were in some respects the period of most extensive direct colonial involvement by Great Britain and France and the ongoing desire for empire on the part of Italy. When the Second World War broke out, both nations would encounter much more nationalist resistance, which following the war would culminate in decolonization. (See Chapter 29.)

Impact of the Peace Settlement on Future Colonial Relations   Many native colonial leaders in Africa and Asia had supported the allied war effort in the hope that their peoples would be rewarded with greater independence and better economic relations with Europe. These hopes were dashed at the peace conference and in the years thereafter. These colonial leaders had hoped they might be allowed to put their case for independence or major administrative reform before the conference, and they had been denied that opportunity. Their disappointment led them over the years to reject engagement with the existing international order and to move in various new directions of disruptive and ultimately successful national anticolonialism.

The European powers themselves had directly contributed to these developments in another fashion. They had sought to stir nationalist uprisings in the lands of their opponents. Here the most significant effort took place among Arab peoples governed by the Ottoman Empire, which had sided with Germany. The British led Arab nationalist groups to believe that they might achieve independence in the wake of an allied victory. T. E. Lawrence, later known popularly as Lawrence of Arabia, led much of this effort on behalf of the British. For their part the Germans had attempted to stir unrest in northern Africa.

A glance at the new map of the post–World War I world could give the impression that the old imperial nations, especially Britain and France, were more powerful than ever, but that impression would be superficial and misleading. The great Western European powers had paid an enormous price in lives, money, and will for their victory in the war. Colonial peoples pressed for the rights that the West proclaimed as universal but denied to their colonies, and some influential minorities in the countries that ruled those colonies sympathized with colonial aspirations for independence. Tension between colonies and their ruling nations was a cause of serious instability in the world the Paris treaties of 1919 created.

EVALUATING THE PEACE

Few peace settlements have undergone more severe attacks than the one negotiated in Paris in 1919. It was natural that the defeated powers should object to it, but the peace soon came under bitter criticism in the victorious countries as well. Many of the French objected that the treaty tied French security to promises of aid from the unreliable Anglo-Saxon countries. In England and the United States, a wave of bitter criticism arose in liberal quarters because the treaty seemed to violate the idealistic and liberal aims that the Western leaders had professed.

The Economic Consequences of the Peace   The most influential economic critic of the treaty was John Maynard Keynes (1883–1946). His book *The Economic Consequences of the Peace* (1920) was a scathing attack, especially on reparations and the other economic aspects of the peace. Keynes argued that the Treaty of Versailles was both immoral and unworkable. He argued it would bring economic ruin and war to Europe unless it was repudiated.

Keynes's argument had a great effect on the British, who were already suspicious of France and glad of an excuse to withdraw from continental affairs. The decent and respectable position came to be one that supported revision of the treaty in favor of Germany. In the United States, the book fed the traditional tendency toward isolationism and gave powerful weapons to Wilson's enemies. Wilson's own political mistakes helped prevent American ratification of the treaty. Thus, America was out of the League of Nations and not bound to defend France. Britain, therefore, was also free from its obligation to France. France was left to protect itself without adequate means to do so for long.

Many of the attacks on the Treaty of Versailles are unjustified. Germany was neither dismembered nor ruined. Reparations could be and were scaled down. Until the great world depression of the 1930s, the Germans recovered prosperity. Complaints against the peace should also be measured against the peace that the victorious Germans had imposed on Russia at Brest-Litovsk and their plans for a European settlement if they had won. Both were far more severe than anything enacted at Versailles. The attempt to achieve self-determination for nationalities was less than perfect, but it was the best effort Europe had ever made to do so.

Divisive New Boundaries and Tariff Walls   The peace, nevertheless, was unsatisfactory in important ways. The elimination of the Austro-Hungarian Empire, however inevitable, created serious problems. Economically, it was disastrous. New borders and tariff walls separated raw materials from manufacturing areas and producers from their markets. In hard times, this separation created friction and hostility that aggravated other quarrels the peace treaties also created. Poland contained unhappy German, Lithuanian, and Ukrainian minorities, and Czechoslovakia and Yugoslavia were collections of nationalities that did not find it easy to live together. Territorial disputes in Eastern Europe promoted further tension.

Moreover, the peace rested on a victory that Germany did not admit. The Germans felt cheated rather than defeated. The high moral principles the Allies proclaimed undercut the validity of the peace, for it plainly fell far short of those principles.

Failure to Accept Reality   Finally, the great weakness of the peace was its failure to accept reality. Germany and Russia must inevitably play an important part in European affairs, yet the settlement and the League of Nations excluded them. Given the many discontented parties, the peace was not self-enforcing, yet no satisfactory machinery to enforce it was established. The League of Nations was never a serious force for this purpose. It was left to France, with no guarantee of support from Britain and no hope of help from the United States, to defend the new arrangements. Finland, the Baltic states, Poland, Romania, Czechoslovakia, and Yugoslavia were expected to be a barrier to the westward expansion of Russian communism and to help deter a revival of German power. Most of these states, however, would have to rely on France in case of danger, and France was simply not strong enough to protect them if Germany revived.

The tragedy of the Treaty of Versailles was that it was neither conciliatory enough to remove the desire for revision, even at the cost of war, nor harsh enough to make another war impossible. The only hope for a lasting peace was that Germany would remain disarmed while the more obnoxious clauses of the peace treaty were revised. Such a policy required continued attention to the problem, unity among the victors, and farsighted leadership, but none of these was consistently present during the next two decades.

SUMMARY

WHY DID the alliance system fail?

Emergence of the German Empire and the Alliance Systems (1873–1890) From 1871 until his dismissal by Kaiser William II in 1890, Bismarck acted as an "honest broker" for peace in Europe. He entered Germany into multiple alliances, some of them secret, in a successful effort to maintain a balance of power in Europe. Bismarck's system of alliances collapsed soon after he left office. Caprivi's incompetence and Kaiser William II's arrogance made an enemy of Britain, which proceeded to enter relationships with France and Russia, creating the Triple Entente. Germany's Triple Alliance (with Austria and Italy) was weak and unstable by comparison. *page 652*

HOW DID conflict in the Balkans lead to the outbreak of general war in Europe?

World War I The 1908 Bosnian crisis, the second Moroccan crisis in 1911, and the First and Second Balkan Wars solidified Europe's alliances and antagonisms and left many of the powers believing they could not afford to repeat various "mistakes" they had made in facing these crises. When the heir to the Austrian throne was assassinated in Sarajevo, Bosnia, Austria was determined to go to war with Serbia. As the crisis dragged on throughout the summer, all the other European powers came to feel they must go to war. Both the Triple Entente (Britain, France, and Russia) and the Central Powers (essentially, Austria and Germany) had reasonable expectations of quick victory. Both sides bungled their strategies, and neither side understood how to take the offensive against machine guns. The land war dragged on with massive casualties and minimal results. On the sea, Germany's fleet served little purpose except, eventually, to help bring the United States into the war against the Central Powers. U.S. entry into the war came only after the Russian Revolution had overthrown the tsar. *page 656*

WHAT FACTORS made the rise of the Bolshrviks to power in Russia possible?

The Russian Revolution The government of Nicholas II was incapable of managing a viable war effort. Nicholas II tried to deal with widespread discontent by adjourning parliament (the Duma) and ruling alone, but that strategy also failed. On March 15, 1917, Russia's last tsar abdicated. The Duma reconvened and formed a provisional government; the provisional government continued the war against Germany. Socialist factions formed *soviets*, councils of workers and soldiers; they did not support the provisional government. The Bolsheviks worked against the provisional government. The Germans helped Lenin get from his Swiss exile to Petrograd. The Bolsheviks attempted a coup in the summer of 1917. In November 1917, a second Bolshevik coup took control. The Bolsheviks nationalized land, factories, banks, and church property; they repudiated the tsarist government's debt; and they withdrew from the war. The Treaty of Brest-Litovsk imposed harsh terms on Russia, but Lenin had to sign. It took the Bolsheviks until 1921 to overcome domestic resistance and a civil war against the White Russians. *page 666*

WHAT WERE the immediate consequences of the end of World War I?

The End of World War I German victory on the eastern front was balanced by the U.S. entry into the war. Germany's last offensive was a fiasco. Kaiser William II abdicated on November 9, 1918, and a republican, socialist-led government signed the armistice on November 11. Most Germans, however, had been prevented from learning the extent of the German army's losses, so the terms of the peace settlement came as an unpleasant surprise; later, the political myth that leftists at home had betrayed the nation became a rallying cry for the right. The Great War was over, at a cost of millions of soldiers' lives and millions of civilians' lives. Europe was transformed forever: The German, Austro-Hungarian, Russian, and Ottoman Empires were all dissolved; the United States became a factor in European affairs; and the nineteenth-century belief in the inevitability of progress was shattered. The Ottoman Empire was dismembered by a treaty between Turkey and the Allies in 1920. Britain and France controlled swaths of the Arab world; Ataturk established the independent republic of Turkey in 1923. *page 668*

WHAT WERE the key weaknesses of the Paris peace settlement?

The Settlement at Paris The Treaty of Versailles was a failure because it was not mild enough to win long-term acceptance by all parties, but it was also not harsh enough to make another war impossible. The victorious Big Four represented constitutional democracies and had to respond to public opinion. In Europe, nationalism reached the status of a secular religion, and Wilson's Fourteen Points had raised unrealistically idealistic expectations; a comprehensive resolution of Europe's nationalist controversies was impossible. Previous agreements and secret treaties could not all be honored and were sometimes mutually exclusive. All the powers feared the spread of communism; France in particular feared a rearmed Germany. The League of Nations was meant to remedy the inevitable shortcomings of the peace set-tlement, but it had no military power to back claims; when the United States failed to ratify the treaty, it also destroyed the league's viability. The most problematic aspect of the treaty was the harshness of its terms toward Germany. The exclusion of Russia from the settlement and the League of Nations reflected a Big Four failure to face realities of European politics. *page 670*

REVIEW QUESTIONS

1. To what areas of the world did Europe extend its power after 1870? How did the New Imperialism (after 1870) compare with previous imperialistic movements? What role in the world did Bismarck envision for the new Germany after 1871? What was Bismarck's attitude toward colonies?

2. Why, at the turn of the century, did Britain abandon its policy of "splendid isolation"? How did developments in the Balkans lead to the outbreak of World War I? Did Germany want a general war?

3. Why did Germany lose World War I? What were the benefits and drawbacks of the Treaty of Versailles? Could it have secured lasting peace in Europe?

4. How did Lenin establish the Bolsheviks in control of Russia? What role did Trotsky play?

KEY TERMS

Fourteen Points (p. 668)   mandate (p. 670)

For additional learning resources related to this chapter, please go to **www.myhistorylab.com**

myhistorylab

27

The Interwar Years: The Challenge of Dictators and Depression

Poster concerning the First Five-Year Plan (1928–1932) with a photograph of Joseph Stalin (1879–1953). The poster declares: "By the end of the Five-Year Plan, the basis of the USSR's collectivization must be completed."

1932 (color litho) by Klutchis (fl. 1932). Deutsches Plakat Museum, Essen, Germany/Archives Charmet/The Bridgeman Art Library

How did Soviet economic policy under Stalin change Soviet society?

uring the two decades that followed the Paris settlement, Europe saw bold experiments in politics and economic life. Two broad sets of factors accounted for these experiments. First, the war, the Russian Revolution, and the peace treaty had transformed the political face of Europe. New political regimes had emerged in the wake of the collapse of the monarchies of Germany, Austria-Hungary, and Russia. These new governments immediately faced the problems of postwar reconstruction, economic dislocation, and nationalistic resentment. Most of these nations also included large groups who questioned the legitimacy of their governments. All the governments and societies of both Western and Eastern Europe believed themselves profoundly threatened by the Soviet Union.

Second, beginning in the early twenties, economic dislocations that led to the economic downturn that became known as the Great Depression began to spread across the world. The Great Depression itself, which began in 1929, was the most severe downturn capitalist economies had ever experienced. Business and political leaders despaired over the market's seeming inability to resolve the crisis. Marxists and, indeed, many other observers thought the final downfall of capitalism was at hand.

European voters looked for new ways out of the doldrums, and politicians sought to escape the pressures that the depression had brought on them. One result of the fight for economic security was the establishment of the Nazi dictatorship in Germany. Another was the piecemeal construction of what became known as the mixed economy; that is, governments became directly involved in making economic decisions alongside business and labor. In both cases, most of the political and economic guidelines of nineteenth-century liberalism were abandoned, and so were decency and civility in political life. Authoritarianism and aggression were not the inescapable destiny of Europe. They emerged from the failure to secure alternative modes of democratic political life and stable international relations and from the inability to achieve long-term economic prosperity. ▪

AFTER VERSAILLES: DEMANDS FOR REVISION AND ENFORCEMENT

WHY DID the Paris settlement fail to bring peace and prosperity to Europe?

The Paris settlement fostered both resentments and discontent. Those resentments counted among the chief political factors in Europe for the next two decades. Germany had been humiliated. The arrangements for reparations led to endless haggling over payments. Many national groups in the successor states of the Austro-Hungarian Empire felt that their rights to self-determination had been violated or ignored. There were strident demands for further border adjustments because significant national minorities, particularly Germans and Magyars, resided outside the national boundaries drawn in Paris. On the other side, the victorious powers, especially France, often believed that the provisions of the treaties were being inadequately enforced. Consequently, throughout the 1920s and into the 1930s, demands either to revise or to enforce the Paris treaties contributed to domestic political turmoil across the Continent.

TOWARD THE GREAT DEPRESSION IN EUROPE

WHAT KEY factors combined to produce the Great Depression?

Along with the move toward political experimentation and the demands for revision of the new international order, there was a widespread yearning to return to the economic prosperity of the prewar years. Unfortunately, during the Great War, Europeans had turned the military and industrial power that they had created during the previous

TABLE 27–1   Total Casualties in the First World War

Country	Dead	Wounded	Total Killed as a Percentage of Population (%)
FRANCE	1,398,000	2,000,000	3.4
BELGIUM	38,000	44,700	0.5
ITALY	578,000	947,000	1.6
BRITISH EMPIRE	921,000	2,090,000	1.7
ROMANIA	250,000	120,000	3.3
SERBIA	278,000	133,000	5.7
GREECE	26,000	21,000	0.5
RUSSIA	1,811,000	1,450,000	1.1
BULGARIA	88,000	152,000	1.9
GERMANY	2,037,000	4,207,000	3.0
AUSTRIA-HUNGARY	1,100,000	3,620,000	1.9
TURKEY	804,000	400,000	3.7
UNITED STATES	114,000	206,000	0.1

Source: Niall Ferguson, *The Pity of War* (New York: Basic Books, 1998).

century against themselves. What had been "normal" in economic and social life before 1914 could not be reestablished.

The casualties from the war numbered in the millions. (See Table 27–1.) This represented not only a waste of human life and talent, but also the loss of producers and consumers.

Three factors originating in the 1920s combined to bring about the intense severity and the extended length of the **Great Depression**. First, a financial crisis stemmed directly from the war and the peace settlement. To this was added a crisis in the production and distribution of goods in the world market. Finally, both of these difficulties became worse than they might have been because no major Western European country or the United States provided strong, responsible economic leadership that might have resulted in some form of cooperation to face the challenge of the depression.

Great Depression   A prolonged worldwide economic downturn that began in 1929 with the collapse of the New York Stock Exchange.

FINANCIAL TAILSPIN

As one of the chief victors in the war, France was determined to collect reparations from Germany for the destruction the war had caused in northern France. The United States was no less determined that its allies repay the money it had lent them during the war. The European allies also owed debts to each other. German reparations were to provide the means of repaying all these debts. Most of the money that the Allies collected from each other also went to the United States.

The quest for payment of German reparations caused one of the major diplomatic crises of the 1920s; that crisis itself resulted in further economic upheaval. In early 1923, the Allies—France in particular—declared Germany to be in technical default of its reparation payments. On January 11, to ensure receipt of the hard-won reparations, French and Belgian troops occupied the Ruhr mining and manufacturing district.

The French invasion of the German Ruhr began a crisis that brought strikes and rampant in-flation in Germany. Here French troops have commandeered a German locomotive during one of the strikes.

UPI/Corbis/BETTMANN

What explains France's aggressive policy toward Germany in the years following the war?

Weimar Republic   German republic that came to power in 1918 embodying the hopes of German liberals.

The **Weimar Republic** ordered passive resistance that amounted to a general strike in Germany's largest industrial region. Confronted with this tactic, the French sent technicians and engineers to run the German mines and railroads. France got its way. The Germans paid, but its victory cost France dearly. The British were alienated by the French heavy-handedness and took no part in the occupation. The cost of the Ruhr occupation, moreover, vastly increased French as well as German inflation and damaged the French economy.

The political and economic turmoil of the Ruhr invasion led to international attempts to ease the German payment of reparations. At the same time, American investment capital was pouring into Europe. However, by 1928 this investment decreased as American money became diverted into the booming New York stock market. The crash of Wall Street in October 1929—the result of virtually unregulated financial speculation—saw the loss of large amounts of money. Credit sharply contracted in the United States as numerous banks failed. Thereafter, little American capital was available for investment in Europe.

As American credit for Europe began to run out, a major financial crisis struck the Continent. U.S. president Herbert Hoover (1874–1964) announced in June 1931 a one-year moratorium on all payments of international debts. The Hoover moratorium was a prelude to the end of reparations. The Lausanne Conference in the summer of 1932 brought, in effect, the era of reparations to a close. The next year the debts owed to the United States were settled either through small token payments or simply through default.

PROBLEMS IN AGRICULTURAL COMMODITIES

In the 1920s the market demand for European goods shrank, leaving much of the Continent's productive capacity idle or underused. This problem originated both within and outside Europe. In both instances the difficulty arose from agriculture. Vast increases in the quantity of grain farmers around the world produced led to record low prices. Although this helped consumers, it decreased the income of European farmers. At the same time, higher industrial wages raised the cost of the industrial goods that farmers or peasants used. These problems were especially acute in central and eastern Europe and increased farmers' disillusionment with liberal politics.

Outside Europe similar problems affected other producers of agricultural commodities, such as coffee, sugar, and wheat. As supply outstripped demand, the prices they received for their products plummeted. The people who produced these goods in underdeveloped nations could no longer make enough money to buy goods from industrial Europe. As world credit collapsed, the economic position of these commodity producers worsened.

The results of the collapse in the agricultural sector of the world economy and the financial turmoil were stagnation and depression for European industry. Coal, iron, and textiles had depended largely on international markets. Unemployment spread from these industries to those producing consumer goods. The policies of reduced spending with which the governments confronted the Depression further weakened domestic demand. By the early 1930s the Depression was feeding on itself.

DEPRESSION AND GOVERNMENT POLICY IN BRITAIN AND FRANCE

The depression did not mean absolute economic decline or total unemployment. But the economic downturn spread potential as well as actual insecurity. People in nearly all walks of life feared the loss of their economic security. The depression also frustrated normal social and economic expectations. Even the employed often seemed to make no progress, and their anxieties created a major source of discontent.

The governments of the late 1920s and the early 1930s were not well suited in either structure or ideology to confront these problems. The electorates demanded action. The governments' responses depended largely on the severity of the depression in a particular country and on the self-confidence of the nation's political system.

Great Britain and France, which because of their vast empires commanded very large economies, undertook moderate political experiments. Under the pressure of the depression and at the urging of King George V (r. 1910–1936), the Labour prime minister Ramsay MacDonald (1866–1937) organized a National Government, which was a coalition of the Labour, Conservative, and Liberal Parties.

The 1920s also saw the establishment of an independent Irish state. On Easter Monday in April 1916, a nationalist uprising occurred in Dublin. The British suppressed the rising but made martyrs of its leaders by executing several of them. Leadership of the nationalist cause quickly shifted from the Irish Party in Parliament to the extremist Sinn Fein, or "Ourselves Alone," movement. On January 21, 1919, they declared Irish independence. Thereafter a civil war broke out between the military wing of Sinn Fein, which became the Irish Republican Army (IRA), and the British army. The conflict ended with a treaty in December 1921, which established the Irish Free State as one of the dominions in the British Commonwealth. The six, predominately Protestant, counties of Ulster, or Northern Ireland, were permitted to remain part of what was now called

Overview Capitalist, Fascist, and Communist Economic Systems

CAPITALISM	• Private ownership of the means of production • Personal profit can be acquired through investment of capital • Limited government intervention in the economy • Free market, based on supply and demand
FASCISM	• Seeks to steer a course between socialism and a liberal laissez-faire system • Corporatism organizes major industries as syndicates of labor and management • Subsidized shipping and protective tariffs are among efforts to become self-sufficient
COMMUNISM	• Central planning sets goals for production and coordinates manufacturing • Focuses on development of heavy industries and infrastructure, not consumer goods • Strictly controlled labor force

the United Kingdom of Great Britain and Northern Ireland, with provisions for home rule. In the 1920s and 1930s, the Free State gradually severed its ties to Britain and declared itself an independent republic in 1949.

The most important French interwar political experiment was the **Popular Front** Ministry, which came to office in 1936. It was composed of Socialists, Radicals, and Communists. Despite fierce resistance from business and conservative groups, the Popular Front enacted major social and economic reforms, but its parliamentary support gradually faded until its final collapse in October 1938.

Popular Front A government of all left-wing parties that took power in France in 1936 to enact social and economic reforms.

THE SOVIET EXPERIMENT

WHAT WAS the relationship between politics and economics in the early decades of the Soviet Union?

The consolidation of the Bolshevik Revolution in Russia established the most extensive and durable of all twentieth-century authoritarian governments. The Communist Party of the Soviet Union retained power from 1917 until the end of 1991, and its presence influenced the political history of Europe and much of the rest of the world, as did no other single factor. (See "Compare & Connect: The Soviets and the Nazis Confront the Issues of Women and the Family," pages 702–703.)

WAR COMMUNISM

Within the Soviet Union the Red Army under the organizational genius of Leon Trotsky (1879–1940) had suppressed internal and foreign military opposition to the new government during the civil war that raged from 1918 to 1920. Within months of the revolution, a new secret police, known as *Cheka,* appeared. Political and economic administration became highly centralized. All major decisions flowed from the top in a nondemocratic manner. Under the economic policy of **"War Communism,"** the revolutionary government confiscated and then operated the banks, the transport facilities, and heavy industry. The state also forcibly requisitioned grain and shipped it from the countryside to feed the army and the urban workers. The Bolsheviks used the need to fight the civil war as justification for suppressing any resistance to these economic policies.

War Communism The economic policy adopted by the Bolsheviks during the Russian Civil War to seize the banks, heavy industry, railroads, and grain.

War Communism helped the Red Army defeat its opponents. The policy, however, generated domestic opposition to the Bolsheviks, who in 1920 numbered only about 600,000. The alliance of workers and peasants forged in 1917 by the Bolsheviks' slogan of "Peace, Bread, and Land" had begun to dissolve. Many Russians were no longer willing to make the sacrifices demanded by the central party bureaucrats. In 1920 and 1921 serious strikes occurred. Peasants were discontented and resisted the requisition of grain. In March 1921 the sailors mutinied at the Kronstadt naval base on the Baltic. The Red Army crushed the rebellion with grave loss of life. Also, by late 1920 it had become clear that revolution was not going to sweep across the rest of Europe.

THE NEW ECONOMIC POLICY

New Economic Policy (NEP) A limited revival of capitalism, especially in light industry and agriculture, introduced by Lenin in 1921 to repair the damage inflicted on the Russian economy by the civil war and War Communism.

Under these difficult conditions Lenin made a strategic retreat. In March 1921, following the Kronstadt mutiny, he outlined the **New Economic Policy**, or NEP. Apart from banking, heavy industry, transportation, and international commerce, considerable private economic enterprise was allowed. In particular, peasants could farm for a profit. They would pay taxes like other citizens, but they could sell their surplus grain on the open market. The NEP was consistent with Lenin's earlier conviction that the Russian peasantry held the key to the success of the revolution. After 1921 the countryside did become more stable, and a secure food supply seemed assured for the cities. Similar free enterprise flourished within light industry and the domestic retail trade. By 1927 industrial production had reached its 1913 level. The revolution seemed to have transformed Russia into a land of small farms and privately owned shops and businesses.

THE THIRD INTERNATIONAL

The onset and consolidation of the Bolshevik revolution in Russia was a transforming event for the history of socialism as well as for Russia and international affairs. In the West, before the war, as discussed in Chapter 23, social democratic parties had regarded the Russian Bolsheviks as eccentric, politically marginal Marxist extremists. The Bolshevik victory forced West European social democrats to rethink their position within the world of international socialism. For their part, the Bolsheviks intended to establish themselves as the international leaders of Marxism and regarded reformist social democrats as enemies and rivals.

In 1919, the Soviet communists founded the Third International of the European socialist movement, better known as the *Comintern.* The Comintern worked to make the Bolshevik model of socialism, as Lenin had developed it, the rule for all socialist parties outside the Soviet Union. In 1920, the Comintern imposed its Twenty-one Conditions on any socialist party that wished to join it. These conditions included acknowledging Moscow's leadership, rejecting reformist or revisionist socialism, repudiating previous socialist leaders, and adopting the Communist Party name. The decision whether to accept these conditions split every major European socialist party. As a result, separate communist and social democratic parties emerged in most countries and fought each other more intensely than they fought either capitalism or conservative political parties.

Anxiety over the spread of the Bolshevik revolution was a fundamental factor of European politics during the 1920s and 1930s. Images like this Soviet portrait of Lenin as a heroic revolutionary conjured fears among people in the rest of Europe of a political force determined to overturn their social, political, and economic institutions.

Bildarchiv Preussischer Kulturbesitz

What was this image meant to convey about Lenin's role in the Russian Revolution?

These Comintern polices and the resulting divisions of the socialist parties directly affected the rise of the fascists and the Nazis in Western Europe. It is difficult to overestimate the fears that Soviet political rhetoric and Communist Party activity aroused in Europe during the 1920s and 1930s. Conservative and right-wing political groups manipulated and exaggerated these fears. The presence of separate communist parties in Western Europe meant that right-wing politicians always had a convenient target they could justly accuse of seeking to overthrow the government and to impose Soviet-style political, social, and economic systems in their nations. Furthermore, right-wing politicians also accused the democratic socialists of supporting policies that might facilitate a communist takeover. The divisions between Communists and democratic socialists also meant that right-wing political movements rarely had to confront a united left.

*NEP
new
economic
Plan*

STALIN VERSUS TROTSKY

The NEP had caused sharp disputes within the Politburo, the highest governing committee of the Communist Party. These frictions increased as Lenin's firm hand disappeared. In 1922 he suffered a stroke and never again dominated party affairs; in 1924 he died. In the ensuing power vacuum, an intense struggle for leadership of the party commenced. Two factions emerged. One was led by Trotsky; the other by Joseph Stalin (1879–1953), who had become general secretary of the party in 1922.

Trotsky, speaking for what became known as the left wing, urged rapid industrialization and looked to voluntary collectivization of farming by poor peasants as a means of increasing agricultural production. He further argued that the revolution in Russia could succeed only if new revolutions took place elsewhere. A right-wing faction led by Stalin opposed Trotsky. In the mid-1920s this group pressed for the continuation of Lenin's NEP and relatively slow industrialization.

In 1924 Stalin enunciated, in opposition to Trotsky, the doctrine of "socialism in one country." He urged that socialism could be achieved in Russia alone. Russian success did not depend on the fate of the revolution elsewhere. Stalin thus nationalized the previously international scope of the Marxist revolution. He cunningly used the apparatus of the party and his control over its Central Committee to edge out Trotsky and his supporters. By 1927 Trotsky had been removed from all his offices, ousted from the party, and exiled to Siberia. In 1929 he was expelled from Russia and eventually moved to Mexico, where he was murdered in 1940 by one of Stalin's agents. With the removal of Trotsky, Stalin was firmly in control of the Soviet state.

THE DECISION FOR RAPID INDUSTRIALIZATION

In 1927 the Party Congress decided to push for rapid industrialization, a sharp departure from the NEP and a rejection of the pockets of relatively free-market operations within the larger Soviet economy. Stalin's goal was to have the Soviet Union overtake the productive capacity of its enemies, the capitalist nations. This policy required the rapid construction of heavy industries, such as iron, steel, and machine-tool making, building electricity-generating stations, and manufacturing tractors. Stalin's organizational vehicle for industrialization was a series of five-year plans, starting in 1928. The State Planning Commission, or *Gosplan*, set goals for production in every area of economic life and attempted to organize the economy to meet them. The task of coordinating all facets of production was immensely complicated and enormous economic disruption occurred as the *Gosplan* built power plants and steel mills and increased the output of mines. The plans consistently favored capital projects over the production of consumer goods. The number of centralized agencies and ministries involved in planning soared, and they often competed with each other.

The rapid expansion of the industrial base created the first genuinely large factory labor force in what had been Russia. Workers were recruited from the countryside and from the urban unemployed. New cities and industrial districts in existing cities arose. Most workers were crowded into shoddy buildings with inadequate sanitation, living space, and nourishment. The results, however, were impressive. Soviet industrial production rose approximately 400 percent between 1928 and 1940. Industries that had never existed in Russia challenged their foreign counterparts. Hundreds of thousands of people populated new industrial cities. The social and human cost of this effort had, however, been appalling.

QUICK REVIEW
Stalin's Rise to Power

- Sided with the opposition to Trotsky in the 1920s
- Used control of the Central Committee to marginalize Trotsky and his supporters
- Emerged from struggle with Trotsky with unchallenged control of the Soviet state

Magnitogorsk was a city that became a monument to Stalin's drive toward rapid industrialization. Located in the Ural Mountains near a vast supply of iron ore, the city became the site of major iron and steel production. It was one of the new industrial cities founded under the Five-Year Plans designed to challenge the capitalist production of the Western nations.

National Archives and Records Administration

Why was the creation of heavy industry so important to Stalin?

THE COLLECTIVIZATION OF AGRICULTURE

Agricultural productivity had always been a core problem for the emerging Soviet economy. Under the NEP, the government purchased a certain amount of grain at prices it set itself. The rest of the grain was then supposed to be sold at market prices, which were higher than the government-set prices. Many peasant farmers of all degrees of wealth tried to circumvent this system, often by keeping grain off the market in hopes that its price would rise. The scarcity of consumer goods available for purchase in the countryside also encouraged hoarding. With little to buy from what they earned by selling their grain, farmers had little incentive to sell it. In 1928 and 1929, as a result of peasants hoarding their grains for better prices, the Soviet government confronted shortfalls of grain on the market and the prospect of food shortages in the cities and social unrest.

Stalin therefore decided to reverse the agricultural policies of the NEP. Stalin decided that Soviet agriculture must be collectivized to produce enough grain for domestic food and foreign export. **Collectivization**—the replacement of private peasant farms with huge state-run and state-owned farms called collectives—would also put the Communist Party firmly in control of the farm sector of the economy and free up peasant labor to work in the expanding industrial sector. To carry out this policy, Stalin portrayed the *kulaks*, the small group of relatively prosperous peasants, as the fundamental cause of the agricultural problems.

Collectivization The bedrock of Stalinist agriculture, which forced Russian peasants to give up their private farms and work as members of collectives, large agricultural units controlled by the state.

Stalin used intimidation and propaganda to support his drive to collectivize Soviet agriculture. Communist Party agitators led groups of peasants, such as these shown above, to demand the seizure of the farms worked by the better-off and more successful farmers known as *kulaks*.

AP/Wide World Photos

Who resisted collectivization? Why?

Party officials with troops at their command carried out the initial campaign of dekulakization and collectivization. Usually they would seek first to remove *kulaks* from a village while confiscating their land and would then attempt to coerce the remaining peasants into organizing a collective farm. Enormous turmoil and violence resulted. Peasants who resisted were killed outright. Others starved to death on their own farms when all the grain that they had produced was seized. Over 2 million peasants were forcibly removed from their homes and deported to distant areas of the Soviet Union or to prison camps where many died from disease, exposure, and malnutrition. Much of the violence of collectivization occurred in Ukraine, where Stalin used the process not only to restructure agricultural production but also to crush any vestiges of Ukrainian nationalism, and many millions of lives were lost as a result.

By 1937, over 90 percent of Soviet grain production had been collectivized. At the cost of millions of peasant lives, Stalin and the Communist Party had won the battle of the grain fields, but they had not solved the problem of producing enough food. That difficulty would plague the Soviet Union until its collapse in 1991 and remains a problem for its successor states.

THE PURGES

In 1933, with turmoil in the countryside and economic dislocation caused by industrialization, Stalin and others in the central Soviet bureaucracy began to fear they were losing control of the country and the party apparatus and that effective rivals to their power and policies might emerge. These apprehensions were largely a figment of Stalin's own paranoia and lust for power, but they resulted in the **Great Purges**.

The pretext for the onset of the purges was the assassination on December 1, 1934, of Sergei Kirov (1888–1934), the popular party chief of Leningrad and a member of the Politburo. In the wake of the shooting, thousands of people were arrested, and still more were expelled from the party and sent to labor camps. Today, many scholars believe that Stalin himself authorized Kirov's assassination because he was afraid of him. The available documentary evidence does not allow us to know for sure whether Stalin was involved, but he quickly used Kirov's death for his own purposes.

QUICK REVIEW

Collectivization

- 1929: Stalin orders collectivization of Soviet agriculture
- Stalin responded to resistance by targeting *kulaks* for elimination
- Collectivization failed to solve the Soviet Union's food supply problem

Great Purges   The arrests, trials, Communist Party expulsions, and executions—beginning with the assassination of Politburo member Sergei Kirov in December 1934—that mainly targeted party officials and reached its climax from 1936 to 1938.

The purges that took place immediately after Kirov's death were just the beginning of a larger and longer process. Between 1936 and 1938, a series of spectacular show trials were held in Moscow. Former high Soviet leaders, including members of the Politburo, publicly confessed to political crimes and were convicted and executed. Other lower-level party members were tried in private and shot. Hundreds of thousands, perhaps millions, of ordinary Soviet citizens received no trial at all and were either executed or deported to slave labor camps where many died. Within the party itself, thousands of members were expelled, and applicants for membership were removed from the rolls. After the civilian party members and leaders had been purged, the prosecutors turned against the government bureaucracy and the Soviet army and navy, convicting and executing thousands of officials and officers, including heroes of the civil war. The exact number of executions, imprisonments, interrogations, and expulsions is unknown, but ran well into the millions. While the purges went on, no one in the Soviet Union, except Stalin himself, was safe.

The rational explanations of the purges—to the extent that mass murder can ever be rationally explained—probably lie in two directions. First, over the several years the purges lasted, different portions of the party leadership moved against others. Initially, Stalin and the central Moscow leadership used the purges to settle old scores and to discipline and gain more control over lower levels of the party in the far-flung regions of the Soviet Union. In addition to increasing Stalin's authority, these central bureaucratic groups wanted to eliminate any opposition to their own positions or policies. By 1937, however, Stalin seems to have become distrustful of the central party elite, his own supporters, and began to find or pretend to find enemies within its ranks. Moreover, by that date, local communist groups were allowed to designate their own victims with little direction from Moscow. Thereafter, a self-destructive cascade of accusations, imprisonments, and executions occurred throughout the party and within its highest levels.

Second, no matter how much tension and rivalry there were among the different levels and regions of the Communist Party, Stalin's primary motive in the purges was almost certainly fear for his own power and a ruthless determination to preserve and increase it. In effect, the purges created a new Communist Party that was absolutely subservient and loyal to Stalin. New, younger recruits replaced the party members who were executed or expelled. The newcomers knew little about old Russia or the ideals of the original Bolsheviks. They had not been loyal to Lenin, Trotsky, or any other Soviet leader, except Stalin himself.

The internal difficulties collectivization and industrialization and his worries about internal opposition caused led Stalin to make an important shift in foreign policy. In 1934, he began to fear the nation might be left isolated against aggression by Nazi Germany. The Soviet Union was not yet strong enough to withstand such an attack. So that year he ordered the Comintern to permit communist parties in other countries to cooperate with noncommunist parties against Nazism and fascism. This reversed the Comintern policy Lenin established as part of the Twenty-one Conditions in 1919. The new Stalinist policy allowed the Popular Front government in France to come to power.

THE FASCIST EXPERIMENT IN ITALY

The first authoritarian political experiment in Western Europe that arose in part from fears of the spread of Bolshevism beyond the Soviet Union occurred in Italy. The general term *fascist*, which has been used to describe the various right-wing dictatorships that arose between the wars, was derived from the Italian Fascist movement of Benito Mussolini (1883–1945).

WHAT DID fascism mean to Mussolini and his supporters?

fascism   System of extreme right-wing dictatorial government.

While scholars still dispute the exact meaning of ***fascism*** as a political term, the governments regarded as fascist were antidemocratic, anti-Marxist, antiparliamentary, and frequently anti-Semitic. They wanted to overcome the class conflict of Marxism and the party conflict of liberalism by consolidating the various groups and classes within the nation for great national purposes. Fascist governments were usually single-party dictatorships characterized by terrorism against, and police surveillance of, both opponents and the general citizenry. These dictatorships were rooted in the base of mass political parties.

THE RISE OF MUSSOLINI

The Italian *Fasci di Combattimento* ("Band of Combat") was founded in 1919 in Milan. Most of its members were war veterans who felt that the sacrifices Italy had made in World War I had not been rewarded at the Paris conference. They feared socialism, inflation, and labor unrest. In 1919, their leader or ***Duce***, Benito Mussolini, was just another Italian politician. His *Fasci* organization was one of many small political groups in a country characterized by such entities. As a politician, Mussolini was an opportunist par excellence. He could change his ideas and principles to suit every new occasion. Action for him was always more important than thought or rational justification. His one real rule was political survival.

Duce   (DO-chay) Meaning "leader." Mussolini's title as head of the Fascist Party.

Postwar Italian politics was a muddle. Many Italians were dissatisfied with the parliamentary system as it then existed. They felt that Italy had emerged from the war as less than a victorious nation, had not been treated as a great power at the peace conference, and had not received the rewards it deserved. Between 1919 and 1921 Italy was also wracked by social turmoil. Numerous industrial strikes occurred, and workers occupied factories. Peasants seized uncultivated land from large estates. Parliamentary and constitutional government seemed incapable of dealing with this unrest.

Initially, Mussolini was uncertain which way the political winds were blowing. He first supported the factory occupations and land seizures. Never one to be concerned with consistency, however, he soon reversed himself. He had discovered that many upper- and middle-class Italians who were hurt by inflation and who feared the loss of their property had no sympathy for the workers or the peasants. They wanted order rather than some vague social justice that might harm their own interests. Consequently, Mussolini and his Fascists took direct action in the face of the government's inaction. They formed local squads who terrorized Socialists. They attacked strikers and farm workers and protected strikebreakers. Conservative land and factory owners were grateful to the terrorists. The officers of the law simply ignored these crimes. By early 1922 the Fascists controlled local government in many parts of northern Italy.

Benito Mussolini became famous for bombastic public speeches delivered in settings surrounded by his fascist followers and military supporters.

AP Wide World Photos

How did Mussolini use public spectacles to shape his public image?

In 1921 Mussolini and thirty-four of his followers had been elected to the Chamber of Deputies. Their importance grew as the local Fascists gained more direct power. The Fascist movement now had hundreds of thousands of supporters. In October 1922 the Fascists, dressed in their characteristic black shirts, began a march on Rome. Intimidated, King Victor Emmanuel III (r. 1900–1946) refused to authorize using the army against the marchers. No other single decision so ensured a Fascist seizure of power. The cabinet resigned in protest. On October 29, the monarch telegraphed Mussolini in Milan and asked him to become prime minister.

THE FASCISTS IN POWER

Mussolini had not really expected to be appointed prime minister. He moved cautiously to consolidate his power. He succeeded because of the impotence of his rivals, his effective use of his office, his power over the masses, and his sheer ruthlessness. On November 23, 1922, the king and Parliament granted Mussolini dictatorial authority for one year to bring order to the lower levels of the government. Wherever possible, Mussolini appointed Fascists to office. Late in 1924, at Mussolini's behest, Parliament changed the election law. Previously parties had been represented in the Chamber of Deputies in proportion to the popular vote cast for them. According to the new election law, the party that gained the largest popular vote (with a minimum of at least 25 percent) received two-thirds of the seats in the chamber. Coalition government, with all its compromises and hesitations, would no longer be necessary. In the election of 1924 the Fascists won a great victory and complete control of the Chamber of Deputies. They used that majority to end legitimate parliamentary life. A series of laws passed in 1925 and 1926 permitted Mussolini, in effect, to rule by decree. In 1926 all other political parties were dissolved, and Italy was transformed into a single-party, dictatorial state.

The Italian dictator made one important domestic departure that brought him significant political dividends. Through the Lateran Accord he signed with the Vatican in February 1929, the Roman Catholic Church and the Italian state made peace with each other. Ever since the armies of Italian unification had seized papal lands in the 1860s, the church had been hostile to the state. The agreement of 1929 recognized the pope as the temporal ruler of the ministate of Vatican City. The Italian government agreed to pay an indemnity to the papacy for confiscated land. The state also recognized Catholicism as the religion of the nation, exempted church property from taxes, and allowed church law to govern marriage. The Lateran Accord brought further respectability to Mussolini's authoritarian regime.

GERMAN DEMOCRACY AND DICTATORSHIP

THE WEIMAR REPUBLIC

The Weimar Republic was born from the defeat of the imperial army, the revolution of 1918 against the Hohenzollerns, and the hopes of German Liberals and Social Democrats. Its name derived from the city in which its constitution was written and promulgated in August 1919. While the constitution was being debated, the republic, headed by the Social Democrats, accepted the humiliating terms of the Versailles Treaty. Although its officials had signed only under the threat of an Allied invasion, the republic was nevertheless permanently associated with the national disgrace and the economic burdens of the treaty. In Germany, more than in other countries, the desire to revise the treaty was closely related to a desire to change the mode of domestic government.

QUICK REVIEW

Mussolini's Rise to Power

♦ Motivated by the desire for power rather than by ideology

♦ Postwar political and economic turmoil provided environment for rise of fascists

♦ October 1922: Black Shirts march on Rome intimidates king into asking Mussolini to become prime minister

WHY DID democracy fail to thrive in postwar Germany?

In 1923, **Germany** suffered from cataclysmic inflation. Paper money became worthless and people used it as fuel for kitchen stoves.

Library of Congress

What were the consequences of hyperinflation in Germany?

The new government suffered major and minor humiliations as well as considerable economic instability. In March 1920, the right-wing Kapp Putsch, or armed insurrection, erupted in Berlin. Led by a conservative civil servant and supported by army officers, the attempted coup failed, but only after government officials had fled the city and workers had carried out a general strike. In the same month, strikes took place in the Ruhr mining district. The government sent in troops. Such extremism from both the left and the right would haunt the republic for all its days. In May 1921, the Allies presented a reparations bill for 132 billion gold marks. The German Republican government accepted this preposterous demand only after new Allied threats of occupation. Throughout the early 1920s there were numerous assassinations or attempted assassinations of important Republican leaders. Violence was the hallmark of the first five years of the republic.

Invasion of the Ruhr and Inflation Inflation brought on the major crisis of this period. The financing of the war and continued postwar deficit spending generated an immense rise in prices. Consequently, the value of German currency fell. By early 1921 the German mark traded against the American dollar at a ratio of 64 to 1, compared with a ratio of 4.2 to 1 in 1914. The German financial community contended that the value of the currency could not be stabilized until the reparations issue had been solved. In the meantime, the printing presses kept pouring forth paper money, which was used to redeem government bonds as they fell due.

The French invasion of the Ruhr in January 1923, to secure the payment of reparations, and the German response of passive economic resistance produced cataclysmic inflation. The Weimar government paid subsidies to the Ruhr labor force, who had laid down their tools. Unemployment soon spread from the Ruhr to other parts of the country, creating a new drain on the treasury and also reducing tax revenues. The printing presses by this point had difficulty providing enough paper currency to keep up with the daily rise in prices. Money was literally not worth the paper it was printed on.

Middle-class savings, pensions, and insurance policies were wiped out, as were investments in government bonds. Simultaneously, debts and mortgages could not be paid off. To the middle and lower-middle classes, the inflation was another trauma coming hard on the heels of the military defeat and the peace treaty. Only when the social and economic upheaval of these months is grasped can one understand the German desire for order and security at almost any cost.

Hitler's Early Career   Late in 1923 Adolf Hitler (1889–1945) made his first significant appearance on the German political scene. The son of a minor Austrian customs official, he had gone to Vienna, where his hopes of gaining admission to an elite art school were soon dashed. Hitler absorbed the rabid German nationalism and extreme anti-Semitism that flourished in Vienna. He came to hate Marxism, which he associated with Jews. During World War I Hitler fought in the German army, was wounded, rose to the rank of corporal, and won the Iron Cross for bravery. The war gave him his first sense of purpose.

After the conflict, Hitler settled in Munich. He soon became associated with a small nationalistic, anti-Semitic political party that in 1920 adopted the name of National Socialist German Workers Party, better known simply as the **Nazis**. It issued a platform, or program, of Twenty-Five Points. Among other things, this platform called for the repudiation of the Versailles Treaty, the unification of Austria and Germany, the exclusion of Jews from German citizenship, agrarian reform, the prohibition of land speculation, the confiscation of war profits, state administration of the giant cartels, and the replacement of department stores with small retail shops.

The "socialism" that Hitler and the Nazis had in mind was not state ownership of the means of production, but the subordination of all economic enterprise to the welfare of the nation. It often implied protection for small economic enterprises. Increasingly, the Nazis discovered their party appealed to virtually any economic group that was at risk and under pressure. They often tailored their messages to the particular local problems these groups confronted in different parts of Germany. The Nazis also found considerable support among war veterans, who faced economic and social displacement in Weimar society.

Soon after the promulgation of the Twenty-Five Points, the storm troopers, or **SA** (*Sturm Abteilung*), were organized under the leadership of Captain Ernst Roehm (1887–1934). The storm troopers were the chief Nazi instrument for terror and intimidation before the party controlled the government. They were a law unto themselves. The organization constituted a means of preserving military discipline and values outside the small army permitted by the Paris settlement. The existence of such a private party army and of a similar one run by the Communists was a sign of the potential for violence in the Weimar Republic and the widespread contempt for the law and the institutions of the republic.

The social and economic turmoil following the French occupation of the Ruhr and the German inflation gave the fledgling party an opportunity for direct action against the Weimar Republic, which seemed incapable of providing military or economic security. By this time, because of his immense oratorical skills and organizational abilities, Hitler personally dominated the Nazi Party. As he established his dominance within the party, he clearly had the model of Mussolini in mind and spoke of the Italian dictator's accomplishments in glowing terms. In late 1923, with the memory of Mussolini's march on Rome still fresh, Hitler attempted to seize power by force.

On November 9, 1923, Hitler and a band of followers, accompanied by General Erich Ludendorff (1865–1937), attempted an unsuccessful putsch from a beer hall in Munich. When the local authorities crushed the rising, sixteen Nazis were killed. Hitler and Ludendorff were arrested and tried for treason. The general was acquitted. Hitler used the trial to make himself into a national figure. He condemned the republic, the Versailles Treaty, the Jews, and the weakened condition of his adopted country. He was convicted and sentenced to five years in prison. He actually spent

Nazis   Members of the National Socialist German Workers' Party that formed in 1920 and supported a mythical Aryan race alleged to be the source of the purest German lineage.

SA   The Nazi parliamentary forces, or storm troopers.

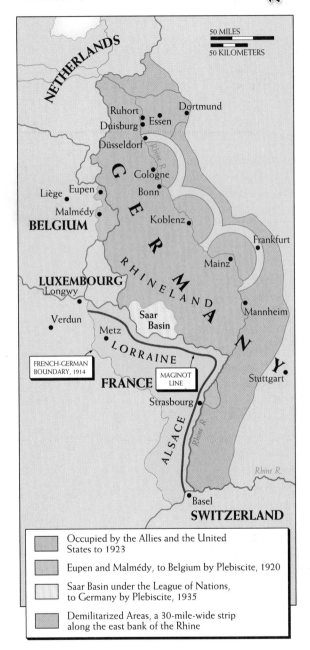

MAP 27–1 Germany's Western Frontier The French-Belgian-German border area between the two world wars was sensitive. Despite efforts to restrain tensions, there were persistent difficulties related to the Ruhr, Rhineland, Saar, and Eupen-Malmédy regions that required strong defenses.

Why were the territorial divisions between France, Germany, and Belgium unsatisfactory?

only a few months in jail before being paroled. During this time, he dictated *Mein Kampf* ("My Struggle"), from which he eventually made a good deal of money. In this book, not taken seriously enough at the time, he outlined key political views from which he never swerved, including a fierce racial anti-Semitism, opposition to Bolshevism, which he associated with Jews, and a conviction that Germany must expand eastward into Poland and Ukraine to achieve greater "living space." Such expansion assumed the resurgence of German military might. In effect, Hitler transferred the foreign policy goals and racial outlooks previously associated with German overseas imperialism to the politics of central and eastern Europe. The natural targets of implementing these ideas would be Jews, the successor states of eastern Europe, the Soviet Union, and any groups within Germany that opposed Hitler's vision of national unity and purpose.

During his imprisonment, Hitler reached two other decisions. First, it appears that this was the moment when he came to see himself as the leader who could transform Germany from a position of weakness to strength. Second, he decided that he and the party must pursue power by legal means, but as Hitler emerged from his imprisonment, he was still a regional politician (albeit one who was transforming himself into a national figure).

The Stresemann Years   The officials of the republic were attempting to repair the damage from the inflation. Gustav Stresemann (1878–1929) was responsible primarily for reconstruction of the republic and for its achievement of a sense of self-confidence. Stresemann abandoned the policy of passive resistance in the Ruhr. The country simply could not afford it. Then, with the aid of banker Hjalmar Schacht (1877–1970), he introduced a new German currency. The rate of exchange was 1 trillion of the old German marks for one new Rentenmark. Stresemann also moved against challenges from both the left and the right. He supported the crushing of both Hitler's abortive putsch and smaller Communist disturbances. In late November 1923, after four months as chancellor, he resigned to become foreign minister, a post he held until his death in 1929. In that office he continued to influence the affairs of the republic.

In 1924 the Weimar Republic and the Allies renegotiated the reparation payments. The Dawes Plan lowered the annual payments and allowed them to fluctuate according to the fortunes of the German economy. The last French troops left the Ruhr in 1925 (see Map 27–1). The same year, Field Marshal Paul von Hindenburg (1847–1934), a military hero and a conservative monarchist, was elected president of the republic. This conservatism was in line with the prosperity of the latter 1920s. Foreign capital flowed into Germany, and employment, which had been poor throughout most of the postwar years, improved smartly. Giant industrial combines spread. The prosperity helped to establish broader acceptance and appreciation of the republic.

In foreign affairs, Stresemann pursued a conciliatory course. He fulfilled the provisions of the Versailles Treaty even as he attempted to revise it by diplomacy. He was willing to accept the settlement in the west but was a determined, if sometimes secret, revisionist in the east. He aimed to recover German-speaking territories lost to Poland and Czechoslovakia and possibly to unite with Austria, chiefly by diplomatic means. The first step, however, was to achieve respectability and economic recovery. That goal required a policy of accommodation and "fulfillment," for the moment at least.

Locarno   These developments gave rise to the Locarno Agreements of October 1925. The spirit of conciliation led foreign ministers Austen Chamberlain (1863–1937) for Britain and Aristide Briand (1862–1932) for France to accept Stresemann's proposal for a fresh start. France and Germany both accepted the western frontier established at Versailles as legitimate. Britain and Italy agreed to intervene against the aggressor if either side violated the frontier or if Germany sent troops into the demilitarized Rhineland. Significantly, no such agreement was made about Germany's eastern frontier, but the Germans made treaties of arbitration with Poland and Czechoslovakia, and France strengthened its ties with those countries. France supported German membership in the League of Nations and agreed to withdraw its occupation troops from the Rhineland in 1930, five years earlier than specified at Versailles.

The Locarno Agreements brought new hope to Europe. The spirit of Locarno was carried even further when the leading European states, Japan, and the United States signed the Kellogg-Briand Pact in 1928, renouncing "war as an instrument of national policy." The joy and optimism were not justified. France had merely recognized its inability to coerce Germany without help. Britain had shown its unwillingness to uphold the settlement in the east. Germany was not reconciled to the eastern settlement. It maintained clandestine military connections with the Soviet Union and planned to continue to press for revision.

In both France and Germany, moreover, the conciliatory politicians represented only a part of the nation. In Germany especially, most people continued to reject Versailles and regarded Locarno as only an extension of it. When the Dawes Plan ran out in 1929, it was replaced by the Young Plan, which lowered the reparation payments, put a term on how long they must be made, and removed Germany entirely from outside supervision and control. The intensity of the outcry in Germany against the continuation of any reparations showed how far the Germans were from accepting their situation. Despite these problems, war was by no means inevitable. Europe, aided by American loans, was returning to prosperity. German leaders like Stresemann would certainly have continued to press for change, but there is little reason to think that they would have resorted to force, much less to a general war. Continued prosperity and diplomatic success might have won the loyalty of the German people for the Weimar Republic and moderate revisionism, but the Great Depression of the 1930s brought new forces to power.

DEPRESSION AND POLITICAL DEADLOCK

The outflow of foreign, and especially American, capital from Germany that began in 1928 undermined the economic prosperity of the Weimar Republic. The resulting economic crisis brought parliamentary government to a halt. In 1928 a coalition of center parties and the Social Democrats governed. All went reasonably well until the depression struck. Then the coalition partners differed sharply on economic policy. The Social Democrats refused to reduce social and unemployment insurance. The more conservative parties, remembering the inflation of 1923, insisted on a balanced budget. The coalition dissolved in March 1930. To resolve the parliamentary deadlock in the *Reichstag*, President von Hindenburg appointed Heinrich Brüning (1885–1970) as chancellor. Lacking a majority in the *Reichstag*, the new chancellor governed through

Mein Kampf   (*My Struggle*) Strategy dictated by Adolf Hitler during his period of imprisonment in 1923 outlining his political views.

Reichstag   (RIKES-stahg) The German parliament, which existed in various forms, until 1945.

emergency presidential decrees, as authorized by Article 48 of the constitution. Party divisions prevented the *Reichstag* from overriding the decrees. The Weimar Republic had become a presidential dictatorship.

German unemployment rose from 2,258,000 in March 1930 to over 6,000,000 in March 1932. The economic downturn and the parliamentary deadlock worked to the advantage of the more extreme political parties. In the election of 1928, the Nazis had won only 12 seats in the *Reichstag*, and the Communists had won 54 seats. Two years later, after the election of 1930, the Nazis held 107 seats and the Communists 77.

The power of the Nazis in the streets was also on the rise. The unemployment fed thousands of men into the storm troopers, which had 100,000 members in 1930 and almost 1 million in 1933. The SA freely and viciously attacked Communists and Social Democrats. For the Nazis, politics meant the capture of power through terror and intimidation as well as through elections. Nazi rallies resembled secular religious revivals. The Nazis paraded through the streets and the countryside. They gained powerful supporters and sympathizers among businessmen, military officers, and newspaper owners. Some intellectuals were also sympathetic. The Nazis transformed this discipline and enthusiasm born of economic despair and nationalistic frustration into impressive electoral results.

HITLER COMES TO POWER

For two years Brüning continued to govern with the backing of Hindenburg. In 1932 the eighty-three-year-old president stood for reelection. Hitler ran against him and forced a runoff. The Nazi leader garnered 30.1 percent of the vote in the first election and 36.8 percent in the second. Although Hindenburg was returned to office, the vote convinced him that Brüning had lost the confidence of conservative German voters. In May 1932 he dismissed Brüning and appointed Franz von Papen (1878–1969) in his place. The new chancellor was one of a small group of extremely conservative advisers on whom the aged Hindenburg had become dependent.

Papen and the circle around the president wanted to draw the Nazis into cooperation with them without giving Hitler effective power. The government needed the popular support on the right that only the Nazis seemed able to generate. The Hindenburg circle decided to convince Hitler that the Nazis could not come to power on their own. Papen removed the ban on Nazi meetings that Brüning had imposed and then called a *Reichstag* election for July 1932. The Nazis won 230 seats and polled 37.2 percent of the vote. Hitler would only enter the Cabinet if he were made chancellor. Hindenburg refused. Another election was called in November, partly to wear down the Nazis' financial resources. The Nazis won only 196 seats, and their percentage of the popular vote dipped to 33.1 percent. The advisers around Hindenburg still refused to appoint Hitler to office.

In early December 1932 Papen resigned, and General Kurt von Schleicher (1882–1934) became chancellor. Schleicher decided to try and fashion a broad-based coalition of conservative groups and trade unionists. The prospect of such a coalition, including groups from the political left, frightened the Hindenburg circle even more than the prospect of Hitler. Consequently, they persuaded Hindenburg to appoint Hitler chancellor. To control him and to see that he did little mischief, Papen was named vice chancellor, and other traditional conservatives were appointed to the cabinet. On January 30, 1933, Adolf Hitler became the chancellor of Germany. It is important to emphasize that this outcome had not been inevitable. Hitler did not come to office on the tide of history, but through the blunders of conservative German politicians who hated the Weimar Republic and its rejection of traditional German political elites and who feared the domestic political turmoil the depression had spawned.

ENCOUNTERING THE PAST

CINEMA OF THE POLITICAL LEFT AND RIGHT

Before television, cinema was the most powerful medium for political propaganda, and brilliant directors served authoritarian regimes of both the left and the right. Sergei Eisenstein (1898–1948) made films for the Soviet Union that, despite their propagandistic content, are acknowledged masterpieces. The Battleship Potemkin, *his most famous work, depicts a mutiny aboard a warship during the Russian Revolution. It portrays the working class as the hero of the story and of history itself. Two other historical epics,* Alexander Nevsky *(a medieval Russian prince who defeated German invaders) and* Ivan the Terrible *(a sixteenth-century despotic tsar), managed remarkably to meet the highest artistic standards and promote reflection on contemporary events—all while pleasing Stalin.*

Nazi Germany's great artistic resource was a female documentary filmmaker, Leni Riefenstahl (1902–2003). After the Nazis took power in 1933, Hitler commissioned her to make documentaries extolling his Third Reich. She produced two dazzling films: *Triumph of the Will* (1934), a record of a Nazi Party rally, and *Olympia* (1938), based on the Olympic Games held in Berlin in 1936. Her innovative, dramatic techniques made her films classics of twentieth-century cinema—and made them perfect vehicles for conveying the theatricality of the Nazi regime. De-

Leni Riefenstahl films the 1936 Olympic Games in Berlin with Hitler on the reviewing stand.
© Bettmann/CORBIS

How did Riefenstahl's films promote Nazi ideology?

spite the support her films gave Hitler, she defended herself as a "pure" artist who (as some scientists have also argued) cannot be held responsible for the use others made of her work.

WHY WERE authoritarian regimes so interested in the cinema? Are artists ethically responsible for the effects of their art?

Hitler had forged a rigidly disciplined party structure and had mastered the techniques of mass politics and propaganda. (See "Encountering the Past: Cinema of the Political Left and Right.") He understood how to touch the raw social and political nerves of the electorate. His support appears to have come from across the social spectrum and not, as historians once thought, just from the lower middle class. Pockets of resistance appeared among Roman Catholic voters in the countryside and small towns. Otherwise, support for Hitler was particularly strong among groups such as farmers, war veterans, and the young, whom the insecurity of the 1920s and the depression of the early 1930s had badly hurt. Hitler promised them security against communists and socialists, effective government in place of the petty politics of the other parties, and a strong, restored, purposeful Germany.

HITLER'S CONSOLIDATION OF POWER

Once in office, Hitler consolidated his control with almost lightning speed. This process had three facets: the capture of full legal authority, the crushing of alternative political groups, and the purging of rivals within the Nazi Party itself. On February 27, 1933, a mentally ill Dutch Communist set fire to the *Reichstag* building in Berlin. The Nazis quickly turned the incident to their own advantage by claiming that the fire proved the existence

QUICK REVIEW

Hitler's Rise to Power

- January 30, 1933: in an effort to hold onto power, Hindenburg appoints Hitler chancellor
- Hitler obtained office legally
- Successfully appealed to broad spectrum of German society

The *Reichstag* fire in 1933 provided Hitler with an excuse to consolidate his power.

Bildarchiv Preussischer Kulturbesitz

How did Hitler use the *Reichstag* fire to advance his political agenda?

Führer (FYOOR-er) Meaning "leader." The title taken by Hitler when he became dictator of Germany.

SS The chief security units of the Nazi state.

of an immediate Communist threat against the government. To the public, it seemed plausible that the Communists might attempt some action against the state now that the Nazis were in power. Under Article 48, Hitler issued an Emergency Decree suspending civil liberties and proceeded to arrest Communists or alleged Communists. This decree remained in force as long as Hitler ruled Germany.

In early March another *Reichstag* election took place. The Nazis still received only 43.9 percent of the vote. However, the arrest of the newly elected Communist deputies and the political fear aroused by the fire meant that Hitler could control the *Reichstag*. On March 23, 1933, the *Reichstag* passed an Enabling Act that permitted Hitler to rule by decree. Thereafter, there were no legal limits on his exercise of power.

In a series of complex moves, Hitler outlawed or undermined various German institutions that might have served as rallying points for opposition. In early May 1933, the offices, banks, and newspapers of the free trade unions were seized, and their leaders arrested. In late June and early July, the other German political parties were outlawed. By July 14, 1933, the National Socialists were the only legal party in Germany. During the same months the Nazis had taken control of the governments of the individual federal states in Germany. By the close of 1933, all major institutions of potential opposition had been eliminated.

The final element in Hitler's personal consolidation of power involved the Nazi Party itself. By late 1933 the SA consisted of approximately 1 million active members and a larger number of reserves. The commander of this party army was Ernst Roehm, a possible rival to Hitler himself. The German army officer corps, on whom Hitler depended to rebuild the national army, was jealous of the SA. Consequently, to protect his own position and to shore up support with the regular army, on June 30, 1934, Hitler ordered the murder of key SA officers, including Roehm. The German army, which was the only institution in the nation that might have prevented the murders, did nothing. A month later, on August 2, 1934, President Hindenburg died. Thereafter, the offices of chancellor and president were combined. Hitler was now the *Führer*, or sole ruler of Germany and of the Nazi Party.

ANTI-SEMITISM AND THE POLICE STATE

Terror and intimidation had helped propel the Nazis to office. As Hitler consolidated his power, he oversaw the organization of a police state. The chief vehicle of police surveillance was the SS (*Schutzstaffel*), or security units, commanded by Heinrich Himmler (1900–1945). In 1933, the SS had approximately 52,000 members. It was the instrument that carried out the blood purges of the party in 1934. By 1936 Himmler had become head of all police matters in Germany.

Nazi Attack on the Jews The police character of the Nazi regime was all-pervasive, but the people who most consistently experienced its terror were the German Jews.

Anti-Semitism had been a key plank of the Nazi program—anti-Semitism based on biological racial theories stemming from late-nineteenth-century thought rather than from religious discrimination. Before World War II the Nazi attack on the Jews went through three stages of increasing intensity. In 1933, shortly after assuming power, the Nazis excluded Jews from the civil service. For a time they also attempted to enforce boycotts of Jewish shops and businesses. The boycotts won relatively little public support. Then in 1935, a series of measures known as the Nuremberg Laws robbed German Jews of their citizenship. The professions and the major occupations were closed to those defined as Jews. Marriage and sexual intercourse between Jews and non-Jews were prohibited. Legal exclusion and humiliation of the Jews became the order of the day.

The persecution of the Jews increased again in 1938. Business careers were forbidden. In November 1938, under orders from the Nazi Party, thousands of Jewish stores and synagogues were burned or otherwise destroyed. The Jewish community itself had to pay for the damage that occurred on this *Kristallnacht* ("Night of Smashed Glass") because the government confiscated the insurance money. In many other ways, large and petty, the German Jews were harassed. This persecution allowed the Nazis to inculcate the rest of the population with the concept of a master race of pure German "Aryans" and also to display their own contempt for civil liberties.

The Final Solution   After the war broke out, Hitler decided in 1942 to destroy the Jews in Europe. It is thought that over 6 million Jews, mostly from eastern European nations, died as a result of that staggering decision, unprecedented in its scope and implementation. This subject will be more fully treated in the next chapter.

Anti-Jewish Policies Soon after seizing power, the Nazi government began harassing German Jewish businesses. Non-Jewish German citizens were urged not to buy merchandise from shops owned by Jews.

Art Resource/Bildarchiv Preussischer Kulturbesitz

Why was anti-Semitism such an important part of Nazi policy?

RACIAL IDEOLOGY AND THE LIVES OF WOMEN

Hitler and other Nazis were less interested in increasing the national population, which was Mussolini's policy in Italy, than in producing racially pure Germans. In their role as mothers, German women had the special task of preserving racial purity and giving birth to pure Germans who were healthy in mind and body. Nazi journalists often compared the role of women in childbirth to that of men in battle. Each served the state in particular social and gender roles. In both cases, the good of the nation was more important than that of the individual. (See "Compare & Connect: The Soviets and the Nazis Confront the Issues of Women and the Family," pages 702–703.)

Nazi policy favored motherhood only for those whom its adherents regarded as racially fit for it. As early as late 1933, the government raised the issue of what kind of persons were fit to bear children for the nation. This policy disapproved of fostering motherhood among those people Nazi racism condemned—particularly the Jews, but also Slavs and Gypsies. During the mass executions of Jews in the Holocaust, Jewish women were specifically targeted for death, in part to prevent them from bearing a new generation.

Nazi theorists also discriminated between the healthy and unhealthy, the desirable and undesirable, in the German population itself. The government sought to prevent "undesirables" from reproducing, a policy that led to both the sterilization and death of many women, often because of an alleged mental "degeneracy." Some pregnant women were forced to have abortions. The Nazis' population policy was, in effect, one of selective breeding, or antenatalism, that profoundly affected the lives of women.

Kristallnacht (KRIS-tahl-NAHKT) Meaning "crystal night" because of the broken glass that littered German streets after the looting and destruction of Jewish homes, businesses, and synagogues across Germany on the orders of the Nazi Party in November 1938.

THE SOVIETS AND THE NAZIS CONFRONT THE ISSUES OF WOMEN AND THE FAMILY

Both the Soviet and Nazi dictatorships intruded deeply into the private lives of their citizens. Some Communist writers in the Soviet Union imagined utopian changes to traditional family life and traditional roles for women. In Germany, the state imposed policies on women that would make their roles of wives and mothers serve the larger political and ideological goals of the Nazi Party. Different and opposed as were these policies of the two dictatorships, both challenged the social roles of women that were emerging in Western Europe and in the United States.

QUESTIONS

1. Why did Kollontai see the restructuring of the family as essential to the establishment of a new kind of Communist society? Would these changes make people loyal to that society?

2. What are the social tasks Hitler assigns to women? How does he attempt to subordinate the lives of women to the supremacy of the state?

3. Why was the present and future role of women such an important topic for both the Communist and the Nazi governments?

I. A COMMUNIST WOMAN DEMANDS A NEW FAMILY LIFE

While Lenin sought to consolidate the Bolshevik Revolution against internal and external enemies, there existed within the young Soviet Union a vast utopian impulse to change and reform virtually every social institution that had existed before the revolution or those Communists associated with capitalist society. Alexandra Kollontai (1872–1952) was a spokesperson of the extreme political left within the early Soviet Union. There had been much speculation on how the end of bourgeois society might change the structure of the family and the position of women. In this passage written in 1920, Kollontai states one of the most radically utopian visions of this change. During the years immediately after the revolution, extreme rumors circulated in both Europe and America about sexual and family experimentation in the Soviet Union. Statements such as this fostered such rumors. Kollontai herself later became a supporter of Stalin and a Soviet diplomat.

There is no escaping the fact: the old type of family has seen its day. It is not the fault of the Communist State, it is the result of the changed conditions of life. The family is ceasing to be a necessity of the State, as it was in the past; on the contrary, it is worse than useless, since it needlessly holds back the female workers from more productive and far more serious work. . . . But on the ruins of the former family we shall soon see a new form rising which will involve altogether different relations between men and women, and which will be a union of affection and comradeship, a union of two equal members of the Communist society, both of them free, both of them independent, both of them workers. No more domestic "servitude" of women. No more inequality within the family. No more fear on the part of the woman lest she remain without support or aid with little ones in her arms if her husband should desert her. The woman in the Communist city no longer depends on her husband but on her work. It is not her husband but her robust arms which will support her. There will be no more anxiety as to the fate of her children. The State of the Workers will assume responsibility for these. Marriage will be purified of all its material elements, of all money calculations, which constitute a hideous blemish on family life in our days. . . .

The woman who is called upon to struggle in the great cause of the liberation of the workers—such a woman should know that in the new State there will be no more room for such petty divisions as were formerly understood: "These are my own children, to them I owe all my maternal solicitude, all my affection; those are your children, my neighbour's children; I am not concerned with them. I have enough to do with my own." Henceforth the worker-mother, who is conscious of her social function, will rise to a point where she no longer differentiates between yours and mine; she must remember that there are henceforth only our children, those of the Communist State, the common possession of all the workers.

The Worker's State has need of a new form of relation between the sexes. The narrow and exclusive affection of the mother for her own children must expand until it embraces all the children of the great proletarian family. In place of the indissoluble marriage based on the servitude of woman, we shall see rise the free union, fortified by the love and mutual respect of the two members of the Workers' State, equal in their rights and in their obligations. In place of the individual and egotistic family there will arise a great universal family of workers, in which all the workers, men and women, will be, above all, workers, comrades.

Source: From Alexandra Kollontai, *Communism and the Family*, as reprinted in *The Family in the USSR*, ed. and trans. by Rudolph Schlesinger (London: Routledge and Kegan Paul, 1949), pp. 67–69. Reprinted by permission.

II. HITLER REJECTS THE EMANCIPATION OF WOMEN

According to Nazi ideology, women's place was in the home producing and rearing children and supporting their husbands. In this speech, Hitler urges this view of the role of women. He uses anti-Semitism to discredit those writers who had urged the emancipation of women from their traditional roles and occupations. Hitler returns here to the "separate spheres" concept of the relationship of men and women. His traditional view of women was directed against views that were associated with the Soviet experiment during the interwar years. Contrast this Nazi outlook on women and the family with the Bolshevik position described by Alexandra Kollontai in the previous document. Ironically, once World War II began, the Nazi leadership demanded that women leave the home and work in factories to support the war effort.

This **Soviet poster** illustrates the role of women in communist society as key players in industrial and agricultural development and progress. This differs greatly from the traditional role assigned to women in Nazi ideology.

Corbis/Bettmann © Swim Inc./CORBIS

What role did Soviet propaganda imagine for women in communist society?

The slogan "Emancipation of women" was invented by Jewish intellectuals and its content was formed by the same spirit. In the really good times of German life the German woman had no need to emancipate herself. She possessed exactly what nature had necessarily given her to administer and preserve; just as the man in his good times had no need to fear that he would be ousted from his position in relation to the woman. . . .

If the man's world is said to be the State, his struggle, his readiness to devote his powers to the service of the community, then it may perhaps be said that the woman's is a smaller world. For her world is her husband, her family, her children, and her home. But what would become of the greater world if there were no one to tend and care for the smaller one? How could the greater world survive if there were no one to make the cares of the smaller world the content of their lives? No, the greater world is built on the foundation of this smaller world. This great world cannot survive if the smaller world is not stable. Providence has entrusted to the woman the cares of that world which is her very own, and only on the basis of this smaller world can the man's world be formed and built up. The two worlds are not antagonistic. They complement each other, they belong together just as man and woman belong together.

We do not consider it correct for the woman to interfere in the world of the man, in his main sphere. We consider it natural if these two worlds remain distinct. To the one belongs the strength of feeling, the strength of the soul. To the other belongs the strength of vision, of toughness, of decision, and of the willingness to act. In the one case this strength demands the willingness of the woman to risk her life to preserve this important cell and to multiply it, and in the other case it demands from the man the readiness to safeguard life. . . .

So our women's movement is for us not something which inscribes on its banner as its programme the fight against men, but something which has as its programme the common fight together with men. For the new National Socialist national community acquires a firm basis precisely because we have gained the trust of millions of women as fanatical fellow-combatants, women who have fought for the common life in the service of the common task of preserving life. . . .

Whereas previously the programmes of the liberal, intellectualist women's movements contained many points, the programme of our National Socialist Women's movement has in reality but one single point, and that point is the child, that tiny creature which must be born and grow strong and which alone gives meaning to the whole life-struggle.

Source: From J. Noakes and G. Pridham, eds., *Nazism, 1919–1945*, Vol. 2, *State, Economy and Society, 1933–39: A Documentary Reader*, Exeter Studies in History No. 8 (Exeter, England: University of Exeter Press, 1984), pp. 449–450.

Young women among an enthusiastic crowd extend the Nazi salute at a party rally in 1938. Nazi ideology encouraged women to favor traditional domestic roles over employment in the workplace and to bear many children. The onset of the war, however, forced the government to recruit women workers.

Bildarchiv Preussischer Kulturbesitz

What appeal might the Nazis have had for German women?

To support motherhood among those whom they believed should have children, the Nazis provided loans to encourage early marriage, tax breaks for families with children, and child allowances) In this respect, Nazi legislation resembled that passed elsewhere in Europe during the decade. The subsidies and other family payments were sent to husbands rather than wives, to make married fatherhood seem preferable to bachelorhood. Furthermore, these policies were administered on the premise that only racially and physically desirable children received support.

Although Nazi ideology emphasized motherhood, in 1930 the party vowed to protect the jobs of working women, and the number of women working in Germany rose steadily under the Nazi regime. The Nazis recognized that in the midst of the depression many women needed to work, but the party urged them to pursue employment that was "natural" to their character as women. Such employment included agricultural labor, teaching, nursing, social service, and domestic service. The Nazis also intended women to be educators of the young. In that role, whether as mothers or as members of the serving professions, women became special protectors of German cultural values.

NAZI ECONOMIC POLICY

Besides consolidating political authority and pursuing anti-Semitic policies, Hitler still had to confront the Great Depression. German unemployment had helped propel him to power. The Nazis attacked this problem with a success that astonished and frightened Europe. By 1936, while the rest of the European economy remained stagnant, the specter of unemployment and other difficulties associated with the Great Depression no longer haunted Germany.

This success was perhaps the most important reason Germans supported his tyrannical regime. Behind the direction of both business and labor stood the Nazi terror and police. The Nazi economic experiment proved that, by sacrificing all political and civil liberty, destroying a free trade-union movement, limiting the private exercise of capital, and ignoring consumer satisfaction, a government could achieve full employment to prepare for war and aggression.

Nazi economic policies supported private property and private capitalism but subordinated all significant economic enterprise and decisions about prices and investment to the goals of the state. Hitler reversed the deflationary policy of the cabinets that had preceded him. He instituted a massive program of public works and vast military spending. From the earliest years of the Nazi regime, government spending and other economic policies served to pursue the cause of rearmament. The government built canals, reclaimed land, and constructed an extensive highway system with clear military uses. It also sent unemployed workers back to farms if they had originally come from them. Other laborers were not permitted to change jobs without official permission.

In 1935, the renunciation of the military provisions of the Versailles treaty led to open rearmament and military expansion with little opposition, as explained in Chapter 28. These measures essentially restored full employment. In 1936, Hitler instructed Hermann Göring (1893–1946), who had headed the air force since 1933, to undertake a four-year plan to prepare the army and the economy for war.

TRIALS OF THE SUCCESSOR STATES IN EASTERN EUROPE

It had been an article of faith among nineteenth-century liberals sympathetic to nationalism that only good could flow from the demise of Austria-Hungary, the restoration of Poland, and the establishment of nation-states throughout eastern Europe. These new states were to embody the principle of national self-determination and to provide a buffer against the westward spread of Bolshevism. They were, however, in trouble from the beginning.

WHAT SHARED challenges faced the successor states in eastern Europe?

ECONOMIC AND ETHNIC PRESSURES

All the new states faced immense postwar economic difficulties. None of them possessed the kind of strong economy that nation-states such as France and Germany had developed in the nineteenth century. Indeed, political independence disrupted the previous economic relationships that each of them had developed as part of one of the prewar empires. None of the new states was financially independent; except for Czechoslovakia, all of them depended on foreign loans to finance economic development. Nationalistic antagonisms often prevented these states from trading with each other, and as a consequence, most became highly dependent on trade with Germany. The successor states of eastern Europe were poor and overwhelmingly rural nations in an industrialized world. The depression hit them especially hard, because they had to import finished goods for which they paid with agricultural exports whose value was falling sharply.

Finally, throughout eastern Europe, the collapse of the old German, Russian, and Austrian empires allowed various ethnic groups—large and small—to pursue nationalistic goals unchecked by any great power or central political authority. The major social and political groups in these countries were generally unwilling to make compromises lest they undermine their nationalist identity and independence. Each state included minority groups that wanted to be independent or to become part of a different nation in the region. Again, except for Czechoslovakia, all these states succumbed to some form of domestic authoritarian government.

POLAND: DEMOCRACY TO MILITARY RULE

The nation whose postwar fortunes probably most disappointed liberal Europeans was Poland. For more than a hundred years, the country had been erased from the map. (See Chapter 17.) When the country was restored in 1919, nationalism proved an insufficient bond to overcome political disagreements stemming from class differences, diverse economic interests, and regionalism. Furthermore, large Ukrainian, Jewish, Lithuanian, and German minorities distrusted the Polish government and resented attempts to force them to adopt Polish culture. The new Poland had been constructed from portions governed by Germany, Russia, and Austria for over a century. Each of those regions of partitioned Poland had different administrative systems and laws, different economies, and different degrees of experience with electoral institutions. A host of small political parties bedeviled the new Polish Parliament, and the executive was weak. In 1926, Marshal Josef Pilsudski (1867–1935) carried out a military coup. Thereafter, he ruled, in effect, personally until his death, when the government passed into the hands of a group of his military followers. The government became increasingly anti-Semitic, and non-Polish minorities suffered various forms of discrimination.

Marshal Josef Pilsudski governed Poland from 1926 to 1935.

Hulton Archive/Getty Images

CZECHOSLOVAKIA: A VIABLE DEMOCRATIC EXPERIMENT

Only one central European successor state escaped the fate of self-imposed authoritarian government. Czechoslovakia possessed a strong industrial base, a substantial middle class, and a tradition of liberal values. After the war, the new government had broken up large estates in favor of small peasant holdings. In the person of Thomas Masaryk (1850–1937), the nation possessed a gifted leader of immense integrity and fairness. The country had a real chance of becoming a viable modern nation-state.

There were, however, tensions between the Czechs and the Slovaks, who were poorer and more rural. Moreover, other non-Czech national groups, including Poles, Magyars, Ukrainians, and especially the Germans of the Sudetenland, which the Paris settlement had placed within Czech borders, resented being part of Czechoslovakia. The parliamentary regime might have been able to work through these problems, but extreme German nationalists in the Sudetenland looked to Hitler, who wanted to expand into eastern Europe, for help. In 1938, at Munich, the great powers first divided liberal Czechoslovakia to appease Hitler's aggressive instincts and then watched passively in early 1939 as he occupied much of the country, gave parts to Poland and Hungary, and manipulated a Slovak puppet state.

HUNGARY: TURN TO AUTHORITARIANISM

Hungary was one of the defeated powers of World War I. In that defeat, it achieved its long-desired separation from Austria, but at a high political and economic price. In Hungary during 1919, Bela Kun (1885–1937), a communist, established a short-lived Hungarian Soviet Republic, which received socialist support. The Allies authorized an invasion by Romanian troops to remove the communist danger. The Hungarian landowners then established Admiral Miklós Horthy (1868–1957) as regent for the Habsburg monarch who could not return to his throne—a position Horthy held until 1944. After the collapse of the Kun government, thousands of Hungarians were either executed or imprisoned.

The Hungarians also deeply resented the territory Hungary had lost in the Paris settlement. The largely agrarian Hungarian economy suffered from a general stagnation. During the 1920s, the effective ruler of Hungary was Count Stephen Bethlen (1874–1947). He presided over a government that was parliamentary in form, but aristocratic in character. In 1932, he was succeeded by General Julius Gömbös (1886–1936), who pursued anti-Semitic policies and rigged elections. After his death in 1936, anti-Semitism lingered in Hungarian politics.

AUSTRIA: POLITICAL TURMOIL AND NAZI OCCUPATION

Austria's situation was little better than that of the other successor states. A quarter of the 8 million Austrians lived in Vienna. Viable economic life was almost impossible, and the Paris settlement forbade union with Germany. Throughout the 1920s, the leftist Social Democrats and the conservative Christian Socialists contended for power. Both groups employed small armies to terrorize their opponents and to impress their followers.

In 1933, the Christian Socialist Engelbert Dollfuss (1892–1934) became chancellor. He tried to steer a course between the Austrian Social Democrats and the German Nazis, who had surfaced in Austria. In 1934, he outlawed all political parties except the Christian Socialists, the agrarians, and the paramilitary groups that composed his own Fatherland Front. He used troops against the Social Democrats but was murdered later that year during an unsuccessful Nazi coup. His successor, Kurt von Schuschnigg (1897–1977), presided over Austria until Hitler annexed it in 1938.

SOUTHEASTERN EUROPE: ROYAL DICTATORSHIPS

In southeastern Europe, revision of the arrangements in the Paris settlement was less of an issue. Parliamentary government floundered there nevertheless. Yugoslavia had been founded by the Corfu Agreement of 1917 and was known as the Kingdom of the Serbs, Croats, and Slovenes until 1929. Throughout the interwar period, the Serbs dominated the government and were opposed by the Croats. The two groups clashed violently, but the Serbs had the advantage of having had an independent state with an army prior to World War I, whereas the Croats and Slovenes had been part of the Austro-Hungarian Empire. The Croats generally were Roman Catholic, better educated, and accustomed to reasonably incorrupt government administration. The Serbs were Orthodox, less well educated, and considered corrupt administrators by the Croats. Furthermore, although each group predominated in certain areas of the country, each had isolated enclaves in other parts of the nation. Bosnia-Herzegovina, in addition to Serbs and Croats, had a significant Muslim population. The Slovenes, Muslims, Albanians, and other small national groups often played the Serbs and the Croats against each other. All the political parties except the small Communist Party represented a particular ethnic group rather than the nation of Yugoslavia. The violent clash of nationalities eventually led to a royal dictatorship in 1929 under King Alexander I (r. 1921–1934), himself a Serb. He outlawed political parties and jailed popular politicians. Alexander was assassinated in 1934, but the authoritarian government continued under a regency for his son.

Other royal dictatorships were imposed elsewhere in the Balkans: in Romania by King Carol II (r. 1930–1940) and in Bulgaria by King Boris III (r. 1918–1943). They regarded their own illiberal regimes as preventing the seizure of power by more extreme antiparliamentary movements and as quieting the discontent of the varied nationalities within their borders. In Greece, the parliamentary monarchy floundered amid military coups and calls for a republic. In 1936, General John Metaxas (1871–1941) instituted a dictatorship under King George II (r. 1935–1947) that, for the time being, ended parliamentary life in Greece.

MAJOR POLITICAL EVENTS OF THE 1920S AND 1930S

1919, August	Constitution of the Weimar Republic promulgated
1920	Kapp Putsch in Berlin
1921, March	Kronstadt mutiny leads Lenin to initiate his New Economic Policy
1922, October	Fascist march on Rome leads to Mussolini's assumption of power
1923, January	France invades the Ruhr
November	Hitler's Beer Hall Putsch
1924	Death of Lenin
1925	Locarno Agreements
1928	Kellogg-Briand Pact; first Five-Year Plan launched in USSR
1929, January	Trotsky expelled from USSR
February	Lateran Accord between the Vatican and the Italian state
October	New York stock market crash
November	Bukharin expelled from his offices in the Soviet Union; Stalin's central position thus affirmed
1930, March	Brüning government begins in Germany; Stalin calls for moderation in his policy of agricultural collectivization because of "dizziness from success"
September	Nazis capture 107 seats in German *Reichstag*
1931, August	National Government formed in Britain
1932, March 13	Hindenberg defeats Hitler for German presidency
May 31	Franz von Papen forms German cabinet
July 31	German *Reichstag* election
November 6	German *Reichstag* election
December 2	Kurt von Schleicher forms German cabinet
1933, January 30	Hitler made German chancellor
February 27	*Reichstag* fire
March 5	*Reichstag* election
March 23	Enabling Act consolidates Nazi power
1934, June 30	Blood purge of the Nazi Party
August 2	Death of Hindenburg
December 1	Assassination of Kirov leads to the beginning of Stalin's purges
1936, May	Popular Front government in France
July–August	Most famous of public purge trials in Russia

SUMMARY

WHY DID the Paris settlement fail to bring peace and prosperity to Europe?

After Versailles: Demands for Revision and Enforcement The Paris settlement fostered both resentments and discontent. Germany had been humiliated. The arrangements for reparations led to endless haggling over payments. There were strident demands for further border adjustments because significant national minorities resided outside the national boundaries drawn in Paris. The victorious powers, especially France, often believed that the provisions of the treaties were being inadequately enforced. *page 682*

WHAT KEY factors combined to produce the Great Depression?

Toward the Great Depression in Europe The severity and length of the Great Depression have three interrelated causes: the financial crisis caused by the Great War and the Paris peace settlement; the global crisis in the production and distribution of goods, especially after 1929; and the failure of the Western European and U.S. governments to respond appropriately to these conditions. The Allies depended on payments from Germany to subsidize their economies and pay their own debts to the United States; the German economy, in turn, had become dependent on U.S. private investment in the mid-1920s. When the U.S. stock market collapsed in 1929, U.S. loans to Europe dried up, and the German economy nearly collapsed. Meanwhile, production and trade faced their own difficulties, including agricultural overproduction; farmers could no longer afford to purchase industrial products, so the manufacture of consumer goods stagnated. This led to a reduction in demand for coal, iron, and textiles, crippling those industries as well. Under the pressure of the depression, Britain's Labour prime minister Ramsay MacDonald (1866–1937) organized a National Government, which was a coalition of the Labour, Conservative, and Liberal Parties. The 1920s also saw the establishment of an independent Irish state. The most important French interwar political experiment was the Popular Front Ministry, which came to office in 1936. It was composed of Socialists, Radicals, and Communists. *page 682*

WHAT WAS the relationship between politics and economics in the early decades of the Soviet Union?

The Soviet Experiment Trotsky led the Red Army to victory over the White Russians. Lenin and the Bolsheviks imposed centralized control over almost all aspects of life, but workers, peasants, and soldiers were all expressing strong discontent by 1921. Lenin responded with the New Economic Policy. In 1922, Lenin suffered a stroke. Trotsky and Stalin competed for control of the party; Stalin won. Comintern policy split Europe's socialist parties, allowing the rise of conservative and right-wing groups. Stalin implemented a plan for rapid industrialization, which led to tremendous economic growth through the 1930s but cost millions of lives. Starting in 1928, a succession of five-year plans set production goals, and the State Planning Commission organized the economy to meet those goals. Meanwhile, in 1929, Stalin had ordered the collectivization of agriculture, so production could be increased under state control and restive peasants could be transformed into obedient industrial laborers in the new factories. Stalin retained his grip on power through the Great Purges and the "show trials" of the mid to late 1930s. *page 686*

WHAT DID fascism mean to Mussolini and his supporters?

The Fascist Experiment in Italy Mussolini's fascist movement was the first to gain power in Western Europe in response to fears of the spread of Bolshevism. Fascist movements opposed more than they stood for, but all were nationalistic and based on mass political parties. In October 1922, after he and his followers had marched on Rome, Mussolini was legally appointed prime minister. By 1926, he had made Italy into a single-party dictatorship. He used propaganda to build a cult of personality. He used violence and terror to consolidate power; he also made peace between the Italian state and the Vatican with the Lateran Accord in 1929. *page 691*

WHY DID democracy fail to thrive in postwar Germany?

German Democracy and Dictatorship The Social Democratic leadership of the Weimar Republic was unfairly blamed for accepting the terms of the Versailles Treaty, when in fact the Allies had offered no choice in the matter. All political groups in Germany wanted to revise the treaty, although they all disagreed about how and to what extent to do so. The enlightened Weimar constitution carried the seeds of its own destruction, because it allowed its liberal institutions to be overthrown. Extremism from both the left and the right, often accompanied by violence, threatened the republic throughout its existence. In the late 1920s, the Nazis were visible on the Weimar political scene but had little influence. In the early 1930s, unemployment soared—as did membership in the Nazi Storm Troopers

(SA). President von Hindenburg appointed Hitler chancellor of Germany in January 1933, hoping to control him. But Hitler consolidated his power by capturing full legal authority, crushing alternative political groups, and purging the Nazi Party of rivals. In March 1933, the Enabling Act allowed Hitler to rule by decree. By the end of 1933, the Nazis had disabled all institutions that might oppose Hitler. Through violence and intimidation, the Nazis created a terrorist police state. The Nuremberg Laws and *Kristallnacht* marked the escalation of official anti-Semitism, which culminated in the Final Solution. Nazi racial ideology encouraged or discouraged women to reproduce, depending on their ethnic and health characteristics, and women were given responsibilities in transmitting the approved culture. Hitler's economic policies achieved great successes. Rearmament and other war preparations spurred economic growth. *page 693*

WHAT SHARED challenges faced the successor states in eastern Europe?

Trials of the Successor States in Eastern Europe Parliamentary governments floundered in most of the eastern European states set up after the dissolution of the Austro-Hungarian Empire. They lacked the economic base and the history of the gradual expansion of liberal democracy that helped provide stability in Great Britain and France. The new states were not financially independent; they were poor and rural nations in an industrialized world. Each state had at least one minority ethnic group living within its new borders. With the exception of Czechoslovakia, all wound up under authoritarian rule. Poland particularly disappointed European liberals, because its recreation had been a celebrated cause among them. *page 705*

REVIEW QUESTIONS

1. What caused the Great Depression? Why was it more severe and why did it last longer than previous economic downturns? Could it have been avoided?

2. How did Stalin achieve supreme power in the Soviet Union? Why did he decide that Russia had to industrialize rapidly? Why did this require the collectivization of agriculture? Was the policy a success? How did it affect the Russian people? Why did Stalin carry out the Great Purges?

3. Why was Italy dissatisfied and unstable after World War I? How did Mussolini achieve power? What were the characteristics of the Fascist state?

4. Why did the Weimar Republic collapse in Germany? How did Hitler come to power? Which groups in Germany supported Hitler and why were they pro-Nazi? How did he consolidate his power? Why was anti-Semitism central to Nazi policy?

5. What characteristics did the authoritarian regimes in the Soviet Union, Italy, and Germany have in common? What role did terror play in each?

6. Why did liberal democracy fail in the successor states of eastern Europe?

KEY TERMS

collectivization (p. 689)
Duce (p. 692)
fascism (p. 692)
Führer (p. 700)
Great Depression (p. 683)
Great Purges (p. 690)
Kristallnacht (p. 701)
Mein Kampf (p. 697)
Nazis (p. 695)

New Economic Policy (NEP) (p. 686)
Popular Front (p. 684)
Reichstag (p. 697)
SA (p. 695)
SS (p. 700)
War Communism (p. 686)
Weimar Republic (p. 682)

For additional learning resources related to this chapter, please go to **www.myhistorylab.com**

myhistorylab

28

World War II

In August 1945, the United States exploded atomic bombs on the Japanese cities of Hiroshima and Nagasaki. A week later Japan surrendered. Without the bombs, the United States would almost certainly have had to invade Japan, and tens of thousands of Americans would have been killed. Still, the decision to use the bomb remains controversial.

© CORBIS

What led to the decision to use atomic bombs against Japan?

I dealistic survivors of the First World War hoped it would be "the war to end all wars," but only twenty years after its conclusion a second and even more terrible global conflict erupted. In Europe and Asia, democracies fought for their lives against militaristic, nationalistic, authoritarian, and totalitarian states. Their victory did not establish world peace but marked the start of an era of Cold War during which the European states were subordinated to the Soviet Union and the United States. ■

AGAIN THE ROAD TO WAR (1933–1939)

HOW DID World War I sow the seeds of World War II?

Nationalism and attention to the social question, along with party discipline, had been the sources of Nazi success. They continued to influence Hitler's foreign policy after he became chancellor in January 1933. Moreover, the Nazi destruction of the Weimar constitution and of political opposition meant that Hitler himself totally dominated German foreign policy. Consequently, it is important to know what his goals were and how he planned to achieve them.

HITLER'S GOALS

From the first expression of his goals in a book written in jail, *Mein Kampf* (*My Struggle*), to his last days in the underground bunker in Berlin where he killed himself, Hitler's racial theories and goals were at the center of his thought. He meant to bring the entire German people—the *Volk*—understood as a racial group, together into a single nation.

The new Germany would include all the Germanic parts of the old Habsburg Empire, including Austria. This virile and growing nation would need more space to live, or **Lebensraum**, that would be taken from the Slavs, who, according to Nazi theory, were a lesser race, fit only for servitude. The removal of the Jews, another inferior race according to Nazi theory, would purify the new Germany. The plans required the conquest of Poland and Ukraine as the primary areas for German settlement and for providing badly needed food. Neither *Mein Kampf* nor later statements of policy were blueprints for action. Rather, Hitler was a brilliant improviser who exploited opportunities as they arose. He never lost sight of his goal, however, which would almost certainly require a major war.

Lebensraum   German for "living space."

Germany Rearms   When Hitler came to power, Germany was far too weak to permit a direct approach to reach his aims. The first problem he set out to resolve was to shake off the fetters of Versailles and to make Germany a formidable military power. In October 1933, Germany withdrew from an international disarmament conference and also from the League of Nations. These acts alarmed the French but were merely symbolic. In January 1934, Germany signed a nonaggression pact with Poland that was of greater concern to France, for it undermined France's chief means of containing the Germans. At last, in March 1935, Hitler formally renounced the disarmament provisions of the Versailles treaty with the formation of a German air force, and soon he reinstated conscription, which aimed at an army of half a million men.

The League of Nations Fails   Growing evidence that the League of Nations could not keep the peace and that collective security was a myth made Hitler's path easier. In September 1931, Japan occupied Manchuria. China appealed to the League of Nations. The league dispatched a commission under a British diplomat, the earl of Lytton (1876–1951). The *Lytton Report* condemned the Japanese for resorting to force, but the powers were unwilling to impose sanctions. Japan withdrew from the League and kept control of Manchuria.

When Hitler announced his decision to rearm Germany, the League formally condemned that action, but it took no steps to prevent it. Hitler had taken a major step toward his goal without provoking serious opposition. Italy's expansionist ambitions in Africa, however, soon brought it into conflict with the Western powers.

ITALY ATTACKS ETHIOPIA

In October 1935, Mussolini, using a border incident as an excuse, attacked Ethiopia. This attack made the impotence of the League of Nations and the timidity of the Allies clear. The League of Nations condemned Italian aggression and, for the first time, voted economic sanctions. It imposed an arms embargo that limited loans and credits to, and imports from, Italy. To avoid alienating Mussolini, however, Britain and France refused to embargo oil, the one economic sanction that could have prevented Italian victory. Even more important, Britain allowed Italian troops and munitions to reach Ethiopia through the Suez Canal. The results of this policy were disastrous. The League of Nations and collective security were discredited, and Mussolini was still alienated. He now turned to Germany, and by November 1, 1936, he spoke publicly of a Rome-Berlin **Axis**.

Axis   Forces (opposed to the Allies) joined together in Europe, including Germany and Italy, before and during World War II.

REMILITARIZATION OF THE RHINELAND

The Ethiopian affair also convinced Hitler that the Western powers were too timid to oppose him forcefully. On March 7, 1936, he took his greatest risk yet, sending a small armed force into the demilitarized Rhineland. This was a breach not only of the Versailles treaty, but also of the Locarno Agreements of 1925—agreements Germany had made voluntarily. It also removed a crucial element of French security. Yet neither France nor Britain did anything but register a feeble protest with the League of Nations. British opinion would not permit support for France, and the French would not act alone. Internal division and a military doctrine that stressed defense and shunned the offensive paralyzed them. A growing pacifism further weakened both countries.

A Germany that was rapidly rearming and had a defensible western frontier presented a completely new problem to the Western powers. Their response was the policy of **appeasement**, based on the assumption that Germany had real grievances and that Hitler's goals were limited and ultimately acceptable. They set out to negotiate and make concessions before a crisis could lead to war.

appeasement   Allied policy of making concessions to Germany based on the belief that Germany's grievances were real and Hitler's goals limited.

Behind this approach was the universal dread of another war. Memories of the horrors of the last war were still vivid, and the prospect of aerial bombardment made the thought of a new war even more terrifying. A firmer policy, moreover, would have required rapid rearmament. British leaders especially were reluctant to pursue this path because of the expense and the widespread belief that the arms race had been a major cause of the last war.

THE SPANISH CIVIL WAR

The Spanish Civil War, which broke out in July 1936, made the new European alignment that found the Western democracies on one side and the fascist states on the other clearer. In 1931, the monarchy had collapsed, and Spain became a democratic republic. The new government followed a program of moderate reform that antagonized landowners, the Catholic Church, nationalists, and conservatives without satisfying the demands of peasants, workers, Catalán separatists, or radicals. Elections in February 1936 brought to power a Spanish Popular Front government ranging from republicans of the left to communists and anarchists. The losers, especially the Falangists, the Spanish fascists, would not accept defeat at the polls. In July, General Francisco Franco (1892–1975) led an army from Spanish Morocco against the republic.

This poster supports General Francisco Franco's Nationalists in the bloody Spanish Civil War, which lasted almost three years and claimed hundreds of thousands of lives.

Courtesy of the Library of Congress

How did the Spanish Civil War come to be seen as a war of contending ideologies?

Anschluss   Union of Germany and Austria.

Thus began the Spanish Civil War, which lasted almost three years, cost hundreds of thousands of lives, and provided a training ground for World War II. Germany and Italy supported Franco with troops, airplanes, and supplies. The Soviet Union sent equipment and advisers to the republicans. Liberals and leftists from Europe and America volunteered to fight in the republican ranks against fascism.

The civil war, fought on blatantly ideological lines, profoundly affected world politics. It brought Germany and Italy closer together, leading to the Rome-Berlin Axis Pact in 1936. Japan joined the Axis powers in the Anti-Comintern Pact, ostensibly directed against international communism, but really a new and powerful diplomatic alliance. Western Europe, especially France, had a great interest in preventing Spain from falling into the hands of a fascist regime closely allied with Germany and Italy. Appeasement reigned, however. Although international law permitted the sale of weapons and munitions to the legitimate republican government, France and Britain forbade the export of war materials to either side, and the United States passed new neutrality legislation to the same end. When Barcelona fell to Franco early in 1939, the fascists had won effective control of Spain.

AUSTRIA AND CZECHOSLOVAKIA

Hitler made good use of his new friendship with Mussolini. He had always planned to annex his native Austria. In 1934, the Nazi Party in Austria assassinated the prime minister and tried to seize power. Mussolini had not yet allied with Hitler and was suspicious of German intentions. He quickly moved an army to the Austrian border, thus preventing German intervention and causing the coup to fail.

In 1938, the new diplomatic situation encouraged Hitler to try again. On March 13, Austrian chancellor Kurt von Schuschnigg (1897–1977) announced a plebiscite for March 13, in which the Austrian people themselves could decide whether to unite with Germany. To forestall the plebiscite, Hitler sent his army into Austria on March 12. To his relief, Mussolini did not object, and Hitler rode to Vienna amid the cheers of his Austrian sympathizers.

The **Anschluss**, or union of Germany and Austria, was another clear violation of Versailles. The treaty, however, was now a dead letter, and the West remained passive. The *Anschluss* had great strategic significance, however, because Germany now surrounded Czechoslovakia, one of the bulwarks of French security, on three sides.

Czechoslovakia contained about 3.5 million Germans who lived in the Sudetenland, near the German border. These Germans had belonged to the dominant nationality group in the old Austro-Hungarian Empire and resented their new minority position. Supported by Hitler and led by Konrad Henlein (1898–1945), they made ever-increasing demands for privileges and autonomy within the Czech state. The Czechs made concessions, but Hitler really wanted to destroy Czechoslovakia.

On September 12, 1938, Hitler made a provocative speech at the Nuremberg Nazi Party rally. His rhetoric led to rioting in the Sudetenland, and the Czechs declared martial law. German intervention seemed imminent. British prime minister Neville Chamberlain (1869–1940) made three flights to Germany between September 15 and September 29 in an attempt to appease Hitler at Czech expense and thus to avoid war. At Hitler's mountain retreat, Berchtesgaden, on September 15, Chamberlain accepted the separation of the Sudetenland from Czechoslovakia, and he and the French premier, Edouard Daladier (1884–1970), forced the Czechs to agree by threatening to abandon them if they did not. A week later, Chamberlain flew yet again to

MAP EXPLORATION

Interactive map: To explore this map further, go to www.myhistorylab.com

MAP 28–1   Partitions of Czechoslovakia and Poland, 1938–1939   The immediate background of World War II is found in the complex international drama unfolding on Germany's eastern frontier in 1938 and 1939. Germany's expansion inevitably meant the victimization of Austria, Czechoslovakia, and Poland. With the failure of the Western powers' appeasement policy and the signing of a German-Soviet pact, the stage for the war was set.

How did appeasement ultimately lead to war?

Germany, only to find that Hitler had raised his demands. He wanted cession of the Sudetenland in three days and immediate occupation by the German army.

MUNICH

Chamberlain returned to England, and France and Britain prepared for war. At Chamberlain's request and at the last moment, Mussolini proposed a conference of Germany, Italy, France, and Britain. It met on September 29 in Munich. Hitler received almost everything he had demanded. (See Map 28–1.) The Sudetenland, the key to Czech security, became part of Germany, thus depriving the Czechs of any chance of self-defense. In return, Hitler agreed to spare the rest of Czechoslovakia.

Even in the short run, the appeasement of Hitler at Munich was a failure. Czechoslovakia did not survive. Soon Poland and Hungary tore more territory from it, and the Slovaks demanded a state of their own. Finally, on March 15, 1939, Hitler broke his promise and occupied Prague, putting an end to the Czech state and to illusions that his only goal was to restore Germans to the Reich. (See "Compare & Connect: The Munich Settlement," pages 716–717.)

QUICK REVIEW

The Occupation of the Sudetenland

- May 1938: Czechs mobilize their army in response to rumors of German invasion
- September 1938: Neville Chamberlain forces Czechs to separate the Sudetenland from Czechoslovakia
- September 29, 1938: Sudetenland is given to Germany at Munich conference

COMPARE & CONNECT

THE MUNICH SETTLEMENT

On September 29–30, 1938, Germany's dictator Adolf Hitler met with the British prime minister Neville Chamberlain, Italy's dictator Benito Mussolini, and France's prime minister Edouard Daladier to settle the fate of Czechoslovakia. The Czechs were not permitted to take part. It was the height of the Western democracies' effort to appease the dictators and resulted in the partition of Czechoslovakia, and the region called the Sudetenland was handed over to Germany, leaving the Czechs without a viable defense. Although Hitler promised to stop there, he took over the rest of the country without firing a shot on March 15, 1939. The following documents present opposite views on the achievement at Munich.

QUESTIONS

1. Why did Chamberlain think the meeting at Munich was a success for Britain?

2. How would he defend his policy of appeasement?

3. What were Churchill's objections to the Munich agreement?

4. What critique would he make of the appeasement policy?

5. Who do you think was right? Why?

I. CHAMBERLAIN'S EVALUATION

The following is an account of Chamberlain's return to England the day after the conference. He was greeted like a hero at the airport by a big crowd. Later that day he stood outside Number 10 Downing Street where again he read from the document and declared that he had brought back "peace with honour. I believe it is peace for our time."

Various shots of Mrs Chamberlain waving and shaking hands with crowds around Downing Street who are offering their support. M/S as Chamberlain's aeroplane finishes its return journey after the conference, taxis and comes to a stop at Heston. M/S of newsreel cameras filming his return from a roof at the aerodrome. M/S as Chamberlain emerges smiling from the door of a British Airways aeroplane to the cheers of the crowd. He shakes hands with a man waiting for him. L/S of crowds watching.

C/U as he makes a speech on the airfield — "The settlement of the Czech problem, which has now been achieved, is, in my view only the prelude to a larger settlement in which all Europe may find peace" (people cheer at this). "This morning I had another talk with the German Chancellor Herr Hitler and here is the paper which bears his name upon it as well as mine." (He holds paper up and waves it about, people cheer again.) "Some of you perhaps have already heard what it contains, but I would just like to read it to you." (He reads — 'We, the German Fuhrer and Chancellor and the British Prime Minister, have had a further meeting today and are agreed in recognising that the question of Anglo-German relations is of the first importance for the two countries, and for Europe. We regard the agreement signed last night and the Anglo-German naval agreement, as symbolic of the desire of our two peoples never to go to war with one another again' (everyone cheers). 'We are resolved that the method of consultation shall be the method adopted' (lots of "hear hears") 'to deal with any other questions that may concern our two countries, and we are determined to continue our efforts to remove possible sources of difference and thus to contribute to assure the peace of Europe.'" Everyone cheers and someone shouts "three cheers for Chamberlain" which they all do as he walks away and gets into the car. Everyone waves as he drives away.

Various shots as his car drives through the crowds to Buckingham Palace, people wave as he passes. M/S as King George VI and Queen Elizabeth (later the Queen Mother) come out onto the balcony of the palace with Neville Chamberlain and his wife. L/S as they wave and crowds wave back. L/S of cars and people blocking the street outside the palace.

Source: British Pathe.com Peace Four Power Conference 983.14.

Agreement at Munich On September 29–30, 1938, Hitler met with the leaders of Britain and France at Munich to decide the fate of Czechoslovakia. The Allied leaders abandoned the small democratic nation in a vain attempt to appease Hitler and avoid war. From left to right in the foreground: British Prime Minister Neville Chamberlain, French Prime Minister Edouard Daladier, Adolf Hitler, Benito Mussolini, and Italian Minister of Foreign Affairs (and Mussolini's son-in-law), Count Ciano.

National Archives and Records Administration

What did Chamberlain hope to accomplish at Munich?

II. CHURCHILL'S RESPONSE TO MUNICH

In the parliamentary debate that followed the Munich conference at the end of September 1938, Winston Churchill was one of the few critics of what had been accomplished. In the following selections from his speech, he expresses his concerns.

I will begin by saying what everybody would like to ignore or forget but which must nevertheless be stated, namely, that we have sustained a total and unmitigated defeat, and that France has suffered even more than we have . . . .

We really must not waste time after all this long debate upon the difference between the positions reached at Berchtesgaden, at Godesberg and at Munich. They can be very simply epitomized if the House will permit me to vary the metaphor. One pound was demanded at the pistol's point. When it was given, £2 were demanded at the pistol's point. Finally, the dictator consented to take £1 17s. 6d. and the rest in promises of good will for the future. . . .

All is over. Silent, mournful, abandoned, broken, Czechoslovakia recedes into the darkness. She has suffered in every respect by her association with the Western democracies and with the League of Nations, of which she has always been an obedient servant. . . .

We have been reduced in these five years from a position of security so overwhelming and so unchallengeable that we never cared to think about it. We have been reduced from a position where the very word "war" was considered one which could be used only by persons qualifying for a lunatic asylum. We have been reduced from a position of safety and power—power to do good, power to be generous to a beaten foe, power to make terms with Germany, power to give her proper redress for her grievances, power to stop her arming if we chose, power to take any step in strength or mercy or justice which we thought right—reduced in five years from a position safe and unchallenged to where we stand now. . . .

The responsibility must rest with those who have had the undisputed control of our political affairs. They neither prevented Germany from rearming, nor did they rearm ourselves in time. They quarreled with Italy without saving Ethiopia. They exploited and discredited the vast institution of the League of Nations and they neglected to make alliances and combinations which might have repaired previous errors, and thus they left us in the hour of trial without adequate national defense or effective international security. . . .

We are in the presence of a disaster of the first magnitude which has befallen Great Britain and France. Do not let us blind ourselves to that. It must now be accepted that all the countries of Central and Eastern Europe will make the best terms they can with the triumphant Nazi power. The system of alliances in Central Europe upon which France has relied for her safety has been swept away, and I can see no means by which it can be reconstituted. The road down the Danube Valley to the Black Sea, the road which leads as far as Turkey, has been opened.

Source: "Churchill's Response to Munich" from Winston S. Churchill, *Blood, Sweat, and Tears* (New York: G. P. Putnam's Sons, 1941), pp. 55–56, 58, 60–61. Reproduced with permission of Curtis Brown Ltd., London on behalf of Winston S. Churchill. Copyright Winston S. Churchill. 1941.

Poland was the next target of German expansion. In the spring of 1939, the Germans put pressure on Poland to restore the formerly German city of Danzig and to allow a railroad and a highway through the Polish Corridor to connect East Prussia with the rest of Germany. When the Poles would not yield, the usual propaganda campaign began, and the pressure mounted. On March 31, Chamberlain announced a Franco-British guarantee of Polish independence. Hitler appears to have expected to fight a war with Poland, but not with the Western allies, for he did not take their guarantee seriously. Moreover, France and Britain had no means to get effective help to the Poles. The French, still dominated by the defensive mentality of the Maginot Line, had no intention of attacking Germany. The only way to defend Poland was to bring Russia into the alliance against Hitler, but a Russian alliance posed many problems. Each side was profoundly suspicious of the other. The French and the British were hostile to communism, and since Stalin's purge of the Red Army, they were skeptical of the military value of a Russian alliance. Besides, the Russians could not help Poland without being given the right to enter Poland and Romania. Both nations, suspicious of Russian intentions—and with good reason—refused to grant these rights. As a result, Western negotiations for an alliance with Russia made little progress.

THE NAZI-SOVIET PACT

The Russians had at least equally good reason to hesitate. They resented being left out of the Munich agreement. The low priority that the West gave to negotiations with Russia, compared with the urgency with which Britain and France dealt with Hitler, annoyed them. The Russians feared, rightly, that the Western powers meant them to bear the burden of the war against Germany. As a result, they opened negotiations with Hitler, and on August 23, 1939, the world was shocked to learn of a Nazi-Soviet nonaggression pact. The secret provisions of the pact, which were easily guessed and soon carried out, divided Poland between the two powers and allowed Russia to occupy the Baltic states and to take Bessarabia from Romania.

The Nazi-Soviet pact sealed the fate of Poland, and the Franco-British commitment guaranteed a general war. On September 1, 1939, the Germans invaded Poland. Two days later, Britain and France declared war on Germany. World War II had begun.

IN WHAT ways was World War II a "total" war?

WORLD WAR II (1939–1945)

World War II was truly global. Fighting took place in Europe, North Africa, and Asia, on the Atlantic and the Pacific Oceans, and in the Northern and Southern Hemispheres. The demand for the fullest exploitation of material and human resources for increased production, the use of blockades, and the intensive bombing of civilian targets made the war of 1939 even more "total"—that is, comprehensive and intense—than that of 1914.

THE GERMAN CONQUEST OF EUROPE

The German attack on Poland produced swift success. The new style of "lightning warfare," or *blitzkrieg*, employed fast-moving, massed armored columns supported by airpower. The speed of the German victory astonished the Russians, who hastened to collect their share of the booty before Hitler could deprive them of it.

On September 17, Russia invaded Poland from the east, dividing the country with the Germans. The Red Army then occupied the encircled Baltic countries of Estonia, Latvia, and Lithuania. In June 1940, the Russians forced Romania to cede Bessarabia. In November 1939, the Russians invaded Finland, but the Finns resisted fiercely for six months. Although they were finally worn down and compelled to yield territory and bases to Russia, the Finns remained independent.

Until the spring of 1940, the western front was quiet. The French remained behind the Maginot Line. Britain rearmed hastily, and the British navy blockaded Germany. Cynics in the West called it the phony war, or *Sitzkrieg*, but Hitler shattered the stillness in the spring of 1940. In April, the Germans invaded Denmark and Norway. A month later, a combined land and air attack struck Belgium, the Netherlands, and Luxembourg.

The British and French armies in Belgium were forced to flee to the English Channel to seek escape on the beaches of Dunkirk. The heroic efforts of hundreds of Britons manning small boats saved more than 200,000 British and 100,000 French soldiers. Casualties, however, were high, and valuable equipment was abandoned.

The Maginot Line ran from Switzerland to the Belgian frontier. Until 1936, the French had expected the Belgians to continue the fortifications along their German border. After Hitler remilitarized the Rhineland without opposition, the Belgians lost faith in their French alliance and proclaimed their neutrality, leaving the Maginot Line exposed on its left flank. Hitler's swift advance through Belgium, therefore, circumvented France's main line of defense.

The French army collapsed. Mussolini, eager to claim the spoils of victory when he thought it was safe to do so, invaded southern France on June 10. Less than a week later, the new French government, under the ancient hero of Verdun, Marshal Henri Philippe Pétain (1856–1951), asked for an armistice.

THE BATTLE OF BRITAIN

If there was any chance the British would consider coming to terms with Germany after the fall of France, it disappeared when Winston Churchill (1874–1965) replaced Chamberlain as prime minister in May 1940. Churchill had been an early and forceful critic of Hitler, the Nazis, and the policy of appeasement. His skill as a speaker and a writer enabled him to inspire the British people with his own courage and determination and to undertake what seemed a hopeless fight. Hitler and his allies, including the Soviet Union, controlled all of Europe. Japan was having its way in Asia. The United States was neutral, dominated by isolationist sentiment, and determined to avoid involvement outside the Western Hemisphere.

One of Churchill's greatest achievements was establishing a close relationship with the American president Franklin D. Roosevelt (1882–1945). Roosevelt found ways to help the British despite strong political opposition. In 1940 and 1941, before the United States was at war, America sent military supplies, traded badly needed warships for leases on British naval bases, and even convoyed ships across the Atlantic to help the British survive.

As weeks passed and Britain remained defiant, Hitler was forced to contemplate an invasion, and that required control of the air. The first strikes by the German air force (**Luftwaffe**), directed against the airfields and fighter planes in southeast England, began in August 1940. In early September, however, seeking revenge for some British bombing raids on German cities, the Luftwaffe switched its main attacks to London. For two months, it bombed London every night. Much of the city was destroyed, and about 15,000 people were killed. Far from shattering British morale, however, the bombings united the British people and made them more resolute.

The Royal Air Force (RAF) inflicted heavy losses on the Luftwaffe. Aided by the newly developed radar and excellent communications, the British Spitfire and Hurricane fighter planes destroyed more than twice as many enemy planes as the RAF lost. Hitler had lost the Battle of Britain in the air and was forced to abandon his plans for invasion.

Luftwaffe The German air force.

THE GERMAN ATTACK ON RUSSIA

The defeat of Russia and the conquest of the Ukraine to provide *Lebensraum*, or "living space," for the German people had always been a major goal for Hitler. In December 1940, even while the bombing of England continued, he ordered his generals to prepare to invade Russia by May 15, 1941. (See Map 28–2.)

MAP 28–2   Axis Europe, 1941   On the eve of the German invasion of the Soviet Union, a German-Italian Axis bestrode most of Europe by annexation, occupation, or alliance—from Norway and Finland in the north to Greece in the south, and from Poland to France. Britain, the Soviet Union, a number of insurgent groups, and, finally, America, had before them the long struggle of conquering this "fortress Europe" of the Axis.

Given the diversity of cultures within the Axis, what were its prospects for maintaining order and stability in Europe over the long term?

Operation Barbarossa, the code name for the invasion of Russia, was aimed to destroy Russia before winter could set in. Success depended, in part, on an early start, but here Hitler's Italian alliance proved costly. Mussolini's invasion of France was a fiasco, even though the Germans were simultaneously crushing the main French forces. Hitler did not allow Mussolini to annex French territory in Europe or North Africa. Mussolini instead attacked the British in Egypt and drove them back some sixty miles. Encouraged by this success, he also invaded Greece from his base in Albania (which he had seized in 1939).

In North Africa, however, the British counterattacked and invaded Libya. The Greeks themselves pushed into Albania. In March 1941, the British sent help to the Greeks, and Hitler was forced to divert his attention to the Balkans and Africa. General Erwin Rommel (1891–1944) went to Africa and soon drove the British back into Egypt. In the Balkans, the German army swiftly occupied Yugoslavia and crushed Greek resistance. The price, however, was a delay of six weeks that would prove costly the following winter in the Russian campaign.

Operation Barbarossa was launched against Russia on June 22, 1941, and it almost succeeded. Despite their deep suspicion of Germany, the Russians were taken quite by surprise. By November, the German army stood at the gates of Leningrad, on the outskirts of Moscow, and on the Don River. Yet the Germans could not deliver the final blow. In August, they delayed their advance while Hitler decided strategy. The German general staff wanted to take Moscow before winter. Hitler, however, diverted a significant force to the south. By the time he was ready to return to the offensive near Moscow, it was too late. Winter devastated the German army, which was not equipped to face it. In November and December, the Russians counterattacked. The *blitzkrieg* had turned into a war of attrition, and the Germans began to have nightmares of duplicating Napoleon's retreat.

HITLER'S PLANS FOR EUROPE

Hitler often spoke of the "new order" that he meant to impose after he had established his **Third Reich** (Empire) throughout Europe. If his organization of Germany before the war is a proper guide, he had no single plan of government but relied on intuition and pragmatism. His organization of a conquered Europe had the same patchwork characteristics. Some conquered territory was annexed to Germany, some was not annexed but administered directly by German officials, and other lands were nominally autonomous but ruled by puppet governments.

Hitler's regime was probably unmatched in history for carefully planned terror and inhumanity. His plan of giving *Lebensraum* to the Germans was to be accomplished at the expense of people he deemed to be inferior. Hitler established colonies of Germans in parts of Poland, driving the local people from their land and employing them as cheap, virtually slave, labor. He had similar plans on an even greater scale for Russia.

Hitler's long-range plans included germanization as well as colonization. In lands people racially akin to the Germans inhabited, like the Scandinavian countries, the Netherlands, and Switzerland, the German nation would absorb the natives. Hitler even had plans to adopt selected people from the lesser races into the master race. For example, the Nazis planned to bring half a million Ukrainian girls to Germany as servants and find German husbands for them.

Hitler regarded the conquered lands as a source of plunder. From Eastern Europe, he removed everything useful, including entire industries. In Russia and Poland, the Germans simply confiscated the land itself. In the West, the conquered countries had to support the occupying army at a rate several times above the real cost. The Germans used the profits to buy up everything desirable, stripping the conquered peoples of most necessities.

Third Reich Hitler's Nazi regime.

JAPAN AND THE UNITED STATES ENTER THE WAR

The U.S. government might not have overcome isolationist sentiment and entered the war in the Atlantic if war had not been thrust on America in the Pacific. Since the Japanese conquest of Manchuria in 1931, American policy toward Japan had been suspicious and unfriendly. The outbreak of the war in Europe emboldened the Japanese to accelerate their drive to dominate Asia. They allied themselves with Germany and Italy, made a treaty of neutrality with the Soviet Union, and forced defeated France to give them bases in Indochina. They also continued their war in China and planned to gain control of Malaya and the East Indies (Indonesia) at the expense of beleaguered Britain and the conquered Netherlands. The only barrier to Japanese expansion was the United States.

The Americans had temporized, unwilling to cut off vital supplies of oil and other materials for fear of provoking a Japanese attack on Southeast Asia and the East Indies. The Japanese occupation of Indochina in July 1941 changed that policy, which had already begun to stiffen. The United States froze Japanese assets and cut off oil supplies; the British and Dutch did the same. Japanese plans for expansion could not continue without the conquest of the Indonesian oil fields and Malayan rubber and tin.

In October, a war faction led by General Hideki Tojo (1885–1948) took power in Japan and decided to risk a war rather than yield. On Sunday morning, December 7, 1941, Japan launched an air attack on Pearl Harbor, Hawaii, the chief American naval base in the Pacific. The attack destroyed much of the American fleet and many airplanes. The American capacity to wage war in the Pacific was negated for the time being. The next day, the United States and Britain declared war on Japan. Three days later, Germany and Italy declared war on the United States.)

THE TIDE TURNS

The Japanese swiftly captured Guam, Wake Island, and the Philippine Islands. By the spring of 1942, they had conquered Hong Kong, Malaya, Burma, and the Dutch East Indies. They controlled the southwest Pacific as far as New Guinea and were poised for an attack on Australia. It seemed that nothing could stop them.

In 1942, the Germans also advanced deeper into Russia, while in Africa Rommel drove the British back into Egypt until they stopped him at El Alamein, only seventy miles from Alexandria. Relations between the democracies and their Soviet ally were not close. German submarine warfare was threatening British supplies. The Allies were being thrown back on every front, and the future looked bleak.

The first good news for the Allied cause in the Pacific came in the spring of 1942. A naval battle in the Coral Sea sank many Japanese ships and gave security to Australia. A month later, the United States defeated the Japanese in a fierce air and naval battle off Midway Island. This victory blunted the chance of another assault on Hawaii and did enough damage to halt the Japanese advance. Soon American marines landed on Guadalcanal in the Solomon Islands and began to reverse the momentum of the war. The war in the Pacific was far from over, but the check to Japan allowed the Allies to concentrate their efforts on Europe.

QUICK REVIEW

The Path to War

- 1931: Japan conquers Manchuria
- July 1941: in response to Japanese occupation of Indonesia, the United States freezes Japanese assets and cuts off oil shipments
- December 7, 1941: Japan launches a surprise attack on Pearl Harbor

The successful Japanese attack on the American base at Pearl Harbor in Hawaii on December 7, 1941, together with simultaneous attacks on other Pacific bases, brought the United States into war against the Axis powers. This picture shows the battleships USS *West Virginia* and USS *Tennessee* in flames as a small boat rescues a man from the water.

U.S. Army Photo

How did the news of the attack on Pearl Harbor change American public opinion?

In 1942, American preparation and production were inadequate to invade Europe. Not until 1944 were conditions right for the invasion, but in the meantime other developments forecast the doom of the Axis. (See "Encountering the Past: Rosie the Riveter and American Women in the War Effort, page 724.")

Allied Landings in Africa, Sicily, and Italy   In November 1942, an Allied force landed in French North Africa. Even before that landing, after stopping Rommel at El Alamein, British field marshal Bernard Montgomery (1887–1976) had begun a drive to the west. Now, the Americans pushed eastward through Morocco and Algeria. The two armies caught the German army between them in Tunisia and crushed it. The Allies now controlled the Mediterranean and could attack southern Europe.

In July and August 1943, the Allies took Sicily. A coup toppled Mussolini, but the Germans occupied Italy. The Allies landed in Italy, and Marshal Pietro Badoglio (1871–1956), the leader of the new Italian government, declared war on Germany. The Germans there resisted fiercely, but the need to defend Italy weakened the Germans on other fronts.

Battle of Stalingrad   The Russian campaign became especially demanding. In the summer of 1942, the Germans resumed the offensive on all fronts but were unable to get far except in the south. (See Map 28–3, page 725.) Their goal was the oil fields near the Caspian Sea. Stalingrad, on the Volga, was a key point on the flank of the German army in the south. The Battle of Stalingrad raged for months with unexampled ferocity. The Russians lost more men in this one battle than the Americans lost in combat during the entire war, but their heroic defense prevailed.

Stalingrad marked the turning point of the Russian campaign. Thereafter, the Americans provided material help. Even more importantly, increased production from their own industry allowed the Russians to gain and keep the offensive. As the Germans' resources dwindled, the Russians inexorably advanced westward.

Strategic Bombing   In 1943, the Allies also gained ground in production and logistics. The industrial might of the United States began to come into full force, and new technology and tactics reduced the submarine menace.

In the same year, the American and British air forces began a series of massive bombardments of Germany by night and day. By 1945, the Allies could bomb at will. Concentrated attacks on industrial targets, especially communication centers and oil refineries, did extensive damage and helped shorten the war. Terror bombing of the civilian population was carried out too, but with no useful result. The bombardment of Dresden in February 1945 was especially savage and destructive. Whatever else it accomplished, the aerial war over Germany took a heavy toll on the German air force and diverted German resources from other military purposes.

THE DEFEAT OF NAZI GERMANY

On June 6, 1944 ("D-day"), American, British, and Canadian troops landed in force on the coast of Normandy. The "second

In the battle of Stalingrad, Russian troops contested every street and building. Although the city was all but destroyed in the fighting and Russian casualties were enormous, the German army in the east never recovered from the defeat it suffered there.

Hulton Archives/Getty Images, Inc.

What made Stalingrad such an important turning point in the war?

Allied troops landed in Normandy on D-day, June 6, 1944.

Courtesy of the Library of Congress

How did American economic power make D-day possible?

ENCOUNTERING THE PAST

ROSIE THE RIVETER AND AMERICAN WOMEN IN THE WAR EFFORT

The huge productive capacity of American industry was essential to Allied victory in the war, and American women helped sustain it. Before the start of the war and despite the unprecedented number of women the Great Depression had forced to seek employment, society was still hostile to the idea of women working outside their homes. World War II changed that. The workforce lost millions of men to the military, and women were needed to take their places.

Factories proliferated to produce the vast amounts of equipment needed for the war, and they eagerly recruited workers from groups they had previously spurned: African Americans from the rural south and women. President Roosevelt in a speech in October 1942 observed, "In some communities employers dislike to hire women. In others they are reluctant to hire Negroes. We can no longer afford to indulge such prejudice."

For some women, patriotism was more important than pay. Their jobs provided them with a way to support their male friends and relatives on the battlefield. A popular song told the story of "Rosie the Riveter," a young woman who made aircraft to protect her Marine boyfriend. A painting by Norman Rockwell for the cover of the *Saturday Evening Post* depicted her holding her rivet gun and resting her foot on a copy of Hitler's *Mein Kampf.*

Rosie the Riveter was one of the best known symbols of the U.S. war effort in World War II.

Printed by permission of the Norman Rockwell Family Agency. Copyright © 1943 the Norman Rockwell Family Entities

What contribution did American women make to the war effort?

HOW DID the war change attitudes about the place of women and minorities in American society?

front" was opened. The German defense was strong, but the Allies established a beachhead and then broke out of it. In mid-August, the Allies also landed in southern France. By the beginning of September, France had been liberated.

The Battle of the Bulge All went smoothly until December, when the Germans launched a counterattack in Belgium and Luxembourg through the Ardennes Forest. Because the Germans pushed forward into the Allied line, this was called the Battle of the Bulge. Although the Allies suffered heavy losses, the Bulge was the last gasp for the Germans in the West. The Allies crossed the Rhine in March 1945, and German resistance crumbled.

MAP 28–3   Defeat of the Axis in Europe, 1942–1945   Here are some of the major steps in the progress toward Allied victory against Axis Europe. From the south through Italy, the west through France, and the east through Russia, the Allies gradually conquered the Continent to bring the war in Europe to a close.

On which of these three fronts—southern, western, or eastern—was World War II fought the longest?

The Capture of Berlin By March 1945, the Russians were near Berlin. Because the Allies insisted on unconditional surrender, the Germans fought on until May. Hitler committed suicide in an underground bunker in Berlin on April 30, 1945. The Russians occupied Berlin by agreement with their Western allies. The Third Reich lasted only a dozen years instead of the thousand Hitler had predicted.

FALL OF THE JAPANESE EMPIRE

The war in Europe ended on May 8, 1945, and by then, victory over Japan was also in sight.

Americans Recapture the Pacific Islands In 1943, the American forces, still small in number, began a campaign of "island hopping." They did not try to

QUICK REVIEW
Key Battles in Europe

- June 6, 1944 (D-day): Allied forces land in Normandy
- December 1944: Germans inflict heavy losses at the Battle of the Bulge but fail to halt Allies' advance
- May 1945: Soviet troops capture Berlin

recapture every Pacific island the Japanese held, but selected major bases and strategic sites along the enemy supply line. (See Map 28–4.) Starting from the Solomon Islands, they moved northeast toward Japan itself. By June 1944, they had reached the Mariana Islands, usable as bases to bomb the Japanese in the Philippines, China, and Japan itself.

In October of the same year, the Americans recaptured most of the Philippines and drove the Japanese fleet back into its home waters. In 1945, Iwo Jima and Okinawa fell, despite fierce Japanese resistance that included kamikaze attacks, suicide missions in which pilots deliberately flew their explosive-filled planes into American warships. From these new bases, closer to Japan, the Americans launched a terrible wave of bombings that destroyed Japanese industry and disabled the Japanese navy. Still the Japanese government, dominated by a military clique, refused to surrender.

Confronted with Japan's determination, the Americans made plans for a frontal assault on the Japanese homeland. They calculated it might cost a million American casualties and even greater losses for the Japanese. At this point, science and technology presented the Americans with another choice.

The Atomic Bomb   Since early in the war, a secret program had been in progress. Its staff, many of whom were exiles from Hitler's Europe, was working to use atomic energy for military purposes. On August 6, 1945, an American plane dropped an atomic bomb on the Japanese city of Hiroshima. The city was destroyed, and more than 70,000 of its 200,000 residents were killed. Two days later, the Soviet Union declared war on Japan and invaded Manchuria. The next day, a second atomic bomb hit Nagasaki. Even then, the Japanese cabinet was prepared to face an invasion rather than give up.

The unprecedented intervention of Emperor Hirohito (r. 1926–1989) finally forced the government to surrender on August 14 on the condition that Japan retain the emperor. Although the Allies had continued to insist on unconditional surrender, President Harry S. Truman (1884–1972), who had come to office on April 12, 1945, on the death of Franklin D. Roosevelt, accepted the condition. Peace was formally signed aboard the USS *Missouri* in Tokyo Bay on September 2, 1945.

THE COST OF WAR

World War II was the most terrible war in history. Military deaths are estimated at some 15 million, and at least as many civilians were killed. If we include deaths linked indirectly to the war, from disease, hunger, and other causes, the number of victims might reach 40 million. Most of Europe and large parts of Asia were devastated. Yet the end of so terrible a war brought little opportunity to relax. The dawn of the atomic age made people conscious that another major war might extinguish humanity. Everything depended on concluding a stable peace, but even as the fighting ended, conflicts among the victors made the prospects of a lasting peace doubtful.

RACISM AND THE HOLOCAUST

WHAT WAS the Holocaust?

The most horrible aspect of the Nazi rule in Europe arose not from military or economic necessity but from the inhumanity and brutality inherent in Hitler's racial doctrines. These were applied to several groups of people in Eastern Europe.

Hitler considered the Slavs *Untermenschen*, subhuman creatures like beasts who need not be treated as people. In parts of Poland, the upper and professional classes

MAP 28–4 World War II in the Pacific   As in Europe, the Pacific war involved Allied recapture of areas that had been quickly taken earlier by the enemy. The enormous area represented by the map shows the initial expansion of Japanese holdings to cover half the Pacific and its islands, as well as huge sections of eastern Asia, and the long struggle to push the Japanese back to their homeland and defeat them.

Could the territories that Japan seized at the start of the war have become a coherent empire?

were entirely removed—jailed, deported, or killed. Schools and churches were closed. The Nazis limited marriage to keep down the Polish birthrate and imposed harsh living conditions.

In Russia, things were even worse. Hitler spoke of his Russian campaign as a war of extermination. Heinrich Himmler (1900–1945), head of Hitler's elite SS formations, planned to eliminate 30 million Slavs to make room for Germans; he formed extermination squads for this purpose. Six million Russian prisoners of war and deported civilians may have died under Nazi rule.

Hitler, however, had envisioned a special fate for the Jews. He meant to make all Europe *Judenrein*, or "free of Jews." The Nazis built extermination camps in Germany and Poland and used the latest technology to achieve the most efficient means to kill millions of men, women, and children simply because they were Jews. The most extensive destruction occurred in Eastern Europe and Russia, but the Nazis and their collaborators in occupied areas of Western Europe, including France, the Netherlands, Italy, and Belgium, also deported Jews from these nations to almost certain death in the east. Before the war was over, perhaps 6 million Jews had died in what has come to be called the **Holocaust**. Only about a million European Jews remained alive, most of them in pitiable condition. (See Map 28–5.)

It is difficult to comprehend the massive Nazi effort to eradicate the Jews of Europe. This destruction took different forms in different regions of the Continent. To explore this central event of twentieth-century European history, we examine the fate of the Polish Jewish community, which before the Second World War was the largest in Europe, consisting of 10 percent of Poland's population.

Holocaust The Nazi extermination of millions of European Jews between 1940 and 1945. Also called the "final solution to the Jewish problem."

MAP 28–5   The Holocaust   The Nazi policy of ethnic cleansing—targeting Jews, Gypsies, political dissidents, and "social deviants"—began with imprisoning them in concentration camps, but by 1943 the *Endlösung*, or *Final Solution*, called for the systematic extermination of "undesirables."

How important were the logistics of rail transportation to the Final Solution?

THE DESTRUCTION OF THE POLISH JEWISH COMMUNITY

A large Jewish community had dwelled within Poland for centuries, often in a climate of religious and cultural anti-Semitism. As a result of this anti-Semitism, Polish Jews had long lived in their own villages and later in their own urban neighborhoods. After the late-eighteenth-century partitions of Poland and the Congress of Vienna, most of Poland came under Russian rule. Through the policy of Official Nationalism (see Chapter 21), the nineteenth-century tsars identified loyalty to their government with membership in the Russian Orthodox Church. Jews were subject to a wide variety of discriminatory legislation. Polish Jews did not experience any of the forms of Jewish emancipation that occurred in Western Europe. (See Chapter 24.)

Language, food, dress, and place of residence as well as religion distinguished Jews from the rest of the Polish population, almost all of whom were Roman Catholics. Many Polish Jews also moved to cities, and Jews were regarded as an urban people in a predominantly rural nation. Moreover, Jews were among the poorest people in Poland, often working as self-employed merchants, peddlers, and craftspeople, or in industries, such as textiles, clothing, and paper, that other Poles identified as Jewish-dominated. Few Polish Jews belonged to trade unions. These conditions made them vulnerable during the economic turmoil of the 1920s and especially of the 1930s.

POLISH ANTI-SEMITISM BETWEEN THE WARS

Discrimination against Jews existed throughout the culture and politics of interwar Poland. During those years, the Polish government, supported by spokesmen for the Polish Roman Catholic Church, pursued policies that were anti-Semitic. The Polish government nationalized the matches, salt, tobacco, and alcohol industries and then enacted legislation that discriminated against hiring Jews for these government monopolies. Other laws made it difficult for Jews to observe the Sabbath while keeping their jobs. Regulations requiring businesses to be closed on Sunday meant Jewish shops had to close two days of the week. By the late 1930s, as ethnic nationalism became stronger, the government required businesses to display their owners' names prominently, which made it easy for people to avoid Jewish shops.

Whatever active anti-Semitism existed in Poland before the German invasion of 1939, it was the Nazis who tried to destroy the Polish Jewish community and Jewish communities elsewhere in Europe that fell under German control. In that respect, the Holocaust constitutes an event driven by German policy within the larger event of the Second World War.

World War II resulted in the near total destruction of the Jews of Europe, victims of the Holocaust spawned by Hitler's racial theories of the superiority and inferiority of particular ethnic groups. Hitler placed special emphasis on the need to exterminate the Jews, to whom he attributed particular wickedness. This picture shows Hungarian Jewish women, after "disinfection" and head shaving, marching to the concentration or death camp at Auschwitz-Birkenau, Poland.

Library of Congress/Photo by Bernhard Walter; source: National Archives and Records Administration

What did the German public know about the Holocaust prior to the end of World War II?

THE NAZI ASSAULT ON THE JEWS OF POLAND

The joint German-Soviet invasion of Poland brought millions of Jews under either German or Soviet authority. By late autumn 1939, the Germans had begun to move against Polish Jews. The Nazi government first thought it might herd virtually all the Jews of occupied Europe into the Lublin region of Poland. By early 1940, the Nazis decided to move as many Jews as possible into ghettos, where they would be separated from the rest of the Polish population. The largest ghettos were Lodz and Warsaw, each of which had populations of several hundred thousand. The Nazis moved Jews from all over Poland and, eventually, other occupied regions by rail into these ghettos and then sealed them off with police guards and walls. Jewish councils, which were torn between responsibility to their communities and the need to respond to German orders, administered the ghettos. The Nazis confiscated and sold the personal property and businesses of the Jews who were herded into the ghettos. Jewish laborers were sent out to work as contract labor while their families remained in the ghettos. By 1941, the Polish Jews had lost their civic standing and property. They had been located in segregated communities within Poland where disease was rampant and the food supply meager. Approximately 20 percent of the population of both the Lodz and Warsaw ghettos died of disease and malnourishment.

The German invasion of the Soviet Union in June 1941 made the situation of Jews in Poland even worse. The advancing German forces killed tens of thousands of Jews in the Soviet Union during 1941 and hundreds of thousands more the next year. During the second half of 1941, the Nazi government decided to exterminate the Jews of Europe. From late 1941 through 1944, the Germans transported Jews from the ghettos by rail to death camps in Poland, including Kulmhof, Belzen, Sobibor, Treblinka, Birkenau, and Auschwitz. In these camps, Jews were systematically killed in gas chambers.

By 1945, approximately 90 percent of the pre-1939 Jewish population of Poland had been destroyed. The tiny minority of Polish Jews who had survived faced bitter anti-Semitism under the postwar Soviet-dominated government. Many immigrated to Israel, leaving only a few thousand Jews within the borders of a nation where they had numbered in the millions and where they had created a rich religious, cultural, and political community. The largest Jewish community in Europe had virtually ceased to exist.

EXPLANATIONS OF THE HOLOCAUST

As interest in the Holocaust has grown since the 1960s, so has debate about its character and meaning. Was it a unique event of unprecedented and unparalleled evil, or was it one specific instance of a more general human wickedness that has found expression throughout history? Are its roots to be found in flaws in human nature as a whole, or are they unique to the experience of the West or, perhaps, to the German people?

Perhaps we should think of the problem from the standpoint of two questions: Why were the Jews the main target of Hitler's policy of extermination? How was it possible to carry out such a vast mass murder? Surely, an essential part of an answer to the first question is the persistence of anti-Semitism in Christianity and Western culture, from the Church Fathers to Luther and to the teachings of churches in modern times. Some would combine this religious and historical anti-Semitism with the coming of the Enlightenment and the social sciences, which gave rise to pseudoscientific racial theories that lent a new twist to the old hatred of the Jews. Pseudoscientific racism appears to have been the most powerful influence on Hitler, but it could not have found widespread support without deeply rooted religious and social anti-Semitism.

As to how it was possible to murder 6 million people, part of the answer must lie in the parochial nationalism that arose during and after the French Revolution. For many people, nationalism divided the world into one's fellow nationals and all others. It encouraged, excused, and even justified terrible and violent acts performed on behalf of one's homeland. Another part of the answer may derive from the utopian visions also unleashed by some Enlightenment writers, who promised to achieve perfect societies through social engineering, regardless of the human cost. To this were added the scientific and technological advances that gave the modern state new power to command its people, to persuade them to obey by controlling the media of propaganda, and to enforce its will with efficient brutality. All of these permitted the creation of a totalitarian state that, for the first time in history, could conduct mass murder on the scale of the Holocaust.

These questions and their possible answers are but suggestions meant to encourage further and deeper thought in what will surely be a continuing debate among scholars and the general public.

THE DOMESTIC FRONTS

WHAT IMPACT did World War II have on European society?

World War II represented an effort at total war by all the belligerents. One result was the carnage that occurred during the fighting. Another was an unprecedented organization of civilians on the home fronts. Each domestic effort and experience was different, but few escaped the impact of the conflict. Everywhere there were shortages, propaganda campaigns, and new political developments.

GERMANY: FROM APPARENT VICTORY TO DEFEAT

Hitler had expected to defeat all his enemies by rapid strokes, or *blitzkriegs*. Such campaigns would have required little change in Germany's society and economy. During the first two years of the war, in fact, Hitler demanded few sacrifices from the German people. Germany's failure to quickly overwhelm the Soviet Union changed everything. Food was no longer available from the east in needed quantities, Germany had to mobilize for total war, and the government demanded major sacrifices.

A great expansion of the army and of military production began in 1942. The government sought the cooperation of major German businesses to increase wartime production. Between 1942 and late 1944, the output of military products tripled. As the war went on, more men were drafted from industry into the army, and military production suffered. As the manufacture of armaments replaced the production of consumer goods, shortages of everyday products became serious. Food rationing began in April 1942, and shortages were severe until the Nazi government seized more food from occupied Europe.

By 1943, labor shortages became severe. The Nazis required German teenagers and retired men to work in the factories, and many women joined them. To achieve total mobilization, the Germans closed retail businesses, raised the age of eligibility of women for compulsory service, shifted non-German domestic workers to wartime industry, moved artists and entertainers into military service, closed theaters, and reduced such basic public services as mail and railways. Finally, the Nazis compelled thousands of non-Germans to do forced labor in Germany.

Hitler assigned women a special place in the war effort. The celebration of motherhood continued, with an emphasis on women who were the mothers of important military figures. Films portrayed ordinary women who became brave and patriotic during the war and remained faithful to their husbands who were at the front. Women were shown as mothers and wives who sent their sons and husbands off to war. The government pictured other wartime activities of women as the natural fulfillment of their maternal roles. Finally, by their faithful chastity, German women were protecting racial purity. They were not to marry or to have sex with non-Germans.

Propaganda minister Josef Goebbels (1897–1945) used both radio and films to boost the Nazi cause. Movies of the collapse of Poland, Belgium, Holland, and France showed German military might. Throughout the conquered territories, the Nazis used the same mass media to frighten inhabitants about the possible consequences of an Allied victory. Later in the war, Goebbels broadcast exaggerated claims of Nazi victories. As the German armies were checked on the battlefield, especially in Russia, propaganda became a substitute for victory. To stiffen German resolve, propaganda now aimed to frighten Germans about the consequences of defeat.

After May 1943, when the Allies began their major bombing offensive over Germany, the German people had much to fear. The bombing devastated one German city after another but did not undermine German morale. The bombing may even have increased German resistance by seeming to confirm the regime's propaganda about the ruthlessness of Germany's opponents.

The war brought great changes to Germany, but what transformed the country most was the experience of physical destruction, invasion, and occupation. Hitler and the Nazis had brought Germany to such a complete and disastrous defeat that only a new kind of state with new political structures could emerge.

FRANCE: DEFEAT, COLLABORATION, AND RESISTANCE

The terms of the 1940 armistice between France, under Pétain, and Germany, signed June 22, allowed the Germans to occupy more than half of France, including the Atlantic and English Channel coasts. Marshal Pétain set up a dictatorial regime at the resort city of Vichy and collaborated with the Germans in hopes of preserving as much autonomy as possible.

Some of the collaborators believed the Germans were sure to win the war and wanted to be on the victorious side. A few sympathized with Nazi ideas and plans.

Many conservatives regarded the French defeat as a judgment on what they saw as the corrupt, secularized, liberal Third Republic. Most of the French were not active collaborators but were demoralized by defeat and German power.

Many conservatives and extreme rightists saw in the Vichy government a way to reshape the French national character and to halt the decadence they associated with political and religious liberalism. The Roman Catholic clergy, which had lost power and influence under the Third Republic, gained status under Vichy. The church supported Pétain, and his government restored religious instruction in the state schools, increased financial support for Catholic schools, and supported the church's positions on social issues.

The Vichy regime also encouraged an intense, chauvinistic nationalism. It exploited prejudice against foreigners working in France and fostered resentment even against French men and women whom it regarded as not genuinely "French," especially French Jews. Even before Germany undertook Hitler's "final solution" in 1942, the French had begun to remove Jews from positions of influence in government, education, and publishing. The Vichy government had no part in the German policies that culminated in the deportation of French Jews to the extermination camps of Eastern Europe, but it made no protest, and its own anti-Semitic policies made the whole process easier to carry out.

Some French men and women, notably General Charles de Gaulle (1890–1969), fled to Britain after the defeat of France. There they organized the French National Committee of Liberation, or "Free French." From London, they broadcast hope and defiance to their compatriots in France. Serious internal resistance to the German occupiers and the Vichy government, however, began to develop only late in 1942. Fear of German retaliation deterred many. Others disliked the violence that resistance to a powerful ruthless nation inevitably entailed. As long as it appeared the Germans would win the war, moreover, resistance seemed imprudent and futile. For these reasons, the organized Resistance never attracted more than 5 percent of the adult French population.

By early 1944, the tide of battle had shifted. The Allies seemed sure to win, and the Vichy government would clearly not survive; only then did a large-scale active movement of resistance assert itself. From Algiers on August 9, 1944, the Committee of National Liberation declared the authority of Vichy illegitimate. French soldiers joined in the liberation of Paris and established a government for Free France. On October 21, 1945, France voted to end the Third Republic and adopted a new constitution as the basis of the Fourth Republic. The French people had experienced defeat, disgrace, deprivation, and suffering. Hostility and quarrels over who had done what during the occupation and under Vichy divided them for decades.

GREAT BRITAIN: ORGANIZATION FOR VICTORY

On May 22, 1940, the British Parliament gave the government emergency powers. Together with others already in effect, this measure allowed the government to institute compulsory military service, rationing, and economic controls.

To deal with the crisis, all British political parties joined in a national government under Winston Churchill. Churchill and the British war cabinet moved as quickly as possible to mobilize the nation. The demand for more planes and other armaments inspired a campaign to reclaim scrap metal. Wrought-iron fences, kitchen pots and pans, and every conceivable metal object were collected for the war effort. This was only one successful example of the many ways the civilian population enthusiastically engaged in the struggle.

By the end of 1941, British production had already surpassed Germany's. To meet the heavy demands on the labor force, factory hours were extended, and many women joined the workforce. Unemployment disappeared, and the working classes had more money to spend than they had enjoyed for many years. To avoid inflation caused by increased demand for an inadequate supply of consumer goods, savings were encouraged, and taxes were raised to absorb the excess purchasing power.

The "blitz" air attacks in 1940–1941 were the most immediate and dramatic experience of the war for the British people. The German air raids killed thousands of people and left many others homeless. Once the bombing began, many families removed their children to the countryside. The government issued gas masks to thousands of city dwellers, who were frequently compelled to take shelter from the bombs in the London subways.

The British made many sacrifices. Transportation facilities were strained simply from carrying enough coal to heat homes and run factories. Food and clothing for civilians were scarce and strictly rationed. Every scrap of land was farmed, increasing the productive portion by almost 4 million acres. Gasoline was scarce, and private vehicles almost vanished.

The British established their own propaganda machine to influence the Continent. The British Broadcasting Company (BBC) sent programs to every country in Europe in the local language to encourage resistance to the Nazis. At home, the government used the radio to unify the nation. Soldiers at the front heard the same programs their families did at home.

Fires destroy a commercial dock in London, England, during the German air raids. Despite many casualties and widespread devastation, the German bombing of London did not break British morale or prevent the city from functioning.

British Information Services

How did strategic bombing impact the course of the war?

Strangely, for the broad mass of the population, the standard of living improved during the war. The general health of the nation also improved, for reasons that are still not clear. These improvements should not be exaggerated, but they did occur, and many connected them with the active involvement of the government in the economy and in the lives of the citizens. This wartime experience may have contributed to the Labour Party's victory in 1945; many feared a return to Conservative Party rule would also mean a return to the economic problems and unemployment of the 1930s.

THE SOVIET UNION: "THE GREAT PATRIOTIC WAR"

The war against Germany came as a great surprise to Stalin and the Soviet Union. The German attack violated the 1939 pact with Hitler and put the government of the Soviet Union on the defensive militarily and politically. It showed the failure of Stalin's foreign policy and the ineptness of his preparation for war. Within days, German troops occupied much of the western Soviet Union. The communist government feared that Soviet citizens in the occupied zones—many of whom were not ethnic Russians—might welcome the Germans as liberators.

No nation suffered more during World War II than the Soviet Union. Perhaps as many as 16 million people were killed, and vast numbers of Soviet troops were taken prisoner. Hundreds of cities and towns and well over half of the industrial and transportation facilities of the country were devastated. From 1942, thousands of Soviet prisoners worked in German factories as forced labor. The Germans also seized grain, mineral resources, and oil from the Soviet Union.

Stalin conducted the war as the virtual chief of the armed forces, and the State Committee for Defense provided strong central coordination. When the war began, millions of citizens entered the army, but the army itself did not grow in influence at the expense of the state and the Communist Party—that is, of Stalin. As the war continued, however, the army gained more freedom of action, and eventually the generals were no longer subservient to party commissars. The power of Stalin and the nature of Soviet government and society, however, still sharply limited the army.

Soviet propaganda was different from that of other nations. Because the Soviet government distrusted the loyalty of its citizens, it confiscated radios to prevent the people from listening to German or British propaganda. In cities, the government broadcast to the people over loudspeakers in place of radios. During the war, Soviet propaganda emphasized Russian patriotism rather than traditional Marxist themes that stressed class conflict. The struggle against the Germans was called "The Great Patriotic War."

Within occupied portions of the western Soviet Union, an active resistance movement harassed the Germans. The swiftness of the German invasion had stranded thousands of Soviet troops behind German lines. Some escaped and carried on guerrilla warfare behind enemy lines. Stalin supported partisan forces in lands the enemy held for two reasons: He wanted to cause as much difficulty as possible for the Germans, and Soviet-sponsored resistance reminded the peasants that the Soviet government had not disappeared. Stalin feared the peasants' hatred of the communist government and collectivization might lead them to collaborate with the invaders. When the Soviet army moved westward, it incorporated the partisans into the regular army.

As its armies reclaimed the occupied areas and then moved across Eastern and Central Europe, the Soviet Union established itself as a world power second only to the United States. Stalin had entered the war a reluctant belligerent, but he emerged a major victor. In that respect, the war and the extraordinary patriotic effort and sacrifice it generated consolidated the power of Stalin and the party more effectively than the political and social policies of the previous decade.

PREPARATIONS FOR PEACE

HOW DID the Allies prepare for a postwar Europe?

The split between the Soviet Union and its wartime allies should cause no surprise. As the self-proclaimed center of world communism, the Soviet Union was openly dedicated to the overthrow of the capitalist nations. The Soviets muted this message, however, when the occasion demanded. On the other side, the Western allies were no less open about their hostility to communism and its chief purveyor, the Soviet Union.

Nonetheless, the need to cooperate against a common enemy and strenuous propaganda efforts helped improve Western feeling toward the Soviet ally. Still, Stalin remained suspicious and critical of the Western war effort, and Churchill was determined to contain the Soviet advance into Europe. Roosevelt perhaps had been more hopeful that the Allies could continue to work together after the war, but even he was losing faith by 1945. Differences in historical development and ideology, as well as traditional conflicts over political power and influence, soon dashed hopes of a mutually satisfactory peace settlement and continued cooperation to uphold it.

THE ATLANTIC CHARTER

In August 1941, even before the Americans were at war, Roosevelt and Churchill met on a ship off Newfoundland and agreed to the Atlantic Charter. This broad set of principles in the spirit of Wilson's Fourteen Points provided a theoretical basis for the peace they sought. When Russia and the United States joined Britain in the war, the three powers entered a purely military alliance in January 1942, leaving all political questions aside. The first political conference was the meeting of foreign ministers in Moscow in October 1943. The ministers reaffirmed earlier agreements to fight on until the enemy surrendered unconditionally and to continue cooperating after the war in a united-nations organization.

TEHRAN: AGREEMENT ON A SECOND FRONT

The first meeting of the leaders of the "Big Three" (the USSR, Britain, and the United States) took place at Tehran, the capital of Iran, in 1943. Western promises to open a second front in France the next summer (1944) and Stalin's agreement to fight Japan when Germany was defeated created an atmosphere of goodwill in which to discuss a postwar settlement. Stalin wanted to retain what he had gained in his pact with Hitler and to dismember Germany. Roosevelt and Churchill were conciliatory but made no firm commitments.

The most important decision was the one that chose Europe's west coast as the main point of attack instead of the Mediterranean. That meant, in retrospect, that Soviet forces would occupy Eastern Europe and control its destiny. At Tehran in 1943, the Western allies did not foresee this clearly, for the Russians were still fighting deep within their own frontiers, and military considerations were paramount.

Churchill and Stalin   By 1944, the situation had changed. In August, Soviet armies were before Warsaw, which had revolted against the Germans in expectation of liberation, but the Russians halted and turned south into the Balkans, allowing the Germans to annihilate the Poles. The Russians gained control of Romania, Bulgaria, and Hungary, advances that centuries of expansionist tsars had only dreamed of achieving. Alarmed by these developments, Churchill went to Moscow and met with Stalin in October. They agreed to share power in the Balkans on the basis of Soviet predominance in Romania and Bulgaria, Western predominance in Greece, and equality of influence in Yugoslavia and Hungary. These agreements were not enforceable without American approval, and the Americans were hostile to such un-Wilsonian devices as "spheres of influence."

Germany   The three powers easily agreed on Germany—its disarmament, de-Nazification, and division into four zones of occupation by France and the Big Three. Churchill, however, began to balk at Stalin's demand for $20 billion in reparations as well as forced labor from all the zones, with Russia to get half of everything. These matters festered and caused dissension in the future.

Eastern Europe   The settlement of Eastern Europe was equally thorny. Everyone agreed the Soviet Union deserved to have friendly neighboring governments, but the West insisted they also be autonomous and democratic. The Western leaders, particularly Churchill, were not eager to see Russia dominate Eastern Europe. They were also, especially Roosevelt, committed to democracy and self-determination.

SIGNIFICANT DATES FROM THE ERA CULMINATING IN WORLD WAR II

1919	(June) The Versailles Treaty
1931	(Spring) Onset of the Great Depression in Europe
1933	(January) Hitler comes to power
1935	(March) Hitler renounces disarmament; (October) Mussolini attacks Ethiopia
1936	(March) Germany remilitarizes the Rhineland; (July) Outbreak of the Spanish Civil War; (October) Formation of the Rome-Berlin Axis
1938	(March) *Anschluss* with Austria; (September) Munich Conference; Partition of Czechoslovakia
1939	(August) The Nazi-Soviet pact; (September) Germany and the Soviet Union invade Poland; Britain and France declare war on Germany; (November) The Soviet Union invades Finland
1940	(April) Germany invades Denmark and Norway; (May) Germany invades Belgium, the Netherlands, Luxembourg, and France; (June) Fall of France; (August) Battle of Britain begins
1941	(June) Germany invades the Soviet Union; (July) Japan takes Indochina; (December) Japan attacks Pearl Harbor; United States enters the war
1942	(June) Battle of Midway
1942	(November) Battle of Stalingrad begins; Allies land in North Africa
1943	(February–August) Allies take Sicily, land in Italy
1944	(June) Allies land in Normandy
1945	(May) Germany surrenders; (August) Atomic bombs dropped on Hiroshima and Nagasaki; (September) Japan surrenders

In February 1945, Churchill, Roosevelt, and Stalin met at Yalta in the Crimea to plan for the organization of Europe after the end of the war. The Big Three are seated. Standing behind President Roosevelt is Admiral William D. Leahy. Behind the prime minister are Admiral Sir Andrew Cunningham and Air Marshal Portal.

U.S. Army Photograph

What were the goals of the "Big Three" at Yalta?

Stalin, however, knew that independent, freely elected governments in Poland, Hungary, and Romania would not be friendly to Russia. He had already established a puppet government in Poland in competition with the Polish government-in-exile in London. Under pressure from the Western leaders, however, he agreed to include some Poles friendly to the West in it. He also signed a Declaration on Liberated Europe, promising self-determination and free democratic elections.

Stalin may have been eager to avoid conflict before the war with Germany was over. He was always afraid the Allies would make a separate peace with Germany and betray him, and he probably thought it worth endorsing some hollow principles as the price of continued harmony. In any case, he wasted little time violating these agreements.

YALTA

The next meeting of the Big Three was at Yalta in Crimea in February 1945. The Western armies had not yet crossed the Rhine, but the Soviet army was within a hundred miles of Berlin. The war with Japan continued, and no atomic explosion had yet taken place. Roosevelt, faced with a prospective invasion of Japan and heavy losses, was eager to bring the Russians into the Pacific war as soon as possible. As a true Wilsonian, he also suspected Churchill's determination to maintain the British Empire and Britain's colonial advantages. The Americans thought Churchill's plan to set up British spheres of influence in Europe would encourage the Russians to do the same and would lead to friction and war. To encourage Russian participation in the war against Japan, Roosevelt and Churchill made extensive concessions to Russia, ceding the Soviets Sakhalin and the Kurile Islands, and accommodating some of their desires in Korea and in Manchuria.

Again in the tradition of Wilson, Roosevelt emphasized a united-nations organization: "Through the United Nations, he hoped to achieve a self-enforcing peace settlement that would not require American troops, as well as an open world without spheres of influence in which American enterprise could work freely." Soviet agreement on these points seemed worth concessions elsewhere.

POTSDAM

The Big Three met for the last time in the Berlin suburb of Potsdam in July 1945. Much had changed since the previous conference. Germany had been defeated, and news of the successful explosion of an atomic weapon reached the American president during the meetings. The cast of characters was also different: President Truman replaced the deceased Roosevelt, and Clement Attlee (1883–1967), leader of the Labour Party that had just won a general election, replaced Churchill as Britain's spokesperson during the conference. Previous agreements were reaffirmed, but progress on undecided questions was slow.

Russia's western frontier was moved far into what had been Poland and included most of German East Prussia. In compensation, Poland was allowed "temporary administration" over the rest of East Prussia and Germany east of the Oder-Neisse River, a condition that became permanent. In effect, Poland was moved about a hundred miles west, at the expense of Germany, to accommodate the Soviet Union. The Allies agreed to divide Germany into occupation zones until the final peace treaty was signed. Germany remained divided until 1990.

A Council of Foreign Ministers was established to draft peace treaties for Germany's allies. Growing disagreements made the job difficult, and Italy, Romania, Hungary, Bulgaria, and Finland did not sign treaties until February 1947. The Russians were dissatisfied with the treaty that the United States made with Japan in 1951 and signed their own agreements with the Japanese in 1956. These disagreements were foreshadowed at Potsdam.

Overview Negotiations Among the Allies

AUGUST 1941	Churchill and Roosevelt meet off Newfoundland to sign Atlantic Charter.	Provides basis for the alliance between Britain and the United States.
OCTOBER 1943	American, British, and Soviet foreign ministers meet in Moscow.	Allies reaffirm to fight until the enemy surrenders and to continue cooperating after the war.
NOVEMBER 1943	Churchill, Roosevelt, and Stalin meet at Tehran.	Britain and the United States agree to open a second front in France; Stalin promises to join war in Japan after Germany is defeated, and Allied offensive begins on Europe's west coast.
OCTOBER 1944	Churchill meets with Stalin in Moscow.	Agree to share power in the Balkans, with Soviet predominance in Romania and Bulgaria, Western predominance in Greece, and equality of influence in Yugoslavia and Hungary.
FEBRUARY 1945	Churchill, Roosevelt, and Stalin meet at Yalta.	Concessions are made to Stalin concerning the settlement of Eastern Europe.
JULY 1945	Attlee, Stalin, and Truman meet at Potsdam.	Polish border moved a hundred miles west to accommodate the Soviet Union; Germany divided into occupational zones; and a Council of Foreign Ministers is established to draft peace treaties for Germany's allies.

SUMMARY

HOW DID World War I sow the seeds of World War II?

Again the Road to War (1933–1939) Hitler and the Nazi Party came to power in Germany through relentless discipline. They were consistent in their nationalism, in their attention to social and economic anxieties faced by Germans, and in their insistence that all of Germany's problems flowed from the Paris peace settlement. Hitler's racial theories and his goal of uniting all German people into one nation drove Nazi Germany's foreign policy. Germany started rebuilding its military in the mid-1930s. Neither the Allies nor the League of Nations took steps to oppose German rearmament. In 1936, Hitler remilitarized the Rhineland; the Western powers responded with appeasement. The 1938 *Anschluss* unified Germany and Austria. Hitler's next target was Czechoslovakia. The British prime minister worked hard to avoid the inevitable, but his policy of appeasing Hitler not only failed to save Czechoslovakia but also earned him history's disapprobation for further encouraging Hitler's aggression. Hitler occupied Prague in 1939. Chamberlain announced Britain and France would guarantee the independence of the country that Germany intended to dismember next, Poland. In August 1939, Germany and the Soviet Union signed the nonaggression pact that allowed them to divide Poland between themselves; on September 1, 1939, Germans invaded Poland; and on September 3, Britain and France declared war on Germany. *page 712*

IN WHAT ways was World War II a "total" war?

World War II (1939–1945) World War II was global, and for the combatants in Europe it was total: Civilians died in numbers equal to soldiers, and all aspects of economic, social, and political life were shaped by the war. In June 1940, the Germans occupied France. Churchill, the newly elected prime minister in Britain, was all that stood between Hitler and continental domination. The Luftwaffe's nightly bombing raids on London in the fall of 1940 were Hitler's first significant wartime blunder: They resulted in substantial losses for the Luftwaffe and stiffened British resistance. Operation Barbarossa was his second. The Germans were defeated by the Russian winter and by the heroism of Stalin's army in the Battle of Stalingrad. Hitler intended for his Third Reich to germanize, colonize, and plunder the rest of Europe. His hopes for keeping the United States out of the war were dashed when Japan bombed Pearl Harbor on December 7, 1941. The United States waited until it was on its way to victory in the Pacific before turning to the war in North Africa, and then Europe. In 1943, the United States and Britain began a massive aerial bombardment campaign against Germany. D-day, June 6, 1944, marked the beginning of the Allied land offensive in France, which resulted in the fall of Berlin in May and Allied victory in Europe. Japan fought on until Emperor Hirohito forced the government to surrender in August 1945, after the United States had dropped atomic bombs on Hiroshima and Nagasaki. *page 718*

WHAT WAS the Holocaust?

Racism and the Holocaust Hitler's racial doctrines resulted in brutality against Jews, Slavs, and other peoples. Approximately 6 million Jews were killed in the Holocaust. Jews made up 10 percent of Poland's prewar population, mostly poor and living in separate communities. The government, church, and society in general were anti-Semitic. Nonetheless, Polish Jews were numerous and included many religious, cultural, and political leaders; they were a prime target for the Nazis. In early 1940, Nazis relocated many Polish Jews to sealed ghettos, where 20 percent of the population died of disease and malnourishment. When Germany invaded the Soviet Union in 1941, Nazi propaganda connected Jews and Bolsheviks, and soon the Nazis adopted the policy of exterminating Jews. By 1945, 90 percent of Poland's pre-1939 population of Jews had been killed. *page 726*

WHAT IMPACT did World War II have on European society?

The Domestic Fronts On the home front, civilians were organized for war to a greater extent than in any previous conflict. In Germany, the economy was redirected to wartime production. Consumer goods became scarce. Women were given many roles in the German war effort. Nazi propaganda permeated society, and there was virtually no popular resistance. Much of Germany's physical and political infrastructure was destroyed by the end of the war. In France, the Vichy government was supported by the church and conservatives. All of Britain's political parties had joined in a national government under Churchill. For most of the population, the standard of living improved during the war, leading some to conclude that active government involvement in the society was a positive force. The Great Patriotic War was most destructive in the Soviet Union, where 16 million people were killed. Stalin won further centralization of authority, and the Soviet Union emerged from the war as a great power, second only to the United States. *page 730*

HOW DID the Allies prepare for a postwar Europe?

Preparations for Peace The fundamental differences between the Soviet Union and the other Allies had been dormant during the fight against Nazi Germany, but they reemerged with a vengeance as soon as the war was over. In 1941, Roosevelt and Churchill had agreed on the Atlantic Charter. The Big Three had entered a purely military alliance in January 1942. At the first meeting between Roosevelt, Churchill, and Stalin, in Tehran in 1943, the three agreed the United States and Britain would open the second front against Germany from the Atlantic coast; this had far-reaching consequences for the geography of the postwar Soviet sphere of influence. By the time the Big Three met again, in February 1945 at Yalta, the situation on the ground was far different. The Soviet Army occupied much of Eastern Europe already. Churchill and Roosevelt ceded much to Stalin; Roosevelt also pressed for a united-nations organization that would help ensure the eventual peace. The final Big Three meeting, at Potsdam in July 1945, gave Russia much of Poland, and Poland a sizable piece of Germany. The seeds of future dissension were sown. *page 734*

REVIEW QUESTIONS

1. What were Hitler's foreign policy aims? Why did Britain and France adopt a policy of appeasement? Did it buy the West valuable time to prepare for war?

2. How was Hitler able to defeat France so easily in 1940? Why was his air war against Britain a failure? Why did he invade Russia? Why did the invasion ultimately fail?

3. Why did Japan attack the United States at Pearl Harbor? What was the significance of American intervention in the war? Did President Truman make the right decision when he ordered the atomic bombs dropped on Japan?

4. What impact did World War II have on the civilian population of Europe? What impact did the "Great Patriotic War" have on the people of the Soviet Union? What was Hitler's "final solution" for Europe's Jewish population?

KEY TERMS

Anschluss (p. 714)
appeasement (p. 713)
Axis (p. 713)
Holocaust (p. 728)

Lebensraum (p. 712)
Luftwaffe (p. 719)
Third Reich (p. 721)

For additional learning resources related to this chapter, please go to **www.myhistorylab.com**

myhistorylab

29

The Cold War Era, Decolonization, and the Emergence of a New Europe

A statue of Queen Victoria is removed from the front of the Supreme Court building in Georgetown, former capital of the British colony of Guyana, in February 1970, in preparation for the transition to independence. Decolonization represented as dramatic a transition in world political relations as had the establishment of European empires in the nineteenth-century Victorian age.

What was the relationship between Britain and its former colonies after decolonization?

Cold War   Period between the end of World War II (1945) and the collapse of the Soviet Union (1991) in which U.S. and Soviet relations were tense, seemingly moments away from actual war at any time during these years.

*S*ince the end of World War II, two often interrelated sets of international political relationships shaped world events: the **Cold War** between the United States and the Soviet Union and the process of decolonization, whereby the peoples of lands dominated by European nations and later by the United States rejected that domination.

From 1945 until the collapse of communist regimes in Eastern Europe between 1989 and 1991, the simmering conflict of the Cold War dominated global politics and threatened the peace of Europe. Decolonization rapidly became enmeshed with the Cold War, as the rivalry of the two nuclear-armed superpowers expanded into a contest for dominance in the postcolonial world, aggravating local conflicts on every continent.

Since the collapse of the Soviet Union in 1991, the United States has remained the world's single superpower. Symbolically identified as embodying modern values of Western civilization, the United States has replaced Europe as the object of anti-Western resistance. A notable result of this new situation is the clash between the United States and radical political Islamism. As the era of European and American colonial dominance came to an end, the reciprocal nature of the relationship between the West and the rest of the global community has intensified. ■

THE EMERGENCE OF THE COLD WAR

WHAT WERE the
origins of the
Cold War?

The tense relationship between the United States and the Soviet Union began in the closing months of World War II. In part, the coldness between the Allies arose from the mutual feeling that each had violated previous agreements. The Russians were plainly asserting permanent control of Poland and Romania under puppet communist governments. The United States was taking a harder line about German reparation payments to the Soviet Union. In retrospect, however, it appears unlikely that friendlier styles on either side could have avoided a split that arose from basic differences of ideology and interest.

The Americans made no attempt to roll back Soviet power where it existed at the close of World War II. In less than a year from the war's end, the Americans had reduced their forces in Europe from 3.5 million to 500,000. The speed of the withdrawal reflected domestic pressure to "get the boys home" but was also fully in accord with America's peacetime plans and goals, which included support for self-determination, autonomy, and democracy in the political sphere, and free trade, freedom of the seas, no barriers to investment, and an Open Door policy in the economic sphere. As the strongest, richest nation in the world—the one with the greatest industrial base and the strongest currency—the United States would benefit handsomely from an international order based on such goals.

Although postwar American hostility to colonial empires created tensions with France and Britain, the main conflict lay with the Soviet Union. The growth in France and Italy of large popular communist parties taking orders from Moscow led the Americans to believe that Stalin was engaged in a worldwide plot to subvert capitalism and democracy. From the Soviet perspective, extending the borders of the USSR and dominating the formerly independent successor states of Eastern Europe would provide needed security and compensate for the fearful losses the Soviet people had endured in the war. The Soviets could thus see American resistance to their expansion as a threat to their security and their legitimate aims.

CONTAINMENT IN AMERICAN FOREIGN POLICY

containment   American foreign policy strategy (beginning in 1947) for countering the communist threat and resisting the spread of Soviet influence.

The resistance of Americans and Western Europeans to what they increasingly perceived as Soviet intransigence and communist plans for subversion and expansion took a clearer form in 1947. The American policy became known as one of **containment**, the purpose of which was to resist the extension of Soviet expansion and influence in the expectation that eventually the Soviet Union would collapse from internal pressures and the burdens of its foreign oppression. This strategy, which American policymakers devised in the late 1940s, would direct the broad outlines of American foreign policy for the next four decades, until the Soviet Union did collapse from exactly such pressures. Containment marked a major departure in American foreign policy and transformed the international situation during the second half of the twentieth century. The execution of the policy led the United States to enter overseas alliances, to make formal and informal commitments of support to regimes around the world it perceived as being anticommunist, to undertake enormous military expenditures, and to send large amounts of money abroad. (See "Compare & Connect: The Soviet Union and the United States Draw the Lines of the Cold War," pages 744–745.)

The Truman Doctrine   Since 1944, civil war had been raging in Greece between the royalist government restored by Britain and insurgents supported by the communist countries, chiefly Yugoslavia. In 1947, Britain informed the United States it could no longer financially support its Greek allies. On March 12, President Truman asked Congress to provide funds to support Greece and Turkey and Congress complied. In a speech to Congress that gave these actions much broader significance, the president set forth what came to be called the Truman Doctrine. He advocated a policy of support for "free people who are resisting attempted subjugation by armed minorities or by outside pressures," by implication, anywhere in the world.

The Marshall Plan   American aid to Greece and Turkey took the form of military equipment and advisers. For Western Europe, where postwar poverty and hunger fueled the menacing growth of communist parties, the Americans devised the European Recovery Program. Named the **Marshall Plan** after George C. Marshall (1880–1959), the secretary of state who introduced it, this program provided broad economic aid to European states on the sole condition that they work together for their mutual benefit. The Marshall Plan restored prosperity to Western Europe and set the stage for Europe's unprecedented postwar economic growth.

Following the declaration of the Truman Doctrine and the announcement of the Marshall Plan, the Soviet Union defined a new era of conflict between the United States and itself. (See "Compare & Connect: The Soviet Union and the United States Draw the Lines of the Cold War," pages 744–745.)

Marshall Plan   The U.S. European Recovery Program introduced by George C. Marshall, American secretary of state, whereby America provided extensive economic aid to the European states, conditional only on their working together for their mutual benefit.

SOVIET DOMINATION OF EASTERN EUROPE

Stalin may have seen containment as a renewed Western attempt to isolate and encircle the USSR. In the autumn of 1947, Stalin called a meeting in Warsaw of all communist parties from around the globe. There they organized the Communist Information Bureau (Cominform), a revival of the old Comintern, dedicated to spreading revolutionary communism throughout the world. In Western Europe the establishment of the Cominform officially ended the era of the popular front during which communists had cooperated with noncommunist parties.

During the late 1940s, the Soviet Union required the subject governments in Eastern Europe to impose Stalinist policies, including one-party political systems, close military cooperation with the Soviet Union, the collectivization of agriculture, Communist Party domination of education, and attacks on the churches. Longtime Communist Party officials were purged and condemned in show trials like those that had taken place in Moscow during the late 1930s. The catalyst for this harsh tightening probably was the success of Marshal Josip (Broz) Tito (1892–1980), the leader of communist Yugoslavia, in freeing his country from Soviet domination. Stalin wanted to prevent other Eastern European states from following the Yugoslav example.

THE SOVIET UNION AND THE UNITED STATES DRAW THE LINES OF THE COLD WAR

Between 1945 and 1950, the lines between the United States and the Soviet Union that became known as the Cold War were drawn. Each country quickly came to define the other as its principal enemy on the world scene. These two documents illustrate the manner in which each nation set its conflict with the other into a larger framework of ideological and political rivalry. Much of the rhetoric of these two documents would characterize the Cold War from its inception until the collapse of the Soviet Union.

QUESTIONS

1. How did the Cominform use the terms "democratic" and "imperialist" to its advantage?

2. Why did it see the Marshall Plan as an act of aggression?

3. How did the National Security Council characterize Soviet policy?

4. What were the goals of containment?

5. Why did the Council urge that the Soviet Union always be given opportunity to save face and to back down with dignity?

6. How does each document indicate that both the Soviet Union and the United States regarded their tensions and conflict as part of a wider global political scene?

I. THE COMINFORM DEFINES CONFLICT BETWEEN THE SOVIET UNION AND THE UNITED STATES

In 1947, under the leadership of the Soviet Union, the leaders of the Soviet and East European Communist Parties formed the Communist Information Bureau, which became known as the Cominform. It was organized in the wake of the Truman Doctrine and Marshall Plan. In September 1947, the Communist Parties constituting the Cominform issued a statement that set forth their view of the emerging conflict between the Soviet bloc and the United States. In doing so, they not only attacked the United States, but also the democratic socialist parties of Western Europe which the Soviet Union had seen as an enemy since the days of Lenin.

Fundamental changes have taken place in the international situation as a result of the Second World War and in the post-war period.

These changes are characterized by a new disposition of the basic political forces operating in the world arena, by a change in the relations among the victor states in the Second World War, and their realignment.

. . . . The Soviet Union and the other democratic countries regarded as their basic war aims the restoration and consolidation of democratic order in Europe, the eradication of fascism and the prevention of the possibility of new aggression on the part of Germany, and the establishment of a lasting all-round cooperation among the nations of Europe. The United States of America, and Britain in agreement with them, set themselves another aim in the war: to rid themselves of competitors on the markets (Germany and Japan) and to establish their dominant position. . . .

Thus two camps were formed—the imperialist and anti-democratic camp having as its basic aim the establishment of world domination of American imperialism and the smashing of democracy, and the anti-imperialist and democratic camp having as its basic aim the undermining of imperialism, the consolidation of democracy, and the eradication of the remnants of fascism. . . .

. . . the imperialist camp and its leading force, the United States, are displaying particularly aggressive activity. . . . The Truman-Marshall Plan is only a constituent part . . . of the general plan for the policy of global expansion pursued by the United States in all parts of the World. . . .

To frustrate the plan of imperialist aggression the efforts of all the democratic anti-imperialist forces of Europe are necessary. The right-wing Socialists are traitors to this cause. . . . and primarily the French Socialists and the British Labourites. . . by their servility and sycophancy are helping American capital to achieve its aims, provoking it to resort to extortion and impelling their own countries on to a path of vassal-like dependence on the United States of America.

This imposes a special task on the Communist Parties. They must take into their hands the banner of defense of the national independence and sovereignty of their countries. . . .

The principle danger for the working class today lies in underestimating their own strength and overestimating the strength of the imperialist camp.

Source: United States Senate, 81st Congress, 1st Session, Document No. 48, *North Atlantic Treaty: Documents Relating to the North Atlantic Treaty* (Washington, DC: U.S. Government Printing Office, 1949), pp. 117–120 as quoted in Katharine J. Lualdi, *Sources of the Making of the West: Peoples and Culture* (Boston: Bedford/St. Martin's, 2009), 2, pp. 248–250.

II. THE UNITED STATES NATIONAL SECURITY COUNCIL PROPOSES TO CONTAIN THE SOVIET UNION

In response to the domination of Eastern Europe by Communist Parties dominated by the Soviet Union and the occupation of these nations by Soviet troops, the United States government in 1950 adopted a policy of "containment" of the Soviet Union. This policy had been debated for many months and had for all practical purposes been in effect since the declaration of the Truman Doctrine in 1947. It was formally set forth after a period of implementation in what became known as the National Security Council Paper 68, arguably the most important statement of American foreign policy of the mid–twentieth century. The paper presented the Soviet Union as a nation determined to pursue an expansionist foreign policy and ideological struggle and as a long-term solution to that challenge proposed a policy of containing the influence of the Soviet Union diplomatically and militarily.

The Allied airlift in action during the Berlin Blockade, which took place from June 1948 until Stalin lifted it in May 1949. Every day during the blockade Western planes supplied the city.

Art Resource/Bildarchiv Preussischer Kulturbesitz

What led to the Soviet blockade of Berlin?

The fundamental design of those who control the Soviet Union and the international communist movement is to retain and solidify their absolute power, first in the Soviet Union and second in the areas now under their control. . . .

The design, therefore, calls for the complete subversion or forcible destruction of the machinery of government and structure of society in the countries of the non-Soviet world and their replacement by an apparatus and structure subservient to and controlled from the Kremlin. . . .

Our overall policy at the present time may be described as one designed to foster a world environment in which the American system can survive and flourish. It therefore rejects the concept of isolation and affirms the necessity of our positive participation in the world community.

This broad intention embraces two subsidiary policies. One is a policy which we would probably pursue even if there were no Soviet threat. It is a policy of attempting to develop a healthy international community. The other is the policy of "containing" the Soviet system. . . .

As for the policy of "containment," it is one which seeks by all means short of war to (1) block further expansion of Soviet power, (2) expose the falsities of Soviet pretensions, (3) induce a retraction of the Kremlin's control and influence, and (4) in general, so foster the seeds of destruction within the Soviet system that the Kremlin is brought at least to the point of modifying its behavior to conform to generally accepted international standards. . . .

One of the most important ingredients of power is military strength. . . . Without superior aggregate military strength . . . a policy of "containment"—which is in effect a policy of calculated and gradual coercion—is no more than a policy of bluff.

At the same time, it is essential to the successful conduct of a policy of "containment" that we always leave open the possibility of negotiation with the USSR . . .

In "containment" it is desirable to exert pressure in a fashion which will avoid so far as possible directly challenging Soviet prestige, to keep open the possibility for the USSR to retreat before pressure with a minimum loss of face and to secure political advantage from the failure of the Kremlin to yield or take advantage of the openings we leave it.

Source: National Security Council, Paper Number 68, *Foreign Relations of the United States* (Washington, DC: U.S. Government Printing Office, 1977), Sections: III, IV, VI. as cited on www.seattleu.edu/artsci/history/us1945/docs/nsc68-1.htm

THE POSTWAR DIVISION OF GERMANY

Soviet actions increased the determination of the United States to go ahead with its own arrangements in Germany.

Disagreements over Germany   During the war, the Allies had never decided how to treat Germany after its defeat. At first they all agreed it should be dismembered, but they differed on how. By the time of Yalta, Churchill had come to fear Russian control of Eastern and central Europe and began to oppose dismemberment.

The Allies also differed on economic policy. The Russians swiftly dismantled German industry in the eastern zone, but the Americans acted differently in the western zone. They concluded that if they followed the Soviet policy, the United States would have to support Germany economically for the foreseeable future. It would also cause chaos and open the way for communism. They preferred, therefore, to try to make Germany self-sufficient, and this meant restoring, rather than destroying, its industrial capacity. To the Soviets, the restoration of a powerful industrial Germany, even in the western zone only, was frightening. The same difference of approach hampered agreement on reparations. The Soviets claimed the right to the industrial equipment in all the zones, and the Americans resisted their demands.

Berlin Blockade   When the Western powers agreed to go forward with a separate constitution for the western sectors of Germany in February 1948, the Soviets walked out of the joint Allied Control Commission. In the summer of that year, the Western powers issued a new currency in their zone. All four powers governed Berlin, though it was well within the Soviet zone. The Soviets chose to seal the city off by closing all railroads and highways that led from Berlin to West Germany. Their purpose was to drive the Western powers out of Berlin.

The Western allies responded to the Berlin blockade by airlifting supplies to the city for almost a year. In May 1949, the Russians were forced to reopen access to Berlin. The incident, however, was decisive. It increased tensions and suspicions between the opponents and hastened the separation of Germany into two states. West Germany formally became the German Federal Republic in September 1949, and the eastern region became the German Democratic Republic a month later.

NATO AND THE WARSAW PACT

Meanwhile, the nations of Western Europe had been drawing closer together. The Marshall Plan encouraged international cooperation. In March 1948, Belgium, the Netherlands, Luxembourg, France, and Britain signed the Treaty of Brussels, providing for cooperation in economic and military matters. In April 1949, these nations joined with Italy, Denmark, Norway, Portugal, and Iceland to sign a treaty with Canada and the United States that formed the North Atlantic Treaty Organization (**NATO**), which committed its members to mutual assistance if any of them was attacked. The NATO treaty transformed the West into a bloc. A few years later, West Germany, Greece, and Turkey joined the alliance. For the first time in history, the United States was committed to defend allies outside the Western Hemisphere.

NATO   North Atlantic Treaty Organization, a mutual defense pact.

A series of bilateral treaties providing for close ties and mutual assistance in case of attack governed Soviet relations with the states of Eastern Europe. In 1949, these states formed the Council of Mutual Assistance (COMECON) to integrate their economies. Unlike the NATO states, the Soviets directly dominated the Eastern alliance system through local communist parties controlled from Moscow and the presence of the Red Army. The **Warsaw Pact** of May 1955, which included Albania, Bulgaria, Czechoslovakia, East Germany, Hungary, Poland, Romania, and the Soviet

Warsaw Pact   Mutual defense agreement among Albania, Bulgaria, Czechoslovakia, East Germany, Hungary, Poland, Romania, and the Soviet Union.

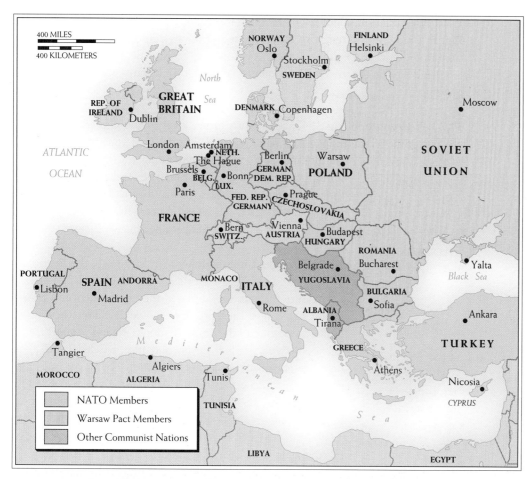

MAP 29–1   Major Cold War European Alliance Systems   The North Atlantic Treaty Organization, which includes both Canada and the United States, stretches as far east as Turkey. By contrast, the Warsaw Pact nations were the contiguous communist states of Eastern Europe, with the Soviet Union, of course, as the dominant member.

Territorially, was NATO or the Warsaw Pact the stronger alliance?

Union, gave formal recognition to this system. Europe was divided into two unfriendly blocs. The Cold War had taken firm shape in Europe. (See Map 29–1.)

THE CREATION OF THE STATE OF ISRAEL

The strategic interests of the United States and the Soviet Union would not, however, permit the Cold War to be limited to the European continent. One of the areas of ongoing regional conflict that became a major point of Cold War rivalry was the Middle East.

British Balfour Declaration   The modern state of Israel was the achievement of the world Zionist movement, founded in 1897 by Theodor Herzl (see Chapter 24) and later led by Chaim Weizmann (1874–1952). In 1917, during World War I, Arthur Balfour (1846–1930), the British foreign secretary, declared that Britain favored establishing a national home for the Jewish people in Palestine, which was then under Ottoman rule. Between the wars, thousands of Jews, mainly from Europe, immigrated to what had become British-ruled Palestine. Arabs already living in Palestine considered the Jewish settlers intruders, and violent conflicts ensued. The British tried, but failed, to mediate these clashes.

This situation might have prevailed longer, except for the outbreak of World War II and Hitler's attempt to exterminate the Jews of Europe. The Nazi persecution united Jews throughout the world behind the Zionist ideal of a Jewish state in Palestine, and it touched the conscience of the United States and other Western powers.

The UN Resolution   In 1947, the British turned over to the United Nations the problem of the relationship of Arabs and Jews in Palestine. That same year, the United Nations passed a resolution dividing the territory into two states, one Jewish and one Arab. The Arabs in Palestine and the surrounding Arab states resisted this resolution. Not unnaturally, they resented the influx of new settlers. Many Palestinian Arabs were displaced and became refugees themselves.

Israel Declares Independence   In May 1948, the British officially withdrew from Palestine, and the Yishuv, the Jewish community in Palestine, declared the independence of a new Jewish state called *Israel* on May 14. Two days later, the United States recognized the new nation. Almost immediately, Lebanon, Syria, Jordan, Egypt, and Iraq invaded Israel. The fighting continued throughout 1948 and 1949. By the end of its war of independence against the Arabs, Israel had expanded its borders beyond the limits the United Nations had originally set forth. Jerusalem was divided between Jordan and Israel. By 1949, Israel had secured its existence, but not the acceptance of its Arab neighbors. (See Map 29–2.)

The Arab-Israeli conflict would inevitably draw in the superpowers. Both the United States and the Soviet Union believed they had major strategic and economic interests in the region. By 1949, the United States had established itself as a firm ally of Israel. Gradually, the Soviet Union began to furnish aid to the Arab nations. The bipolar tensions that had settled over Europe were thus transferred to the Middle East.

THE KOREAN WAR

Between 1910 and 1945, Japan, as an Asian colonial power, had occupied and exploited the formerly independent kingdom of Korea, but at the close of World War II, the United States and the Soviet Union expelled the Japanese and divided Korea into two parts along the thirty-eighth parallel of latitude. Korea was supposed to be reunited. By 1948, however, two separate states had emerged: the Democratic People's Republic of Korea in the north, supported by the Soviet Union, and the Republic of Korea in the south, supported by the United States.

In late June 1950, after border clashes, North Korea invaded South Korea across the thirty-eighth parallel. The United States intervened, at first unilaterally and then under the authority of a UN resolution. For the United States, the point of the Korean conflict was to contain the spread and halt the aggression of communism.

MAP 29–2   Israel and Its Neighbors in 1949   The territories gained by Israel in 1949 did not secure peace in the region. In fact, the disposition of those lands and the Arab refugees who live there have constituted the core of the region's unresolved problems to the present day.

What challenges does Israel face in terms of territory and self-defense?

Late in 1950, the Chinese, responding to the approach of UN forces near their border, sent troops to support North Korea. The American forces had to retreat. The U.S. policymakers believed, mistakenly, that the Chinese, who, since 1949, had been under the communist government of Mao Zedong (1893–1976), were simply Soviet puppets. Accordingly, the Americans viewed the movement of Chinese troops into Korea as another example of communist pressure against a noncommunist state, similar to what had previously happened in Europe. On June 16, 1953, the Eisenhower administration concluded an armistice ending the Korean War and restoring the border near the thirty-eighth parallel. Thousands of American troops, however, are still stationed in Korea.

The formation of NATO and the Korean conflict capped the first round of the Cold War. In 1953, Stalin's death and the armistice in Korea fostered hopes that international tensions might ease. In early 1955, Soviet occupation forces left Austria after that nation accepted neutral status. Later that year, the leaders of France, Great Britain, the Soviet Union, and the United States held a summit conference in Geneva. Nuclear weapons and the future of a divided Germany were the chief items on the agenda. Despite public displays of friendliness, the meeting produced few substantial agreements, and the Cold War soon resumed.

THE KHRUSHCHEV ERA IN THE SOVIET UNION

WHAT WERE the three crises of 1956, and how did they affect world order?

Many Russians had hoped the end of World War II would signal a reduction in the scope of the police state and a redirection of the economy away from heavy industry to consumer products. They were disappointed. Stalin did little or nothing to modify the character of the regime he had created. If anything, his determination to centralize his authority and a desire to undertake a new wave of internal purges continued until his death on March 6, 1953.

For a time, no single leader replaced Stalin. Rather, the *presidium* (the renamed Politburo) pursued a policy of collective leadership. Gradually, however, power and influence began to devolve on Nikita Khrushchev (1894–1971), who had been named party secretary in 1953. Three years later, he became premier. Khrushchev's rise ended collective leadership, but he never commanded the extraordinary powers of Stalin.

KHRUSHCHEV'S DOMESTIC POLICIES

The Khrushchev era, which lasted until the autumn of 1964, witnessed a retreat from Stalinism, though not from authoritarianism. Khrushchev sought to reform the Soviet system but to maintain the dominance of the Communist Party. Intellectuals were somewhat freer to express their opinions. Khrushchev also made modest efforts to meet the demand for more consumer goods and decentralize economic planning. In agriculture, he removed many of the more restrictive regulations on private cultivation and sought to expand the area available for growing wheat.

The Secret Speech of 1956 In February 1956, at the Twentieth Congress of the Communist Party, Khrushchev gave a secret speech (later published outside the Soviet Union) in which he denounced Stalin and his crimes against socialist justice during the purges of the 1930s. The speech stunned party circles, but it also opened the way for genuine, if limited, internal criticism of the Soviet government and for many of the changes in intellectual and economic life cited earlier. Khrushchev's speech, however, had repercussions well beyond the borders of the Soviet Union. Communist leaders in

Eastern Europe took it as a signal that they could govern with greater leeway than before and retreat from Stalinist policies. Indeed, Khrushchev's speech was simply the first of a number of extraordinary events in 1956.

THE THREE CRISES OF 1956

The Suez Intervention   In July 1956, President Gamal Abdel Nasser (1918–1970) of Egypt nationalized the Suez Canal. Great Britain and France who had controlled the private company that had run the canal feared that this action would close the canal to their supplies of oil in the Persian Gulf. In October 1956, war broke out between Egypt and Israel. The British and French seized the opportunity to intervene militarily; however, the United States refused to support their action. The Soviet Union protested vehemently. The Anglo-French forces had to be withdrawn, and Egypt retained control of the canal.

The Suez intervention proved that without the support of the United States the nations of Western Europe could no longer impose their will on the rest of the world. It also appeared that the United States and the Soviet Union had restrained their allies from undertaking actions that might result in a wider conflict. The fact that neither of the superpowers wanted war constrained both Egypt and the Anglo-French forces.

Polish Efforts Toward Independent Action   The autumn of 1956 also saw important developments in Eastern Europe that demonstrated similar limitations on independent action among the Soviet bloc nations. When the prime minister of Poland died, the Polish Communist Party leaders refused to replace him with Moscow's nominee. In the end, Wladyslaw Gomulka (1905–1982) emerged as the new Communist leader of Poland. He was the choice of the Poles, and he proved acceptable to the Soviets because he promised continued economic and military cooperation, and particularly because he continued Polish membership in the Warsaw Pact. Within those limits he halted the collectivization of Polish agriculture and improved relations with the Polish Roman Catholic Church.

The Hungarian Uprising   Hungary provided the third trouble spot for the Soviet Union. In late October, demonstrations of sympathy for the Poles in Budapest led to street fighting. The Hungarian communists installed a new ministry headed by former premier Imre Nagy (1896–1958). Nagy was a Communist who sought a more independent position for Hungary. He went much further in his demands than Gomulka, calling for the removal of Soviet troops, the ultimate neutralization of Hungary, and for Hungarian withdrawal from the Warsaw Pact. These demands were wholly unacceptable to the Soviet Union. In early November, Soviet troops invaded Hungary; deposed Nagy, who was later executed; and imposed Janos Kadar (1912–1989) as premier.

LATER COLD WAR CONFRONTATIONS

HOW DID the Berlin Wall and the Cuban missile crisis strain relations between the United States and the Soviet Union?

After 1956, the Soviet Union began to talk about "peaceful coexistence" with the United States. By 1959, tensions had relaxed sufficiently for Western leaders to visit Moscow and for Khrushchev to tour the United States. A summit meeting was scheduled for May 1960, and President Eisenhower was to go to Moscow. Just before the Paris Summit Conference, the Soviet Union shot down an American U-2 aircraft that was flying reconnaissance over Soviet territory. Khrushchev demanded an apology from Eisenhower for this air surveillance. Eisenhower accepted full responsibility for the surveillance policy but refused to apologize publicly. Khrushchev then refused to take part in the summit conference.

The Soviets did not scuttle the summit meeting on the eve of its opening simply because of the American spy flights. They had long been aware of these flights and had other reasons for protesting them when they did. By 1960, the communist world itself had split between the Soviets and the Chinese, who were portraying the Russians as lacking revolutionary zeal. Destroying the summit was, in part, a way to demonstrate the Soviet Union's hard-line attitude toward the capitalist world.

THE BERLIN WALL

The aborted Paris conference opened the most difficult period of the Cold War. Throughout 1961, thousands of refugees from East Germany crossed the border into West Berlin. This outflow of people embarrassed East Germany, hurt its economy, and demonstrated the Soviet Union's inability to control Eastern Europe. Consequently, in August 1961, the East Germans, with Soviet support, erected a concrete wall along the border between East and West Berlin, separating the two parts of the city. Despite speeches and symbolic support from the West, the wall halted the flow of refugees and brought the U.S. commitment to West Germany into doubt.

THE CUBAN MISSILE CRISIS

The most dangerous days of the Cold War occurred during the Cuban missile crisis of 1962. In 1957, Fidel Castro (b. 1926) launched an insurgency in Cuba, which toppled the dictatorship of Flugencio Batista (1901–1973) on New Year's Day of 1959. Thereafter Castro established a communist government, and Cuba became an ally of the Soviet Union. These events caused enormous concern within the United States.

In 1962, the Soviet Union secretly began to place nuclear missiles in Cuba. In response, the American government, under President John F. Kennedy (1917–1963), blockaded Cuba, halted the shipment of new missiles, and demanded the removal of existing installations. After a tense week, during which nuclear war seemed a real possibility, the Soviets backed down, and the crisis ended. This adventurism in foreign policy undermined Khrushchev's credibility in the ruling circles of the Soviet Union and caused other non-European communist regimes to question the Soviet commitment to their security and survival. It also increased the influence of the People's Republic of China in communist circles and convinced Soviet military leaders of the need to strengthen their forces, so that they would be as strong as, or stronger than, those of the United States in any future confrontation.

If the Cuban missile crisis had led to war, the United States could have launched missiles over Europe or from European bases into the Soviet Union. The crisis thus threatened Europe directly, but it was the last major Cold War confrontation to do so. In 1963, the United States and the Soviet Union concluded a nuclear test ban treaty. This agreement marked the beginning of a lessening in the overt tensions between the two powers.

QUICK REVIEW

The Cuban Missile Crisis

- 1959: Fidel Castro comes to power as a result of the Cuban revolution
- 1962: Khrushchev orders construction of missile bases in Cuba
- Tense negotiations resulted in the Soviets backing down and removing the missiles

Cuban Missile Crisis of 1962. The American ambassador to the United Nations displayed photographs to persuade the world of the threat to the United States less than one hundred miles from its own shores.
© CORBIS

How did the Cuban missile crisis raise Cold War tensions?

THE BREZHNEV ERA

WHAT IMPACT did Brezhnev have on the Soviet Union and Eastern Europe?

By 1964, many in the Soviet Communist Party had concluded that Khrushchev had tried to do too much too soon and had done it poorly. On October 16, 1964, Khrushchev was forced to resign. He was replaced by Alexei Kosygin (1904–1980) as premier and Leonid Brezhnev (1906–1982) as party secretary. Brezhnev eventually emerged as the dominant figure.

1968: THE INVASION OF CZECHOSLOVAKIA

In 1968, during what became known as the Prague Spring, the government of Czechoslovakia, under Alexander Dubcek (1921–1992), began to experiment with a more liberal communism. In the summer of 1968, the Soviet government and its allies in the Warsaw Pact sent troops into Czechoslovakia and replaced Dubcek with communist leaders more to its own liking.

Brezhnev Doctrine   Asserted the right of the Soviet Union to intervene in domestic politics of communist countries.

At the time of the invasion, Soviet party chairman Brezhnev, in what came to be termed the **Brezhnev Doctrine**, declared the right of the Soviet Union to interfere in the domestic politics of other communist countries. No further direct Soviet interventions occurred in Eastern Europe after 1968, yet the invasion of Czechoslovakia showed that any attempt at a greater liberalization could trigger Soviet military repression.

THE UNITED STATES AND *DÉTENTE*

Foreign policy under Brezhnev combined attempts to reach an accommodation with the United States with continued efforts to expand Soviet influence and maintain Soviet leadership of the communist movement.

détente   Relaxation of tensions between the United States and Soviet Union that involved increased trade and reduced deployment of strategic arms.

Under President Richard Nixon (1969–1974), the United States began a policy of *détente* with the Soviet Union, and the two countries concluded agreements on trade and on reducing strategic arms. Despite these agreements, Soviet spending on defense, and particularly on its navy, grew, damaging the consumer sectors of the economy.

During Gerald Ford's presidency (1974–1977), both the United States and the Soviet Union along with other European nations signed the Helsinki Accords. The accords recognized the Soviet sphere of influence in Eastern Europe, but they also recognized the human rights of the signers' citizens, which every government, including the Soviet Union, agreed to protect. President Jimmy Carter (1977–1981), a strong advocate of human rights, sought to induce the Soviet Union to comply with this commitment, a policy that cooled relations between the two countries.

In the summer of 1968, Soviet tanks rolled into Czechoslovakia, ending that country's experiment in liberalized communism. This picture shows defiant flag-waving Czechs on a truck rolling past a Soviet tank in the immediate aftermath of the invasion.

Hulton Archive Photos/Getty Images, Inc.

Why did the leaders of the Soviet Union think it was so important to suppress liberalization in Soviet Bloc countries?

Throughout this period of *détente*, in addition to its military presence in Eastern Europe, the Soviet Union pursued an activist foreign policy around the world. During the 1970s, it financed Cuban military intervention in Angola, Mozambique, and Ethiopia. Soviet funds flowed to the Sandinista forces in Nicaragua and to Vietnam, which permitted the Soviets to use naval bases after North Vietnam conquered the south in 1975. The Soviet Union also provided funds and weapons to various Arab governments for use against Israel. By the early 1980s, the Soviet Union possessed the largest armed force in the world and had achieved virtual nuclear parity with the United States.

THE INVASION OF AFGHANISTAN

It was at this moment of great military strength in 1979 that the Brezhnev government decided to invade Afghanistan, a strategic decision of enormous long-range consequences for the future of the Soviet Union as well as the United States. The invasion brought a sharp response from the United States. The U.S. Senate refused to ratify a second Strategic Arms Limitation agreement that President Carter had signed earlier that year. The United States also embargoed grain shipments to the Soviet Union, boycotted the 1980 Olympic Games in Moscow, and sent aid to the Afghan rebels through various third parties, as did Pakistan, Saudi Arabia, and other Islamic nations. The U.S. Central Intelligence Agency became directly involved with the Afghan resistance forces, some of whom were radical Muslims. China, which felt threatened by the invasion, also helped the rebels.

Eventually, the Soviet forces bogged down in Afghanistan and could not defeat their guerrilla enemies. At first, few Soviets knew about the problems in Afghanistan, but during the 1980s, the military failure became common knowledge in the Soviet Union. Although the Afghan war did not make daily headline news in the Western press, it sapped Soviet strength for ten years and demoralized the Soviet Union not unlike the way the Vietnam conflict did the United States.

COMMUNISM AND SOLIDARITY IN POLAND

Events in Poland commencing in 1980—a time when the Soviet government was becoming increasingly rigidified and involved in Afghanistan—challenged both the authority of the Polish Communist Party and the influence of the Soviet Union.

In 1978, the election of Karol Wojtyla, cardinal archbishop of Kraków, as Pope John Paul II (d. 2005) proved important for Polish resistance to communist control and Soviet domination. An outspoken Polish opponent of communism now occupied a position of authority and enormous public visibility well beyond the reach of Soviet or communist control. The new pope visited his homeland in 1979 and received a tumultuous welcome.

In July 1980, the Polish government raised meat prices, leading to hundreds of protest strikes across the country. On August 14, workers occupied the Lenin shipyard at Gdansk on the Baltic coast. The strike soon spread to other shipyards, transport facilities, and factories connected with the shipbuilding industry. The strikers, led by Lech Walesa (b. 1944), refused to negotiate through any of the government-controlled unions. The Gdansk strike ended on August 31 after the government promised the workers the right to organize an independent union called Solidarity. In September, the head of the Polish Communist Party was replaced, the Polish courts recognized Solidarity as an independent union, and the state-controlled radio broadcast a Roman Catholic mass for the first time in thirty years. The summer of 1981 saw events that were no less remarkable occur within the Polish Communist Party itself. For the first time in any European communist state, secret elections for the party congress were permitted with real choices among the candidates.

QUICK REVIEW
Détente

- Brezhnev sought accommodation with the United States while continuing to extend Soviet influence
- Brezhnev and President Nixon agreed to a policy of *détente* that increased trade and reduced deployment of strategic arms
- 1975: United States and Soviet Union signed the Helsinki Accords

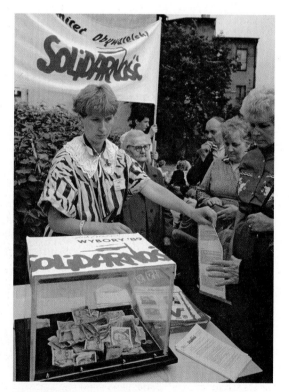

The Polish trade union "Solidarity" in 1989 successfully forced the Polish communist government to hold free elections. In June of that year, Solidarity, whose members here are collecting funds for their campaign, won overwhelmingly.
Bernard Bisson/CORBIS/Bettmann

Why did Poland's government find it so hard to defeat Solidarity?

This extraordinary Polish experiment, however, ended abruptly. In 1981, General Wojciech Jaruzelski (b. 1923) became head of the Polish Communist Party, and the army imposed martial law in December. The leaders of Solidarity were arrested. Martial law remained in effect until late in 1983, but the Polish Communist Party could not solve Poland's major economic problems.

RELATIONS WITH THE REAGAN ADMINISTRATION

Early in the administration of President Ronald Reagan (1981–1989), the United States relaxed its grain embargo on the Soviet Union and placed less emphasis on human rights. At the same time, however, Reagan intensified Cold War rhetoric, famously describing the Soviet Union as an "evil empire." More importantly, the Reagan administration increased U.S. military spending, slowed arms limitation negotiations, deployed a new missile system in Europe, and proposed the Strategic Defense Initiative (dubbed "Star Wars" by the press), involving a high-technology space-based defense against nuclear attack. Star Wars and the Reagan defense spending forced the Soviet Union to increase its own defense spending when it could ill afford to do so and contributed to the economic problems that helped bring about its collapse.

DECOLONIZATION: THE EUROPEAN RETREAT FROM EMPIRE

HOW DID World War II serve as a catalyst for decolonization?

At the founding of the United Nations in 1945, approximately one-third of the population of the world was subject to the government of colonial powers. Since that time, more than eighty of those then non-self-governing territories have been admitted to UN membership as independent states. (See Map 29–3.)

The catalyst for this transformation was World War II. The war drew the military forces of the colonial powers back to Europe. The Japanese overran European possessions in East Asia and demonstrated thus that the European presence there might not be permanent. After the dislocations of the war came the immediate postwar European economic collapse, which left the European colonial powers less able to afford to maintain their military and administrative positions abroad. Consequently, in less than a century after the great nineteenth-century drive toward empire, European imperialists found themselves in retreat around the globe.

The liberal-democratic war aims of the Allies had also undermined colonialism. It was difficult to fight against tyranny in Europe while maintaining colonial dominance abroad. The United States opposed the continuation of the colonial empires. This policy was, in part, a matter of principle, but it also recognized that both the political and economic interests of the United States were more likely to prosper in a decolonized world. The founding of the United Nations also assured the presence of an international body opposed to colonialism.

The Cold War complicated the process of decolonization. Both the United States and the Soviet Union opposed the old colonial empires, but both also worried about the potential alignment of the new nations and moved to create spheres of influence and, in some cases, alliances with the newly independent states. Certain nations, such as India, fiercely pursued policies of neutrality in hopes of receiving aid and support from both sides.

Decolonization was a worldwide event lasting throughout the second half of the twentieth century and beyond. The two largest colonial empires were the British and the French. Their retreat from empire produced the most far-reaching repercussions not only in former colonial nations, but also in both Europe and the United States.

MAP EXPLORATION

Interactive map: To explore this map further, go to **www.myhistorylab.com**

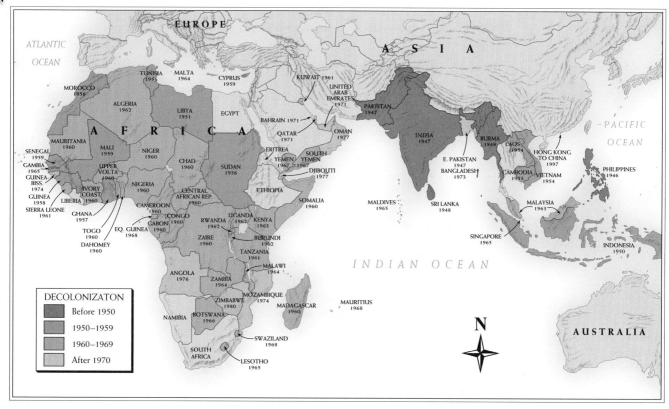

MAP 29–3   Decolonization Since World War II   The Western powers' rapid retreat from imperialism after World War II is graphically shown on this outline map covering half the globe—from West Africa to the Southwest Pacific.

What patterns are noticeable about the time when South Asian, Southeast Asian, and African countries gained their independence?

INDIA

As early as 1885, politically active Hindu Indians founded the Indian National Congress with the goals of modernizing Indian life and liberalizing British policy. Muslims organized the Muslim League in 1887, which for a time cooperated with the National Congress but eventually sought an independent Muslim nation. After World War I, the Indian nationalist movement grew steadily in strength, in part because of British blunders, but more importantly because remarkable leaders pursued effective strategies.

Chief among these leaders was Mohandas Gandhi (1869–1948), who had studied law in Britain and there began to encounter the ideas of liberal Western thinkers, including the American Henry David Thoreau (1817–1862) from whom he learned the concept of passive resistance. In 1893 Ghandi went to South Africa where for over twenty years he worked on behalf of Indian immigrants. Gandhi returned to India in 1915 and soon distinguished himself as a leader of Indian nationalism by his insistence on religious toleration. From the 1920s to the mid-1940s, he inspired a growing movement of passive resistance to British rule in India. In 1930, he lead a famous march to break the British salt monopoly by collecting salt from the sea. He was repeatedly arrested and jailed by the British authorities. To embarrass the British during these

Ghandi led Indian resistance to British colonial rule. Part of his appeal was the simplicity of his life and dress.

How did Ghandi use the celebration of traditional Indian culture in his fight for Indian independence?

imprisonments and to gain worldwide publicity, he undertook long protest fasts during which he nearly died. In 1942, during World War II, Gandhi called on the British Government to leave India. In 1947, the British Labor government, weary of the incessant agitation and uncertain of its ability to maintain control in India, decided to do so.

Gandhi and the Congress Party succeeded in forcing the British from India. However, they did not succeed in creating a single nation. Parallel to Gandhi's drive for an India characterized by diverse religions living in mutual toleration, the Muslim League led by Ali Jinnah (1876–1948) sought a distinctly Muslim state. What occurred in 1947 as the British left India was a partition of the country into the states of India and Pakistan. Intense sectarian warfare and hundreds of thousands of deaths marked the partition. A Hindu extremist assassinated Gandhi himself in 1948.

FURTHER BRITISH RETREAT FROM EMPIRE

The British surrender of India marked the beginning of a long, steady retreat from empire. Generally speaking, the British accepted the loss of empire as inevitable. British decolonization sought first to maintain whatever links were economically and politically possible without conflict. Indeed, during the 1940s and 1950s, the British undertook various development programs in their remaining Asian, African, and Caribbean colonies. These investments paradoxically made the British government and public more aware of the actual costs of empire and may have led both to accept more easily the end of empire. Second, throughout decolonization the British hoped to oversee the creation of institutions in their former colonies that would assure representative self-government once they had departed.

In 1948, Burma and Sri Lanka (formerly Ceylon) became independent. As already observed, the formation of the state of Israel and Arab nationalist movements forced Britain to withdraw from Palestine. During the 1950s, the British tried, belatedly, to prepare their tropical colonies for self-government. Ghana (formerly the Gold Coast) and Nigeria—which became self-governing in 1957 and 1960, respectively—were the major examples of planned decolonization. In other areas, such as Cyprus, Kenya, and Aden (now part of Yemen), the British withdrew under the pressure of militant nationalist movements. In many areas, violence between the British and the forces demanding independence hastened this retreat.

The development of these former colonies in the second half of the twentieth century has followed two distinct paths. In general, political instability and poverty have characterized the history of the independent states in Africa. By contrast, Asia has been an area of overall political stability and remarkable economic growth, challenging the economies of both the United States and Western Europe.

THE TURMOIL OF FRENCH DECOLONIZATION

WHY WAS France so reluctant to decolonize?

Although the British retreat from empire involved violence, at no point did the British "make a stand." Such was not the case with France. Having been defeated by the Nazis and then liberated by the allied forces, France believed it must reassert its position as a great power. This determination led it into two disastrous attempts to maintain its colonial empire, in Algeria and Vietnam.

FRANCE AND ALGERIA

Over the decades, as France consolidated and extended its position in Algeria, French soldiers and hundreds of thousands of Europeans from France and other Mediterranean countries settled there, primarily in the cities and on small farms. By the close of World War I, approximately 20 percent of the population was of European descent. Collectively these immigrants were termed the *pieds noirs* (meaning "black feet," a derogatory term). The voting structure was set up to give the French settlers as large a voice as the majority Arab Muslim population. Algerian Muslims were not given posts in the administration. Shortly after World War I, the French extended the rights of full French citizenship to Algerian Muslims who had fought in the war, who were literate in French, or who owned land, but this rewarded only a few thousand of them.

In May 1945, during celebrations of the Allied victory in World War II, a violent clash broke out at Sétif between Muslims and French settlers. Matters rapidly got out of hand, and people on both sides were killed, but the French repressed the Muslims with a considerable loss of life. The incident robbed the French administration of legitimacy and marked the beginning of conscious Algerian nationalism. To placate Muslim opinion, in 1947, the French established a structure for limited political representation of the Muslim population and undertook economic reforms. Not unsurprisingly, these steps proved ineffective.

Algerian nationalists soon founded the National Liberation Front (FLN). In late 1954, insurrections and soon open civil war broke out in Algeria as the FLN undertook highly effective guerrilla warfare. Thereafter a war lasting until 1962 ground on between the Algerian nationalists and the French. Both sides committed atrocities; hundreds of thousands of Algerians were killed. The war divided France itself with many French citizens, often of left-wing political opinion, objecting to the war, and the French military, still smarting from its defeats in World War II and in Indochina, determined to fight on. The presence of more than 1 million European settlers in Algeria, who saw any settlement with the nationalists as a betrayal, exacerbated the situation. The French government itself became paralyzed and lost control of the army. There was fear of civil war in France itself or of a military takeover. In Algeria, violence was spreading.

In the midst of this turmoil, General Charles de Gaulle (1890–1970), who had led the Free French forces during World War II and had briefly governed France immediately after the war, reentered French political life largely at the urging of the military. His condition for taking office was the end of the Fourth Republic and the promulgation of a new constitution, which enhanced the power of the president and created the Fifth Republic. The voters ratified this, and de Gaulle became president of France in December 1958. He then undertook a long strategic retreat from Algeria. The process was neither peaceful nor easy. In 1962, however, de Gaulle held a referendum in Algeria on independence, which passed overwhelmingly. Algeria became independent on July 3, 1962.

FRANCE AND VIETNAM

In its push for empire, France had occupied Indochina (which contained Laos, Cambodia, and Vietnam) between 1857 and 1893. By 1930, Ho Chi Minh (1892–1969) had turned a nationalist movement against French colonial rule into the Indochina Communist Party, which the French, for a time, succeeded in suppressing. World War II, however, provided new opportunities for Ho Chi Minh and other nationalists as they fought both the Japanese who occupied Indochina in 1941 and the pro-Vichy French colonial administration that collaborated with the Japanese until 1945. The war thus established Ho Chi Minh as a major anticolonial, nationalist leader.

In September 1945, Ho Chi Minh declared the independence of Vietnam under the Viet Minh, a coalition of nationalists that the communists soon dominated. By 1947, a full-fledged civil war had erupted in Vietnam. (Cambodia and, to a lesser extent, Laos remained quiescent under pro-French or neutralist monarchies.)

Until 1949, the United States displayed minimal concern about the Indochina war. The establishment of the Communist People's Republic of China that year dramatically changed the U.S. outlook. The United States now saw the French colonial war against Ho Chi Minh as an integral part of the Cold War conflict. The U.S. support for France in southeast Asia also served to gain French support for the establishment of NATO. Even though the United States supported the French effort in Vietnam financially, it was not prepared, despite divisions among policymakers, to intervene militarily. In the spring of 1954, during an international conference in Geneva on the future of Vietnam, the French military stronghold of Dien Bien Phu fell to Viet Minh forces after a prolonged siege. France lost the will to continue the struggle, which had become increasingly unpopular with the French people.

By late June, a complicated and unsatisfactory peace accord divided Vietnam at the seventeenth parallel of latitude. North of the parallel, centered in Hanoi, the Viet Minh were in charge; below it, centered in Saigon, the French were in charge. This was to be a temporary border. By 1956, elections were to be held to reunify the country. In effect, the conference attempted to transform a military conflict into a political one.

VIETNAM DRAWN INTO THE COLD WAR

Unhappy with these arrangements, the United States, in September 1954, formed the Southeast Asia Treaty Organization (SEATO), a collective security agreement that somewhat resembled the European NATO alliance, but without the integration of military forces or inclusion of all states in the region. Its membership consisted of the United States, Great Britain, France, Australia, New Zealand, Thailand, Pakistan, and the Philippines.

U.S. Troops Engaged in Combat in Vietnam At the war's peak, more than 500,000 American troops were stationed in South Vietnam. The United States struggled in Vietnam for more than a decade, seriously threatening its commitment to Western Europe.

U.S. Army Photo

What led to the escalation of American involvement in Vietnam?

In 1955, French troops began to withdraw from South Vietnam. As they left, the various Vietnamese political groups began to fight for power among themselves. The United States stepped into the turmoil in Vietnam with military and economic aid. Among the Vietnamese politicians, it chose to support was Ngo Dinh Diem (1901–1963). In October 1955, Diem established a Republic of Vietnam in the territory for which the Geneva conference had made France responsible. Diem announced that the Geneva agreements would not bind his newly established government and that elections would not be held in 1956. The American government, which had not signed the Geneva documents, supported his position.

In 1960, the National Liberation Front was founded, with the goals of overthrowing Diem, unifying the country, reforming the economy, and ousting the Americans. It was anti-colonial, nationalist, and communist. Its military arm was called the Viet Cong and was aided by the government of North Vietnam. Diem, a Roman Catholic, also faced mounting criticism from Buddhists and the army. His response to these pressures was further repression and dependence on an ever-smaller group of advisers.

DIRECT UNITED STATES INVOLVEMENT

The Eisenhower and Kennedy administrations continued to support Diem while demanding reforms in his government. The American military presence grew from about 600 advisers in early 1961 to more than 16,000 troops in late 1963. The political situation in Vietnam became increasingly unstable. On November 1, 1963, an army coup in which the United States was deeply involved overthrew and murdered Diem. The United States hoped a new government in South Vietnam would generate popular support. Thereafter, the United States sought to find a leader who could fulfill that hope. It finally settled on Nguyen Van Thieu (1923–2001), who governed South Vietnam from 1966 to 1975.

President Kennedy was assassinated on November 22, 1963. His successor, Lyndon Johnson (1963–1969), vastly expanded the commitment to South Vietnam. In August 1964, after an attack on an American ship in the Gulf of Tonkin, Johnson authorized the first bombing of North Vietnam. In February 1965, major bombing attacks began. They continued, with only brief pauses, until early in 1973. The land war grew until more than 500,000 Americans were stationed in South Vietnam.

In 1969, President Richard Nixon began a policy known as *Vietnamization*, which involved the gradual withdrawal of American troops from Vietnam while the South Vietnamese army took over the full military effort. Peace negotiations had begun in Paris in the spring of 1968, but a cease-fire was not finally arranged until January 1973. American troops left South Vietnam, and North Vietnam released its American prisoners of war. On April 30, 1975, Saigon (renamed Ho Chi Minh City) fell to the Viet Cong and the North Vietnamese army. Vietnam was finally united. (See Map 29–4.)

The U.S. intervention in Vietnam, which grew out of a power vacuum left by French decolonization, affected the entire Western world. For a decade after the Cuban missile crisis, Vietnam largely diverted the attention of the United States from Europe. American prestige suffered, and the U.S. policy in Southeast Asia made many Europeans question the wisdom of the American government and its commitment to Western Europe. Within the United States, the Vietnam conflict produced enormous divisions and debates over American involvement in the rest of the world that persist to the present day.

MAP EXPLORATION
Interactive map: To explore this map further, go to
www.myhistorylab.com

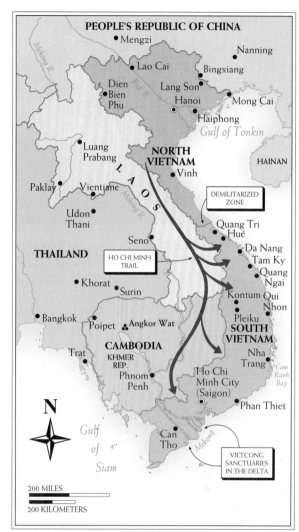

MAP 29–4 **Vietnam and Its Southeast Asian Neighbors**
The map identifies important locations associated with the war in Vietnam.
How did the Ho Chi Minh Trail affect the outcome of the war?

THE COLLAPSE OF EUROPEAN COMMUNISM

The withdrawal of Soviet influence from Eastern Europe and the internal collapse of the Soviet Union are the most important European historical events of the second half of the twentieth century. Many of the factors leading to the Soviet collapse remain murky, but here is a relatively clear narrative of what occurred.

Under Brezhnev, who governed from 1964 to 1982, the Soviet government became markedly more repressive at home, suggesting a return to Stalinist policies. This internal repression gave rise to a dissident movement. Certain Soviet citizens dared to criticize the regime in public and accused the government of violating the human

WHY DID European communism collapse?

President Ronald Reagan and Communist Party general secretary Mikhail Gorbachev confer at a summit meeting in December 1987.

AP Wide World Photos

What made it possible for Gorbachev and Reagan to find common ground?

perestroika   ("restructuring") Means by which Gorbachev wished to raise his country's standard of living.

glasnost   ("openness") Gorbachev's policy of opening the way for unprecedented public discussion and criticism of Soviet history and the Communist Party. Censorship was relaxed and dissidents were released from prison.

rights provision of the 1975 Helsinki Accords. The Soviet government responded with further repression, placing some opponents in psychiatric hospitals and others under what amounted to house arrest. During the same period the structures of the Communist Party became both rigidified and corrupt, which increasingly demoralized younger Soviet bureaucrats and party members.

GORBACHEV ATTEMPTS TO REFORM THE SOVIET UNION

Although economic stagnation, party corruption, and the lingering Afghan war had long been undermining Soviet authority, what brought these forces to a head and began the dramatic collapse of the Soviet Empire was the accession to power of Mikhail S. Gorbachev (b. 1931) in 1985 after both of Brezhnev's two immediate successors, Yuri Andropov (1914–1984) and Konstantin Chernenko (1911–1985), died within thirteen months of each other. In what proved to be the last great attempt to reform the Soviet system, Gorbachev immediately began the most remarkable changes that the Soviet Union had witnessed since the 1920s. (See "Encountering the Past: Rock Music and Political Protest.")

Economic *Perestroika*   Gorbachev's primary goal was to revive the Russian economy to raise the country's standard of living. Initially, he and his supporters, most of whom he had appointed himself, challenged traditional party and bureaucratic management of the Soviet government and economy. Under the policy of ***perestroika***, or "restructuring," they reduced the size and importance of the centralized economic ministries.

By early 1990, in a clear abandonment of traditional Marxist ideology, Gorbachev began to advocate private ownership of property and liberalization of the economy toward free market mechanisms. Despite many organizational changes, the Soviet economy remained stagnate and even declined. The failure of Gorbachev's economic policies affected his political policies. To some extent, he pursued bold political reform because he failed to achieve economic progress.

Glasnost   Gorbachev allowed an extraordinary public discussion and criticism of Soviet history and Soviet Communist Party policy. This development was termed ***glasnost***, or openness. Workers were permitted to criticize party officials and the economic plans of the party and the government. Censorship was relaxed and free expression encouraged. Dissidents were released from prison. In the summer of 1988, Gorbachev presided over a party congress that witnessed full debates.

Gorbachev soon applied *perestroika* to the political arena. In 1988, a new constitution permitted openly contested elections. After real political campaigning—a new experience for the Soviet Union—the Congress of People's Deputies was elected in 1989. After lively debate, the Supreme Soviet, another elected body—although one the Communist Party dominated—formally elected Gorbachev president in 1989.

The policy of open discussion allowed national minorities within the Soviet Union to demand political autonomy. Throughout its history, the Soviet Union had remained a vast empire of subject peoples. *Glasnost* quickly brought to the foreground the discontent of all such peoples. Gorbachev proved inept in addressing these ethnic complaints. He badly underestimated the unrest that internal national discontent could generate.

ENCOUNTERING THE PAST

ROCK MUSIC AND POLITICAL PROTEST

The political scene in many parts of the modern world has been powerfully influenced by the rock music pioneered in the United States in the 1950s by African American, working-class, and folk musicians. In America it served as a vehicle for protesting the Vietnam War and for demanding civil rights. Europeans also took it up and set their own stamp on it. Britain's Beatles were the most successful of the early European rock bands, but the lyrics of their songs were minimally political.

Rock music acquired its hard edge as social commentary in the 1970s with the appearance of punk rock groups with provocative names such as the Sex Pistols. Pluralistic Western societies took its antiestablishment message in stride, but in Eastern Europe and the Soviet Union, it was literally revolutionary. During the 1970s and 1980s, it offered social and political critics a major outlet. Rock stars were celebrated for their personal heroism in openly attacking communist governments, and their music expressed and spread the disaffection

The Russian rock group "Dynamic" performs in Moscow in 1987.
R. Podemi/TASS/Sovfoto/Eastfoto

How did *glasnost* change Soviet society?

that contributed to the collapse of communist regimes throughout Eastern Europe.

WHAT IS the source of the mass appeal of rock music? Why did it become antiestablishment? How did it undermine communism?

1989: REVOLUTION IN EASTERN EUROPE

Solidarity Reemerges in Poland In the early 1980s, Poland's government relaxed martial law, and it eventually released all the Solidarity prisoners, although Jaruzelski remained president. In 1988, new strikes surprised even the leaders of Solidarity. This time, the communist government could not reimpose control. After consultations between the government and Solidarity, the union was legalized. Lech Walesa again took center stage, as a kind of mediator between the government and the more independent elements of the trade union movement he had founded.

Jaruzelski began some political reforms with the tacit consent of the Soviet Union. When free elections were held in 1989, the communists lost overwhelmingly to Solidarity candidates. Late in the summer, Jaruzelski, unable to find a communist who could forge a majority coalition in parliament, turned to Solidarity and appointed the first noncommunist prime minister of Poland since 1945. Gorbachev expressly approved the appointment.

German youth breach the Berlin Wall in November 1989, an act that days earlier would have been unthinkable and deadly; the breach of the wall was the most symbolic moment in the collapse of European communism.

R. Bossu/Sygma/CORBIS

Why did communism in Eastern Europe collapse so rapidly?

Toward Hungarian Independence   Throughout 1989, as these events unfolded within Poland, one Soviet-dominated state after another in Eastern Europe moved toward independence. Early in the year, the Hungarian government opened its border with Austria, permitting free travel between the two countries. This breach in the Iron Curtain immediately led thousands of East Germans to move through Hungary and Austria to West Germany. The Hungarian Communist Party changed its name to the Socialist Party, permitted other parties to engage openly in politics, and promised free elections by October.

German Reunification   In the autumn of 1989, popular demonstrations erupted in East German cities. Adding to the pressure, Gorbachev told the leaders of the East German Communist Party that the Soviet Union would not use force to support them. In November 1989, in one of the most emotional moments in European history since 1945, the government of East Germany ordered the opening of the Berlin Wall. That week, tens of thousands of East Berliners crossed into West Berlin to celebrate, to visit their families, and to shop with money the West German government gave them. Shortly thereafter, free travel began between East and West Germany.

Within days of these dramatic events, West Germany and the other Western nations faced the issue of German reunification. Helmut Kohl (b. 1930), the chancellor of West Germany, became the leading force in moving toward full unification. Late in 1989, the European Economic Community accepted, in principle, the unification of Germany. By February 1990, some form of reunification had become a forgone conclusion, accepted by the United States, the Soviet Union, Great Britain, and France.

The Velvet Revolution in Czechoslovakia   Revolution in Czechoslovakia rapidly followed the breach of the Berlin Wall. The popular new Czech leader who led the forces against the party was Václav Havel (b. 1936), a playwright of international standing whom the communist government had imprisoned. In December 1989, Havel's group, known as Civic Forum, forced Gustav Husak (b. 1913), who had been president of Czechoslovakia since 1968, to resign. On December 28, 1989, Alexander Dubcek became chairman of the parliament, and the next day, Havel was elected president.

Violent Revolution in Romania   The only revolution of 1989 that involved significant violence occurred in Romania. There, in mid-December, the forces of President Nicolae Ceausescu (1918–1989), who had governed without opposition since 1965, fired on crowds that were protesting conditions in the country. By December 22, Bucharest was in full revolt. Ceausescu and his wife attempted to flee, but were captured, secretly tried, and shot on December 25.

The Soviet Stance on Revolutionary Developments   None of the revolutions of 1989 could have taken place unless the Soviet Union had refused to intervene militarily, in contrast to 1956 and 1968. For the first time since the end of World War II, Eastern Europeans could shape their own political destiny without the fear of Soviet military intervention. Once they realized the Soviets would not act, thousands of ordinary citizens took to the streets to denounce Communist Party domination and assert their desire for democracy. The major question facing the Soviet Union became the peaceful withdrawal of its troops from Eastern Europe. The haphazard nature of that withdrawal and the general poverty to which those troops returned were other factors undermining the Soviet armed forces.

THE COLLAPSE OF THE SOVIET UNION

Gorbachev clearly believed, as his behavior toward Eastern Europe in 1989 showed, that the Soviet Union could no longer afford to support communist governments in that region or intervene to uphold their authority while seeking to restructure its own economy. He also had concluded that the Communist Party in the Soviet Union must restructure itself and its relationship to the Soviet state and society.

Renunciation of Communist Political Monopoly In early 1990, Gorbachev formally proposed to the Central Committee of the Soviet Communist Party that the party abandon its monopoly of power. After intense debate, the committee abandoned the Leninist position that only a single elite party could act as the vanguard of the revolution and forge a new Soviet society.

New Political Forces Gorbachev confronted challenges from three major political forces by 1990. One consisted of those groups—considered conservative in the Soviet context—whose members wanted to preserve the influence of the Communist Party and the Soviet army. The country's economic stagnation and political and social turmoil deeply disturbed them. They appeared to control significant groups in the economy and society. During late 1990 and early 1991, Gorbachev, who himself seems to have been disturbed by the nation's turmoil, began to appoint members of these factions to key positions in the government. In other words, he seemed to be making a strategic retreat.

Gorbachev initiated these moves because he was now facing opposition from a second group—those who wanted much more extensive and rapid change. Their leading spokesman was Boris Yeltsin (1931–2007). He and his supporters wanted to move quickly to a market economy and a more democratic government. In 1990, he was elected president of the Russian Republic, the largest and most important of the Soviet Union's constituent republics. In the new political climate, that position gave him a firm political base from which to challenge Gorbachev's authority and increase his own.

The third force that came into play from 1989 onward was growing regional unrest in some of the republics of the Soviet Union. Initially, the greatest unrest came from the three Baltic republics

SIGNIFICANT DATES FROM THE ERA OF THE COLD WAR

1945	Yalta Conference; founding of the United Nations
1946	Churchill's Iron Curtain speech
1947	(March) Truman Doctrine; (June) announcement of Marshall Plan
1948	Communist takeovers in Czechoslovakia and Hungary; State of Israel proclaimed
1948–1949	Berlin Blockade
1949	NATO founded; East and West Germany emerge as separate states
1950–1953	Korean conflict
1953	Death of Stalin
1955	Warsaw Pact founded; Austria established as a neutral state
1956	(February) Khrushchev's secret speech denouncing Stalin; (October) Suez crisis and the Hungarian uprising
1957	*Sputnik* launched
1961	Berlin Wall erected
1962	Cuban missile crisis
1963	Test Ban Treaty (Soviet Union and the United States)
1964	Gulf of Tonkin Resolution; America in Vietnam
1967	Six Days' War, Arab-Israeli conflict
1968	Soviet invasion of Czechoslovakia
1972	Strategic Arms Limitation Treaty
1973	Yom Kippur War
1975	Saigon falls to North Vietnam; Helsinki Accords
1978	Camp David Accords
1979	Soviet invasion of Afghanistan
1981	Solidarity founded in Poland
1982	Israel invades Lebanon; death of Brezhnev
1985	Israel withdraws from Lebanon
1987	Arab uprising on the West Bank commences
1988	PLO accepts Israel's right to exist
1993	Israel and PLO agree to phase out self-rule in the West Bank and Gaza
1995	Israeli prime minister Rabin assassinated

of Estonia, Latvia, and Lithuania, which had been independent states until 1940 when the Soviet Union had occupied them in accord with secret provisions of the Soviet-German nonaggression pact of 1939. In these republics, many local communist leaders began to see themselves as national leaders rather than as party stalwarts.

During 1989 and 1990, the parliaments of the Baltic republics tried to decrease Soviet control, and Lithuania actually declared independence. Gorbachev used military force to resist these moves. Discontent also arose in the Soviet Islamic republics in Central Asia and the Caucasus. Riots broke out in Azerbaijan and Tajikistan, where the army was used as a police force against Soviet citizens. Throughout 1990 and 1991, Gorbachev sought to negotiate new constitutional arrangements between the republics and the central government. His failure to effect such arrangements may have been the single most important reason for the rapid collapse of the Soviet Union.

The August 1991 Coup   The turning point in all these events came in August 1991, when the conservative forces that Gorbachev had brought into the government attempted a coup. Troops occupied Moscow, and Gorbachev was placed under house arrest while on vacation in the Crimea. The day of the coup, Boris Yeltsin climbed on a tank in front of the Russian Parliament building to denounce the coup and ask the world for help to maintain the Soviet Union's movement toward democracy.

Within two days, the coup collapsed and a humiliated Gorbachev returned to Moscow. From that point on, Yeltsin steadily became the dominant political figure in the nation. The Communist Party, compromised by its participation in the coup, collapsed as a political force. The constitutional arrangements between the central government and the individual republics were revised. In December 1991, the Soviet Union ceased to exist, Gorbachev left office, and the Commonwealth of Independent States came into being. (See Map 29–5.)

THE YELTSIN DECADE

Boris Yeltsin emerged as the strongest leader within the new commonwealth. As president of Russia, he was head of the largest and most powerful of the new states. His popularity was high both in Russia and in the commonwealth in 1992, but within a year, he faced serious economic and political problems. The Russian Parliament, most of whose members were former communists, opposed Yeltsin personally and his policies of economic and political reform. In September 1993, Yeltsin suspended parliament, which responded by deposing him. Parliament leaders tried to incite popular uprisings against Yeltsin in Moscow. The military, however, backed Yeltsin, and he surrounded the parliament building with troops and tanks. On October 4, 1993, after pro-parliament rioters rampaged through Moscow, Yeltsin ordered the tanks to attack the parliament building, crushing the opposition.

These actions consolidated Yeltsin's authority. The major Western powers, deeply concerned by the turmoil in Russia, supported him. In December 1993, Russians voted for a new parliament and approved a new constitution. By 1994, the central government found itself at war in the Islamic province of Chechnya in the Caucasus. Under Yeltsin, Russian forces held off a rebel victory, but the war reached no clear conclusion.

During the mid-1990s, to dismantle the Soviet state and economy, former state-owned industries were privatized. This complicated process involved much corruption and opportunism by individuals determined to profit from the emerging economic organization. One result was the creation of a small group of enormously wealthy individuals, whom the press dubbed "the oligarchs." While these people amassed vast wealth, the general Russian economy remained stagnant. The economic downturn contributed

MAP 29–5 The Commonwealth of Independent States In December 1991, the Soviet Union broke up into its fifteen constituent republics. Eleven of these were loosely joined in the Commonwealth of Independent States. Also shown is the autonomous region of Chechnya, which has waged two bloody wars with Russia in the last decade.

What does the breakup of the Soviet Union say about nationalism in the modern era?

to further political unrest. In the face of these problems and in declining health, Yeltsin resigned the presidency in a dramatic gesture just as the new century opened. His hand-picked successor was Vladimir Putin (b. 1952), a relatively unknown figure at the time. Putin would lead the Russian Federation in new economic and political directions. Before considering Putin's role, it is necessary to examine the events that occurred during the 1990s in southeastern Europe.

THE COLLAPSE OF YUGOSLAVIA AND CIVIL WAR

Yugoslavia was created after World War I. Its borders included seven major national groups—Serbs, Croats, Slovenes, Montenegrins, Macedonians, Bosnians, and Albanians—among whom there have been ethnic disputes for centuries. The Croats and Slovenes are Roman Catholic and use the Latin alphabet. The Serbs, Montenegrins, and Macedonians are Eastern Orthodox and use the Cyrillic alphabet. The Bosnians and

HOW DID ethnic tensions lead to civil war in Yugoslavia?

Albanians are mostly Muslims. Most members of each group reside in a region with which they are associated historically—Serbia, Croatia, Slovenia, Montenegro, Macedonia, Bosnia-Herzegovina, and Kosovo—and these regions constituted individual republics or autonomous areas within Yugoslavia. Many Serbs, however, lived outside Serbia proper.

Tito (1892–1980) had acted independently of Stalin in the late 1940s and pursued his own foreign policy. To mute ethnic differences, he encouraged a cult of personality around himself and instituted complex political power sharing among these different groups. After his death, economic difficulties undermined the authority of the central government, and Yugoslavia gradually dissolved into civil war.

In the late 1980s, the old ethnic differences came to the foreground again in Yugoslav politics. Nationalist leaders—most notably Slobodan Milosevic (b. 1941–2006) in Serbia and Franjo Tudjman (b. 1922) in Croatia—gained authority. During the summer of 1990, in the wake of the changes in the former Soviet bloc nations, Slovenia and Croatia declared independence from the central Yugoslav government, and several European nations, including, most importantly, Germany, immediately granted them recognition. The full European community soon did likewise.

From this point on, violence escalated. Serbia—concerned about Serbs living in Croatia and about the loss of lands and resources there—was determined to maintain a unitary Yugoslav state that it would dominate. Croatia was equally determined to secure independence. By June 1991, full-fledged war had erupted between the two republics.

The conflict took a new turn in 1992 when Croatian and Serbian forces determined to divide Bosnia-Herzegovina. The Muslims in Bosnia—who had lived alongside Serbs and Croats for generations—soon became crushed between the opposing forces. The Serbs in particular, pursuing a policy called "ethnic cleansing," a euphemism redolent of some of the worst horrors of World War II, killed or forcibly removed many Bosnian Muslims.

More than any other single event, the unremitting bombardment of Sarajevo, the capital of Bosnia-Herzegovina, brought the violence of the Yugoslav civil war to the attention of the world. The United Nations attempted unsuccessfully to mediate the conflict and imposed sanctions that had little affect. Early in 1994, however, a shell exploded in the marketplace in Sarajevo, killing dozens of people. Thereafter, NATO forced the Serbs to withdraw their artillery from around Sarajevo.

The events of the civil war came to a head in 1995 when NATO forces carried out strategic air strikes. Later that year, under the leadership of the United States, the leaders of the warring forces negotiated a peace agreement in Dayton, Ohio. The agreement was of great complexity but recognized an independent Bosnia. NATO troops, including those from the United States, have enforced the terms of the agreement.

Toward the end of the 1990s, Serbian aggression against ethnic Albanians in the province of Kosovo again drew NATO into Yugoslav affairs. For months, the world watched the Serbian military deport Albanians from Kosovo where Albanians constituted a majority of the population. There were many casualties, atrocities, and deaths. Early in 1999, NATO again carried out an air campaign and sent troops into Kosovo to safeguard the ethnic Albanians. In 2000, a revolution overthrew Slobodan Milosevic.

Destruction of Sarajevo An elderly parishioner walks through the ruins of St. Mary's Roman Catholic Church in Sarajevo. The church was destroyed by Serb shelling in May 1992.

Reuters/CORBIS/ Bettmann

Why did the fall of communism lead to civil war in Yugoslavia?

The disintegration of the former Yugoslavia took still another important turn in February 2008 when Kosovo with its Albanian majority population declared its independence from Serbia. The United States, a majority of the nations composing the European Union, and all Kosovo's neighbors except Serbia have recognized the independence of Kosovo. The Russian Federation, a longtime supporter of Serbia, immediately and strongly condemned the independence of Kosovo. The issue of Kosovo's independence, as will be seen in the next section, led to Russian military actions in the region of the Black Sea later in 2008.

PUTIN AND THE RESURGENCE OF RUSSIA

WHAT VISION does Putin have of Russia's place in the world?

Vladimir Putin, who had become president of the Russian Federation in 2000, immediately moved to establish his position as a national and nationalistic leader of the federation. He vigorously renewed the war against the rebels in Chechnya, which resulted in heavy casualties and enormous destruction there, but also strengthened Putin's political support in Russia itself. By the middle of the decade, however, Russian forces had clearly established the upper hand over the Chechen rebels and the drive toward independence was firmly checked at a very high cost in lives on both sides.

In the wake of the Chechen war and as part of his determination that the central government will dominate Russia's economy and political life, Putin has sought to diminish local autonomy and centralize power in his own hands. The central government has also moved against leading oligarchs and other businessmen with some being imprisoned. Putin used the attacks on these enormously wealthy and economically powerful figures to generate support from the broad Russian public who regard the oligarchs as thieves and one of the causes of the economic hardship of the 1990s. Putin also imprisoned political critics and opponents and moved against independent newspapers and television stations as well.

During Putin's presidency the Russian economy genuinely began to improve. Foreign debts were paid. The Russian ruble came to be regarded as a serious currency. Many more consumer goods were available. Much of this relative prosperity was the result of the oil resources available to the Russian Federation and the rising price of oil on the world market. Under Putin a clear trade-off occurred between political freedom and economic and political stability. In 2008 Putin left the elected presidency at the end of his second four-year term, turning the office over to his own handpicked successor Dmitri Medvedev (b. 1965). At the same time, however, Putin assumed the office of prime minister and clearly remained the chief political figure in the country.

Putin both as president and now prime minister has been determined to use the nation's economic recovery and new wealth to allow Russia to reassert its position as a major power on both the regional and world scene. After the terrorist attacks on the United States in September 2001, Putin supported the American assault on Afghanistan, largely because the Russian government was afraid that Islamic extremism would spread beyond Chechnya to other regions in Russia and to the largely Muslim nations that bordered Russia in Central Asia and the Caucasus. This period of cooperation proved short-lived. Putin became one of the leading voices against the American-led invasion of Iraq and has continued to criticize American policy in the region. Putin has also been sharply critical of the ongoing expansion of NATO, which has embraced nations directly bordering the Russian Federation. His government continued to attempt to exert influence in various of the new nations, such as the former Soviet republics of Ukraine and Georgia, that came into existence with the collapse of the former Soviet Union.

The aftermath of an attack by a Russian warplane on an apartment block in Gori, Georgia, during the conflict in South Ossetia in August 2008. Here a Georgian man cradles the body of a relative killed during the bombing, which killed at least five people.

Gleb Garanich/Corbis/Reuters America LLC

How has the world responded to Russia's aggressive foreign policy during the Putin era?

This determination to assert Russian domination over recently independent nations once part of the former Soviet Union dramatically displayed itself in August 2008. That month troops of the Russian Federation invaded the republic of Georgia. What had provoked this attack was Georgia's having shortly before sent troops into South Ossetia. Russian troops first drove the Georgians out of South Ossetia and then continued into Georgia itself. South Ossetia itself a part of the former Soviet Union had been divided into regions dominated by Russia and Georgia. Georgia sought to assert further influence only to be immediately and overwhelmingly blocked by Russian forces. Russia eventually withdrew after a cease-fire but had succeeded in demonstrating its power in the region and in creating potential instability in postwar Georgia.

The Russian invasion of Georgia marked a new departure in post-Soviet Russian foreign policy and a resurgence of Russian international influence following the collapse of the Soviet Union nearly twenty years earlier. During that period both the European Union and NATO had moved to expand their memberships by expanding into Eastern Europe and into regions previously dominated by or part of the former Soviet Union. Discussions had taken place about the possibility of bringing both Ukraine and Georgia into NATO. The United States had indicated support for such inclusion. Putin and other leaders of the Russian Federation had witnessed the manner in which various regions of the former Yugoslavia, most recently Kosovo in February 2008, had broken away from Serbia and established their own independence. The Russia Federation feared the example of Kosovo and the international recognition its independence had achieved might serve as a pattern for potential break-away regions in the Russian Federation. It also feared encirclement by NATO member nations where the United States might locate military bases. The action taken against Georgia served to demonstrate the ability of the Russian Federation to take military action on its borders and to give warning to other nations in the region of its capacity to intervene. At the same time the absence of any effective resistance to Russian actions in Georgia from either the United States or the European Union nations raised doubts about the capacity of either to influence events in the region of the Black Sea. Moreover, the action also demonstrated Russian willingness to take advantage of American involvement in Iraq and Afghanistan to reassert its potential authority in those regions it has dominated since the wars of Catherine the Great in the eighteenth century.

In late 2008 another question suddenly confronted Russia. As one element in the worldwide financial crisis, commodity prices dropped sharply. These included the price of oil on the world market. It remains to be seen whether Russia will be able to maintain its economic growth and political resurgence in the face of dropping income from the sale of oil, which had financed its new international influence during the past decade.

WHAT FORCES gave rise to radical political Islamism?

THE RISE OF RADICAL POLITICAL ISLAMISM

On September 11, 2001, Islamic terrorists attacked the United States, crashing hijacked civilian domestic aircraft into the twin towers of the World Trade Center in New York City, the Pentagon in Washington, D.C., and a Pennsylvania field with a vast loss of life and property. These events and those flowing from them have not only transformed American foreign policy toward the Middle East but have also changed European relations with the United States.

In retrospect, we can see that those attacks were the result of forces that had been affecting not only the United States but also the Western world for at least a half century. The end of the Cold War has been succeeded by a new political world in which both the United States and the nations of Europe, including the Russian Federation, are endangered by terrorist attacks from nongovernmental or non-state-based organizations. These groups are guided by ideologies in the Islamic world that have filled a political and ideological vacuum left by the end of the Cold War.

Radical Islamism is the term scholars use to describe an interpretation of Islam that came to have a significant impact in the Muslim world during the decades of decolonization. It is only one—and by no means the most popular—interpretation of Islam. The ideas informing radical Islamism extend back to the 1930s and resistance to British rule in Egypt, but for many years, those had little impact on the politics of the Middle East.

ARAB NATIONALISM

Radical Islamism arose primarily in reaction to the secular Arab nationalism that developed in countries like Egypt and Syria in the 1920s and 1930s. Although Arab and other Middle Eastern nationalists, like nineteenth-century modernizers in the Ottoman Empire, believed that the path to independence and strength lay in adopting the technology and imitating the political institutions of the West, these advocates of radical Islamism wanted to reject Western ideas and create a society based on a rigorous interpretation of Islam and its teachings. (See Chapter 22.)

In the wake of World War II, many of the foremost leaders of Arab nationalism against Western direct and indirect dominance, such as Gamal Abdul Nasser of Egypt, were sympathetic to socialism or to the Soviet Union. Because socialism and communism were Western ideologies, left-leaning Arab nationalism was no less Western in its orientation than were nationalists friendly to the United States. Moreover, Soviet communism was overtly atheistic and hence doubly offensive to devout Arab Muslims.

Arab governments defining themselves according to the values of nationalism worked out arrangements with local Muslim authorities. For example, the Saudi royal family turned over its educational system to adherents of a rigorist, puritanical form of Islam called *Wahhabism* while modernizing the country's infrastructure. The Egyptian government attempted to play different Islamic groups off against one another. These governments retained the support of prosperous, devout middle-class Muslims while doing little about the plight of the poor. In general, Muslim religious leaders were hostile to the Soviet Union and its influence in the Islamic world.

THE IRANIAN REVOLUTION

The Iranian Revolution of 1979 transformed the Middle East. The Ayatollah Ruhollah Khomeini (1902–1989) managed to unite both the middle and lower classes of a major Middle Eastern nation to overthrow a repressive but a modernizing government that had long cooperated with the United States. Iran's revolutionary government was a theocracy; that is, there was no separation of religion and government or, in European terms, of church and state. The Iranian constitution gave the clergy the final say in all matters.

By challenging the Westernization of Iranian society, the Iranian Revolution shocked the world. It also challenged the largely secular presuppositions of Arab nationalists in states such as Egypt, Saudi Arabia, and Algeria that had failed to satisfy

Overview The Rise of Radical Political Islamism

1979	Iranian Revolution
1979	Russian invasion of Afghanistan
1981	Assassination of President Anwar Sadat
1991	Persian Gulf War
1993	Bombing of the World Trade Center in New York City
1996	Bombing of U.S. army barracks in Saudi Arabia
1998	Bombing of U.S. embassies in East Africa
2000	Bombing of USS *Cole* in the Yemeni port of Aden
2001	September 11 terrorist attacks on American soil

the needs of their own underclasses. In the mid-twentieth century, Arabs and other Middle Eastern peoples had turned to nationalism in reaction against European colonial powers. Those who grew up under nationalist leadership and still found themselves politically and economically disadvantaged, however, reacted against nationalism. The Iranian Revolution, which many thought would spread throughout the Islamic world, attracted them.

The Iranian Revolution both embodied and emboldened the forces of what is commonly called Islamic *fundamentalism* but is more correctly termed Islamic or Muslim *reformism*. This is the belief that a reformed or pure Islam must be established in the contemporary world. Most adherents of this point of view would emphasize personal piety and religious practice. However, a minority wish to see their states strictly governed the way Iran purports to be by Islamic law or the Shari'a. (In fact, the Iranian clergy made numerous compromises to the practical demands of everyday government and the oil industry.)

The conservative Arab governments feared the Iranian Revolution would challenge their legitimacy. They consequently began to pay much more attention to their own religious authorities and cracked down on radical reformist or fundamentalist Muslims. In Egypt, such actions followed the assassination in 1981 of President Anwar Sadat (b. 1918) by a member of the Muslim Brotherhood.

AFGHANISTAN AND RADICAL ISLAMISM

The Russian invasion of Afghanistan of 1979, discussed earlier in this chapter, introduced a major new component into this already complicated picture, illustrating the convergence of Cold War and Islamist politics. The Soviet Union sought to impose a communist, and hence both Western and atheist, government in Afghanistan. Muslim religious authorities declared *jihad*, literally meaning "a struggle" but commonly interpreted as a religious war, against the Soviet Union. The Afghan resistance to the Soviets thus became simultaneously nationalistic, universalistic, and religious.

jihad A struggle; interpreted as a call for religious war.

Thousands of Muslims, mostly fundamentalist in outlook, arrived in Afghanistan from across the Islamic world to oust the Soviets and their Afghan puppets. Conservative Arab states and the United States supported this effort, which succeeded when all Soviet forces withdrew in 1989. The conservative Arab states saw the Afghan war as an opportunity both to resist Soviet influence and to divert the energies of their own religious extremists. The United States saw the Afghan war as another round in the Cold War. The militant Muslim fundamentalists saw it as a religious struggle against an impious Western power.

The Taliban and Al Qaeda   The Soviet withdrawal created a power vacuum in Afghanistan that lasted almost a decade. By 1998, however, rigorist Muslims known as the *Taliban* had seized control of the country. They imposed their own version of Islamic law, which involved strict regimentation of women and public executions, floggings, and mutilations for criminal, religious, and moral offenses. The Taliban also allowed groups of Muslim terrorists known as *Al Qaeda*, which means "Base," to establish training camps in their country. The terrorists who attacked the United States on September 11, 2001, came from these camps.

Taliban fighters brandish machine-guns and rocket launchers near the Tora Bora mountains in Afghanistan, the site of a major battle with U.S. forces in late 2001.

Knut Mueller/Das Fotoarchiv/Peter Arnold, Inc.

What makes Afghanistan so attractive to terrorist organizations?

The ideology of these groups had emerged over several decades from different regions of the Islamic world but had been inculcated in Pakistan. The Pakistani government had long assigned considerable control over education to Islamic schools, or *madrasas*, that taught reformed Islam, rejection of liberal and nationalist secular values, intolerance toward non-Muslims, repudiation of Western culture, hostility to Israel, and hatred of the United States.

Jihad **Against the United States**   Once the *jihad* against the Soviet Union had succeeded, radical Muslims, largely educated in these Pakistani schools, turned their attention to the United States, the other great Western power. The event that brought about this redirection was the Persian Gulf War of 1991. The occasion for that conflict was the invasion of Kuwait by Iraq, under Saddam Hussein (1937–2006). The conservative Arab governments, most importantly Saudi Arabia, not only supported the United States but also permitted it to construct military bases on their territory. Islamic extremists who had fought in Afghanistan, one of whom was Osama Bin Laden (b. 1957), saw the establishment of U.S. bases in Saudi Arabia, which was the home of the prophet Muhammed and contained Islam's two holiest cities, Mecca and Medina, as a new invasion by Western Crusaders. The bases added a new grievance to the already long list of radical Muslim complaints against the United States.

The United States became a target because of its secular public morality, its international wealth and power, its military strength, its ongoing support for Israel, and its adherence to the UN sanctions imposed on Iraq after the Gulf War. Certain Muslim religious authorities declared a *jihad* against the United States, thus transforming opposition to American policies and culture into a religious war. Through the 1990s, terrorist attacks were directed against targets in or associated with the United States. These included bombings of the World Trade Center in New York City in 1993, of a U.S. army barracks in Saudi Arabia in 1996, of U.S. embassies in East Africa in 1998, and of the USS *Cole* in the Yemeni port of Aden in 2000. These attacks resulted in a considerable loss of life.

A TRANSFORMED WEST

HOW DID the events
of September 11, 2001,
transform the West?

The attacks on the United States on September 11, 2001, transformed and redirected American foreign policy into what the administration of President George W. Bush (b. 1946) termed "a war on terrorism." In late 2001, the United States attacked the Taliban government of Afghanistan, rapidly overthrowing it. The defeat of the Taliban destroyed Al Qaeda's Afghan bases but not its leadership, which survived, although it was dispersed and remains in hiding. By 2008, there was evidence that the Taliban had regrouped and again become active.

Following the Afghan campaign, the Bush administration set forth a policy of preemptive strikes and intervention against potential enemies of the United States. The administration argued that the danger of weapons of mass destruction developed by governments such as that of Iraq falling into the hands of international terrorist organizations posed so severe a danger to the security of the United States that the nation could not wait to respond to an attack but must take preemptive action. This argument, which aroused controversy both at home and abroad, marked a major departure from previous United States foreign policy. It is a direct result of the attacks on the United States that occurred on September 11.

In 2002, the Bush administration turned its attention to Saddam Hussein's government in Iraq. Since the defeat of Iraq in 1991 by an international coalition led by the United States, Saddam Hussein, contrary to widespread expectations, had remained in power and had continued to oppress his own people. Throughout the 1990s, the Iraqi government had also resisted the work of United Nations inspectors charged with discovering and destroying weapons of mass destruction found in Iraq or facilities capable of manufacturing such weapons. The Iraqis eventually expelled the United Nations inspectors in 1998, and the United Nations was unable to reinsert them for almost five years.

In the wake of the September 11, 2001, attacks the Bush administration determined to overthrow Saddam Hussein and remove any threat from supposed Iraqi weapons of mass destruction. In late 2002 and early 2003, the United States and British governments sought to obtain passage of United Nations Security Council resolutions that would require Iraq to disarm on its own or to be disarmed by military force. Nonetheless, the United States and Great Britain, backed by token forces or other support from over thirty other nations, invaded Iraq in late March 2003. After three weeks of fighting, the Iraqi army and with it the government of Saddam Hussein collapsed. The announced goals of the invasion, in addition to toppling the Iraqi regime, were to destroy Iraq's capacity to manufacture or deploy weapons of mass destruction and to bring consensual government to the Iraqi people. The latter goal has remained elusive as Iraq has been violently split by deadly internal political conflict.

The invasion of Iraq was undertaken in the face of considerable opposition from France, Germany, and Russia. It also provoked large antiwar demonstrations in the United States and throughout the world. Both the war and the diplomatic difficulties preceding it disrupted the long-standing Atlantic alliance. Moreover, French and German opposition to the war created strains within Europe and particularly within NATO and the European Union, as other European governments either strongly supported or opposed the United States and Britain. As a result, the war in Iraq marked a new and divisive era in relations between the United States and Europe, and between the United States and the rest of the world.

Once the invasion of Iraq had been carried out and the occupation commenced, Al Qaeda terrorists struck in Europe itself. On March 11, 2004, at least 190 people were killed in train bombings in Madrid, Spain. The terrorist attack occurred just before the Spanish election. The Spanish government, which had supported the American invasion of Iraq, unexpectedly lost the election. The new government then soon

On July 7, 2005, a series of bombs rocked the London transport system with the loss of over fifty lives. This photo shows the remains of a London bus on which a suicide bomber took more than a dozen lives near Russell Square, London.

Sion Touhig/CORBIS/Bettmann

How do Europeans and Americans differ in their views on the best ways to combat terrorism?

withdrew Spanish troops from Iraq. The Madrid bombings were the largest act of terrorism against civilians in Europe since World War II. The attack demonstrated that terrorist attacks can directly influence European political processes.

The Iraq War and the bloody insurgency that followed generated enormous controversy. The coalition forces found no weapons of mass destruction in Iraq. Government commissions in the United States and Britain have criticized the intelligence information used to justify the invasion. In 2004, however, President Bush was reelected. In March 2005, thousands of Iraqis braved threats to vote in the first meaningful election held in Iraq since the 1950s; in October 2005, they voted to ratify a new constitution. In 2006, Saddam Hussein was tried and executed for crimes against humanity. Meanwhile, in May 2005, the British government of Prime Minister Tony Blair was also reelected, though with a much reduced parliamentary majority. However, on July 7, 2005, terrorist bombings struck the London bus and subway system with a considerable loss of life. Once more, as in Spain, terrorism struck a major European city. The British government, unlike the Spanish, continued to retain its armed forces in Iraq.

The Iraq war, which has witnessed the death of more than 4,000 American troops and thousands of Iraqis, continued to cause controversy in the United States and between the United States and its NATO allies. However, in early 2007, the Bush administration increased the number of troops committed to Iraq. The purpose of the increase in troops, called "the surge" in the press, was to bring about greater internal stability in the country and most particularly in Baghdad. Over the months the level of violence did subside. By 2008, the United States under the Bush administration and the Iraq government were negotiating the future status of American troops in Iraq with the goal of significantly reducing their numbers in upcoming years. Somewhat surprisingly, issues of the economy more than those of Middle East involvement dominated the 2008 U.S. presidential campaign. Early in 2009 after assuming the presidency, President Barack Obama undertook a policy to establish an orderly withdrawal of most American combat troops from Iraq by the late summer of 2010.

SUMMARY

WHAT WERE the origins of the Cold War?

The Emergence of the Cold War

The Cold War was based on the fundamental opposition between the ideologies of the Soviet Union and the Western democracies. An "Iron Curtain" separated Western Europe from the satellite states of the USSR. Germany was divided, and in 1949, most nations of Western Europe joined the United States, Canada, and the island states of the Atlantic to form NATO. The Soviet Union responded in 1955 with the Warsaw Pact. Israel's independence in 1948, and the Arab response, brought the Cold War to the Middle East. The Korean conflict (1950–1953) was motivated by the West's policy of containing the spread of communism. *page 742*

WHAT WERE the three crises of 1956, and how did they affect world order?

The Khrushchev Era in the Soviet Union

Stalin strengthened his hold over the Soviet Union during World War II. Nikita Khrushchev, who succeeded him in 1953, was less powerful. He allowed more intellectual and economic freedom but preserved the Communist Party's dominance. In 1956, the war that followed Egyptian president Nasser's nationalization of the Suez Canal prompted the United States to curtail intervention by the Western European powers in affairs beyond Europe. The USSR permitted modest political reforms in Poland, as long as Poland remained a member of the Warsaw Pact, but in Hungary, it toppled an independent communist government. *page 749*

HOW DID the Berlin Wall and the Cuban missile crisis strain relations between the United States and the Soviet Union?

Later Cold War Confrontations

Tensions continued to simmer between the United States and the USSR in the late 1950s. In August 1961 the Berlin Wall was erected, and in 1966 the Cuban missile crisis brought the Cold War to the Americas. In 1968 the USSR invaded Czechoslovakia to suppress the Prague Spring. *page 750*

WHAT IMPACT did Brezhnev have on the Soviet Union and Eastern Europe?

The Brezhnev Era

Brezhnev led the Soviet Union from 1964 to 1982. In 1968 the USSR invaded Czechoslovakia to suppress the Prague Spring in the last major Soviet military action in Eu-

rope of the Cold War. The Helsinki Accords recognized the Soviet sphere of influence in Eastern Europe but protected human rights. By the early 1980s, Soviet armed forces were the largest in the world, and the USSR's nuclear arsenal nearly equaled that of the United States. The Soviet invasion of Afghanistan in 1979 sapped much of that strength. In July 1980, a shipyard workers' strike at Gdansk in Poland created Solidarity, an independent union. The Soviets responded by increasing their own military spending, a tactic that accelerated the end of the regime. *page 752*

HOW DID World War II serve as a catalyst for decolonization?

Decolonization: The European Retreat from Empire

World War II accelerated the decolonization process. Mohandas Gandhi utilized Western liberal ideas and the passive resistance strategy of Henry David Thoreau to gain Indian independence in 1947. Britain generally succeeded in establishing representative self-governments in its former colonies. *page 754*

WHY WAS France so reluctant to decolonize?

The Turmoil of French Decolonization

France ended its colonial era more slowly and painfully than did Britain. In Algeria, nationalists demanded civic equality and fought a civil war until 1962, when a referendum ordered by President Charles de Gaulle approved Algerian independence. In Vietnam, Ho Chi Minh fought for independence from France, but in 1955, when the French began to withdraw from South Vietnam, the United States entered the Vietnam War. Many Europeans, Americans, and others questioned U.S. motives and goals. *page 756*

WHY DID European communism collapse?

The Collapse of European Communism

Gorbachev took power in 1985 and attempted to reform the Soviet system, but his reforms set off a cascade of consequences. Revolutions swept Eastern Europe in 1989. Poland elected a Solidarity government, Hungary opened its borders with Austria and promised free elections, and East Germany opened the Berlin Wall. By late 1990, Gorbachev had allied with conservatives, and Yeltsin became the spokesman for a rival group that wanted to move quickly to a market economy and greater democratization. Gorbachev left office, and on December 25, 1991, the Commonwealth of Independent States replaced the Soviet Union, with Boris Yeltsin as president of the Russian Federation. *page 759*

HOW DID ethnic tensions lead to civil war in Yugoslavia?

The Collapse of Yugoslavia and Civil War Yugoslavia was created after World War I. Its major national groups have been involved in ethnic disputes for centuries. After Tito's death in 1980, Yugoslavia gradually dissolved into civil war. By June 1991, full-fledged war had erupted between Serbia and Croatia. Bosnian Muslims were caught between the two sides. The Serbs in particular killed or forcibly removed many Bosnian Muslims. The intervention of NATO forces led to the negotiation of a peace agreement in Dayton, Ohio, in 1995. Toward the end of the 1990s, Serbian aggression against ethnic Albanians in the province of Kosovo again drew NATO into Yugoslav affairs. In 2008, Kosovo with its Albanian majority population declared its independence from Serbia. *page 765*

WHAT VISION does Putin have of Russia's place in the world?

Putin and the Resurgence of Russia Vladimir Putin, who had become president of the Russian Federation in 2000, sought to diminish local autonomy and centralize power in his own hands. Putin also imprisoned political critics and opponents and moved against independent newspapers and television stations as well. During Putin's presidency the Russian economy genuinely began to improve, largely as the result of rising oil prices on the world market. Putin has been determined to use Russia's economic recovery and new wealth to allow Russia to reassert its position as a major power on both the regional and world scene. The 2008 Russian invasion of Georgia marked a new departure in post-Soviet Russian foreign policy. *page 767*

WHAT FORCES gave rise to radical political Islamism?

The Rise of Radical Political Islamism Radical Islamism is a reaction to early-twentieth-century Arab secular nationalism. Most nationalist leaders of Muslim countries satisfied their religious critics by giving them some control over social institutions, but the Iranian Revolution of 1979 subjected a major state to Islamist domination. Afghanistan in 1998 was taken over by the Muslim-led Taliban, and radical Pakistani-educated Muslims targeted the United States after the 1991 Persian Gulf War, which they saw as an assault on the Muslim Holy Land. *page 768*

HOW DID the events of September 11, 2001, transform the West?

A Transformed West Terrorist attacks, incuding those of September 11, 2001, targeted the United States for its military and economic strength and its Western values. The U.S. military response against Afghanistan was widely supported by Europe, but only Great Britain supported the Bush administration's actions against Iraq. Despite lack of support by the United Nations, the invasion of Iraq succeeded in removing the government of Saddam Hussein after only three weeks of fighting. The Iraq War and the bloody insurgency that followed generated enormous controversy. In early 2007, the Bush administration increased the number of troops committed to Iraq. By 2008, the United States under the Bush administration and the Iraq government were negotiating the future status of American troops in Iraq with the goal of significantly reducing their numbers in upcoming years. Issues of the economy more than those of Middle East involvement dominated the 2008 U.S. presidential campaign. *page 772*

REVIEW QUESTIONS

1. How did Europe come to be dominated by the United States and the Soviet Union after 1945? How would you define the policy of containment? What were some of the global events in the period from 1945 to 1982 that were influenced by this American policy?

2. Why did the nations of Europe give up their empires? How did the United States become involved in Vietnam?

3. What internal political pressures did the Soviet Union experience in the 1970s and early 1980s? How did Gorbachev's reforms contribute to the collapse of the Soviet Union?

4. What were the major events in Eastern Europe that contributed to the collapse of communism? What was Poland's role in this process?

5. How has radical political Islamism developed? How has it been affected by the invasion of Afghanistan and recent military conflicts in the Middle East?

KEY TERMS

Brezhnev Doctrine (p. 752)
Cold War (p. 742)
containment (p. 742)
détente (p. 752)
glasnost (p. 760)

jihad (p. 770)
Marshall Plan (p. 743)
NATO (p. 746)
perestroika (p. 760)
Warsaw Pact (p. 746)

For additional learning resources related to this chapter, please go to **www.myhistorylab.com**

PEARSON
myhistorylab

30

The West at the Dawn of the Twenty-First Century

The most important accomplishment of the European Community was the launching on January 1, 1999, of the euro, a single monetary unit that replaced the national currencies of most of its member nations. In Frankfurt, Germany, people crowded around a symbol of the new currency. The world financial crisis that commenced in 2008 has placed many internal pressures on the European Community and upon its currency.

AP Wide World Photos

Why was the establishment of the euro such an important step on the road to European unification?

777

uring the second half of the twentieth century, the Cold War influenced life in the West—for individuals as well as states. It closed vast areas to travel and sealed off most of Eastern Europe from the era's material and technological advances. It did not, however, impede the developments that remarkably transformed the Western European countries and the United States. They achieved unprecedented prosperity and technological progress. Europe also took unprecedented steps toward economic cooperation and political union. ∎

THE TWENTIETH-CENTURY MOVEMENT OF PEOPLES

HOW HAS migration changed the face of Europe?

In the twentieth century, the movement of peoples transformed European society and the character of many European communities. The most pervasive trend in this movement of peoples was the continuing shift from the countryside to the cities. Today, except for Albania, at least one-third of the population of every European nation lives in large cities. In Western Europe, city dwellers are approximately 75 percent of the population.

Other vast forced movements of peoples by governments, however, were little discussed during the Cold War. During the century, millions of Germans, Hungarians, Poles, Ukrainians, Bulgarians, Serbs, Finns, Chechens, Armenians, Greeks, Turks, Balts, and Bosnian Muslims were displaced. These forced displacements transformed parts of Europe. Stalin literally moved whole nationalities from one area of the Soviet Union to another and killed millions of people in the process. The Nazis first displaced the Jews and then sought to exterminate them. Throughout Eastern Europe, cities that once had large Jewish populations and a vibrant Jewish religious and cultural life lost any Jewish presence. The displacement of Germans from Eastern Europe back into Germany immediately after World War II transformed cities that had been German into places almost wholly populated by Czechs, Poles, or Russians.

DISPLACEMENT THROUGH WAR

World War II created a vast refugee problem. An estimated 46 million people were displaced in central and Eastern Europe and the Soviet Union alone between 1938 and 1948. Many cities in Germany and in central and Eastern Europe had been bombed or overrun by invading armies. The Nazis had moved hundreds of thousands of foreign workers into Germany as slave laborers. Millions more were prisoners of war. Some of these people returned to their homeland willingly; others, particularly Soviet prisoners fearful of being executed by Stalin, had to be forced to go back, and many were executed. Hundreds of thousands of Baltic, Polish, and Yugoslav prisoners found asylum in Western Europe.

Changes in political borders after the war also uprooted many people. For example, Poland, Czechoslovakia, and Hungary forcibly expelled millions of ethnic Germans from their territories to Germany. In another case of forced migration, hundreds of thousands of Poles were transferred to within Poland's new borders from territory the Soviet Union annexed. Other minorities, such as Ukrainians in Poland and Italians on the Yugoslav coast, were driven into their ethnic homelands.

EXTERNAL AND INTERNAL MIGRATION

Between 1945 and 1960, approximately half a million Europeans left Europe each year. In the second half of the nineteenth century, most immigrants were from rural areas. After World War II, they often included educated city dwellers. Immediately after the war, some governments encouraged migration because they were afraid that, as in the 1930s, their economies would not be able to provide adequate employment for all their citizens.

Decolonization in the postwar period led many European colonials to return to Europe from overseas. Decolonization also led non-European inhabitants of the former colonies to migrate to Europe. Great Britain, for example, received thousands of immigrants from its former colonies in the Caribbean, Africa, and the Indian subcontinent. France received many immigrants from its empire in Africa, Indochina, and the Arab world. This influx has proved to be a long-term source of social tension and conflict. In Britain, racial tensions were high during the 1980s. France faced similar difficulties, which contributed to the emergence of the National Front, an extreme right-wing group led by Jean-Marie Le Pen (b. 1928) that sought to exploit the resentment many working-class voters felt toward North African immigrants. Similar pressures have arisen in Germany, Austria, Italy, the Netherlands, and even Denmark. Such tension did not result only from immigration from Africa and Asia; internal European migration—from the Balkans, Turkey, and the former Soviet Union, often of people in search of jobs—also changed the social and economic face of the Continent and led to a backlash. In recent years, internal immigration within the European Union has seen the movement of significant numbers of people. However, the growing Muslim presence in Europe has produced some of the most serious ethnic and political tensions.

THE NEW MUSLIM POPULATION

Until recently most Europeans paid little direct attention to Islam as a domestic matter. That indifference began to change in the 1960s and had dissolved by the end of the twentieth century as a sizable Muslim population settled in Europe. This highly diverse immigrant community had become an issue in Europe even before the events of September 11, 2001.

The immigration of Muslims into Europe, and particularly Western Europe, arose from two chief sources: European economic growth and decolonization. As the economies of Western Europe began to recover in the quarter century after World War II, a labor shortage developed. To fill this demand, Western Europe imported laborers, many of whom came from Muslim nations. For example, Turkish "guest workers" were invited to move to West Germany—on a temporary basis, it was presumed—in the 1960s, and Britain welcomed Pakistanis. The aftermath of decolonization and the quest for a better life led Muslims from East Africa and the Indian subcontinent to settle in Great Britain. The Algerian war brought many Muslims to France. Today there are approximately 1.3 million Muslims in Great Britain, 3.2 million in Germany, and 4.2 million in France.

These Muslim immigrant communities share certain social and religious characteristics. Originally, many Muslims came to Europe expecting they would eventually return to their homes, an expectation their host countries shared. Moreover, except for Great Britain, where all immigrants from the Commonwealth may vote immediately upon settling there, European governments made it difficult for Muslim, or any other, immigrants to take part in civic life. The Muslim communities have, therefore, generally remained unassimilated and self-contained. This apartness has

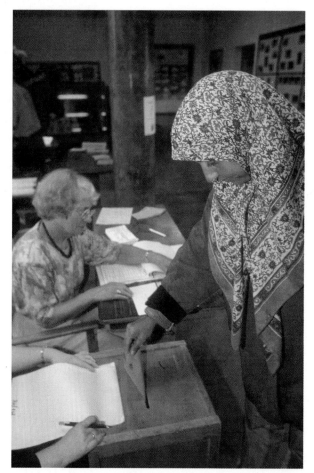

A Muslim woman wearing a traditional headscarf in Hamburg, Germany, votes in the Bundestag elections. The presence of foreign-born Muslims whose labor is necessary for the prosperity of the European economy is an important issue in contemporary Europe. Many of these Muslims live in self-contained communities.
Peter Arnold, Inc.

What is the relationship between Muslim communities in Europe and the larger societies of which they are a part?

provided internal community support for Muslim immigrants but has also prevented them from fully engaging with the societies in which they live.

Yet the world around these communities has changed. Many of the largely unskilled jobs that the immigrants originally filled have disappeared. Most of the Muslim immigrants to Europe, unlike many who have settled in the United States and Canada, were neither highly skilled nor professionally educated. As a result, they and their adult children who may have grown up in Europe find it difficult to get jobs in the modern service economy. Furthermore, as European economic growth has slowed, European Muslims have become the target of politicians, such as Le Pen in France, who seek to blame the immigrants for a host of problems from crime to unemployment.

The radicalization of parts of the Islamic world has also touched the Muslim communities in Europe. The July 7, 2005, suicide bombings in London were carried out by four young Muslims, three of whom had been born in the United Kingdom and one in Jamaica. By contrast, the French government has exerted more control over its Muslim population. However, that policy appeared to have failed badly when in the autumn of 2005 immigrant youth, largely Muslim, carried out riots in various parts of France. These were the most serious civil disturbances in France since 1968. There have also been sharp disputes in France over attempts by the government to forbide young Muslim women from wearing headscarves while attending secular government schools.

Nonetheless, European Muslims are not a homogeneous group. They come from different countries, have different class backgrounds, and espouse different Islamic traditions. At the same time, these Muslim communities, so often now marked by deep poverty and unemployment, have become a major concern for European social workers, who disagree among themselves about how their governments should respond to them. What has become clear, however, is that European governments cannot regard their Muslim populations as passive communities; rather European governments and societies must engage them as a permanent fact in the life of early-twenty-first-century Europe.

EUROPEAN POPULATION TRENDS

During the past quarter century, the population of Europe, measured in terms of the European birthrate, has stabilized in a manner that has deeply disturbed many observers. Europeans are having so few children that they are no longer replacing themselves. There is no consensus on why the European birthrate has declined. One reason often cited is that women are postponing having children until later in their childbearing years.

This falling birthrate means that Europe will face the prospect of an aging population. The energy and drive that youth can provide may shift to the other side of the Atlantic. An aging population is unlikely to give rise to economic innovation. The internal European market, now larger than the internal American market, will shrink. In contrast to the late nineteenth century (see Chapter 23), Europe itself will have fewer Europeans, and Europe's share of the world's population will also decline.

WHAT EFFECT did the Great Depression and World War II have on the way Europeans viewed the role of government in social and economic life?

TOWARD A WELFARE STATE SOCIETY

During the decades spanning the Cold War, the U.S. involvement in Vietnam, and the Soviet domination of Eastern Europe, the nations of Western Europe achieved unprecedented economic prosperity and maintained or inaugurated independent, liberal democratic governments. Most of them also confronted problems associated with decolonization and with maintaining economic growth. The Great Depression had shown that democracy requires a social and economic base, as well as a political structure. Most Europeans came to believe that government ought to ensure economic prosperity and social security.

CHRISTIAN DEMOCRATIC PARTIES

Except for the British Labour Party, the vehicles of the new postwar politics were not, as might have been expected, the democratic socialist parties. Outside Scandinavia, those parties generally did not prosper after the onset of the Cold War. Both communists and conservatives opposed them. Rather, various **Christian democratic parties**, usually leading coalition governments, introduced the new policies.

These parties were a major new feature of postwar politics. They were largely Roman Catholic in leadership and membership. Until the 1930s, Catholic parties had been conservative and had protected the social, political, and educational interests of the church. The postwar Christian democratic parties of Germany, France, Austria, and Italy, however, were progressive and welcomed non-Catholic members. Democracy, social reform, economic growth, and anticommunism were their hallmarks.

The most immediate postwar domestic problems included not only those the physical damage of the conflict created, but often also those that had existed in 1939. The war, however, opened new opportunities to solve those prewar difficulties.

THE CREATION OF WELFARE STATES

The Great Depression, the rise of authoritarian states in the wake of economic dislocation and mass unemployment, and World War II, which involved more people in a war effort than ever before, changed how many Europeans thought about social welfare. Governments began to spend more on social welfare than they did on the military. This reallocation of funds was a reaction to the state violence of the first half of the century and was possible because the NATO defense umbrella, which the United States primarily staffed and funded, protected Western Europe.

The modern European welfare state was broadly similar across the Continent. Before World War II, except in Scandinavia, the two basic models for social legislation were the German and the British. In both the German and British systems, workers were insured only against the risks from disease, injury on the job, and old age. Unemployment was assumed to be only a short-term problem and often one that workers brought on themselves. People higher up in the social structure could look out for themselves and did not need government help.

After World War II, the concept emerged that social insurance against predictable risks was a social right and should be available to all citizens. Paradoxically, making coverage universal appealed to conservatives as well as socialists. If medical care, old-age pensions, and other benefits were available to all, they would not become a device to redistribute income from one part of the population to another.

The first major European nation to begin to create a welfare state was Britain, in 1945–1951 under the Labour Party ministry of Clement Attlee (1883–1967). The most important element of this early legislation was the creation of the National Health Service. France and Germany did not adopt similar health care legislation until the 1970s, because their governments initially refused to make coverage universal.

The spread of welfare legislation (including unemployment insurance) within Western Europe was related to both the Cold War and domestic political and economic policy. The communist states of Eastern Europe were promising their people social security as well as full employment. The capitalist states came to believe they had to provide similar security for their people, but, in fact, the social security of the communist states was often more rhetoric than reality.

Christian democratic parties
Post–World War II political parties that, although predominately Roman Catholic, welcomed non-Catholic members and fought for democracy, social reform, and economic growth.

QUICK REVIEW
The Welfare State

- Great Britain was the first European nation to create a welfare state
- France and Germany followed Britain's lead in the 1970s
- European attitudes toward the welfare state have fluctuated with the European economy

MARGARET THATCHER AND TONY BLAIR DEBATE GOVERNMENT'S SOCIAL RESPONSIBILITY FOR WELFARE

Toward the close of the twentieth century, and the turn of the twenty-first century, many of the assumptions that had informed the creation of mid-twentieth-century European welfare states came under criticism and redefinition. Nowhere was the debate sharper than in the United Kingdom where the modern welfare state had essentially been invented through social policies enacted in the aftermath of World War II. Margaret Thatcher's government raised serious questions about the role of government in society. By the turn of the century, even the British Labour Party led by Tony Blair had come to modify its own understanding of government social responsibility.

QUESTIONS

1. How and why does Thatcher contend that there is no such thing as society? How does she emphasize the reciprocal character of social relationships?

2. How does Thatcher argue in favor of personal and private charity to aid persons in need? Does she criticize all government aid to citizens?

3. How is it clear in Blair's speech that he is trying to lead a traditional party of the left toward a new understanding of government social responsibility?

4. What does Blair portray as duties of government? How does he seek to mesh government help for individuals with still assigning responsibility to the individuals receiving that help?

5. Though Thatcher and Blair differ in their views of policy, what social and political values do they share despite those differences?

I. MARGARET THATCHER ASSERTS THE NEED FOR INDIVIDUAL RESPONSIBILITY

No single European political figure so challenged and criticized the assumptions of the welfare state and of state intervention in general than Margaret Thatcher, British prime minister from 1979 to 1990. Known as the "Iron Lady," Mrs. Thatcher repeatedly demanded that people take individual responsibility rather than rely on state-sponsored support. Yet her administration did not dismantle the key structures of the British welfare state. The discussion below is from an interview by Mrs. Thatcher in October 1987.

I think we have gone through a period when too many children and people have been given to understand "I have a problem, it is the Government's job to cope with it!" or "I have a problem, I will go and get a grant to cope with it!" "I am homeless, the Government must house me!" and so they are casting their problems on society and who is society? There is no such thing! There are individual men and women . . . there are families and no government can do anything except through people and people look to themselves first. It is our duty to look after ourselves and then also to help look after our neighbour and life is a reciprocal business and people have got the entitlements too much in mind without the obligations, because there is no such thing as an entitlement unless someone has first met an obligation and it is, I think, one of the tragedies in which many of the benefits we give, which were meant to reassure people that if they were sick or ill there was a safety net and there was help, that many of the benefits which were meant to help people who were unfortunate—"It is all right. We joined together and we have these insurance schemes to look after it." That was the objective . . . But it went too far. If children have a problem, it is society that is at fault. There is no such thing as society. There is living tapestry of men and women and people and the beauty of that tapestry and the quality of our lives will depend upon how much each of us is prepared to take responsibility for ourselves and each of us prepared to turn round and help by our own efforts those who are unfortunate.

Source: This extract derives from a transcript of the original interview rather than the published text. Reprinted with permission from margaretthatcher.org, the official Web site of the Margaret Thatcher Foundation.

II. TONY BLAIR SEEKS TO REDEFINE THE BRITISH WELFARE STATE

Tony Blair (b. 1953) served as Labour Party prime minister of the United Kingdom from 1997 to 2007. During his time in office he championed what he termed "New Labour" and sought to redefine the British welfare state while still preserving many of its most basic outlines. In June 2002, he outlined his new understanding of the character of the welfare state and its role in promoting individual responsibility. In many respects his view of welfare and government social responsibility had been influenced by Margaret Thatcher's attack on earlier understandings of welfare and government social responsibility.

In welfare, for too long, the right had let social division and chronic unemployment grow; the left argued for rights but were weak on responsibilities. We believe passionately in giving people the chance to get off benefit and into work. . . .

It's right for them, for the country, for society. But with the chance, comes a responsibility on the individual — to take the chance, to make something of their lives and use their ability and potential to the full. . . .

We must give the unemployed youth the skills to find a job; give the single mother the childcare she needs to go out and work; give the middle-aged man on a disability benefit the support and confidence to go back into the office.

And we must not only lift people out of poverty. We must transform their horizons, aspirations and hopes as well — through helping people get the skills they need for better jobs, and through giving them chance to save and build up a nest egg.

Only in this way will we drive up social mobility, the great force for equality in dynamic market economies.

To do all that, ours has to be an enabling welfare state — one which helps people to help themselves. . . .

Government has a responsibility to provide real opportunities for individuals to gain skills and to get into work that pays. But individuals also have a responsibility to grasp those opportunities.

We are now seeing the beginnings of a sea-change in how people view our welfare state. There is growing public support for a welfare state that tackles poverty at its source; that gets people into work; that offers people hope — in exchange for a commitment to help themselves. . . .

This is a welfare state which reflects all our responsibilities: the responsibility we have to engage actively with the jobless to provide them with opportunities; their responsibility to engage actively with us and take those opportunities. . . .

All of our reforms have the same underlying principles — opportunity, fairness and mutual responsibility. We want to give people the chance to fulfill their potential. We want to raise people's expectations and their self-belief, by giving them the tools to help themselves.

Source: Tony Blair, June 10, 2002, as made available at www.guardian.co.uk/society/2002/jun/10/socialexclusion.politics1

RESISTANCE TO THE EXPANSION OF THE WELFARE STATE

Western European attitudes toward the welfare state have reflected three periods that have marked economic life since the end of the war. The first period was one of reconstruction from 1945 through the early 1950s. It was followed by the second period—almost twenty-five years of generally steady and expanding economic growth. The third period brought first an era of inflation in the late 1970s and then one of relatively low growth and high unemployment from the 1990s to the present. During each of the first two periods, a general conviction existed, based on Keynesian economics, that the foundation of economic policy was government involvement in a mixed economy. From the late 1970s, more people came to believe the market should be allowed to regulate itself and that government should be less involved in, though not completely withdraw from, the economy.

The most influential political figure in reasserting the importance of markets and resisting the power of labor unions was Margaret Thatcher (b. 1925) of the British Conservative Party who served as prime minister from 1979 to 1990. She cut taxes and sought to curb inflation. She and her party were determined to roll back many of the socialist policies that Britain had enacted since the war. Her administration privatized many industries that Labour Party governments had nationalized. She also curbed the power of the trade unions in a series of bitter and often violent confrontations. Although her administration roused enormous controversy, she was able to push these policies through Parliament. Furthermore, over time the British Labour Party under the leadership of Tony Blair (b. 1953) itself largely came to accept what was at the time known as the Thatcher Revolution. (See "Compare & Connect: Margaret Thatcher and Tony Blair Debate the Government Social Responsibility for Welfare," pages 782–783.)

While Thatcher redirected the British economy, the government-furnished welfare services now found across continental Europe began to encounter resistance. The funding on which they are based assumed a growing population and low unemployment, conditions that no longer exist. As the proportion of the population consuming the services of the welfare state—the sick, the injured, the unemployed, and the elderly—increases relative to the number of able-bodied workers who pay for them, the costs of those services have risen.

The general growth of confidence in the ability of market forces rather than government intervention to sustain social cohesion has also spread in the past twenty-five years and has raised questions about the existing welfare structures. Governments across the Continent, including those normally associated with left-of-center politics, such as the British Labour Party and the German Social Democratic Party, have limited further growth of the welfare state and have reduced benefits.

Margaret Thatcher, a shopkeeper's daughter who became the first female prime minister of Great Britain, served in that office from May 1979 through November 1990. Known as the "Iron Lady" of British politics, she led the Conservative Party to three electoral victories and carried out extensive restructuring of the British government and economy.

AP Wide World Photos

Why did Thatcher attempt to roll back Britain's welfare state?

NEW PATTERNS IN WORK AND EXPECTATIONS OF WOMEN

HOW DID the status of women in business, politics, and the professions change in Europe in the second half of the twentieth century?

Since World War II, the work patterns and social expectations of European women have changed enormously. In all social ranks, women have begun to assume larger economic and political roles. More women have entered the "learned professions," and more are filling major managerial positions than ever before in European history. Yet certain more or less traditional patterns continue to describe the position of women in both family and economic life.

FEMINISM

Since World War II, European feminism, although less highly organized than in America, has set forth a new agenda. The most influential postwar work on women's issues was Simone de Beauvoir's (1908–1986) *The Second Sex*, published in 1949. In that work, de Beauvoir explored the difference being a woman had made in her life. She and other European feminists argued that, at all levels, European women experienced distinct social and economic disadvantages. Divorce and family laws, for example, favored men. European feminists also called attention to the social problems that women faced, including spousal abuse.

In contrast to earlier feminism, recent feminism has been less a political movement pressing for specific rights than a social movement offering a broader critique of European culture. An emphasis on women controlling their own lives may be the most important element of recent European feminism. Whereas in the past feminists sought and, in significant measure, gained legal and civil equality with men, they are now pursuing personal independence and issues that are particular to women. In this sense, feminism is an important manifestation of the critical tradition in Western culture.

MORE MARRIED WOMEN IN THE WORKFORCE

One of the patterns that seemed firmly established in 1900 has reversed itself. The number of married women in the workforce has risen sharply. Both middle-class and working-class married women have sought jobs outside the home. Some factories changed their work shifts to accommodate the needs of married women. Consumer conveniences and improvements in health care also made it easier for married women to enter the workforce by reducing the demands child care made on their time. At the same time, all surveys indicate that the need to provide care for their children is the most important difficulty women face in the workplace. This situation is a main reason why so many women remain in part-time employment.

In the twentieth century, children were no longer expected to contribute substantially to family income. They now spend more than a decade in compulsory education. When families need more income than one worker can provide, both parents work, bringing many married women with children into the workforce. Such financial necessity led many married women back to work. Evidence also suggests that married women began to work to escape the boredom of housework and to enjoy the companionship of other adult workers.

NEW WORK PATTERNS

The work pattern of European women was far more consistent in the twentieth century than it was in the nineteenth century. Single women enter the workforce after their schooling and continue to work after marriage. They may stop working to care for their young children, but they return to work when the children begin school. Several factors created this new pattern, but women's increasing life expectancy is one of the most important.

When women died relatively young, child rearing filled a large proportion of their lives. As a longer life span has shortened that proportion, women throughout the West are seeking ways to lead satisfying lives after their children have grown. Decisions about when to have children and how many also shaped the late-twentieth-century work pattern for women. Many women have begun to limit the number of children they bear or to forgo childbearing and child rearing altogether. The age at which women have decided to bear children has risen, to the early twenties in Eastern Europe and to the late twenties in Western Europe. In urban areas, women have fewer children and have them later in life than rural women do. These various personal decisions leave many years free to develop careers and stay in the workforce.

Simone de Beauvoir, here with her companion, the philosopher Jean-Paul Sartre, was the major feminist writer in postwar Europe.

Keystone_Paris/ Getty Images Inc./Hulton Archive Photos

How has European feminism changed in the decades since World War II?

WOMEN IN THE NEW EASTERN EUROPE

Many paradoxes surround the situation of Eastern European women now that communists no longer govern the region. Under communism, women generally enjoyed social equality, as well as a broad spectrum of government-financed benefits. Most women worked in these societies. No significant women's movements existed, however, because communist governments regarded them with suspicion, as they did all independent associations.

The new governments of the region are free but have shown little concern with women's issues. Indeed, the economic difficulties the new governments face may endanger their funding of health and welfare programs that benefit women and children. Moreover, the high proportion of women in the workforce could leave them more vulnerable than men to the region's economic troubles. Women may be laid off before men and hired later than men for lower pay.

TRANSFORMATIONS IN KNOWLEDGE AND CULTURE

HOW WAS cultural and intellectual life transformed in Europe during the twentieth century?

Knowledge and culture in Europe were rapidly transformed in the twentieth century. Institutions of higher education enrolled a larger and more diverse student body, making knowledge more widely available than ever before. Also, movements such as existentialism challenged traditional intellectual attitudes. Environmental concerns also raised new issues. Throughout this ferment, representatives of the Christian faith tried to keep their religion relevant.

COMMUNISM AND WESTERN EUROPE

Until the final decade of the twentieth century, Western Europe had large, organized communist parties, as well as groups of intellectuals sympathetic to communism.

The Intellectuals　During the 1930s, as liberal democracies floundered in the face of the Great Depression and as right-wing regimes spread across the Continent, many people saw communism as a vehicle for protecting humane and even liberal values. European university students were often affiliated with the Communist Party. During the late 1920s and the 1930s, communism became a substitute religion for some Europeans.

Four events proved crucial to the intellectuals' disillusionment: the great Soviet public purge trials of the late 1930s, the Spanish Civil War (1936–1939), the Nazi-Soviet pact of 1939, and the Soviet invasion of Hungary in 1956. Yet disillusionment with the Soviet Union or with Stalin did not always mean disillusionment with Marxism or with radical socialist criticisms of European society. Some writers and social critics looked to the establishment of alternative communist governments based on non-Soviet models. During the decade after World War II, Yugoslavia provided such an example. Beginning in the late 1950s, radical students and a few intellectuals found inspiration in the Chinese Revolution. Other groups hoped a European Marxist system would develop. The thinking of non-Soviet communists became important to Western European communist parties, such as the Italian Communist Party, that hoped to gain office democratically.

Another way to accommodate Marxism within mid-twentieth-century European thought was to redefine the basic message of Marx himself. During the 1930s, many of Marx's previously unprinted essays were published. These books and articles, written before the *Communist Manifesto* of 1848, are abstract and philosophical. They make the "young Marx" appear to belong more nearly to the humanist than to the revolutionary tradition of European thought. They allowed some people to consider themselves sympathetic to Marxism without also seeing themselves as revolutionaries or supporters of the Soviet Union. With the collapse of the communist governments of Eastern Europe and the Soviet Union, what influence Marxism will continue to have on European intellectual life in the future is unclear.

EXISTENTIALISM

The intellectual movement that perhaps best captured the predicament and mood of mid-twentieth-century European culture was **existentialism**. Existentialism was badly divided; most of the philosophers associated with it disagreed with each other on major issues. The movement represented, in part, a continuation of the revolt against reason that began in the nineteenth century.

Roots in Nietzsche and Kierkegaard   Friedrich Nietzsche (1844–1900), discussed in Chapter 24, was a major forerunner of existentialism. Another was the Danish writer Søren Kierkegaard (1813–1855), who received little attention until after World War I. He maintained that the truth of Christianity could be grasped only in the lives of those who faced extreme situations, not in creeds, doctrines, and church structures. Kierkegaard also criticized Hegelian philosophy and, by implication, all academic rational philosophy. Philosophy's failure, he felt, was the attempt to contain life and human experience within abstract categories. Kierkegaard spurned this faith in the power of mere reason.

The intellectual and ethical crisis of World War I brought Kierkegaard's thought to the foreground and also created new interest in Nietzsche's critique of reason. The war led many people to doubt whether human beings were actually in control of their own destiny. Its destructiveness challenged faith in human rationality and improvement. Indeed, the war's most terrible weapons—poison gas, machine guns, submarines, high explosives—were the products of rational technology.

Questioning of Rationalism   Existentialist thought thrived in this climate and received further support from the trauma of World War II. The major existential writers included the Germans Martin Heidegger (1889–1976) and Karl Jaspers (1883–1969) and the French Jean-Paul Sartre (1905–1980) and Albert Camus (1913–1960). Although they frequently disagreed with each other, they all, in one way or another, questioned the primacy of reason and scientific understanding as ways to come to grips with the human situation.

The Romantic writers of the early nineteenth century had also questioned the primacy of reason, but their criticisms were much less radical than those of the existentialists. The Romantics emphasized the imagination and intuition, but the existentialists dwelled primarily on the extremes of human experience. Death, fear, and anxiety provided their themes.

According to the existentialists, human beings are compelled to formulate their own ethical values and cannot depend on traditional religion, rational philosophy, intuition, or social customs for ethical guidance. The opportunity and need to define values endow humans with a dreadful freedom.

European intellectuals were attracted to communism and existentialism before and just after World War II, but in the 1960s, the turmoil over Vietnam and the youth rebellion brought other intellectual and social issues to the fore. Even before the collapse of communism, these had begun to redirect European intellectual interests.

QUICK REVIEW

Factors Leading to Disillusionment with Communism and the Soviet Union

- Purges of the 1930s
- Spanish Civil War
- Alliance between Russia and Germany in 1939
- Soviet invasion of Hungary in 1956

existentialism   Philosophy that maintains that human beings are compelled to formulate their own ethical values and cannot depend on traditional religion, rational philosophy, intuition, or social customs for ethical guidance.

In 1968 a student rebellion in Paris threatened to bring down the government of Charles de Gaulle. This was only one example of the explosion of student activity that rocked the West in the late 1960s.

© Bettmann/CORBIS

What role did universities play in the social upheaval of the 1960s?

EXPANSION OF THE UNIVERSITY POPULATION AND STUDENT REBELLION

As rapid changes in communications technology vastly expanded access to information, more Europeans received some form of university education. In 1900, only a few thousand people were enrolled in universities in any major European country. By 2000, that figure had risen to hundreds of thousands, although university education is still less common in Europe than in the United States. Higher education is now available to people from a variety of social and economic backgrounds, and, for the first time, to women.

One of the most striking and unexpected results of this rising post–World War II population of students and intellectuals was the student rebellion of the 1960s. Student uprisings began in the early 1960s in the United States and grew with opposition to the war in Vietnam. The student rebellion then spread into Europe and other parts of the world. It was almost always associated with a radical political critique of the United States, although Eastern European students resented the Soviet Union even more. The movement was generally antimilitarist. Students also questioned middle-class values and traditional sexual mores and family life.

The student movement peaked in 1968, when American students demonstrated forcibly against U.S. involvement in Vietnam. In the same year, students at the Sorbonne in Paris almost brought down the government of Charles de Gaulle, and in Czechoslovakia, students were in the forefront of the liberal socialist experiment.

By the early 1970s, the era of student rebellion seemed to have passed. Students remained active in European movements against nuclear weapons and particularly against the placement of American nuclear weapons in Germany and elsewhere in Europe. From the mid-1970s, however, although often remaining political radicals, they generally abandoned the disruptive protests that had marked the 1960s.

THE AMERICANIZATION OF EUROPE

During the past half century, through the Marshall Plan, the leadership of NATO, the stationing of huge military bases, student exchanges, popular culture, and tourism, the United States has exerted enormous influence on Europe, especially Western Europe. The word *Americanization*, an often pejorative term in European publications, refers, in part, to this economic and military influence but also to concerns about cultural loss. Many Europeans feel that American popular entertainment, companies, and business methods threaten to extinguish Europe's unique qualities. Many American firms now have European branches. Shopping centers and supermarkets, first pioneered in America, are displacing neighborhood markets in European cities. American television programs, movies, computer games, and rock and rap music are readily available. Furthermore, as Europe moves toward greater economic cooperation, English has become the common language of business, technology, and even some academic fields—and it is American English, not British. (See "Encountering the Past: Toys from Europe Conquer the United States.")

A CONSUMER SOCIETY

Although European economies came under pressure during the 1990s and experienced high levels of unemployment, the consumer sector has expanded to an extraordinary degree during most of the last half century.

The consumer orientation of the Western European economy emerged as one of the most important characteristics differentiating it from Eastern Europe. Those differences produced political results. In the Soviet Union and the nations it dominated in Eastern Europe, economic planning overwhelmingly favored capital investment and military production. These nations produced inadequate food for their people and few

ENCOUNTERING THE PAST

TOYS FROM EUROPE CONQUER THE UNITED STATES

Europeans often complain about American influences on their culture, but European products have also shaped life in America. At least one European toy, the LEGO building block, has had an effect on childhood comparable to that of the American Disney Corporation's cartoon characters.

In 1932, Ole Kirk Christiansen founded a company in Denmark to manufacture household goods and wooden toys. The toys did so well that in 1934 the company adopted the name LEGO (from Danish, *Leg godt*, "Play well"). The first LEGO building block sets were produced in 1955. The ingenious interlocking design of the LEGO block allowed children to build all kinds of things, and the sets were a hit when they went on sale in the United States in 1961. Subsequent editions were improved by the addition of new forms (such as wheels) that allowed children even freer range for their imaginations.

In 1968, the LEGO Company followed the lead of the Disney organization and began to open amusement parks with rides that resembled large LEGO toys. By the 1990s, it had become the largest toy manufacturer in Europe, and LEGO blocks were established as staples of popular culture. Museums now house structures made from them, and contests are held at which their builders compete. Some management gurus have even urged business executives to play with LEGO blocks to clarify their thinking.

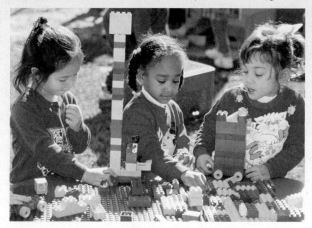

Children across the world play with LEGO toys.

Tom Prettyman/PhotoEdit Inc.

Why do so many Europeans fear Americanization?

WHY HAS the influence of LEGO on America been less controversial than that of American fast-food chains on Europe?

---

consumer goods. By contrast, by the early 1950s, Western Europeans enjoyed an excellent food supply that has continued to improve. Western Europe has enjoyed a similar expansion of consumer goods and services.

This vast expansion of consumerism, which, as we noted in Chapter 15, began in the eighteenth century, became a defining characteristic of Western Europe in the late twentieth century. It stood in marked contrast to the consumer shortages in Eastern Europe. Yet through even the limited number of radios, televisions, movies, and videos available to them, people in the East grew increasingly aware of the discrepancy between their lifestyle and that of the West. They associated Western consumerism with democratic governments, free societies, and economic policies that favored the free market and limited government planning. Thus, the expansion of consumerism in the West, which many intellectuals and moralists deplored, helped generate the discontent that brought down communism in Eastern Europe and the Soviet Union.

ENVIRONMENTALISM

After World War II, shortages of consumer goods created a demand that fueled postwar economic reconstruction and growth into the 1950s and 1960s. In those expansive times, public debate about the ethics of economic expansion and efficiency and their effects on the environment was muted. Concerns about pollution began to grow in the

1970s, and by the 1980s, environmentalists had developed real political clout. Among the most important environmental groups were the German Greens. The Greens formed a political party in 1979 that immediately became an electoral force.

Several developments lay behind this new concern for the environment. The Arab oil embargo of 1973–1974 pressed home two messages to the industrialized West: Natural resources are limited, and foreign, potentially hostile, countries control critical resources. By the 1970s, too, the environmental consequences of three decades of economic expansion were becoming increasingly apparent. Finally, long-standing worries about nuclear weapons merged with concerns about their environmental effects, strengthening antinuclear groups and generating opposition to the placement of nuclear weapons in Europe.

Green movement   Made up, in part, of members from the radical student groups of the 1960s, this movement was anticapitalistic, peace oriented, in opposition of nuclear arms, and condemned business for producing pollution. Unlike earlier student groups, though, the Greens opted to compete in the electoral process.

The German **Green movement** originated among radical student groups in the late 1960s. Like them, it was anticapitalist, blaming business for pollution. The Greens and other European environmental groups were also strongly antinuclear. Unlike the students of the 1960s, the Greens avoided violence and mass demonstrations, seeking instead to become a significant political presence through the electoral process.

The 1986 disaster at the Chernobyl nuclear reactor in the Soviet Union heightened concern about environmental issues and raised questions that no European government could ignore. The Soviet government had to confront casualties at the site and relocate tens of thousands of people. Radioactive fallout spread across Europe. Environmentalists had always contended that their issues transcended national borders. The Chernobyl fire proved them right.

After Chernobyl, European governments, East and West, began to respond to environmental concerns. Economic and political integration opens the possibility of transnational cooperation on environmental matters. As the European Economic Community solidifies, it and its member nations will likely impose more environmental regulations on business and industry. The nations of Eastern Europe have been forced to face the cleanup of vast areas of industrial development polluted during the communist era and to try to combine environmental protection with economic growth.

ART SINCE WORLD WAR II

HOW DID the Cold War shape Western art in the second half of the twentieth century?

It is impossible to cover even briefly the expansive and varied world of Western art since the end of World War II. However, we can note how both the Cold War and the memory of the horrors of the Second World War influenced Western art.

CULTURAL DIVISIONS AND THE COLD WAR

Although they may seem like products from different centuries, the Soviet painter Tatjiana Yablonskaya's (b. 1917) sun-strewn *Bread* (1949) and the American Jackson Pollock's (1912–1956) dizzyingly abstract *One* (Number 31, 1950) were painted only one year apart. The stark differences between these two works mirror the cultural divisions of the early Cold War.

socialist realism   Doctrine of Soviet art and literature that sought to create figurative, traditional, optimistic, and easily intelligible scenes of a bold socialist future of prosperity and solidarity.

Bread, measuring over six feet high and twelve feet wide, is a monumental example of **socialist realism**. Established, on Stalin's orders, as the official doctrine of Soviet art and literature in 1934, socialist realism sought to create optimistic and easily intelligible scenes of a bold socialist future, in which prosperity and solidarity would reign.

The looping skeins of paint in *One* (Number 31, 1950)—on display at the Museum of Modern Art in New York—may seem completely different from the kind of "realistic" propaganda visible in *Bread*, but Pollock's painting is in fact a central document of postwar American cultural life. Flinging paint from sticks and brushes onto his floor-bound canvas, Pollock freed his lines from representing any figure or outline. In the politically charged atmosphere of the early Cold War, critics saw Pollock's exuberant "drip" paintings as the embodiment of American cultural freedom and celebrated the

Wyoming-born Pollock as a kind of artist cowboy. As skeptical as many viewers might have been about the merits of abstract art, many people in the West saw it as the antithesis of socialist, realist totalitarianism.

Indeed, New York City—not Paris—emerged as the international center of modern art after World War II, a position it retains today. Just as American political and economic structures became models for the postwar redevelopment of Western Europe, so did American cultural developments. By the time Pollock's first posthumous retrospective toured Europe in 1958, much European painting resembled an elegant imitation of his frenetic lines.

Yablonskaya and Pollock together illustrate the two central poles of twentieth-century art: realism and abstraction. Although artistic style is no longer as closely associated with political programs as it once was, these two poles still frame the work of countless artists today.

Tatjiana Yablonskaya, *Bread,* 1949.

Ria Novosti/Sovfoto/Eastfoto

Why were paintings such as this one favored by Soviet leaders in the years after World War II?

MEMORY OF THE HOLOCAUST

The British sculptor Rachel Whiteread (b. 1963) is one of the leading artists of today's Europe. Her work illustrates how European art is breaking out of the modernist contours that were set at the beginning of the twentieth century. On one hand, Whiteread's art returns to what seem like familiar forms; on the other, it forces us to view these forms in ways that are as new to us as cubism was to the public in its day.

Whiteread's work is associated with minimalism in contemporary art. This movement, which originated in architecture and interior design, seeks to remove from the object being portrayed as many features as possible while retaining the object's form and the viewer's interest. Minimalist art aims to be as understated as possible.

Whiteread's most important public work is *Nameless Library,* the Judenplatz Holocaust Memorial in Vienna, which commemorates the deaths of 65,000 Austrian Jews under the Nazis. This memorial, which resembles a vast haunting tomb, is cast in concrete and embodies the outline of books whose spines are turned inward, thus remaining forever unread and as unopenable as the library's huge concrete doors are. Whiteread has said the molded, unopened books, which have been compared to the ghost of a library, symbolize the loss both of Jewish contributions to culture and of Jewish lives in the Holocaust.

Whiteread's *Nameless Library* in Vienna commemorates the thousands of Austrian Jews killed in the Nazi Holocaust.

© Reuters NewMedia Inc./CORBIS

What does this monument tell us about the ongoing cost of the Holocaust?

THE CHRISTIAN HERITAGE

In most ways, Christianity in Europe continued to be as hard-pressed during the twentieth century as it had been in the late nineteenth. Material prosperity, political ideologies, environmentalism, gender politics, and simple indifference have replaced religious faith for many people. Still, despite the loss of much of their popular support and legal privileges and the low rates of church attendance, the European Christian churches continue to exercise social and political influence.

In Western Europe, religious affiliation provided much of the initial basis for the Christian Democratic parties. The churches have also raised critical questions about colonialism, nuclear weapons, human rights, war, and other issues. Consequently, even in this most secular of ages, Christian churches have influenced state and society.

HOW HAS the Christian heritage of the West been affected by events of the twentieth century?

NEO-ORTHODOXY

Liberal theologians of the nineteenth century often softened the concept of sin and portrayed human nature as close to the divine. The horror of World War I destroyed that optimistic faith. Many Europeans felt that evil had stalked the Continent.

The most important Christian response to World War I appeared in the theology of Karl Barth (1886–1968). Barth portrayed God as wholly other than, and different from, humankind. In a sense, Barth was returning to the Reformation theology of Luther, but the work of Kierkegaard had profoundly influenced his reading of the reformer. Like the Danish writer, Barth regarded the lived experience of men and women as the best testimony to the truth of Luther's theology.

This view challenged much nineteenth-century writing about human nature. Barth's theology, which came to be known as neo-Orthodoxy, proved influential throughout the West in the wake of new disasters and suffering.

LIBERAL THEOLOGY

Neo-Orthodoxy did not, however, sweep away liberal theology, which had a strong advocate in Paul Tillich (1886–1965). This German-American theologian tended to regard religion as a human, rather than a divine, phenomenon. Whereas Barth saw God as dwelling outside humankind, Tillich believed that evidence of the divine had to be sought in human nature and human culture. Other liberal theologians, such as Rudolf Bultmann (1884–1976), continued to work on the problems of naturalism and supernaturalism that had troubled earlier writers. Another liberal Christian writer from Britain, C. S. Lewis (1878–1963), attracted millions of readers during and after World War II.

ROMAN CATHOLIC REFORM

Among Christian denominations, the most significant postwar changes have been in the Roman Catholic Church. In 1959, Pope John XXIII (r. 1958–1963) summoned the Twenty-First Ecumenical Council (the Emperor Constantine had called the first council in the fourth century), which came to be called Vatican II. The council finished its work in 1965 under John's successor, Pope Paul VI (r. 1963–1978). Among many changes in Catholic liturgy the council introduced, Mass was now celebrated in the vernacular languages rather than in Latin. The council also encouraged freer relations with other Christian denominations, fostered a new spirit toward Judaism, and gave more power to bishops. In recognition of the growing importance to the church of the world outside Europe and North America, Pope Paul appointed several cardinals from the former colonial nations, transforming the church into a truly world body.

In contrast to these liberal changes, however, Pope Paul and his successors have firmly upheld the celibacy of priests, maintained the church's prohibition on contraception and abortion, and opposed moves to open the priesthood to women. The church's unyielding stand on clerical celibacy has caused many men to leave the priesthood and many men and women to leave religious orders. The laity has widely ignored the prohibition on contraception.

Elected in 1978, John Paul II (1920–2005), the former Karol Wojtyla, archbishop of Kraków in Poland, pursued a three-pronged policy during his long pontificate. First, he maintained traditionalist doctrine, stressing the authority of the papacy and attempting to limit doctrinal and liturgical experimentation. Second, taking a firm stand against communism, he supported the spirit of freedom in Eastern Europe that brought down the communist regimes. Third, John Paul II encouraged the growth of the church in the non-Western world, stressing the need for social justice, but limiting the political activity of priests.

The pope's concern for the expansion of Roman Catholicism beyond Europe and North America recognized and encouraged what appears to be a transformation in Christianity as a world religion. Whereas in Europe Christian observance whether Roman Catholic, Protestant, or Orthodox had declined sharply during the twentieth century, Christianity has grown rapidly and fervently in Africa and Latin America. Observers estimate that within a few years, over half of the world's Christians will live in those two continents.

Pope John Paul II kisses a copy of the Qu'ran. Pope John Paul II and his successor, Pope Benedict XVI, made an effort to reach out to other religions and cultures.

National Archives and Records Administration

QUICK REVIEW

Pope John Paul II

- 1978: Karol Wojtyla, archbishop of Cracow, becomes Pope John Paul II
- Defended traditional doctrines, stressed papal authority, and opposed doctrinal and liturgical experimentation
- Worked hard to promote church in non-Western nations

LATE-TWENTIETH-CENTURY TECHNOLOGY: THE ARRIVAL OF THE COMPUTER

During the twentieth century, technology crossed international borders the way popular culture did. As with other areas of European life and society, American technology had an unprecedented impact on the Continent. It seems certain that no single American technological achievement of the twentieth century will so influence Western life on both sides of the Atlantic, as well as throughout the rest of the world, as the computer.

WHAT IMPACT has the computer had on twentieth-century society?

THE DEMAND FOR CALCULATING MACHINES

Starting in the late nineteenth century, the governments of the consolidating nation-states of Europe and of the United States confronted new administrative tasks that involved collecting and organizing vast amounts of data about national censuses, tax collection, economic statistics, and the administration of pensions and welfare legislation. During the same years, private businesses sought calculating machinery to handle and organize growing amounts of economic and business data. Such machines became technologically possible through the development of complex circuitry for electricity, the most versatile mode of energy in human history. Moreover, inventions that were dependent on electricity, including the telephone, the telegraph, underwater cables, and the wireless, created a new communications industry that in and of itself also required the organization of large databases of customer information to deliver their services. By the late 1920s, companies like National Cash Register, Remington Rand, and International Business Machines Corporation (IBM) had begun to manufacture such business machinery.

The earliest computers were very large. Here in a 1946 photograph J. Presper Eckert and J. W. Mauchly stand by the Electronic Numerical Integrator and Computer (ENIAC), which was dedicated at the University of Pennsylvania Moore School of Electrical Engineering.

CORBIS/Bettmann

What role did governments play in the development of computers in the twentieth century?

EARLY COMPUTER TECHNOLOGY

As has happened so often in history, warfare was the chief catalyst of change. After World War I and during World War II, the major powers developed new weapons that required exact mathematical ballistic calculations to effectively strike targets with bombs delivered by aircraft or long-range guns.

The first machine genuinely recognizable as a modern digital computer was the Electronic Numerical Integrator and Computer (ENIAC), built and designed at Moore Laboratories of the University of Pennsylvania and put into use by the U.S. Army in 1946 for ballistics calculation. Further computer engineering occurred at the Institute for Advanced Research in Princeton, New Jersey, in laboratories at the Massachusetts Institute of Technology, and in other laboratories the U.S. government and private businesses, especially IBM, ran. The other primary sites for computer development were laboratories in Britain.

THE DEVELOPMENT OF DESKTOP COMPUTERS

During the 1950s, the **transistor** revolutionized electronics, permitting a miniaturization of circuitry that made vacuum tubes obsolete and allowed computers to become smaller. Yet computers still had to be programmed with difficult computer languages by persons expertly trained to use them.

transistor Miniaturized electronics circuitry making the vacuum tube obsolete.

By the late 1960s, however, two innovations transformed computing technology. First, control of the computer was transferred to a bitmap covering the screen of a computer monitor. The mouse, invented in 1964, eased the movement of the cursor around the computer screen. Second, engineers at the Intel Corporation—then a California start-up company—invented the microchip, which became the heart of all future computers.

The bitmap on the screen, operated through the mouse, in effect embedded complicated computer language in the machine, hidden from the user, who simply manipulated images on the screen with the mouse. Almost anyone could thus learn to operate computers. At the same time, the tiny microchip, itself a miniature computer or microprocessor, permitted computer technology to abandon the mainframe and move to still smaller computers. By the mid-1980s, for a relatively modest cost (and one that has continued to drop), individuals had available for their own personal use in their offices or homes computers with far more power than the old mainframes. Computers became objects of everyday life and, by being so, began to transform everyday life itself. Nonetheless, the chief contemporary users of computers remain governments followed by the telephone industry, banking and finance, automobile operation, and airline reservation systems.

Despite the potential democratizing character of computer technology, the computer revolution has also introduced new concepts of "haves" and "have-nots" to societies around the world. Whether in poor school districts in the United States or in poor countries of the former Soviet bloc, students who graduate without computer skills will have difficulty making their way in the world's rapidly computerizing economy. Some commentators also fear that boys are more likely than girls to receive technological training in computers. Nations whose governments and businesses become networked into the world of computers will prosper more fully than those whose access to computer technology is deficient. In that regard, the possession of computers and the ability to use them will probably determine future economic competition, just as they have determined recent military competition.

THE CHALLENGES OF EUROPEAN UNIFICATION

WHAT LED to Western European unification following World War II?

The unprecedented steps toward economic cooperation and unity Western European nations took during the second half of the twentieth century were the single most important European success story of that era.

POSTWAR COOPERATION

The mid-twentieth-century Western European movement toward unity could have occurred in at least three ways: politically, militarily, or economically. Economic cooperation, unlike military and political cooperation, involved little or no immediate loss of sovereignty by the participating nations. Furthermore, it brought material benefits to all the states involved, increasing popular support for their governments. Moreover, the administration of the Marshall Plan and the organization of NATO gave the countries involved new experience in working with each other and demonstrated the productivity and efficiency that mutual cooperation could achieve.

The first effort toward economic cooperation was the formation of the European Coal and Steel Community in 1951 by France, West Germany, Italy, and the Benelux countries (Belgium, the Netherlands, and Luxembourg). The community both benefited from and contributed to the immense growth of material production in Western Europe during this period. Its success reduced the suspicions of government and business groups about coordination and economic integration.

THE EUROPEAN ECONOMIC COMMUNITY

It took more than the prosperity of the European Coal and Steel Community to draw European leaders toward further unity, however. The unsuccessful Suez intervention of 1956 and the resulting diplomatic isolation of France and Britain persuaded many Europeans that only by acting together could they significantly influence the United States and the Soviet Union or control their own national and regional destinies. So, in 1957, through the Treaty of Rome, the six members of the Coal and Steel Community agreed to form a new organization: the **European Economic Community (EEC)**. The members of the Common Market, as the EEC was soon known, sought to achieve the eventual elimination of tariffs, a free flow of capital and labor, and similar wage and social benefits in all their countries.

European Economic Community (EEC) European nations as members of the "Common Market" pledging to eliminate tariffs, guarantee unimpeded flow of capital and labor, and establish uniform wage scales and social benefits.

The Common Market achieved stunning success during its early years. By 1968, well ahead of schedule, the six members had abolished all tariffs among themselves. Trade and labor migration among the members grew steadily. Moreover, nonmember states began to copy the EEC and, later, to seek to join it. In 1973, Great Britain, Ireland, and Denmark became members. Throughout the late 1970s, however, and into the 1980s, momentum for expanding EEC membership slowed. Norway and Sweden, with relatively strong economies, declined to join. Although in 1982, Spain, Portugal, and Greece applied for membership and were eventually admitted, sharp disagreements and a sense of stagnation within the EEC continued.

THE EUROPEAN UNION

In 1988, the leaders of the EEC reached an important decision. By 1992, the EEC was to be a virtual free-trade zone with no trade barriers or other restrictive trade policies among its members. In 1991, the Treaty of Maastricht made a series of specific proposals that led to a unified EEC currency (the euro) and a strong central bank. The treaty was submitted to referendums in several European states. Denmark initially rejected it, and it passed only narrowly in France and Great Britain, making clear that it needed wider popular support. When the treaty finally took effect in November 1993, the EEC was renamed the **European Union**. Throughout the 1990s, the Union's influence grew. Its most notable achievement was the launching in early 1999 of the **euro**, which by 2002 had become the common currency in twelve of the member nations. In May 2004, the European Union added ten new nations raising the total number of members to twenty-five. (See Map 30–1.)

DISCORD OVER THE UNION

The 2004 expansion of the European Union may mark for some time the high point of European integration. During that year the leaders of the member nations adopted a new constitutional treaty for the Union. This treaty, generally known as the **European Constitution**, was a long, detailed, and highly complicated document involving a bill of rights

European Union Formerly the European Economic Community (EEC), renamed in 1993.

euro Launched in 1999 by the EU, a single currency circulating in most of Western Europe.

European Constitution Treaty that would transfer considerable decision-making authority from governments of the individual states to the Union's central institutions.

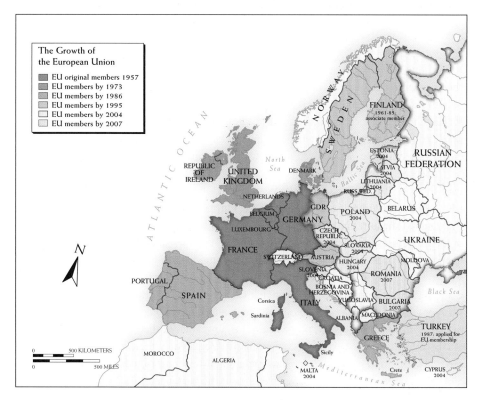

MAP 30–1 The Growth of the European Union This map traces the growth of membership in the European Union from its founding in 1957 through the introduction of its newest members in 2007. Note that Turkey, though having applied for membership, has not yet been admitted.

Given the political, social, historical, and demographic differences among its member states, how successful will EU enlargement and integration be?

Overview   Steps Toward European Unification

EUROPEAN COAL AND STEEL COMMUNITY	• Formed in 1951 by France, West Germany, Italy, Belgium, the Netherlands, and Luxembourg • Benefited from and contributed to the growth of material production in postwar Western Europe
EUROPEAN ECONOMIC COMMUNITY (EEC)	• Formed in 1957 by members of the Coal and Steel Community • Also known as the Common Market • Sought to achieve the elimination of tariffs, free flow of capital and labor, and similar wage and social benefits in member countries • Membership expanded in the 1970s and 1980s to include Great Britain, Ireland, Denmark, Spain, Portugal, and Greece
EUROPEAN UNION (EU)	• Replaced EEC in 1993 when the Treaty of Maastricht (1991) took effect • European common currency, the euro, launched in 1999 • Ten new members added in 2004 bringing total number of members to twenty-five
EUROPEAN CONSTITUTION	• Adopted by the leaders of EU nations in 2004 • Would have transferred considerable authority from member states to central institutions of the EU • Failure of voters to ratify the Constitution in many members states has slowed movement toward greater European unity

On Friday, May 27, 2005, two days before the vote on France's referendum on the EU constitution, a woman stands between a "yes" and a "no" campaign poster in a street of Rennes, western France.

AP Wide World Photos

Why has public opinion in Europe turned against the European Constitution?

and complex economic and political agreements among all the member states. It would have transferred considerable decision-making authority from the governments of the individual states to the central institutions of the European Union, many of which are located in Brussels, Luxembourg, and Strasbourg. To become effective, all the member states had to ratify the constitution either by their parliaments or through national referendums.

To the surprise of many in the European elite, in the spring of 2005, referendums held in France and the Netherlands heavily defeated the new constitutional treaty. Britain, where support for further European integration was lukewarm at best, immediately postponed holding its own referendum. Public opinion in other nations also soured on the constitutional treaty. Furthermore, immediately after these events, discord erupted over the Union's internal budget. These events marked an unprecedented crisis for the European Union and for the project of European integration. A similar crisis erupted in 2008 when a referendum in Ireland failed to support changes in the European Union that would create shared institutions of foreign policy formulation and military policy.

Several factors appear to have brought the European Union to this pass. First, for at least the past fifteen years, a gap has been growing between the European political elites, who have led the drive toward unity, and the European voting public. The former have either ignored the latter or have moved the project along with only narrow majorities. Second, the general Western European economy has stagnated for the last decade with relatively high rates of unemployment, especially among the young. Voting against the constitution was a way to voice discontent with this situation. Third, many of the smaller member states of the European Union have felt that France and Germany have either ignored them or taken them for granted. Fourth, some nations have come to believe that they were placed at an economic disadvantage when the euro replaced their former national currencies because the rates of exchange were unfairly calculated. Fifth, many people in the various states, large and small, have become increasingly reluctant to cede national sovereignty and the authority to make economic decisions to the bureaucracy in Brussels.

Finally, another large issue has informed the internal skeptics of the current European Union. Over the past several years, the leaders of the major member states have grown more favorable to the eventual admission of Turkey as a member state. If Turkey were admitted, Europe would have to integrate into the Union a state whose population is larger and much poorer than that of any other member state. Furthermore, although the Turkish government has long been seen as adamantly secular, the Turkish people are overwhelmingly Muslim. This "Islamic factor" has become increasingly controversial among those Europeans who, whether they are religiously observant or not, believe European culture to be Christian, and among those secular Europeans who are deeply concerned about the political, economic, and social implications of the Continent's already significant Muslim population.

It seems inconceivable that the effort to unify in Europe will either halt or be reversed. At the present time, however, it also seems certain that all future developments will move much more slowly and will require increasingly complicated negotiations. Moreover, the future of the European Union has become enmeshed in often bitter and divisive debates within the member states over social policies, the future of their economies, and what role the state should play in economic affairs.

NEW AMERICAN LEADERSHIP AND FINANCIAL CRISIS

WHY MIGHT 2008 prove to be a turning point in the relationship between the United States and Europe?

Much of the first decade of the twenty-first century witnessed considerable strain between the new post–Soviet Union Europe and the United States. The events leading up to the U.S. Iraq invasion in 2003 and the violence occurring since that invasion caused considerable strain between the United States and Europe, especially in terms of popular opinion. Europeans through their press and to some extent through their governments voiced much criticism over what they regarded as unilateral action by the United States in its foreign policy.

Three events in 2008 may have begun to change this situation and possibly to lessen those tensions. The first was the Russian invasion of Georgia discussed in Chapter 29. The United States and the European Union agreed in condemning that action. Second, the American presidential election of 2008 saw the strong victory of Barack Obama, the Democratic Party candidate. Obama is the first African American to be elected to the presidency. He ran on a platform critical of the Iraq invasion and American unilateralism. Even though he also voiced strong support for the war in Afghanistan, Obama has generated enormous popular support across Europe. Third, during the second half of 2008 a major international financial crisis potentially of the dimensions of that of the 1930s overwhelmed the American, transatlantic, and world economies. The crisis originated in the United States mortgage market where numerous major banks found themselves holding mortgages that could not be paid. Several major financial institutions in the United States failed as did some banks in Europe. The United States and some European governments intervened deeply in areas of the economy where they had previously generally refrained from intervening. Stock markets around the world lost a third or more of their value. The interconnectedness of world markets demonstrated itself as never before with financial panic displaying itself around the globe.

The financial crisis and its broad fallout even more than the wars in Iraq and Afghanistan will be the major issues confronting the new Obama administration. The financial problems even more than matters of traditional and foreign policy may for the next several years determine the relationship of the United States and Europe and hence the role of the West in the world.

Barack Obama shakes hands with supporters in Berlin, Germany, on July 24, 2008, following a speech he gave before a crowd of tens of thousands at the Victory Column in Tiergarten Park.

Reuters/Jim Young/Landov Media

What explains Barack Obama's extraordinary popularity in Europe?

SUMMARY

HOW HAS migration changed the face of Europe?

The Twentieth-Century Movement of Peoples Significant numbers of people relocated in Europe during the twentieth century. Millions of Europeans also emigrated, European colonials returned from overseas, and non-European peoples migrated to the former colonial powers. Europe's immigrant Muslim communities are often segregated, poorly assimilated, and discriminated against. The declining European birthrate will undoubtedly have profound consequences for future developments. *page 778*

WHAT EFFECT did the Great Depression and World War II have on the way Europeans viewed the role of government in social and economic life?

Toward a Welfare State Society After World War II, most Western European nations endorsed principles of liberal democracy, and many Europeans wanted their governments to take responsibility for ensuring prosperity and social security. Christian democratic parties took the lead in introducing new policies. A Labour Party ministry introduced universal health care in Britain in 1945, and welfare legislation spread across Western Europe. Through the postwar reconstruction period and the quarter century that followed many Europeans endorsed government management of the economy. Since then, confidence in free markets has grown, and some social welfare programs have been scaled back. Margaret Thatcher was the foremost proponent of a freer market economy. *page 780*

HOW DID the status of women in business, politics, and the professions change in Europe in the second half of the twentieth century?

New Patterns in Work and Expectations of Women Gender inequality persists in Europe, despite expanding economic and political roles for women. Recent feminism has focused on helping women as individuals take control of their lives. European women now have fewer children and more time to develop careers. Women in Eastern Europe are adapting to free-market, democratic systems. *page 784*

HOW WAS cultural and intellectual life transformed in Europe during the twentieth century?

Transformations in Knowledge and Culture Most Western European intellectuals have become disillusioned with Soviet communism. Interest in existentialism, a philosophy that questions rationalism, has been encouraged by distrust of the pride in rational achievement that has produced so much suffering and warfare. Social concerns prompted student rebellions in the 1960s, and the economic and military influence of the United States has threatened European culture. *page 786*

HOW DID the Cold War shape Western art in the second half of the twentieth century?

Art Since World War II The Second World War and the Cold War influenced art in the twentieth century. Socialist realism was the dominant official form of art in the Soviet Union and communist bloc, while abstract art, like that of Jackson Pollock, reflected postwar cultural freedom in the West. Minimalist art returns to familiar forms while it compels new ways of viewing the objects being portrayed. *page 790*

HOW HAS the Christian heritage of the West been affected by events of the twentieth century?

The Christian Heritage Christian churches have continued to be influential even in an increasingly secularized Europe. The Roman Catholic Church changed significantly under Pope John XXIII, but subsequent papacies have been more traditionalist and have furthered the spread of Christianity as a world religion. *page 791*

WHAT IMPACT has the computer had on twentieth-century society?

Late-Twentieth-Century Technology: The Arrival of the Computer Most of the development work for computers was done in the United States and Britain. Calculating machines started to become available in the 1920s. The U.S. Army used the first digital computer, ENIAC, for ballistics computations starting in 1946. By the 1980s, desktop computers were becoming everyday objects. *page 793*

WHAT LED to Western European unification following World War II?

The Challenges of European Unification Economic unification was easier for European nations than military or political union. In 1951 six nations formed the European Coal and Steel Community, which in 1957 became the European Economic Community or the Common Market. In 1973 membership was increased, and in 1998 the EEC created a free-trade zone. In 1999 a common currency was decreed, and the EEC was renamed the European Union. Its euro became the currency of most of Western Europe in 2001. In 2004, the European Union admitted ten more member nations, but discord spread over the details of a constitution designed to regulate relations among members. *page 794*

WHY MIGHT 2008 prove to be a turning point in the relationship between the United States and Europe?

New American Leadership and Financial Crisis Much of the first decade of the twenty-first century witnessed considerable strain between the new post–Soviet Union Europe and the United States. Three events in 2008 may have begun to change this situation and possibly to lessen those tensions: the Russian invasion of Georgia, the election of Barack Obama to the American presidency, and the emergence of a major international financial crisis. The financial crisis may for the next several years determine the relationship of the United States and Europe and hence the role of the West in the world. *page 797*

REVIEW QUESTIONS

1. How did migration affect twentieth-century social life in Europe? In what ways was Europe "Americanized" in the second half of the century?

2. How and why did European attitudes toward the welfare state and free-market economics change from the end of World War II to the dawn of the twenty-first century?

3. How did women's social and economic roles change in the second half of the twentieth century? What problems have new patterns of work created for women?

4. How did the pursuit and diffusion of knowledge change during the twentieth century? In what sense was existentialism a response to the crises of the twentieth century?

5. What kind of artistic styles arose in the mid– and late-twentieth century and how did World War II and the Cold War influence those styles?

6. How did Western Christian theology develop in the twentieth century? What changes are computers most likely to bring?

7. How did the nations of Western Europe move toward economic and political unity? What challenges face further European integration?

KEY TERMS

Christian democratic parties (p. 781)

euro (p. 795)

European Constitution (p. 795)

European Economic Community (EEC) (p. 794)

European Union (p. 795)

existentialism (p. 787)

Green movement (p. 790)

socialist realism (p. 790)

transistor (p. 793)

For additional learning resources related to this chapter, please go to **www.myhistorylab.com**

PEARSON
myhistorylab

Academy School founded by Plato in Athens to train statesmen and citizens.

Acropolis At the center of the city of Athens, the most famous example of a citadel.

Act of Supremacy Act of 1534 proclaiming Henry VIII "the only supreme head on earth of the Church of England."

agape Common meal, or "love feast," that was the central ritual of the church in early Christianity.

agora Place for markets and political assemblies.

Ahura Mazda The chief deity of Zoroastrianism, the native religion of Persia. Ahura Mazda is the creator of the world, the source of light, and the embodiment of good.

Albigensians Heretical sect that advocated a simple, pious way of life following the example set by Jesus and the Apostles, but rejecting key Christian doctrines.

Anabaptists ("rebaptizers") The most important of several groups of Protestants forming more radical organizations that sought a more rapid and thorough restoration of the "primitive Christianity" described in the New Testament.

anarchists Those who opposed any cooperation with industry or government.

Anschluss Union of Germany and Austria.

anti-Semitism Prejudice against Jews often displayed through hostility.

apartheid (a-PAR-tid) An official policy of segregation, assignment of peoples to distinct regions, and other forms of social, political, and economic discrimination based on race associated primarily with South Africa.

appeasement Allied policy of making concessions to Germany based on the belief that Germany's grievances were real and Hitler's goals limited.

Aramaic Semitic language spoken widely throughout the Middle East in antiquity.

Areopagus Council heading Athens's government comprised of a group of nobles that annually chose the city's nine *archons*, the magistrates who administered the *polis*.

arete The highest virtue in Homeric society: the manliness, courage, and excellence that equipped a hero to acquire and defend honor.

Arianism Belief that Christ was the first of God the Father's creations and the being through whom the Father created all other things.

aristocratic resurgence Eighteenth-century resurgence of nobles that mantained the exclusiveness of noble rank, made it difficult to obtain, reserved powerful posts to nobles, and protected nobles from taxation.

Attica Region (about 1,000 square miles) that Athens dominated.

Augsburg Confession Moderate Protestant creed endorsed by the Schmalkaldic League (a defensive alliance of Lutherans).

Augustus ("revered") Name by which the Senate hailed Octavian for his restoration of the republic.

Avignon Papacy Period from 1309 to 1377 when the papal court was situated in Avignon, France, and gained a reputation for greed and worldly corruption.

Axis Forces (opposed to the Allies) joined together in Europe, including Germany and Italy, before and during World War II.

banalities Monopolies maintained by landowners giving them the right to demand that tenants pay to grind all their grain in the landowner's mill and bake all their bread in his oven.

baroque Artistic and architectural styles that were naturalistic rather than idealized to involve observer on an emotional level through dramatic portrayals.

Beguines Sisterhoods of pious, self-supporting single women.

Black Death Virulent plague that struck in Sicily in 1347 and spread through Europe. It discolored the bodies of its victims. By the early fifteenth century, the plague may have reduced the population of Western Europe by two-fifths.

Bolsheviks ("majority") Lenin's turn-of-the-century Russian faction favoring a party of elite professionals who would provide the working class with centralized leadership.

boyars Wealthy landowners among the freemen in late medieval Russia.

Brezhnev Doctrine Asserted the right of the Soviet Union to intervene in domestic politics of communist countries.

Bronze Age (3100–1200 B.C.E.) Began with the increasing importance of metal that also ended the Stone Ages.

Caesaropapism Emperor acting as if he were pope as well as caesar.

caliphate Office of the leader of the Muslim community.

categorical imperative Kant's view that all human beings possess an innate sense of moral duty, an inner command to act in every situation as one would have other people act in that same situation.

catholic ("universal") As in "universal" majority of Christians.

censors Men of unimpeachable reputation, chosen to carry the responsibility for enrolling, keeping track of, and determining the status and tax liability of each citizen.

Chartism The London Working Men's Association's 1838 proposal for political reform featuring the Six Points.

Christian democratic parties Post–World War II parties that welcomed non-Catholic members and fought for democracy, social reform, and economic growth.

civilization Stage in the evolution of organized society that has among its characteristics urbanism, long-distance trade, writing systems, and accelerated technological and social development.

civilizing mission The concept that Western nations could bring advanced science and economic development to non-Western parts of the world that justified imperial administration.

clientage The custom in ancient Rome whereby men became supporters of more powerful men in return for legal and physical protection and economic benefits.

Cold War Period between the end of World War II (1945) and the collapse of the Soviet Union (1991) in which U.S. and Soviet relations were tense, seemingly moments away from actual war at any time during these years.

collectivization The bedrock of Stalinist agriculture, which forced Russian peasants to give up their private farms and work as members of collectives, large agricultural units controlled by the state.

coloni Tenant farmers who were bound to the lands they worked.

concentration camps Camps first established by Great Britain in South Africa during the Boer War to incarcerate noncombatant civilians; later, camps established for political prisoners and other persons deemed dangerous to the state in the Soviet Union and Nazi Germany. The term is now primarily associated with the camps established by the Nazis during the Holocaust.

condottieri Military brokers from whom one could hire a mercenary army.

Congregationalists The more extreme Puritans who believed every congregation ought to be autonomous, a law unto itself controlled by neither bishops nor presbyterian assemblies.

conquistadores "Conquerors."

conservatism Form of political thought that, in mid-nineteenth-century Europe, promoted legitimate monarchies, landed aristocracies, and established churches.

Consulate A republican facade for one-man government by Napoleon.

consuls Elected magistrates from patrician families chosen annually to lead the army, oversee the state religion, and sit as judges.

containment American foreign policy strategy (beginning in 1947) for countering the communist threat and resisting the spread of Soviet influence.

Convention The newly elected French body that met on September 21, 1792, whose first act was to declare France a republic—a nation governed by an elected assembly without a king.

Counter-Reformation A reorganization of the Catholic Church that equipped it to meet the challenges posed by the Protestant Reformation.

Creole Merchants, landowners, and professional people of Spanish descent.

Crusades Campaigns authorized by the church to combat heresies and rival faiths.

cubism Autonomous realm of art with no purpose beyond itself. Includes as many different perspectives, angles, or views of the object as possible.

culture Way of life invented by a group and passed on by teaching.

cuneiform Developed by the Sumerians as the very first writing system ever used, it used several thousand characters, some of which stood for words and some for sounds.

deism The *philosophes'* theology. A rational religion, a faith without fanaticism and intolerance that acknowledged the sovereign authority of reason.

Delian League Pact joined in 478 B.C.E. by Athenians and other Greeks to continue the war with Persia.

détente Relaxation of tensions between the United States and Soviet Union that involved increased trade and reduced deployment of strategic arms.

"divine right of kings" The belief that God appoints kings and that kings are accountable only to God for how they use their power.

domestic system of textile production Means by which urban merchants obtained their wares. They bought wool or other unfinished fiber for distribution to peasant workers who took it home, spun it into thread, wove it into cloth, and returned the finished product to the merchants for sale.

Duce (DO-chay) Meaning "leader." Mussolini's title as head of the Fascist Party.

ego Among Freud's three entities of the mind, the *ego* mediates between the impulsive id and the self-denying superego.

émigrés French aristocrats and enemies of the revolution who fled to countries on France's borders and set up bases for counterrevolutionary activities.

empiricism The use of experiment and observation derived from sensory evidence to construct scientific theory or philosophy of knowledge.

encomienda Legal grant of the right to the labor of a specific number of Indians for a particular period of time. This was used as a Spanish strategy for exploiting the labor of the natives.

Enlightenment The eighteenth-century movement led by the *philosophes* that held that change and reform were both desirable through the application of reason and science.

Epicureans People who believed the proper pursuit of humankind is undisturbed withdrawal from the world.

equestrians Men rich enough to qualify for cavalry service.

Estates General Assembly of representatives from France's propertied classes.

Etruscans A people of central Italy who exerted the most powerful external influence on the early Romans. Etruscan kings ruled Rome until 509 B.C.E.

Eucharist ("thanksgiving") Celebration of the Lord's Supper in which bread and wine were blessed and consumed.

euro Launched in 1999 by the EU, a single currency circulating in most of Western Europe.

European Constitution Treaty that would transfer considerable decision-making authority from governments of the individual states to the European Union's central institutions.

European Economic Community (EEC) European nations as members of the "Common Market" pledging to eliminate tariffs, guarantee unimpeded flow of capital and labor, and establish uniform wage scales and social benefits.

European Union (EU) Formerly the European Economic Community (EEC), renamed in 1993.

existentialism Maintains that the human condition is greater than the sum of its parts and can only be grouped as whole.

fascism System of extreme right-wing dictatorial government.

fiefs ("lands") Granted to cavalry men to fund their equipment and service.

Fourteen Points President Woodrow Wilson's idealistic principles articulated as America's goals in World War I, including self-determination for nationalities, open diplomacy, freedom of the seas, disarmament, and establishment of a league of nations to keep the peace.

Fronde Widespread rebellions in France between 1649 and 1652 (named after a slingshot used by street ruffians) aimed at reversing the drift toward absolute monarchy and preserving local autonomy.

Führer (FYOOR-er) Meaning "leader." The title taken by Hitler when he became dictator of Germany.

Gallican Liberties The French Roman Catholic Church's ecclesiastical independence of papal authority in Rome.

Gaul Area that is now modern France.

ghettos Separate districts in cities and entire villages in the countryside where Jews lived apart from Christians in eighteenth-century Europe.

glasnost ("openness") Gorbachev's policy of opening the way for unprecedented public discussion and criticism of Soviet history and the Communist Party. Censorship was relaxed and dissidents were released from prison.

"Glorious Revolution" Parliament's bloodless 1688 declaration of a vacant throne and proclamation that William and Mary were its heirs.

Golden Bull Arrangements agreed to by the Holy Roman Emperor and the major German territorial rulers in 1356 that helped stabilize Germany.

Great Depression A prolonged worldwide economic downturn that began in 1929 with the collapse of the New York Stock Exchange.

Great Purges The arrests, trials, Communist Party expulsions, and executions—beginning with the assassination of Politburo member Sergei Kirov in December 1934—that mainly targeted Party officials and reached its climax from 1936 to 1938.

Great Trek The migration by Boer (Dutch) farmers during the 1830s and 1840s from regions around Cape Town into the eastern and northeastern regions of South Africa that ultimately resulted in the founding of the Orange Free State and Transvaal.

Green movement Made up, in part, of members from the radical student groups of the 1960s, this movement was anticapitalistic, peace oriented, in opposition of nuclear arms, and condemned business for producing pollution. Unlike earlier student groups, though, the Greens opted to compete in the electoral process.

guild An association of merchants or craftsmen that offered protection to its members and set rules for their work and products.

hacienda Large landed estate that characterized most Spanish colonies.

Hegira Forced flight of Muhammad and his followers to Medina, 240 miles north of Mecca. This event marks the beginning of the Islamic calendar.

Hellenistic Term that describes the cosmopolitan civilization, established under the Macedonians, that combined aspects of Greek and Middle Eastern cultures.

Helots Slaves to the Spartans that revolted and nearly destroyed Sparta in 650 B.C.E.

heretics "Takers" of contrary positions, namely in Christianity.

hieroglyphs ("sacred carving") Greek name for Egyptian writing. The writing was often used to engrave holy texts on monuments.

Holocaust The Nazi extermination of millions of European Jews between 1940 and 1945. Also called the "final solution to the Jewish problem."

Holy Roman Empire The domain of the German monarchs who revived the use of the Roman imperial title during the Middle Ages.

home rule Government of a country or locality by its own citizens.

hoplite A true infantry soldier who began to dominate the battlefield in the late eighth century B.C.E.

Homo sapiens Our own species, which dates back roughly 200,000 years.

hubris Arrogance produced by excessive wealth or good fortune.

Huguenots French Protestants, named after Besançon Hugues, the leader of the revolt that won Geneva its freedom at that time.

humanitas Wide-ranging intellectual curiosity and habits of critical thinking that are the goals of liberal education.

iconoclasm Opposition to the use of images in Christian worship.

id Among Freud's three entities of the mind, the *id* consists of innate, amoral, irrational drives for sexual gratification, aggression, and sensual pleasure.

Iliad Homer's poem narrates a dispute between Agamemnon the king and his warrior Achilles, whose honor is wounded and then avenged.

imperator "Commander in chief."

imperialism The extension of a nation's authority over other nations or areas through conquest or political or economic hegemony.

Imperialism of Free Trade The advance of European economic and political interests in the nineteenth century by demanding that non-European nations allow European nations, most particularly Great Britain, to introduce their manufactured goods freely into all nations or to introduce other goods, such as opium into China, that allowed those nations to establish economic influence and to determine the terms of trade.

imperium Right held by a Roman king to enforce commands by fines, arrests, and corporal and capital punishment.

impressionism Focuses on social life and leisured activities of the urban middle and lower-middle classes; a fascination with light, color, and representation of momentary experience of social life or of landscape.

indulgence Remission of the obligation to perform a "work of satisfaction" for a sin.

Industrial Revolution Term coined by early-nineteenth-century observers to describe the changes that the spreading use of powered machinery made in society and economics.

Inquisition Formal ecclesiastical court dedicated to discovering and punishing heresy.

Intolerable Acts Series of laws passed by Parliament in 1774 that closed the port of Boston, reorganized the government of Massachusetts, quartered soldiers in private homes, and transferred trials of customs officials accused of crimes to England.

Ionia Western coast of Asia Minor.

Islam New religion appearing in Arabia in the sixth century in response to the work of the Prophet Muhammad.

Jacobins The best organized of the political clubs, they embraced the most radical of the Enlightenment's political theories, and they wanted a republic, not a constitutional monarchy.

Jacquerie (From "Jacques Bonhomme," a peasant caricature) Name given to the series of bloody rebellions that desperate French peasants waged beginning in 1358.

Jansenism Appearing in the 1630s, it followed the teachings of St. Augustine, who stressed the role divine grace played in human salvation.

jihad A struggle; interpreted as a call for religious war.

Junkers (Prussian nobles) They were allowed to demand absolute obedience from the serfs on their estates in exchange for their support of the Hohenzollerns.

jus gentium Law of all peoples as opposed to the law that reflected only Roman practice.

jus naturale Law of nature that enshrined the principles of divine reason that Cicero and the Stoics believed governed the universe.

Ka'ba One of Arabia's holiest shrines located in Mecca, the birthplace of Muhammad.

Keynesian economics Economic theories and programs ascribed to John M. Keynes and his followers advocating government monetary and fiscal policies that increase employment and spending.

Kristallnacht (KRIS-tahl-NAHKT) Meaning "crystal night" because of the broken glass that littered German streets after the looting and destruction of Jewish homes, businesses, and synagogues across Germany on the orders of the Nazi Party in November 1938.

Kulturkampf ("cultural struggle") An extreme church-state conflict waged by Bismarck in Germany during the 1870s in response to a perceived threat to German political unity from the Roman Catholic Church.

laissez-faire Policy of noninterference, especially the policy of government noninterference in economic affairs or business.

latifundia Great estates that produced capital-intensive cash crops for the international market.

Latium Region located in present-day Italy that included the small town of Rome.

Lebensraum German for "living space."

levée en masse Order for total military mobilization of both men and property.

liberal arts The medieval university program that consisted of the *trivium* (TRI-vee-um): grammar, rhetoric, and logic, and the *quadrivium* (qua-DRI-vee-um): arithmetic, geometry, astronomy, and music.

Lower Egypt The Nile's one-hundred-mile deep, triangularly shaped delta.

Luftwaffe The German air force.

Lyceum School founded by Aristotle in Athens that focused on the gathering and analysis of data from all fields of knowledge.

Magna Carta ("Great Charter") Document spelling out limitations on royal authority agreed to by John in 1215. It created foundation for modern English law.

mandate Territory under the aegis of the League of Nations but actually ruled as a colony.

mannerism Reaction against the simplicity, symmetry, and idealism of High Renaissance art. It made room for the strange, even the abnormal, and gave free reign to the subjectivity of the artist. The name reflects a tendency by artists to employ "mannered" ("affected") techniques—distortions that expressed individual perceptions and feelings.

manor A self-sufficient rural community that was a fundamental institution of medieval life.

Marshall Plan The U.S. European Recovery Program introduced by George C. Marshall, American secretary of state, whereby America provided extensive economic aid to the European states, conditional only on their working together for their mutual benefit.

Marxism Socialist movement begun by Karl Marx in the mid–nineteenth century that differed from competing socialist views primarily in its claim to a scientific foundation and in its insistence on reform through revolution.

Mein Kampf (*My Struggle*) Strategy dictated by Adolf Hitler during his period of imprisonment in 1923 outlining his political views.

Mensheviks ("minority") Turn-of-the-century Russian faction that wanted to create a party with a large mass membership (like Germany's SPD).

mercantilism Economic theory in which governments heavily regulated trade and promoted empires in order to increase national wealth.

Methodism Movement begun in England by John Wesley, an Oxford-educated Anglican priest, the first major religion to embody romanticism. It emphasized religion as a "method" for living more than a set of doctrines.

millets Communities of the officially recognized religions that governed portions of the Ottoman Empire.

Minoan Civilization of Crete (2100–1150 B.C.E.), and the Aegean's first civilization, named for a legendary king on the island.

modernism Movement of the 1870s criticizing middle-class society and traditional morality.

Monophysites Believers in a single, immortal nature of Christ; not both eternal God and mortal man in one and the same person.

monotheism Having faith in a single God.

Mycenaean Civilization occupying mainland Greece during the Late Helladic era (1580–1150 B.C.E.).

nationalism The belief that the people who share an ethnic identity (language, culture, and history) should also be recognized as having a right to a government and political identity of their own.

NATO North Atlantic Treaty Organization, a mutual defense pact.

natural selection Darwin and Wallace's theory that those species with a unique trait that gives them a marginal advantage in the struggle for existence change the nature of their species by reproducing more successfully than their competitors; the fittest survive to pass on their unique characteristics.

naturalists Authors who tried to portray nature and human life without sentimentality.

Nazis Members of the National Socialist German Workers' Party that formed in 1920 and supported a mythical Aryan race alleged to be the source of the purest German lineage.

neo-Gothic Style that idealized nature and portrayed it in all its power.

neoclassicism Style that embodied a return to figurative and architectural models drawn from the Renaissance and the ancient world.

Neolithic "New Stone" Age, dating back 10,000 years to when people living in some parts of the Middle East made advances in the production of stone tools and shifted from hunting and gathering to agriculture.

New Economic Policy (NEP) A limited revival of capitalism, especially in light industry and agriculture, introduced by Lenin in 1921 to repair the damage inflicted on the Russian economy by the Civil War and war communism.

New Imperialism The extension in the late nineteenth and early twentieth centuries of Western political and economic dominance to Asia, the Middle East, and Africa.

nomes Egyptian districts ruled by regional governors who were called nomarchs.

Odyssey Homer's epic poem that tells of the wanderings of the hero Odysseus.

oikos The Greek household, always headed by a male.

Old Regime Eighteenth-century era marked by absolutist monarchies, agrarian economies, tradition, hierarchy, corporateness, and privilege.

optimates ("the best men") Opponents of Tiberius and defenders of the traditional prerogatives of the Senate.

orthodox ("correct") As in "correct" faith in Christianity.

Ottoman Empire The authority Istanbul's Ottoman Turkish sultan exercised over the Balkans, the Middle East, and North Africa from the end of the Middle Ages to World War I.

Paleolithic Greek for "old stone"; the earliest period in cultural development that began with the first use of stone tools about a million years ago and continued until about 10,000 B.C.E.

Panhellenic (All Greek) Sense of cultural identity that all Greeks felt in common with one other.

papal infallibility Assertion that the pope's pronouncements on matters of faith and morals could not be questioned.

Papal States Central part of Italy where Pope Stephen II became the secular ruler when confirmed by the Franks in 755.

parlements Regional courts allowed considerable latitude by Louis XIV to deal with local issues.

parliamentary monarchy English rule by a monarch with some parliamentary guidance or input.

patricians Upper class of Roman families that originally monopolized all political authority. Only they could serve as priests, senators, and magistrates.

Peloponnesian Wars Series of wars between Athens and Sparta beginning in 460 B.C.E.

Peloponnesus Southern half of the Greek peninsula.

perestroika ("restructuring") Means by which Gorbachev wished to raise his country's standard of living.

petite bourgeoisie New lower-middle class made up of white-collar workers such as secretaries, retail clerks, and lower-level bureaucrats.

phalanx Tight military formation of men eight or more ranks deep.

pharaoh The god-kings of ancient Egypt.

Pharisee Member of a Jewish sect known for strict adherence to the Jewish law.

Phoenicians Seafaring people (Canaanites and Syrians) who scattered trading colonies from one end of the Mediterranean to the other.

plebeians Commoner class of Roman families, usually families of small farmers, laborers, and artisans who were early clients of the patricians.

political absolutism Government by a ruler with absolute authority.

politique Ruler or person in a position of power who puts the success and well-being of his or her state above all else.

polytheists Name given those who workship many gods and/or goddesses.

Popular Front A government of all left-wing parties that took power in France in 1936 to enact social and economic reforms.

populares Politicians who followed Tiberius's example of politics and governing.

positivism Comte's philosophy that all knowledge should be the kind of knowledge common to the physical sciences.

postimpressionism Focuses more on form and structure to bring painting of modern life back in touch with earlier artistic traditions.

Pragmatic Sanction Document recognizing Charles VI's daughter Maria Theresa as his heir.

Presbyterians Puritans who favored a national church of semiautonomous congregations governed by representative presbyteries.

proconsulships Extension of terms for consuls who had important work to finish.

protectorate A non-Western territory administered by a Western nation without formal conquest or annexation, usually a de facto colony.

Ptolemaic system Astronomical theory, named after Greek astronomer Ptolemy, that assumed Earth was the center point of a ball-shaped universe composed of concentric layers of rotating crystalline spheres to which the heavenly bodies were attached.

Puritans English Protestants who wanted simpler forms of church ceremony and strictness and gravity in personal behavior.

Qur'an Sacred book comprised of a collection of the revealed texts that God had chosen Muhammad to convey.

racism Belief that some peoples are innately superior to others.

realists Authors who tried to describe human behavior with scientific objectivity, rejecting the Romantic idealization of nature, poverty, love, and polite society, and portraying the hypocrisy, physical and psychic brutality, and the dullness that underlay bourgeois life.

regular clergy Those clergy living under a *regula*, the rule of a monastic order.

Reichstag (RIKES-stahg) The German parliament, which existed in various forms, until 1945.

Reign of Terror Extreme measures employed by the French government in an effort to protect the revolution.

rococo Style that embraced lavish, often lighthearted decoration with an emphasis on pastel colors and the play of light.

romanticism Reaction against the rationalism and scientism of the Enlightenment, insisting on the importance of human feelings, intuition, and imagination as supplements for reason in the human quest to understand the world.

SA The Nazi parliamentary forces, or storm troopers.

sans-culottes Parisians (shopkeepers, artisans, wage earners, and factory workers who had been ignored by the Old Regime) who, along with radical Jacobins, began the second revolution in France.

Scholasticism Method of study associated with the medieval university.

scientific revolution The emergence in the sixteenth century of rational and empirical methods of research that challenged traditional thought and promoted the rise of science and technology.

second Industrial Revolution Started after 1850, it expanded the production of steel, chemicals, electricity, and oil.

secular clergy Clergy, such as bishops and priests, who lived and worked among the laity in the *saeculum* ("world").

Sejm Central legislative body to which the Polish nobles belonged.

September Massacres The execution ordered by the Paris Commune of approximately 1,200 aristocrats, priests, and common criminals who, because they were being held in city jails, were assumed to be counterrevolutionaries.

serf Peasant bound to the land he worked.

Shi'a The "party" of Ali. They believed Ali and his descendants were Muhammad's only rightful successors.

social Darwinism Spencer's argument (coming close to claiming that might makes right) used to justify neglect of the poor and the working class, exploitation of colonial peoples, and aggressive competition among nations.

socialist realism Doctrine of Soviet art and literature that sought to create figurative, traditional, optimistic, and easily intelligible scenes of a bold socialist future of prosperity and solidarity.

Sophists Professional teachers who emerged in Greece in the mid–fifth century B.C.E. who were paid to teach techniques of rhetoric, dialectic, and argumentation.

spheres of influence A region, city, or territory where a non-Western nation exercised informal administrative influence through economic, diplomatic, or military advisers.

spinning jenny Invented by James Hargreaves in 1765, this machine spun sixteen spindles of thread simultaneously.

SS The chief security units of the Nazi state.

Stoics People who sought freedom from passion and harmony with nature.

studia humanitas (humanism) Scholarship of the Renaissance that championed the study of Latin and Greek classics and Christian church fathers as an end in itself and as a guide to reforming society. Some claim it is an un-Christian philosophy emphasizing human dignity, individualism, and secular values.

Sturm und Drang ("Storm and Stress") Movement in German romantic literature that emphasized feeling and emotion.

suffragettes Derisive name for members of the Women's Social and Political Union, who lobbied for votes for women.

Sunnis Followers of the *sunna*, "tradition." They emphasize loyalty to the fundamental principles of Islam.

superego Among Freud's three entities of the mind, the *superego* internalizes the moral imperatives that society and culture impose on the personality.

symposium A men's drinking party at the center of aristocratic social life in archaic Greece.

Table of Ranks Issued by Peter the Great to draw nobles into state service, it made rank in the bureaucracy or military, not lineage, the determinant of an individual's social status.

tabula rasa (a blank page) John Locke's *An Essay Concerning Human Understanding* (1690) theorized that at birth the human mind is a tabula rasa.

taille The direct tax on the French peasantry.

ten lost tribes Israelites who were scattered and lost to history when the northern kingdom of Israel fell to the Assyrians in 722 B.C.E.

tetrarchy Coalition of four men, each of whom was responsible for a different part of the empire, established by Diocletian.

Thermidorian Reaction Tempering of revolutionary fervor that led to the establishment of a new constitutional regime.

Third Estate Members of the commercial and professional middle classes, or everyone but the clergy (the First Estate) and the nobility (the Second Estate).

Third Reich Hitler's regime of Nazis.

three-field system Developed by medieval farmers, a system in which three fields were utilized during different growing seasons to limit the amount of nonproductive plowing and to restore soil fertility through crop rotation.

transistor Miniaturized electronics circuitry making the vacuum tube obsolete.

transubstantiation Christian doctrine which holds that, at the moment of priestly consecration, the bread and wine of the Lord's Supper become the body and blood of Christ.

tribunes Officials elected by the plebeian tribal assembly given the power to protect plebeians from abuse by patrician magistrates.

ulema ("Persons with correct knowledge") Scholarly elite leading Islam.

Upper Egypt Narrow valley extending 650 miles from Aswan to the border of Lower Egypt.

utilitarianism Maintained that people should always pursue the course that promotes the greatest happiness for the greatest number.

utopian socialists Early critics of industrialism whose visionary programs often involved plans to establish ideal societies based on noncapitalistic values.

vassal A person granted an estate or cash payments in return for rendering services to a lord.

Vulgate Latin translation of the Bible that became the standard text for the Catholic Church.

War Communism The economic policy adopted by the Bolsheviks during the Russian Civil War to seize the banks, heavy industry, railroads, and grain.

Warsaw Pact Mutual defense agreement among Albania, Bulgaria, Czechoslovakia, East Germany, Hungary, Poland, Romania, and the Soviet Union.

water frame Invented in 1769 by Richard Arkwright, this water-powered device produced a 100 percent cotton fabric rather than the standard earlier blend of cotton and linen.

Weimar Republic German republic that came to power in 1918 embodying the hopes of German liberals.

Zionism Movement based on the theory that if Jews were unacceptable as citizens of European nations, their only safety lay in establishing a nation of their own.

Chapter 1

C. ALDRED, *The Egyptians* (1998). Probably the best one-volume history of the subject.

P. BRIANT, *From Cyrus to Alexander: A History of the Persian Empire* (2002). A scholarly account of ancient Persia with greater knowledge of the Persian evidence than is usual.

T. BRYCE, *The Kingdom of the Hittites* (1998). A fine new account.

M. EHRENBERG, *Women in Prehistory* (1989). Discusses the role of women in early times.

B. M. FAGAN, *People of the Earth: An Introduction to World Prehistory*, 11th ed. (2003). A narrative account of human prehistory up to the earliest civilizations.

W. W. HALLO AND W. K. SIMPSON, *The Ancient Near East: A History*, rev. ed. (1998). A fine survey of Egyptian and Mesopotamian history.

A. KAMM, *The Israelites: An Introduction* (1999). A brief, excellent, and accessible account.

R. MATTHEWS, *Archaeology of Mesopotamia: Theories and Approaches* (2003). A fascinating investigation of the theories, methods, approaches, and history of Mesopotamian archaeology from its origins in the nineteenth century up to the present day.

J. B. PRITCHARD, ED., *Ancient Near Eastern Texts Relating to the Old Testament* (1969). A good collection of documents in translation with useful introductory material.

R. RUDGLEY, *The Lost Civilizations of the Stone Age* (1999). A bold new interpretation that claims that many elements of civilization were already present in the Stone Age.

H. W. F. SAGGS, *Babylonians* (1995). A general account of ancient Mesopotamia by an expert scholar.

I. SHAW, ED., *The Oxford History of Ancient Egypt* (2000). An up-to-date survey by leading scholars.

W. K. SIMPSON ET AL., *The Literature of Ancient Egypt: An Anthology of Stories, Instructions, Stelae, Autobiographies, and Poetry* (2003). A fine collection of writings from ancient Egypt.

D. C. SNELL, *Life in the Ancient Near East, 3100–332 B.C.E.* (1997). A social history with emphasis on culture and daily life.

Chapter 2

E. K. ANHALT, *Solon the Singer* (1993). A fine study of the Athenian poet-politician.

W. BURKERT, *The Orientalizing Revolution: Near Eastern Influence on Greek Culture in the Early Archaic Age* (1992). A study of the Eastern impact on Greek literature and religion from 750 to 650 B.C.E.

J. CHADWICK, *The Mycenaean World* (1976). A readable account by an author who helped decipher Mycenaean writing.

R. DREWS, *The Coming of the Greeks* (1988). A fine study of the arrival of the Greeks as part of the movement of Indo-European peoples.

J. V. A. FINE, *The Ancient Greeks* (1983). An excellent survey that discusses historical problems and the evidence that gives rise to them.

M. I. FINLEY, *World of Odysseus*, rev. ed. (1965). A fascinating attempt to reconstruct Homeric society.

V. D. HANSON, *The Other Greeks* (1995). A revolutionary account of the invention of the family farm by the Greeks and the central role of agrarianism in shaping the Greek city-state.

V. D. HANSON, *The Western Way of War* (1989). A brilliant and lively discussion of the rise and character of the *hoplite* phalanx and its influence on Greek society.

J. M. HURWIT, *The Art and Culture of Early Greece* (1985). A fascinating study of the art of early Greece in its literary and cultural context.

W. K. LACEY, *The Family in Ancient Greece* (1984). A valuable survey of family life in ancient Greece.

P. B. MANVILLE, *The Origins of Citizenship in Ancient Athens* (1990). An examination of the origins of citizenship in the time of Solon of Athens.

J. F. McGLEW, *Tyranny and Political Culture in Ancient Greece* (1993). A study of tyranny and its effect on Greek political tradition.

S. G. MILLER, *Ancient Greek Athletics* (2004). The best available account.

R. OSBORNE, *Greece in the Making, 1200–479 B.C.* (1996). An up-to-date, well-illustrated account of early Greek history.

S. PRICE, *Religions of the Ancient Greeks* (1999). A valuable survey from early times through the fifth century B.C.E.

R. SALLARES, *The Ecology of the Ancient Greek World* (1991). A valuable study of the Greeks and their environment.

D. M. SCHAPS, *Economic Rights of Women in Ancient Greece* (1981). Exploration of the economic conditions of ordinary free Greek women.

B. STRAUSS, *The Battle of Salamis: The Naval Encounter That Saved Greece—and Western Civilization* (2004). A lively account of the great Persian invasion of Greece.

C. G. THOMAS AND C. CONANT, *Citadel to City-State: The Transformation of Greece, 1200–700 B.C.E.* (1999). A good account of Greece's emergence from the Dark Ages into the world of the *polis*.

H. VAN WEES, *Greek Warfare: Myths and Realities* (2004). An account of Greek fighting that challenges traditional understandings.

Chapter 3

J. BUCKLER, *Aegean Greece in the Fourth Century BC* (2003). A political, diplomatic, and military history of the Aegean Greeks of the fourth century B.C.E.

W. BURKERT, *Greek Religion* (1985). A fine general study.

P. CARTLEDGE, *Alexander the Great: The Hunt for a New Past* (2004). A learned and lively biography.

P. CARTLEDGE, *Spartan Reflections* (2001). A collection of valuable essays by a leading scholar of ancient Sparta.

G. CAWKWELL, *Philip of Macedon* (1978). A brief but learned account of Philip's career.

Y. GARLAN, *Slavery in Ancient Greece* (1988). An up-to-date survey.

R. GARLAND, *Daily Life of the Ancient Greeks* (1998). A good account of the way the Greeks lived.

P. GREEN, *From Alexander to Actium* (1990). A brilliant synthesis of the Hellenistic period.

P. GREEN, *The Greco-Persian War* (1996). A lively account by a fine scholar with a keen feeling for the terrain.

E. S. GRUEN, *Heritage and Hellenism: The Reinvention of Jewish Tradition* (1998). A fine account of the interaction between Jews and Greeks in Hellenistic times.

C. D. HAMILTON, *Agesilaus and the Failure of Spartan Hegemony* (1991). An excellent biography of the king who was the central figure in Sparta during its domination in the fourth century B.C.E.

R. JUST, *Women in Athenian Law and Life* (1988). A good study of the place of women in Athenian life.

D. KAGAN, *The Peloponnesian War* (2003). An analytic narrative of the great war between Athens and Sparta.

D. KAGAN, *Pericles of Athens and the Birth of Athenian Democracy* (1991). An account of the life and times of the great Athenian statesman.

B. M. W. KNOX, *The Heroic Temper: Studies in Sophoclean Tragedy* (1964). A brilliant analysis of tragic heroism.

D. M. LEWIS, *Sparta and Persia* (1977). A valuable discussion of relations between Sparta and Persia in the fifth and fourth centuries B.C.E.

C. B. PATTERSON, *The Family in Greek History* (1998). An interesting interpretation of the relationship between family and state in ancient Greece.

J. J. POLLITT, *Art and Experience in Classical Greece* (1972). A scholarly and entertaining study of the relationship between art and history in Classical Greece, with excellent illustrations.

J. J. POLLITT, *Art in the Hellenistic Age* (1986). An extraordinary analysis that places the art in its historical and intellectual context.

R. W. SHARPLES, *Stoics, Epicureans, and Sceptics. An Introduction to Hellenistic Philosophy* (1996). A brief and useful introduction.

B. S. STRAUSS, *Athens after the Peloponnesian War* (1987). An excellent discussion of Athens's recovery and of the nature of Athenian society and politics in the fourth century B.C.E.

I. WORTHINGTON, *Demosthenes, Statesman and Orator* (2000). A useful collection of essays on the career and importance of the Athenian political leader.

Chapter 4

G. BARKER AND T. RASMUSSEN, *The Etruscans* (2000). A valuable new study of a mysterious people.

R. BAUMANN, *Women and Politics in Ancient Rome* (1995). A study of the role of women in Roman public life.

A. H. BERNSTEIN, *Tiberius Sempronius Gracchus: Tradition and Apostasy* (1978). An interpretation of Tiberius's place in Roman politics.

T. J. CORNELL, *The Beginnings of Rome: Italy and Rome from the Bronze Age to the Punic Wars* (1995). A fine new study of early Rome.

T. CORNELL AND J. MATTHEWS, *Atlas of the Roman World* (1982). Presents a comprehensive view of the Roman world in its physical and cultural setting.

J-M. DAVID, *The Roman Conquest of Italy* (1997). A good analysis of how Rome united Italy.

E. S. GRUEN, *The Hellenistic World and the Coming of Rome* (1984). A new interpretation of Rome's conquest of the eastern Mediterranean.

W. V. HARRIS, *War and Imperialism in Republican Rome, 327–70 B.C.E.* (1975). An analysis of Roman attitudes and intentions concerning imperial expansion and war.

T. HOLLAND, *Rubicon: The Last Years of the Roman Republic* (2004). A lively account of the fall of the republic.

S. LANCEL, *Carthage, A History* (1995). A good account of Rome's great competitor.

H. MOURITSEN, *Plebs and Politics in the Late Roman Republic* (2001). A new study of Roman republican politics and the place of the common people in them.

J. POWELL AND J. PATTERSON, *Cicero the Advocate* (2004). A careful study of the Roman statesman's legal career.

H. H. SCULLARD, *A History of the Roman World 753–146 B.C.E.*, 4th ed. (1980). An unusually fine narrative history with useful critical notes.

Chapter 5

W. BALL, *Rome in the East* (2000). A study of the eastern parts of the empire and how they interacted with the West.

A. A. BARRETT, *Livia: First Lady of Imperial Rome* (2004). Biography of Augustus's powerful and controversial wife.

P. BROWN, *The Rise of Western Christendom: Triumph and Diversity, 200–1000*, 2nd ed. (2003). A vivid picture of the spread of Christianity by a master of the field.

A. FERRILL, *The Fall of the Roman Empire, The Military Explanation* (1986). An interpretation that emphasizes the decline in the quality of the Roman army.

K. GALINSKY, *Augustan Culture* (1996). A work that integrates art, literature, and politics.

E. GIBBON, *The History of the Decline and Fall of the Roman Empire*, 2nd ed. 7 vols., ed. by J. B. Bury (1909–1914). A masterwork of the English language.

D. JOHNSTON, *Roman Law in Context* (2000). Places Rome's law in the context of its economy and society.

D. KAGAN, ED., *The End of the Roman Empire: Decline or Transformation?*, 3rd ed. (1992). A collection of essays on the problems of the decline and fall of the Roman Empire.

C. KELLY, *Ruling the Later Roman Empire* (2004). A study of the complexities of Roman government in the last centuries of the empire.

J. LENDON, *Empire of Honour: The Art of Government in the Roman World* (1997). A brilliant study that reveals how an aristocratic code of honor led the upper classes to cooperate in Roman rule.

R. W. MATHISON, *Roman Aristocrats in Barbarian Gaul: Strategies for Survival* (1993). An unusual slant on the late empire.

S. MATTERN, *Rome and the Enemy: Imperial Strategy in the Principate* (1999). A study of Rome's foreign and imperial policy under the Principate.

F. G. B. MILLAR, *The Emperor in the Roman World, 31 B.C.–A.D. 337* (1977). A study of Roman imperial government.

H. M. D. PARKER, *A History of the Roman World from A.D. 138 to 337* (1969). A good survey.

D. S. POTTER, *The Roman Empire at Bay: A.D. 180–395* (2004). An account of the challenges to Rome in the third and fourth centuries and how the Romans tried to meet them.

M. I. ROSTOVTZEFF, *Social and Economic History of the Roman Empire*, 2nd ed. (1957). A masterpiece whose main thesis is much disputed.

V. RUDICH, *Political Dissidence under Nero, The Price of Dissimulation* (1993). A brilliant exposition of the lives and thoughts of political dissidents in the early empire.

G. E. M. DE STE. CROIX, *The Class Struggle in the Ancient World* (1981). An ambitious interpretation of all of classical civilization from a Marxist perspective.

R. SYME, *The Roman Revolution* (1960). A brilliant study of Augustus, his supporters, and their rise to power.

Chapter 6

K. ARMSTRONG, *Muhammad: A Biography of the Prophet* (1992). Substantial popular biography.

G. BARRACLOUGH, *The Origins of Modern Germany* (1963). Originally published in 1946 and still the best survey of medieval Germany.

R. BARTLETT, *The Making of Europe* (1993). How migration and colonization created Europe.

G. W. BOWERSOCK ET AL., *Interpreting Late Antiquity: Essays on the Postclassical World* (2001). Introductory essays presenting a unified interpretation of the centuries between 250 C.E. and 800 C.E.

P. BROWN, *Augustine of Hippo: A Biography* (1967). Late antiquity seen through the biography of its greatest Christian thinker.

P. BROWN ET AL., EDS., *The Rise of Western Christendom: Triumph and Diversity* (1997). Sweeping, detailed summary.

VIRGINIA BURRUS, ED., *A Peoples' History of Christianity, II* (2005). Substantial and accessible.

R. COLLINS, *Charlemagne* (1998). Latest biography.

J. W. CURRIER, *Clovis, King of the Franks* (1997). Biography of founder of first Frankish dynasty.

F. L. GANSHOF, *Feudalism* (1964). The most profound brief analysis of the subject.

P. GODMAN ET AL., EDS., *Charlemagne's Heir: New Perspectives on Louis the Pious (814–40)* (1990). Latest research on the king whose divided kingdom set the boundaries of modern Europe.

S. GUTHRIE, *Arab Social Life in the Middle Ages* (1995). How Arab society holds itself together.

A. HOURANI, *A History of the Arab Peoples* (1991). Comprehensive with overviews of the origins and early history of Islam.

B. LEWIS, *The Middle East: A Brief History of the Last 2,000 Years* (1995). An authoritative overview.

R. MCKITTERICK, ED., *Carolingian Culture: Emulation and Innovation* (1994). The culture from which Western Europe was born.

R. J. MORRISSEY, *Charlemagne and France: A 1000 Years of Mythology* (2002). The European argument over who owns Charlemagne.

J. J. NORRIS, *Byzantium: The Decline and Fall* (1995). The final volume in an essential three-volume history of Byzantium.

P. RICHE, *The Carolingians: A Family Who Forged Europe* (1993). Readable account of the dynasty from start to finish.

P. SAWYER, *Kings and Vikings: Scandinavia and Europe A.D. 700–1100* (1994). Raiding Vikings and their impact on Europe.

W. WALTHER, *Woman in Islam* (1981). One hour spent with this book teaches more about the social import of Islam than days spent with others.

Chapter 7

J. W. BALDWIN, *The Government of Philip Augustus* (1986). The standard work.

S. FLANAGAN, *Hildegard of Bingen, 1098–1179: A Visionary Life* (1998). Latest biography of a powerful religious woman.

S. D. GOITEIN, *Letters of Medieval Jewish Traders* (1973). Rare first-person accounts.

E. M. HALLAM, *Capetian France 987–1328* (1980). Good on politics and heretics.

J. C. HOLT, *Magna Carta*, 2nd ed. (1992). Succeeding generations interpret the famous document.

K. LEYSER, *Medieval Germany and Its Neighbors, 900–1250* (1982). Basic and authoritative.

H. E. MAYER, *The Crusades*, trans. by John Gilligham (1972). The best one-volume account.

W. MELCZER, *The Pilgrim's Guide to Santiago de Compostela* (1993). Do's and dont's, and what the medieval pilgrim might expect along the way.

C. MORIARITY, ED., *The Voice of the Middle Ages: In Personal Letters, 1100–1500* (1989). Rare first-person accounts.

J. B. MORRALL, *Political Thought in Medieval Times* (1962). Readable, elucidating account.

J. RICHARD, *Saint Louis: Crusader King of France* (1992). Biography of Louis IX and an exploration of the mental, political, and religious world of the thirteenth century.

J. RILEY-SMITH, *The Oxford Illustrated History of the Crusades* (1995). Sweeping account.

C. TYERMAN, *Fighting for Christendom* (2004). Brief and accessible.

Chapter 8

E. AMT, ED., *Women's Lives in Medieval Europe: A Sourcebook* (1993). Outstanding collection of sources.

P. ARIES, *Centuries of Childhood: A Social History of Family Life* (1962). Influential pioneer effort on the subject.

J. W. BALDWIN, *The Scholastic Culture of the Middle Ages: 1000–1300* (1971). Good brief synthesis.

M. BLACK, *The Medieval Cookbook* (1992). Dishing it up in the Middle Ages.

M. T. CLANCHY, *Abelard: A Medieval Life* (1998). The biography of the famous philosopher and seducer of Héloïse.

L. GRANE, *Peter Abelard: Philosophy and Christianity in the Middle Ages* (1970). Places Abelard in his philosophieal and theological context.

B. A. HANAWALT, *Growing Up in Medieval London* (1993). Positive portrayal of parental and societal treatment of children.

D. HERLIHY, *Women, Family, and Society in Medieval Europe: Historical Essays, 1978–91* (1995). A major historian's collected essays.

A. HOPKINS, *Knights* (1990). Europe's warriors and models.

D. KRUEGER, ED., *Byzantine Christianity* (2006).

E. MALE, *The Gothic Image: Religious Art in France in the Thirteenth Century* (1913). An enduring classic.

L. DE MAUSE, ED., *The History of Childhood* (1974). Substantial essays on the inner as well as the material lives of children.

R. I. MOORE, *The Formation of a Persecuting Society: Power and Deviance in Western Europe, 950–1250* (1987). A sympathetic look at heresy and dissent.

J. T. NOONAN, *Contraception: A History of Its Treatment by the Catholic Theologians and Canonists* (1967). Fascinating account of medieval theologians' take on sex.

S. OZMENT, *Ancestors: The Loving Family in Old Europe* (2001). A sympathetic look at families past.

S. SHAHAR, *The Fourth Estate: A History of Women in the Middle Ages* (1983). A comprehensive survey, making clear the great variety of women's work.

Chapter 9

C. ALLMAND, *The Hundred Years' War: England and France at War, c. 1300–c. 1450* (1988). Overview of the war's development and consequences.

P. R. BACKSCHEIDER ET AL., EDS., *A Journal of the Plague Year* (1992). The Black Death at ground level.

R. BARBER, ED., *The Pastons: Letters of a Family in the War of the Roses* (1984). Rare revelations of English family life in an age of crisis.

E. H. GILLETT ET AL., *Life and Times of John Huss: The Bohemian Reformation of the Fifteenth Century* (2001). The latest biography.

J. HUIZINGA, *The Waning of the Middle Ages: A Study of the Forms of Life, Thought, and Art in France and the Netherlands in the Dawn of the Renaissance* (1924). Exaggerated, but engrossing study of mentality at the end of the Middle Ages.

P. KAHN ET AL., *Secret History of the Mongols: The Origins of Ghingis Kahn* (1998). Introduction to the greatest Mongol ruler.

S. OZMENT, *The Age of Reform, 1250–1550* (1980). Highlights of late medieval intellectual and religious history.

E. PERROY, *The Hundred Years' War*, trans. by W. B. Wells (1965). Still the most comprehensive one-volume account.

M. SPINKA, *John Huss's Concept of the Church* (1966). Lucid account of Hussite theology.

W. R. TRASK, ED./TRANS., *Joan of Arc in Her Own Words* (1996). Joan's interrogation and self-defense.

P. ZIEGLER, *The Black Death* (1969). Highly readable account.

Chapter 10

D. ABULAFIA, *The Discovery of Mankind: Atlantic Encounters in the Age of Columbus* (2008). Emphasizes contact between peoples in its exploration of European colonization of the Americas.

L. B. ALBERTI, *The Family in Renaissance Florence*, trans. by R. N. Watkins (1962). A contemporary humanist, who never married, explains how a family should behave.

K. ATCHITY, ED., *The Renaissance Reader* (1996). The Renaissance in its own words.

H. BARON, *The Crisis of the Early Italian Renaissance*, vols. 1 and 2 (1966). A major work on the civic dimension of Italian humanism.

G. A. BRUCKER, *Giovanni and Lusanna: Love and Marriage in Renaissance Florence* (1986). Love in the Renaissance shown to be more Bergman than Fellini.

J. BURCKHARDT, *The Civilization of the Renaissance in Italy* (1958). Modern edition of an old nineteenth-century classic that still has as many defenders as detractors.

R. E. CONRAD, *Children of God's Fire: A Documentary History of Black Slavery in Brazil* (1983). Not for the squeamish.

L. HANKE, *Bartholomé de Las Casas: An Interpretation of His Life and Writings* (1951). Biography of the great Dominican critic of Spanish exploitation of Native Americans.

J. HANKINS, *Plato in the Renaissance* (1992). A magisterial study of how Plato was read and interpreted by Renaissance scholars.

D. HERLIHY AND C. KLAPISCH-ZUBER, *Tuscans and Their Families* (1985). Important work based on unique demographic data that give the reader a new appreciation of quantitative history.

J. C. HUTCHISON, *Albrecht Dürer: A Biography* (1990). A solid biography of the German artist.

L. MARTINES, *Power and Imagination: City States in Renaissance Italy* (1980). Stimulating account of cultural and political history.

S. E. MORRISON, *Admiral of the Ocean Sea: A Life of Christopher Columbus* (1946). Still the best Columbus read.

E. PANOFSKY, *Meaning in the Visual Arts* (1955). Eloquent treatment of Renaissance art.

J. H. PARRY, *The Age of Reconnaissance* (1964). A comprehensive account of exploration in the years 1450 to 1650.

I. A. RICHTER, ED., *The Notebooks of Leonardo da Vinci* (1985). The master in his own words.

A. WHEATCROFT, *The Habsburgs* (1995). The dynasty that ruled the center of late medieval and early modern Europe.

C. C. WILLARD, *Christine de Pizan* (1984). Demonstration of what an educated woman could accomplish in the Renaissance.

Chapter 11

H. BLOOM, *Shakespeare: The Invention of the Human* (1998). An analysis of the greatest writer in the English language.

T. A. BRADY, JR., ED., *Handbook of European History: Late Middle Ages, Renaissance, Reformation* (1995). Essays summarizing recent research on aspects of the Reformation.

P. COLLINSON, *The Reformation* (2004). Portrays the Reformation as creating religious pluralism and civil liberty despite itself.

E. DUFFY, *The Stripping of the Altars: Traditional Religion in England, 1400–1580* (1992). Strongest of recent arguments that popular piety survived the Reformation in England.

M. DURAN, *Cervantes* (1974). Detailed biography.

B. S. GREGORY, *Salvation at Stake: Christian Martyrdom in Early Modern Europe* (1999). Massive, enthralling study of religion.

R. HOULBROOKE, *English Family Life, 1450–1716. An Anthology from Diaries* (1988). A rich collection of documents illustrating family relationships.

J. C. HUTCHISON, *Albrecht Dürer: A Biography* (1990). An art historian chronicles both the life and work of the artist.

H. JEDIN, *A History of the Council of Trent*, vols. 1 and 2 (1957–1961). Still the gold standard.

P. JOHNSTON AND R. W. SCRIBNER, *The Reformation in Germany and Switzerland* (1993). Reformation from the bottom up.

D. MACCOLLOCH, *The Reformation* (2004). Finds old Catholics and non-Protestant Evangelicals to be the forerunners of modern religion.

H. A. OBERMAN, *Luther: Man between God and the Devil* (1989). Perhaps the best account of Luther's life, by a Dutch master.

J. O'MALLEY, *The First Jesuits* (1993). Detailed account of the creation of the Society of Jesus and its original purposes.

S. OZMENT, *The Age of Reform, 1250–1550: An Intellectual and Religious History of Late Medieval and Reformation Europe* (1980). A broad survey of major religious ideas and beliefs.

B. ROBERTS, *Through the Keyhole: Dutch Child-Rearing Practices in the 17th and 18th Centuries* (1998). A study of three elite families.

Q. SKINNER, *The Foundations of Modern Political Thought II: The Age of Reformation* (1978). A comprehensive survey that treats every political thinker and tract.

D. STARKEY, *Elizabeth: The Struggle for the Throne* (2000). Details the early years of Elizabeth's life.

L. STONE, *The Family, Sex, and Marriage in England 1500–1800* (1977). Controversial, but enduring in many respects.

G. STRAUSS, ED. AND TRANS., *Manifestations of Discontent in Germany on the Eve of the Reformation* (1971). Rich collection of both rural and urban sources.

F. WENDEL, *Calvin: The Origins and Development of His Religious Thought*, trans. by P. Mairet (1963). The best treatment of Calvin's theology.

H. WUNDER, *He Is the Sun, She Is the Moon: A History of Women in Early Modern Germany* (1998). A model of gender history.

Chapter 12

F. BRAUDEL, *The Mediterranean and the Mediterranean World in the Age of Philip the Second*, vols. 1 and 2 (1976). Widely acclaimed "big picture" by a master historian.

N. Z. DAVIS, *Society and Culture in Early Modern France* (1975). Essays on popular culture.

R. DUNN, *The Age of Religious Wars, 1559–1689* (1979). Excellent brief survey of every major conflict.

J. H. FRANKLIN, ED. AND TRANS., *Constitutionalism and Resistance in the Sixteenth Century: Three Treatises by Hotman, Beza, and Mornay* (1969). Three defenders of the right to resist tyranny.

J. GUY, *Tudor England* (1990). The standard history and a good synthesis of recent scholarship.

D. LOADES, *Mary Tudor* (1989). Authoritative and good storytelling.

G. MATTINGLY, *The Armada* (1959). A masterpiece resembling a novel in style.

J. E. NEALE, *The Age of Catherine de Médicis* (1962). Short, concise summary.

A. SOMAN, ED., *The Massacre of St. Bartholomew's Day: Reappraisals and Documents* (1974). Essays from an international symposium on the anniversary of the massacre.

C. WEDGWOOD, *William the Silent* (1944). Eloquent political biography of William of Orange.

A. B. WEIR, *The Life of Elizabeth I* (1998). Detailed portrayal of a successful ruler.

J. WORMALD, *Mary, Queen of Scots: A Study in Failure* (1991). Mary portrayed as out of touch with her country and her times.

Chapter 13

W. BEIK, *Louis XIV and Absolutism: A Brief Study with Documents* (2000). An excellent collection by a major scholar of absolutism.

T. Blanning, *The Pursuit of Glory: Europe 1648–1815* (2007). The best recent synthesis of the emergence of the modern European state system.

J. BREWER, *The Sinews of Power: War, Money and the English State, 1688–1783* (1989). An important study of the financial basis of English power.

P. BURKE, *The Fabrication of Louis XIV* (1992). Examines how Louis XIV used art to forge his public image.

C. CLARK, *The Rise and Downfall of Prussia 1600–1947* (2006). A stunning survey.

R. CUST, *Charles I* (2007). The definitive biography.

P. COLLINSON, *The Religion of Protestants: The Church in English Society, 1559–1625* (1982). Remains the best introduction to Puritanism.

N. DAVIS, *God's Playground: A History of Poland: The Origins to 1795* (2005). The recent revision of a classic survey.

J. DE VRIES AND A. VAN DER WOUDE, *The First Modern Economy* (1997). Compares Holland to other European nations.

P. G. DWYER, *The Rise of Prussia 1700–1830* (2002). An excellent collection of essays.

S. FAROQHI, *The Ottoman Empire and the World Around It* (2006). Emphasizes the various interactions of the empire with both Asian and European powers.

R. I. FROST, *The Northern Wars: War, State and Society in Northeastern Europe, 1558–1721* (2000) A survey of an often neglected subject.

D. GOFFMAN, *The Ottoman Empire and Early Modern Europe* (2002). An accessible introduction to a complex subject.

T. HARRIS, *Restoration: Charles II and His Kingdom, 1660–1685* (2006). A major exploration of the tumultuous years of the restoration of the English monarchy after the civil war.

L. HUGHES, *Russia in the Age of Peter the Great* (2000). A major overview of the history and society of Peter's time.

C. IMBER, *The Ottoman Empire, 1300–1650: The Structure of Power* (2003). A sweeping analysis based on a broad range of sources.

C. J. INGRAO, *The Habsburg Monarchy, 1618–1815* (2000). The best recent survey.

J. I. ISRAEL, *The Dutch Republic: Its Rise, Greatness, and Fall, 1477–1806* (1995). The major work of the subject.

M. KISHLANSKY, *A Monarchy Transformed: Britain, 1603–1714* (1996). An important overview.

J. A. LYNN, *The Wars of Louis XIV* (1999). The best recent treatment.

J. LUKOWSKI AND H. ZAWADZKI, *A Concise History of Poland* (2006). A straightforward survey.

D. MCKAY, *The Great Elector: Frederick William of Brandenburg–Prussia* (2001). An account of the origins of Prussian power.

P. K. MONOD, *The Power of Kings: Monarchy and Religion in Europe, 1589–1715* (1999). An important and innovative examination of the roots of royal authority as early modern Europe became modern Europe.

G. PARKER, *The Military Revolution: Military Innovation and the Rise of the West (1500–1800)* (1988). A classic work on the impact of military matters on the emergence of centralized monarchies.

H. PHILLIPS, *Church and Culture in Seventeenth-Century France* (1997). A clear examination of the major religious issues confronting France and their relationship to the larger culture.

S. PINCUS, *England's Glorious Revolution 1688–1689: A Brief History with Documents* (2005). A useful collection by an outstanding historian of the subject.

G. TREASURE, *Louis XIV* (2001). The best, most accessible recent study.

Chapter 14

R. ASHCRAFT, *Revolutionary Politics and Locke's Two Treatises of Government* (1986). A major study emphasizing the radical side of Locke's thought.

J. BARRY, M. HESTER, AND G. ROBERTS, EDS., *Witchcraft in Early Modern Europe: Studies in Culture and Belief* (1998). A collection of recent essays.

M. BIAGIOLI, *Galileo Courtier: The Practice of Science in the Culture of Absolutism* (1993). A major revisionist work.

J. A. CONNER, *Kepler's Witch: An Astronomer's Discovery of Cosmic Order Amid Religious War, Political Intrigue, and the Heresy Trial of His Mother* (2005). Fascinating account of Kepler's effort to vindicate his mother against charges of witchcraft.

P. DEAR, *Revolutionizing the Sciences: European Knowledge and Its Ambitions, 1500–1700* (2001). A broad-ranging study of both the ideas and institutions of the new science.

M. FEINGOLD, *The Newtonian Moment: Isaac Newton and the Making of Modern Culture* (2004). A superb, well-illustrated volume.

S. GAUKROGER, *The Emergence of a Scientific Culture: Science and the Shaping of Modernity* (2007). A challenging book exploring the differing understanding of natural knowledge in early modern European culture.

S. GAUKROGER, *Francis Bacon and the Transformation of Early-Modern Philosophy* (2001). An excellent, accessible introduction.

J. GLEIK, *Isaac Newton* (2003). Highly accessible to the general reader.

I. HARRIS, *The Mind of John Locke: A Study of Political Theory in Its Intellectual Setting* (1994). The most comprehensive recent treatment.

J. L. HEILBRON, *The Sun in the Church: Cathedrals as Solar Observatories* (2000). Explores uses made of Roman Catholic cathedrals to make astronomical observations.

K. J. HOWELL, *God's Two Books: Copernican Cosmology and Biblical Interpretation in Early Modern Science* (2002). The clearest discussion of this important subject.

L. JARDINE, *Ingenious Pursuits: Building the Scientific Revolution* (1999). A lively exploration of the interface of personalities, new knowledge, and English society.

A. C. KORS AND E. PETERS, EDS., *European Witchcraft, 1100–1700* (1972). Classics of witch belief.

T. S. KUHN, *The Copernican Revolution: Planetary Astronomy in the Development of Western Thought* (1957). Remains the classic work.

B. LEVACK, *The Witch Hunt in Early Modern Europe* (1986). Lucid survey.

P. MACHAMER, ED., *The Cambridge Companion to Galileo* (1998). Essays that aid the understanding of the entire spectrum of the new science.

J. MARSHALL, *John Locke, Toleration and Early Enlightenment Culture* (2006). A magisterial and challenging survey of the background of seventeenth-century arguments for and against toleration.

J. R. MARTIN, *Baroque* (1977). A classic introduction to baroque art.

M. OSLER, *Rethinking the Scientific Revolution* (2000). A collection of revisionist essays particularly exploring issues of the interrelationship of the new science and religion.

R. POPKIN, *The History of Scepticism: From Savonarola to Bayle* (2003). A classic study of the fear of loss of intellectual certainty.

L. PYENSON AND S. SHEETS-PYENSON, *Servants of Nature: A History of Scientific Institutions, Enterprises, and Sensibilities* (1999). A history of the settings in which the creation and diffusion of scientific knowledge have occurred.

J. REPCHECK, *Copernicus' Secret: How the Scientific Revolution Began* (2007). A highly accessible biography of Copernicus.

L. SCHIEBINGER, *The Mind Has No Sex? Women in the Origins of Modern Science* (1989). A major study of the subject.

S. SHAPIN, *The Scientific Revolution* (1996). A readable brief introduction.

W. R. SHEA AND M. ARTIGAS, *Galileo in Rome: The Rise and Fall of a Troublesome Genius* (2003). Argues that Galileo in part brought about his own condemnation.

T. SORELL, *The Cambridge Companion to Hobbes* (1994). Excellent essays on the major themes of Hobbes's thought.

Chapter 15

J. BLUM, *Lord and Peasant in Russia from the Ninth to the Nineteenth Century* (1961). Remains a classic discussion.

J. BURNET, *Gender, Work and Wages in Industrial Revolution Britain* (2008). A major revisionist study of the wage structure for work by men and women.

P. M. DEANE, *The First Industrial Revolution* (1999). A well-balanced and systematic treatment.

P. EARLE, *The Making of the English Middle Class: Business, Community, and Family Life in London, 1660–1730* (1989). The most careful study of the subject.

M. W. FLINN, *The European Demographic System, 1500–1820* (1981). Remains a major summary.

E. HOBSBAWM, *Industry and Empire: The Birth of the Industrial Revolution* (1999). A survey by a major historian of the subject.

K. HONEYMAN, *Women, Gender and Industrialization in England, 1700–1850* (2000). Emphasizes how certain work or economic roles became associated with either men or women.

O. H. HUFTON, *The Poor of Eighteenth-Century France, 1750–1789* (1975). A brilliant study of poverty and the family economy.

A. KAHAN, *The Plow, the Hammer, and the Knout: An Economic History of Eighteenth-Century Russia* (1985). An extensive and detailed treatment.

D. I. KERTZER AND M. BARBAGLI, *The History of the European Family: Family Life in Early Modern Times, 1500–1709* (2001). Broad-ranging essays covering the entire Continent.

S. KING AND G. TIMMONS, *Making Sense of the Industrial Revolution: English Economy and Society, 1700–1850* (2001). Examines the Industrial Revolution through the social institutions that brought it about and were changed by it.

F. E. MANUEL, *The Broken Staff: Judaism Through Christian Eyes* (1992). An important discussion of Christian interpretations of Judaism.

K. MORGAN, *The Birth of Industrial Britain: Social Change, 1750–1850* (2004). A useful brief overview.

M. OVERTON, *Agricultural Revolution in England: The Transformation of the Agrarian Economy, 1500–1850* (1996). A highly accessible treatment.

J. R. RUFF, *Violence in Early Modern Europe 1500–1800* (2001). An excellent survey of an important and disturbing topic.

P. STEARNS, *The Industrial Revolution in World History* (2007). A broad interpretive account.

D. VALENZE, *The First Industrial Woman* (1995). An elegant, penetrating volume.

E. A. WRIGLEY, *Continuity, Chance and Change: The Character of the Industrial Revolution in England* (1994). A major conceptual reassessment.

Chapter 16

F. ANDERSON, *Crucible of War: The Seven Years' War and the Fate of Empire in British North America, 1754–1766* (2001). A splendid narrative account.

B. BAILYN, *The Ideological Origins of the American Revolution* (1992). An important work illustrating the role of English radical thought in the perceptions of the colonists.

C. A. BAYLY, *Imperial Meridian: The British Empire and the World, 1780–1830* (1989). A major study of the empire after the loss of America.

I. BERLIN, *Many Thousands Gone: The First Two Centuries of Slavery in North America* (1998). The most extensive recent treatment emphasizing the differences in the slave economy during different decades.

R. BLACKBURN, *The Making of New World Slavery from the Baroque to the Modern, 1492–1800* (1997). An extraordinary work.

M. A. BURKHOLDER AND L. L. JOHNSON, *Colonial Latin America* (2004). A standard synthesis.

L. COLLEY, *Britons: Forging the Nation, 1707–1837* (1992). Important discussions of the recovery from the loss of America.

D. B. DAVIS, *Inhuman Bondage: The Rise and Fall of Slavery in the New World* (2006). A splendid overview by a leading scholar.

D. B. DAVIS, *The Problem of Slavery in the Age of Revolution, 1770–1823* (1975). A major work on both European and American history.

J. ELLIOTT, *Empires of the Atlantic: Britain and Spain in America 1492–l830* (2006). A brilliant and accessible comparative history.

J. J. ELLIS, *His Excellency: George Washington* (2004). A biography that explores the entire era of the American Revolution.

R. HARMS, *The Diligent: A Voyage through the Worlds of the Slave Trade* (2002). A powerful narrative of the voyage of a French slave trader.

H. S. KLEIN, *The Atlantic Slave Trade* (1999). A succinct synthesis based on recent literature.

P. LANGFORD, *A Polite and Commercial People: England, 1717–1783* (1989). An excellent survey covering social history, politics, the overseas wars, and the American Revolution.

P. MAIER, *American Scripture: Making the Declaration of Independence* (1997). Replaces previous works on the subject.

A. PAGDEN, *Lords of All World: Ideologies of Empire in Spain, Britain, and France, 1492–1830* (1995). One of the few comparative studies of the empires during this period.

M. REDIKER, *The Slave Ship: A Human History* (2007). An exploration of the harrowing experience of slave transportation across the Atlantic.

M. REDIKER, *Villains of All Nations: Atlantic Pirates in the Golden Age* (2008). A serious historical treatment of the subject.

J. THORNTON, *Africa and the Africans in the Making of the Atlantic World, 1400–1800*, 2nd ed. (1998). A discussion of the role of Africans in the emergence of the transatlantic economy.

J. WINIK, *The Great Upheaval: America and the Birth of the Modern World, 1788–1800* (2007). Sets the founding of the American republic in a transatlantic political context.

G. S. WOOD, *The American Revolution: A History* (2002). A major interpretation.

Chapter 17

D. D. BIEN, *The Calas Affair: Persecution, Toleration, and Heresy in Eighteenth-Century Toulouse* (1960). The standard treatment of the famous case.

T. C. W. BLANNING, *The Culture of Power and the Power of Culture: Old Regime Europe 1660–1789* (2002). A remarkable synthesis of the interaction of political power and culture in France, Prussia, and Austria.

P. BLOOM, *Enlightening the World: Encyclopedie, The Book That Changed the Course of History* (2005). A lively, accessible introduction.

J. BUCHAN, *Crowded with Genius: The Scottish Enlightenment* (2003). A lively, accessible introduction.

L. DAMROSCH, *Rousseau: Restless Genius* (2007). The best recent biography.

I. DE MADARIAGA, *Russia in the Age of Catherine the Great* (1981). The best discussion in English.

S. FEINER, *The Jewish Enlightenment* (2002). An extensive, challenging pan-European treatment of the subject.

P. GAY, *The Enlightenment: An Interpretation*, 2 vols. (1966, 1969). A classic.

D. GOODMAN, *The Republic of Letters: A Cultural History of the French Enlightenment* (1994). Concentrates on the role of salons.

C. HESSE, *The Other Enlightenment: How French Women Became Modern* (2004). Explores the manner in which French women authors created their own sphere of thought and cultural actiavity.

J. ISRAEL, *Enlightenment Contested: Philosophy, Modernity, and the Emancipation of Man 1670–1752* (2006). A challenging major revisionist history of the subject.

J. I. ISRAEL, *Radical Enlightenment: Philosophy and the Making of Modernity* (2001). A controversial account of the most radical strains of thought in Enlightenment culture.

C. A. KORS, *Encyclopedia of the Enlightenment* (2002). A major reference work on all of the chief intellectual themes of the era.

J. P. LEDONNE, *The Russian Empire and the World, 1700–1917* (1996). Explores the major reasons for Russian expansion from the eighteenth to the early twentieth centuries.

G. MACDONAGH, *Frederick the Great* (2001). A thoughtful and accessible biography.

D. MACMAHON, *Enemies of the Enlightenment: The French Counter-Enlightenment and the Making of Modernity* (2001). A fine exploration of French writers critical of the *philosophes*.

J. V. H. MELTON, *The Rise of the Public in Enlightenment Europe* (2001). Explores the social basis of print culture with an excellent bibliography.

S. MUTHU, *Enlightenment Against Empire* (2003). A challenging volume covering the critique of the empire.

R. PEASON, *Voltaire Almighty: A Life in Pursuit of Freedom* (2005). An accessible biography

R. PORTER, *The Creation of the Modern World: The Untold Story of the British Enlightenment* (2000). Seeks to shift the center of the Enlightenment from France to England.

P. RILEY, *The Cambridge Companion to Rousseau* (2001). Excellent accessible essays by major scholars.

E. ROTHCHILD, *Economic Sentiments: Adam Smith, Condorcet, and the Enlightenment* (2001). A sensitive account of Smith's thought and its relationship to the social questions of the day.

J. SHEEHAN, *The Enlightenment Bible* (2007). Explores the Enlightenment treatment of the Bible.

S. SMITH, *Spinoza, Liberalism, and the Question of Jewish Identity* (1997). A clear introduction to a challenging thinker.

A. M. WILSON, *Diderot* (1972). A splendid biography of the person behind the *Encyclopedia* and other major Enlightenment publications.

L. WOLFF, *Inventing Eastern Europe: The Map of Civilization on the Mind of the Enlightenment* (1994). A remarkable study of how Enlightenment writers recast the understanding of this part of the Continent.

Chapter 18

D. ANDRESS, *The Terror: The Merciless War for Freedom in Revolutionary France* (2006). The best recent survey of the reign of terror.

N. ASTON, *Christianity and Revolutionary Europe c. 1750–1830* (2002). Continent-wide survey of the impact of revolution on religion.

T. C. BLANNING, *The Revolutionary Wars, 1787–1802* (1996). Essential for understanding the role of the army and the revolution.

S. DESAN, *The Family on Trial in Revolutionary France* (2004). An important analysis of how the revolution impacted French domestic life.

W. DOYLE, *The Oxford History of the French Revolution* (2003). A broad, complex narrative with an excellent bibliography.

A. FORREST, *Revolutionary Paris, the Provinces and the French Revolution* (2004). A clear presentation of the tensions between the center of the revolution and the provinces.

C. HAYDEN AND W. DOYLE, EDS., *Robespierre* (1999). Essays evaluating Robespierre's ideas, career, and reputation.

P. HIGONNET, *Goodness beyond Virtue: Jacobins During the French Revolution* (1998). An outstanding work that clearly relates political values to political actions.

D. JORDON, *The King's Trial: Louis XVI vs. the French Revolution* (1979). A gripping account of the event.

E. KENNEDY, *A Cultural History of the French Revolution* (1989). An important examination of the role of the arts, schools, clubs, and intellectual institutions.

S. E. MELZER AND L. W. RABINE, EDS., *Rebel Daughters: Women and the French Revolution* (1997). Essays exploring the role and image of women in the revolution.

S. Neely, *A Concise History of the French Revolution* (2008). The best of the numerous brief accounts.

C. C. O'Brien, *The Great Melody: A Thematic Biography of Edmund Burke* (1992). A deeply thoughtful biography

R. R. Palmer, *The Age of Democratic Revolution: A Political History of Europe and America, 1760–1800*, 2 vols. (1959, 1964). Still an impressive survey of the political turmoil in the transatlantic world.

M. Price, *The Road from Versailles: Louis XVI, Marie Antoinette, and the Fall of the French Monarchy* (2004). A lively narrative that brings the personalities of the king and queen into focus.

R. Scurr, *Fatal Purity: Robespierre and the French Revolution* (2007). A compelling analysis of a personality long difficult to understand.

T. Tackett, *Becoming a Revolutionary: The Deputies of the French National Assembly and the Emergence of a Revolutionary Culture (1789–1790)* (1996). The best study of the early months of the revolution.

Chapter 19

M. H. Abrams, *The Mirror and the Lamp: Romantic Theory and the Critical Tradition* (1958). A classic on romantic literary theory.

E. Behler, *German Romantic Literary Theory* (1993). A clear introduction to a difficult subject.

D. Bell, *The First Total War: Napoleon's Europe and the Birth of Warfare as We Know It* (2007). A consideration of the Napoleonic conflicts and the culture of warfare.

G. E. Bentley, *The Stranger from Paradise: A Biography of William Blake* (2001). Now the standard work.

N. Boyle, *Goethe* (2001). A challenging two-volume biography.

M. Broers, *Europe under Napoleon 1799–1815* (2002). Examines the subject from the standpoint of those Napoleon conquered.

T. Chapman, *Congress of Vienna: Origins, Processes, and Results* (1998). A clear introduction to the major issues.

P. Dwyer, *Napoleon: The Path to Power, 1769–1799* (2008). A major study of the subject.

P. Dwyer, *Talleyrand* (2002). A useful account of his diplomatic influence.

S. Englund, *Napoleon: A Political Life* (2004). A thoughtful recent biography.

C. Esdaile, *The Peninsular War: A New History* (2003). A narrative of the Napoleonic wars in Spain.

A. Forrest, *Napoleon's Men: The Soldiers of the Revolution and Empire* (2002). An examination of the troops rather than their commander.

H. Honour, *Romanticism* (1979). Still the best introduction to romantic art, well illustrated.

F. Kagan, *The End of the Old Order: Napoleon and Europe, 1801–1805* (2006). A masterful narrative.

S. Körner, *Kant* (1955). A classic brief, clear introduction.

J. Lusvass, *Napoleon on the Art of War* (2001). A collection of Napoleon's own writings.

J. J. McGann and J. Soderholm, eds., *Byron and Romanticism* (2002). Essays on the poet who most embodied romantic qualities to the people of his time.

R. Muir, *Tactics and the Experience of Battle in the Age of Napoleon* (1998). A splendid account of troops in battle.

T. Pinkard, *Hegel: A Biography* (2000). A long but accessible study.

N. Roe, *Romanticism: An Oxford Guide* (2005). A series of informative essays.

P. W. Schroeder, *The Transformation of European Politics, 1763–1848* (1994). A major synthesis of the diplomatic history of the period, emphasizing the new departures of the Congress of Vienna.

I. Woloch, *Napoleon and His Collaborators: The Making of a Dictatorship* (2001). A key study by one of the major scholars of the subject.

A. Zamoyski, *Rites of Peace: The Fall of Napoleon and the Congress of Vienna* (2007). A lively analysis and narrative.

Chapter 20

B. Anderson, *Imagined Communities*, rev. ed. (2006). An influential and controversial discussion of nationalism.

M. S. Bell, *Toussaint Louverture: A Biography* (2007). An outstanding new biography.

M. Berdahl, *The Politics of the Prussian Nobility: The Development of a Conservative Ideology, 1770–1848* (1988). A major examination of German conservative outlooks.

A. Briggs, *The Making of Modern England* (1959). Classic survey of English history during the first half of the nineteenth century.

A. Craitu, *Liberalism under Siege: The Political Thought of the French Doctrinaires* (2003). An outstanding study of early-nineteenth-century French liberalism.

M. F. Cross and D. Williams, eds., *French Experience from Republic to Monarchy, 1792–1824: New Dawns in Politics, Knowledge and Culture* (2000). Essays on French culture from the revolution through the restoration.

D. Dakin, *The Struggle for Greek Independence* (1973). An excellent explanation of the Greek independence question.

L. Dubois, *Avengers of the New World: The Story of the Haitian Revolution* (2004). An analytic narrative likely to replace others.

E. J. Evans, *Britain Before the Reform Act: Politics and Society, 1815–1832* (2008). Explores the forces that resisted and pressed for reform.

W. Fortescue, *Revolution and Counter-Revolution in France, 1815–1852* (2002). A helpful brief survey.

E. Gellner, *Nations and Nationalism* (1983). A classic theoretical work.

L. Greenfeld, *Nationalism: Five Roads to Modernity* (1992). A major comparative study.

R. Harvey, *Liberators: Latin America's Struggle for Independence* (2002). An excellent, lively treatment.

E. J. Hobsbawm, *Nations and Nationalism since 1780: Programme, Myth, Reality*, rev. ed. (1992). Emphasizes intellectual factors.

C. JELAVICH AND B. JELAVICH, *The Establishment of the Balkan National States, 1804–1920* (1987). A standard survey.

G. A. KELLY, *The Humane Comedy: Constant, Tocqueville, and French Liberalism* (2007). The best introduction to the subject.

M. B. LEVINGER, *Enlightened Nationalism: The Transformation of Prussian Political Culture, 1806–1848* (2002). A clear and expansive coverview on the most recent scholarship.

J. LYNCH, *Simon Bolivar: A Life* (2006). Now the standard biography.

C. A. MACARTNEY, *The Habsburg Empire, 1790–1918* (1971). Remains an important survey.

N. V. RIASANOVSKY, *Nicholas I and Official Nationality in Russia, 1825–1855* (1959). Remains a lucid discussion of the conservative ideology that made Russia the major opponent of liberalism.

J. SHEEHAN, *German History, 1770–1866* (1989). A long work that is now the best available survey of the subject.

A. SKED, *Metternich and Austria: An Evaluation* (2008). A thoughtful restoration of Metternich to the position of leading diplomat of his age.

A. B. ULAM, *Russia's Failed Revolutionaries* (1981). Contains a useful discussion of the Decembrists as a background for other nineteenth-century Russian revolutionary activity.

B. WILSON, *The Making of Victorian Values: Decency and Dissent in Britain: 1789–1837* (2007). A very lively overview of the cultural factors shaping early-nineteenth-century British society.

Chapter 21

B. S. ANDERSON AND J. P. ZINSSER, *A History of Their Own: Women in Europe from Prehistory to the Present*, vol. 2 (1988). A wide-ranging survey.

I. BERLIN, *Karl Marx: His Life and Environment*, 4th ed. (1996). A classic introduction.

R. B. CARLISLE, *The Proffered Crown: Saint-Simonianism and the Doctrine of Hope* (1987). The best treatment of the broad social doctrines of Saint-Simonianism.

J. COFFIN, *The Politics of Women's Work* (1996). Examines the subject in France.

I. DEAK, *The Lawful Revolution: Louis Kossuth and the Hungarians, 1848–1849* (1979). The most significant study of the topic in English.

R. J. EVANS, *The Revolutions in Europe, 1848–1849: From Reform to Reaction* (2002). A series of essays by major experts.

J. F. C. HARRISON, *Quest for the New Moral World: Robert Owen and the Owenites in Britain and America* (1969). The standard work.

D. I. KERTZER AND M. BARBAGLI, EDS., *Family Life in the Long Nineteenth Century, 1789–1913: The History of the European Family* (2002). Wide-ranging collection of essays.

K. KOLAKOWSKI, *Main Currents of Marxism: Its Rise, Growth, and Dissolution*, 3 vols. (1978). A classic, comprehensive survey.

D. LANDES, *The Unbound Prometheus: Technological Change and Industrial Development in Western Europe from 1750 to the Present* (1969). Classic one-volume treatment of technological development in a broad social and economic context.

H. PERKIN, *The Origins of Modern English Society, 1780–1880* (1969). A provocative attempt to look at the society as a whole.

J. D. RANDERS-PEHRSON, *Germans and the Revolution of 1848–1849* (2001). An exhaustive treatment of the subject.

W. H. SEWELL, JR., *Work and Revolution in France: The Language of Labor from the Old Regime to 1848* (1980). A fine analysis of French artisans.

J. SPERBER, *The European Revolution, 1841–1851* (2005). An excellent synthesis.

E. P. THOMPSON, *The Making of the English Working Class* (1964). A classic work.

F. WHEEN, *Karl Marx: A Life* (2001). An accessible work that emphasizes the contradictions in Marx's career and personality.

D. WINCH, *Riches and Poverty: An Intellectual History of Political Economy in Britain, 1750–1834* (1996). A superb survey from Adam Smith through Thomas Malthus.

Chapter 22

V. AKSAN, *Ottoman Wars, 1700–1870: An Empire Besieged* (2007). Explores the impact of war on the weakening of the Ottoman Empire.

R. ALDOUS, *The Lion and the Unicorn: Gladstone vs. Disraeli* (2008). An accessible volume tracing the great political rivalry of the mid-Victorian age.

I. T. BEREND, *History Derailed: Central and Eastern Europe in the Long Nineteenth Century* (2003). The best one-volume treatment of the complexities of this region.

P. BEW, *Ireland: The Politics of Enmity 1789–2006* (2007). A major, new, outstanding survey of the sweep of modern Irish history.

E. F. BIAGINI, *British Democracy and Irish Nationalism 1876–1906* (2007). Explores impact of the Irish question on British political structures themselves.

D. BLACKBOURN, *The Long Nineteenth Century: A History of Germany, 1780–1918* (1998). An outstanding survey.

R. BLAKE, *Disraeli* (1967). Remains the best biography.

J. BREUILLY, *Austria, Prussia and Germany, 1806–1871* (2002). Examines the complex relations of these states leading up to German unification.

C. CLARK, *Iron Kingdom: The Rise and Downfall of Prussia, 1600–1947* (2006). Now the standard survey.

M. CLARK, *The Italian Risorgimento* (1998). A brief overview.

R. B. EDGERTON, *Death or Glory: The Legacy of the Crimean War* (2000). Multifaceted study of a mismanaged war that transformed European politics.

C. J. EICHNER, *Surmounting the Barricades: Women in the Paris Commune* (2004). Explores the impact of women's journalism and organizing in the Commune and wider radical political tradition.

B. EKLOF AND J. BUSHNELL, *Russia's Great Reforms, 1855–1881* (1994). A clear analysis.

M. A. HANIOGLU, *A Brief History of the Late Ottoman Empire* (2008). An accessible introduction.

R. KEE, *The Green Flag: A History of Irish Nationalism* (2001). A lively, accessible account.

D. LANGEWIESCHE, *Liberalism in Germany* (1999). A broad survey that is particularly good on the problems unification caused for German Liberals.

H. C. G. MATTHEW, *Gladstone, 1809–1898* (1998). A superb biography.

D. MOON, *Abolition of Serfdom in Russia: 1762–1907* (2001). Analysis with docments.

W. G. MOSS, *Russia in the Age of Alexander II, Tolstoy and Dostoyevsky* (2002). Emphaises the cultural background.

N. M. NAIMARK, *Terrorists and Social Democrats: The Russian Revolutionary Movement under Alexander III* (1983). Useful discussion of a complicated subject.

P. G. NORD, *The Republican Moment: Struggles for Democracy in Nineteenth-Century France* (1996). A major examination of nineteenth-century French political culture.

J. PARRY, *The Politics of Patriotism: English Liberalism, National Identity and Europe, 1830–1886* (2006). An excellent overview of English Liberalism and how its values determined mid-Victorian relations with the Continent.

J. P. PARRY, *The Rise and Fall of Liberal Government in Victorian Britain* (1994). An outstanding study.

O. PFLANZE, *Bismarck and the Development of Germany*, 3 vols. (1990). A major biography and history of Germany for the period.

R. PRICE, *The French Second Empire: An Anatomy of Political Power* (2001). This volume along with the following title are the most comprehensive recent study.

R. PRICE, *People and Politics in France, 1848–1870* (2004). Examines the rise of Louis Napoleon Bonaparte and his use of political power.

E. RADZINSKY, *Alexander II: The Last Great Tsar* (2005). An accessible biography.

L. RIALL, *Garibaldi: Invention of a Hero* (2007). An exploration of a nationalist hero's reputation in his own day and later.

A. SCIROCCO, *Garibaldi: Citizen of the World: A Biography* (2007). An admiring account.

D. SHAFER, *The Paris Commune: French Politics, Culture, and Society at the Crossroads of the Revolutionary Tradition and Revolutionary Socialism* (2005). Excellent in relating the Commune to previous and later revolutionary traditions.

A. SKED, *Decline and Fall of the Habsburg Empire 1815–1918* (2001). A major, accessible survey of a difficult subject.

D. M. SMITH, *Cavour* (1984). An excellent biography.

Chapter 23

A. ASCHER, *P. A. Stolypin: The Search for Stability in Late Imperial Russia* (2000). A broad-ranging biography based on extensive research.

P. BIRNBAUM, *Jewish Destinies: Citizenship, State, and Community in Modern France* (2000). Explores the subject from the French Revolution to the present.

T. W. CLYMAN AND J. VOWLES, *Russia through Women's Eyes: Autobiographies from Tsarist Russia* (1996). A splendid collection of relatively brief memoirs.

G. CROSSICK AND S. JAUMAIN, EDS., *Cathedrals of Consumption: The European Department Store, 1850–1939* (1999). Essays on the development of a new mode of distribution of consumer goods.

D. ELLENSON, *After Emancipation: Jewish Religious Responses to Modernity* (2004). A volume that explores numerous examples of this response across Europe.

A. GEIFMAN, *Thou Shalt Kill: Revolutionary Terrorism in Russia, 1894–1917* (1993). An examination of political violence in late imperial Russia.

R. F. HAMILTON, *Marxism, Revisionism, and Leninism: Explication, Assessment, and Commentary* (2000). A contribution by a historically minded sociologist.

J. HARSIN, *Policing Prostitution in Nineteenth-Century Paris* (1985). A major study of this significant subject in French social history.

G. HIMMELFARB, *Poverty and Compassion: The Moral Imagination of the Late Victorians* (1991). The best examination of late Victorian social thought.

E. HOBSBAWM, *The Age of Empire, 1875–1914* (1987). A stimulating survey that covers cultural as well as political developments.

S. S. HOLTON, *Feminism and Democracy: Women's Suffrage and Reform Politics in Britain, 1900–1918* (1986). An excellent treatment of the subject.

T. HOPPEN, *The Mid-Victorian Generation, 1846–1886* (1998). The most extensive treatment of the subject.

S. KOVIN, *Slumming: Sexual and Social Politics in Victorian London* (2004). Explores the complexities of the extension of charity and social services in late Victorian London.

M. MALIA, *Russia under Western Eyes: From the Bronze Horseman to the Lenin Mausoleum* (2000). A brilliant work on how Western intellectuals understood Russia.

E. D. RAPPAPORT, *Shopping for Pleasure: Women in the Making of London's West End* (2001). A study of the rise of department stores in London.

H. ROGGER, *Jewish Policies and Right-Wing Politics in Imperial Russia* (1986). A learned examination of Russian anti-Semitism.

M. L. ROZENBLIT, *The Jews of Vienna, 1867–1914: Assimilation and Identity* (1983). Covers the cultural, economic, and political life of Viennese Jews.

R. SERVICE, *Lenin: A Biography* (2002). Based on new sources and will no doubt become the standard biography.

D. SORKIN, *The Transformation of German Jewry, 1780–1840* (1987). An examination of Jewish emancipation in Germany.

G. P. STEENSON, *Not One Man! Not One Penny!: German Social Democracy, 1863–1914* (1999). An extensive survey.

N. STONE, *Europe Transformed* (1984). A sweeping survey that emphasizes the difficulties of late-nineteenth-century liberalism.

A. THORPE, *A History of the British Labour Party* (2001). From its inception to the twenty-first century.

J. R. WALKOWITZ, *Prostitution and Victorian Society: Women, Class, and the State* (1980). A work of great insight and sensitivity.

Chapter 24

C. ALLEN, *The Human Christ: The Search for the Historical Jesus* (1998). A broad survey of the issue for the past two centuries.

M. D. BIDDIS, *Father of Racist Ideology: The Social and Political Thought of Count Gobineau* (1970). Sets the subject in the more general context of nineteenth-century thought.

P. BOWLER, *Evolution: The History of an Idea* (2003). An outstanding survey.

J. BROWNE, *Charles Darwin*, 2 vols. (1995, 2002). A stunning biography.

J. BURROW, *The Crisis of Reason: European Thought, 1848–1914* (2000). The best overview available.

F. J. COPPA, *The Modern Papacy since 1789* (1999). A straightforward survey.

F. J. COPPA, *Politics and Papacy in the Modern World* (2008). A broad-ranging exploration.

B. DENVIR, *Post-Impressionism* (1992). A brief introduction.

M. FRANCIS, *Herbert Spence and the Invention of Modern Life* (2007). Now the standard biography.

P. GAY, *Modernism: The Lure of Heresy* (2007). A broad interdisciplinary exploration.

R. HARRIS, *Lourdes: Body and Soul in a Secular Age* (1999). A sensitive discussion of Lourdes in its religious and cultural contexts.

R. HELMSTADTER, ED., *Freedom and Religion in the Nineteenth Century* (1997). Major essays on the relationship of church and state.

J. HODGE AND G. RADICK, *The Cambridge Companion to Darwin* (2003). A far-ranging collection of essays with a good bibliography.

A. HOURANI, *Arab Thought in the Liberal Age 1789–1939* (1967). A classic account, clearly written and accessible to the nonspecialist.

J. KÖHLER, *Zarathustra's Secret: The Interior Life of Friedrich Nietzsche* (2002). A controversial new biography.

W. LACQUEUR, *A History of Zionism* (2003). The most extensive one-volume treatment.

M. LEVENSON, *The Cambridge Companion to Modernism* (1999). Excellent essays on a wide range of subjects.

B. LIGHTMAN, *Victorian Popularizers of Science: Designing Nature for New Audiences* (2007). A study that adds numerous new dimensions to the subject.

G. MAKARI, *Revolution in Mind: The Creation of Psychoanalysis* (2008). A major, multidimensional survey.

A. PAIS, *Subtle Is the Lord: The Science and Life of Albert Einstein* (1983). The most accessible biography.

P. G. J. PULZER, *The Rise of Political Anti-Semitism in Germany and Austria* (1989). A sound discussion of anti-Semitism and central European politics.

F. QUINN, *The Sum of All Heresies: The Image of Islam in Western Thought* (2008). An interesting and clear overview of this important subject.

R. ROSENBLUM, *Cubism and 20th Century Art* (2001). A well-informed introduction.

C. E. SCHORSKE, *Fin de Siècle Vienna: Politics and Culture* (1980). Classic essays on the creative intellectual climate of Vienna.

W. SMITH, *Politics and the Sciences of Culture in Germany, 1840–1920* (1991). A major survey of the interaction between science and the social sciences.

F. M. TURNER, *Contesting Cultural Authority: Essays in Victorian Intellectual Life* (1993). Explorations in issues relating to Victorian science and religion.

D. VITAL, *A People Apart: The Jews in Europe 1789–1939* (1999). A broad and deeply researched volume.

A. N. WILSON, *God's Funeral* (1999). Explores the thinkers who contributed to religious doubt during the nineteenth and twentieth centuries.

Chapter 25

M. ADAS, *Machines as the Measure of Men: Science, Technology, and Ideologies of Western Dominance* (1989). The best single volume on racial thinking and technological advances as forming ideologies of European colonial dominance.

R. ALDRICH, *Greater France: A History of French Overseas Expansion* (1996). Remains the best overview.

C. BAYLY, *Imperial Meridian: The British Empire and the World: 1780–1830* (1989). Places the British expansion in India into larger imperial contexts.

D. BROWER, *Turkestan and the Fate of the Russian Empire* (2003). A concise treatment of a case study in Russian imperialism in Asia.

A. BURTON, *Burdens of History: British Feminists, Indian Women, and Imperial Culture, 1865–1915* (1994). Explores the relationship of women in Britain's Indian empire.

A. CONKLIN, *A Mission to Civilize: The Republican Idea of Empire in France and West Africa, 1895–1930* (2000). An in-depth analysis of a case history of the civilizing mission.

F. COOPER AND A. L. STOLER, EDS., *Tensions of Empire: Colonial Cultures in a Bourgeois World* (1997). Explores difficulties of accommodating ideas and realities of empire to domestic middle-class values and outlooks.

J. COX, *Imperial Fault Lines: Christianity and Colonial Power in India, 1818–1940* (2002). The best treatment of British missionaries in India.

J. P. DAUGHTON, *An Empire Divided: Religion, Republicanism, and the Making of French Colonialism, 1880–1914* (2008). A superb discussion of the interaction of religion, empire, and domestic French politics.

N. P. DIRKS, *The Scandal of Empire: India and the Creation of Imperial Britain* (2006). An elegant study of the interaction of British political sensibilities and the emergence of the British empire in India.

R. DRAYTON, *Nature's Government: Science, Imperial Britain, and the "Improvement" of the World* (2000). The best volume on the relationship of science and imperialism.

M. H. EDNEY, *Mapping an Empire: The Geograhical Constuction of British India, 1765–1843* (1997). Discusses how the science of cartography contributed to the British domination of India.

N. ETHERINGTON, ED., *Misions and Empire* (2005). An excellent collection of essays.

D. HEADRICK, *The Tools of Empire: Technology and European Imperialism in the Nineteenth Century* (1981). Remains an important work of analysis.

A. HOCHSCHILD, *King Leopold's Ghost: A Study of Greed, Terror, and Heroism in Colonial Africa* (1999). A well-informed account of a tragedy.

I. HULL, *Absolute Destruction: Military Culture and the Practices of War in Imperial Germany* (2006). Excellent account of destructive German actions in East Africa.

R. HYAM, *Britain's Imperial Century 1815–1914: A Study of Empire and Expansion* (2002). The single best one-volume analysis.

T. JEAL, *Livingstone* (2001). This and the following title recount the lives of the two persons most associated in the popular mind with the exploration of Africa.

T. JEAL, *Stanley: The Impossible Life of Africa's Greatest Explorer* (2008). A fascinating portrait of the famous explorer.

A. KAPPELLER, *The Russian Empire: A Multiethnic History* (2001). A straightforward overview that is very clear on the concepts behind Russian expansionist policy.

D. C. LIEVAN, *The Russian Empire and Its Rivals* (2001). Explores the imperial side of Russian government.

K. E. MEYER AND S. B. BRYSA, *Tournament of Shadows: The Great Game and the Race for Empire in Central Asia* (1999). A lively account of the conflict between Great Britain and Russia.

W. J. MOMMSEN, *Theories of Imperialism* (1980). A study of the debate on the meaning of imperialism.

M. A. OSBORNE, *Nature, the Exotic, and the Science of French Colonialism* (1994). Explores the impact of French horticultural gardens and imperialism.

B. PORTER, *The Absent-Minded Imperialists: Empire, Society, and Culture in Britain* (2006). Discusses the relatively few people actually involved in Britain imperialism and how imperialism often had a low profile in the British Isles.

B. PORTER, *The Lion's Share: A Short History of British Imperialism, 1850–2004* (2004). A lively narrative.

L. PYENSON, *Civilizing Mission: Exact Sciences and French Overseas Expansion, 1830–1940* (1993). A major work of the history of both science and imperialism.

R. ROBINSON, J. GALLAGHER, AND A. DENNY, *Africa and the Victorians: The Official Mind of Imperialism* (2000). A classic analysis that continues to bear rereading.

P. J. TUCK, *French Catholic Missionaries and the Politics of Imperialism in Vietnam, 1857–1914* (1987). Includes both narrative and documents.

H. L. WESSELING, *Divide and Rule: The Partition of Africa, 1889–1914* (1996). A clear narrative and analysis of a complicated topic.

H. L. WESSELING, *The European Colonial Empires: 1815–1919* (2004). The best recent overview of the entire nineteenth-century European colonial ventures.

E. R. WOLF, *Europe and the People Without History* (1990). A classic, highly critical account.

A. ZIMMERMAN, *Anthropology and Antihumanism in Imperial Germany* (2001). Discusses the manner in which anthropology in conjunction with imperialism challenged humanistic ideas in German intellectual life.

Chapter 26

L. ALBERTINI, *The Origins of the War of 1914*, 3 vols. (1952, 1957). Discursive, but invaluable.

V. R. BERGHAHN, *Germany and the Approach of War in 1914* (1973). Stresses the importance of Germany's naval program.

S. B. FAY, *The Origins of the World War*, 2 vols. (1928). The best and most influential of the revisionist accounts.

N. FERGUSON, *The Pity of War* (1999). An analytic study of the First World War with controversial interpretations, especially of why it began and why it ended.

O. FIGES, *A People's Tragedy: The Russian Revolution: 1891–1924* (1998). The best recent analytic narrrative.

F. FISCHER, *Germany's Aims in the First World War* (1967). An influential interpretation that stirred an enormous controversy by emphasizing Germany's role in bringing on the war.

D. FROMKIN, *Europe's Last Summer: Who Started the Great War in 1914?* (2004). A lively and readable account of the outbreak of the war based on the latest scholarship.

D. FROMKIN, *A Peace to End All Peace: The Fall of the Ottoman Empire and the Creation of the Modern Middle East* (1989). A well-informed narrative of a complicated process.

R. F. HAMILTON AND H. H. HERWIG, *The Origins of World War I* (2003). An extensive collection of recent essays examining the subject from a number of differing perspectives.

H. HERWIG, *The First World War: Germany and Austria, 1914–18* (1997). A fine study of the war from the losers' perspective.

J. N. HORNE, *Labour at War: France and Britain, 1914–1918* (1991). Examines a major issue on the home fronts.

J. JOLL, *The Origins of the First World War* (2006). Most recent revision of a classic study.

J. KEEGAN, *The First World War* (1999). A vivid and readable narrative.

P. KENNEDY, *The Rise of the Anglo-German Antagonism, 1860–1914* (1980). An unusual and thorough analysis of the political, economic, and cultural roots of important diplomatic developments.

D. C. B. LIEVEN, *Russia and the Origins of the First World War* (1983). A good account of the forces that shaped Russian policy.

M. MACMILLAN, *Paris 1919: Six Months That Changed the World* (2003). The most extensive recent treatment.

E. MANELA, *The Wilsonian Moment: Self Determination and the International Origins of Anticolonial Nationalism* (2007).

A major exploration of how Wilson's foreign policy at Versailles raised colonial expectations and revolts in Egypt, India, China, and Korea.

A. MOMBAUER, *The Origins of the First World War: Controversies and Consensus* (2002). A discussion and evaluation of historians' shifting views regarding the responsibility for the outbreak of the war.

Z. STEINER, *Britain and the Origins of the First World War* (2003). A perceptive and informed account of British foreign policy before the war.

D. STEVENSON, *Cataclysm: The First World War as Political Tragedy* (2004). Analyzes the bankruptcy of reason that precipitated the war and kept it going.

N. STONE, *The Eastern Front 1917–1917* (2004). A study of the often neglected region of the war.

H. STRACHAN, *The First World War* (2004). A one-volume version of the massive three-volume magisterial account now underway.

S. R. WILLIAMSON, Jr., *Austria-Hungary and the Origins of the First World War* (1991). A valuable study of a complex subject.

Chapter 27

L. AHAMED, *Lords of Finance: The Bankers Who Broke the World* (2009). A lively narrative of the banking collapse leading to the Great Depression.

W. S. ALLEN, *The Nazi Seizure of Power: The Experience of a Single German Town, 1930–1935*, rev. ed. (1984). A classic treatment of Nazism in a microcosmic setting.

A. APPLEBAUM, *Gulag: A History* (2003). A superbly readable account of Stalin's system of persecution and resulting prison camps.

I. T. BEREND, *Decades of Crisis: Central and Eastern Europe before World War II* (2001). The best recent survey of the subject.

R. J. BOSWORTH, *Mussolini* (2002). A major new biography.

R. J. BOSWORTH, *Mussolini's Italy: Life Under the Fascist Dictatorship, 1915–1945* (2007). A broad-based study of both fascist politics and the impact of those politics on Italian life.

M. BURLEIGH AND W. WIPPERMAN, *The Racial State: Germany 1933–1945* (1991). Emphasizes the manner in which racial theory influenced numerous areas of policy.

I. DEUTSCHER, *The Prophet Armed* (1954), *The Prophet Unarmed* (1959), and *The Prophet Outcast* (1963). Remains the major biography of Trotsky.

B. A. ENGEL AND A. POSADSKAYA-VANDERBECK, *A Revolution of Their Own: Voices of Women in Soviet History* (1998). Long interviews and autobiographical recollections by women who lived through the Soviet era.

R. EVANS, *The Coming of the Third Reich* (2004) and *The Third Reich in Power, 1933–1939* (2005). Superb narratives.

G. FELDMAN, *The Great Disorder: Politics, Economics, and Society in the German Inflation, 1914–1924* (1993). The best work on the subject.

S. FITZPATRICK, *Stalin's Peasants: Resistance and Survival in the Russian Village After Collectivization* (1994). A pioneering study.

F. FURET, *The Passing of an Illusion: The Idea of Communism in the Twentieth Century* (1995). A brilliant account of how communism shaped politics and thought outside the Soviet Union.

R. GELLATELY, *Lenin, Stalin, and Hitler: The Age of Social Catastrophe* (2007). A major new study of the Soviet and Nazi dictatorships.

R. GELLATELY AND N. STOLTZFUS, *Social Outsiders in Nazi Germany* (2001). Important essays on Nazi treatment of groups the party regarded as undesirables.

J. A. GETTY AND O. V. NAUMOV, *The Road to Terror: Stalin and the Self-Destruction of the Bolsheviks, 1932–1939* (1999). A remarkable collection of documents and commentary on Stalin's purges.

R. HAMILTON, *Who Voted for Hitler?* (1982). An examination of voting patterns and sources of Nazi support.

J. JACKSON, *The Popular Front in France: Defending Democracy, 1934–1938* (1988). An extensive treatment.

P. KENEZ, *The Birth of the Propaganda State: Soviet Methods of Mass Mobilization, 1917–1929* (1985). An examination of the manner in which the Communist government inculcated popular support.

B. KENT, *The Spoils of War: The Politics, Economics, and Diplomacy of Reparations, 1918–1932* (1993). A comprehensive account of the intricacies of the reparations problem of the 1920s.

I. KERSHAW, *Hitler*, 2 vols. (2001). Replaces all previous biographies.

C. KINDLEBERGER, *The World in Depression, 1929–1939* (1986). A classic, accessible analysis.

B. LINCOLN, *Red Victory: A History of the Russian Civil War* (1989). An excellent narrative account.

M. McAULEY, *Bread and Justice: State and Society in Petrograd, 1917–1922* (1991). A study that examines the impact of the Russian Revolution and Leninist policies on a major Russian city.

R. McKIBBIN, *Classes and Cultures: England, 1918–1951* (2000). Viewing the era through the lens of class.

R. PIPES, *The Unknown Lenin: From the Secret Archives* (1996). A collection of previously unpublished documents that indicated the repressive character of Lenin's government.

P. PULZER, *Jews and the German State: The Political History of a Minority, 1848–1933* (1992). A detailed history by a major historian of European minorities.

R. SERVICE, *Stalin: A Biography* (2005). The strongest of a host of recent biographical studies.

J. STEPHENSON, *Women in Nazi Germany* (2001). Analysis with documents.

A. TOOZE, *The Wages of Destruction: The Making and Breaking of the Nazi Economy* (2006). A wide-ranging, accessible study of the politics and ideology behind Nazi economic policy.

E. WEBER, *The Hollow Years: France in the 1930s* (1995). Examines France between the wars.

L. YAHIL, *The Holocaust: The Fate of European Jewry, 1932–1945* (1990). A major study of this fundamental subject in twentieth-century history.

Chapter 28

O. BARTOV, *Mirrors of Destruction: War, Genocide, and Modern Identity* (2000). Remarkably penetrating essays.

A. BEEVOR, *The Spanish Civil War* (2001). Particularly strong on the political issues.

R. S. BOTWINICK, *A History of the Holocaust*, 2nd ed. (2002). A brief but useful account of the causes, character, and results of the Holocaust.

C. BROWNING, *The Origins of the Final Solution: The Evolution of the Nazi Jewish Policy* (2004). The story of how Hitler's policy developed from discrimination to annihilation.

W. S. CHURCHILL, *The Second World War*, 6 vols. (1948–1954). The memoirs of the great British leader.

A. CROZIER, *The Causes of the Second World War* (1997). An examination of what brought on the war.

J. C. FEST, *Hitler* (2002). Probably the best Hitler biography.

R. B. FRANK, *Downfall: The End of the Imperial Japanese Empire* (1998). A thorough, well-documented account of the last months of the Japanese Empire and why it surrendered.

J. L. GADDIS, *We Now Know: Rethinking Cold War History* (1998). A fine account of the early Cold War using new evidence emerging since the collapse of the Soviet Union.

J. L. GADDIS, P. H. GORDON, AND E. MAY, EDS., *Cold War Statesmen Confront the Bomb: Nuclear Diplomacy since 1945* (1999). Essays on the effect of atomic and nuclear weapons on diplomacy since World War II.

M. GILBERT, *The Holocaust: A History of the Jews of Europe during the Second World War* (1985). The best and most comprehensive treatment.

M. HASTINGS, *The Second World War: A World in Flames* (2004). A fine account by a leading student of contemporary warfare.

A. IRIYE, *Pearl Harbor and the Coming of the Pacific War* (1999). Essays on how the Pacific war came about, including a selection of documents.

J. KEEGAN, *The Second World War* (1990). A lively and penetrating account by a master military historian.

W. F. KIMBALL, *Forged in War: Roosevelt, Churchill, and the Second World War* (1998). A study of the collaboration between the two great leaders of the West.

M. KNOX, *Common Destiny, Dictatorship, Foreign Policy, and War in Fascist Italy and Nazi Germany* (2000). A brilliant comparison between the two dictatorships.

M. KNOX, *Mussolini Unleashed* (1982). An outstanding study of fascist Italy in World War II.

S. MARKS, *The Illusion of Peace* (1976). A good discussion of European international relations in the 1920s and early 1930s.

W. MURRAY, *The Change in the European Balance of Power 1938–1939* (1984). A brilliant study of the relationship among strategy, foreign policy, economics, and domestic politics.

W. MURRAY AND A. R. MILLETT, *A War to Be Won: Fighting the Second World War* (2000). A splendid account of military operations.

P. NEVILLE, *Hitler and Appeasement: The British Attempt to Prevent the Second World War* (2005). A defense of the British appeasers of Hitler.

R. OVERY, *Why the Allies Won* (1997). An analysis of the reasons for the Allied victory with emphasis on technology.

N. RICH, *Hitler's War Aims*, 2 vols. (1973–1974). The best study of the subject in English.

D. VITAL, *A People Apart: The Jews in Europe, 1789–1939* (1999). A major survey with excellent discussions of the interwar period.

R. WADE, *The Russian Revolution, 1917* (2000). A fine account that includes political and social history.

G. L. WEINBERG, *A World at Arms: A Global History of World War II* (1994). An excellent narrative.

Chapter 29

A. AHMED, *Discovering Islam. Making Sense of Muslim History and Society*, rev. ed (2003). An excellent and readable overview of Islamic–Western relations.

C. BAYLY, *Forgotten Wars: Freedom and Revolution in Southeast Asia* (2007). An important volume on decolonization by a master historian of the region.

R. BETTS, *France and Decolonization* (1991). Explores the complexities of the French case.

A. BROWN, *The Gorbachev Factor* (1996). Reflections by a thoughtful observer.

C. ELKINS, *Imperial Reckoning: The Untold Story of Britain's Gulag in Kenya* (2005). A study of the violence involved in Britain's eventual departure from Kenya.

M. ELLMAN AND V. KONTOROVICH, *The Disintegration of the Soviet Economic System* (1992). An overview of the economic strains in the Soviet Union during the 1980s.

G. FULLER, *The Future of Political Islam* (2003). A good overview of Islamist ideology by a former CIA staff member.

J. L. GADDIS, *The United States and the Origins of the Cold War, 1941–1947* (1992). A major discussion.

M. GLENNY, *The Balkans, 1804–1999: Nationalism, War and the Great Powers* (1999). A lively narrative by a well-informed journalist.

D. HALBERSTAM, *The Coldest Winter: America and the Korean War* (2007). A superb narrative by a gifted journalist.

M. I. GOLDMAN, *Petrostate: Putin, Power, and the New Russia* (2008). A thoughtful, but critical analysis.

W. HITCHCOCK, *Struggle for Europe: The Turbulent History of a Divided Continent, 1945–2002* (2003). The best overall narrative now available.

A. HORNE, *A Savage War of Peace: Algeria 1954–1962* (1987). A now dated but still classic narrative.

R. HYAM, *Britain's Declining Empire: The Road to Decolonization, 1918–1968* (2007). The best one-volume treatment.

T. JUDAH, *The Serbs: History, Myth and the Destruction of Yugoslavia* (1997). A clear overview of a complex event.

J. KEAY, *Sowing the Wind: The Seeds of Conflict in the Middle East* (2003). A thoughtful account.

N. R. KEDDIE, *Modern Iran: Roots and Results of Revolution* (2003). Chapters 6–12 focus on Iran from 1941 through the 1978 revolution.

J. KEEP, *Last of the Empires: A History of the Soviet Union, 1945–1991* (1995, 2007). An outstanding one-volume survey.

G. KEPEL, *Jihad: The Trail of Political Islam* (2002). An extensive treatment by a leading French scholar.

Y. KHAN, *The Great Partition: The Making of India and Pakistan* (2008). An important recent study of a difficult issue.

P. KHANNA, *The Second World: Empires and Influence in the New Global Order* (2008). A volume that seeks to provide a broad global analysis of recent events.

W. R. LOUIS, *Ends of British Imperialism: The Scramble for Empire, Suez, and Decolonization* (2007). A major study that captures the intensity and passions of the events.

R. MANN, *A Grand Delusion: America's Descent into Vietnam* (2001). The best recent narrative.

K. E. MEYER AND S. B. BRYSAC, *Kingmakers: The Invention of the Modern Middle East* (2008). A lively narrative of the past two centuries of British and then American influence in the Middle East.

D. E. MURPHY, S. A. KONDRASHEV, AND G. BAILEY, *Battleground Berlin: CIA vs. KGB in the Cold War* (1997). One of the best of a vast literature on Cold War espionage.

W. E. ODOM, *The Collapse of the Soviet Military* (1999). A study more wide ranging than the title suggests.

M. OREN, *Power, Faith, and Fantasy: America in the Middle East: 1776 to the Present* (2007). A thoughtful, balanced analysis.

B. PAREKH, *Gandhi: A Very Short Introduction* (2001). A useful introduction to Gandhi's ideas.

T. R. REID, *The United States of Europe: The New Superpower and the End of American Supremacy* (2004). A journalist's exploration of the impact of the European Union on American policy.

T. SHEPARD, *The Invention of Decolonization: The Algerian War and the Remaking of France* (2008). Explores the impact of the Algerian War on French politics.

L. SHEVTSOVA, *Russia—Lost in Transition: The Yeltsin and Putin Legacies* (2007). A major analysis and meditation on the past two decades.

J. SPRINGHALL, *Decolonization since 1945: The Collapse of European Empires* (2001). Systematic treatment of each major former colony.

B. STANLEY, *Missions, Nationalism, and the End of Empire* (2003). Discusses the often ignored role of Christian missions and decolonization.

M. THOMAS, *The French Empire Between the Wars: Imperialism, Politics and Society* (2005). Useful background to postwar decolonization.

M. VIORST, *In the Shadow of the Prophet: The Struggle for the Soul of Islam* (2001). Explores the divisions in contemporary Islam.

L. WRIGHT, *The Looming Tower: Al Qaeda and the Road to 9/11* (2007). A compelling narrative.

Chapter 30

G. AMBROSIUS AND W. H. HUBBARD, *A Social and Economic History of Twentieth-Century Europe* (1989). An excellent one-volume treatment of the subject.

B. S. ANDERSON AND J. P. ZINSSER, *A History of Their Own: Women in Europe from Prehistory to the Present*, vol. 2 (1988). A broad-ranging survey.

G. BOCK AND P. THANE, EDS., *Maternity and Gender Politics: Women and the Rise of the European Welfare States, 1880s–1950s* (1991). Explores the emergence of welfare legislation.

E. BRAMWELL, *Ecology in the 20th Century: A History* (1989). Traces the environmental movement to its late-nineteenth-century origins.

P. E. CERUZZI, *A History of Modern Computing* (2003). A comprehensive survey.

S. COLLINSON, *Beyond Borders: West European Migration Policy and the 21st Century* (1993). Explores a major contemporary European social issue.

R. CROSSMAN, ED., *The God That Failed* (1949). Classic essays by former communist intellectuals.

D. DINAN, *Europe Recast: A History of the European Union* (2004). A major overview.

C. FINK, P. GASERT, AND D. JUNKER, *1968: The World Transformed* (1998). The best collection of essays on a momentous year.

B. GRAHAM, *Modern Europe: Place, Culture, Identity* (1998). Thoughtful essays on the future of Europe by a group of geographers.

H. S. HUGHES, *Sophisticated Rebels: The Political Culture of European Dissent, 1968–1987* (1988). Thoughtful essays on recent cultural critics.

P. JENKINS, *Mrs. Thatcher's Revolution: The Ending of the Socialist Era* (1988). The best work on the subject.

P. JENKINS, *The Next Christendom: The Coming of Global Christianity* (2002). A provocative analysis.

T. JUDT, *Past Imperfect: French Intellectuals, 1944–1956* (1992). An important study of French intellectuals and communism.

T. JUDT, *Pastwar: A History of Europe Since 1945* (2005). The most recent authoritative overview.

R. MALTBY, ED., *Passing Parade: A History of Popular Culture in the Twentieth Century* (1989). Essays on a topic just beginning to receive scholarly attention.

R. MARRUS, *The Unwanted: European Refugees in the 20th Century* (1985). An important work on a disturbing subject.

D. MEYER, *Sex and Power: The Rise of Women in America, Russia, Sweden, and Italy* (1987). A lively, useful survey.

N. NAIMARK, *Fires of Hatred: Ethnic Cleansing in Twentieth-Century Europe* (2002). A remarkably sensitive treatment of a tragic subject.

M. POSTER, *Existential Marxism in Postwar France* (1975). An excellent and clear work.

H. ROWLEY, *Tête-á-Tête: Simone de Beauvoir and Jean-Paul Sartre* (2005). A highly critical joint biography.

S. STRASSER, C. MCGOVERN, AND M. JUDT, *Getting and Spending: European and American Consumer Societies in the Twentieth Century* (1998). An extensive collection of comparative essays.

F. THEBAUD, ED., *A History of Women in the West*, vol. 5: *Toward a Cultural Identity in the Twentieth Century* (1994). A collection of wide-ranging essays of the highest quality.